ROUTLEDGE HANDBOOK OF INTERNATIONAL EDUCATION AND DEVELOPMENT

This timely Handbook takes stock of the range of debates that characterise the field of international education and development and suggests key aspects of a research agenda for the next period. It is deliberately divergent in its approach, recognising the major ideological and epistemological divides that characterise a field that draws on many traditions. Leading and emergent voices from different paradigms and contexts are afforded a space to be heard, and each section puts current debates in larger historical contexts.

The Handbook is divided into four parts and book-ended by an introduction and a conclusion, the latter oriented towards the implications that the volume has for future research agendas. The first part explores major strands of debates about education's place in development theory. The second acknowledges the disciplining of the field by the Education for All movement and examines the place that learning, teaching and schools play in development. Part three looks beyond schools to consider early years, adult and vocational education but focuses particularly on the return to thinking about higher education's role in development. The final part considers the changing, but still important, role that international cooperation plays in shaping education in developing countries.

Featuring over thirty chapters written by leading international and interdisciplinary scholars, the *Routledge Handbook of International Education and Development* offers the first comprehensive and forward-looking resource for students and scholars.

Simon McGrath is Professor of International Education and Development at the University of Nottingham, UK. He is also an Extraordinary Professor at the University of the Western Cape, South Africa, and a research associate of the Human Sciences Research Council of South Africa.

Qing Gu is Associate Professor at the University of Nottingham, UK. She is Vice Chair of the British Association for International and Comparative Education.

ROUTLEDGE HANDBOOK OF INTERNATIONAL EDUCATION AND DEVELOPMENT

Edited by Simon McGrath and Qing Gu

Routledge
Taylor & Francis Group

LONDON AND NEW YORK

First published 2016 by Routledge

2 Park Square, Milton Park, Abingdon, Oxon OX14 4RN
711 Third Avenue, New York, NY 10017, USA

Routledge is an imprint of the Taylor & Francis Group, an informa business

First issued in paperback 2017

Copyright © 2016 Simon McGrath and Qing Gu

The right of the editors to be identified as the authors of the editorial
material, and of the authors for their individual chapters, has been asserted
in accordance with sections 77 and 78 of the Copyright, Designs and
Patents Act 1988.

British Library Cataloguing in Publication Data

A catalogue record for this book is available from the British Library

Library of Congress Cataloging-in-Publication Data
Routledge handbook of international education and development / edited
by Simon McGrath and Qing Gu.
pages cm
Includes bibliographical references and index.
1. Education—Economic aspects—Handbooks, manuals, etc.   2. Economic
development—Effect of education on—Handbooks, manuals, etc.
I. McGrath, Simon A., editor.
LC65.R68 2015
338.4'737—dc23
2015005116

ISBN: 978-0-415-74754-7 (hbk)
ISBN: 978-1-138-07076-9 (pbk)

Typeset in Bembo
by Apex CoVantage, LLC

CONTENTS

Contents

LIST OF BOXES

LIST OF FIGURES

LIST OF TABLES

ACKNOWLEDGMENTS

Elsevier for permission to reproduce Robin Alexander (2014) Teaching and learning for all? The quality imperative revisited. *International Journal of Educational Development* 40: 250–258.

Kate Raworth for permission to reproduce Figure 32.1.
Cadena, Suarez & Al Borde for permission to reproduce Figure 15.2.
White Architects for permission to reproduce Figure 15.3.
ESALA, University of Edinburgh for permission to reproduce Figure 15.5.
ESALA, University of Edinburgh for permission to reproduce Figure 15.6.

LIST OF ABBREVIATIONS

AAI	ActionAid International
ACER	Australian Council for Educational Research
ADEA	Association for the Development of Education in Africa
AERA	American Education Research Association
AIDS	auto immune deficiency syndrome
AIMS	Africa, Indian Ocean, Mediterranean and South China Sea
AOSIS	Alliance of Small Island States
APL	assessment of prior learning
ASER	Annual Status of Education Report
ATT	average treatment effect on the treated
AusAID	Australian Agency for International Development
BICS	basic interpersonal communicative skills
BMI	body mass index
BMZ	German Federal Ministry for Economic Cooperation and Development
BRAC	Bangladesh Rural Action Committee
CA	capability approach
CAADP	Comprehensive Africa Agriculture Development Programme
CALP	cognitive academic language proficiency
CARE	Christian Action Research and Education
CCNGO/EFA	Collective Consultation of NGOs on EFA
CCT	conditional cash transfer
CEF	Commonwealth Education Fund
CFS	child-friendly schools
CFT	competency framework for teachers
CIBV	Centre for Infant Wellbeing
CLASS	classroom assessment scoring system
CONFEMEN	Conference of Francophone Ministers of Education
CREATE	Consortium for Research on Educational Access, Transitions and Equity
CSER	Centre for the Study of Existential Risk

CSO	civil society organisation
DAAD	German Academic Exchange Service
DAC	Development Assistance Committee
DDR	disarmament, demobilisation and reintegration
DESD	Decade for Education for Sustainable Development
DFID	Department for International Development
DIBELS	Dynamic Indicators of Basic Early Literacy Skills
DMR	diminishing marginal returns
DPEP	District Primary Education Programme
DRC	Democratic Republic of Congo
ECCE	early childhood care and education
ECD	early childhood development
ECDI	early child development index
ECEC	early childhood education and care
EDGE	education and gender
EDI	Early Development Instrument
EDI	education development index
EFA	Education for All
EFA SC	Education for All Steering Committee
EGMA	Early Grade Math Assessment
EGRA	Early Grade Reading Assessment
ERASMUS	European Community Action Scheme for the Mobility of University Students
ESD	education for sustainable development
EU	European Union
EUA	European Universities Association
FAO	Food and Agriculture Organisation
FDI	foreign direct investment
FODI	Children's Development Fund
FRESH	focusing resources on effective school health
FSQL	fundamental school quality level
FTI	Fast Track Initiative
FYP	five-year plan
GAD	gender and development
GADN	Gender and Development Network
GAP	Global Action Programme
GATS	General Agreement on Trade in Services
GBC-E	Global Business Coalition for Education
GCE	Global Coalition for Education
GDP	gross domestic product
GEFI	Global Education First Initiative
GEI	gender equity index
GII	gender inequality index
GIZ	German Agency for International Cooperation
GMR	Global Monitoring Report
GNP	gross national product
GoI	Government of India
GPE	Global Partnership for Education

GSFP	Ghana School Feeding Programme
GUNI	Global University Network for Innovation
GVC	global value chain
H/L	Heyneman/Loxley
HDI	human development index
HDR	Human Development Report
HforA	height for age
HGSF	home grown school feeding
HIV	human immunodeficiency virus
HLM	hierarchical linear modelling
HLP	High Level Panel
HRD	human resource development
IALS	International Adult Literacy Survey
IAU	International Association of Universities
ICCS	International Civics and Citizenship Study
ICDF	International Cooperation and Development Fund
ICS	Research Centre for International and Comparative Studies
ICT	information and communications technology
IDA	International Development Agency
IDTs	international development targets
IEA	International Association for the Evaluation of Educational Achievement
IET	International Education Team (ActionAid)
IFAD	International Fund for Agricultural Development
IFC	International Finance Corporation
IIE	Institute of International Education
IJED	International Journal of Educational Development
ILO	International Labour Organisation
IMF	International Monetary Fund
INGO	international non governmental organisation
INRULED	International Research and Training Centre for Rural Education
IPCC	Intergovernmental Panel on Climate Change
IQ	intelligence quotient
IRC	International Rescue Committee
ITEC	Indian Technical Economic Cooperation Programme
ITERS	infant/toddler environment rating scale
JEI	Jordan Education Initiative
JOCVs	Japanese Overseas Cooperation Volunteers
J-PAL	Abdul Latif Jameel Poverty Action Lab
KICE	Korea Institute of Curriculum and Evaluation
KOICA	Korean International Cooperation Agency
L1	first language (mother tongue)
L2	subsequent language
LAMP	Literacy Assessment and Monitoring Programme
LFP	low-fee private
LLECE	Latin-American Laboratory for the Evaluation of the Quality of Education
LMTF	Learning Metrics Task Force

MD	managing director
MDG	Millennium Development Goals
MEPSP	Ministry for Primary, Secondary and Vocational Education
MICS	multiple indicator cluster survey
MLE	multilingual education
MNC	multinational corporation
MNPs	micronutrient powders
MOOCs	massive open online courses
MSF	Médecins Sans Frontières (Doctors Without Borders)
MSPs	multi stakeholder partnerships
MTB-MLE	mother tongue-based multilingual education
NAM	Non-Aligned Movement
NEET	not in employment, education and training
NEPAD	New Partnership for Africa's Development
NFE	non formal education
NGO	non governmental organisation
NORRAG	Network for International Policies and Cooperation in Education and Training
NRC US	National Research Council
NRP	National Reading Panel
NTD	neglected tropical disease
ODA	official development assistance
OECD	Organisation for Economic Co-operation and Development
OLS	ordinary least square
OMS	Oxford Martin School
OWG	Open Working Group on Sustainable Development Goals
PACES	Plan for the Expansion of Coverage of Secondary Education
PASEC	Programme for the Analysis of Education Systems of CONFEMEN
PCD	Partnership for Child Development
PIAAC	Programme for International Assessment of Adult Competencies
PIDI	Integrated Project for Infant Development
PIRLS	Progress in International Reading Literacy Study
PISA	Programme for International Student Assessment
PPP	public-private partnership
PPVT	Peabody picture vocabulary test
PRIDI	Regional Programme of Indicators for Infant Development
R&D	research and development
RBA	rights-based approach
RTI	Research Training Institute
SABER	systems approach for better education results
SACMEQ	Southern and Eastern Africa Consortium for Monitoring Educational Quality
SC	scheduled castes
SCAAP	Special Commonwealth Assistance for Africa Programme
SDG	Sustainable Development Goal
SD	sustainable development
SDOH	social determinants of health
SES	socio economic status

SICOLE-R-Primaria	multi media early years reading assessment
SIDS	small island developing states
SSA	Sarva Shiksha Abhiyan (The Education for All Movement (India))
SSC	South-South cooperation
ST	scheduled tribes
STEM	science, technology, engineering and mathematics
TCD	Technical Cooperation Division
TCDC	Technical Cooperation between Developing Countries
TED	Technology, Entertainment, Design
TIMSS	Trends in International Mathematics and Science Study
TNC	transnational corporation
TVET	technical and vocational education and training
TVSD	technical and vocational skills development
UCL	University College London
UCLA	University of California, Los Angeles
UCT	University of Cape Town
UDHR	Universal Declaration of Human Rights
UIS	UNESCO Institute of Statistics
UK	United Kingdom
UN	United Nations
UNDESA	United Nations Department of Economic and Social Affairs
UNDP	United Nations Development Programme
UNECA	United Nations Economic Commission for Africa
UNESCO	United Nations Educational, Scientific and Cultural Organisation
UNESCO-IIEP	UNESCO International Institute for Educational Planning
UNGEI	United Nations Global Education Initiative
UNHCR	Office of the United Nations High Commissioner for Refugees
UNICEF	United Nations Children's Fund
UNU	United Nations University
UPE	universal primary education
US	United States
USA	United States of America
USAID	United States Agency for International Development
VET	vocational education and training
VSO	Voluntary Service Overseas
WCARO	West and Central Africa Regional Office (UNICEF)
WCEFA	World Conference on Education for All
WFP	World Food Programme
WHO	World Health Organisation
WID	Women in Development
YL	Young Lives

LIST OF CONTRIBUTORS

Robin Alexander, University of Cambridge
Kate Anderson, Brookings Institution
Lesley Bartlett, University of Wisconsin
Colin Brock, University of Oxford
Phillip Brown, Cardiff University
Donald Bundy, World Bank
Carmen Burbano, United Nations World Food Programme
Nicholas Burnett, Results for Development Institute
Sheng-Ju Chan, National Chung Cheng University
I-Hsuan Cheng, National Chi Nan University
Joan DeJaeghere, University of Minnesota
Mariachiara Di Cesare, Imperial College London
Lesley Drake, Partnership for Child Development and Imperial College London
Alexandra Draxler, independent consultant
Julia Frazier, International Rescue Committee and Hunter College
Qing Gu, University of Nottingham
Clive Harber, University of Birmingham
Stephen Heyneman, Vanderbilt University
Fiona Hunter, Università Cattolica del Sacro Cuore
Analía Jaimovich, Inter-American Development Bank
Kenneth King, University of Edinburgh
Jane Knight, University of Toronto
Hugh Lauder, University of Bath
Guy Le Fanu, Sightsavers International
Tristan McCowan, University College London
Simon McGrath, University of Nottingham and University of the Western Cape
Bronwen Magrath, University of Nottingham
Susan Nyaga, SIL Africa
Lesley Powell, University of Nottingham
Barry Reilly, University of Sussex
Anna Robinson-Pant, University of East Anglia

Alan Rogers, University of East Anglia and University of Nottingham
Pauline Rose, University of Cambridge
Ricardo Sabates, University of Sussex
Rebecca Schendel, University College London
Michele Schweisfurth, University of Glasgow
Terra Sprague, University of Bristol
Milan Thomas, Results for Development Institute
James Tooley, University of Newcastle
Barbara Trudell, SIL Africa
Ola Uduku, University of Edinburgh
Emiliana Vegas, Inter-American Development Bank
Melanie Walker, University of the Free State
Rebecca Winthrop, Brookings Institution
Hans de Wit, Università Cattolica del Sacro Cuore, Amsterdam University of Applied Sciences and Nelson Mandela Metropolitan University
Catherine Young, SIL International

Introduction

1

INTERNATIONAL EDUCATION AND DEVELOPMENT

Using multiple lenses or remaining in multiple silos?

Simon McGrath and Qing Gu

Introduction

The contributions that comprise this Handbook represent a set of test pits dug into the complex field of international education and development. As with archaeological test pits, the chapters may provide important insights into what the field looks like as a whole, but it is possible, indeed likely, that important details are missing. Nonetheless, even from this fragmentary picture, it is immediately obvious that the field of international education and development is characterised by great diversity.

Such diversity itself is multidimensional. There is no single research tradition in the field but rather multiple traditions that only partially align to disciplinary delineations or to the logics of ontology, epistemology and methodology. Thus, in this Handbook, we see approaches that draw on economics, medical sciences, political science, history, philosophy, human geography and sociolinguistics, to name but a sample of the disciplinary traditions on show. There are a great range of theoretical concepts employed, most of which have origins in other disciplinary spaces. We have work that is analysing policy documents, experiments and epidemiological data, as well as work that is essentially nonempirical. Positivist, interpretivist and critical paradigms are all employed. There is much pragmatism that never speaks of theoretical or epistemological traditions, though these can often times be traduced from the text. There are huge variations in the scale of research in the field: from multimillion, multiyear, multicountry, multimethods and multiresearcher studies to small, unfunded, solo projects including literature reviews and think pieces. Much of the work is funded by major international development agencies, and some authored by their staff, but there is much that is explicitly critical of the agencies and of the development orthodoxy.

Crucially, the explicit and imagined contexts of the contributions vary hugely. This is not just a matter of scale and/or the attitudes of different traditions to universality versus context-specificity. Rather, there is a sense that the "development space" is understood in very different ways. Some chapters clearly see this as global, both in terms of generalisability of data and in terms of theoretical or policy messages. Others, however, are clearly working with some notion of "developing countries" or are focused on a particular region, type of state (e.g., small island developing states) or country. As we sit in 2015 with a new global development agenda, notions of whom and where development is about and for are particularly salient.

To deploy a different metaphor, there is a plurality of voices in the book, even if we would have wished for (and indeed planned for) even greater diversity. However, one of the biggest questions that we want to pose is about the nature of this plurality. A brief reading of the reference lists of the chapters is quite instructive. Rather than a set of authors coming together from different traditions and issue sets to discuss common concerns in international education and training and constructing a shared corpus of literature, it is apparent that there is more of a practice of authors staying largely within separate traditions. Only a handful of names are apparently important enough to transcend traditions: Psacharopoulos and Hanushek from the human capital tradition and Sen and Nussbaum from the capability approach. Even here, the way that they are mobilised is noteworthy. Whilst Sen is cited with approval both within economics and outside, Psacharopoulos is often cited in order to delineate a position to be critiqued rather than really deeply engaged with. Strikingly, not one contributor to the Handbook appears more than ten times in the reference lists of others. Thus, there is an overwhelming sense of a set of "invisible colleges" (Crane 1972) bounded by high walls.

This leads to the question contained in the title of the chapter: are we talking here of a coherent field that is enriched by multiple traditions and perspectives or rather a field on which different factions have encamped that try to keep themselves apart from the "others"? Of course, this leads to further questions as to whether the latter, if true, matters; and, if so, whether there is anything that can be done about it.

Whilst there is no real sense of fertile interactions between different traditions, there are a number of flashpoints represented within the Handbook. These include disputes over the nature of development; the definition of and means of ensuring quality education; and the relative roles to be played by the public and private sectors in the funding and delivery of education.

The Handbook is organised into four sections, which also highlight four key questions asked across the volume. However, these questions are not neatly contained by the artificial logic of sections and seep across the boundaries throughout.

What is the nature of the relationship between education and development?

This question underpins the whole volume and the decisions that were made in commissioning papers. It is apparent that authors hold differing views about the nature and purpose of education, of development, and of the relationship between them. In Section 1, some important perspectives on these issues are explored. Human capital theory provides the most influential account of the education–development relationship, but its importance has often led to oversimplified accounts being propagated by supporters and critics alike. Thus, it is important, as Thomas and Burnett do, to look very carefully at the evolution of the approach and how it has developed new methodological and theoretical tools over time.

Other traditions that have policy purchase at the moment include human rights and sustainable development perspectives; these, too, are explored in Section 1 through Brock's consideration of the humanitarian case for education and Sprague's exploration of sustainable education and education for sustainability in the specific context of small island developing states.

As can be seen from across the Handbook as a whole, human development and capability accounts are of growing significance in the field of international education and development. This approach informs DeJaeghere's chapter, in which she makes clear the links between capability thinking and justice approaches. She also brings a strong gender lens to bear on the question of education and development, reminding us that the issues embedded in the relationship are experienced in highly differentiated ways.

Robinson-Pant puts rural development and learning beyond schools more firmly on the Handbook's agenda, a further illustration of the importance of contextualisation and analytical differentiation.

Much of the education for development debate, particularly in the policy and advocacy spheres, is focused on the positive nature of education's contribution to development. Whilst several of these authors touch on the negative effects of educational exclusion and violence within education, Harber's use of a political science lens brings to the forefront the complex and often problematic relationship between education and the state. Such an approach insists on the complex playing out of power in the educational space and on the inevitable complicity of formal education with structural inequalities.

How do we improve education?

A number of chapters in Section 2, and much of the wider policy debate at national and international levels, sidestep these larger philosophical issues about education and development for a focus on improving education. However, this is also the section where the debates are at their hottest. Whilst authors share concerns about improving the quality of education, they differ hugely on how to achieve this. Anderson and Winthrop argue the case for a new set of global learning tests, designed to drive a revolution in the quality of teaching and learning. However, Bartlett and Frazier focus on the weaknesses of existing international testing regimes. Alexander notes the recent attention to both quality learning and teaching in recent Global Monitoring Reports but develops a powerful critique of the conceptual weaknesses of the approach. He argues that there is a wealth of research on pedagogy already available but an apparent inability of the international policy community to access and utilise this. Trudell, Young and Nyaga call for a greater focus on issues of language of instruction as a major element both in the drive towards improving educational quality and as a key vector of thinking about identity, culture and development.

Heyneman takes this debate about education quality to a different level of aggregation by revisiting the long-standing question of the relative weight of "in-school" and "out-of-school" factors in determining educational achievement. In the international education and development field, this debate has been centred on the "Heyneman-Loxley effect," named after a paper that Steve cowrote 30 years ago. It is a particular pleasure, therefore, to have him revisit this literature in the Handbook. In his chapter, he reflects on the rise of international testing (see the discussion of the previous paragraph) and the continued effects that poverty has on educational performance.

Heyneman's insistence on understanding the effect of nonschool factors on educational performance is reflected also in the policies, practices and literatures around nutrition and education. These are rarely discussed within the international education and development field, but Drake, Burbano and Bundy show the importance of thinking about nutrition and learning. The nutrition-development and education-development debates are then bridged in a chapter by Sabates, Di Cesare and Reilly, who look at the relationship between educational exclusion and child health. This is done by building a conversation between two large DFID-funded research projects, combining data from Young Lives with a conceptual framework developed by the Consortium for Research on Educational Access, Transitions and Equity.

If nutrition is a metaphorical building block for education, then school architecture is a more literal one. Uduku revisits the educational quality debate through the lens of her profession of architecture to consider the question of how we build more effective learning spaces to support quality and inclusive education.

The section concludes with two very different perspectives on the question of educational quality, although both are focused on the question of inclusion. First, from the inclusive education tradition, Le Fanu examines how international agency policies and the international education and development literature conceptualise inclusive education. He cautions against the dangers of global, top-down models that define inclusion in ways that actually exclude local inclusion and agencies in agenda setting. Finally, Tooley asks whether low-cost private schooling may be a highly effective mechanism for including the poorest into schooling. He critically evaluates recent literature on the issue and argues that such schooling reflects the agency of the poor and needs to be taken very seriously as a result.

What is the role of education (not just schooling) in development?

The wording of this question may appear rather clumsy, but it reflects a problem with an educational orthodoxy in which schooling has come to be seen as synonymous with both learning and education. This tendency has been strengthened immeasurably by the Education for All (EFA) and Millennium Development Goal (MDG) processes, even though this was not the intention of the former (as King notes in Section 4).

Section 3 in particular talks back to this orthodoxy. In doing so, it includes chapters on early childhood, adult, vocational and higher education and notes the importance of informal and nonformal learning. Vegas and Jaimovich review the evidence from both economics and neuroscience suggesting that early childhood education is a highly effective intervention, both in terms of generating income and in reducing inequality. However, they note that access to early childhood interventions is both very limited and extremely unequal. Thus they place early childhood firmly at the centre of our consideration of the origins of and responses to inequality.

Rogers takes issue with some of the discourse that was at the heart of Section 2: the claim that many millions of young people are not learning. Taking as his starting point a Global Monitoring Report claim that "Today, all over the world, 115 million girls are doing no learning", Rogers shows how this statement is based on the aforementioned assumption that learning = schooling but reviews a literature that shows this is simply not true. Rather, he notes that because they are human beings, these girls (and boys experiencing inadequate schooling) are learning from others and through reflection on their own life experiences. They are learning school-related knowledge but also a range of other useful knowledges and skills. This existing fund of knowledge needs to be the starting point for formal education interventions.

Vocational education and training (VET) has been neglected within the international agency orthodoxy yet has ascended domestic policy agendas both north and south in recent years. However, McGrath and Powell point to the dangers of this, arguing that there is an inadequate theory of VET's contribution to development. Indeed, they suggest that there is a critical need for a reimagining both of VET and of development. In order to advance this project, they draw upon the human development and capability approach, as do a number of other chapters across the book. This leads them to resist the instrumentalism that is so engrained in thinking about VET. Rather than a focus on the needs of the economy, they call for an approach that starts from the needs of people and that is attentive both to their aspirations and the ways in which their dreams and experiences are limited by structural injustices.

Higher education has also fallen from grace amongst the development community. From being a central tool of national development in the 1960s and an important tool of Cold War international relations, by the 1980s it had become stereotyped by the development community as an expensive way of reproducing elites. Indeed, from the time of the World Conference on Education for All in Jomtien in 1990, it has been established that public resources should be shifted from higher education to primary schooling.

However, important countercurrents have been building up. The growth of primary enrolments since 1990 has filtered through eventually to significant increases in upper-secondary-school-leaver numbers. Rising prosperity, particularly amongst enlarged middle classes in many countries of the South, is also fuelling demand. At the same time, the discourse of the global knowledge economy and recent human capital data suggesting that returns to higher education are greater than those for primary schooling have also made governments more willing to see economic as well as political benefits in higher education expansion. This has resulted in massive increases in higher education participation and enrolment rates, particularly in Africa. UNESCO data shows that the tertiary gross enrolment rate (GER) for sub-Saharan Africa doubled from 4% to 8% between 1999 and 2011. At the national level there have been rapid expansions both in low and high participation countries. Ethiopia's tertiary GER grew from 1% to 8%, whilst Mauritius increased its GER from 10% to 40%. In absolute numbers, several countries saw a more than ten-fold expansion of students in higher education: e.g., Angola 7,000–140,000; Ethiopia 50,000–700,000; Rwanda 5,000–70,000; Mozambique 10,000–110,000. The Association for Commonwealth Universities has launched a campaign to assert the importance of higher education in development, and there are a number of hints about its importance in the key post-2015 documents.

It is in the light of these shifts in attention to higher education that this Handbook includes several chapters on the issue. McCowan and Schendel present a systematic review of the literature on higher education's impact on development and conclude with persuasive evidence that higher education is essential for economic growth, prosperity and competitiveness. However, Lauder questions the neoclassical orthodoxy on which such arguments are based, suggesting that they underplay the importance of national varieties of capitalism, with their distinct models of educational and labour market institutions, and fail to engage theoretically or methodologically with the changing nature of globalisation and the role of nation states therein. In contrast to both, Walker insists on the status of higher education as a public good, with far broader benefits for human development.

The recent rise of national university systems in the South is taking place at the same time the North is increasingly trying to export its higher education provision. This is achieved through diverse mechanisms, including recruitment of international students to attend Northern universities, the growth in online learning offerings and the emergence of international branch campuses and for-profit cross-border education programmes. This phenomenon of the internationalisation of higher education is not normally given attention in the international education and development literature but is highly salient to the concerns of the field. Two accounts of the emergence of this field of activity provided by Knight and de Wit and Hunter reveal that internationalisation has, without a shadow of a doubt, become integral to the financial health of many institutions in the world of higher education. Its sustained development and expansion in the North, and increasingly the South, is closely linked with national political and economic drivers for economic and innovation competitiveness and the great brain/talent race. Gu and Schweisfurth's analysis of the experiences of international mobile students adds to the wider debate about the transnational flows of knowledge and skills and raises some critical questions as to whether the evidence about international student mobility is universally applicable in the new context of emphasis on sustainable development.

What is the future of international cooperation in education?

2015 marks a symbolic transition point in development thinking and, hence, in international education cooperation. Whether or not that becomes a genuine transformation is unknowable at this point, but there is an overall discourse of an end to an era of international cooperation being thought of simply in terms of multilateral and (Northern) bilateral agencies, official development assistance and strong conditionalities.

Section 4 begins with reflections about the past and future of international cooperation in education. King reviews the long sweep of cooperation history and takes a broad view of education, whilst Rose looks at the specific case of the Education for All movement. McGrath begins with a critique of EFA and the MDGs but then shifts to a focus on the emerging post-2015 development agenda as it had progressed by the end of 2014. This leads him into a final discussion of the implications the new agenda might have for the field of international education and development, an issue to which we will return in the concluding chapter of this Handbook.

New dynamics already evident in the international cooperation in education field are the subject of three further chapters. Cheng and Chan look at the rise of new bilateral actors, specifically South Korea, Taiwan and India. They show how their own experiences of development have shaped profoundly their approaches to development cooperation. Cheng and Chan highlight the particular importance that they attach to human resources development, seeing this as essential to the building of a dynamic economy and the achievement of social development goals. Magrath considers the role of civil society in education for development and the problematic ways in which national and international civil society organisations have come to mirror the discourses and practices of official international cooperation. Her analysis of large international NGOs in particular illustrates the ways in which they influence the discourse of global educational governance and reinforce the power imbalance embedded in civil society advocacy networks operating in the international and development education field. Draxler critiques the way in which public–private partnership has become a core of much of the recent international cooperation in education and asks hard questions about whose interests are served by this approach.

A final invitation

This introduction can only scratch the surface of the richness of the discussions that follow. In the coming pages, you will find approaches that clash with each other in multiple ways. We hope that readers will find this useful in reminding them, if that is needed, that issues of education and development are so important that they are always contested and that they will be encouraged to look at the field through unfamiliar lenses that could enrich their existing work. We invite you to read on.

Reference

Crane, D., 1972. *Invisible Colleges: Diffusion of Knowledge in Scientific Communities*. University of Chicago Press, Chicago.

SECTION 1

Rethinking the relationship between education and development

2

HUMAN CAPITAL AND DEVELOPMENT

Milan Thomas with Nicholas Burnett

Introduction

This chapter reviews theory and evidence on the economics of human capital, with an emphasis on the education aspect of human capital and its impact on economic growth in developing countries. We focus our discussion on development as measured by economic growth (i.e., change in gross domestic product) while recognising that there is a range of other dimensions that human capital accumulation influences, such as social development and health.

Tracking the evolution of economic thought on this topic from its origins to its inclusion in macroeconomic growth models, we first review the concept of human capital and then labour market research on its relationship with individual earnings before turning to its impact on aggregate income. We review evidence primarily from human capital's inclusion in neoclassical growth models rather than endogenous growth models because the former is relatively strong at explaining cross-country differences in national income while the latter is more pertinent to advanced economies in the global technological frontier (Barro and Lee 2013). We also consider how the estimation of education's impact on development has changed due to recent advances in the measurement of human capital.

Understanding the nuances of human capital's role in development is not an academic exercise. Evidence on it can guide public policy and encourage it so that scarce resources are channelled to impactful investments in human productive capacity that will accelerate economic growth and poverty reduction. In addition to reviewing research on human capital's impact on growth through labour force productivity, we highlight emerging evidence on the importance of human capital investment for promoting equity and environmental sustainability – both of which will be critical for sustaining economic growth through the 21st century.

Economics and human capital

Sparked by the Industrial Revolution in Britain, the last two hundred years have been an era of unprecedented global economic development. After millennia of global economic stagnation (Clark 2007), gross domestic product (GDP) in today's advanced economies grew from $1,000 per capita in 1820 to $21,000 in 2000 (Maddison 2001). Meanwhile, GDP per capita in today's developing countries grew only fivefold over that period. Thus, while average standards

11

of living measured by income, life expectancy and other development indicators show unambiguous improvement in the global average standard of living, the benefits of growth have been unevenly distributed within and among nations (Ostry, Berg and Tsangarides 2014).

Although the income gap between early industrialisers and today's developing economies remains large, over the past fifty years developing countries have exhibited growth rates far exceeding the average growth of Western Europe since industrialisation (1.7% per year, Maddison 2001). Between 1980 and 2012, average annual GDP per capita growth was 2.8% in low- and middle-income countries, compared to 1.8% in high-income countries (World Bank database). However, there has been wide divergence in rates of development since 1960, when per capita income in some East Asian economies (Taiwan, South Korea) was comparable to that of poor African countries like Ghana, Senegal and Mozambique (Rodrik 1995). In the following decades, some East Asian incomes have grown rapidly to reach the level of leading Western economies, while GDP per capita in sub-Saharan Africa is less than 5% of the average income in high-income countries (US$37,000).

In response to these global disparities, growth accounting has emerged as a major branch of modern macroeconomics. This subfield analyses the drivers and mechanisms behind economic growth to understand why average national or subnational incomes diverge over time. Similarly at the microeconomic level, labour economics focuses on understanding variation in earnings of individual economic agents.

Central to both of these subfields of economics is the concept of human capital. Capital refers to factors of production that generate goods or services in an economy – the various inputs that produce economic output. For decades, mainstream economic theory had emphasised physical, tangible capital (machinery, natural resources, factories, equipment, etc.) as the strongest source of short-run economic growth, with exogenous and inexplicable technological change serving as the catalyst for long-term growth.

However, intangible capital also has a role in the history of economic thought. As far back as 1776, Adam Smith formally recognised the productive capabilities of the populace as part of a nation's capital stock in *An Inquiry into the Nature and Causes of the Wealth of Nations*. Nelson and Phelps (1966) emphasised the role of human capital in enabling economies to adopt technologies and new ideas discovered elsewhere, while Romer (1989) identified the causal role of human capital as the generation of ideas and development of new products. Mankiw (1995) defines 'knowledge' as the sum total of technological and scientific discoveries (written in textbooks, scholarly journals, websites, etc.), and defines 'human capital' as the stock of knowledge that has been transmitted from those sources into human brains through learning. More recently, Frank and Bernanke (2007: 355) define human capital as "an amalgam of factors such as education, experience, training, intelligence, energy, work habits, trustworthiness, and initiative that affect the value of a worker's marginal product." In short, human capital includes anything that contributes to the productive capacity of the workforce.

Still, from its foundations in the early modern work of Ricardo, Mills and Malthus until the 1960s, economic thought on the wealth of nations has been dominated by the study of tangible capital accumulation, and the human element of economic growth was largely neglected. Led by Schultz (1961), Denison (1962), Becker (1964) and others, there was a renaissance for human capital in economics in the 1960s, from which emerged a debate on the role of education in development. There is a broad distinction between theories by which observable measures of human capital like schooling are directly useful to economic productivity (Becker 1964; Nelson and Phelps 1966) and those in which they are not. According to Marxian critiques, the positive relationship between education and earnings reflects schooling's role in building workers' capacity to obey orders and adapt in capitalist societies (Bowles and Gintis 1975).

At the other extreme of the productive human capital theory of education is the signalling theory, in which education serves as a signal of inherent ability and is not independently useful in production processes (Spence 1973). By this set of theories, education does not increase the productive capacity of an economy but instead overcomes labour market information imperfections. Individuals with high levels of innate ability elect to invest in education to signal to employers that they are of high skill and deserving of higher wages. The disutility of education is prohibitive for low-ability workers, so they do not invest in education and earn lower wages. Although the bulk of empirical studies support education as a productivity-enhancing investment (as we discuss below), evidence does not unambiguously support human capital theory over signalling theory nor are the theories necessarily mutually exclusive.

Human capital and the labour market

While the central economic role of education had been posited centuries before, human capital did not take off in economic modelling until the 1960s, in part because of difficulties with measurement. Among the earliest applications of human capital in economics was explaining differences in wages in developed economies. Mincer (1974) proposed that years of schooling could be used as a measure of human capital, claiming that the primary reason that children attend school is for labour market preparedness. Based on that idea, he formulated the human capital earnings function below:

$$\ln y = \ln y_0 + rS + \beta_1 X + \beta_2 X^2$$

where ln is the natural log operator, y is an individual's labour market earnings, s is the individual's years of schooling, X is years of labour market experience and y_0 is the expected base wage of a person with no experience and no education. The variables r and B_1 are the average returns to education and work experience respectively, which the earnings function is designed to estimate.

This type of equation has been specified in a number of ways, including different characteristics such as ethnicity and sex, and is the basis for a vast literature testing the relationship between education and earnings. For decades to follow, empirical analysis of human capital would be largely based on education attainment as measured by years of schooling (for micro studies) and average years of schooling (for macro studies).

Psacharopoulos and Patrinos (2004) analyse the wealth of evidence that emerged from applying the Mincerian approach to a variety of labour markets. Their review finds a 10% increase in earnings for an extra year of education at the mean of the distribution (i.e., $r = 0.1$). A survey by Card (1999) similarly finds a 6–10% return to an additional year of education. However, the marginal return to a year of schooling varies substantially by geography, by level of education, by demographic group and over time. Psacharopoulos and Patrinos (2004) find a premium to female education (9.8% return to a year of female education versus 8.7% for male education). Psacharopoulos and Patrinos (2008) show that returns to education are higher in low-income areas; labour market evidence for working males from the 1960s to the 1990s suggested that in developing countries, primary education provided the highest returns, with the marginal benefit from education diminishing in years of schooling.

However, more recent evidence from the 1990s and 2000s (summarised by Colclough, Kingdon and Patrinos 2009) suggests that there has been a shift in the relative returns of different education levels, with postprimary returns rising above primary school returns in developing countries. For example, Behrman, Birdsall and Szekely (2003) find that for a sample of 18

Latin American countries, returns to tertiary education increased greatly throughout the 1990s while returns to primary and secondary education fell. This could be interpreted as evidence that skill-biased technological change has increased demand for workers with higher education (lowering the relative wages of low-skilled workers), that expansion of primary education has saturated labour markets with workers with basic education (increasing the premium for workers with postprimary education), that the quality of primary education has declined (reducing the productivity gains associated with primary school completion) or some combination of these explanations.

There is also growing evidence that early childhood education yields high economic returns (Heckman 2011). Based on longitudinal data from the High/Scope Perry randomised controlled experiment, Schweinhart et al. (2005) find that American children raised in poverty that completed a high-quality preschool program had significantly higher rates of employment in adulthood than individuals in the control group. Median annual income for the preschooled group was also 36% higher at age 40. Furthermore, comparison of the two groups' propensity for crime and health suggests large public externalities of early childhood education. Similar evidence for developing countries is scarce.

While Mincer-type studies provide empirical evidence that education accounts for much of the variation in individual earnings in developing countries, they face several limitations. The approach only allows the study of formal employment with wage data (often for males) and thus does not capture the returns to education within the informal economy. However, there is emerging evidence that education increases informal sector productivity (e.g., De Brauw and Rozelle 2006 for rural China; Nguetse Tegoum 2009 for Cameroon; Arbex et al. 2010 for Brazil; and Yamasaki 2012 for South Africa), as well as ability to secure employment in the growing digital economy (Results for Development Institute 2013). There is also an established literature (reviewed in Huffman 2001) showing that schooling improves farm yields, particularly in settings where farmers are able to benefit from their education by accessing affordable agricultural technologies.

Furthermore, the Mincerian approach was critiqued by Heckman, Lochner and Todd (2003) for not being able to capture the complexity of modern labour markets. Mincerian returns do not capture the value of education in increasing a worker's employment stability (discussed for the US case in Cairo and Cajner 2014), which is particularly relevant in postrecession economies with high unemployment rates. In addition, it is unclear that years of schooling (which do not account for quality of education) are the optimal measure of an individual's human capital. There is growing focus on microeconomic data that captures skill levels acquired through education (an output of education) rather than years spent in school (an input into education). This measurement issue with respect to human capital is discussed further later in this chapter.

Human capital and economic growth

In the 1950s, Solow (1956) and Swan (1956) investigated the divergence in economic production of nations using exogenous growth models, which specify per capita income as a function of physical capital, size of the labour force, assumed (exogenous) rates of technological progress, saving, population growth and residual total factor productivity (which augments the productivity of capital and labour). All inputs into economic production are thus tangible (physical capital and labour). The basic exogenous growth model is applied to data by regressing log per capita income on log savings rate and log of the sum of the depreciation rate, technological growth rate and population growth rate.

As discussed in Mankiw, Romer and Weil (1992), empirical testing shows that the basic exogenous growth model has promising features but is ultimately inconsistent with reality. A typical

Solow-Swan regression explains half of the variation in per capita income, with the remaining half attributed to the residual (total factor productivity). However, the estimated magnitudes of the effects of saving and labour force growth are too great. The difference in income between India and the USA, for example, could only be explained by implausibly huge differences in physical capital stock. By the basic specification, the implied value of capital's share of income is 0.6, but globally the true value of capital's share of income is about 0.3.

$$Y(t) = K(t)^{\alpha} \left(A(t) L(t) \right)^{1-\alpha}$$

where $Y(t)$ is output for time period t, $K(t)$ is the physical capital stock at time t, $L(t)$ is the size of the labour force at time t, $A(t)$ is a residual, catchall variable, and α is the elasticity (respon-siveness) of output with respect to physical capital. A and L grow over time at exogenous rates g and n, respectively, while a constant fraction of output s is saved in each period and invested in physical capital.

These weaknesses suggest that the basic Solow-Swan model omits key variables that account for economic growth. Given the strong evidence that education is a central determinant of earnings at the individual level, it should follow that human capital is a determinant of income and growth of nations and thus should be included in Solow-Swan-type growth account-ing exercises. This idea was tested empirically by Mankiw, Romer and Weil (1992), who aug-mented the Solow-Swan exogenous growth model with the inclusion of human capital. They tested the relationship between investment in human capital and economic development using cross-country regressions that included human capital as a factor of production along with labour and physical capital. The rate of accumulation of human capital is proxied in their aug-mented model by a country's proportion of youth (age 12–17) currently enrolled in secondary school multiplied by the fraction of the working-age population that is of secondary-school age (15–19). They find that for nonoil based economies, a 1% increase in their proxy measure raises GDP per working-age person by 0.66%. This effect is highly statistically significant.

$$Y(t) = K(t)^{\alpha} H(t)^{\beta} \left(A(t) L(t) \right)^{1-\alpha-\beta}$$

where $Y(t)$ is output for time period t, $K(t)$ is the physical capital stock at time t, $L(t)$ is the size of the labour force at time t, $H(t)$ is the human capital stock at time t, $A(t)$ is a residual, catchall variable, α is the elasticity of output with respect to physical capital and β is the elasticity of output with respect to human capital, while constant fractions of output s_k and s_h are saved in each period and invested in physical and human capital, respectively.

Accounting for human capital eliminates the original Solow-Swan model's issues. The aug-mented model explains 80% of the cross-country variation in per capita income. The implied value of alpha falls to a more reasonable 0.33 in the augmented model. The elasticity of output with respect to saving rises from 0.5 in the original version to 1, so implausibly large differences in physical capital stocks are no longer needed to explain the difference in income between poor and rich countries (negating the India-USA issue described earlier).

Following Mankiw et al. (1992), there has been a wealth of research on the relationship between human capital and development at the macro level, using various proxies for human capital. Psacharopoulos and Arriagada (1986) proposed average years of schooling as a proxy for human capital in 1986, and Barro and Lee developed a dataset on average years of schooling for the working-age population in 146 countries since 1950 (first published in 1993). That dataset has become a dominant proxy for human capital in cross-country growth modelling. For exam-ple, Glaeser et al. (2004) use average years of schooling to proxy for human capital and estimate a 25–35% return for an additional year of schooling for the average worker, while Barro (2013) adds additional variables to the model (e.g., rule-of-law, trade openness, government spending) and estimates a lower return of 19%.

These macroeconomic estimates of the return to human capital tend to be two to three times higher than the returns estimated in microeconomic studies (see above). Some of the difference between micro- and macroestimates of the return to human capital can be ascribed to externalities of education. Wage-based estimates of the return only capture the benefit to the individual who receives the education. But when one person is educated, the economic benefits extend beyond the individual. Knowledge is a public good – nonrivalled and nonexcludable (Arrow 1962). It was for this reason that Lucas (1988) modelled human capital with externalities in his endogenous growth model so that every individual is more productive if surrounded by highly skilled workers.

As at the micro level, there is evidence at the macro level that the effect of education varies by level of education, by demographic group and by initial level of development. Barro (2013) finds for a sample of 100 countries, primary education has no discernible impact on growth, but the large sample may mask country-specific nuances. For example, in a case study of India, Self and Grabowski (2004) find strong growth effects of primary education using data from 1966 to 1996, with weaker evidence of growth effects for higher levels of education. Petrakis and Stamatakis (2002) suggest that the relationship between attainment at different levels of education and growth depends on the development level of the country. They conclude that basic education is critical for catch up (giving workers the skills necessary to apply technologies at the global frontier); for advanced economies, growth is dependent on higher education (which gives workers the skills to innovate and push the global technological frontier forward). As with the microevidence discussed earlier, there is evidence of a growth premium to female education on top of higher earnings – 0.2% of GDP per year – in part due to the demographic dividend (lower total fertility rates) and better childcare associated with female education (Lawson 2008).

One possible issue with these studies based on cross-country regressions is the measures of human capital that they use. Mankiw et al., for example, use secondary school enrolment of working-age people as a proxy for human capital. This limits the model's implications for developing countries because it omits the variation in primary school enrolment among them. More generally, enrolment and years of schooling are flawed measures of human capital. They record inputs, rather than the outputs of an education system, and quality of education is unaccounted for. Indeed, as we discuss in the following section, the results of economic growth models are sensitive to the choice of human capital measure, and thus reliably supporting human capital theory with empirical evidence hinges on the ability to accurately measure human capital.

Measurement of human capital

Although the studies discussed in the previous section support a strong role of human capital in development, robustly identifying that relationship has been fraught with methodological difficulties. The first is an econometric issue, while the second is a measurement issue. Great strides in addressing both issues have been made over the past two decades.

The first obstacle to estimating the impact of human capital accumulation on development is the question of endogeneity. Does a positive association between education indicators and development reflect that education fuels growth, or rather is it a result of countries investing in education only after they have developed the economic means to do so? Easterlin (1981) uses historical data (1830–1975) from 25 large countries to demonstrate a link between primary school enrolment and economic growth, noting that the spread of public schooling preceded economic take off in industrializing nations and that in many countries high growth was not followed by a surge in primary enrolment. Barro (1997) uses lagged variables to arrive at the same conclusion.

More recently, econometricians have been able to address this sequencing issue formally. Advances in econometric methodology (panel methods, instrumental variables), coupled with improvement in data from developing countries, have enabled human capital to be included in economic modelling in a way that was not previously possible and strengthened the evidence on the relationship between human capital and development. In a recent example, Barro and Lee (2010) control for the simultaneity of education and development using the 10-year lag of parents' education as an instrumental variable for the current level of education and estimate a 5–12% macroeconomic return for an additional year of average schooling. Gennaioli et al. (2013) apply a newly constructed panel dataset on regional education attainment and growth to a variation of the Lucas model of human capital externalities. They conclude that human capital has strong explanatory power for regional variation in incomes, providing a regional-level extension of national-level studies of the 1990s and 2000s.

The second modelling issue is with measurement of human capital. Enrolment ratios and years of schooling (the two most common proxies of human capital stock) are inputs into the production of human capital rather than an output of an individual's education. Furthermore, in attempting to identify the relationship between human capital and economic growth based on cross-country data on years of schooling, modelling implicitly assumes that the value of a year of schooling in the United States and the Democratic Republic of Congo is the same. It also values a year in primary school identically to a year in a PhD programme (Aghion et al. 2009).

Massive expansion of education in developing countries and rising average school lifespans have not led to economic growth across the board (Hanushek 2013). Net enrolment rates in developing countries have increased markedly over the past two decades (UNESCO 2013), with the adjusted net primary enrolment rate in developing countries rising from 80% in 1990 to 90% in 2011 (UN 2013). Domestic and donor resources devoted to education have also increased drastically, reflecting a growing recognition of the importance of basic education for development. Between 2002 and 2010, overseas development assistance for basic education more than doubled from $1.7 billion in 2012 constant dollars to $3.8 billion in 2010 (OECD DAC 2014). Education expenditure as a share of total government spending in developing countries increased from 4.3% in 1999 to 4.7% in 2011 (UNESCO 2013). However, commensurate economic growth has not clearly followed in many cases. This is not necessarily an indictment of human capital theory, but it does raise questions about how human capital can be modelled to capture the true benefits of education. Quality of education cannot be proxied by easily measured inputs to education like pupil-teacher ratios and per capita education expenditure because these variables are not closely linked to student performance (Glewwe et al. 2011).

Due to these concerns, years of schooling is no longer the unequivocal standard measure for estimating rates of return to human capital. In recent years, there has been a shift to measuring human capital through outcomes of education rather than inputs. Underscoring the importance of accounting for quality of education in human capital measures, Hanushek and Wössmann (2007) estimate a strong relationship between education achievement (an output of the education system) and economic growth using internationally comparable mathematics and science test scores (TIMSS and PISA) as a proxy for quality of education. Deficits in human capital are much more pronounced between high- and low-income countries when taking into account skills rather than years of schooling, and regressions using education achievement have three times more explanatory power than regressions using education attainment to measure human capital. Hanushek (2013) estimates that a one standard deviation difference in test performance raises a country's average GDP per capita growth by 2% per year.

Box 2.1. Human capital through the ages

Following its development and application to modern economies, human capital theory has been applied to premodern periods. Initially, a major critique of human capital theory was that it was not applicable to the Industrial Revolution because there was no discernible link between literacy and economic growth in early modern Europe (Allen 2003). However, research from the past decade is overturning this conclusion using alternative measures of human capital and looking at other periods of economic history.

Using panel data on regional enrolment rates from 1816 to 1882, Becker et al. (2009) find that formal education played a key role in the Industrial Revolution, with relatively high preindustrial levels of education accelerating the adoption of technology in Prussia. Squicciarini and Voigtlander (2014) also attempt to resolve the puzzle of human capital being a strong predictor of economic development today but apparently not during the Industrial Revolution. They ascribe the failure to detect the impact of workforce skills on economic growth in previous studies to their lack of attention to the top of the skills distribution – entrepreneurs and engineers who spurred early modern economies from stagnation to growth. Using data from France, they find that the presence of knowledge elites strongly predicts regional economic growth after 1750. This highlights one of the shortcomings of using population averages (even for measures of skills rather than years of schooling) – they fail to account for the distribution of education (see Hanushek and Wössmann 2007 for a discussion of the effects of the distribution of education on economic growth).

The link between education and growth has also been demonstrated for other periods of economic history. Saller (2008) looks at the experience of the Roman Empire and argues that investment in human capital, which was higher than at any time in Europe before 1500, was responsible for the empire's economic growth. Meiji Japan's rapid and widespread adoption of Western technology was enabled by its educated workforce (World Bank 1991), and Botticini and Eckstein (2004) provide a human capital interpretation of Jewish economic history. Becker and Wössmann (2009) show that Protestant economic prosperity in the late 19th century can be attributed to high levels of literacy, while Boustan et al. (2013) discuss the role of education in increasing labour productivity and labour participation over the course of American history. Finally, a number of studies highlight the importance of broad-based human capital accumulation in fuelling the East Asian economic miracles between the 1960s and 1990s (Tilak 2002).

Critically, Hanushek and Wössmann (2012) find that attainment measured by years of schooling becomes statistically insignificant in explaining national differences in per capita income if measures of achievement are included in the model. This means that education is only a determinant of growth insofar as schooling leads to acquisition of skills and that it is cognitive skill acquisition, rather than time spent in school, that drives earnings and economic growth. There is also some evidence that certain subjects have greater impact on growth than others. Barro (2013) finds a strong impact of performance on science tests in particular on economic growth.

Indeed, these measurement issues can go a long way to explain evidence against human capital theory. For example, the apparent paradox of a large stock of human capital (measured by years of schooling) and the economic collapse of the Soviet Union (Meliantsev 2004) may be explained by the deteriorating quality of education in the late Soviet era (Didenko et al. 2013).

Signalling theory (see above) has some traction at higher levels of education – for example, Holmes (2013) finds that, using education attainment, the expansion of higher education has no statistically significant relationship with economic growth. However, this result is sensitive to the proxy used for human capital. Technical skills at the end of compulsory education and number of researchers employed are strong predictors of growth, and both of these are related to the quality of higher education. When human capital is properly measured such that it captures variation in skills imparted by education, the relationship between education and development is robust. That relationship is likely to become even clearer if advances in measurement and data collection allow nonformal education, lifelong learning and training to be accounted for.

In this context, the work of the UIS-Brookings Task Force on Learning Metrics is highly relevant. Established to develop metrics for a possible post-2015 education goal, this task force recommends expanding the set of measures of global education progress to include learning (rather than just access). It calls for education systems to offer children the opportunity to master competencies across seven domains of learning (physical well-being, social and emotional, culture and the arts, literacy and communication, learning approaches and cognition, numeracy and mathematics, and science and technology) and proposes that a small set of learning indicators be tracked in all countries (Learning Metrics Task Force 2013). It remains to be seen if these recommendations will be adopted, but their very preparation is indicative of the paradigm shift from focus on years of schooling to the emphasis on learning outcomes.

Human capital and the quality of growth

As was discussed earlier, the late modern era (since the Industrial Revolution) has been one of unprecedented average economic growth. In addition to being unevenly distributed geographically, that growth has been highly uneven over time, scattered with booms and deep depressions. Disruptions in growth have caused massive welfare losses in advanced and developing economies alike, from the Great Depression in the 1930s to the Global Recession of the late 2000s. Droughts and floods also pose a threat to growth in developing countries that are ill-prepared to mitigate the effects of extreme weather events. Thus far, the discussion has centred on the impact of human capital accumulation and economic development as measured by growth rates of GDP per capita, primarily through the improvement of labour force productivity. However, there are other channels through which human capital could improve economic growth, especially given recent global trends – equity and disaster resilience.

The first channel is the interaction between equity and education. Income inequality has been increasing over the past several decades in developing and advanced economies alike. Ostry, Berg and Tsangarides (2014) find lower net inequality is strongly associated with faster and more durable growth. Inequality in education is a significant source of income inequality. A study of Brazil (World Bank 2004) found that 29% of Brazil's excess income inequality (relative to the United States' income inequality, which is itself high by global standards) was due to education inequality, 32% was due to skill premia (the wage differential by skill level in Brazil is 50% higher than in the United States) and 39% was due to public transfers (e.g., urban subsidies, retirement pensions). Since skill premia are influenced in part by distribution of education (education influences the relative supply of skills), the majority of income inequality in Brazil stems from education. To the extent that equity is growth enhancing, human capital also makes a contribution to economic growth through its impact on equity (Patrinos and Psacharopoulos 2011). There is also some support for the notion that economic inequality plays a causal role in economic crises (Atkinson and Morelli 2011), which have periodically disrupted the global economy for centuries.

Fifty-seven million children of primary school age are out of school, mostly in the poorest countries. Of the 700 million that are in school, 250 million are not learning the basic skills expected from primary education (UNESCO 2013). Out-of-school children represent the most extreme form of education inequality, and recent estimates show that they impose a significant economic loss in the poorest countries. Using Mincerian wage premium estimates collected by Psacharopoulos and Patrinos (2004), Thomas and Burnett (2013) estimate that countries with the highest rates of out-of-school children will forfeit as much as 10% of GDP per year when today's out-of-school children join the labour force, due to lost earnings. The loss is even greater when accounting for nonmarket externalities of education.

The rising threat of climate change presents a second channel through which education promotes quality of growth. The Fifth Intergovernmental Panel on Climate Change (IPCC 2013) assessment report concludes that climate change will result in more intense droughts and heatwaves, causing food and water shortages, with a 2°C increase in global mean temperature resulting in the economic loss of about 1% of annual GDP. Blankespoor et al. (2010) demonstrate that controlling for income and weather patterns, developing countries with high levels of female education fare better against natural disaster so that economic growth is not reversed by climate change.

These recent studies on equity and disaster resilience support Thomas et al.'s view that by ensuring that high growth rates in developing countries are sustainable and durable, a strong and equitable human capital stock is essential not only for the quantity of growth but also for the quality of growth (Thomas et al. 2000).

Conclusion

Sen (1999) argues that development is the progressive activation of a range of freedoms, including political rights and choice, freedom from coercion and freedom from income poverty. Through education, individuals can acquire the capabilities needed to exercise many freedoms and access fundamental human rights (Sen 2005). Thus, education is both a means and an end to development (UNESCO and UNICEF 2007). This chapter has focused on theory and evidence on education as a means for economic growth, reviewing evidence on the channels that have a causal impact on development. Quality education not only gives individuals the tools they need to earn a living and support their families (Psacharopoulos and Patrinos 2004) but generates social externalities that benefit communities, nations and the world (Barro 2013) – especially the education of adolescent girls (Lloyd 2009). In short, human capital is an essential contributor to both the quantity and quality of growth in developing countries.

The evidence reviewed in the chapter shows that human capital theory, by which investment in human productive capacity "leads to a more mobile, adaptable, autonomous, creative workforce that is capable of learning new tasks and applying technologies and equipment to boost production" (Dickens et al. 2006), is a compelling explanation for economic growth. However, it is not the only explanation. The geographical view of development (Kamarck 1976; Sachs 2003; Collier 2006) emphasises the importance of ecology, climate and disease environment. By the institutional view of development (e.g., Acemoglu, Gallego and Robinson 2014), the organisation of society, and the incentives for production that it provides to individuals and firms, is a key driver of economic growth. By social capital theory (Putnam 1995; Dasgupta 2000), trust and social cohesion drive economic growth by enabling economic transactions. These views are not mutually exclusive and should be seen as complementary to human capital theory. While human capital accumulation is an essential ingredient for social progress, in recent decades the economic records of the Indian state of Kerala, the Philippines, Sri Lanka (Tan 1999) and Cuba (Madrid-Aris 1998) have shown that it is not sufficient for economic growth. It must be combined with inclusive institutions and policies that enable individuals to apply their education to economic opportunities.

The question of human capital sits at the nexus of the debate on equity versus efficiency in economic development. Growing evidence (discussed above) suggests that no such trade-off exists and that equity and growth are development goals that may be pursued in tandem. This makes investment in education (and especially basic education in developing economies) a clear priority. Schooling is heavily subsidised in developing and advanced economies alike, and the strong evidence on private and public returns to human capital supports public spending on education. On top of this, there are nonmarket aspects of well-being that are influenced by the accumulation of human capital, such as health and civic engagement (reviewed in Burnett, Guison-Dowdy and Thomas 2013), that are not accounted for in GDP per capita growth (although they may influence economic growth).

Since the 1960s, human capital has established a firm role in economic theory. Our understanding of the central role that human capital plays across the dimensions of economic development continues to evolve, and measurement issues continue to be addressed. The latest economic research shows that education that imparts productive skills plays a key role in strengthening and accelerating economic development. It is thus essential that policymakers and education specialists collaborate to ensure that quality education is provided to build the stock of human capita, and raise the level and quality of economic growth where it is needed most.

References

Acemoglu, D., Gallego, F., Robinson, J., 2014. Institutions, human capital and development. *Annual Reviews of Economics* 6, 875–912.

Aghion, P., Boustan, L., Hoxby, C., Vandenbussche J., 2009. Causal impact of education on economic growth: evidence from US. In: Roemer, P. and Wolfers, J. (Eds.) *Brookings Papers on Economic Activity*. Brookings Institution, Washington.

Allen, R., 2003. Progress and poverty in early modern Europe. *Economic History Review* 56, 3, 403–443.

Arbex, M., Galvao, A., Gomes, F., 2010. Heterogeneity in the returns to education and informal activities. Insper Working Paper No. 221/2010, IBMEC, Sao Paulo.

Arrow, K., 1962. Economic welfare and the allocation of resources for invention. In: Groves, H. (Ed.) *The Rate and Direction of Inventive Activity*. Princeton University Press, Princeton.

Atkinson, A., Morelli, S., 2011. Economic crises and inequality. Human Development Research Paper No. 106, UNDP, New York.

Barro, R., 1997. *Determinants of Economic Growth*. MIT Press, Cambridge, MA.

Barro, R., 2013. Education and economic growth. *Annals of Economics and Finance* 14, 2, 301–328.

Barro, R., Lee, J., 2013. A new data set of educational attainment in the world, 1950–2010. *Journal of Development Economics* 104, 184–198.

Becker, G., 1964. *Human Capital*. Columbia University Press, New York.

Becker, S., Wössmann, L., 2009. Was Weber wrong? A human capital theory of Protestant economic history. *Quarterly Journal of Economics* 124, 2, 531–596.

Behrman, J., Birdsall, N., Szekely, M., 2003. Economic policy and wage differentials in Latin America. Center for Global Development Working Paper No. 29, Center for Global Development, Washington.

Blankespoor, B., Dasgupta, S., Laplante, B., Wheeler, D., 2010. Adaptation to climate extremes in developing countries: the role of education. World Bank Policy Research Working Papers No. 5342, World Bank, Washington.

Botticini, M., Eckstein, Z., 2004. From farmers to merchants: a human capital interpretation of Jewish economic history. Centre for Economic Policy Research Discussion Papers No. 5571, Centre for Economic Policy Research, London.

Boustan, L., Frydman, C., Bureau, N., Margo, R.A., 2013. *Human Capital in History: The American Record*. University of Chicago Press, Chicago.

Bowles, S., Gintis, H., 1975. The problem with human capital theory: a Marxian critique. *American Economic Review* 65, 2, 74–82.

Burnett, N., Guison-Dowdy, A., Thomas, M., 2013. *A Moral Obligation, an Economic Priority: The Economic Cost of Out-of-School Children.* Education Above All Foundation, Doha.

Cairo, I., Cajner, T., 2014. Human capital and unemployment dynamics: why more educated workers enjoy greater employment stability. Federal Reserve Board Finance and Economics Discussion Series No. 2014–9, Federal Reserve, Washington.

Card, D., 1999. The causal effect of education on earnings. In: Ashenfelter, O. and Card, D. (Eds.) *Handbook of Labor Economics.* Volume 3A. Elsevier, Amsterdam.

Clark, G., 2007. *A Farewell to Alms: A Brief Economic History of the World.* Princeton University Press, New Jersey.

Colclough, C., Kingdon, G., Patrinos, H., 2009. The pattern of returns to education and its implications. Research Consortium on Educational Outcomes and Poverty Policy Brief No. 4, University of Cambridge.

Collier, P., 2006. Africa: geography and growth. *TEN* Fall, 18–21.

Dasgupta, P., 2000. Economic progress and the idea of social capital. In: Dasgupta, P. and Serageldin, I. (Eds.) *Social Capital: A Multifaceted Perspective.* World Bank, Washington.

De Brauw, A., Rozelle, S., 2006. Reconciling the returns to education in off-farm wage employment in rural China. Department of Economics Working Papers No. 2006–03, Williams College.

Denison, E., 1962. The sources of economic growth in the US and the alternatives before us. *Economic Journal* 72, 288, 935–938.

Dickens, W., Sawhill, I., Tebbs, J., 2006. *The Effects of Investing in Early Education on Economic Growth.* The Brookings Institution, Washington.

Didenko, D., Foldvari, P., Van Leeuwen, B., 2013. The spread of human capital in the former Soviet Union area in a comparative perspective: exploring a new dataset. *Journal of Eurasian Studies* 4, 123–135.

Easterlin, R.A., 1981. Why isn't the whole world developed? *The Journal of Economic History* 41, 1, 1–19.

Frank, R., Bernanke, B., 2007. *Principles of Microeconomics.* McGraw-Hill/Irwin, New York.

Gennaioli, N., Shleifer, A., 2013. Human capital and regional development. *The Quarterly Journal of Economics* 128, 1, 105–164.

Glaeser, E., LaPorta, R., López-de-Silanes, F., Shleifer, A., 2004. Do institutions cause growth? *Journal of Economic Growth* 9, 3, 271–303.

Glewwe, P., Hanushek, E., Humpage, S., Ravina, R., 2011. School resources and educational outcomes in developing countries: a review of the literature from 1990 to 2010. NBER Working Paper No. 17554, National Bureau of Economic Research, Washington.

Hanushek, E., 2013. Economic growth in developing countries: the role of human capital. *Economics of Education Review* 37, 204–212.

Hanushek, E., Wössmann, L., 2007. The role of education quality in economic growth. World Bank Policy Research Working Paper No. 4122, World Bank, Washington.

Hanushek, E., Wössmann, L., 2012. Do better schools lead to more growth? Cognitive skills, economic outcomes, and causation. *Journal of Economic Growth* 17, 4, 267–321.

Heckman, J., 2011. The economics of inequality: the value of early childhood education. *American Educator* Spring, 31–47.

Heckman, J., Lochner, L., Todd, P., 2003. Fifty years of Mincer earnings regressions. National Bureau of Economic Research Working Paper No. 9732, National Bureau of Economic Research, Washington.

Holmes, C., 2013. Has the expansion of higher education led to greater economic growth? *National Institute Economic Review* 224, 1, R29–47.

Huffman, W., 2001. Human capital: education and agriculture. In: *Handbook of Agricultural Economics.* Volume 1. Elsevier, Amsterdam.

Intergovernmental Panel on Climate Change Working Group, 2013. *Climate Change 2013: The Physical Science Basis.* Fifth Assessment Report, Stockholm.

Kamarck, A., 1976. *The Tropics and Economic Development.* Johns Hopkins University Press, Baltimore.

Lawson, S., 2008. Women hold up half the sky. Goldman Sachs Global Economics Paper No. 164, Goldman Sachs, New York.

Learning Metrics Task Force, 2013. *Toward Universal Learning: Recommendations from the Learning Metrics Task Force.* UNESCO Institute for Statistics, Montreal, and Center for Universal Education at the Brookings Institution, Washington.

Lloyd, C., 2009. *New Lessons: The Power of Educating Adolescent Girls.* Population Council, Washington.

Lucas, R., 1988. On the mechanics of economic development. *Journal of Monetary Economics* 22, 3–42.

Maddison, A., 2001. *The World Economy: A Millennial Perspective.* OECD Development Centre, Paris.

Madrid-Aris, M., 1998. Investment, human capital, and technological change: evidence from Cuba and its implications for growth models. In: *Cuba in Transition.* Volume 8. Association for the Study of the Cuban Economy, Miami.

Mankiw, N., 1995. The growth of nations. *Brookings Papers on Economic Activity* 1, 275–326.

Mankiw, N.G., Romer, D., Weil, D.N., 1992. A contribution to the empirics of economic growth. *The Quarterly Journal of Economics* 107, 2, 407–437.

Meliantsev, V., 2004. Russia's economic development in the long run. *Social Evolution and History* 3, 1, 106–136.

Mincer, J., 1974. *Schooling, Experience and Earnings.* National Bureau of Economic Research, New York.

Nelson, R., Phelps, E., 1966. Investment in humans, technological diffusion, and economic growth. *American Economic Review* 51, 2, 69–75.

Nguetse Tegoum, P., 2009. Estimating the returns to education in Cameroon informal sector. Paper presented at GLOBELICS Conference, Dakar, October.

OECD DAC, 2014. Stat Aid statistics database.

Ostry, J., Berg, A., Tsangarides, C., 2014. Redistribution, inequality, and growth. IMF Staff Discussion Note No. 14/02, IMF, Washington.

Patrinos, H., Psacharopoulos, G., 2011. Education: past, present and future global challenges. World Bank Policy Research Working Paper Series No. 5616, World Bank, Washington.

Petrakis, P., Stamatakis, D., 2002. Growth and educational levels: a comparative analysis. *Economics of Education Review* 21, 5, 513–521.

Psacharopoulos, G., Arriagada, A., 1986. The educational composition of the labour force: an international comparison. *International Labour Review* 125, 5, 561–574.

Psacharopoulos, G., Patrinos, H., 2004. Returns to investment in education: a further update. *Education Economics* 12, 2, 111–134.

Psacharopoulos, G., Patrinos, H., 2008. Education and human capital. In: Dutt, A. and Ros, J. (Eds.) *International Handbook of Development Economics.* Edward Elgar, Cheltenham.

Putnam, R., 1995. Bowling alone: America's declining social capital. *Journal of Democracy* 6, 1, 65–78.

Results for Development Institute, 2013. *Training Models for Employment in the Digital Economy.* Results for Development Institute, Washington.

Rodrik, D., 1995. Getting interventions right: how South Korea and Taiwan grew rich. *Economic Policy* 20, April, 55–107.

Romer, P., 1989. Human capital and growth: theory and evidence. National Bureau of Economic Research Working Paper No. 3173, National Bureau of Economic Research, Washington.

Sachs, J., 2003. Institutions don't rule: direct effects of geography on per capita income. National Bureau of Economic Research Working Paper No. 9490, National Bureau of Economic Research, Washington.

Saller, R., 2008. Human capital and the growth of the Roman economy. Princeton / Stanford Working Papers in Classics.

Schultz, T., 1961. Investment in human capital. *American Economic Review* 51, 1–19.

Schweinhart, L., Montie, J., Xiang, Z., Barnett, W., Belfield, C., Nores, M., 2005. *Lifetime Effects: The High/Scope Perry Preschool Study Through Age 40.* High/Scope Press, Ypsilanti.

Self, S., Grabowski, R., 2004. Does education at all levels cause growth? India, a case study. *Economics of Education Review* 23, 1, 47–55.

Sen, A., 1999. *Development as Freedom.* Oxford University Press, Oxford.

Sen, A., 2005. Human rights and capabilities. *Journal of Human Development* 6, 2, 151–166.

Smith, A., 1776. *Inquiry into the Nature and Causes of the Wealth of Nations.* Knopf, New York.

Solow, R., 1956. A contribution to the theory of economic growth. *Quarterly Journal of Economics* 70, 1, 65–94.

Spence, M., 1973. Job market signaling. *Quarterly Journal of Economics* 87, 3, 355–374.

Squicciarini, M., Voigtländer, N., 2014. Human capital and industrialization: evidence from the Age of Enlightenment. National Bureau of Economic Research Working Paper No. 20219, National Bureau of Economic Research, Washington.

Swan, T., 1956. Economic growth and capital accumulation. *Economic Record* 32, 2, 334–361.

Tan, J., 1999. Human capital formation as an engine of growth: the East Asian experience. Institute of Southeast Asian Studies, Singapore.

Thomas, M., Burnett, N., 2013. *Exclusion from Education: The Economic Cost of Out-of-School Children in 20 Countries.* Education Above All Foundation, Doha.

Thomas, V., Dailami, M., Dhareshwar, A., López, R., Kaufmann, D., Kishor, N., Wang, Y., 2000. *The Quality of Growth.* Oxford University Press, New York.

Tilak, J., 2002. *Building Human Capital in East Asia: What Others Can Learn*. World Bank, Washington.

UNESCO, UNICEF, 2007. *A Human Rights-based Approach to Education for All*. UNESCO, Paris.

UNESCO, 2013. *Teaching and Learning: Achieving Quality for All*. Education for All Global Monitoring Report 2013/2014. UNESCO, Paris.

United Nations, 2013. *The Millennium Development Goals Report 2013*. United Nations, New York.

World Bank, 1991. *World Development Report 1991: The Challenge of Development*. World Bank, Washington.

World Bank, 2004. *Inequality and Economic Development in Brazil*. World Bank, Washington.

Yamasaki, I., 2012. The effect of education on earnings in the informal sector in South Africa. Paper presented at the annual meeting of the Comparative and International Education Society, San Juan, April.

3

EDUCATION AS A HUMANITARIAN RESPONSE AS A GLOBAL OBJECTIVE

Colin Brock

Man is without doubt the most intriguing fool there is.

(Mark Twain 1909)

Introduction

There is also no doubt that education is a human right, as declared by the United Nations early in its existence (1948). The problem is that what was in mind was formal education, with basic schooling as the minimum, but schooling is not the same as education. Indeed it is only a small part of the education of an individual and then only if it can be obtained at all. Successive Global Monitoring Reports (GMRs), covering the progress of the international policy Education for All (EFA) since the onset of the third millennium, continue to show that many countries have yet to achieve universal basic education. Gender parity at that level, a Millennium Development Goal (MDG) target for 2015, is also far from being achieved.

However, Article 26 of the Universal Declaration of Human Rights (UDHR) is worth looking at in detail because it provides a benchmark for what was regarded by the UN as a humanitarian response to educational need. Article 26 of the declaration has three parts and reads as follows:

1. *Everyone has the right to education. Education shall be free, at least in the elementary and fundamental stages. Elementary education shall be compulsory. Technical and professional education shall be made generally available and higher education shall be equally accessible to all on the basis of merit.*
2. *Education shall be directed to the full development of the human personality and to the strengthening of human rights and fundamental freedoms. It shall promote understanding, tolerance and friendship among all nations, racial and religious groups, and shall further the activities of the United Nations for the maintenance of peace.*
3. *Parents have a prior right to choose the kind of education that shall be given to their children.*

It is immediately clear that this article of the universal declaration is problematic in terms of its own internal consistency as well as in its relation to a concept of education as a humanitarian response that has to do with such situations as conflict and post conflict; refugees and internally displaced peoples; disadvantaged children; natural disasters; and indigenous minorities, nomads and other travelling communities. Such a notion lay behind the decision of the writer to name his UNESCO Chair at the University of Oxford (2005–12) *Education as a Humanitarian Response* and to give that title also to one of what is today called the 'impacts' of the project: a series of 13 books, only two of which remain to be published at the time of writing (see, for example: Paulson 2012; Demirdjian 2012; Smith-Ellison and Smith 2013; Smawfield 2013; Griffin 2014). In all these, and other relatively short-term responses to need, the objective is nearly always the restoration of the *status quo ante*. This means that the opportunity to reform educational provision, usually formal schooling, is missed. But the replacement of the existing system is what recipient governments expect and require. Humanitarian agencies, whether multinational or bilateral, have no authority to reform in relation to possible future needs of the country concerned.

However, the core book introducing the series, *Education as a Global Concern* (Brock 2012), takes a much broader and more fundamental view that, in effect, responds to aspects of Article 26 in the Universal Declaration of Human Rights, though it was not directly designed so to do. The aim of this chapter is also to take this broader, indeed global, view of education as a humanitarian response to the unprecedented and mostly imminent challenges of the twenty-first century. These are challenges to human and environmental survival and sustainability (Martin 2006). Some are widely known and contended in the wider media, such as climate change and biodiversity survival. Others relate to the equally challenging effects of powerful political and corporate self-interest on educational policy that severely constrain the potential contribution of education, in all its forms, to play its crucial part in reaching the fundamental goal in saving planet Earth and its human populations.

Education is not a panacea, yet much of the widespread conventional wisdom thinks it is. But in its different forms, it is an essential dimension of survival. In this holistic sense, it has to be humane to play its vital part. This is the wider scenario of education as a humanitarian response.

Homo sapiens, wisdom and education

Arguably the most outrageous and arrogant act of humankind has been to designate its own species as 'sapiens': wise. Successive writers, including Orr (1994) and Martin (2006), have illustrated this delusion in respect of what education should be for.

> Much of the current debate about educational standards and reforms, however, is driven by the belief that we must prepare the young only to compete in the global economy. That done, all will be well, or so it is assumed. But there are better reasons to reform education which have to do with the rapid decline of the habitability of the earth. The kind of discipline-centred education that enabled us to industrialise the earth will not necessarily help us to heal the damage cause by industrialisation.
>
> (Orr 1994: 2)

Orr goes on to quote Kennedy (1993), who calls for "nothing less than the re-education of humankind" (p. 331). That education needs, by definition, to be humanitarian.

Yet education, that is to say 'learning and teaching', is clearly something that already sets humankind well above all other forms of animal life. Unfortunately, humans do not see themselves as animals even though they are more destructive of their own species, and of the environmental systems on which they depend, than is any other species. Current (2014) bloodletting in the Middle East, Ukraine and Central Africa testify to this. Article 26/2 of the abovementioned UN declaration calls for education to work for the maintenance of peace between nations and racial and religious groups. But the UN is a club of nations, as implied in Article 26/1, regarding the provision of formal education, and Article 26/3 potentially compromises this by stating that parents should have the right to choose the kind of education their children receive.

Certainly education of all forms can lead to the acquisition of knowledge and skills. A crucial question is, what has this led to? There seem to be three main products: data, cleverness and technological advance, and these are not being utilised wisely. Morozov (2014) outlines this in the title of his book: *To Save Everything Click Here: Technology, Solutionism and the Urge to Fix Problems that Don't Exist.* Or, as Orr puts it:

> The truth is that without significant precautions, education can equip people merely to be more effective vandals of the earth. If one listens carefully, it may even be possible to hear the Creation groan every year in late May when another batch of smart, degree-holding, but ecologically illiterate Homo Sapiens who are eager to succeed are launched into the biosphere.
>
> (Orr 1994: 5)

Ironically the most crucial product of education is missing, wisdom. Without that, there can be no true species called *Homo sapiens.* Somehow education has to be reformed to enable that essentially humane quality to emerge, and fast. Otherwise it will not only be those currently disadvantaged by poverty, as well as disasters, that need education as a humanitarian response. In fact, we all already do, but Article 26 of the UDHR is unrealistic and unhelpful in this regard, largely due to issues constraining education, especially nationalism, that had developed and become entrenched long before the UN became a belated, though well-meaning, institution.

Issues of scale, imperialism and convention

Education – formal, nonformal and informal – operates on a range of scales from 1) local to 2) internally regional (e.g., the provinces of Canada) to 3) national to 4) externally regional (e.g., the European Union) to 5) global. This has to do with place and space as well as scale, in other words the geography of education (Brock 2013). We need also to consider the temporal scale of educational activity.

One of the roots of the humanitarian problem is the way in which a near global curriculum has emerged over centuries, become a convention serving the interests of nationalism, corporatism and competition and spread by imperialism (Carnoy 1974). This also includes educational aid distributed as part of humanitarian responses to need (Hayter 1971). Indeed Hayter (1981) goes further in identifying humanitarian aid as a significant contribution to world poverty. According more recently to Birrell (2014), major NGOs are now complicit, favouring "lucrative work on modish concepts such as conflict resolution, capacity-building and governance" (p. 18). He continues: "highly paid charity chiefs cuddle up to governments to promote the illusion they can spur democracy and development despite evidence that torrents of foreign aid prop up repressive regimes, fuel corruption and foster conflict." Birrell's analysis comes directly from the 2014 Report of Médecins Sans Frontières (MSF), an aid agency that is certainly humanitarian and includes health education in its work. The labelling of major aid agencies and NGOs as proxy corporations is certainly true of the multilaterals and bilaterals. Others, officially nonpolitical, have simply grown too big, with massive bureaucracies and management systems derived from the business world. On the other hand, there are thousands of small NGOs throughout the world that operate on a local scale and engender self-help, such as *Practical Action.* The majority are indigenous, local, and are of course exempt from the criticism of MSF.

Practical Action, based at Rugby, UK, and formerly known as *Intermediate Technology*, was founded by E.F. Schumacher, author of *Small Is Beautiful: A Study of Economics as if People Mattered*

(1973). Schumacher's basic tenet was that "production from local resources for local needs is the most rational way of economic life". This could be applied to education, as it is a curious by-product of globalisation in the form of Information Communications Technology (ICT) that a global/local direct connection has developed. This has the potential to bypass the intermediate scale, that of the national. We shall return to that later but first need to consider the dead, and correspondingly inhumane, hand of nationalism on educational development.

The national scale of operation has dominated formal education since the advent of modern Western nation-states in the eighteenth and nineteenth centuries (Green 1990). With respect to Europe, Dodgson (1987) described this development in political geography as moving from control over groups of people to control over territory containing people. Emergent states developed formal education systems using majority vernaculars such as English in England and German in Prussia rather than the exclusive Latin of the privileged minority. Compulsory schooling up to the secondary level with centrally devised, and controlled curricula became the norm. The grip of the churches was gradually overcome so that natural sciences and humanities became part of a curriculum model spread by European colonialism to nearly all parts of the world (Taylor and Flint 2000). The few nations hardly touched by what Altbach and Kelly (1978) termed "classical colonialism", i.e., occupation, such as China and Japan, chose to acquire the European model, termed by Mallinson (1980) the *Western European Idea of Education,* as part of their modernisation revolutions in the late nineteenth century. Thus a virtually universal schooling and curricular model became a near-global convention. The recent advent and increasing influence of the Paris-based Organisation for Economic Co-operation and Development's (OECD) *Programme for International Student Assessment* (PISA) is serving to fortify and spread this conventional curriculum. Indeed it narrows it even further by concentrating on a few subjects that are, purely by conventional wisdom, deemed to be more important than others. According to Meyer and Benavot (2013), most industrialised counties and an increasing number of less developed are operating under the 'global governance' of PISA.

This is highly problematic because it strengthens and exports the conventional idea that a group of subjects, with an elite core, constitute a curriculum. They don't, as Belth (1965) explained half a century ago:

> In addition to the innumerable unconscious absorptions which occur, whatever modes of thinking the student may use are made available to him by the curriculum which is woven about him in the activities of education.
>
> (p. 261)

By education, Belth does not mean only schooling. He means the totality of the learning experience, informal and nonformal as well as formal. In other words, the experience of humanity. School is not society; neither is it community. Consequently, it is not humane in itself, not necessarily in an oppressive sense but in a more subtly invidious way, because the curriculum has become a convention driven by nationalism and competition. It is not fit in terms of meeting the imminent and unprecedented challenges of the twenty-first century (Brock 2014b).

It is also inhumane in that the purpose of formal education has become a cog in the neo-liberal corporatist project devoted to increasing profit for the few. Curiously, the educational establishment seems to accept this, but other more perceptive voices do not, such as the author and playwright Alan Bennett (2014):

> I have no time for the ideology masquerading as pragmatism that would strip the state of its benevolent functions and make them occasions for profit. And why roll back the

state only to be rolled by the corporate entities that have been allowed, nay encouraged, to take its place?

(p. 35)

Neoliberalism has become entrenched as a near-global convention not only since its popularisation among the political elite of the USA and UK from the 1980s but in fact dates back at least to the incorporation of state education from the late nineteenth century, beginning in the USA. Indeed, it goes back even further in the sense that the beginnings of formal schooling in medieval Europe emerged under the combined influence of a wealthy, near-universal Catholic Church, with universities devoted to serving that church and merchants seeking numerate and literate employees (Brock 2010). The state education systems that emerged from this became increasingly selective as populations grew with industrialisation and economic diversification. Seeking to serve the economy became a dominant function to the detriment of a liberal education, as Grayling (2002) has observed:

> Education, and especially 'liberal education', is what makes civil society possible. That means it has an importance even greater than its contribution to economic success, which, alas, is all that politicians seem to think it is for.

(p. 157)

As national populations have grown, the condition of increasing anonymity has led to credentialism as the basis for selection for professional and technical employment. This is in harness with other indicators of selection that act as mediators, such as those identified by Hopper (1968) as: 1) aristocratic (by birth); 2) paternalistic (by favour); 3) meritocratic (on pure merit); and 4) collectivistic (by general agreement). Oxenham's (1984) perceptive title *Education Versus Qualifications* also rightly infers that formal teaching and learning have become merely instrumental and technocratic. Certainly they no longer, if they ever did, relate to the call in Article 26/2 of the UDHR that "education shall be devoted to the full development of the human personality", an aspiration that certainly qualifies as humanitarian on a global scale. Being devoted to instrumental ends is unwise, as implied by Martin (2006) in the culminating and overarching of his seventeen challenges of the twenty-first century, namely closing the "skills-wisdom gap".

Global challenges of the twenty-first century

Martin is not the only prominent figure to stress the urgency of identifying and preparing to meet these challenges, but he is the only one to spell out a comprehensive list – seventeen in all – of challenges that face humankind in the short and medium term. But we need first to acknowledge his practical actions, and those of others, in seeking to engender a wider understanding of unprecedented but very likely events.

James Martin, a physicist turned computer scientist, founded and endowed the Oxford Martin School (OMS) in 2005. According to its current website, it now has more than 300 researchers at Oxford and elsewhere "working to address the most pressing global challenges and opportunities of the 21st century". It is necessarily interdisciplinary and requires that "research must tackle issues of a global scale", adding that the OMS was "founded with the belief that this century, and specifically the next two decades, is a crucial turning point for humanity". It has many affiliates, including the Future of Humanity Institute in the Faculty of Philosophy at Oxford, that enquire, according to its website, into the "big-picture questions about humanity and its prospects". That Institute is also connected with The Centre for the Study of Existential

Risk at the University of Cambridge (CSER), founded in 2011 and headed by the eminent cosmologist and astronomer Martin Rees of Trinity College. It could be that James Martin was inspired to act by the book *Our Final Century: Will the Human Race Survive the Twenty-First Century?* (Rees 2003) and the TED lecture of Martin Rees in 2005 on *Is This Our Final Century?* (Rees 2005). At the time, Rees gave the human species a 50/50 chance of surviving this century.

According to its website, CSER "is an interdisciplinary research centre focussed on the study of human-extinction level risks that may emerge from technological advances" by engaging "the best minds across disciplines to tackle the greatest challenge of the coming century: safely harnessing our rapidly developing technological power". Its cofounders, Rees together with Hugh Price (a philosopher) and Jann Tallin (cofounder of Skype), are the subject of an article in *Guardian Weekend* (Martin 2014) by Andrew Martin that also includes Sir Patha Dasgupta, an economist and Cambridge advisor of CSER. It contains some engaging and instructive insights into the risks involved, including an extract from the 2005 Rees TED Lecture:

> In our interconnected world, novel technology could empower just one fanatic, or some weirdo with the mindset of those who now design computer viruses, to trigger some kind of disaster.
>
> (p. 37)

Four other 'worst case possibilities' are discussed: the *disaffected lab worker* who spreads viruses through global air travel; the *termination risk* caused by stratospheric aerosol geo-engineering; *distributed manufacturing* leading to nanoscale manufacture of military grade missiles; *artificial intelligence escaping into the Internet* with devices communicating between themselves. Andrew Martin describes a computer as "a sort of idiot savant". This is important with regard to what has been termed *The Singularity*, "the point at which humans build their last machine, all subsequent ones being built by other machines" (Martin 2014: 41). We will no longer be able to switch them off.

At the level of higher education, but only a tiny part of it in a few universities, there is a hopeful, rapidly emergent sector that recognises the urgency of the range of threats to human and environmental survival, some of them in the very near future. What is also needed is an engagement at all other levels of education with these challenges. Martin (2006: 226–236) has identified the following, presented here in paraphrased form:

1. *The Earth:* stop actions leading to climate change, polluting rivers and lakes, breaching the ozone layer, wasting fresh water.
2. *Poverty:* all nations need to reach a "decent literacy rate" and adequate levels of employment.
3. *Population:* overpopulation needs to be curbed by raising the educational levels of women and improving lifestyles.
4. *Lifestyles:* twentieth century lifestyles cannot be sustained, but technology has the potential to support new, comfortable lifestyles in keeping with sustaining the environment.
5. *War:* the existence of weapons capable of ending civilisation makes this a very different century from any before. Weapons control and eradication is essential for survival.
6. *Globalism:* this is already here but must be adjusted to allow unique cultures to survive. Localism is vital to sustainability. The global/local link is fundamental.
7. *The Biosphere:* global management of the biosphere is essential, including a computer-inventoried knowledge of all species.
8. *Terrorism:* all grade uranium and plutonium must be locked. Causes of terrorism must be eradicated, including mutual respect of all religions for each other to prevent their perversion.

9. *Creativity:* creativity must be supported by current and future levels of technology in the interest of innovative interventions to progress sustainability.
10. *Disease:* increasing potential for pandemics (including terrorist generated) must be resisted by appropriate defences.
11. *Human Potential:* most people today "fall outrageously short of their potential".
12. *The Singularity:* this is the chain reaction of computer intelligence. It needs to be controlled to enable appropriate education of young people to cope with self-evolving technologies.
13. *Existential Risk:* there are risks that could lead to the termination of the human species and demand immediate resolution as to controlling science. This is essential because current estimates give us only a 50/50 chance.
14. *Transhumanism:* nanotechnology will change human capability, creating advanced civilizations, but also an increasingly wider gap between rich and poor.
15. *Advanced Civilization:* this will permeate cyberspace and affect decisions relating to the management of planet Earth.
16. *Gaia:* we must learn to live within the constraints of the Earth's natural balance of species and environments. Failure to do so will be catastrophic.
17. *The Skill-Wisdom Gap:* science and technology are accelerating furiously, but wisdom is not. We need more interdisciplinarity in education and less corporate greed in the economy.

Clearly, the conventional and near-global view as to what education is for is totally inappropriate if we subscribe to the current view that it is for the support of national and corporate wealth, power and competition. Lack of substantial and rapid reform towards enabling education to meet the challenges listed above would, in effect, be a crime against humanity. Richard Aldrich (2010), the distinguished historian of education, has identified two phases of the purpose of education to date and a third that needs to be activated without delay. They are: education for salvation, education for development and education for survival. We are still in the second phase; to enable us to move into the third, we need nothing short of a curricular revolution on a global scale, one that will serve "a notion of wealth that includes natural capital" (Martin 2014: 41) and not just global neoliberalism with its purely economic objective of profit. To consider this, we need to briefly reprise the issue of selection and move on to subjects and curriculum.

Selection, subjects and curriculum

The nature of curriculum, defined in the *Oxford English Dictionary* both as "a collection of subjects" and "any educational activity," is determined by the aforementioned underlying function of education systems to be selective. This may be explicit, where the outcome of examinations of various kinds determine different pathways with clear titles such as 'academic' and 'technical/vocational'. Or they may be implicit as described by Sir Ken Robinson when, in his celebrated TED lecture of 2006, he illustrated the higher status of the 'academic' by suggesting that the ultimate product of selection turns out to be university professors. As we have seen above with reference to the Oxford Martin School and the Centre for the Study of Existential Risk, it is at this level that vital information about the imminent challenges of the twenty-first century is being illuminated. But to meet those challenges on a global scale involves a distillation to the level of curricula in schools. But at this level, selection is never purely on educational grounds, as encapsulated in the question posed by Timmons (1988): "Selection, educational or social?", and the duplicity involved:

> Educational systems in highly industrialized countries face a constant and probably insoluble problem. They have to provide at least a semblance of equality of educational

opportunity and they have also to ensure that occupations of various levels of responsibility and skill are catered for. In other words they have to act as sorting houses. They
are vast selection mechanisms.

(p. 157)

Despite Article 26/3 of the UDHR, Timmons contends that "selection cannot remain solely
parental" (p. 158), though in England, certainly, parental wealth and social class, working through
a private sector that is uniquely large, this is a determining factor. For the majority, however,
progressive selection through schooling is determined by examination scores and the capacity of
institutions at each successive stage. Even if fair, these tests tell us only a tiny proportion of what
each individual actually knows. In reality, one of the basic problems of humanity dealing with
itself in a fair way is that we just don't know what any individual actually knows nor often what
talents lie latent. Howard Gardner (1983) made a valuable and humane contribution to dealing
with this problem with his concept of multiple intelligences, but it has rarely been embraced by
the educational establishment. Somehow we have to subvert the global conventional curriculum
from within.

The first problem to be faced is that of subjects, or as Hunt (1970) put it: "the tyranny of
subjects". His main argument is that individual subjects do not fit with the way people, and
especially children, learn most effectively, cutting into the more natural way in which skills are
acquired: "a skill is a useful technique: you acquire it when you need it for a tangible purpose.
A subject is something that educational tradition says you ought to learn whether it is useful or
not" (p. 45), beginning with reading.

Reading has become a subject. You see it as "work", something separate from your
normal play activities. Soon, other subjects are added. By the time you reach secondary
school, you are confronted with a bewildering array of them. They take up most of
your day and they tend to come at you in forty minute slabs. You are expected to be
equally interested in all of them. But not too interested because soon the bell will go:
"Put your books away and get ready for the next lesson". . . . At the end of five years,
if you collect enough certificates, you will be recognized as an educational success. But
what will you really have learned?

(Hunt 1970: 45–46)

Another way of critiquing the concept and practice of subjects is to consider them against
the notion of the seamless coat of learning advocated by Alfred North Whitehead (1929), who
strongly advised against what he called "scraps of information." Evans (1998) encapsulated
Whitehead's contribution in the following terms:

Whitehead wrote of many aims of education but one strikes me as paramount and to
lead to the rest. That aim, which I choose to identify as the principal Whiteheadian
goal, is to achieve a balanced education, the fruit of which is wisdom. Balanced education, as Whitehead advocated it, is one of the right mix of necessary specialisation and
equally important generalisation.

(p. 90)

So there are precedents for advocating a more humane curriculum for what the writer
described as "The Dysfunctional Mainstream" (Brock 2012), but they have been trampled by
the stampede towards international competition based on league tables. All this is leading in the

wrong direction in the face of the challenge of twenty-first century survival, by far the largest humanitarian project yet.

> A radical reform is required not a 'tweaking' here and there because the existing curricular structure has slowly emerged to support numerous nationalisms. So a logical place to begin is to relate Martin's seventeen 21st century challenges to a new curricular scheme. Some can be conflated but none ignored, nor can the fundamental requirement of sufficient levels of literacy and numeracy.
>
> (Brock 2014a: 135)

As the subject components are so conventionally embedded, and also as the timeframe for reform is short, we need to relate clusters of current curricular components to key themes in the discourse of those working on the frontiers of the human and environmental threats in such outposts as The Oxford Martin School and the Cambridge Centre for the Study of Existential Risk. The writer has proposed four clusters for initial discussion (Brock 2014a: 135–136): A. *Communication; B. Gaia and the Biosphere;* C. *Poverty and Population; D. War and Terrorism.* They are all interconnected in that new forms of communication such as advanced ICT and social media are involved, for example, in researching and teaching, formally and informally, about rapid environmental degradation; population pressures due to increasing fertility and massive migration; and violent conflict relating to such issues as religious fundamentalism, water resources and land grabs. We may visit each cluster in turn.

The cluster Communication services everything else. It means a more sophisticated idea of literacy and numeracy that would comprise language, mathematics and ICT in an integrated way, rather than as two 'subjects'. Currently, mathematics is seen as being primarily related to science whereas it is simply a form of communication that uses numbers and symbols rather than words and sounds. Challenge number eleven (11) in Martin's list (the majority of humankind failing massively to reach their full potential) is very clear in terms of mathematics partly because it is seen as something that goes with science in the school curriculum rather than being a form of language and communication. Selected modern languages would be included in this cluster, as would expressive and performing arts. This cluster should be maintained as part of the school curriculum throughout, from primary school to the end of compulsory schooling, as it carries with it the tools of creativity. In the title of his 2006 TED lecture, Sir Ken Robinson asked '*Do Schools Kill Creativity?*' The answer, is, as he argued, 'yes'. Communication skills to serve creativity should also be at the core of further and adult education.

The cluster Gaia and the Biosphere would comprise an integration of the four basic natural sciences. Currently, only three figure in most curricula: biology, chemistry and physics. Geology should be added and act as the core, incorporating physical geography and climatology in providing an environmental context ranging from the edge of the earth's atmosphere to the contents of the earth's crust, or lithosphere. The concept of 'Gaia' put forward by James Lovelock and Lynn Margulis in the 1970s should be the central theme: being a self-regulating complex of organic and inorganic forms that maintains the balance of all forms of life to survive. It is threatened by the reckless activities of Homo sapiens in search of wealth and profit, hence the aforementioned call for an understanding of 'natural capital'. Accepting and understanding climate change, as outlined in *The Goldilocks Planet: The Four Billion Years Story of Earth's Climate* (Zalasiewicz and Williams 2012), is essential at the school level and is perfectly feasible, as well as the necessary balance between the human, animal, plant and marine components of the earth. As Martin (2006) has warned:

> Perhaps the greatest catastrophe that could befall us would be that we inadvertently push Gaia so that positive feedback causes it to become unstable or to change to a

different state. Our Earth may become a roasted planet with tundra, inhabitable only by a small number of humans – probably near the poles.

(p. 234)

He adds: 'Gaia does its own thing and we must learn to live within its constraints' (p. 235).

The third cluster, Poverty and Population, would be served by the social sciences, with demography in the lead assisted by human geography and anthropology, history, economics, politics and sociology. The number of people on the Earth already, together with, in global terms, an exponential rate of growth, likely to reach 10 billion by 2050 (Emmott 2013), is one of the main factors threatening human and environmental survival. Population change and structure should be included rather than just crude overall figures. Issues such as gender balance, age structure, occupational structure and religious affiliation should be included. Of course, this threat of overpopulation, as with that of climate change, is differential in its likely level as between different parts of the world. In crude terms, the already favoured temperate latitudes, including North America, much of Northern and Western Europe and East Asia, may well even benefit from the climate change that seems to be likely. This is engendering complacency and leading to political inaction, a very unwise stance when looked at in terms of the growth of poverty and related human migration.

The final cluster, War and Terrorism, is important because of the propensity of Homo sapiens for violent conflict, destruction and sheer inhumanity on an enormous scale. This is celebrated in conventional curricula lauding success in battles, empire building and subjection. There is a great deal of misinformation in history syllabuses on such issues. To most people, films and television programmes showing violence are widely popular, as are murder mysteries in print. While routine religious issues would be in the previous cluster, issues of fundamentalist and extremist religious views need to be here, both in a historical and contemporary perspective. Terrorism is a feature of modern human society that needs to be studied at this level so as to distinguish it from legitimate defence, as do the actions of some countries to take, or settle in, the territory of others with impunity.

Some might think that the above clusters are no different from existing subjects, but the central point is that they are not being focussed in the same way. It is not beyond the wit of modern humankind, with sophisticated computers at their disposal, to develop school timetables that will allow for a combination of specialist classes in the various disciplines and integrated thematic classes alongside. The balance between these two curricular components would depend on the nature of different subjects, as some require sequential learning and others do not. Certain life-supporting processes such as soil formation, photosynthesis and biodiversity can and should be introduced at the earliest possible stage. They are perfectly amenable to simple and attractive explanation with young children, including field work on site or nearby. The main objective is to shift the meaning of formal schooling from solely preparing for employment in a way that, it is imagined, can contribute to economic capital to add an understanding of the crucial and urgent need to value natural capital.

Conclusion

The discourse above may not have been what most readers had expected from a chapter on education as a humanitarian response. There is nothing wrong with education being part of humanitarian responses to need in situations of disaster or disadvantage such as those listed at the beginning of this chapter. Such work needs to continue and indeed increase, but the argument presented here is that unprecedented challenges that are almost upon us threaten humanity itself. Most of them are the result of human actions. This means that the prime purpose of learning and teaching must be the greatest humanitarian education exercise ever, to save itself and the environment of planet Earth. Ironically, one of the most sophisticated tools yet devised by the cleverness of humankind, the computer, could become the imposter or the saviour. That depends on whether we can control it and avoid the Singularity. If we can, then technological advances may help save us and the planet. If we cannot, then we are doomed, as Emmott (2013) predicts.

James Martin (2006) concluded that the most crucial of his challenges of the twenty-first century is to close the skills-wisdom gap. He was right. Human cleverness can deal with skills development, but only wisdom may save us. We need to earn the title 'sapiens' through bringing creativity to the core of our education, and fast. There is not much time left to exercise education as a humanitarian response for our meaningful survival beyond this century. If we fail, then 'sapiens' will be seen to have been a mere soubriquet.

References

Aldrich, R., 2010. Education for survival: an historical perspective. *History of Education* 39, 1, 1–14.

Altbach, P., Kelly, G., 1978. *Education and Colonialism*. Longman, New York.

Belth, M., 1965. *Education as a Discipline*. Allyn and Bacon, Boston.

Bennett, A., 2014. A private dysfunction. *The Independent,* 19th June, 35–37.

Birrell, I., 2014. The aid corporations. *The Guardian,* 8th August, 28.

Brock, C., 2010. Spatial dimensions of Christianity and education in Western European history, with legacies for the present. *Comparative Education* 46, 3, 289–306.

Brock, C., 2012. *Education as a Global Concern*. Continuum, London and New York.

Brock, C., 2013. The geography of education and comparative education. *Comparative Education* 49, 3, 275–289.

Brock, C., 2014a. Global curricular legacies and challenges for the Twenty-First Century. *Journal of International and Comparative Education* 3, 1, 126–138.

Brock, C., 2014b. Will a neo-liberal economic climate permit education to assist human and environmental survival in the Twenty-First Century? Proceedings of the 2014 Conference of the Southern African Comparative and History of Education Society (SACHES). Forthcoming.

Carnoy, M., 1974. *Education as Cultural Imperialism*. David Mckay & Co., New York.

Demirdjian, L. (Ed.), 2012. *Education, Refugees and Asylum Seekers*. Continuum, London and New York.

Dodgson, R.A., 1987. *The European Past: Social Evolution and the Spatial Order*. Macmillan, Basingstoke.

Emmott, S., 2013. *10 Billion*. Penguin, London.

Evans, M.D., 1998. *Whitehead and Philosophy of Education: The Seamless Coat of Learning*. Rodopi, Amsterdam and Atlanta.

Gardner, H., 1983. *Frames of Mind: The Theory of Multiple Intelligences*. Basic, New York.

Grayling, A.C., 2002. *The Meaning of Things: Applying Philosophy to Life*. Phoenix, London.

Green, A., 1990. *Education and State Formation: The Rise of Education Systems in England, France and the USA*. St Martin's Press, New York.

Griffin, R. (Ed.), 2014. *Education in Indigenous, Nomadic and Travelling Communities*. Bloomsbury, London and New York.

Hayter, T., 1971. *Aid as Imperialism*. Pelican, London.

Hayter, T., 1981. *The Creation of World Poverty*. Pluto, London.

Hopper, E.I., 1968. A typology for the classification of education systems. *Sociology* 2, 1, 29–46.

Hunt, A., 1970. The tyranny of subjects. In: Rubonstein, D. and Stoneman, C. (Eds.) *Education for Democracy*. Penguin, Harmondsworth.

Kennedy, P., 1993. *Preparing for the Twenty-First Century*. Random House, New York.

Mallinson, V., 1980. *The Western European Idea of Education*. Elsevier, Oxford.

Martin, A., 2014. Saviours of the universe. *Guardian Weekend*, 30th August, 35–41.

Martin, J., 2006. *The Meaning of the 21st Century: A Vital Blueprint for Ensuring Our Future*. Transworld Books/Eden Project, London.

Meyer, H.-D., Benavot, A. 2013. *PISA, Power and Policy: The Emergence of Global Educational Governance*. Symposium Books, Oxford.

Morozov, A., 2014. *To Save Everything Click Here: Technology, Solutionism, and the Urge to Fix Problems that Don't Exist*. Penguin, London.

Orr, D.W., 1994. *Earth in Mind: On Education, Environment and the Human Prospect*. Island Press, Washington.

Oxenham, J. 1984. *Education Versus Qualifications*. Allen and Unwin, London.

Paulson, J., 2012. *Education and Reconciliation: Exploring Conflict and Post-Conflict Situations*. Continuum, London and New York.

Rees, M., 2003. *Our Final Century: Will the Human Race Survive the Twenty-First Century?* Basic, New York.

Rees, M., 2005. Is This Our Final Century? http://www.ted.com/talks/martin_rees_asks_is_this_our_final_century

Robinson, K. 2006. Do Schools Kill Creativity? http://www.ted.com/talks/ken_robinson_says_schools_kill_creativity

Schumacher, E.F., 1973. *Small is Beautiful: A Study of Economics as if People Mattered*. Blond and Briggs, London.

Smawfield, D., 2013. *Education and Natural Disasters*. Bloomsbury, London and New York.

Smith Ellison, C., Smith, A., 2013. *Education and Internally Displaced Persons*. Bloomsbury, London and New York.

Taylor, P.J., Flint, C., 2000. *Political Geography. World Economy, Nation-State and Locality*. Prentice Hall, Harlow.

Timmons, G., 1988. *Education, Industrialisation and Selection*. Routledge, London.

Whitehead, A.N., 1929. *The Aims of Education and Other Essays*. Macmillan, London.

Zalasiewicz, J., Williams, M., 2012. *The Goldilocks Planet: the Four Billion Year Story of the Earth's Climate*. Oxford University Press, Oxford.

4

EDUCATION AND POLITICAL DEVELOPMENT

Contradictions and tensions in relationships between education, democracy, peace and violence

Clive Harber

But of all the safeguards that we hear spoken of as helping to maintain constitutional continuity the most important, but most neglected today, is education, that is educating citizens for the way of living that belongs to the constitution in each case. It is useless to have the most beneficial rules of society fully agreed upon by all who are members of the politeia, if individuals are not going to be trained and have their habits formed for that politeia, that is to live democratically if the laws of the society are democratic, oligarchically if they are oligarchic.

(Aristotle 1962: 215–6)

Introduction

Since the end of the cold war in 1989, democracy has increasingly been seen as *the* goal of international political development. The 2010 *Human Development Report*, for example, contained the following indicators of 'empowerment': political freedom and democracy, human rights violations, press freedom, journalists imprisoned, corruption victims, democratic decentralisation and political engagement (UNDP 2010: 164–7). As this suggests, the UNDP now has an explicit model of political development in which the goal for all countries is the attainment, sustainability and consolidation of democracy. Strongly influenced by the ideas of Amartya Sen on human capabilities (Sen wrote the introduction to the twentieth edition), the 2010 report continues its long-term explicit support for democracy:

> The 1990 HDR began with a clear definition of human development as a process of "enlarging people's choices", emphasising the freedom to be healthy, to be educated and to enjoy a decent standard of living. But it also stressed that human development and well-being went far beyond these dimensions to encompass a much broader range

of capabilities, including political freedom, human rights and, echoing Adam Smith, "the ability to go about without shame".

(UNDP 2010: 2)

It notes with approval that the proportion of formal democracies has increased from less than a third of all countries in 1970 to half in the mid-1990s to three-fifths in 2008 and that many hybrid forms have also emerged. Overall, it argues that,

> While real change and healthy political functioning have varied, and many formal democracies are flawed and fragile, policy-making is much better informed by the views and concerns of citizens. Local democratic processes are deepening. Political struggles have led to substantial change in many countries, greatly expanding the representation of marginalised people, including women, the poor, indigenous groups, refugees and sexual minorities.

(UNDP 2010: 6)

Others such as Smith, while acknowledging a broad trend in the direction of democracy, are somewhat less optimistic about the extent to which a process of democratisation has genuinely and consistently taken place in developing countries. He also notes that the Arab Middle East has a huge democratic deficit with no states being rated as 'free' by Freedom House in 2006 (though this situation began to change in 2011). He notes that all but four countries rated as 'not free' in 2006 were developing countries (Smith 2009: 14). Nevertheless, Smith does also recognise that, despite the problems often actually experienced in establishing and maintaining democracies in developing countries, democracy ought to be the goal of political development because of its potential to provide government regarded as legitimate by a population. However, this definition of political development *as* democratisation has not always been so clear and unambiguous, or sometimes even present, in academic and theoretical debates about the nature of political development.

There are many different definitions of democracy (Davies 1999), but the following captures its salient features:

> Democracy embodies the ideal that decisions affecting an association as a whole would be taken by all its members and that they would each have equal rights to take part in such decisions. Democracy entails the twin principles of popular control over collective decision-making and equality of rights in the exercise of that control.

(Beetham and Boyle 1995: 1)

However, what most definitions seem to have in common is a concern with:

- Rights: a set of entitlements that are protected and common to all individuals
- Participation: the free involvement of individuals in the decision-making process
- Equity: fair and equal treatment of individuals and groups
- Informed Choice: the tools to make decisions that are based on relevant information and reason (Davies, Harber and Schweisfurth 2002: 4–9).

Authoritarianism, on the other hand, is a type of political system where the government is not representative of the people and where the final power to remove a government is not in the hands of citizens as voters as there are no genuinely free and fair elections. There is no free political choice, and the government is not accountable to the people for its actions. As the government is not accountable, it is free to do as it wishes; there are therefore no guaranteed human rights. Citizens have little say in how the country is run, and rule is by edict and diktat. Single party and military regimes fall into this category. The surrounding political culture in which such regimes exist is not characterised by full information, regular discussion and encouragement of a range of viewpoints. Diversity, critical thought and participation are not encouraged or are suppressed. The leaders know they have the right answers, and the role of the people is to obey and do what they are told. Those who do not obey are punished accordingly. Communication is top-down and hierarchical. The ideal citizen is one who is submissive, behaves according to the wishes of the regime, respects authority and doesn't ask questions.

Education, political modernisation and democracy

For early post-war political development theorists, a 'modern' state was seen as neither democratic nor nondemocratic. For Coleman, for example, a modern state is a participatory state, but this can either be participation in the coerced, centrally directed and monolithic fashion of an authoritarian state or equally by free and voluntary association in a democratic state. The contribution of education to political development in this case would be the mass inculcation of bureaucratic skills:

> Formal education has a cardinal role to play in producing the bureaucratic, managerial, technical and professional cadres required for modernisation. Moreover, literacy helps a government with penetration, i.e., the population will be sufficiently literate to understand what the government wants them to do.
>
> (Coleman 1965: 17)

While political modernisation theorists were primarily concerned with what constituted the modern polity, the work of Alex Inkeles (1969a, 1969b; Inkeles and Smith 1974) focused much more on individual modernity: what a modern individual might look like and which socialisation agencies most contribute to individual modernity. For him, a modern citizen is one who takes an active interest in public affairs, is informed about important events and participates in civic affairs. Most importantly, the citizen must understand the ways in which bureaucratic rules and impersonal judgement replace treatment based mainly on personal qualities, on family ties or friendship and connections, for the modern polity is "suffused with bureaucratic rationality" (Inkeles 1969a: 1122), whether this citizen lives in a democratic or authoritarian state. In his empirical work, he found education to have the strongest relationship of all variables to the possession of modern (i.e., bureaucratic) attitudes, values and behaviour. This is partly because the pupil at school learns new skills such as reading, writing and arithmetic so that he or she will be able to "read directions and instructions and to follow events in the newspaper," but also because of the bureaucratic nature of the hidden curriculum:

> School starts and stops at fixed times each day. Within the school day there generally is a regular sequence for ordering activities: singing, reading, writing, drawing, all have their scheduled and usually invariant times. Teachers generally work according to this

plan. . . . Thus, principles directly embedded in the daily routine of the school teach the value of planning ahead and the importance of maintaining a regular schedule.

(Inkeles and Smith 1974: 141)

More recently, and reflecting the discussion concerning increased democratisation discussed in the introduction, the development of modern, organisational and bureaucratic skills and attitudes has been seen as a necessary basis for the subsequent development of democratic states and political systems. Leftwich (1998), for example, returns to modernisation theory to argue that unless certain socioeconomic and political preconditions exist that are associated with development towards a 'modern' society, such as an ethic of science and rationality, industrialisation, urbanisation, bureaucratisation, differentiation and specialisation of social structures, the principles of individualism and political stability, then democracy will not take root and succeed. Without an existing, relatively modern social and economic infrastructure and accompanying values and behaviours, attempts at political democratisation will fail as they will not have the required social foundations to build on. He argues:

> And the history of developing societies in the last 30 years suggests that it would be foolhardy to ignore some of the insights of that large body of theoretical and empirical scholarship on modernisation. . . . For whatever its many limitations, modernisation theory in general terms assumed the intimacy of politics with other social and economic processes, especially in the course of change, not its extrusion from them.
>
> (1996: 21)

The true extent to which schools in developing countries can actually perform this role of modernising bureaucratic socialisation is open to some question, considering that they themselves are not completely sealed off from the surrounding society and inevitably also reflect both its 'traditional' and 'modern' norms and behaviours in their daily practices (Harber 2014). However, if formal education potentially contributes to democracy mainly indirectly through providing the basic, modern bureaucratic and organisational skills, attitudes and behaviours upon which more explicitly democratic values might then be built, then its role is necessary but not sufficient and there is a need for a more explicitly democratic role for education. Onto a modern, efficient bureaucratic institutional base must be added knowledge and experience of explicitly democratic values and practices in order to contribute to a democratic political culture as well as a bureaucratic, modern one for, as Diamond (1993) has argued:

> Prominent theories of democracy, both classical and modern, have asserted that democracy requires a distinctive set of political values and orientations from its citizens: moderation, tolerance, civility, efficacy, knowledge, participation.
>
> (p. 1)

A review of empirical evidence examining possible links between education and democracy (Harber and Mncube 2012) concluded that the weight of the evidence seemed to point generally in a positive direction between more education and more stated support for democracy and to a positive relationship between higher levels of educational provision and a greater chance of the existence and maintenance of a democratic system of government. However, these studies largely left unclear exactly *how* education contributes to democracy. What macro cross-national studies carried out by economists and political scientists tend to exclude is consideration of what goes on *inside* education. Crucial here is the *type* of education experienced; of particular importance in this regard is the relationship between the internal micropolitical structures, processes and cultures of formal education and the type of people and citizens that result.

Education and types of political learning

Does education contribute to the learning of democratic skills and values? Here we must initially distinguish between three different types of political learning – political indoctrination, political socialisation or political education. We can define political indoctrination as an attempt to intentionally inculcate values and beliefs as facts or truths. The process may involve deliberately falsifying or ignoring evidence, as well as presenting it in a biased way. Historically, this process has been associated with authoritarian/totalitarian states such as Nazi Germany and Soviet Russia where individuals have little access to alternative viewpoints. Political socialisation is the learning of preferences and predispositions towards political values and attitudes, though often in contexts where other viewpoints are available. It is just that some ideas and values are taken more seriously than others. The ethos of schools in a particular country, for example, might sometimes provide cooperative experiences for children or even teach about the benefits of cooperation. Nevertheless, at the same time an overwhelmingly daily emphasis and priority is given to examinations, class rankings, prizes and competitive sports children experience and learn that competition is far more important in life than cooperation. Both indoctrination and socialisation assume a 'correct' answer to social and political questions that young people must learn to accept as correct and the only right answer – the answer provided by those with power and authority.

Schools can, and do, attempt to socialise or indoctrinate a whole series of messages about, for example, nationalism and national identity, attitudes towards other nations, gender, race and ethnicity, religion, economic systems, equality and inequality, war and peace, political participation and leadership. They can do this through the selection of subjects taught in the curriculum, through the content and interpretation of each subject, through the values in textbooks, through the talk and behaviour of teachers, through teaching methods, through the organisational structure and processes of the school, through the symbols displayed in the school (flags, posters, pictures), or through the content of assemblies and the nature of extracurricular activities (for numerous further detailed examples how political socialisation takes place in schools in developing countries see Dawson, Prewitt and Dawson 1977; Fagerlind and Saha 1989; Harber 1989; Bush and Salterelli 2000; Harber 2004).

Unlike political indoctrination and socialisation, a genuine education for democracy is not a form of social and political control. It does not aim for the inculcation of a right answer or a particular viewpoint. It is an attempt to create critical awareness of a political phenomenon by open, balanced discussion of a range of evidence and opinions. It encourages individuals to make up their own minds about issues after considering the arguments and evidence. Education for democracy is not neutral – no education is neutral – but it does not, either deliberately or by default, transmit one-sided views of substantive values (e.g., in relation to controversial issues such as privatisation, the environment, nuclear weapons or abortion) as 'true.' Its values are procedural and concerned with how issues are discussed and how people relate to each other, and it operates according to democratic citizenship values such as the celebration of social and political diversity, mutual respect between individuals and groups, regarding all people as having equal social and political rights as human beings, respecting evidence in forming their own opinions and respecting the opinions of others based on evidence, being open to changing one's mind in the light of new evidence and possessing a critical and analytical stance towards information. Democratic citizenship values include having a proclivity to reason, open-mindedness and fairness and the practice of cooperation, bargaining, compromise and accommodation.

Education for democracy?

To what extent then do schools in developing countries actually educate for democracy – or is their role more one of authoritarian socialisation? Let us begin by describing what a democratic school might look like based on Davies, Harber and Schweisfurth (2002, 2005), Trafford (2003), Davies and Kirkpatrick (2000) and Davies (1995). However, it is important to bear in mind that no two democratic schools will be identical as, by definition, certain aspects and characteristics will be decided within the school itself.

First of all, a democratic school would make clear and explicit its commitment to the values of education for democracy in its published documents – its prospectus, mission statement, etc. These would stress the procedural values of democracy, including the regular, free but polite exchange of views and opinions. Its structures and practices would then involve a significant sharing of power over decision making between key groups – staff, pupils and parents. In practice – in most schools in most countries – this would mean a significant shifting of power away from senior management and staff to others, particularly pupils. At the whole-school level, this might well necessitate some form of freely elected school council where, depending on the size of the school, pupils and staff were represented and some form school governing body where staff, pupils and parents were represented. Such bodies would have some power of decision making and rule making over meaningful educational areas of concern such as budgets, staffing, curriculum, pupil and staff discipline/codes of conduct and the use of premises, not just more minor matters like social events or the school tuck shop. The operation of such bodies in terms of language used and scope of decision making might well vary according to the age of the pupils involved, but age is not a reason for excluding pupils from decision making.

A democratic school culture or ethos would also be characterised by democratic relationships built on trust and mutual respect, and therefore corporal punishment would be absent as would other forms of physical punishment and all forms of bullying, whether staff to pupil, pupil to pupil, or pupil to staff. More peaceful forms of discipline such as peer mediation and restorative justice would tend to prevail instead. At the classroom level, pupils would have a say in making class rules for classroom behaviour – a learning contract – and some say about curriculum content (what was to be learned and when), which classroom teaching methods were used and which methods of assessment were used. As a result, more democratic schools tend to be characterised by more classroom variety and engagement. Also, in the classroom, teaching and learning would not shy away from controversial issues, but there would be a clear understanding of the ways they were to be discussed and debated by both staff and pupils. As well as experiencing more democratic relationships in the classroom as a result of the above, knowledge of how wider democracy works would also form part of the curriculum.

For all this to work, staff, students and parent governors would need to be explicitly trained in democratic skills or capabilities such as speaking skills and putting a case, listening skills, chairing skills, organising and planning skills, assertiveness and conflict resolution skills. No single school would probably ever completely match this model, and each would have its own characteristics, some less democratic and some perhaps even more so.

Harber and Mncube (2012) provide examples of such democratic schools from India and Ecuador before discussing an evaluation of UNICEF Child Friendly Schools in 150 public or state schools in six developing countries – Nigeria, South Africa, the Philippines, Thailand, Guyana and Nicaragua (Osher et al. 2009). UNICEF based the CFS framework on the 1990 Convention of the Rights of the Child, as well as other international human rights instruments and declarations. CFS are based on three interrelated principles:

- Democratic participation – as rights holders, children and those who facilitate their rights should have a say in the form and substance
- Child-centeredness – central to all decision making in education is safeguarding the interest of the child
- Inclusiveness – all children have a right to education.

There was a great deal of evidence that heads and teachers speak the language of CFS and that most schools in the six countries encouraged students' active engagement with teachers using child-centred instructional techniques and creating environments that encourage active learning as well as trust and respect. However, 'although teachers endorse active learning, traditional notions of effective instruction persist' (Harber and Mncube 2012: 74), and school heads and teachers identified the lack of trained teachers who can implement child-centred instructional methods as a challenge in all six countries. Moreover, specific UNICEF/CFS in-service training on participatory and student-centred teaching seemed to have been the main catalyst for change and was necessary because of poor quality initial teacher education in this respect. Student or learner support for the idea that they experienced various forms of child-centred teaching ranged from 73% to 92% across countries (Harber and Mncube 2012: 81).

There was also evidence of students taking an increasing role in decision-making activities through bodies like school councils or school committees, though it is important to note that the examples of activities that were used were limited to fundraising, celebratory activities, beautifying the school compound and peer tutoring. Interestingly, when asked about how safe, inclusive and respectful the school was, between 19% and 56% of the students opted for 'needs improvement' while only 0–8% of head teachers and 7–53 % of teachers (7–21% excluding South Africa) did (Harber and Mncube 2012: 23–26). Again perceptions of gender inclusivity and equality were much less marked among pupils than teachers and heads (Harber and Mncube 2012: 29). More than two-thirds of students in each country reported that adults in their schools supported them, listened to them and cared about them (though obviously a third did not think this).

A further review of key aspects of education: educational policy; democratic school leadership; whole-school decision making and pupil voice; curriculum decision making; methods of classroom teaching and learning; democratic discipline; democratic teacher professionalism; explicit programmes of civic education; the development of a democratic school culture; teacher education; and school inspection found many positive examples of democratic practice in developing countries. However, throughout the discussion of positive examples of what can be done, it had to be noted that these remain in a minority and that there remain many obstacles to the democratic reform, or perhaps democratic transformation, of education in developing countries (Harber and Mncube 2012: 3).

Authoritarian education

For many, probably most, learners in schools in developing countries, education is more of an authoritarian form of political socialisation. Whereas elite private schools socialise their pupils in terms of confidence, experience and expectations of leadership and social connections (Caddell 2006; Kitaev 2007), the authority structure of formal education for many is quite different:

> In terms of schooling, the dominant or hegemonic model globally, with exceptions that will be discussed later in the book, is authoritarian rather than democratic. Education for and in democracy, human rights and critical awareness is not a primary characteristic of the majority of schooling. While the degree of harshness and despotism within authoritarian schools varies from context to context and from institution to institution, in the majority of schools power over what is taught and learned, how it is taught and learned, where it is taught and learned, when it is taught and learned and what the general learning environment is like is not in the hands of pupils. It is predominantly government officials, headteachers and teachers who decide, not learners. Most schools are essentially authoritarian institutions, however benevolent or benign that authoritarianism is and whatever beneficial aspects of learning are imparted.
>
> (Harber 2004: 24)

A review of literature on schooling in the same book that included Africa, Asia, the Middle East, South and Central America and the Caribbean provided considerable evidence in support of this argument. In many such countries, an additional factor was the colonial history of education. By the 1930s, colonialism had exercised its sway over 84.6% of the land surface of the globe (Loomba 1998: 15). When formal education was eventually provided, missionary schools and those of the colonial state were used to control local populations by teaching the superiority of the culture of the colonising power and by supplying the subordinate personnel necessary for the effective functioning of the colonial administration (Altbach and Kelly 1978). In a study of the ex-British colony of Trinidad and Tobago, for example, the author argues that:

> Schooling was intended to inculcate into the colonised a worldview of voluntary subservience to the ruling groups, and a willingness to continue to occupy positions of on the lowest rungs of the occupational and social ladder. A number of effective strategies were used in the process, but the most significant among these was the instructional programmes and teaching methodologies used in colonial schools . . . Values, attitudes and behaviour were highlighted such as the habits of obedience, order, punctuality and honesty.
>
> (London 2002: 57)

Some of the characteristics of colonial schooling in Trinidad and Tobago outlined by London include mindlessness, verbatim repetition, character development, mastery of rules as a prerequisite for application, use of abstract illustrations, monotonous drill, inculcation of specified norms for cleanliness and neatness and harsh discipline. He concludes by arguing that schooling is one of the places where colonial forms and practices have persisted and remained essentially the same throughout the postcolonial period.

A similar authoritarian stress on conformity and obedience existed, for example, in British India (Alexander 2000: 92), Francophone Africa (Moumouni 1968) and Portuguese Mozambique (Azevedo 1980; Searle 1981; Barnes 1982). In a study of contemporary schooling in India, Mali, Lebanon, Liberia, Mozambique, Pakistan, Mongolia, Ethiopia and Peru for DFID/Save the Children, the authors emphasise the continuation of models of classroom discipline and teaching methodology first instigated under colonialism (Molteno et al. 2000: 13).

Further detailed, a review of schooling in developing countries (Harber and Mncube 2012; Harber 2014) suggested that there is a significant authoritarian historical legacy and that serious obstacles remain to more democratic forms of education at the school level. Examination of whole school organisation, ethos and culture; school discipline and corporal punishment; classroom teaching methods and assessment; teacher education; continued use of colonial language of instruction; and politics, resources and culture concluded that while:

> Schools can potentially contribute to democracy and democratisation in a number of ways. If efficiently organised and run, pupils can learn the bureaucratic organisational skills necessary for the functioning of any modern institution. On top of, or as well as this, schools can also operate not only in an efficient and competent manner but also more democratically through shared power of decision-making. Unfortunately . . . many (probably the majority) of schools in developing countries do not at present provide a sufficiently robust or consistent model or experience of a well organised democracy to make a significant contribution to the development of a more democratic political culture. There are still many barriers and obstacles to overcome before formal education can play a significant part in exposing the majority of young people to education for democracy.
>
> (Harber and Mncube 2012: 128)

Hawkins (2007) further argues that the traditional, nondemocratic model of schooling persists, is dominant and is taken for granted. In discussing what he terms 'The Intractable Dominant Educational Paradigm,' he recounts a research project in Ethiopia where he was regularly reminded by Ethiopians that they were one of the only African nations never to be colonised by the West and that therefore they did not suffer from many of the postcolonial legacies found in other African and developing countries. Yet visits to schools and colleges revealed little that was truly Ethiopian – indeed, they were like schools anywhere in the world, only poorer. When pressed as to the rationale of models from the West (or global north), the answer almost invariably was "so we can develop like them" (Hawkins 2007: 137).

Hawkins argues that the features of this dominant paradigm that exists almost everywhere, despite the political nature of the regime, are that:

- An authoritarian relationship often lies at the core of the teacher-learner interaction;
- Teachers are generally insecure because of a lack of training and poor remuneration;
- Teaching methods do not generally benefit from knowledge of cognitive psychology and child development;
- Teachers generally discourage discussion and questioning, and adhere to textbooks;
- A principal function of schooling is to select entrants to the next educational level;
- The selection is through a highly competitive examination system that requires the reproduction of rote learning rather than critical thought;
- The main activities of the formal school system are directed towards preparing pupils for these examinations; and
- Students and parents are preoccupied with certificate status rather than with the essence of what is taught (Hawkins 2007: 150–1).

The problem, according to Hawkins, is that this model of schooling has come, almost universally, to be regarded as the only possibility, the only model of a 'real' school.

Authoritarian schooling and violent conflict

This predominantly authoritarian school structure and ethos also has implications for peace and violent conflict. Many, if not most, violent conflicts in recent decades have occurred in 'developing' countries. Much conflict has taken place in what are often referred to as 'fragile states,' i.e., where the state and government are not seen as providing the functions and services that would be expected of a 'normal' or more secure or developed state, e.g., Somalia (Bengtsson 2011). The 2011 Education for All Global Monitoring Report was entitled *The Hidden Crisis; Armed Conflict and Education* (UNESCO 2011) and specifically looked at the issue, both in terms of the impact of war on education and education's role in either helping to increase or decrease the chance of violent conflict.

In terms of the impact on education, over the decade to 2008, 35 countries experienced armed conflict, of which 30 were low- and middle-income countries. 42% of out-of-school children live in conflict-affected, low-income countries. The average duration of violent conflicts in these countries is twelve years, the entire primary and secondary school cycle. Only 79% of young people are literate in conflict-affected poor countries, compared to 93% in other poor countries. Schools and schoolchildren are often seen by combatants as legitimate targets, in clear violation of international law. Over 43 million people have been displaced by armed conflict, and refugees and internally displaced people face major barriers to education. In 2008, only 69% of primary school-age refugee children in UNHCR camps were attending primary school (UNESCO 2011: 2).

It has been argued for some time that formal education has the contradictory potential to contribute both to peace and violent conflict by, for example, promoting a culture of democracy and peace on the one hand and militarisation and ethnic conflict on the other (Bush and Salterelli 2000; Harber 2004). As UNESCO put it,

> Education has the potential to act as a force for peace – but too often schools are used to reinforce the social divisions, intolerance and prejudices that lead to war. No country can hope to live in peace and prosperity unless it builds mutual trust between its citizens, starting in the classroom. . . . Schools should be seen first and foremost as places for imparting the most vital of skills: tolerance, mutual respect and the ability to live peacefully with others.
>
> (UNESCO 2011: 3)

The authoritarian structure of schooling has been seen to contribute to violent conflict in a number of contexts. Matsumoto's (2011) study of postconflict Sierra Leone asks whether education is making a positive contribution to development there. Matsumoto is critical of prewar schooling for contributing indirectly towards the war because of its divisive and elitist nature and because of the gap between the expectations created and the realities of the labour market. He describes the postwar educational changes that have taken place, including an attempt at greater vocationalism, but is doubtful whether they will work because of the prevalence of 'Sababu' or social connections in getting employment – who you know is more important than what you know. However, at one point he touches on a significant internal aspect of schooling in Sierra Leone that has resonance elsewhere. Good students – those with a 'blessing' – are perceived to be those that obey teachers, the principal and others. Elsewhere, Wright (1997) is very critical of the prewar education system in Sierra Leone for having an overemphasis on conformity and sycophancy that has helped to facilitate a population that is too docile in the face of dictatorial leaders, even noting that the very violent Revolutionary Front had "an unusually high proportion of ex-teachers and ex-students in its ranks" (1997: 25).

Paulson (2011) examined the 20-year violent conflict between governments and Shining Path guerrillas in Peru where there was a Truth and Reconciliation Commission following the end of the fighting. Shining Path had a great deal of support membership among teachers and:

> It helped that Shining Path indoctrination mirrored the authoritarian, didactic and unquestionable pedagogic style that had long characterised teaching and learning in Peru's state schools.
>
> (Paulson 2011: 130)

The Truth and Reconciliation recommended a move away from such authoritarian practices to greater democratisation in school in its final report in 2003, but nothing much has happened subsequently – "a real contribution to reconciliation via education reform is not evident in Peru" (Paulson 2011: 145).

Even studies that have examined the potential role of schooling in 'building back better' in postviolent conflict countries have found problems in going beyond restoring conventional forms of schooling. For example, the final three chapters of Paulson's book on education, conflict and development (2011) all focus on northern Uganda. The section makes clear the enormous demands made on teachers in simply coping with and trying to help traumatised children when the teachers themselves have not been well trained in such areas and lack motivation and morale. The discussions also pose fundamental questions about whether the present, predominantly authoritarian schools in Northern Uganda are contributing, or could contribute, to peace building in the sense of developing a more peaceful society in the medium and longer terms. The continued use of corporal punishment doesn't help. Indeed, a separate study of an explicit peace education programme in Northern Uganda (Najjuma 2011) found only limited impact, largely because of incompatibilities between the values and practices of peace education and the 'normalities' of formal schooling (e.g., a stress on 'factual' knowledge as opposed to the affective or interpersonal skills, pupils having very little say in school decision making, a reluctance to teach controversial issues or to engage in social science, an emphasis on competition and hierarchy rather than cooperation and equality).

Kearney (2011) examines the Ingando Peace and Solidarity Camp in Rwanda, which exists to strengthen Rwandan identity as opposed to ethnic ties. The argument of this study is that the top-down, authoritarian and unequivocal approach of the camp is more a method of establishing unity and social cohesion through a single view of history rather than an attempt at reconciliation through discussion and open debate. Moreover, this authoritarian style is reinforced by intense military training involving physical punishment.

A study of peace education in Sri Lanka (Lopes Cardoso and May 2009) notes that peace education is supposed to be integrated into all subjects in formal schooling. However, the problem is that "the system appears to be anti-minorities, because the Sinhala nationalist ideology is persistent in some textbooks" (Lopes Cardoso and May 2009: 208).

They note that while:

> [T]rainee teachers are expected to develop the skills of empathetic listening, democratic leadership, developing children's self-esteem and conflict resolution . . . these expectations might be too high, given the often poor quality of teacher training.
>
> (Lopes Cardoso and May 2009: 209)

Moreover, the Sri Lankan educational system continues to be organised along ethnically segregated lines. As the authors note, democratically organised schools "are still the exception in Sri Lanka," where "There has been only limited attention to the promotion of peaceful relations and democratic values and attitudes" (Lopes Cardoso and May 2009: 210).

In the literature on education and violent conflict overall, there is only very limited evidence of the structures and processes of schools themselves being changed in any significantly peaceful and democratic way by, during or after the crisis of violent conflict and of this having an impact. There is much more evidence of successful attempts to return to the 'normality' of providing access to conventional schooling. The evidence tends to suggest that schools might stop doing the harm that they do and be better able to help pupils 'cope and hope,' but at the moment there is little sign or evidence of them successfully educating for a more peaceful future via their organisation, pedagogy and curricula emphases. Indeed, Shah (2012), writing on postconflict Timor-Leste, argues that the political and administrative conditions necessary for such educational change are rarely present in fragile states shortly after the end of hostilities or turmoil. It appears then that serious change is very difficult, and on the whole tends not to take place, in formal education in and after violent conflict. Genuinely different, nonauthoritarian approaches are more likely to take place outside of mainstream schooling.

Conclusion

The increased emphasis on democracy as the goal for political development begs the question of the role of education in either facilitating the values and behaviours of a supportive political culture or being an obstacle to greater democratisation. Certainly education has a role to play in developing the organisational skills and behaviours that a modern democratic state needs to function, but on top of this it also needs to help to develop specifically democratic values, skills and behaviours. While there is some evidence that schools in developing countries can provide an educational experience that encourages a more democratic disposition, the dominant model of schooling in developing countries continues to be essentially authoritarian. Not only does this mean that schools are not playing a particularly significant role in developing democracy but they are also doing little to build for peace in the future in countries affected by violent conflict, the majority of which are developing countries.

References

Alexander, R., 2000. *Culture and Pedagogy.* Blackwell, Oxford.

Altbach, P., Kelly, G., 1978. *Education and Colonialism.* Longman, London.

Aristotle, 1962. *The Politics.* Penguin, Harmondsworth.

Azevedo, M., 1980. A century of colonial education in Mozambique. In: Mugomba, A. and Nyaggah, M. (Eds.) *Independence Without Freedom.* ABC-Clio, Santa Barbara.

Barnes, B., 1982. Education for socialism in Mozambique. *Comparative Education Review* 26, 3, 406–19.

Beetham, J., Boyle, K., 1995. *Introducing Democracy.* Polity Press/UNESCO, London and Paris.

Bengsston, S., 2011. Fragile states, fragile concepts: a critical reflection on the terminology in the field of education in emergencies. In: Paulson, J. (Ed.) *Education, Conflict and Development.* Symposium, Oxford.

Bush, K., Saltarelli, D. (Eds.), 2000. *The Two Faces of Education in Ethnic Conflict.* UNICEF, Florence.

Caddell, M., 2006. Private schools as battlefields: contested visions of learning and livelihood in Nepal. *Compare* 36, 4, 463–80.

Coleman, J., 1965. *Education and Political Development.* Princeton University Press, Princeton.

Davies, L., 1995. International indicators of democratic schools. In: Harber, C. (Ed.) *Developing Democratic Education.* Education Now, Ticknall.

Davies, L., 1999. Comparing definitions of democracy in education. *Compare* 29, 2, 127–40.

Davies, L., Harber, C., Schweisfurth, M., 2002. *Democracy Through Teacher Education*. CIER/CfBT, Birmingham.

Davies, L., Harber, C., Schweisfurth, M., 2005. *Democratic Professional Development*. CIER/CfBT, Birmingham.

Davies, L., Kirkpatrick, G., 2000. *The EURIDEM Project: A Review of Pupil Democracy in Europe*. Children's Rights Alliance, London.

Dawson, R., Prewitt, K., Dawson, K., 1977. *Political Socialisation*. Little Brown, Boston.

Diamond, L., 1993. *Political Culture and Democracy in Developing Countries*. Lynne Reiner, Boulder.

Fagerlind, I., Saha, L., 1989. *Education and National Development*. Pergamon, Oxford.

Harber, C., 1989. *Politics in African Education*. Macmillan, London.

Harber, C., 2004. *Schooling as Violence*. RoutledgeFalmer, London.

Harber, C., 2014. *Education and International Development*. Symposium, Oxford.

Harber, C., Mncube, V., 2012. *Education, Democracy and Development*. Symposium, Oxford.

Hawkins, J., 2007. The intractable dominant educational paradigm. In: Mason, M., Hershock, P. and Hawkins, J. (Eds.) *Changing Education*. Comparative Education Research Centre, University of Hong Kong.

Inkeles, A., 1969a. Participant citizenship in six developing countries. *American Political Science Review* 43, 1122–33.

Inkeles, A., 1969b. Making men modern. *American Journal of Sociology* 75, 208–25.

Inkeles, A., Smith, D., 1974. *Becoming Modern*. Heinemann, London.

Kearney, J., 2011. A unified Rwanda? Ethnicity, history and reconciliation in the Ingando Peace and Solidarity Camp. In: J. Paulson (Ed.) *Education and Reconciliation*. Continuum, London.

Kitaev, I., 2007. Education for all and private education in developing and transitional countries. In: Srivastava, P. and Walford, G. (Eds.) *Private Schooling in Less Economically Developed Countries*. Symposium, Oxford.

Leftwich, A., 1998. Forms of the democratic developmental state. In: Robinson, M. and White, G. (Eds.) *The Democratic Developmental State*. Oxford University Press, Oxford.

London, N., 2002. Curriculum convergence: an ethno-historical investigation into schooling in Trinidad and Tobago. *Comparative Education* 38, 1, 53–72.

Loomba, A., 1998. *Colonialism/Postcolonialism*. Routledge, London.

Lopes Cardoso, M., May, A., 2009. Teaching for peace – overcoming division? In: Nicolai, S. (Ed.) *Opportunities for Change*. IIEP-UNESCO, Paris.

Matsumoto, M., 2011. Expectations and realities of education in post-conflict Sierra Leone. In: Paulson, J. (Ed.) *Education, Conflict and Development*. Symposium, Oxford.

Molteno, M., Ogadhoh, K., Cain, E., Crumpton, B., 2000. *Towards Responsive Schools*. Department for International Development/Save the Children, London.

Moumouni, A., 1968. *Education in Africa*. Andre Deutsch, London.

Najjuma, R., 2011. *Peace Education in the Context of Post-Conflict Formal Schooling*. Unpublished PhD Thesis, University of Birmingham.

Osher, D., Kelly, D., Tolani-Brown, N., Shors, L., Chen, C.-S., 2009. *UNICEF Child Friendly Schools Programming: Global Evaluation Final Report*. American Institutes for Research, Washington.

Paulson, J., 2011. Reconciliation through educational reform? In: Paulson, J. (Ed.) *Education, Conflict and Development*. Symposium, Oxford.

Searle, C., 1981. *We're Building the New School!* Zed Press, London.

Shah, R., 2012. Goodbye conflict, hello development? Curriculum reform in Timor-Leste. *International Journal of Educational Development* 32, 1, 31–38.

Smith, B., 2009. *Understanding Third World Politics*. Palgrave Macmillan, Basingstoke.

Trafford, B., 2003. *School Councils, School Democracy and School Improvement*. SHA, Leicester.

UNDP, 2010. *Human Development Report 2010*. Oxford University Press, New York.

UNESCO, 2011. *The Hidden Crisis*. UNESCO, Paris.

Wright, C., 1997. Reflections on Sierra Leone. In: UNESCO (Ed.) *Final Report and Case Studies of the Workshop on Educational Destruction and Reconstruction in Disrupted Societies*. UNESCO, Paris.

5

EDUCATION FOR SUSTAINABLE DEVELOPMENT

The rising place of resilience and lessons from small island developing states

Terra Sprague

Introduction

This Handbook takes shape during a period of significant change in the field of international education and development. Indeed, one of the purposes of the volume is to reflect upon the current international debates in education and development at this key moment in the history of the field. As we approach the 2015 end date of the Millennium Development Goals (MDGs) and the Education for All (EFA) goals, the landscape of education and development is quickly shifting with a global architecture under reconstruction. One of the hallmarks of this reconstruction phase, often referred to as the post-2015 process, has been an opening up of debate through wider global consultation than had previously been seen in 1990 at Jomtien (leading to the World Declaration on Education for All) or in 2000 at Dakar or New York (leading to the Dakar Framework for Action and the Millennium Development Goals, respectively). Arguably, the post-2015 process has remained a largely Northern-led initiative (King and Palmer 2013) and has been met by some criticism about the consultation processes as being tokenistic and lacking in genuine opportunity for stakeholder engagement that truly counts towards post-2015 goal and target development (Green 2013; Stecher 2013).

Meanwhile, the Education for Sustainable Development (ESD) community is also facing transition, with the Decade for Education for Sustainable Development (DESD) having ended in 2014. While ESD is an international debate and movement of pertinence to all nations and global citizens, it similarly remains a largely Northern construct. Sustainable development certainly has wider implications for development beyond the field of education and has firmly made its way into the renewal of the MDGs by way of the proposed Sustainable Development Goals; with these simultaneous transition periods, we are currently seeing a stronger coalescence between international development, education and sustainability than has previously been exhibited.

Despite the criticisms made about these resent processes of renewal, they have driven many to take stock of the lessons learnt in the recent eras of international goal and target setting (see later chapters from King, McGrath and Rose). This allows us to seek lessons from a range of contexts and groups. Small Island Developing States (SIDS) is one such group. SIDS have demonstrated considerable deliberation and experience with ESD. They have also been some of the first to feel the effects of global environmental change, including sea level rise, extreme weather events, groundwater salination and associated challenges to food production. Meanwhile, their perspectives from the 'sharp end' of global environmental change (Louisy 2014; Sprague, Crossley and Holmes 2014; Sprague and Crossley 2013) have often been overlooked in the international debates and discourse surrounding ESD. Before expounding upon these matters, this chapter first briefly recaps the ESD movement, introduces SIDS as a whole, and then provides examples of their ESD experience from which the international community can learn. The chapter concludes by proposing that resilience is an emerging priority area in the international development discourse – for and beyond SIDS. As with ESD, much can be learnt from the SIDS experience or resilience, both beyond the Decade for ESD and into a post-2015 era of Sustainable Development Goals.

Education for sustainable development

The Sustainable Development (SD) movement is most often traced back to the Brundtland Report, within which SD is defined as "development that meets the needs of the present without compromising the ability of future generations to meet their own needs" (United Nations 1987: 41). SD is characterised by the pillars of environment, economy and society, with culture as the underlying foundation, or in some cases a fourth pillar. It is important to note that while there may be 'definitions' of SD and ESD, these concepts are evolving, with differing and sometimes divergent views and movements (Fein and Tilbury 2002) including education for sustainability and sustainability education.

In order to help implement the values of SD, a Decade for Education for Sustainable Development (DESD) was pronounced in 2005. The overall goal of this decade was to "integrate the principles, values, and practices of sustainable development into all aspects of education and learning", with the hope that it would "encourage changes in behaviour that will create a more sustainable future in terms of environmental integrity, economic viability and a just society for present and future generations" (Toh 2006: 9).

There was an early tendency to view ESD as 'green' or environmental education, which was often treated as a stand-alone subject. Looking at the historical background, this is somewhat understandable, given that SD had grown out of an environmental movement characterised by the 1972 World Environmental Conference in Stockholm, which led to the establishment of the UN Environmental Programme.[1] Throughout the DESD, however, the global understandings and practices of SD and ESD have become more holistic and less focused on the environmental pillar alone, managing to better integrate aspects of society, economics and culture. This inclusivity has progressed the thinking of ESD as a stand-alone subject to being an approach to learning about sustainability and SD concepts across the traditional teaching subjects, in formal and nonformal settings, as a lifelong learning aim through participatory teaching and learning methods (UNESCO 2014a).

The year 2014 marked the end of the DESD, which was concluded in a UNESCO World Conference on ESD held in Aichi-Nagoya, Japan. The 'Learning Today for a Sustainable Future' conference (UNESCO 2014b) was the second of its kind, with an earlier such conference in Bonn, Germany, in 2009 (UNESCO 2009). In addition to celebrating the achievements of the DESD and learning lessons from the decade, the conference rallied support towards the launching of the Global Action Programme (GAP) on ESD[2] (UNESCO 2014c). The GAP is intended to strengthen efforts towards the scaling up of learning to contribute to sustainable development. It aims to reorient this learning through five priority action areas aimed at strategic stakeholder involvement and stresses that this learning is for all human beings.

Beyond ESD being a movement that will carry on in its own right through the momentum of the GAP, it is furthermore embedded into the proposed Post-2015 Sustainable Development Goals. This is acknowledged in the Aichi-Nagoya Declaration on Education for Sustainable Development, which welcomes:

> [T]he growing international recognition of ESD as an integral and transformative element of inclusive quality education and lifelong learning and an enabler for sustainable development, as demonstrated by the inclusion of ESD as a target in the Muscat Agreement adopted at the 2014 Global Education For All Meeting and in the proposal for Sustainable Development Goals (SDGs) by the Open Working Group of the UN General Assembly on SDGs.
>
> (UNESCO 2014d: 1)

While they are still under debate at the time of writing this chapter, the Open Working Group's (OWG) proposed Sustainable Development Goals (UNDESA 2014a) greatly increase the attention of sustainability issues within the international development agenda. Beyond the use of 'sustainable' in their collective title, nearly all of the 16 proposed goals explicitly mention sustainability. The Education for All (EFA) Global Monitoring Report, meanwhile, is also highlighting ways in which education can support the OWG's proposed goals in more sophisticated ways beyond matters of ESD, curriculum and pedagogy (UNESCO 2014e). In this way, we currently see the issues of sustainability becoming more closely aligned with international development and education in a post-2015 era than was perhaps seen in the 2000–2015 period.

Small island developing states

Small Island Developing States (SIDS) are part of a wider classification of small states, for which there is an increasing body of research and literature in the fields of education, development and beyond (see Bacchus 2008; Brock and Crossley 2013; Commonwealth Secretariat 1998; Crossley, Bray and Packer 2011; Current Issues in Comparative Education 2012). With a broad range of economic, political and geographical characteristics, small states are usually identified by population and include both landlocked and island states. The World Bank and the Commonwealth, for example, use a 1.5 million population threshold when identifying small states but with notable exceptions such as Jamaica and Papua New Guinea being countries that share similar characteristics, albeit larger populations.

As a subcategory of small states, SIDS are rather easier to identify. They were recognised as a distinct group of countries in 1992 at the UN Conference on Environment and Development. The United Nations Department of Economic and Social Affairs (UNDESA) maintains a list of 52 SIDS. While UNDESA does not have official criteria for its SIDS classification, they tend to be low-lying coastal countries that share similar challenges to sustainable development, including fragility, remoteness, natural resources limitations, vulnerability to external shock, susceptibility to natural disaster and dependence on international trade. Many SIDS are part of the Alliance of Small Island States (AOSIS), which is an umbrella organisation that functions within the United Nations as a lobbying group.

While they share some similar characteristics, it is important to recognise that SIDS are not a homogeneous group. While all are classified as 'developing', some SIDS are additionally recognised as least developed countries (LDCs) and not all are members of the United Nations. Geographically, they come from very distinct regions and are typically categorised into three: the

Caribbean; the Pacific; and Africa, Indian Ocean, Mediterranean and South China Sea (AIMS), the latter being more a cluster of subregions.

Given their distinctive characteristics, SIDS have been some of the first to experience challenges associated with climate change, which include sea level rise, groundwater salination and associated challenges to food security as well as increases in frequency and severity of extreme weather events (Crossley and Sprague 2014; Nath, Roberts and Madhoo 2010; Sem 2007; Sprague et al. 2014). Sustainable development is therefore an especially urgent agenda for SIDS. The international development community has been increasingly responsive to these needs, as evidenced by the growing number of global conferences, programmes and declarations devoted to sustainable development in SIDS, some of which are seen in Table 1 and further expounded upon by Crossley and Sprague (2014). In addition to these activities, there has also been an increasing body of research and literature on SD in SIDS (Springer and Roberts 2011; Strachan and Vigilance 2008, 2011; Vigilance and Roberts 2011). Much of this has been supported by the Commonwealth, over 50% of whose membership is comprised of small states.

Table 5.1 Sustainable development and SIDS: key international documents and conferences

Date	SD documents and **associated conferences**	Key points
1987	**Our Common Future**, a Report of the World Commission on Environment and Development (the Brundtland Commission)	Commonly used definition of Sustainable Development
1992	**Agenda 21**, including the **The Rio Declaration on Environment and Development** adopted by the world community at the *United Nations Conference on Environment and Development 'Earth Summit'*	Reflects a global consensus and commitment to development and environment
1994	**Barbados Programme of Action for the Sustainable Development of SIDS (BPOA)** from the *Global Conference on Sustainable Development of SIDS*	Translated Agenda 21 into specific policies, creating 14 priority areas for SD in SIDS and identified cross-sectorial areas for implementation
2002	**Johannesburg Plan of Implementation** at the *World Summit on Sustainable Development*	Proposal for Education for Sustainable Development (chapter 7 on SIDS)
2005	**Mauritius Strategy** at the *International Meeting to Review the Implementation of the Programme of Action for the Sustainable Development of Small Island Developing States*	Further implementation of the 1994 BPOA, expanding the 14 priority areas 20
2009	**AOSIS Climate Change Declaration** at the *AOSIS Climate Change Summit*	Calls upon international community to take 'urgent, ambitious, and decisive action' concerning climate change.
2012	**The Future We Want** at the *Rio+20 United Nations Conference on Sustainable Development*	Assessing the progress to date and renewing the global commitment to sustainable development
2014	**SIDS Accelerated Modalities of Action (SAMOA) Pathway** at the *Third International Conference on Small Island Developing States* within The International Year of SIDS	Wide-ranging 19-section outcome document reaffirming commitment to the sustainable development of SIDS through genuine and durable partnerships

One initiative that has most recently helped to raise the profile and voice of this group has been the 2014 International Year of SIDS (United Nations 2014a). Highlighting the challenges faced by SIDS and the innovation of these countries, the International Year raised awareness of the Third International Conference on SIDS, held in September in Samoa, which focused upon building partnerships for sustainable development (United Nations 2014b).

SIDS contributions to ESD

Also during the year of SIDS, held in advance of the UN international conference in Samoa, was a two-day multidisciplinary event that examined the realities of living with environmental change in SIDS to identify implications for ESD. The 'Living at the Sharp End of Environmental Uncertainty in SIDS' day conference and research workshop at the University of Bristol coincided with the 20th anniversary of the Education in Small States Research Group (www.smallstates.net), a specialist group within the Research Centre for International and Comparative Studies (ICS). This multidisciplinary event brought together different sectors and regions to highlight the many messages which the environmental research and international development communities can learn from SIDS' early experiences in dealing with environmental change. SIDS offer a multitude of experience with ESD practice, yet most of this blossoms within non-formal and informal educational settings.

In her keynote address at the Sharp End conference, Dame Pearlette Louisy (2014), Governor General and Head of State of Saint Lucia, highlighted that there is an absence of attention to ESD within the 2011–2012 Education Strategy formulated by the Organisation of Eastern Caribbean States and in the five-year education sector plan for Saint Lucia. She argued that ESD has failed to sufficiently take hold within the formal education sector in the Caribbean region, a finding supported by a recent study by the Commonwealth Secretariat on ESD in Small Island Developing States of the Commonwealth (2013). Meanwhile, the nonformal sector has been helping to fill the gap. In particular, Sandwatch serves as one prominent example that began as an initiative in the Caribbean in 1999 and has turned into an international project with UNESCO support. This multidisciplinary coastal monitoring project brings together school children, teachers and communities to observe and think critically about environmental changes in beaches and coastal areas brought about by climate change. The project is being scaled up to act as a cross-regional initiative through the creation of handbooks, training videos and a database for collected data and currently involves countries in all three SIDS regions. Sandwatch exemplifies one way in which others can learn from the early experiences of SIDS, as the project can be applied to coastal communities in larger states and indeed has participants in countries of Africa, Asia, Europe, and South America alike.

One of the basic challenges of learning from the early experiences of SIDS is a simple matter of accessibility to information. By contrast to the Caribbean region, ESD initiatives in the Pacific are arguably becoming more visible. Work supported by The University of the South Pacific, a regional university servicing 12 member countries, has brought Pacific thinking and practice of ESD to the international stage through the publication of a three-book series (Furivai 2010; Koya, Nabobo-Baba and Teadero 2010; Nabobo-Baba, Koya and Teadero 2010). Similar to the Caribbean region, Pacific ESD finds strength in nonformal and informal approaches. In fact, this series pushes to further break down the typically held divisions between these areas of learning and problematises the separation between the ESD pillars by "challenging the conceptions that compartmentalise the environment and the economy from the personal and cultural life experience" (Koya, Nabobo-Baba and Teadero 2010) through examples of adaptation, continuity and survival within vulnerable environments. The authors remind us that this has been the life experience of Pacific Islanders for thousands of years, and, as a result, ESD in the Pacific makes ample space for indigenous knowledge through acknowledgement of cultural knowledge and traditional and contemporary art forms coupled with reflective analysis of traditional practice.

Within the AIMS region, the nonformal sector again brings us examples of ESD practice, particularly within the SIDS of the Indian Ocean. By contrast to the Pacific initiatives described here, which have emphasised a holistic approach to sustainability within ESD and have called for attention to philosophical underpinnings, this project in the Indian Ocean has focused predominantly upon ESD content and pedagogy. In 2011, the Indian Ocean Commission, through the ISLANDS Project, launched an ESD initiative with Comoros, Mauritius, Madagascar, Reunion, Seychelles and Zanzibar. This project aims to support the implementation of the Mauritius Strategy (United Nations 2005). The result has produced a series of publically available educational materials including a comic book, teachers' guides and an online platform for teaching ESD in a regionally specific way (Indian Ocean Commission 2013). Public outreach has also been accomplished through puppet shows, the production of a cartoon DVD and the public airing of a cartoon series in 2013 to increase children's awareness of environmental protection.

It has been argued elsewhere (Crossley and Sprague 2014) that the ESD experience of SIDS holds a bitter irony. In brief, this argument contends that international education agendas have not always been in line with the self-identified educational priorities of SIDS (Crossley, Bray and Packer 2011) and that early sustainable development work within SIDS did not sufficiently focus upon education. Ironically, now that more international aid and attention is being placed upon the education component of SD in SIDS (Heibert 2012), these are the countries that are now in such a dire position due to climate change and recent economic woes that, at least anecdotally, some international agencies have 'given up' on the islands (McNamara et al. 2014). Helpfully, in recent months, the SIDS EDS experience seems to be having a stronger impact in international deliberations with greater recognition in declarations, such as the Aichi-Nagoya Declaration from the 2014 ESD conference. Within this declaration, explicit recognition is made that ESD is a concern and a priority activity for developed and developing countries, specifically small island developing states whereby participants:

> STRESS that ESD is an opportunity and a responsibility that should engage both developed and developing countries in intensifying efforts for poverty eradication, reduction of inequalities, environmental protection and economic growth, with a view to promoting equitable, more sustainable economies and societies benefiting all countries, especially those most vulnerable such as Small Island Developing States and Least Developed Countries.
>
> (UNESCO 2014d: 2)

From ESD to learning for resilience

In contrast to the 'Living at the Sharp End' conference, which was exploring implications for ESD from amongst examples of living with environmental uncertainty in small island states (University of Bristol Cabot Institute 2014), the agenda of the UN SIDS conference in Samoa (UNDESA 2014b) included surprisingly little about ESD. As a conference with the theme of "sustainable development of small island developing States through genuine and durable partnerships", one could easily question this near absence of ESD. What was in abundance, however, was attention to resilience in many forms and relating to numerous domains, *inter alia* climate change and ocean threats, animal and community protection, macrofiscal approaches, resource management and maritime transport. Presentations on resilience were given by nation-states, regional bodies and international development organisations alike.

Resilience is quickly emerging as a dominant development discourse (Chandler 2013). Helen Clark, UNDP Administrator, puts it "at the heart of the development agenda" (Clark 2012), and it has made its way firmly into many of the OWG's proposed Sustainable Development Goals (UNDESA 2014a). Yet, if resilience is to become a widely used tool of sustainable development practice, we ought first to understand what resilience *is* before coming to promote its development. Furthermore, we ought to consider how it can be learnt, taught and integrated into ESD.

Resilience is widely accepted and promoted as a desirable trait that should be strengthened within individuals, communities and nation-states, particularly in the face of environmental change and uncertainty, yet there appears to be very little research within the international development community to understand the *meaning* of resilience. Instead, there has been a quick uptake of this buzzword and a push to promote resilience strengthening without first examining its essence beyond the most basic understanding. In its simplest and most commonly expressed form, resilience is understood as the ability to 'bounce back' from shock. There is much more that can be unpacked from this, however, including its types; sites; forms of expression; and ways of operating in different locations, contexts and domains. Understanding this complexity is an essential to step being able to build it through learning and teaching.

One project that is unpicking some of these questions is being undertaken by a UN SIDS Partnership, launched at the Samoa SIDS conference in September 2014. The 'Learning from the Sharp End of Environmental Uncertainty in SIDS' Partnership (See UNDESA 2014c) is comprised of more than 20 postsecondary, tertiary education institutions, specialists and international organisations across the three SIDS regions. The objective is to support a wider global process of learning from sharp-end experiences of SIDS relating to environmental uncertainty and climate change. One of the projects within the Partnership is an investigation into the concept of resilience in SIDS, which seeks to understand the unique nature of resilience in SIDS, including how it is learnt and taught, in order to bring these perspectives to the global debates and discourse surrounding resilience in the international development community.

Understanding resilience

Resilience is a robust field of enquiry in its own right, emerging from ecology and the work of C.S. Holling in the 1960s, that sought to identify an ecological stability theory and has been progressed largely through the work of the Stockholm Resilience Centre. More recently, socioecological resilience has emerged as a way of understanding how individuals and groups adapt to environmental change (Adger 2000). Like sustainable development and ESD, resilience is an evolving field that has multiple conceptions and for which varying definitions exist. In ecology, resilience has been defined as "a measure of how fast a system returns to an equilibrium state after a disturbance" (Walker et al. 2006: 1). In sociology, this concept is extended to mean "the ability of human communities to withstand external shocks to their social infrastructure, such as environmental variability, or social, economic and political upheaval" (Folke, Colding and Berkes 2002: 354). Resilience studies have gone on to influence a number of fields outside of ecology including nonlinear dynamics, environmental psychology, cultural theory, management and even property rights (Folke 2006). Within education and development studies, educational resilience has recently been defined by UNESCO and UNICEF as "the ability of an education system (at different levels) to minimise disaster and conflict risks, to maintain its functions during an emergency, and to recover from shocks" (2014: 221).

From vulnerability to resilience: the small island state shift

Small island states have long been characterised as vulnerable due to their isolation, challenges of economies of scale, often heavy dependence upon external aid and their susceptibility to natural disaster (Commonwealth Secretariat 1985, 1997, 1998; Sem 2007). Extensive work since the early 1990s has been undertaken to develop an index of small state vulnerability, particularly when the United Nations and Commonwealth bodies realised that "the concept of vulnerability needed to be operationalised and measured in the form of an index relating to the extent to which economies were prone to harm by external shocks" (Briguglio 2014: 12). Much of this work has consequently focused predominantly upon economics (Briguglio and Kisanga 2004; Commonwealth Secretariat 1998). This propensity to characterise small island states as vulnerable has been met with considerable critique. A counternarrative stresses that positioning small island states as vulnerable is negatively deterministic and frames them as weak (Baldacchino 2012; Baldacchino and Bertram 2008). While the vulnerability argument often results in greater political attention to the challenges of small island states, it can also result in "unintended (and damaging) attitudes and consequences" (McNamara et al. 2014). Pointing to what are seen as flaws in vulnerability argument, Baldacchino instead highlights the many benefits of smallness, such as their distinct cultural fabric and sense of natural identity, their capacity for rapid policy development and their ability to respond to opportunity and adversity (Baldacchino 2000).

Recently, however, the vulnerability discourse in this area has begun to shift. Some are working to reframe islands as 'champions of resilience' by highlighting certain characteristics in SIDS, including local and traditional knowledge of environmental systems; natural resource management strategies; abilities to respond to real-time threats; responsive governments; and the ability to innovate and take risks (Laban 2014; McNamara et al. 2014). Recent work in small states research has begun to take account of resilience indicators through a revised vulnerability/resilience framework (Briguglio 2014; Commonwealth Secretariat 2014). This revised framework helpfully expands beyond economic measures of vulnerability/resilience to include social and environmental aspects of development (Lewis-Bynoe 2014). These aspects, however, are often still done with reference to economic measures. For example, environmental management is linked to its potential to result in eco industry or green jobs. There is still some way to go in these efforts. Notions of resilience, when applied to SIDS, most often refer to a narrow definition of withstanding external shocks. There are other ways, perhaps not easily measurable for the purposes of index building, in which resilience in SIDS can be examined and appreciated.

Which of the many sociological components of resilience, if examined better from a SIDS perspective, might be applied to understandings of environmental or economic resilience? These might reflect some of the counterarguments to vulnerability in SIDS such as a willingness to take risks, group perseverance and strategies for overcoming adversity. Some of these qualities are indeed considered to be inborn or culturally cultivated characteristics. At the recent UN SIDS conference, resilience was certainly referred to as an intrinsic trait amongst the Pacific Islanders (Government of Tonga 2014). Stories of travellers rowing thousands of kilometres in open boats known as outriggers are part of the cultural fabric of Pacific Islanders in particular (Underwood, Andreas and Nabobo-Baba 2014). Postcolonial perspectives might also lend helpful insight: from the physical resilience of islanders who encountered disease brought during colonial encounters (Dorovolomo 2010) to powerful sites of resistance that insist on the place of cultural knowledge and epistemologies in postcolonial education systems to achieve meaningful learning and regional development for livelihoods (Thaman 2014, 1993). With greater attention, these experiences might be understood through a resilience lens in a way that can be learnt and appreciated by others.

Learning resilience

If resilience is in part down to an inherent nature and cultural embeddedness, there is nothing keeping the education sector from treating it as a skill that can be taught. It is certainly a trait that the education sector wishes to see strengthened in young people, as evidenced by the attention to developing interventions and promoting resilience during school years (NCH 2007). Within this is an assumption that resilience must be a characteristic that can be learnt. Should this be the case, ESD seems one site where resilience might be embedded in educational settings. Where it is already identified in the education sector in SIDS, this is generally in reference to disaster preparedness. Recent case studies by UNESCO and UNICEF (2012), for example, point to ways in which Maldives, Fiji and the British Virgin Islands have developed curriculum, pedagogy and educational policy to safeguard future generations against natural hazards, thereby strengthening sustainable development.

Yet, resilience as an educational concept is most assuredly a wider notion than disaster preparedness. If it is an innate or culturally embedded trait, as some suggest, and one that those living in small island states must exercise regularly because of their position at the sharp end, then there is much the international development community, as well as educational policymakers in larger nation-states, can learn from the type of resilience exhibited by SIDS. In order to access this knowledge, further attention is needed to unpack the concept from the perspective of SIDS in a way that respectfully acknowledges their cumulative experience.

Conclusions

Similar to the vulnerability argument, the resilience thesis does not go without critique. With notions of resilience emerging around us in everyday settings, it is easy to consider it a universal good that we must all strive to achieve. From overcoming personal challenges in our careers to making our children more resilient in school, from improving public health to strengthening technology systems, resilience is a term all around us and emerges in most domains of life (Chandler 2013). It has become a buzzword that denotes a personal endeavour to get us through hardship, as well as a community goal to respond to change and something for nation-states to build through policy development. Yet, there are counterarguments that point to a negative side in which resilience has come to be operationalised.

Critiques of the recent proliferation of resilience discourse point to ways in which it shifts responsibility and how it causes society to think that shock is an undeniable way of contemporary life. These point to resilience as a neoliberal tool of government used to "responsibilise risk away from the state and onto individuals and institutions" (Welsh 2014: 15) in a world where human life is in constant vulnerability and where our purpose is simply to survive (Evans and Reid 2014). Applied to SIDS, there seems to be growing concern, at least anecdotally, that the recent mandate amongst the international development community for resilience building in SIDS is a transference of responsibility, which small states must do for themselves in order to respond to and prepare for further environmental change and uncertainty.

As with the ESD story, there exists an irony in this situation. The Intergovernmental Panel on Climate Change (IPCC) has stated conclusively that humans are contributing to climate change, largely through greenhouse gas emissions (Field et al. 2014; IPCC 2014). Industrial nations contribute more to these emissions and commit less to cutting them. SIDS have committed to cutting their greenhouse gases by 45% by 2020: considerably more than the world's richest countries, which have pledged 12–18% (Vidal 2012). While they suffer the effects of climate change and contribute more to reversing it, they simultaneously receive mandates from the international development community that they must become more resilient in order to survive. It has even been proposed that SIDS exhibit strengthened resilience as a condition of aid (Commonwealth Secretariat 2014: 26). The growth of the resilience discourse in some ways works to shift the risk of climate uncertainty and adaptation in SIDS away from those powerful states who have contributed most to climate change, leaving SIDS to focus on the task of survival.

To date, SIDS have been very careful to challenge the resilience movement in international development. At the UN conference in Samoa, countries were quick to showcase examples of resilience through their improved resilience indicators (Lewis-Bynoe 2014) their regional cooperation (Indian Ocean Commission 2014), community-based adaptations (UNDP 2012), and integrated climate change and disaster risk management plans (ADPC 2013: 68). Yet they remained cautious to question the increasing mandate to improve and demonstrate this. Typically as takers, not makers, of international aid, they may be understandably slow to support the critiques of today's resilience narrative.

SIDS have withstood the tests of time (Baldacchino 2012). They have been some of the first to deal with the challenges of climate change and have provided exemplars of ESD. Their experiences have much to offer the international development community, including perspectives on resilience as we move into a post-2015 development era and new international agreement on ESD. The imperative to respond and adapt to climate change is undeniable, yet there remains room for questioning the ways in which resilience is being operationalised within the international development community, particularly within SIDS. If SIDS can withstand this current irony in the imperative for resilience in this age of climate uncertainty, that may exhibit the greatest resilience of all.

Notes

1 This historical timeline is well documented by UNESCO and nation-states. See, for example, Toh 2006.
2 The GAP was endorsed by UNESCO Member States through the adoption of 37 C/Resolution 12.

References

Adger, W., 2000. Social and ecological resilience: are they related? *Progress in Human Geography* 24, 347–364.
ADPC, 2013. *Integrating Disaster Risk Management into Climate Change Adaptation*. Disaster Risk Management Practitioners Series, ADPC, Bangkok, Thailand.
Bacchus, M., 2008. The education challenges facing small nation states in the increasingly competitive global economy of the twenty-first century. *Comparative Education* 44, 127–145.
Baldacchino, G., 2000. The challenge of hypothermia: a six-proposition manifesto for small island territories. *Round Table* 89, 65–79.
Baldacchino, G., 2012. Meeting the tests of time: small states in the 21st century. *Current Issues in Comparative Education* 15, 14–25.
Baldacchino, G., Bertram, G., 2008. The beak of the finch: insights into the economic development of small economies. *Round Table* 98, 141–160.
Briguglio, L., 2014. A vulnerability and resilience framework for small states. In: Lewis-Bynoe, D. (Ed.) *Building the Resilience of Small States: A Revised Framework*. Commonwealth Secretariat, London.
Briguglio, L., Kisanga, E., 2004. *Economic Vulnerability and Resilience of Small States*. Commonwealth Secretariat, London.
Brock, C., Crossley, M., 2013. Revisiting scale, comparative research and education in small states. *Comparative Education* 49, 388–403.
Chandler, D., 2013. Editorial. *Resilience* 1, 1–2.
Clark, H., 2012. Putting Resilience at the Heart of the Development Agenda. http://www.undp.org/content/undp/en/home/presscenter/speeches/2012/04/16/helen-clark-putting-resilience-at-the-heart-of-the-development-agenda/

Commonwealth Secretariat, 1985. *Vulnerability: Small States in the Global Society.* Commonwealth Secretariat, London.

Commonwealth Secretariat, 1997. *A Future for Small States: Overcoming Vulnerability.* Commonwealth Secretariat, London.

Commonwealth Secretariat, 1998. *Small States and Development: A Composite Index of Vulnerability.* Commonwealth Secretariat, London.

Commonwealth Secretariat, 2013. *Education for Sustainable Development in Small Island Developing States.* Commonwealth Secretariat, London.

Commonwealth Secretariat, 2014. *Proceedings Report: The Third Global Biennial Conference on Small States: Building Resilience in Small States. Saint Lucia, March 2014.* Commonwealth Secretariat, London.

Crossley, M., Bray, M., Packer, S., 2011. *Education in Small States: Policies and Priorities.* Commonwealth Secretariat, London.

Crossley, M., Sprague, T., 2014. Education for sustainable development: implications for small island developing states (SIDS). *International Journal of Educational Development* 35, 86–95.

Current Issues in Comparative Education, 2012. Education in Small States: Fragilities, Vulnerabilities, and Strengths. Special Issue 15, 1.

Dorovolomo, J., 2010. An unfit and malnourished Pacific: challenges and opportunities in sustainability. In: Nabobo-Baba, U., Koya, C.F. and Teaero, T. (Eds.) *Education for Sustainable Development: Continuity and Survival in the Pacific.* School of Education, University of the South Pacific and Asia-Pacific Cultural Centre for UNESCO, Suva and Tokyo.

Evans, B., Reid, J., 2014. *Resilient Life: The Art of Living Dangerously.* Polity, Cambridge.

Fein, J., Tilbury, D., 2002. The global challenge of sustainability. In: Tilbury, D., Stevenson, R., Fein, J. and Schreuder, D. (Eds.) *Education and Sustainability: Responding to the Global Challenge.* Commission on Education and Communication, IUCN, Gland and Cambridge.

Field, C., Barros, V., Dokken, D., Mach, K., Mastrandrea, M., Bilir, T., . . . White, L., 2014. Summary for Policymakers. In: IPCC (Eds.) *Climate Change 2014: Impacts, Adaptation and Vulnerability Part A: Global and Sectoral Aspects, Contribution of Working Group II to the Fifth Assessment Report of the Intergovernmental Panel on Climate Change.* IPCC, Geneva.

Folke, C., 2006. Resilience: the emergence of a perspective for social-ecological systems analyses. *Global Environmental Change* 16, 253–267.

Folke, C., Colding, J., Berkes, F., 2002. Synthesis: building resilience and adaptive capacity in social-ecological systems. In: Berkes, F., Colding, J. and Folke, C. (Eds.) *Navigating Social-Ecological Systems: Building Resilience for Complexity and Change.* Cambridge University Press, Cambridge.

Furivai, P., 2010. *Education for Sustainable Development: An Annotated Bibliography.* School of Education, University of the South Pacific & Asia-Pacific Cultural Centre for UNESCO, Suva and Tokyo.

Government of Tonga, 2014. *Building Pacific Resilience: Strategy for Climate and Disaster Resilient Development in the Pacific.* Government of Tonga, Nuku'alofa.

Green, D., 2013. Panels of the Poor: What Would Poor People Do if They Were in Charge of the Post-2015 Process? http://oxfamblogs.org/fp2p/panels-of-the-poor-what-would-poor-people-do-if-they-were-in-charge-of-the-post-2015-process/

Heibert, M., 2012. *Islands of Inspiration: Education for Sustainable Development in Small Island Developing States.* Commonwealth Secretariat, London.

Indian Ocean Commission, 2013. ISLANDS Resources. http://commissionoceanindien.org/activites/islands/nos-ressources/

Indian Ocean Commission, 2014. *The Indian Ocean Commission and its Development Partners: 10 Years of Cooperation.* Indian Ocean Commission, Mauritius.

IPCC, 2014. *Concluding Instalment of the Fifth Assessment Report: Climate Change Threatens Irreversible and Dangerous Impacts, but Options Exist to Limit Its Effects.* IPCC, Geneva.

King, K., Palmer, R., 2013. Post-2015 agendas: Northern tsunami, southern ripple? The case of education and skills. *International Journal of Educational Development* 33, 409–425.

Koya, C., Nabobo-Baba, U., Teadero, T. (Eds.), 2010. *Education for Sustainable Development: Pacific Stories of Sustainable Living.* School of Education, University of the South Pacific and Asia-Pacific Cultural Centre for UNESCO, Suva and Tokyo.

Laban, S., 2014. Building resilient communities in Vanutau. *Outreach* 4.

Lewis-Bynoe, D. (Ed.), 2014. *Building the Resilience of Small States: A Revised Framework.* Commonwealth Secretariat, London.

Louisy, P., 2014. Living on the sharp end of environmental uncertainty in a small island developing state: challenges and strategies from Saint Lucia and the Caribbean. Paper presented at the Living at the Sharp End Conference, Bristol, July.

McNamara, K., Henly-Shepard, S., De Souza, R.-M., Fernando, N., 2014. Re-framing islands as champions of resilience. *Outreach* 3.

Nabobo-Baba, U., Koya, C., Teadero, T. (Eds.), 2010. *Education for Sustainable Development: Continuity and Survival in the Pacific*. School of Education, University of the South Pacific and Asia-Pacific Cultural Centre for UNESCO, Suva and Tokyo.

Nath, S., Roberts, J., Madhoo, Y., 2010. *Saving Small Island Developing States: Environmental and Natural Resource Challenges*. Commonwealth Secretariat, London.

NCH, 2007. *Literature Review: Resilience in Children and Young People*. Bridge Child Care Development Service, London.

Sem, G., 2007. *Vulnerability and Adaptation to Climate Change in Small Island Developing States*. United Nations Development Programme, New York.

Sprague, T., Crossley, M., 2013. Learning from the sharp end: education for sustainable development in small states. PolicyBristol Hub.

Sprague, T., Crossley, M., Holmes, K., 2014. At the sharp end: Education for sustainable development in small states. In: Jones-Parry, R. and Robertson, A. (Eds.) *Commonwealth Education Partnerships 2014–15*. Nexus/Commonwealth Secretariat, Cambridge.

Springer, C., Roberts, J., 2011. *Partnerships for Sustainable Development in Small States*. Commonwealth Secretariat, London.

Stecher, L., 2013. 15 Seconds of Fame: Why Post-2015 Doesn't Need More "Participation." http://think africapress.com/development/15-seconds-fame-why-post-2015-doesnt-need-more-participation

Strachan, J., Vigilance, C. (Eds.), 2008. *Sustainable Development in Small Island Developing States: Issues and Challenges*. Commonwealth Secretariat, London.

Strachan, J., Vigilance, C., 2011. *Integrating Sustainable Development into National Frameworks: Policy Approaches for Key Sectors in Small States*. Commonwealth Secretariat, London.

Thaman, K., 1993. Culture and the curriculum. *Comparative Education* 20, 249–260.

Thaman, K., 2014. Pacific island countries: an overview. In: Crossley, M., Hancock, G. and Sprague, T. (Eds.) *Education in Australia, New Zealand and the Pacific*. Bloomsbury, London.

Toh, S.H., 2006. Integrating Education for Sustainable Development & Education for International Understanding: Conceptual issues and pedagogical principles for Teacher Education to address sustainability (No. Paper No. 6), UNESCO Bangkok Occasional Paper Seires. UNESCO Asia-Pacific Centre of Education for International Understanding.

Underwood, R., Andreas, R., Nabobo-Baba, U., 2014. Micronesia: an overview of the Federated States of Micronesia. In: Crossley, M., Hancock, G. and Sprague, T. (Eds.) *Education in Australia, New Zealand and the Pacific*. Bloomsbury, London.

UNDESA, 2014a. Proposal for Sustainable Development Goals. http://sustainabledevelopment.un.org/sdgsproposal.html

UNDESA, 2014b. Calendar of Activities in Samoa: 2014 Third International Conference on Small Island Developing States. http://www.sids2014.org/index.php?menu=1587

UNDESA, 2014c. Learning from the Sharp End of Environmental Uncertainty in SIDS. http://www.sids2014.org/index.php?page=view&type=1006&nr=2705&menu=1507

UNDP, 2012. *20 Years: Community Action for the Global Environment: The GEF Small Grants programme*. UNDP, New York.

UNESCO, 2009. World Conference on Education for Sustainable Development – Moving into the Second Half of the UN Decade. http://www.esd-world-conference-2009.org/en/about-world-conference-on-esd.html

UNESCO, 2014a. What Is ESD? http://www.unesco.org/new/en/unesco-world-conference-on-esd-2014/resources/what-is-esd/

UNESCO, 2014b. UNESCO World Conference on Education for Sustainable Development. http://www.unesco.org/new/en/unesco-world-conference-on-esd-2014/

UNESCO, 2014c. *UNESCO Roadmap for Implementing the Global Action Programme on Education for Sustainable Development*. UNESCO, Paris.

UNESCO, 2014d. *Aichi-Nagoya Declaration on Education for Sustainable Development*. UNESCO, Paris.

UNESCO, 2014e. *Sustainable Development Begins with Education: How Education Can Contribute to the Proposed Post-2015 Goals*. UNESCO, Paris.

UNESCO, UNICEF, 2012. *Disaster Risk Reduction in School Curricula: Case Studies from Thirty Countries.* UNESCO and UNICEF, Paris and New York.

UNESCO, UNICEF, 2014. *Towards a Learning Culture of Safety and Resilience: Technical Guidance for Integrating Disaster Risk Reduction in the School Curriculum.* UNESCO and UNICEF, Paris and New York.

United Nations, 1987. *Report of the World Commission on Environment and Development. Our Common Future.* Oxford University Press, New York.

United Nations, 2005. *Mauritius Strategy for the Further Implementation of the Programme of Action for Sustainable Development in Small Island Developing States.* United Nations, Port Louis.

United Nations, 2014a. International Year of Small Island Developing States. http://www.un.org/en/events/islands2014/

United Nations, 2014b. Small Island Developing States Accelerated Modalities of Action (Samoa Pathway). http://www.sids2014.org/index.php?menu=1537

University of Bristol Cabot Institute, 2014. Small Island States – Living at the Sharp End of Environmental Uncertainty. http://www.bristol.ac.uk/cabot/research/casestudies/2014/57.html

Vidal, J., 2012. Small Island States in Clean Energy Race. http://www.theguardian.com/environment/2012/may/10/small-island-states-clean-energy-race

Vigilance, C., Roberts, J. (Eds.), 2011. *Tools for Mainstreaming Sustainable Development in Small States.* Commonwealth Secretariat, London.

Walker, B., Anderies, J., Kinzing, A., Ryan, P., 2006. Exploring resilience in social-ecological systems through comparative studies and theory development: introduction to the special issue. *Ecology and Society* 11.

Welsh, M., 2014. Resilience and responsibility: governing uncertainty in a complex world. *Geographical Journal* 180, 15–26.

6

REFRAMING GENDER AND EDUCATION FOR THE POST-2015 AGENDA

A critical capability approach

Joan DeJaeghere[1]

Framing gender and education in development agendas

The large and diverse body of scholarship and practice on gender, education and development illustrates how the field is shaped by divergent paradigms, discourses and methodologies that frame gender equality. Studies on gender and education draw on empiricist and economic, Marxist and critical, sociocultural and interpretative, and postcolonial and antifoundational perspectives. Despite these diverse paradigms, the development agenda is dominated by an assumption of universalism in which redistributing access and completion of education will foster gender equality universally; by extension, gender equality will promote other development goals.

Even as organisations continue to assess 'progress' and call for alternatives with regard to gender equality and the post-2015 development agenda (see, for example, GADN 2013; OECD n.d.), the High Level Panel Report (HLP) (2013) makes it clear that the post-2015 development agenda will be universal in scope. While this statement is primarily political, it has conceptual and methodological implications. The HLP Report also states the importance of seeking consensus on goals, assumedly through participation of people representing international-, national- and local-level concerns. Finally, the Report includes girls and women as a cross-cutting issue, stating that "gender equality is integrated across all of the goals, both in specific targets and by making sure that targets are measured separately for women and men, or girls and boys, where appropriate". This reference to the disaggregation of targets by sex continues to narrow the goals, practices and measures toward gender equality even as other terms, such as discrimination and empowerment, are used in the agendas.

In response to the dominant discourse of the international development regime, scholarship from postcolonial and critical feminist perspectives critiques and troubles meanings of gender equality, calling for more than multiple frameworks but also for perspectives that come from and reflect different local realities (e.g., Epstein and Morrell 2012; Fennell and Arnot 2008). For instance, Nnaemeka (2004) considers how people in local communities resist universal frameworks, and she argues for "the possibilities, desirability, and pertinence of a space clearing that allows a multiplicity of different but related frameworks from different locations to touch, intersect, and feed off of each other in a way that accommodates different realities and histories" (p. 353). The disjunctures between the dominant approach of the global agenda and the perspectives of those working on gender issues in specific sites illustrate what Nnaemeka (2004) refers to as "the double apartheid of social and epistemological exclusions" (p. 359). These exclusions are apparent, on the one hand, when local communities resist or reshape educational practices linked with measures generated in international agendas (see, for example, Unterhalter and Dorward 2013) and, on the other hand, when scholars conducting research, particularly from paradigms and methodologies that assume universalism, are blind to locally contested meanings of gender and education work.

The aim of this chapter is to show how two mechanisms, gender mainstreaming and gender and education indicators, used to advance gender equality in and through education are implemented in top-down approaches through international organisations that often assume universality. While these two approaches are distinct in the ways that gender equality is conceptualised, I illustrate an assumed universality by first explaining how a rights-based approach became linked with gender mainstreaming as an institutional mechanism. Gender mainstreaming in education also became articulated with gender equality targets and measures of EFA and the MDGs, and these measures have an assumed universality through a methodological stance of empiricism. In contrast to this universal stance, I employ Santos, Nunes and Menses's (2007) idea of an "ecology of knowledges" and epistemic dialogue to allow for local conceptualisations and practices of working toward gender equality within global agendas. In the final section, I discuss how a capability approach as an evaluative space focuses on equality as necessary for human well-being while it also allows for diverse epistemological approaches that elucidate our ways of knowing and equitable actions toward gender equality in specific sites. Before examining these gender equality mechanisms, I review the dominant approaches for conceptualising gender and education in international development.

In a 2005 chapter titled *Fragmented Frameworks?* Elaine Unterhalter summarises the different approaches used in gender, education and development work, noting their distinctions and their influences on education and development scholarship and practices. She proposes that the field needs to move forward with a combination of approaches, drawing on the contributions of each. Extending this idea, the argument made here is that the global agenda, in particular, and scholar and practitioners working to implement strategies for gender equality need to draw on a more inclusive paradigm that allows for new epistemologies and multiple methodologies to elucidate meanings of and processes toward gender equality in local contexts.

Gender and development scholars have long noted the dominance of the Women in Development (WID) approach in the global agenda (Unterhalter 2005; Vavrus and Richy 2003). Based in an economic and empiricist epistemology, a WID perspective identifies gender inequality as a gap in women's representation. It was first used to achieve parity in the labour market, and then it was later applied to other domains, such as education. Some scholars have argued this approach has contributed greatly to addressing gender inequalities in education by getting more girls in school, which has been shown to be related to other social development outcomes (e.g., Schultz 2002; Tembon and Fort 2008). Others have disputed WID's narrow conceptualisation of access to education, which does not necessarily address gender discrimination reproduced by daily practices in schools, and its lack of focus on social transformation within families and communities (Aikman and Unterhalter 2005; Chisamya et al. 2012; Vavrus and Richy 2003). Despite these critiques, the MDG and EFA targets set for gender equality and education goals are primarily about redistribution and the achievement of parity of access.

Gender and Development (GAD), with a conceptual focus on changing structures of oppression, has also influenced development agendas and work in gender equality and education. One

GAD approach that received considerable traction in global conventions is the identification of gender inequalities with patriarchal state institutions and laws (e.g., Stromquist 1990, 2008). Attention to redressing gender inequalities through state institutions became central to numerous conferences held on gender, as well as rights and education during the 1990s. For example, the Jomtien World Declaration of Education for All (WCEFA; 1990) and later the Dakar Framework of EFA (2000), which had broadly framed gender inequalities (Unterhalter 2014), drew heavily on a rights discourse linked with GAD's focus on redressing discriminatory practices. While GAD scholars have been concerned with how structures of oppression affect women differently in different contexts, the linkage with a rights discourse shifted the approach to one that assumed universality of gender oppression through institutions. For instance, the preamble to the WCEFA (1990) starts with a reference to the Universal Declaration of Human Rights, asserting that "everyone has a right to education", and the first of five points in its vision stresses the need to universalise access to education to promote equity. Gender equality in the Beijing Platform for Action (1995) was also framed from a GAD perspective, with its overall purpose as women's empowerment. However, a key mechanism for promoting gender equality and empowerment is gender mainstreaming in government and civil society institutions, an institutional approach, and access to education was one of the areas of critical concern. This conflation of a rights discourse with GAD's attention to institutional structures tended to emphasise the promotion of individual rights to education through a universal and institutional approach (see, for example, Greany 2008).

Another approach among GAD scholars is empowerment of women and girls by changing the social relations that allowed individual women or girls to assert their voice and make decisions that could, in turn, shift inequalities in family and interpersonal relations, as well as in other domains in society (Kabeer 1999; Maslak 2008; Parpart, Rai and Staudt 2002). From this perspective, education is advocated as a critical way for girls and women to claim their voice and be empowered. However, the discourse of empowerment was appropriated by international organisations in ways that limited the emphasis on changing gender relations within societal relations to one in which the "autonomous female subject" is responsible for changing inequalities and for advancing societal development (Vavrus 2002). For example, the Millennium Development Goal 3 refers to promoting gender equality and empowerment. However, the targets for this goal aim to eliminate gender disparities in education at all levels, which focuses on an outcome rather than processes of empowerment. Appropriating a GAD construction, empowerment was assumed possible through access to education, as measured by gender and education parity measures.

In contrast to WID and GAD frameworks, poststructural perspectives have had less influence on education and development work and agendas. Unterhalter (2005) notes that poststructuralism has developed more prominently in Western academic settings and has been applied to gender issues in the North. The lack of influence of these perspectives may be in part because poststructuralism is seen as coming "from the margins" (Strega 2005), and it is marginalised because it is less pointed in contributing to policy and in generating 'what works' for programmes. However, poststructural scholars who epistemologically and methodologically frame inequalities within historically situated relations and draw on local situated perspectives have much to contribute to framing and redressing gender inequality (Epstein and Morrell 2012).

The capability approach (CA), while used extensively in broader development scholarship and practice, has been undertheorised, and, therefore, it has been difficult to utilise to inform gender equality and education scholarship and practice. Nussbaum (2000), Robeyns (2003), Walker (2007) and Unterhalter (2007) among others have advanced the CA theoretically to contribute to the field of gender and education, arguing for identifying contextually specific capabilities that foster gender equality as well as locally relevant education pedagogies for fostering well-being. However, the capability approach is used by development scholars drawing on a diverse set of methodologies with different epistemological and ontological assumptions, including historical and philosophical argumentation (Unterhalter and Brighouse 2007); post-positivist inquiry that quantifies measures of well-being and equality, such as the Human Development Index (HDI) or the Gender Inequality Index (GII); and action-oriented applications for policies and programmes (e.g., Frediani, Boni and Gasper 2014; Unterhalter 2014). Some empirical uses of a CA, such as the GII, while multidimensional and more nuanced to relate to local contexts, risk framing capabilities and functionings as universals. Therefore, a critical capability approach used as an evaluative framework, as I argue in a later section, is necessary for identifying and debating contextually specific conditions and policies for fostering gender equality within structural constraints that vary in different contexts.

Despite the dominant framing of gender equality and education in the MDGs and EFA goals, they are also sites of contestation in which the mechanism of gender mainstreaming utilises different meanings of gender equality as it is debated and translated through different scales into political action and research (Fraser 2009; Unterhalter and North 2011; Ong 2011). In addition, some research and practice, such as that of ActionAid and CARE, has sought to define and develop alternative gender and education indicators. In thinking toward the post-2015 development agenda and subsequent political and scholarly work on gender and education, there is an opportunity to not only assess achievements at a point in time but also to reconsider the epistemological and discursive framing of gender equality goals.

To reframe gender equality, I argue for a need to draw on critical feminist and postcolonial scholars of knowledge production that call for an "ecology of knowledges" (Santos, Nunes and Menses 2007) and epistemic dialogue. An "ecology of knowledges" perspective recognises the value of different kinds of knowledges – scientific, popular and other – and an epistemic dialogue negotiates these different perspectives in specific sites and times to achieve a just society. Epistemic dialogue does not negate a normative ethical approach to equality nor does it necessarily advocate for epistemological relativism. A capability approach takes a normative ethical stance in which attention to injustices and inequality is fundamental to development and human well-being; however, there is considerable space within CA for epistemic diversity and dialogue drawing on different forms of knowledge. Before turning to these possibilities, I first summarise the underlying epistemological assumptions of gender mainstreaming and gender indicators in education as central mechanisms for implementing the current development agenda.

Mechanisms of gender and education in development agendas

Gender mainstreaming in education

Gender mainstreaming in development has been an ongoing effort for several decades, and much of the early work focused on mainstreaming gender commitments, goals and analysis through the state and international organisations (see Unterhalter and North 2010 for a brief history of gender mainstreaming; Mehra and Gupta 2006; Moser and Moser 2005). While education is one sector of the state, gender mainstreaming in education became more visible following the proclamation of EFA and MDGs, which were an attempt to mainstream gender within specific goals and targets for gender equality in education.

The instruments and techniques for mainstreaming gender in education are broad, allowing initiatives to be taken up in different ways. They can include a gender focal person or unit in the ministry of education, gender audits of education systems, policies that require 'gender' to be included in all education projects, gender institutional analyses and policies to prevent harassment and discrimination, gender-responsive training for teachers, gender analyses of curriculum and gender disaggregated data. In addition to different instruments for mainstreaming, there are also different frameworks used to guide this work. For instance, Leach's (2003) *Practising Gender Analysis in Education* discusses several frameworks, such as Longwe's Women's Empowerment Framework or the Harvard Framework, for analysing gender inequalities, drawing on views of empowerment and efficiency, respectively. These frameworks illustrate the different epistemological assumptions of 'what' gender equality is and how to achieve it.

In the past decade or so, international organisations have developed specific frameworks for mainstreaming gender in education programmes. Miske, Meagher and DeJaeghere (2010) summarise what they call "the education and gender (EDGE) frameworks" that have been developed by UNICEF (2001) and USAID (2007), among others, to explicitly look at different components of education with a gender lens. These frameworks are designed to address complexities of gender equality in different contexts. However, I suggest that because they also draw on a rights discourse (e.g., UNICEF's Quality of Education), and institutional approaches to implement them, assumptions about how to 'best' achieve gender equality have become universalised. For example, one issue that has been taken up extensively in education projects aimed at gender equality is the existence of toilets for girls, which is regarded as a necessary component of a school environment to ensure girls' privacy and hygiene. While important to increase initial participation in schooling, toilets have not been shown to necessarily affect girls' overall participation and empowerment (Unterhalter et al. 2013). The argument made here is that while gender mainstreaming frameworks draw on multiple components for fostering gender equality, the institutional and universal ways in which they are implemented may not sufficiently address local realities. In addition, the influence of a rights discourse shapes what is deemed as necessary for gender equality in diverse sites.

A common critique of gender mainstreaming has been that it is implemented in a technicist manner, drawing on toolkits and how-to manuals that assume rationale and linear planning and implementation steps rather than negotiation of different perspectives on gender equality or on differences between global frameworks and national and local-level policies related to equity and social change (Morley 2010). In addition, gender mainstreaming has also been critiqued for a lack of attention to processes at different levels in which gender inequalities are addressed. Miske, Meagher and DeJaeghere (2010) note that existing gender analysis frameworks used for mainstreaming gender rarely attend to educational processes in schools and classrooms, nor programme operations within NGOs. Without opening the black box of schools and institutions, we have little understanding of how these institutional mechanisms get implemented and translated.

Unterhalter and North (2010), in a special issue on gender mainstreaming in education, point out that in different educational contexts, "meanings of gender, mainstreaming, and equality are reinterpreted, negotiated, and contested as they move between global and local spaces" (p. 401). While gender mainstreaming is often implemented top-down through an institutional approach of transnational organisations, rather than through national institutions or even local schools (Walby 2005), a closer examination reveals the cracks in which resistance to and openings for gender equality take place at local levels. For example, Sharma, Verma and Arur (2013) show how an indicator framework used to mainstream gender throughout an NGO and its programmes was negotiated and translated into practice, often in different ways, among staff. Similarly, DeJaeghere and Pellowski Wiger (2013) illustrate how teachers utilised WID and GAD meanings of gender equality in schools in rural Bangladesh, and both advanced social transformations in small but important ways within their communities.

In addition, gender mainstreaming often excludes perspectives and practices of gender equality from the very level that it most aims to affect: girls and boys, as well as teachers and other actors in specific local contexts. Silfver (2010) argues in her analysis of a gender mainstreaming project between Sweden and Laos that Swedish notions of a woman as mother, wife and citizen were both reproduced in Laos and disrupted as women used the local system of *nayobay* to marry into families that would secure good futures for their children. She argues that despite these different social categories present in framing gender in Laos, gender mainstreaming was most often advanced as a technical tool and was not negotiated and translated into the local context. Understanding local social-cultural and political-economic meanings of gender equality and how it is potentially promoted and disrupted is not a common approach of institutional gender mainstreaming.

In many discussions and briefings leading up to the post-2015 agenda, scholars and activists argue that gender mainstreaming is important in order to address seemingly intractable inequalities, but it is not sufficient (GADN 2013; OECD n.d.). Gender mainstreaming approaches provide legal and institutional incentives, and while there is considerable translation that happens in implementing these approaches, local perspectives are often absent. In addition, the effects of such mainstreaming efforts on individuals' lives are not often well understood by those purporting frameworks or implementing them.

Measures of gender and education

Similar to the gender mainstreaming scholarship and practice, more has been written on gender and development measures outside of education. For example, the Gender Equity Index (GEI) and the Gender Inequality Index (GII) are multidimensional measures that include education indicators to assess 'progress' toward gender equality at the national level. More specifically, gender measures of education have been defined by and operationalised within the EFA goals and MDGs. For example, the Millennium Development Goal promote gender equality and empowerment – has a specific target for "eliminating gender disparity" at all levels of education – and this goal is measured through indicators of sex-disaggregated data on primary and secondary enrolment, retention and completion (see, for example, the World Development Report 2012). Similarly, the Education for All Goal 5 specifies gender equality in education as "girls' equal access to and achievement in basic education of good quality". While this goal presumes the need to attend to equality through quality education, requiring gender analysis of schools and curricula as well as teacher training, it also narrowed the meaning of gender to girls' representation in education. Unterhalter (2014) notes considerable conceptual differences in the early framing of EFA and the MDGs, but in practice, as these goals became implemented, the measures reported in the Global Monitoring Report and the World Development Report are not that distinguishable. For example, the EFA Global Monitoring Report (2003/4) on Gender Equality notes the distinction between equality of opportunities (measured usually in access), equality in learning processes and equality of outcomes. However, to date most indicators used and data reported focus on what is usually referred to as inputs and outputs of education: enrolment, completion and transition rates. As we move toward the post-2015 agenda, there is a shift in emphasis to learning outcomes, often still assessed by sex-disaggregated data. It is to be seen whether measures will assess gendered pedagogical and learning processes.

Measures of inputs (access) and outputs (achievement) have been justifiably critiqued for assuming that redistribution (parity of girls and boys) of access and achievement would lead to empowerment. Aikman and Unterhalter's (2005) book, *Beyond Access*, calls for moving beyond parity to undertake more comprehensive and transformative approaches to gender equality.

They advocate the need for a wider framing of the MDGs and show how particular factors make schooling and education gender inequitable. They argue that "women and girls are not a homogenous category and that women themselves need to participate in decision making about their own education, to ensure that it is flexible and meets a wide range of different needs" (p. 6). While considerable research has shown the limits of gender and education measures for fostering gender equality, few alternatives have been developed, possibly because an assumption of such measures is their universality and their a priori nature of defining what gender equality looks like.

In cases where parity has been achieved according to these measures, claims have arisen that suggest the end of a 'gender problem' or a reverse gender problem, meaning that boys are not represented in schooling in equal numbers (Al-Samarrai 2009). However, Chisamya et al. (2012) show how, in Bangladesh and Malawi, gender parity as measured by enrolment and completion indicators does not address gender inequalities in the process of learning or in applying schooling to one's future livelihood. The use of these indicators and targets limits meanings of gender equality and empowerment within the international development agenda discourse. These measures are also applied universally without consideration of what a good quality education means and what empowerment in and through education is in places as distinct as nomadic communities (Dyer 2001), among diverse ethnic and castes in India (Bajaj 2012) or in communities where schooling is marked by considerable gender-based violence (Parkes and Heslop 2011).

A few examples of gender measures have emerged in an attempt to capture the multidimensional nature of gender equity through education. For example, Unterhalter, Heslop and Mamedu's (2013) work in Tanzanian and Nigerian schools develops three measures related to gender equality and schooling: a gender profile score, a gender management score and a teacher qualification score. These different measures are analysed to examine the relationships between resource distribution – human and economic – in schools and girls' empowerment. In another example of developing measures for an international NGO's work related to gender equality and empowerment, Miske and DeJaeghere (2013) report on a set of measures that assess changes in gendered norms related to schooling, asking girls and boys, teachers and communities their beliefs about which sex is more intelligent and better at school. Less has been done to develop measures of empowerment as an outcome of education, possibly due to the many diverse ways empowerment is exercised in different contexts and at different developmental stages. Studies that examine empowerment in specific contexts tend to draw on rich qualitative data to reveal microlevel changes in the interactions between girls and boys, their families, or their teachers. For example, Murphy-Graham (2008, 2012) and Bajaj (2009) have described how an agency is enacted by girls in settings in and outside schools, illustrating the many contingent ways that structures and people with whom they interact affect greatly how they are able to enact their agency.

The inability of current gender and education measures to capture the complexities of gender equality and empowerment are in part due to their positivistic and universal assumptions. Hochfeld and Bassadien (2007) note that universal, quantified and static indicators do not allow for debates to occur about how education is valued for fostering gender equality. As Kabeer (2005) eloquently argues:

> [G]ender inequalities are multi-dimensional and cannot be reduced to some single and universally agreed set of priorities. Any attempt to do so will run the danger of being either too narrow (as the MDGs have been accused of being) or a wish list that is too long and complex to act on. However, gender relationships are not internally

cohesive . . . a shift in one aspect of social relations can initiate a series of changes in other aspects, with unpredictable consequences.

(p. 23)

Framing the limitations of an empiricist epistemology to explain complex social change, Santos (2004) says: "because there is no single principle of social transformation, it is not possible to determine, in abstract, the articulations or hierarchies among the different social experiences and their conceptions of social transformation" (p. 182). Santos is arguing against a singular theoretical or epistemological approach to inform and explain social transformation. He suggests that we must look for the meanings and actions in local practices that have transformative possibility while also reading/translating these local meanings and practices across different times and space.

In sum, these two mechanisms attend to different levels of gender equality – institutional and individual – leaving a considerable gap in attending to how gender equality is fostered through pedagogical processes and local practices – or the spaces in which much negotiation and translation occurs. In the case of gender mainstreaming, which draws on many different conceptualisations of gender equality, it is implemented through an institutional approach often linked with a universal discourse of human rights, which reduces its translatability to local contexts. Gender measures and gender mainstreaming, when implemented in a technicist manner, do not often allow for the contested conceptualisations of gender equality in local contexts. While there is considerable interpretation and related actions that broaden the meanings and scope of gender mainstreaming and, less so, gender indicators, these usually occur in the translation of practices at the different levels (Unterhalter and North 2011). In addition, these local interpretations and practices seem to get lost or are made invisible as they move back up the levels to the development agenda.

Reframing gender and education for the post-2015 agenda and practice: a critical capability approach

In this section, I consider how a critical capability approach could allow for epistemic diversity and debate about how to foster gender equality in specific contexts. The capability approach has been used by scholars from many different epistemological, theoretical and methodological perspectives. One critique of the CA is that it is a "loose paradigm", undertheorised and lacking in epistemic clarity, particularly in relation to gender equality (Robeyns 2003; Alkire 2008). In response to this critique, Robeyns (2005) and Alkire (2008) discuss the capability approach as a normative and evaluative framework, distinct from theoretical uses of it, in which policies and social actions related to gender equality can be considered and taken. In this section, I use a CA as an evaluative framework that allows for bringing different epistemological orientations, and theoretical and methodological approaches, into the dialogue and use it to identify ways of redressing gender inequalities. Sen (2009) acknowledges his approach is both philosophical in intent and partial in conceptual and procedural considerations of equality and justice. However, for purposes of identifying and transforming gender inequalities, an evaluative approach is useful to take a step back from specific theories, methods or practices that a priori define equality and consider what equality means for individuals or groups in specific contexts. Used in this way, I posit that a CA, from a critical perspective, can provide ontological and epistemological guidance on the relationship of individuals and societies, including how to understand what equality could mean in different contextual and dynamic relationships. These ontological and epistemological orientations of a CA can be useful in framing gender equality in global agendas.

As an underspecified approach to justice, Deunelin, Nebel and Sagovsky (2006) critique a CA as being neutral as a political project, which, on the one hand, has allowed for it to be extensively employed through multiple epistemologies and methods; on the other hand, this has led to contradictory interpretations and uses. While I don't agree fully that Sen's CA is necessarily neutral, a common approach of employing it has tended to theorise and identify capabilities, without due attention to structural injustices in economic, political and cultural institutions and to the effects of power that flows through individuals and institutions (see Deneulin, Nebel and Sagovsky 2006; Hill 2003). Scholars employing a CA that do not give much attention to structural injustices, I suggest, misread or misuse Sen's ontological focus on individual well-being embedded within social relations. These studies tend to delink the concept of capabilities from the expansion of freedoms within the larger sociocultural and political-economic environment. For example, Walby (2012, cited in Unterhalter et al. 2013) has argued that the concepts of freedom and choice and the focus on the individual are "open signifiers" that can be easily tied to neoliberal agendas of the state. From this perspective, a capability and its related functionings are individual outcomes achieved through greater opportunities and enacting choice, and little attention is given to the processes of public debate and action necessary to transform structures of inequality.

A critical reading of Sen, I suggest, calls for attention to social structures and the injustices perpetuated by them. Sen (2009) writes, in response to Rawls's focus on just institutions, "Any theory of justice has to give an important place to the role of institutions ... however ... we have to seek institutions that promote justice, rather than treating the institutions as themselves manifestations of justice" (p. 82). Sen's position on institutions and social structures is similar to that of his rejection of Nussbaum's specific list of capabilities. He argues that both individual capabilities and institutions matter in realising justice, but the focus should be less on the right institutions or capabilities and more on the process of realising justice through social structures. However, because he does not specify the necessary conditions for fostering justice through institutions nor for enhancing capabilities, a capability approach has sometimes been used to identify more minimal meanings of the "good life" (Walker 2012) or is "too thin to offer guidelines for action to transform unjust structures" (Deneulin, Nebel and Sagovsky 2006: 9). A critical capability approach, distinct from some uses of it, ontologically situates individuals' and groups' well-being within societal structures that are unequal, including economic and political institutions as well as sociocultural norms that influence the conversion of capabilities to well-being.

Epistemologically, a critical capability approach allows for diverse perspectives to be brought to bear to both illuminate inequalities and to debate how to redress them so that unequal power structures and norms can shift in society. While Sen does not specify all the conditions for fostering justice, he does suggest that public debate and action are critical to transforming inequalities. However, the role of public debate and action in CA has not been given as much theoretical attention as have other concepts, such as capabilities (see DeJaeghere 2012; Alkire 2006). This perspective on public debate and action to identify and alter injustices stands in contrast to Nussbaum's approach, positioned within political liberalism, that identifies a minimal threshold of specific capabilities that the state should uphold to ensure well-being, particularly women's equality. While Nussbaum's approach brings a particular theoretical view to ensuring a specific set of capabilities, the development of a capability list has been much debated for the risk of being applied universally, even while most acknowledge it as a starting point for identifying specific capabilities in contexts (Nussbaum 2011; Walker 2007). A critical capability approach draws on an epistemology that is antiessentialist and inclusive, seeking ways to include diverse perspectives and values toward achieving equality and development. CA's emphasis on individuals' and groups' well-being in different contexts and times has important implications for gender approaches and measures that have often assumed universality. In the following paragraphs, I discuss the use of a critical capability approach as an evaluative space with a normative basis for considering gender equality in the post–2015 agenda, which provides ontological and epistemological guidance for situating gender equality in specific contexts and diverse perspectives.

The normative basis of a capability approach is that policies or programmes should advance equality and improve human well-being for all; this provides a rationale for a "universal" commitment to equality without necessarily applying universalism epistemologically or methodologically. Sen (1992) says the underlying question for development, and one that should be debated, is: equality of what and for whom. Such questions of development should focus on the impact policy and programme decisions have on individuals and groups, not solely on institutions or the nation-state more largely. For example, consider how transforming inequalities in a context in which girls and women are experiencing gender-based violence from teachers or adults as a result of being in school would prompt a debate about different policy and programme alternatives, and different ways to 'measure' equality, than in a situation in which girls and boys are supported financially and emotionally in their schooling but girls face different challenges than boys in obtaining employment after completing their education (see, for example, Jeffery and Jeffery 1994; Jeffrey, Jeffery and Jeffery 2008). Therefore, the question of how to advance equality is not only with regard to the ends achieved, such as getting an education or being employed, but also the means of achieving a valued end.

A critical reading of the capability approach ontologically and epistemologically links an individual's well-being with social relations at many levels. CA is a relational approach that does not attribute inequality simply to characteristics of an individual, such as a poor woman; instead, these inequalities are imbedded in larger societal and institutional relations, such as gender relations. For example, Sen (1992) discusses gender inequalities with regard to many different social relations in both low- and high-income societies. He suggests that underlying causes of gender inequalities are related to intrafamily relations (including mothers/fathers and siblings); societal economic relations and opportunities, such as labour market segregation; and international mobility and migration. This implies that educational interventions and measures toward gender equality cannot focus on the individual nor societal institutions as discrete areas for change. For example, measure of education participation and completion or of the existence of a gender discrimination policy are insufficient to demonstrate the transformation in gender inequalities. A relational approach considers how the girl or woman experiences inequalities with regard to the institution, such as schooling, and in turn how schooling affects the specific inequalities experienced. Such complex relationships necessitate an inclusive epistemology that allows for different methods and perspectives to explain inequality in contextually specific social relations. Drawing on diverse ways of seeing gender inequalities may also reveal new ways of transforming them.

An epistemological and political orientation that a critical capability approach brings to considering gender in the post–2015 agenda involves the role of public debate and dialogue in identifying what equality means, how it is being constrained and how to transform inequalities in specific contexts through policies and practices. Sen (2009) suggests that the means of expanding freedoms entails debate about how to achieve equality, and this debate is ongoing and does not necessarily reach a consensus. He argues against a unique set of principles for making choices and decisions and notes the importance of "possible plurality of robust and impartial reasons that can emerge" (p. 201). This perspective has important epistemological implications in that it suggests the importance of a plurality of not only actors but, importantly, ideas and perspectives. Public debate of different actors and ideas as an epistemological orientation is not a call for relativism. Sen grounds his arguments on democratic practice and debate in a neo-Marxist perspective that conflict exists within societies and there may not always be consensus, but there are better and worse policies and political actions for promoting equality within specific contexts. He states: "One implication of this line of reasoning (of a plurality of reasons) is the recognition that a broad theory of justice that makes room for non-congruent considerations ... need not thereby make itself incoherent, or unmanageable, or useless. Definite conclusions can emerge despite the plurality" (Sen 2009: 397). He goes on to argue that such a plurality of ideas can bring about definitive conclusions, even if partial, without there being a necessity of the "best or right choice in seeking justice" (p. 398). Thus, the use of public debate can and should allow for epistemic dialogue and, if grounded in a critical and relational ontology, offers some room for bringing different perspectives to bear on gender issues without succumbing to minimal meanings of equality.

To further Sen's idea of public debate within the context of global agendas as they are interpreted and enacted in national and local contexts, Fraser's (2009) concept of representation at different scales is useful. A critique of international debates and agenda setting, and particularly the MDGs, is that a plurality of voices is not represented. In addition, national and local educational policies are driven by international agendas more than by local perspectives on the value of education. This is one use of Fraser's concept in which she refers to an ordinary-political representation of having one's voice represented in local, national or international fora where decisions that affect one's well-being are taken. From this perspective, those who are involved in defining and deciding the post-2015 agenda argue that they have attempted to include multiple voices and perspectives. However, Fraser also describes representation as the framing or "mis-framing" of the boundaries of debate in which the perspectives by which the debate is framed already exclude alternative perspectives. For example, framing of gender equality in education through access or completion, which national governments had to include in their education strategies and report on to international organisations, results in epistemological and social exclusion of other forms of gender inequalities. An implication of Fraser's second perspective on representation related to the post-2015 agenda is to encourage ongoing public debate at multiple levels so that contextually specific practices, goals and targets can be identified and implemented.

This epistemological orientation of epistemic diversity relates to Santos' work on critical approaches to knowledge creation and application in the global South. He suggests that an epistemological principle for social transformation should be that it is "artisanal rather than architectural work" (Santos 2013: 51), meaning ideas emerge from and are embedded, translated, enlarged and reframed rather than imposed from elsewhere. Such artisanal work would allow for enlarging the theoretical and methodological approaches used in specific contexts to address contested realities about gender inequalities. While Sen does not explicitly call for multiple epistemologies to inform development agendas, practices and measures, his own work draws on diverse perspectives and epistemologies, including Indian and Western philosophy, economics, legal studies, and feminist analysis. In addition, Sen (1992) emphasises the "incompleteness in inequality evaluation" in which he argues a conclusive or right approach or measure to equality may not be possible; he suggests that even with this incompleteness, inequalities can be made "visible from different angles, and not by lumping them together with more fine-tuned presumptions" (p. 135). His approach gives a strong critique of singular and universal approaches to and measures of gender equality in education that have dominated the international agendas. In sum, the international agenda should take into account the potentially contradictory and socially embedded values that individuals and communities hold for gender equality that are situated in distinctly different social and historical relations.

Considerations for policymaking, research and practice

In this chapter, I have suggested that a critical capability approach as an evaluative space onto-logically positions individuals' and groups' well-being in relation to broader social structures, without specifying the theoretical explanations of which relations matter in which contexts. Epistemologically, a critical CA calls for diverse perspectives and epistemic dialogue to illuminate what gender equality means and how it can be achieved in specific sites. From an ethical perspective, CA provides a normative basis for development and education agendas to focus on questions and debates about equality rather than, for example, poverty reduction or economic growth. The normative basis of a critical CA provides for a global commitment to gender equality in the post-2015 agenda, without specifying targets and measures that either narrow its scope or limit its meanings. These ontological and epistemological orientations that a critical capability approach offers also provide for some partial starting points for the political and conceptual work of gender equality in the post-2015 development agenda.

First, CA's relational ontology can be further enhanced with relational frameworks and approaches to move beyond the institutional and individual binary represented by the dominant emphasis on gender mainstreaming and education and gender measures. However, as Santos and Nnaemeka have argued, relational theories from 'elsewhere' should not be applied to local contexts. Nnaemeka asserts that when epistemologies and concepts from elsewhere are applied to other local settings, they may not allow for learning from the 'the other' or local people's specific experiences. Instead, scholars and educators need to make these relational explanations translatable to the specific experiences of women/girls and men/boys and the social conditions that constrain them. For instance, girls and boys, families and communities may not regard sexual abuse of girls by male teachers, for example, as best addressed by ensuring the right to bodily integrity protected by the state or as exemplified by a reduction in the number of girls experiencing such violence. This gender injustice is part of a larger web of social relations between men and women in communities, and norms and institutional structures regarding who is seen as capable of learning in school, who is regarded as powerful in the school or community, who 'needs' economic support to pay for school and who should act on sexual desire. By drawing on local knowledges, practices and lived experiences, a more holistic sense of how gender inequalities are experienced and the ways in which they can be redressed can be understood. In addition, engaging epistemic dialogues among those who are affected and concerned about gender relations and equity can further what Unterhalter and Dorward (2013) refer to as "the missing middle" in gender equality scholarship and practice – or the spaces in which gender equality gets negotiated and international goals are translated by local communities or teachers and administrators. Such epistemic dialogues are distinctly different from universal approaches that aim to define 'what works' to achieve specific predefined outcomes.

Second, targets and measures will continue to play a role in demonstrating change toward equality in the post-2015 agenda (Subrahmanian 2005). However, specific targets and measures illustrate broad trends at best, and they can misguide subsequent action or generate negative repercussions at worst (see also Fukuda-Parr 2014 for more on the methodological limitations and distortions of targets). For example, indicators that show that gender parity in education has been achieved from a narrow definition of enrolment can wrongly reallocate funding and programmes to other areas or can trigger negative responses to programmes that continue to focus on women and girls. A critical capability approach suggests that targets and measures might best be negotiated at multiple levels, including within NGO programmes, by local and national governments and by funders in dialogue with local participants. Methodologically, a critical capability approach posits that there are diverse ways in which humans experience inequalities and diverse-valued well-being outcomes, suggesting that utilising mixed methodologies and multiple indicators as measures of gender equality may better represent local realities. While some scholars (e.g., Beetham and Demitriades 2007) have called for qualitative, ethnographic and participatory approaches to get at locally constructed meanings and processes, there remains a scant body of literature that share local methods and measures. An epistemic dialogue that draws on an "ecology of knowledges" to inform the international agenda and its implementation in local contexts could go a long way toward understanding and transforming gender inequalities in education globally.

Note

1 I wish to thank Bindu Timiri and Aditi Arur for the contributions they made to this chapter. I am grateful to comments from Simon McGrath and anonymous reviewers, which have strengthened the chapter.

References

Aikman, S., Unterhalter, E. (Eds.), 2005. *Beyond Access: Transforming Policy and Practice for Gender Equality in Education*. Oxfam, Oxford.

Alkire, S., 2006. Structural injustice and democratic practice: the trajectory in Sen's writings. In: Deneulin, S., Nebel, M. and Sagovsky, N. (Eds.) *Transforming Unjust Structures: The Capability Approach*. Springer, Dordrecht.

Alkire, S., 2008. Using the capability approach: prospective and evaluative analyses. In: Comim, F., Qizilbash, M. and Alkire, S. (Eds.) *The Capability Approach: Concepts, Measures and Applications*. Cambridge University Press, Cambridge.

Al-Samarrai, S., 2009. Education spending and equity in Bangladesh. In: Narayan, A. and Zaman, H. (Eds.) *Breaking Down Poverty in Bangladesh*. The University Press, Dhaka.

Bajaj, M., 2009. "I have big things planned for my future": The limits and possibilities of transformative agency in Zambian schools. *Compare* 39, 4, 551–568.

Bajaj, M., 2012. From "time pass" to transformative force: school-based human rights education in Tamil Nadu, India. *International Journal of Educational Development* 32, 1, 72–80.

Beetham, G., Demetriades, J., 2007. Feminist research methodologies and development: overview and practical application. *Gender and Development* 15, 2, 199–216.

Chisamya, G., DeJaeghere, J., Kendall, N., Khan, M., 2012. Gender and Education for All: progress and problems in achieving gender equity. *International Journal of Educational Development* 32, 6, 743–755.

DeJaeghere, J., 2012. Public debate and dialogue from a capabilities approach: can it foster gender justice in education? *Journal of Human Development and Capabilities* 13, 3, 353–372.

DeJaeghere, J., Pellowski Wiger, N., 2013. Gender discourses in an NGO education project: openings for transformation toward gender equality in Bangladesh. *International Journal of Educational Development* 33, 6, 557–565.

Deneulin, S., Nebel, M., Sagovsky, N. (Eds.), 2006. *Transforming Unjust Structures: The Capability Approach*. Springer, Dordrecht.

Dyer, C., 2001. Nomads and Education for All: education for development or domestication? *Comparative Education* 37, 3, 315–327.

Epstein, D., Morrell, R., 2012. Approaching Southern theory: explorations of gender in South African education. *Gender and Education* 24, 5, 469–482.

Fennell, S., Arnot, M., 2008. Decentring hegemonic gender theory: the implications for educational research. *Compare* 38, 5, 525–538.

Fraser, N., 2009. *Scales of Justice: Reimagining Political Space in a Globalizing World*, Columbia University Press, New York.

Frediani, A., Boni, A., Gasper, D., 2014. Approaching development projects from a human development and capability perspective. *Journal of Human Development and Capabilities* 15, 1, 1–12.

Fukuda-Parr, S., 2014. Global goals as policy tool: intended and unintended consequences. *Journal of Human Development and Capabilities* 15, 2–3, 118–131.

Gender and Development Network, 2013. *Achieving Gender Equality and Women's Empowerment in the Post-2015 Framework*. www.gadnetwork.org.uk

Greany, K., 2008. Rhetoric versus reality: exploring the rights-based approach to girls' education in rural Niger. *Compare* 38, 5, 555–568.

Hill, M., 2003. Development as empowerment. *Feminist Economics* 9, 2, 117–135.

Hochfeld, T., Bassadien, S.R., 2007. Participation, values, and implementation: three research challenges in developing gender-sensitive indicators. *Gender and Development* 15, 2, 217–230.

Jeffrey, C., Jeffery, P., Jeffery, R., 2008. *Degrees without Freedom? Education, Masculinities, and Unemployment in North India.* Stanford University Press, Stanford.

Jeffery, P., Jeffery, R., 1994. Killing my heart's desire: education and female autonomy in rural north India. In: Kumar, N. (Ed.) *Women as Subjects: South Asian Histories.* University Press of Virginia, Charlottesville.

Kabeer, N., 1999. Resources, agency, achievements: reflections on the measurement of women's empowerment. *Development and Change* 30, 3, 435–464.

Kabeer, N., 2005. Gender equality and women's empowerment: a critical analysis of the third Millennium Development Goal 1. *Gender and Development* 13, 1, 13–24.

Leach, F.E., 2003. *Practising Gender Analysis in Education.* Oxfam, Oxford.

Maslak, M.A. (Ed.), 2008. *The Structure and Agency of Women's Education.* SUNY Press, Albany.

Mehra, R., Gupta, G.R., 2006. *Gender Mainstreaming: Making It Happen.* International Center for Research on Women, Washington.

Miske, S., DeJaeghere, J., 2013. Measuring gender and educational quality: the need for social learning outcomes. Paper presented at the Comparative and International Education Society Conference, Toronto.

Miske, S., Meagher, M., DeJaeghere, J., 2010. Gender mainstreaming in education at the level of field operations: the case of CARE USA's indicator framework. *Compare* 40, 4, 441–458.

Morley, L., 2010. Gender mainstreaming: myths and measurement in higher education in Ghana and Tanzania. *Compare* 40, 4, 533–550.

Moser, C., Moser, A., 2005. Gender mainstreaming since Beijing: a review of success and limitations in international institutions. *Gender and Development* 13, 2, 11–22.

Murphy-Graham, E., 2008. Opening the black box: women's empowerment and innovative secondary education in Honduras. *Gender and Education* 20, 1, 31–50.

Murphy-Graham, E., 2012. *Opening Minds, Improving Lives: Education and Women's Empowerment in Honduras.* Vanderbilt University Press, Nashville.

Nnaemeka, O., 2004. Negro-feminism: theorizing, practicing, and pruning Africa's way. *Signs* 29, 2, 357–385.

Nussbaum, M., 2000. Women's capabilities and social justice. *Journal of Human Development* 1, 2, 219–247.

Nussbaum, M.C., 2011. *Creating capabilities.* Harvard University Press.

OECD, n.d. *Gender Equality and Women's Rights in the Post-2015 Agenda: A Foundation for Sustainable Development. Element 3, Paper 1.* OECD, Paris.

Ong, A., 2011. Translating gender justice in Southeast Asia: situated ethics, NGOs, and bio-welfare. *Hawwa* 9, 1/2, 1–2.

Parkes, J., Heslop, J., 2011. *Stop Violence Against Girls in School: A Cross Country Analysis of Baseline Research from Ghana, Kenya and Mozambique.* Institute of Education and ActionAid International, London.

Parpart, J., Rai, S., Staudt, K. (Eds.), 2002. *Rethinking Empowerment: Gender and Development in a Global/Local World.* Routledge, London and New York.

Robeyns, I., 2003. Sen's capability approach and gender inequality: selecting relevant capabilities. *Feminist Economics* 9, 2/3, 61–92.

Robeyns, I., 2005. The capability approach: a theoretical survey. *Journal of Human Development* 6, 1, 93–117.

Santos, B. de S., 2004. A critique of lazy reason: against the waste of experience. In: Wallerstein, I. (Ed.) *The Modern World System in the Longue Durée.* Paradigm, Boulder.

Santos, B. de S., Nunes, J.A., Menses, M.P., 2007. Opening up the canon of knowledge and recognition of difference. In: Santos, B. de S. (Ed.) *Another Knowledge is Possible: Beyond Northern Epistemologies.* Random House, New York.

Santos, B. de S., 2013. Public sphere and epistemologies of the South. *Africa Development* 37, 1, 43–67.

Schultz, P., 2002. Why governments should invest more to educate girls. *World Development* 30, 2, 207–225.

Sen, A., 1992. *Inequality Reexamined.* Oxford University Press, Oxford.

Sen, A., 2009. *The Idea of Justice.* Harvard University Press, Cambridge, MA.

Sharma, P., Verma, G., Arur, A., 2013. Negotiating meanings of gender justice: critical reflections on dialogs and debates in a non-governmental organization (NGO). *International Journal of Educational Development* 33, 6, 576–584.

Silfver, A.L., 2010. Emancipation or neo-colonisation? Global gender mainstreaming policies, Swedish gender equality politics and local negotiations about putting gender into education reforms in the Lao People's Democratic Republic. *Compare* 40, 4, 479–495.

Strega, S., 2005. The view from the poststructural margins. In: Brown, L. and Strega, S. (Eds.) *Research as Resistance: Critical, Indigenous and Anti-oppressive Approaches.* Canadian Scholars' Press, Toronto.

Stromquist, N.P., 1990. Gender inequality in education: accounting for women's subordination. *British Journal of Sociology of Education* 11, 2, 137–153.

Stromquist, N.P., 2008. The intersection of public policies and gender: understanding state action in education. In: Maslak, M.A. (Ed.) *The Structure and Agency of Women's Education.* SUNY Press, Albany.

Subrahmanian, R., 2005. Gender equality in education: definitions and measurements. *International Journal of Educational Development* 25, 4, 395–407.

Tembon, M., Fort, L., 2008. *Girls' Education in the 21st century: Gender Equality, Empowerment, and Economic Growth.* World Bank, Washington.

United Nations Children's Fund, 2001. Defining Quality in Education. Working Paper UNICEF/PD/ED/00/02, UNICEF, New York.

United States Agency for International Development, 2007. *Gender Equality in Education: A Dynamic Framework.* Washington, DC: MSI International. http://www.usaid.gov/our_work/cross-cutting_programs/wid/ed/equate.html

Unterhalter, E., 2005. Fragmented frameworks? Researching women, gender, education and development. In: Aikman, S. and Unterhalter, E. (Eds.) *Beyond Access: Transforming Policy and Practice for Gender Equality in Education.* Oxfam, Oxford.

Unterhalter, E., 2007. Global values and gender equality in education. In: Fennell, S. and Arnot, M. (Eds.) *Gender Education and Equality in a Global Context.* Routledge, New York.

Unterhalter, E., 2014. Measuring education for the Millennium Development Goals: Reflections on targets, indicators, and a post-2015 framework. *Journal of Human Development and Capabilities* 15, 1, 1–12.

Unterhalter, E., Brighouse, H., 2007. Distribution of what for social justice in education? The case of Education for All by 2015. In: Walker, M. and Unterhalter, E. (Eds.) *Amartya Sen's Capability Approach and Social Justice in Education.* Palgrave Macmillan, New York.

Unterhalter, E., Dorward, A., 2013. New MDGs, development concepts, principles and challenges in a post-2015 world. *Social Indicators Research* 113, 2, 609–625.

Unterhalter, E., Heslop, J., Mamedu, A., 2013. Girls claiming education rights: reflections on distribution, empowerment and gender justice in Northern Tanzania and Northern Nigeria. *International Journal of Educational Development* 33, 6, 566–575.

Unterhalter, E., North, A., 2010. Assessing gender mainstreaming in the education sector: Depoliticized technique or a step towards women's rights and gender equality? *Compare* 41, 4, 389–404.

Unterhalter, E., North, A., 2011. Responding to the gender and education Millennium Development Goals in South Africa and Kenya: reflections on education rights, gender equality, capabilities and global justice. *Compare* 41, 4, 495–511.

Vavrus, F., 2002. Constructing consensus: The feminist modern and the reconstruction of gender. *Current Issues in Comparative Education* 5, 1, 51–63.

Vavrus, F., Richey, L.A., 2003. Women and development: rethinking policy and reconceptualizing practice. *Women's Studies Quarterly* 3/4, 6–18.

Walby, S., 2005. Gender mainstreaming: productive tensions in theory and practice. *Social Politics* 12, 3, 321–343.

Walker, M., 2007. Selecting capabilities for gender equality in education. In: Walker, M. and Unterhalter, E. (Eds.) *Amartya Sen's Capability Approach and Social Justice in Education.* Palgrave McMillan, New York.

Walker, M., 2012. A capital or capabilities education narrative in a world of staggering inequalities? *International Journal of Educational Development* 32, 3, 384–393.

World Bank, 2012. *World Development Report 2012: Gender Equality and Development.* World Bank, Washington.

World Conference on Education for All, 1990. *World Declaration on Education for All and Framework for Action to Meet Basic Learning Needs.* Interagency Commission, New York.

7

EDUCATION AND RURAL DEVELOPMENT

Proposing an alternative paradigm[1]

Anna Robinson-Pant

Introduction

"Educated men and women are more likely to find work"

"Education narrows pay gaps between men and women"

"Schooling can save the planet: higher levels of education lead to more concern about the environment"

"Education keeps hunger away: mothers' education improves children's nutrition"

"Educated people are more tolerant"

These statements in UNESCO's (2013a) *Education Transforms Lives* are backed up by statistical data illustrating, for instance, the wage gap between women with secondary education as compared to women with primary education only. The graphics in this publication extrapolate from such statistics to show what the situation might be if Education for All were to be achieved – for example, if all women completed primary education in sub-Saharan Africa, there could be a 70% reduction in mothers dying in childbirth. The breakdown of country data implies the mechanism by which this reduction might be achieved – "In Cameroon, 54% of literate mothers from poor households have the benefit of a skilled attendant, compared with 19% of mothers who are not literate". The UNESCO document thus puts forward a powerful case that education "needs to be a central part of any post-2015 global development framework", and that "to unlock the wider benefits of education, all children need the chance to complete not only primary school but also lower secondary school" (p. 2).

This argument that education can solve the problems of poverty, health and even political conflict is so strong within education and international development policy and research that it is difficult to consider other perspectives. Any critical discussion of the link between education and the perceived social and economic benefits can often appear to challenge or deny the importance and value of education. This chapter sets out to look at the assumptions behind the dominant research and policy paradigm and propose alternative ways of looking at both education and development. By focusing specifically on education in relation to rural livelihoods, I explore how policymakers could take greater account of the complexity of relationships between diverse forms and practices of learning, education and livelihoods. In contrast to the dominant paradigm informed by quantitative evidence of the relationships between education and development, this alternative perspective on education and development relies on qualitative, and particularly ethnographic data, for the analysis.

What is wrong with the dominant paradigm?

Statistical evidence demonstrating the relationship between education and development often conflates causation and correlation – overlooking, for instance, that a positive relationship between education and political participation indicators might be caused by a third factor (such as income/socioeconomic status). Many such studies have been conducted, analysing the relationship between literacy and maternal and child health (LeVine, LeVine and Schnell 2009, LeVine et al 2004), literacy and fertility rates (Cochrane 1979) and literacy and income (St. Clair 2010). This chapter is, however, more concerned with the assumptions about education that underlie the dominant paradigm.

In particular, this model of analysis relies on a notion of measurable inputs and outcomes: educational inputs (schools, classes, programmes – with education usually being regarded as synonymous with schooling) and outcomes (measurable competencies, literacy rates, school examination passes). Similarly, development indicators to be correlated with educational achievement are measurable and need to be indisputably 'benefits' (such as lower child and maternal mortality), rather than contested development indicators such as migration rates. Recent major cross-national surveys (such as Programme for International Student Assessment (PISA), Programme for International Assessment of Adult Competencies (PIAAC), International Adult Literacy Survey (IALS), Literacy Assessment and Monitoring Programme (LAMP) and Southern and Eastern Africa Consortium for Monitoring Education Quality (SACMEQ)[2]) have demonstrated some of the difficulties involved in producing comparative statistical measures – not least the tendency to focus on the learning outcomes that are easiest to measure rather than the skills that are most needed by the economy or even by respondents themselves. For instance, the PIAAC (OECD 2013) survey of adult skills in 24 countries (OECD, Cyprus and the Russian Federation) assessed only reading skills, not writing – although research indicates that most adults join literacy programmes to learn to write.

By focusing narrowly on the relationship between educational outcomes and development, little attention is paid to what kind of education and what kind of development is being measured. In fact, as Joshi and Ghose (2012) point out in their account of shifts in the adult educational policy discourse in India, there have been significant changes in the kind of education being promoted – from "education as a universal good for men and women" in the 1950s/60s to the instrumentalist "functional literacy" of the 1970s and literacy for empowerment in the 1980s/90s. From 2000 onwards, they suggest that there has been a shift from a 'socially transformative agenda' to market-oriented agendas, with an emphasis on skills to train and prepare adults for the market. Despite these indications of changes in curriculum objectives, schooling (and this includes formal approaches to adult education) tends to be treated as uniform across cultural contexts and institutions, often conflating 'literate' and 'educated'. Research demonstrating the relationship between education and development may actually be reporting on different kinds of education. For instance, UNESCO (2014a: 147) cites evidence that educated farmers were likely to make better use of technologies (irrigation technology in China, soil conservation measures in Nepal and increased fertiliser use in Ethiopia) and move into higher value crops. The studies cited varied according to whether the measure of 'educated' was schooling (for instance, completion of primary school in the Nepal study) or literacy (which could have been acquired informally). Within policy contexts, correlations between development and women's literacy rates are frequently taken as evidence to promote adult literacy programmes for improved female or child health. However, such studies rarely disaggregate the effect of girls' schooling from that of adult learning (see Bown 1990) – with the implication that women's literacy programmes may not influence health knowledge in the same way as girls' schooling.

The dominant paradigm of education and rural development is not only informed by the notion of a linear relationship but is also based on an assumed hierarchy of skills/knowledge: for instance, that basic numeracy and literacy skills should precede vocational learning. Much research on rural development and education has built on Lockheed, Jamison and Lau's (1980) seminal finding that four years of schooling makes a difference to a farmer's productivity. Consequent studies have aimed to provide more evidence that schooling is a necessary foundation for any further learning: for instance, Brooks et al. (2013: 31) cite recent research showing "that more educated farmers are the first to adopt new seeds, tillage practices, fertilizers and animal breeds". The UNESCO Global Monitoring Report on EFA *Youth and Skills: Putting Education to Work* (2012a: 14) develops this idea further with a model of three different types of skill development – foundational skills (literacy and numeracy skills "necessary for getting work that can pay enough to meet daily needs"), transferable skills ("needed to adapt to different work environments", such as the ability to solve problems) and technical/vocational skills ("specific technical know-how" for certain jobs like growing vegetables). There is an implied hierarchy of skills and knowledge through the term 'foundation' skills. These ideas around a linear progression and hierarchy of skills have informed much policy on education and rural development and support the 'literacy first' approach critiqued by Rogers (2000) to vocational skill training and agricultural extension. Nonschooled adults can be excluded from such extension programmes, due to lack of literacy skills or school certificates (see IFAD-UNESCO 2014).

Due to the prioritising of Universal Primary Education (UPE), adult literacy remains the most neglected educational goal and consequently is underresourced and marginalised within most countries' educational and development agendas (Wagner 2011). Debates on the relationship between education and development thus assume that the key target group for policymakers are school-aged children and young people. Within policy discourse in differing contexts, Te Lintelo (2012: 99) suggests that youth are constructed variously as "passive clients, constrained decision makers and autonomous agents" – none of which takes full account of young people's diverse and often multiple identities, roles and experiences. In the dominant education and development paradigm, young people are positioned primarily as "passive clients" with little control over the kind of education and development they desire. Sumberg et al. (2012) suggest that many governments take an 'instrumental' approach to engaging the young as future agents of change – rather than considering their role in the 'here and now'. This would seem to be the case in the education sector, where debates focus on how to prepare them as future citizens who can contribute effectively to economic growth. The almost exclusive focus on schooling within the dominant policy and research paradigm means that young people's other current roles are often overlooked, notably as agricultural workers. Above all, such analysis fails to take account of the informal learning in which they engage during everyday activities in their communities. This seems the greatest limitation of the dominant paradigm – that by focusing on the relationship between schooling and development, no consideration is given to the informal learning already taking place within and outside educational institutions.

The above analysis has highlighted some assumptions implicit in the dominant discourse on education and development: the prioritisation of schooling and formal learning above other forms of learning; a focus on education for children and the construction of youth as a time of preparation; the notion of education as a linear process leading to development; and learning as a hierarchical structure of skills/knowledge, starting with basic numeracy and literacy skills.

Turning to rural development specifically, research has shown that the school curriculum is often not appropriate to the needs of rural economies and can serve to undermine indigenous values and agricultural knowledge and skills. This may be conveyed through the hidden curriculum by teachers who have themselves left behind agricultural work and their identities as rural agricultural workers. For instance, Biriwasha's (2012) research in Zimbabwe revealed that agriculture was presented by teachers as a profession for men not women and as "unsophisticated and backward" as compared to an "exciting, modern livelihood or career choice". Perpetuation of such stereotypes – in a world where at least 70% of the poorest people are living in rural areas (IFAD 2010) – suggest an urgent need to reconceptualise the relationship between education and development. Our first step could be to challenge the assumption that education should be informed by Western values and curricula (as implied by the aim to have comparative indicators of educational attainment across nations) or lead necessarily out of rural livelihoods.

Reconceptualising education and rural development

The next section offers three different perspectives on learning, young people and schooling in rural areas in order to develop an alternative model for examining rural development and education. Adopting this approach would imply promoting a more participatory approach to research and policy processes, which can respond to people's experiences (both inside and outside educational programmes) and seek to give greater voice to their views and perspectives on learning.

A wider perspective on learning in rural communities

Schools and educational programmes are not the only or even major sites where learning takes place in rural communities. Taking a wider perspective on education and development involves investigating informal learning through everyday activities and how such learning is being transformed through technological and social changes in rural economies. Informal and intergenerational transfer of skills and knowledge has always been an important – though sometimes unrecognised – process within rural development. In many economies, however, formal education has tended to be valued above informal learning. Rather than seeing the relationship between informal and formal learning as hierarchical and polarised, Colley, Hodkinson and Malcolm (2003) suggest that it is "more accurate to conceive of formality and informality as attributes present in all circumstances of learning". Rogers (2013) proposes informal and formal learning as "lying on a continuum ranging from accidental/incidental learning, through task-conscious learning, through self-directed learning to non-formal and formal learning" (p. 5). Our attention is then shifted to considering the kind of learning taking place through different activities and institutions, and this raises questions about whether informal learning can be assessed or evaluated in the same way as formal learning. Rogers (p. 5) distinguishes between purposeful, planned and 'learning-conscious learning' ('measured by learning') as compared to informal, accidental/incidental learning 'measured by task'.

Understanding and researching informal learning presents particular challenges, as people do not always recognise or know themselves how they learned a particular skill or task. As Rogers and Street (2012: 36) noted from their ethnographic research into literacy practices, many people did not see informal learning as 'learning': 'it was seen simply as "doing" something, completing some task that they needed or wished to do. They did not say at the end, "I have learned this and that"; 'they simply said, "I have done that well (or not so well)"'. Polyani's (1967) term 'tacit knowledge' (defined as "that which we know but cannot tell") identifies the difficulty of discussing this kind of knowledge and learning process in tangible ways. It is clearly easier to measure and take account of formal learning and education (as in the dominant paradigm) than to try to attempt to capture the many different kinds of informal learning taking place in rural communities.

Recognising that learning takes place outside educational institutions and planned interventions can lead us to investigate farms, factories, households, community gatherings, religious institutions and market places as learning spaces. The related concepts of 'situated learning' (Lave and Wenger 1991), 'situated literacies' (Barton, Hamilton and Ivanic 2000) and 'social literacies' (Street 1995) are important for exploring how people are learning traditional and new skills, including new literacies, in these spaces. The starting point for investigating embedded literacies is the view that

> [L]iteracy is not practised in a vacuum: it is always embedded within some socio-cultural set of activities, and it is these activities, not the literacy itself, which provide the material for the analysis of literacy practices.
>
> (Rogers and Street 2012: 17)

Such research has investigated how apparently 'illiterate' people engage with multiple literacy practices and literacies in their lives, analysing informal networks and the meanings associated with different domains of literacy practice (such as business literacies as compared to religious literacies). In particular, young people are learning digital literacies in rural communities through interaction with peers and developing their own strategies, for instance using visual symbols to recognise caller names and numbers (Kelemu et al. – Ethiopia country study in IFAD-UNESCO 2014). In a study in Kenya, Njenga, Mugo and Opiyo (2012) noted that 'most of the youth can manoeuvre most of the ICTs including accessing the internet using mobile phones'. These findings show that when people recognise the value of new technology, they quickly learn and share the knowledge with others. Informal and embedded learning needs to be viewed as social and collaborative, in contrast to a conceptualisation of learning as an individualised activity (as implicit in the dominant paradigm with its emphasis on individual performance and outcomes).

Globalisation and technological, environmental and climate change are increasingly influencing livelihood strategies in rural economies, with implications not only for what people see as 'development' but also for the kind of informal learning taking place in these communities. Changing patterns of land ownership – particularly large-scale development by foreign investors and the growth of 'super farms' – mean that young people are less likely to work on their family's land as smallholder farmers (see Chinsinga and Chasukwa 2012). Brooks et al. (2013: 13) identify four distinctive agricultural career paths followed by young people: full-time on existing family holdings, full-time on new holdings, part-time combined with household enterprise (such as sale of services) and off-farm wage work. Each of these options involves different skills and learning opportunities – both formal and informal learning through work. As new forms of social and economic organisation are developing in rural areas, people need to acquire different skills. Analysing foreign agricultural investment contracts in sub-Saharan Africa, Fernandez (2012) reveals the tendency for governments to use the land of smallholders, displacing local communities, and notes that there has been unbalanced bargaining power with local stakeholders having little voice in such decisions. This analysis suggests the importance of soft-skill development alongside new technical expertise.

It is important to develop a gendered perspective on learning in rural communities – in terms of the skills that women and men are learning informally, how these are shaped by gendered relations, and also gendered access to formal educational opportunities. In the context of increasing male migration to cities, Collett and Gale (2009) noted the wider variety of agricultural tasks that women in which were becoming involved, including traditional 'male' areas of work. They suggested that women smallholder farmers in particular:

> [N]ot only require the technical skills to improve their productivity, but they also need to be equipped with skills to negotiate rapidly changing agricultural markets and adapt their productive activities in response to the new niches it creates.
>
> (p. 13)

In this section, I have outlined ways in which rural communities are being rapidly transformed, influencing the kinds of learning and knowledge being practised informally. Taking a wider lens on learning involves looking at informal and formal learning processes and outcomes in everyday situations as well as in educational programmes – focusing on social practices in these communities rather than using the entry point of 'education'. A gendered analysis of rural livelihood practices can reveal not only how women's and men's learning experiences differ but also how changing gender relations and practices (such as women moving into traditional 'male' skill areas) might be taken into account in educational and development policy.

Recognising young people as active citizens

Within much educational policy informed by human capital theory, young people tend to be positioned as students (or as 'out-of-school' youth) and as recipients of skills and knowledge required by society/the economy. Although most governments have moved on from the traditional learner as 'empty vessel' stance critiqued by Freire (1970), there is still a sense in which educationalists are concerned with shaping young people as future citizens. This policy perspective does not take account of the fact that many young people (including those at school) are already active in shaping their lives and contributing to household economies. Youth also tend to be defined as a homogeneous group in policy, with a lack of acknowledgement of their differences according to gender, poverty, age, geography and ethnicity. Although youth were singled out as the key target group for MDG target 16 ("to develop and implement strategies for decent and productive work for youth"), the emphasis has been largely on urban youth, rarely the poorer young people or women in rural communities. As te Lintelo (2012) argues:

> As long as youth are seen as an undifferentiated and problematic mass that is to be acted upon, to be protected, reformed and directed. . . . Agricultural policies are likely to prescribe one-size-fits-all solutions (e.g., modernisation) that are insensitive to the varied needs and instrumental ways in which young people engage in agriculture.
>
> (p. 100)

Within the educational sector, too, there has been a tendency to assume that all young people should attend school in order to acquire the skills required for enhanced rural livelihoods. As I will discuss later, schools have sometimes proved particularly problematic in terms of the gap between the curriculum and the needs of rural economies.

Traditionally, youth has been seen as a transition from childhood into adulthood, from dependence to independence (White 2012), and these assumptions of young people as passive and dependent on elders informs much educational policy. Bennell (2010) points out, however, that this transition stage hardly exists in many developing countries, where children are expected to engage in subsistence or paid work from an early age (in rural Ethiopia, 80% of children aged

5–14 years old work) and marry early. Research into young people's experiences in rural areas offers a more holistic perspective on the relationship between learning, agriculture and social change than that which underpins the dominant education and development paradigm. For instance, recent ethnographic-style research in Cambodia, Egypt and Ethiopia suggested that young people viewed family farming as a 'given' within a variety of livelihood strategies, which could also provide financial support to continue in formal education – so for them, it was not necessarily a question of choosing between education or farm work (IFAD-UNESCO 2014). Rather than seeing farm and nonfarm activities as separate and discrete, there is increasing recognition of their interdependence and more discussion instead of what the combination of farm and nonfarm activities should be (see UNESCO 2012a). Bennell (2010: 12) points to rural people's views that nonfarm employment can be a "ladder from under employment to regular wage employment and to the formal sector". Given the important role of remittances sent back from nonfarm employment outside the local area, he suggests that policymakers need to "revise their negative perceptions of migration" (p. 12).

As well as adopting a more holistic perspective on young people's livelihoods, which acknowledges their active economic roles from an early age, we need to recognise how their voice and autonomy may be influenced by gender and vary across the life cycle. For instance, whereas a young man may have increased autonomy over his life cycle, opening up new opportunities for employment, land ownership and training, a young woman may face increased dependency after education and marriage. Bennell (20101: 21) emphasises how land ownership issues are intensified for women as male relatives 'grab' widows' and orphans' land. Young women are also likely to suffer lack of access to secondary education when compared to boys. All these factors can later influence their roles in paid agricultural employment and their decision making/bargaining power in the household and society. As King and Palmer (2010) point out, women are often excluded from male trades or activities, have less control over resources and are more likely to be confined to the informal sector and subsistence agriculture. Social expectations around gendered roles and relation can strongly influence informal learning opportunities for young women. For instance, researchers in the Fayoum district of Egypt discovered that women were not allowed to own mobile phones until they married, meaning that – unlike young men – they were unable to learn these skills at home (Moheb el Rafei et al., Egypt country study in IFAD-UNESCO 2014). In Yabello, a pastoralist community in Ethiopia, restrictions on young women's mobility once they reached adolescence prevented them from attending community meetings where they could have learned valuable soft skills of negotiation and confidence in public debates (Kelemu et al. in IFAD-UNESCO 2014).

Starting from the viewpoint that young people are active citizens in their communities implies a shift away from looking first at their educational needs and preparation for future careers. Although it is important to consider how their existing skills and knowledge can be extended through educational interventions, the focus should be on understanding their current livelihood and learning practices. Rather than positioning young people primarily as students within a formal educational system, I suggest that we need to find ways of valuing their existing knowledge and enhancing their voice in educational and development decision making.

School as a contested site in rural areas

The success of the Education for All agenda can be seen in the increasing numbers of children and young people enrolling in schools. Within the dominant policy discourse, school is viewed as an undisputed good – although high dropout and retention rates have led to the current emphasis on the need for 'quality' education (UNESCO 2014a). However, I suggest in this section that we also need to consider how schooling interacts with informal and formal learning in rural communities.

Much research on the role of education in rural development has identified schools and formal curricula as serving to alienate young people from the land (White 2012). Anyidoho, Leavy and Asenso-Okyere (2012) discuss the tensions that school students felt between their identities as farmers and as students in Ghana. Tadele and Gelle (2012) discovered in Ethiopia a strong gender dimension in that girls at school were more negative about farming than boys and felt an even greater disconnect between their family lives and school experiences. These studies suggest that we need to look at schooling not only in terms of improving and supporting economic opportunities but also as introducing alternative value systems and identities. Hailu's (2007) ethnographic research in a rural community in Ethiopia identifies an "opposition that exists between the worldview and value systems underlying formal education and those that the community holds" (p. vii). As well as exploring how schooling has interrupted traditional household roles (through the physical absence of children on the land, for instance), Hailu suggests that values associated with the school (such as materialism) are becoming more important to the community than traditional spiritual values.

Despite beliefs – particularly amongst older community members – that schooling is disrupting and transforming traditional cultural practices and values, a majority of parents and young people appear to view formal education positively, as evidenced by high school enrolment rates around the world. However, the link between schooling and rural development has proved a more complex matter than simply providing the skills required to access better employment. In Uganda, Ngaka (in Rogers and Street 2012) found that formal literacy did not transfer easily into rural occupations – market sellers who had sent their daughters to school reported that they now preferred to sit at home and read, rather than using their numeracy and literacy skills in the market. This relates also to issues around the relevance of the school curriculum to the local context. In the very different context of a Canadian coastal community, Corbett (2007: 273) suggested that 'the prevailing idea of standardised curriculum, standardised texts and standardised tests will continue to render school irrelevant for large numbers of students in rural, northern and coastal communities'. As Bartlett (2010: 156) explored in her ethnographic study of literacy in Brazil, many students saw literacy instruction as fostering economic opportunity – "not for its provision of skills, but rather for the opportunity to enhance their 'educated' persona and extend their social networks". This suggests that we need to look beyond skills to issues around identity and social capital when considering the relationship between schooling and rural livelihoods.

This section has outlined the importance of looking critically at the impact of schooling on rural communities – in a wider sense than only measuring academic achievement through examination passes or learning outcomes. As the ethnographic evidence cited above suggests, we need to consider the influence of schooling on indigenous practices and values, as well as young people's aspirations for change. Through looking at school in terms of informal learning as well as formal learning outcomes, we can compare schooling to other sites of social learning where new identities and values are being constructed, such as factories in the private sector. This more critical perspective on schooling can enable us to identify other new processes facilitating learning – such as migration – that are contributing to rapid social and cultural change in these rural communities.

Implications for future policy and research

This chapter proposes adopting a more nuanced view of the relationship between learning, schooling and rural livelihoods than that put forward within many educational and development policy documents. I have not set out to undermine the importance of formal education within rural communities but rather to contextualise schooling in relation to other learning spaces and practices. I have suggested that by focusing almost exclusively on formal schooling for children, the dominant education and development paradigm disregards informal learning – both within school and in everyday life/work – and considers young people only in their role as potential/ current students or future citizens. Despite the rapid social, political, technological and economic transformation taking place in many rural communities, it appears that schools have remained remarkably unchanged – in terms of the kind of education and skills offered, learning structures, goals, teacher-student relationships and teaching practices.

Although many young people are engaging with new digital literacies and taking advantage of new economic opportunities, they are doing this through their own initiative, learning the skills and attributes required through informal interaction with peers. Where policymakers have taken note of the growing importance of mobile technologies and informal learning, a common response has been to offer more formal learning opportunities. A recent report on *Reading in the Mobile Era* (UNESCO 2014b: 79) proposes providing "programmes and trainings that emphasise the benefits of mobile reading and help potential users adopt a positive mindset towards reading on their mobile phones". The challenge for policymakers and programmes is how to support and encourage the new literacy practices that people are already learning informally without imposing formal structures such as 'one-day training seminars' (p. 79). Perhaps this is where policymakers need to listen and learn from how young people engage with new livelihood and communication practices. In some rural communities, private providers have led the way in developing client-led, individualised approaches to learning, as recent research in Cambodia on contract pig rearing revealed (see Luch et al., Cambodia country study in IFAD-UNESCO 2014).

This chapter has illustrated that policy and research paradigms are intrinsically connected. The dominant policy paradigm has both sponsored and been informed by statistical evidence on the link between literacy/education and development. Making a paradigm shift is not just about adopting an alternative theoretical understanding of education and development but also about valuing different kinds of research evidence. The ethnographic data discussed in this chapter does not set out to answer the research questions posed within the dominant paradigm (see Robinson-Pant 2001) but may contribute greater understanding into the difference between the effect of schooling as compared to literacy (which is rarely disaggregated in statistical analysis – see Basu, Maddox and Robinson-Pant 2009). However, the main contribution of ethnographic research could be to develop theorisation around the purpose of education in rural economies.

The post-2015 agenda

This alternative perspective on education and rural development has particular relevance as we move towards formulation of the post-2015 education and development agenda. At this stage, it seems likely that there will be a continued emphasis on early childhood, primary and secondary education within the EFA goals. UNESCO (2012b: 1) notes the 'limited progress so far in narrowing inequality gaps in education', meaning that the poorest, girls, those with disabilities and those in rural areas have often missed out on education. Significantly, the guiding principles for setting the post-2015 education goals that are set out in this draft document include a recognition that learning (particularly for the most marginalised groups) need not only take place in schools or formal institutions: "The goals should recognise the learning needs at each stage of a person's life, and that learning takes place in nonformal as well as formal settings" (p. 2).

This discussion document proposes five individual goals, of which the first two focus explicitly on formal schooling – the completion and quality of early childhood education, primary education and lower secondary education. The emphasis here and in the document as a whole is on "measurable learning outcomes, especially in literacy and numeracy" (p. 3), though this document acknowledge the challenges that this will involve. This document does not suggest any difficulties in determining/having consensus on what 'the basics' are across varying countries and learning contexts. It discusses instead the technicalities of how to measure foundation skills in literacy and numeracy, transferable skills (such as problem-solving skills) and technical/vocational skills. We can see that though there is recognition here that learning can take place outside the formal system, the main emphasis is on 'schooled' knowledge/skills ('the basics'), implying a hierarchical notion of foundational and other skills, formal and nonformal learning (as outlined in the first section of this chapter with regard to the dominant paradigm). Nonformal and skills-training programmes are positioned as alternatives for groups marginalised from formal education ('second-chance programmes', p. 3) and a way of addressing inequalities.

Alongside the attention to providing quality schooling for all, post-2015 debates (including UNESCO 2013b) have proposed a broader consideration of 'skills' to respond to the pressures to develop the links between EFA and jobs, productivity and growth (see King and Palmer 2013). UNESCO (2012b) emphasises the potentially transformative role of skills for life and for work as part of a strategy for achieving sustainable human development. The latest *EFA Global Monitoring Report* (UNESCO 2014a: 49) recommends that young people should learn not just foundation skills but transferable skills (critical thinking, problem solving, advocacy and conflict resolution) as part of becoming 'responsible global citizens'. The distinction in the early research literature between 'basic skills' and 'vocational skills' has now been expanded to embrace a wider range of capacities and the broader notion of 'skills development'. As UNESCO/INRULED (2012: 10) outlined, within this definition, skills development should not be seen as "an isolated and self-contained area of activity". This more holistic view of skills development as connected with the formal education system, as well as with nonformal and informal learning, also needs to engage with other sectors, too (such as to ensure access to microcredit or agricultural technology).

Reflecting on the proposed direction of the post-2015 EFA agenda, several assumptions underpinning the dominant paradigm outlined at the beginning of this paper can be identified. In particular, there is the focus on schooling, prioritising measurable literacy and numeracy learning outcomes and an economistic discourse. Nonformal education is considered as a 'catch-up' mechanism for hard-to-reach groups, but there is no recognition of informal and indigenous learning/knowledge already taking place. Returning to the three areas explored in relation to my proposed alternative paradigm on education and rural development, the shift towards seeing skills development in terms of lifelong learning signals a more holistic perspective on education than in previous decades (see section 3(i), A wider perspective on learning in rural communities). There is also increasing understanding that educational policy needs to respond to the rapid changes in communities (the 'global trends' such as greater urbanisation, increasing importance of technology and shifting population patterns, noted in UNESCO 2013b). However, what is lacking from current debates on EFA is the notion of children and adolescents as active citizens (see 3(ii)) who should have a voice within, as well as a right to, education. Linked to this point is the assumption within all EFA policy documents that schooling is an undisputed good (see 3(iii)) with the same projected learning outcomes, aims and forms across diverse cultures. Given the attention to equity in the proposed EFA post-2015 goals, there is an urgent need to consider the school as a contested site of learning in many rural communities. Ethnographic findings presented in this chapter suggest that if marginalised groups are to enrol and succeed in formal education, young people will need greater say regarding the kind of learning, values and objectives promoted by these institutions.

Notes

1 This chapter draws on a literature review conducted for the IFAD-UNESCO project, 'Learning knowledge and skills for agriculture to improve rural livelihoods', in my role as Global Research Coordinator. The full report 'Reviewing the Field' (Feb. 2014) is available at: http://www.unesco.org/new/en/education/themes/education-building-blocks/technical-vocational-education-and-training-tvet/learning-knowledge-and-skills-for-agriculture-and-rural-livelihoods/
2 There is a growing critical literature on politics, practices and assumptions around such surveys; see Meyer and Benavot 2013.

References

Anyidoho, N., Leavy, J., Asenso-Okyere, K., 2012. Perceptions and aspirations: a case study of young people in Ghana's cocoa sector. *IDS Bulletin* 43, 6, 20–32.

Bartlett, L., 2010. *The Word and the World: The Cultural Politics of Literacy in Brazil*. Hampton, New Jersey.

Barton, D., Hamilton, M., Ivanic, R., 2000. *Situated Literacies: Reading and Writing in Context*. Routledge, London.

Basu, K., Maddox, B., Robinson-Pant, A. (Eds.), 2009. *Interdisciplinary Approaches to Literacy and Development*. Routledge, London.

Bennell, P., 2010. *Investing in the Future: Creating Opportunities for Young Rural People*. IFAD, Rome.

Biriwasha, L., 2012. Agriculture and the school curriculum in Zimbabwe. Paper presented at International Conference on the future of the Agrifood sector in Africa, Accra, March.

Bown, L., 1990. *Preparing the Future: Women, Literacy and Development*. ActionAid, London.

Brooks, K., Zorya, S., Gautam, A., Goyal, A., 2013. Agriculture as a sector of opportunity for young people in Africa. Sustainable Development Network Policy Research Working Paper No. 6473, World Bank, Washington.

Chinsinga, B., Chasukwa, M., 2012. Youth, agriculture and land grabs in Malawi. *IDS Bulletin* 43, 6, 67–77.

Cochrane, S., 1979. *Fertility and Education*. Johns Hopkins University Press, Baltimore.

Collett, K., Gale, C., 2009. *Training for Rural Development: Agricultural and Enterprise Skills for Women Smallholders*. City and Guilds Centre for Skills Development, London.

Colley, H., Hodkinson P., Malcolm, J., 2003. *Informality and Formality in Learning*. University of Leeds.

Corbett, M., 2007. *Learning to Leave: The Irony of Schooling in a Coastal Community*. Fernwood Publishing, Black Point.

Fernandez, L., 2012. Land policies and labour markets in Sub-Saharan Africa: a law and economics analysis. *IDS Bulletin* 43, 6, 78–89.

Freire, P., 1970. *Pedagogy of the Oppressed*. Herder and Herder, New York.

Hailu, D., 2007. *Implications of Formal Education for Rural Communities in Ethiopia: The Case of Woyisso-Qancaara Kebele, Oromia Region*. Social Anthropology Dissertation Series No. 16, Department of Sociology and Social Anthropology, Addis Ababa University.

IFAD, 2010. *Rural Poverty Report 2011*. IFAD, Rome.

IFAD-UNESCO, 2014. *Learning Knowledge and Skills for Agriculture to Improve Rural Livelihoods*. UNESCO, Paris.

Joshi, S., Ghose, M., 2012. India: literacy and women's empowerment, a tracer study. In: ASPBAE (Ed.) *The Power of Literacy: Women's Journeys in India, Indonesia, Philippines and Papua New Guinea*. ASPBAE, Manila.

King, K., Palmer, R., 2010. *Planning for Technical and Vocational Skills Development*. International Institute for Educational Planning, UNESCO, Paris.

King, K., Palmer, R., 2013. Post-2015 agendas: northern tsunami, southern ripple? The case of education and skills. Working Paper No. 4, NORRAG, Geneva.

Lave, J., Wenger, E., 1991. *Situated Learning*. Cambridge University Press, Cambridge.

LeVine, R., LeVine, S., Rowe, M., Schnell-Anzola, B., 2004. Maternal literacy and health behavior: a Nepalese case study. *Social Science and Medicine* 58, 4, 863–877.

LeVine, R., LeVine, S., Schnell, B., 2009. 'Improve the women': mass schooling, female literacy and worldwide social change. *Harvard Educational Review* 71, 1, 1–51.

Lockheed, M., Jamieson, D., Lau, L., 1980. Farmer education and farm efficiency: a survey. In King, T. (Ed) *Education and Income.* World Bank, Washington.

Meyer, H., Benavot, A. (Eds.), 2013. *Power and Policy.* Symposium, Oxford.

Njenga, P., Mugo, F., Opiyo, J., 2012. *Youth and Women Empowerment Through Agriculture in Kenya.* VSO, Nairobi.

OECD, 2013. *Skilled for Life? Key Findings from the Survey of Adult Skills.* OECD, Paris.

Polyani, M., 1967. *The Tacit Dimension.* Doubleday, New York.

Robinson-Pant, A., 2001. Women's literacy and health: can an ethnographic researcher find the links? In: Street, B. (Ed) *Literacy and Development.* Routledge, London.

Rogers, A., 2000. Literacy comes second: working with groups in developing societies. *Development in Practice* 10, 2, 236–240.

Rogers, A., 2013. The classroom and the everyday: the importance of informal learning for formal learning. *Investigar Em Educacao* 1, 1, 7–34.

Rogers, A., Street, B., 2012. *Adult Literacy and Development.* NIACE, Leicester.

St. Clair, R., 2010. *Why Literacy Matters.* NIACE, Leicester.

Street, B., 1995. *Social Literacies.* Longman, London.

Sumberg, J., Anyidoho, N., Leavy, J., te Lintelo, D., Wellard, K., 2012. Introduction: the young people and agriculture 'problem' in Africa. *IDS Bulletin* 43, 6, 1–8.

Tadele, G., Gella, A., 2012. 'A last resort and often not an option at all': farming and young people in Ethiopia. *IDS Bulletin* 43, 6, 33–42.

Te Lintelo, D., 2012. Young people in African (agricultural) policy processes? What national youth policies can tell us. *IDS Bulletin* 43, 6, 90–102.

UNESCO, 2012a, *Youth and Skills: Putting Education to Work. Education for All Global Monitoring Report 2012.* UNESCO, Paris.

UNESCO, 2012b. *Transforming Technical and Vocational Education and Training: Building Skills for Work and Life.* Main Working Document for the Third International Congress on Technical and Vocational Education and Training, Shanghai, May.

UNESCO, 2013a. *Education Transforms Lives.* UNESCO, Paris.

UNESCO, 2013b. Proposed post–2015 education goals: emphasising equity, measurability and finance. EFA Global Monitoring Report, Initial draft for discussion, March 2013.

UNESCO, 2014a. *Teaching and Learning: Achieving Quality for All. Education for All Global Monitoring Report 2013/4.* UNESCO, Paris.

UNESCO, 2014b. *Reading in the Mobile Era: A Study of Mobile Reading in Developing Countries.* UNESCO, Paris.

UNESCO/INRULED, 2012. *Education and Training for Rural Transformation: Skills, Jobs, Food and Green Future to Combat Poverty.* UNESCO, Beijing.

Wagner, D., 2011. What happened to literacy? Historical and conceptual perspectives on literacy in UNESCO. *International Journal of Educational Development* 31, 319–323.

White, B., 2012. Agriculture and the generation problem: rural youth, employment and the future of farming. *IDS Bulletin* 43, 6, 9–19.

SECTION 2

Learning, teaching and schooling for development

8

BUILDING GLOBAL CONSENSUS ON MEASURING LEARNING

Debates and opportunities

Kate Anderson and Rebecca Winthrop

The global learning crisis

The EFA goals established in Jomtien, Thailand, in 1990 demonstrated a global commitment to meeting basic learning needs. This commitment was restated in 2000 in the Dakar Framework for Action, in which Goal 6 calls for "improving every aspect of the quality of education, and ensuring their excellence so that recognised and measurable learning outcomes are achieved by all, especially in literacy, numeracy and essential life skills" (World Education Forum 2000). However, there was no consensus on what those outcomes should be or how they should be measured. The MDGs initiated in 2000 also included a focus on education, with Goal 2 being the completion of primary schooling for all children and youth.

Although in the past decades much progress has been made regarding access to education, levels of learning still remain significantly low. The most recent estimates show that 250 million school-age children worldwide fail to reach minimum reading and numeracy outcomes, even though half of them had spent at least four years in school (UNESCO 2012b). This number rises above 50 percent in the poorest countries and regions. Similarly, a study focused on 13 Arab countries estimates that 56 percent of primary students and 48 percent of lower secondary school students are not learning basic competencies, as measured by literacy and numeracy scores on international tests (Steer, Ghanem and Jalbout 2014). The latest results from the OECD Programme for International Student Assessment (PISA) indicate that 32 percent of 15-year-old students in all participating countries do not reach the baseline level of performance (Level 2) in mathematics (OECD 2013). This means that one-third of participating students cannot extract relevant information from a single source and cannot use basic procedures to solve problems involving whole numbers. The full scale of this crisis is unknown, however, as the available international data leaves out many low-income countries and typically focuses on just two domains: literacy and mathematics.

As with enrolment rates, gender, race, geographical and income gaps are also present in learning outcomes. For example, in Colombia, the richest quintile of Grade 8 students scored close to 100 points higher on an international math test than those from the poorest quintile, according to the Trends in International Mathematics and Science Study (TIMSS). In Tanzania, urban students in Grade 3 are three times more likely than their rural counterparts to meet literacy and numeracy standards (van der Gaag and Putcha 2013). These gaps reinforce inequalities in child and youth development as well as broaden the income disparities among countries.

With a new set of global development goals on the post-2015 horizon, key multilateral organisations, governments and civil society organisations have reclaimed the access *plus* learning agenda established in the EFA goals with a focus on making education and learning equitable (Save the Children 2013b; The World We Want 2013; UNESCO 2013; United Nations 2013; United Nations 2014). This shift is also evident in the priorities of the United Nations Secretary-General's Global Education First Initiative, which seeks to 1) put every child in school, 2) improve the quality of learning, and 3) foster global citizenship (GEFI 2013).

Once the internationally agreed education goals have been decided, how will we know whether we are making progress? Learning metrics are critical to demonstrating that efforts to improve education access and quality are making an impact.

Why focus on learning outcomes?

While there is widespread agreement that learning outcomes are important to measure, the reasons for focusing on measurement stem from different yet overlapping arguments.

The human rights argument. Education, and implicitly, learning, is a fundamental human right, inherent to all human beings, that should be guaranteed to all, regardless of gender, nationality, religion, ethnicity, income level and other status. The right to education is stated and reaffirmed in numerous international and regional treaties, including the Universal Declaration on Human Rights (Article 26), the Convention on the Rights of the Child and the UNESCO Convention against Discrimination in Education. In addition, this right does not only imply free and compulsory primary education and the availability of secondary education for all but also the right to quality education. As such, the full realisation of the right to education involves the accomplishment of adequate learning outcomes by all.

The human rights approach has also been used to argue against learning outcomes as a globally agreed goal, citing the unintended consequences of focusing on a narrow set of outcomes (e.g., literacy and numeracy), the difficulty of developing approaches that are relevant to national and local contexts and the risk of further marginalising the most vulnerable (Grey 2013). However, the Right to Education Project offers three ways these risks can be mitigated: 1) defining learning outcomes broadly to support the aims of education identified in human rights frameworks, including cognitive and noncognitive; 2) learning assessments are adapted to national and local contexts and evolve over time; and 3) assessments are used to identify and support marginalised populations and are monitored to ensure they do not contribute to further exclusion (Right to Education Project 2013).

The economics argument. Many education stakeholders, including economists, argue that learning outcomes are the real driver of the economic benefits of education. Several studies have found that learning outcomes have a larger effect on economic outcomes than years of education. Hanushek and Wössmann (2007, 2009) find, for instance, that a one standard deviation increase in scores on international assessments has been associated with a two percent increase in annual growth rates of GDP per capita. In addition, in an earlier study, Hanushek and Kimko (2000) estimate that the effects of years of schooling on GDP per capita is greatly reduced when considering differences in quality of education. Additionally, the noncognitive, or "character skills", learned in education programmes such as engagement, initiative and persistence learned as early as preprimary have been shown to have an even greater impact on long-term economic, health and well-being outcomes for both individuals and society than academic competencies (Heckman, Pinto and Savelyev 2013).

The 'measure what you treasure' argument. If we truly value learning, then measuring proxy indicators such as teacher-pupil ratios, textbooks, etc. are not sufficient. What gets measured gets resources. Many argue that setting clear targets for learning outcomes – in addition to targets on key inputs such as teachers, facilities, financing and learning materials – can drive resources to the education sector that are necessary for meeting these goals (LMTF 2013c). In fact, following the Millennium Declaration, ODA increased from $72 to $128 billion in the period 2000–2009. In addition, the shift in allocation of aid flows suggests a greater concentration on MDG priority areas and countries (Kenny and Sumner 2011). However, this argument also calls attention to the consequences of selecting a small set of global goals and targets: the learning outcomes left out, especially those that are difficult to measure in an internationally comparable way, may be deemphasised.

Risks of assessing learning

Measurement can play a crucial role in improving the quality of education and learning, but there are risks involved. While measureable learning outcomes are one component of a healthy education system, they must not be treated as the only measurable indicators. Consistent with this idea, UNESCO developed a General Education Quality Diagnosis Framework (UNESCO 2012a) that provides a set of tools that go beyond international and national examinations to help countries assess, diagnose and improve education quality. This framework adopts a comprehensive approach to education quality, which pushes countries to a systematic analysis of the resources and processes related to learning outcomes. Teaching, learning and assessment are identified as the core processes, which in turn result from a set of core resources or inputs, including learners, curriculum, teachers and teaching environment. According to this model, all of these elements interrelate and interact with each other to shape education quality in a given country.

Assessment should not be conducted for its own sake. Available evidence suggests that the use of national and international assessment data is not widespread and that developing countries in particular experience barriers to using assessment data in policymaking (Kellaghan, Greaney and Murray 2009; Best et al. 2013). Classroom assessments can also be an important lever for improving quality (Black 2004) but are underutilised in many classrooms around the world (LMTF 2013c). There are several commonly identified reasons for this underuse of assessment: lack of training for teachers on how to develop and use assessments, problems with the technical quality of the assessment programme, inadequate dissemination of results to the public and education stakeholders, lack of analysis to determine the appropriate interventions, and lack of ability or willingness by education stakeholders to act upon the results (Best et al. 2013; LMTF 2013c).

Kelleghan, Greaney and Murray (2009) describe four conditions that assessments must meet in order to accurately reflect student achievement and serve the needs of users:

1. The assessment has enough items to comprehensively assess the knowledge and skills within a given domain.
2. The assessment measures knowledge and skills at an appropriate level for the students taking it (i.e., it is neither too difficult nor too easy for the majority of students).
3. The assessment's ability to measure knowledge in one domain should not depend on students' abilities in other domains, which is especially important for students who are tested in a language other than the one they primarily use.
4. The assessment instruments are designed so that comparison over time is possible.

Clearly, a one-size-fits-all approach is not feasible at the global level if the goal is to have meaningful data that can be used to improve learning in addition to data for global monitoring. In that case, a hybrid approach is useful in determining what should be measured: a large amount of competencies assessed in the classroom, a smaller subset measured at the national level and an even smaller subset of areas of measurement at the global level in which each country selects the tools and methods according to their needs.

Determining what to measure

Motivated by the global education challenges of low learning levels and the lack of robust data on learning achievement, the Learning Metrics Task Force (LMTF) was convened by the UNESCO Institute for Statistics and the Center for Universal Education at the Brookings Institution with the ultimate objective of improving learning outcomes for children and youth around the world. Task force members included national and regional governments, teachers' organisations, EFA-convening agencies, regional political bodies, civil society organisations, donor agencies and the private sector. The task force engaged more than 1,700 experts, practitioners, education ministry representatives, and other education stakeholders in 118 countries in an 18-month-long process to make recommendations on the following three questions:

What learning is important for all children and youth? In the first phase, the task force took a step back from measurement and sought to determine whether there are key competencies that are important for all children and youth based on research, policy review and global consultations. The task force agreed on a broad set of global competencies across seven domains: Physical Well-Being, Social and Emotional, Culture and the Arts, Literacy and Communication, Learning Approaches and Cognition, Numeracy and Mathematics, and Science and Technology (LMTF 2013a). The resulting Global Framework of Learning Domains and corresponding sub-domains span early childhood through early adolescence as shown in Figure 8.1 below.

How should learning outcomes be measured? In the second phase, the task force investigated how learning outcomes should be measured across countries. The most frequently measured of the seven domains identified by the LMTF are *Literacy & communication* and *Numeracy &*

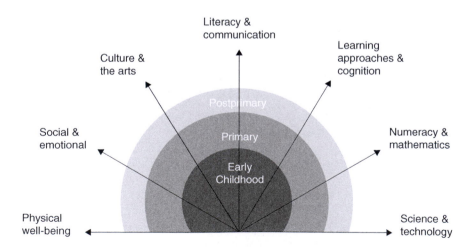

Figure 8.1 LMTF global framework of learning domains
Source: LMTF 2013a.

mathematics. In an analysis of publicly available data on 142 national assessments and examinations in 35 developing countries, the domains of *Literacy & communication* and *Numeracy & mathematics* appeared in 99 percent of assessments. Other domains were represented far less – *Science & technology* appeared in 52 percent of the assessments analysed, *Culture & the arts* in 36 percent; *Social & emotional* in 18 percent, and *Physical Well-being* and *Learning approaches & cognition* each in less than one percent (Cheng and Gale 2014).

However, there is a high demand in many countries to track progress in other areas beyond literacy and communication, such as early learning and development, problem-solving skills and critical thinking (LMTF 2013b). In response, the task force selected a diverse set of areas for global measurement, some in which a critical mass of measurement efforts existed and could be better coordinated to monitor global progress and others that required additional commitment and investment to develop. Rather than being limited by the current capacity for measurement, the task force took a long-term view, allowing for changing needs and future innovations in technology and assessment (LMTF 2013b). Seven measurement areas, described in Table 8.1, represent the vision of the task force for how learning could be measured across countries, with the understanding that this would require significant improvements in assessment capacity in many countries. Beyond this small set of areas, the task force recommended that countries should decide which additional competencies within the seven domains to measure and track based on national priorities.

Similar calls for a diverse set of learning indicators were evident in the Open Working Group and Education for All Steering Committee documents at the time of writing this paper. They all include some areas of measurement that are widely measured in most countries, such as literacy and numeracy, and some areas that are not measured on a wide scale but viewed as important to

Table 8.1 LMTF recommended areas of global measurement

Area of Measurement	Description
Learning for All	Percentage of all children who complete a cycle of education with adequate learning outcomes. This measurement area relies on measures of school completion and learning (e.g., reading or mathematics proficiency) in one indicator.
Age and Education Matter for Learning	To ensure a focus on learning does not exclude those still out of school, measurement in this area relies on school data on timely entry, progression and completion of schooling, and population-based data to capture those who do not enter school or leave early.
Reading	Measure foundational skills before Grade 3 and proficiency by the end of primary school.
Numeracy	Measure foundational skills before the end of primary school and proficiency by lower secondary school.
Ready to Learn	Measure acceptable levels of early learning and development across multiple domains by the time a child enters primary school.
Citizen of the World	Measure among youth the demonstration of values and skills necessary for success in their communities and the world.
Breadth of Learning Opportunities	Track exposure to high-quality learning opportunities across all seven domains of learning by examining national policies and classroom practices.

Source: LMTF 2013a.

global education and development goals, such as readiness to learn in early childhood and global citizenship. Coming up with global indicators is challenging in both cases.

How can measurement of learning be implemented to improve education quality? In the third phase, the task force examined how countries assess learning and in which domains, how assessment results are used, the specific needs of countries to measure learning and the use of assessments to improve the quality of education. The task force also investigated the feasibility of a multistakeholder partnership that could bring together existing efforts to support countries to measure and improve learning.

Through examining available research and consultation feedback from 85 countries, the task force identified three key supports that are necessary for a successful learning measurement system and are in high demand worldwide: technical expertise, institutional capacity, and political will.

- **Technical expertise:** Countries need the technical tools and expertise to carry out quality learning assessments. A significant amount of developmental work involving multiple actors is required to generate and pilot the tools needed for countries to measure learning, including in the areas identified by the LMTF. Additionally, countries need technical experts from within their education systems to implement large-scale assessments and provide guidelines for formative assessments.
- **Institutional capacity:** In parallel with the technical work, stakeholders involved in measuring learning must develop strong institutional capacity to build and sustain a robust system for measuring learning. This requires collaboration across multiple agencies and nongovernmental stakeholders.
- **Political will:** In order to develop and sustain efforts to improve learning, there must be political will to invest in learning measurement and translate the data into action. Political support for assessment is important at all levels, including at the school, district, provincial, national and global levels.

Taken together, these three components support a successful learning measurement system and provide important input into a dynamic education system. The lack of any of these supports can lead to the entire system being inefficient, weak or irrelevant. This can be likened to a three-legged stool, in which the absence of any of the three 'legs' prevents the entire stool from functioning.

The ambitious agenda set forth by the task force raises two sets of issues when determining global indicators for learning: 1) How do we produce a global picture of learning where there are many actors measuring things differently, such as in the domains of reading and numeracy? and 2) How do we produce a global picture of learning where very few countries are currently measuring learning but there is a high demand for this information, such as readiness to learn in primary school and global citizenship? The following section describes how multiple education actors worked together to reach consensus on indicators and the challenges and opportunities in each situation.

Measuring what is most commonly measured

At least 150 countries administer national assessments or examinations of learning achievement, the overwhelming majority of which measure reading and/or numeracy (Guadalupe 2013; Cheng and Gale 2014). However, the way these assessments are currently designed does not allow for global monitoring of learning achievement. This section describes the challenges and opportunities of using existing primary school reading and numeracy assessments to measure progress toward global indicators. It highlights efforts to bring together the multiple actors involved in international, regional and cross-national assessments of learning.

Reading

There are three regional assessments that measure competencies in reading toward the end of primary school in a comparable way: the Southern and Eastern Africa Consortium for Monitoring Educational Quality (SACMEQ), the Programme d'Analyse des Systèmes Éducatifs de la CONFEMEN (PASEC) in Francophone Africa, and the Laboratorio Latinoamericano de Evaluación de la Calidad de la Educación (LLECE). The International Association for the Evaluation of Educational Achievement (IEA) Progress in International Reading Literacy Study (PIRLS) also measures reading at this level, primarily in high- and upper-middle-income countries, making internationally or regionally comparable data available on reading at the end of primary in 90 countries.

However, even by taking into account all of these assessments, we would be far from establishing a global baseline for reading. Some of the most marginalised children in the world live in countries not participating in these studies and are affected by conflict, disasters, poverty and gender disparities. The end-of-primary reading assessments are typically administered in one or two of the national languages, and therefore performance in any subject is dependent on a students' reading ability. These assessments are administered in schools, leaving out children who are not in attendance on testing day, enrolled in a nonformal education programme or have left schooling altogether. Furthermore, many of these tools are too difficult for the majority of children to complete even the most basic items (called a 'floor effect'). These issues, while present in all countries, are amplified in low- and middle-income countries and in some cases impact the majority of test-takers (LMTF 2013c). Because of these problems, countries are increasingly seeking assessment tools that diagnose reading problems early, with less of an emphasis on international comparability.

There are multiple reading measures designed to measure foundational reading skills, which are typically used to help teachers and policymakers understand children's reading abilities in the early grades, such as the Early Grade Reading Assessment (EGRA) administered in more than 60 developing countries; Annual Status of Education Report (ASER) in India and Pakistan; Uwezo in Kenya, Tanzania and Uganda; Literacy Boost, a tool developed by Save the Children and used in more than 25 countries; and SICOLE-R-Primaria in Chile, Guatemala, Mexico and Spain (LMTF 2013b). These tools are often administered in local languages and are not internationally comparable, except for the ability to compare the percentage of children who cannot perform a task at all (also called 'zero scores'). Some are administered in classrooms and others in the home.

Deciding between the myriad existing measures requires examining the policy questions a country seeks to answer. For example:

- At Grade X (usually in upper primary), what percentage of students are proficient readers? What percentage are advanced? Many national assessments and tools such as the PIRLS, pre-PIRLS or the regional end-of-primary assessments can answer this. However, if a significant proportion of students do not reach the lowest benchmark on the test, additional assessments of foundational skills may be needed to better understand the learning needs of all children.
- At Grade X (usually around Grade 1–3), what percentage of our students can read at a basic level? Tools such as the EGRA or Literacy Boost can answer this question and can capture children's reading ability in multiple languages.

- At what age are *all* of our children, including those not in school, learning to read? Measures such as ASER, which uses Grade 2 reading material and is administered to children ages 5–16 in the household, can answer that question.

In April 2014, the UIS and the World Bank brought together assessment, education and reading experts in Montreal, Canada, to reach a technical consensus on goals, targets and indicators that could be used to promote learning and inform the post-2015 target-setting agenda (UIS and World Bank forthcoming). The focus of this meeting was reading indicators in the early grades and at the end of primary school. The three criteria decided upon by participants as important for any global reading indicators were:

- Technical strength: Indicators should be statistically robust and based on the state of the art in assessment. Indicators should be based on high-quality, accurate, reliable and valid data.
- Ease of communication: Targets and indicators should yield information that is not only understood by policymakers but also readily grasped by other education stakeholders, especially by nonexperts.
- Contextual relevance and flexibility: Indicators should recognise context and should be led by local priorities and needs.

The group deliberated on how to recommend reading indicators that were realistic yet reflected standards high enough to ensure children leaving primary school were able to read independently. This is especially important in countries where a large number of the most marginalised children do not continue on to lower secondary. The deliberations resulted in the following proposed goals, targets and indicators, which were intended to provide a snapshot of reading at a global level:

Early Grade Reading
- Goal: All children able to read by the end of Grade 2.
- Indicator: Ability to read a simple story and answer one or two questions.
- Options for targets: Reduce number of children unable to read by X percent; increase number of children able to read by X percent; reduce gaps between girls and boys by X percent.

End of Primary Reading
- Goal: All children read proficiently by the end of Grade 6.
- Indicators: Ability to read narrative text/documents and answer questions.
- Options for targets: Reduce number of children unable to read proficiently by X percent; increase number of children able to read proficiently by X percent; reduce gaps between girls and boys by X percent.

The UIS/World Bank report recommended that in the short term, countries report on these indicators based on their own country curricular standards, set targets based on how much change they envision in a given number of years and use their own measurement tools to set specific cut points. Longer-term efforts to develop a common global metric and align international and regional assessment efforts are described later in this chapter.

Numeracy and mathematics

Many of the issues identified in the previous section on reading apply to measurement of numeracy and mathematics. The regional assessments – SACMEQ, PASEC and LLECE – measure numeracy and mathematics near the end of primary school. The IEA's Trends in International Mathematics and Science Study (TIMSS) and TIMSS Numeracy also measure numeracy and mathematics at this level, primarily in high- and upper-middle-income countries. There are some measures designed to measure foundational numeracy skills, which are less widely used than the foundational reading assessments but expanding in global coverage. These include the Early Grade Math Assessment (EGMA) administered in 11 developing countries; the Annual Status of Education Report (ASER) in India and Pakistan; Uwezo in Kenya, Tanzania and Uganda; and Save the Children's Numeracy Boost, used in Malawi and Bangladesh. Still, there is no mechanism for combining the data from these disparate assessments into a global picture of learning achievement.

Building from the UIS/World Bank recommendations on reading, a concurrent process to develop indicators for numeracy and mathematics was coordinated by the Deutsche Gesellschaft für Internationale Zusammenarbeit (GIZ) on behalf of the German Federal Ministry for Economic Cooperation and Development (BMZ) and the Korea Institute of Curriculum and Evaluation (KICE) (2014). This working group, convened in April and May 2014, brought together international experts in the field of mathematics education to share existing knowledge and to develop recommendations for goals, targets and indicators for measuring learning outcomes in mathematics at the primary level. The numeracy group adopted the same key criteria for global indicators as the UIS/World Bank reading group, namely that they are technically strong, easily communicated and contextually relevant and flexible. The numeracy working group identified an additional criterion of "coverage," or the extent to which all members of the school-age population, whether in or out of school, are included in the indicator (GIZ/KICE 2014).

The working group reviewed national curricula and assessment specifications and determined that there was a large degree of international consensus that students need to be proficient in knowledge and application of skills and concepts across three core domains: 1) number sense and operations; 2) geometry and spatial sense; and 3) measurement and data. The group acknowledged that mathematics is multidimensional and children can progress at different rates in the various subdomains, but this progression is typically correlated and it is possible to identify a child's approximate level of mathematical competency across subdomains. The group proposed the following goal for numeracy and mathematics learning achievement at the primary level:

- Goal: All children are proficient in basic mathematics by the time of end of primary age.
- Indicator: Two assessments of learning outcomes, one at the end of Grade 2 and another at Grades 4–6 in the subdomains of number sense and operations, geometry and spatial sense, and measurement and data.
- Options for targets: Define four benchmarks of progressive achievement and set targets for moving a percentage of children i) below or at a given benchmark from X percent to Y percent in T years or ii) above or at a benchmark from R percent to S percent in T years, with the specific percentages and years defined by the country.

As with reading, the assessments and targets for measuring numeracy and mathematics should be determined by the countries and be fit for national decision-making purposes. In the longer term, a common global metric could link the existing national, regional and international assessments to aid in global monitoring.

Linking existing assessments to form a common metric

Statistically speaking, the easiest way to develop a global metric for reading or numeracy is for all countries to use a comparable assessment, but this is neither politically feasible nor would it provide data fit for national policy purposes. However, there is a way forward to generate data that are useful to countries as well as global monitoring. The development of a single common continuum of skills from basic to advanced, or a common metric, was proposed by the Australian Council for Educational Research (ACER) to equate the results from national, regional and international assessments (UIS/World Bank forthcoming). This proposed metric would be able to assess the status of learning achievement despite the degree of variability in terms of age or grade. The focus of this metric would not be country rankings but would include socio-demographic and school-level correlates of learning proficiency to help diagnose systems and provide guidance for policy action. At the time of writing this paper, the UIS, World Bank and various LMTF member organisations were working to identify the financial resources, political engagement and partnership structure among existing assessment agencies and coordinating mechanisms to support a common global metric for reading. Once developed, the methodology for this common metric for reading could be applied to numeracy and other domains, including those that have not been widely measured to date.

Measuring what has not been widely measured

The previous section described the challenges to global measurement of learning in areas where most countries currently have some type of national assessment. In this section, we describe the challenges and opportunities of developing measurement in new areas, namely readiness to learn upon primary school entry and global citizenship.

Readiness to learn at primary school entry

There is growing interest in measuring young children's development. In addition to the LMTF's recommendations on measuring "readiness to learn" as part of the global education measurement agenda, the WHO initiated an effort in 2013, in partnership with UNESCO and UNICEF, to integrate health, nutrition and education together in the creation of a measurement framework for children aged birth to eight years.

There are multiple existing regional and international tools for measuring early learning and development. UNICEF's Multiple Indicator Cluster Survey (MICS) Early Child Development Index (ECDI) is a household survey containing 10 items administered to caregivers to measure children's development and learning between the ages of three and five years. MICS ECDI is administered in 55 countries. The Early Development Instrument (EDI) is a teacher report of readiness to learn in primary school across multiple domains administered in 24 countries. Several regional surveys of early learning and development have been validated in the past five years, including the Programa Regional de Indicadores de Desarrollo Infantil (PRIDI) in Latin America; the East Asia Pacific Child Development Scales; and the West and Central Africa Regional Office (WCARO) prototype developed by UNICEF. Nonprofit organisations and universities have also developed and validated national measures in a large number of countries, including Korea, India and Hong Kong (LMTF 2013b).

Given the complexity of child development, a holistic measure across several domains is the best way to capture learning at this stage. All of these existing and emerging assessments measure early learning and development across multiple domains, typically including physical well-being, social and emotional, early literacy and communication, early numeracy and mathematics, and learning approaches and cognition.

Decisions on the tools and methodologies for assessing early learning and development should be context specific. For example, in a classroom of 20–30 Grade 1 students, it is likely that the teacher has developed a relationship with each child and can be a reliable source of information on their abilities. In a classroom of more than 100 children, which is not uncommon in many developing countries, it is unlikely that a teacher can reliably report on the abilities of all children, and an outside observer administering tasks to the child might be a more accurate source of data. Similarly, reporting by parents or caregivers can be inaccurate if the interviewee does not spend a significant amount of time with the child each day and can be subjective. Multiple sources of child data combined with information about the quality of the learning environment can provide a more complete picture of early development and learning.

As with reading and numeracy at the primary level, global measurement will be dependent on countries selecting and implementing tools according to national purposes. Across the existing and emerging assessments described above, there is an opportunity to collaborate and share items and data to produce a global baseline of early learning and development. By coordinating these efforts in the early stages of development and making tools and data open-source, measurement in this area could expand rapidly in response to a post-2015 target on readiness to learn in primary school.

Global citizenship

Several initiatives have emphasised the role of global citizenship and related thematic areas as a priority for education and learning. According to UNESCO (2013):

> Education in a globalised world is increasingly putting emphasis on the importance of values, attitudes, and communication skills as a critical complement to cognitive knowledge and skills. The education community is also paying increasing attention to the relevance of education in understanding and resolving social, political, cultural, and global issues. This includes the role of education in supporting peace, human rights, equity, acceptance of diversity, and sustainable development.

The UN Secretary-General's Global Education First Initiative (GEFI) includes *global citizenship education* as one of its three priorities. Additionally, a recent Resolution of the 37th session of UNESCO's General Conference endorsed a Global Action Programme on Education for Sustainable Development (ESD) as a follow up to the UN Decade of ESD with the objective "to reorient education and learning so that everyone has the opportunity to acquire the knowledge, skills, values and attitudes that empower them to contribute to sustainable development." Within the context of youth skills, there is an opportunity to include global citizenship education in the post-2015 development agenda as part of the knowledge, skills and competencies that learners require in the 21st century.

At the same time, there is currently a lack of consensus about what competencies constitute global citizenship. Through a series of consultations, UNESCO (2014) identified the following core competencies as common outcomes of global citizenship education:

* An attitude supported by an understanding of multiple levels of identify, and the potential for a collective identity that transcends individual cultural, religious, ethnic or other differences;

103

- A deep knowledge of global issues and universal values such as justice, equality, dignity and respect;
- Cognitive skills to think critically, systematically and creatively, including adopting a multi-perspective approach that recognises different dimensions, perspectives and angles of issues;
- Noncognitive skills, including social skills such as empathy and conflict resolution, and communication skills and aptitudes for networking and interacting with people of different backgrounds, origins, cultures and perspectives; and
- Behavioural capacities to act collaboratively and responsibly to find global solutions to global challenges and to strive for the collective good.

The LMTF consultations on this topic revealed a similar set of competencies with a specific focus on issues related to climate change, environmental awareness, leadership and digital literacy (LMTF 2013b). Defining the key competencies are the first step in coming to consensus on global citizenship education, and there is agreement that youth must be a key constituency involved in these decisions.

Global experts and youth leaders have emphasised a need to measure aspects of global citizenship education (UNESCO 2014), but the traditional ways of testing may not be appropriate for measuring global citizenship and could stifle innovation and creativity. Measures of civics and citizenship, such as national assessments and the IEA's International Civics and Citizenship Study (ICCS), can provide some information, although coverage is limited in low- and middle-income countries. There is an opportunity to build on these efforts yet move beyond traditional methods and redefine how learning is measured in the context of global citizenship. More research is required on how to leverage technology to provide better data on learning achievement across all domains, including via mobile phones, social media and learning analytics.

Equity considerations for global indicators

One of the cross-cutting themes that emerged from global conversations on the post-2015 agenda is the need to reduce, and ultimately eliminate, differences in opportunities associated with ethnicity, sex, geography, disability, race or socioeconomic status. The UN Secretary-General's High Level Panel report, for example, asserts at the outset that the transformative shift of leaving no person behind is central to its vision; addressing inequality transcends all goals.

A focus on learning must include a concomitant focus on equity, with particular attention to rising inequalities within countries. Learning data should be collected and reported to describe progress over time and across population groups, rather than only by average achievement levels in a country (LMTF 2013b; Right to Education Project 2013; United Nations Girls Education Initiative [UNGEI] 2013).

While aggregate reports on learning outcomes at the country level can be useful for international comparisons, more nuanced information is also needed to improve learning outcomes for the most marginalised children and youth. Because education is a universal aspiration and a right, measures of access and learning at any level (global, national or subnational) should reveal information about aggregate measures of overall conditions (e.g., enrolment, achievement), as well as disparities between student subpopulations (LMTF 2013b).

Out-of-school children and youth must be considered in determining which equity dimensions a country should measure, as 57 million children were still out of primary school worldwide in 2011, and 69 million were out of lower secondary (UNESCO 2013). It is important to understand the characteristics of these children and what factors led to their leaving (or never entering) school. A large proportion of out-of-school children and youth live in poverty, conflict areas and/or disaster contexts and other hard-to-reach areas (Save the Children 2013a). These children face daily challenges that require them to use a higher order of thinking skills to solve problems, make critical decisions, learn persistence and think creatively – skills that are essential for their survival. They must also develop leadership skills, awareness of their environment and the dangers that surround them, as well as knowledge of local culture and customs. As learning takes place both inside and outside formal school settings, household-based assessments with sound sampling and testing procedures would ensure that the learning levels of out-of-school children are measured and taken into account.

To ensure that interventions reach the most marginalised children and youth, countries must also collect data on sociodemographic dimensions, such as sex, age, urban or rural residence; socioeconomic status; mother tongue; ethnicity; citizenship status; disabilities and emergency situations. These data should be analysed with information about inputs, such as class size, teacher qualifications, school facilities, availability of learning materials and other contextual factors. Each country should identify which dimensions are particularly relevant in their own context and design measurements and interventions that take these variables into account (LMTF 2013b).

Assessment as a public good

There is considerable debate internationally about how data are produced, managed and used (LMTF 2014). While education statistics systems and national and international data are public goods (i.e., funded with public resources to serve a public purpose), this is not always the case for learning assessments. For assessment data to be made a public good, these basic elements must be taken into account:

- Full documentation of studies that are funded with public resources should be publicly available. Documentation should include data sets, instruments and procedures used to generate the data.
- Informed and explicit consent by participants in the studies should be properly guaranteed.
- The body responsible for conducting the studies must have the independence to make technical decisions on what is publishable and what is not.
- Collaboration among different agencies should be promoted as a way of ensuring that a diversity of interests, perspectives and needs is embedded in the development of the studies from the outset.
- Collaboration among public and private assessment agents can take different forms, ranging from the codevelopment of a given study to agreement on technical procedures that would make one study comparable to another.

The LMTF recommended that any products or services used for global tracking of learning achievement should be considered public goods, with tools, documentation and data made freely available (LMTF 2013c). While certain assessment items cannot be in the public domain because doing so would invalidate the test, the education community, including assessment companies, must ensure that no country is precluded from measuring learning due to the costs associated with purchasing and administering tests.

To accomplish this, an international platform could be developed to provide technical and financial support to the countries that most need it (i.e., those that are both the poorest and lacking rigorous learning assessment systems), promote linkages between regional and international groups and initiatives, identify key individuals or groups that can provide the required technical expertise and disseminate relevant tools and resources. It could also provide financial support to regional assessment initiatives that contribute to enhancing national information and capacity with regard to learning quality in developing nations. This support would, over time, contribute to building internal capacity, hence ultimately reducing reliance on international expertise.

Conclusion

Having international data on learning outcomes is a big step forward for the education community, but one that comes with hard decisions and trade-offs. In order to ensure that any efforts for international tracking of learning are useful to national governments and provide data that can be used to improve learning, country actors must make decisions on what to measure, when to measure it, how to measure and what tools to use. Furthermore, a broad range of domains should be assessed to prevent global measurement from limiting national curricula. Individual child characteristics and information on the school environment should be collected to analyse with learning achievement data. Any monitoring system for global learning goals must be revisited frequently to incorporate new technologies and research. Finally, a significant effort must be made by global actors to demystify learning assessment and make the tools and data more accessible to teachers, students, parents, government, and other key decision makers.

References

Best, M., Knight, P., Lietz P., Lockwood, C., Nugroho, D., Tobin, M., 2013. *The Impact of National and International Assessment Programmes on Education Policy, Particularly Policies Regarding Resource Allocation and Teaching and Learning Practices in Developing Countries.* Final report, EPPI-Centre, Social Science Research Unit, Institute of Education, University of London.

Black, P., 2004. *Working Inside the Black Box: Assessment for Learning in the Classroom.* Granada Learning, London.

Cheng, X., Gale, C., 2014. *EPDC National Learning Assessments Mapping: Phase 1.* EPDC, Washington.

Deutsche Gesellschaft für Internationale Zusammenarbeit, Korea Institute of Curriculum and Evaluation (GIZ/KICE), 2014. *Indicators for Monitoring Learning Outcomes in Mathematics as Part of a Post-2015 Education Agenda.* GIZ, Eschborn.

Global Education First Initiative, 2013. Priorities. Accessed June 13, 2014. http://www.globaleducationfirst.org/priorities.html

Grey, B., 2013. Ensuring Accountability in Post-2015: Potential Threats to Education Rights. Accessed June 13, 2014. http://www.right-to-education.org/fr/node/87

Guadalupe, C., 2013. Access Plus Learning: Age Matters. Accessed June 2, 2014. http://www.brookings.edu/blogs/education-plus-development/posts/2013/08/29-access-plus-learning-guadalupe

Hanushek, E., Kimko, D., 2000. Schooling, labor force quality, and the growth of nations. *American Economic Review* 90, 5, 1184–1208.

Hanushek, E., Wössmann, L., 2007. The Role of School Improvement in Economic Development. Accessed June 13, 2014. http://www.hks.harvard.edu/pepg/PDF/Papers/PEPG0701_Hanushek_Wössmann.pdf

Hanushek, E., Wössmann, L., 2009. Do better schools lead to more growth? National Bureau of Economic Research Working Paper No. 14633, Washington.

Heckman, J., Pinto R., Savelyev P., 2013. Understanding the mechanisms through which an influential early childhood program boosted adult outcomes. *American Economic Review* 103, 6, 2052–2086.

Kellaghan, T., Greaney, V., Murray, S., 2009. *Using the Results of a National Assessment of Educational Achievement. National Assessments of Educational Achievement Series.* Volume 5. World Bank, Washington.

Kenny, C., Sumner A., 2011. More money or more development: what have the MDGs achieved? CGD Working Paper 278, Center for Global Development, Washington.

Learning Metrics Task Force, 2013a. Toward universal learning: what every child should learn. Report No. 1 of the Learning Metrics Task Force. UNESCO Institute for Statistics and Center for Universal Education, Montreal and Washington.

Learning Metrics Task Force, 2013b. Toward universal learning: a global framework for measuring learning. Report No. 2 of the Learning Metrics Task Force. UNESCO Institute for Statistics and Center for Universal Education, Montreal and Washington.

Learning Metrics Task Force, 2013c. *Toward Universal Learning: Recommendations from the Learning Metrics Task Force.* UNESCO Institute for Statistics and Center for Universal Education, Montreal and Washington.

Learning Metrics Task Force, 2014. Implementing Assessment to Improving Learning. UNESCO Institute for Statistics and Center for Universal Education at the Brookings Institution, Montreal and Washington, DC. Available from: http://www.brookings.edu/research/reports/2014/07/implementing-assessment-improve-learning

OECD, 2013. PISA 2012 Results in Focus. What 15-Year-Olds Know and What They Can Do with What They Know. Accessed June 13, 2014. http://www.oecd.org/pisa/keyfindings/pisa-2012-results-overview.pdf

Right to Education Project, 2013. Learning Outcomes Assessment: A Human Rights Perspective. Accessed June 13, 2014. http://www.right-to-education.org/sites/right-to-education.org/files/resource-ttachments/RTE_Learning_Outcomes_Assessments_HR_perspective_2013.pdf

Save the Children, 2013a. Attacks on Education. The Impact of Conflict and Grave Violations on Children's Futures. Accessed June 13, 2014. http://www.savethechildren.org/atf/cf/%7B9def2ebe-10ae-432c-9bd0 df91d2eba74a%7D/ATTACKS_ON_EDUCATION_FINAL.PDF

Save the Children, 2013b. Equitable Learning for All in the Post-2015 Development Agenda. Accessed June 13, 2014. http://www.savethechildren.org/atf/cf/%7B9def2ebe-10ae432c-9bd0-df91d2eba74a%7D/EQUITABLE_LEARNING_FOR_ALL_POST2015_FRAMEWORK.PDF

Steer, L., Ghanem, H., and Jalbout, M., 2014. *Arab Youth: Missing Educational Foundations for a Productive Life?* Center for Universal Education, Brookings Institution, Washington.

The World We Want, 2013. Envisioning Education in the Post-2015 Development Agenda. Global Thematic Consultation on Education in the Post-2015 Development Agenda (executive summary). Accessed June 13, 2014. http://en.unesco.org/post2015/sites/post2015/files/Post-2015.

UNESCO, 2012a. General Education System Quality Analysis/Diagnosis Framework. Accessed May 6, 2014. http://www.unesco.org/new/en/education/themes/strengthening-education-systems/quality-framework/background/

UNESCO, 2012b. *Youth and Skills: Putting Education to Work. 2012 Education for all Global Monitoring Report.* Oxford University Press, Oxford.

UNESCO, 2013. Thematic Consultation on Education in the Post-2015 Development Agenda. Summary of Outcomes. Accessed June 13, 2014. http://www.unesco.org/new/fileadmin/MULTIMEDIA/HQ/ED/pdf/post-2015-summaryoutcomes.pdf

UNESCO, 2014. *Global Citizenship Education: Preparing Learnings for the Challenges of the 21st Century.* UNESCO, Paris.

UNESCO Institute for Statistics and World Bank, forthcoming. Reading indicators for monitoring the Post-2015 education agenda. Meeting summary, UIS, Montreal.

United Nations, 2013. *A New Global Partnership: Eradicate Poverty and Transform Economies through Sustainable Development.* Report of the High-Level Panel of Eminent Persons on the Post-2015 Development Agenda, New York.

United Nations, 2014. *An Action Agenda for Sustainable Development: Network Issues Report Outlining Priority Challenges.* Report of the Leadership Council of the Sustainable Development Solutions Network, New York.

United Nations Girls Education Initiative (UNGEI), 2013. Exploring the Gendered Dimensions of Teaching and Learning – Background Paper for the Education for All Global Monitoring Report 2013, New York. Available from: http://www.ungei.org/resources/index_5659.html

Van der Gaag, J., Putcha V., 2013. *From Enrollment to Learning: The Way Forward.* Center for Universal Education, Brookings Institution, Washington.

World Education Forum, 2000. *The Dakar Framework for Action: Education for All: Meeting Our Collective Commitments.* UNESCO, Paris.

9

LITERACY AND DEVELOPMENT

Lesley Bartlett and Julia Frazier

Introduction

As steady gains were made toward the Education for All (EFA) goal to provide universal access to primary education by 2015, a consensus quickly formed around a focus on early grade literacy as a way to address quality. At that time, USAID invested significant funds to develop the Early Grade Reading Assessment, or EGRA. In 2011, as part of their Education Strategy, USAID announced an audacious goal: "improved reading skills for 100 million children in primary grades by 2015". Other donors have joined them in this focus. USAID, World Vision, and AusAID launched the multiyear initiative, "All Children Reading: A Grand Challenge for Development," which includes a multidonor grant-making mechanism for innovative projects. By 2008, a 'reading consensus' was emerging among various institutions, including the Global Partnership for Education, USAID, DFID, the William and Flora Hewlett Foundation, and the Bill and Melinda Gates Foundation, that early grade reading was the primary way to address educational quality. When millions of dollars began suddenly flowing into early grade literacy programmes, EGRA exerted a definite and, in the opinion of some, disproportionate influence over the shape those programmes took.

Early grade reading efforts have introduced important changes to the way the relationship between education and development is conceptualised and addressed. They provide a valuable focus for educational quality efforts because reading is the foundation upon which future learning is built. They have also set a clear and quantifiable agenda for educational quality. They have offered a set educational target and encouraged donors to invest in primary education for children and even early childhood education. International reading efforts have marshalled extensive, improved pedagogical development for early grade teachers and they have helped to expand the available teaching and learning materials in many of the poorest parts of the world.

What, though, may be some of the limitations of this focus? This chapter examines how EGRA, a reading assessment tool based largely on an American reading assessment called DIBELS, has shaped the agenda of the educational quality debate in developing countries. Based on practitioner experience in the Democratic Republic of the Congo and Pakistan, as well as interviews with literacy practitioners, this piece identifies significant challenges raised by the current framing of emergent literacy in international educational development circles.

To do so, the chapter first considers how concerns for educational quality came to be defined as a narrow and problematic version of early grade reading. Next, it offers a reflection on field experience in the DRC and Pakistan to show how literacy practitioners are wrestling with the shortcomings of early grade reading as currently framed and practiced. The chapter then highlights a number of challenges in early grade reading assessment before concluding with questions to stimulate debate on the future of literacy and international educational development, especially in light of discussions within the Learning Metrics Task Force to make early grade reading the central indicator of educational quality in the post-2015 agenda.

Background

In 2000, in the wake of significant "Reading Wars" that pitted those who preferred a phonics-based approach against those who emphasised a more holistic approach, the US National Reading Panel (NRP) issued an influential report, *Teaching Children to Read* (NRP 2000). The National Reading Panel privileged cognitive and psychological studies with experimental designs and routinely failed to include more sociological findings, claiming they were not scientific enough (Coles 2000); further, the NRP based its recommendations on research published in English and conducted primarily on learning to read in English, including few studies of second language literacy. Finally, the National Reading Panel Summary reduced the massive metareview, at times contradicting the evidence available in its longer report (Allington 2002; Garan 2002).

The Report, *Teaching Children to Read,* controversially canonised five "pillars" of reading:

- phonemic awareness, or the ability to identify the individual sounds in spoken words;
- phonics, or the correspondence of letters (graphemes) to sounds (phonemes);
- fluency, which is the ability to read text accurately and quickly, with natural prosody;
- vocabulary; and
- comprehension, which is the ability to understand and communicate meaning from what is read.

The report simplified very complex debates about these key terms, especially phonics (Garan 2002), fluency (Krashen 2002), and the relationship between phonics and comprehension (Coles 2000). Further, the report tended to ignore other crucial literacy factors and, more generally, the importance of context, such as pedagogical histories, multilingual situations, etc.

Definitions of the core components of English-language literacy are debated in the field of literacy studies. While the importance of phonics, phonemic awareness, vocabulary, fluency, and comprehension for learning to read alphabetic writing is indisputable, scholars have critiqued the way that scientific evidence has been "reviewed, distorted, and misrepresented" in the NRP Report and subsequent policies that have drawn upon it (Allington 2002: 4). The "five core components" (or the "five pillars") to literacy do not include essential features of reading, such as concepts about print and lexical knowledge (Allington 2002). Further, the Report offers an abridged representation of core components like fluency and comprehension (Krashen 2002; Garan 2002). While some reading scholars favour a stage-wise approach, insisting on starting with the 'parts' like letters and phonemes, most concur that oral vocabulary must be built from the earliest ages for reading success, that writing is essential to literacy learning, and that literacy is best promoted through "balanced" approaches that incorporate explicit skills instruction with authentic texts and a focus on comprehension (Samuels and Farstrup 2011). As Goodman (2006) explains, reading is ultimately a qualitative practice of making meaning from text.

The version of reading represented in the National Reading Panel report served as the foundation for the Dynamic Indicators of Basic Early Literacy Skills (DIBELS) assessment (the precursor of EGRA, as discussed in depth below), a continuous assessment tool that reduces reading to discrete skills and then condenses those skills to isolated, quantitative measures. DIBELS consists of a set of short, timed tests meant to measure phonemic awareness, alphabetic principle, fluency, reading comprehension, and vocabulary. DIBELS has been roundly criticised by highly respected literacy researchers for making claims not based in evidence, distorting the skills required to read and then testing only a fragment of those skills, emphasising speed over accuracy, proving difficult to administer consistently, and benefiting financially from the inappropriate promotion of tests as part of the federal Reading First programme (see, e.g., Goodman 2006; Riedel 2007; Samuels 2007).

The emergence of EGRA

On the heels of the successful Health for All campaign of the 1980s, in 1990 the World Bank, key UN organisations, and many others met and set aspirational goals of Education for All (Chabbott 2009). At that meeting 164 governments pledged to meet six key goals by 2015. As stated, the Education for All goals are remarkably broad, and in reality donors and organisations focused predominantly on access at first.

However, when access expanded rapidly in the 1990s, it placed significant strain on educational systems, causing teacher and facility shortages and high student-teacher ratios, particularly in the early grades; these shifts had significant implications for the quality of education on offer. A 2006 evaluation of primary education programmes found that "only about one in five projects had an explicit objective to improve student learning outcomes" (World Bank 2006: 16).

How, though, to define and measure quality? Hints of how the learning agenda narrowed to reading are identifiable in the literature. The achievement of "mastery levels" in early primary proved hard to measure and were not really comparable. However, reading seemed an appealing indicator, given that it is foundational to future learning and seems easy to measure. For example, the World Bank's 2006 report on the shift from access to learning as the "unfinished agenda" looked at learning measures among 12 countries where the evaluation undertook field studies and ultimately focused on reading. Measurement pressures made reading seem appealing as a learning indicator. Beginning in 2003, literacy expert Dan Wagner emphasised the importance of developing "smaller, quicker, cheaper" learning assessments that could be used to "pinpoint the nature of children's difficulties and to do so with a precision and timing that will allow for potential intervention before it is too late" (2011: 141). His work focused primarily on reading assessments (see also Wagner 2003, 2010).

In the 2000s, influential actors within the World Bank began engaging tests of reading in places like Mali, Peru, and Brazil, and they found very low levels of learning (World Bank 2002; Bender 2005; Abadzi et al. 2005). Drawing on cognitive neuroscience, one influential actor, Helen Abadzi, emphasised fluency, specifically reading speed and automaticity, over other facets, such as comprehension. She recommended words-per-minute benchmarks for reading competency, and this view became widespread for some time, with implementing partners debating whether 60 or 45 words per minute were sufficient to secure literacy and governments adopting specific words-per-minute goals (see, e.g., Abadzi 2008 and the presentation of Liberia's Deputy Minister of Instruction at Brookings). Such moments indicate that, while there were debates among those promoting EGRA, EGRA was rolled out as a fairly influential and unitary policy tool.

In 2006, Colette Chabbott completed a desk review of early grade reading for USAID. The review drew heavily upon the National Research Council's *Preventing Reading Difficulties in Young Children* and the National Reading Panel's *Teaching Children to Read,* adopting their reduced model of reading. The resulting recommendations endorsed tasks developed for English monolinguals and relied on indicators like "words per minute," but they also emphasised the importance of prereading skills, reading materials, one-to-one contact with more expert reader mentors (such as teachers or paraprofessionals), and the importance of mother-tongue literacy and oral development in the target language. In other words, this version of "early grade reading" was broader than what eventually emerged.

Also in 2006, USAID, through its Education Data for Decision Making (EdData II) project, contracted with RTI International staff (many of whom had previously been affiliated with the World Bank) to develop an instrument for assessing early grade reading. Notably, the majority of the core members of this original, influential group were not themselves reading specialists or experts on mother-tongue education and multilingual literacies (Gove and Cvelich 2010). Within the group, the dominant disciplines were cognitive science, economics, and sociology, and the dominant research methodologies were quantitative and experimental in nature. The consultation process was broader than this core group, but consultants had less influence over the tool, and those with a reading background tended to favour phonics-based approaches (see www.eddataglobal.org for a summary of the 2006 workshop). As a consequence, the resulting assessment highlights the cognitive aspects of reading. The group, heavily influenced by the National Reading Panel, conceptualised reading using the "five pillars" model.

Ultimately, RTI essentially adopted adapted tasks from DIBELS as an individual, oral assessment of students' reading skills. It is rather surprising, given the solid and widespread critiques of DIBELS, that it became the foundation of a multimillion dollar international campaign for early grade reading. RTI took the DIBELS subtests, modified them slightly to different languages, and field tested them, resulting in a suite of short, adaptable, timed tests that have come to be known as Early Grade Reading Assessment, or EGRA (RTI 2009; Gove and Cvelich 2010). EGRA includes tests such as letter naming, the pronunciation of letter sounds, nonsense word reading, familiar word reading, and comprehension questions based on a short passage. Different tasks can be adapted or excluded in different locations. The assessment focuses on what it calls the "three early stages of reading acquisition", noting that "the rate at which children pass through these phases varies by country and language" but that, nonetheless, the tests provide "rough guidance for when most children should acquire these skills" (RTI 2009: 12). Those "stages" and relevant test components are:

- Emergent – explored through phonemic awareness and listening comprehension
- Decoding – focusing on letter name and sound, with a mixture of testing nonsense and familiar words
- Confirmation and fluency – with testing by paragraph reading with comprehension, and dictation.

It is important to note that the idea that reading is acquired in "stages" is not universally embraced; many reading experts insist that comprehension and fluency must be taught simultaneously with decoding skills.

In practice, most of the EGRA tests implemented to date have focused on phonemic awareness and the items listed under decoding, in part because comprehension scores are regularly too low to warrant measurement. Thus, the assessments have promoted interventions that stress phonics and phonemic awareness more than, for example, comprehension. For example, the task that has children read "nonsense words" pits phonics against comprehension.

Applications of the tool expanded slowly in the late 2000s, including a 2007 application in Senegal and The Gambia, funded by the World Bank; one in Nicaragua, funded by USAID;

and the use of certain subtasks by national governments, USAID missions, and NGOs in South Africa, Kenya, Haiti, Afghanistan, and Bangladesh (with and without the involvement of RTI) (Gove and Wetterberg 2011: 7–8). A 2008 EGRA workshop, convened by RTI and funded by USAID and the World Bank, marked a turning point. The workshop included results from pilot tests in The Gambia, Senegal, and Nicaragua, as well as case studies from South Africa, Kenya, Mali, Niger, Bangladesh, and Liberia. Based on enthusiasm shared by actors at the World Bank, USAID, and RTI, EGRA expanded rapidly. By 2011, it had been adapted and applied in 50 countries and 70 languages (for updated figures, see the EGRA tracker at www.eddataglobal. org). DIBELS, controversial as it may have been, was designed as a continuous assessment tool to be used by teachers in classrooms; EGRA, in contrast, was rolled out as a policy mechanism to be used by RTI and partner organisations in multiple sites to demonstrate to people within Ministries of Education just how little students were learning in the early grades. This focus, along with the desire for USAID funds, earned support within Ministries of Education for reading interventions that were built around the assessment. The low scores on assessment resulted in Country Missions rapidly developing reading-focused RFPs built around the reduced "five pillars" notion of reading. As funding for reading interventions became more available, RTI and other organisations in the industry expanded by promoting EGRA as an assessment tool driving early grade reading interventions. Such efforts influenced USAID's declaration, in its 2011–2015 Education Strategy, of a remarkable goal: "improved reading skills for 100 million children in primary grades by 2015".

As the educational development field stands poised on the cusp of a reading revolution, and as momentum for using an early grade reading assessment as the primary learning goal for the post-2015 agenda, it is an important moment to question the achievements and limitations of this model of literacy. In what follows, we draw upon Frazier's extensive field experience with literacy programmes, and specifically her work for the International Rescue Committee (IRC) in the Democratic Republic of Congo and in Pakistan, to describe some of the challenges EGRA poses to literacy practitioners. This reflection is also informed by an ongoing, interview-based study conducted by Bartlett with literacy scholars and practitioners.

EGRA in the field: two experiences

DRC

In an early grade education project in DRC, the donor asked IRC to support the teaching and learning of reading in French in Grades 1–6 and required the use of EGRA to measure outcomes in a randomised, controlled trial. The IRC faced challenges implementing this project as planned because of tensions between the IRC's beliefs about the teaching of reading, USAID's requirements and priorities, and the DRC Ministry of Education's (MEPSP) existing curriculum and pedagogical standards. These tensions came through most strongly in planning for the assessment and in the curriculum design for the intervention.

In DRC, the language of instruction in Grades 1 and 2 is a local language; in grade 3, it changes to French. French is taught orally in Grades 1 and 2, but basic literacy skills are taught in the local language in these years. The decision was made to assess Grades 2, 4, and 6. For Grade 2, however, only EGRA subtests that did not require French reading and writing could be used because written French had not yet been formally introduced to students. Therefore, the subtests for second grade were letter identification, identification of initial sounds, receptive vocabulary, and listening comprehension. On the letter identification subtest, second grade students were permitted to say the letter or digraph in either French or Swahili (the predominant local language in the project zones). The remaining subtests (initial sound identification, receptive vocabulary, and listening comprehension) were administered in French with instructions given in a local language. Although this assessment helped identify some basic preliteracy skills and needs among the Grade 1 and 2 students and helped signal the students' weak command of oral French after two years of daily oral French classes, it did not help IRC, the MEPSP, teachers, or language of instruction. Because the DRC MEPSP curriculum for the first two grades of primary school places a priority on teaching foundational reading skills in a local language, which is considered good practice, it would have been more informative to assess children's skills in those languages. The appropriateness of a French-medium EGRA as a literacy assessment is questionable. A better use of assessment time might be to consider students' oral, reading, and writing proficiency in L1 and their oral language development in French. Such assessments would better inform the development of interventions that would help students build on their existing skills.

Another tension emerged during the design of the curriculum to be used in the continuing professional development programme for teachers in the intervention. The IRC developed a lesson planning workbook for teachers to use to guide them through methods of reading pedagogy, such as explicitly teaching sound-symbol correspondence and decoding skills and emphasising meaning making by connecting vocabulary and comprehension to children's lived experiences. A scope and sequence had been developed that integrated IRC's approach to teaching reading (with a dual focus on alphabetic principle and meaning making – similar in philosophy to balanced literacy but modified for a low-resource context) with DRC's existing textbooks and curriculum. This scope and sequence addressed the "five pillars" (phonemic awareness, phonics, vocabulary, fluency, and comprehension) plus writing in each week of the school year for each grade level. Using the scope and sequence, IRC intended to provide for teachers a lesson planning workbook with model reading lesson plans that integrated the component skills of reading and linked to a text for the week that would highlight target sounds and vocabulary words.

When the sample lesson plans were presented to the MEPSP, the inspectors were not happy. They explained that their curriculum specifies that each day of the week be dedicated to a specific skill area: reading, vocabulary, spelling, recitation, and writing. They did not want an integrated approach, and they were not using a "five pillars" model of reading. Working with them, IRC agreed to focus on these skills, using the reading lesson for comprehension, spelling time for phonemic awareness and phonics, and recitation for oral language and fluency. Although IRC staff members believe that integrated reading lessons are ideal, the group was able to design lessons that focused on one of these skills for the principle activity of the day. In retrospect, it may have been easier for teachers to learn this way because each day they only had to focus on one key skill related to the text, words, and sounds of the week. This also meant that what IRC staff members were introducing was closer to the skills the teachers already understood and to what the textbooks and curriculum were designed to teach. Designing lessons this way actually allowed IRC to exploit a more balanced approach to focus on the component skills of reading without removing them from the context of a meaningful text. Each day of the week focused on a different component skill; the text tied the lessons together into a meaningful instructional unit each week.

Pakistan

In Pakistan, USAID hired a contractor to conduct an EGRA in both English and Urdu across the country (even though the Annual Status of Education Report, ASER, is a widely used assessment that has been developed and carried out by civil society in that country for nearly a decade). The EGRAs used for English and Urdu comprised the same subtests, regardless of linguistic differences between the two languages. From the EGRA results, it is very difficult to ascertain which aspects Urdu students find difficult because the Urdu version of the test did not address some skills that may be useful for assessing Urdu reading skills. For example, in Urdu, many words begin with a vowel sound, making it hard for a child to hear and identify the initial sound. Asking students to identify the final sound might be more appropriate. Further, as noted above, Urdu letters change shape depending on their position in the word (like Arabic). The EGRA in Pakistan isolated letters from different positions in the word by writing a full word that included the letter and then blocking out the letters that came before or after so that, on the student stimulus, only the isolated letter appeared. Asking students to identify these letters is inauthentic; students would not see, for example, a letter in the medial position without other letters surrounding it. The reading of Urdu demonstrates the interaction between the alphabetic principle and meaning that occurs in reading. Asking students to read syllables instead of isolated letters would come closer to representing what they will need to be able to do to decode and read in Urdu.

IRC is the lead organisation of a consortium that USAID hired to implement an early grade reading programme, of which a significant component is pre- and in-service teacher professional development. When IRC was drafting the teacher in-service curriculum, comprehension and vocabulary were introduced early in the programme, after print concepts and basic phonics. Partner organisations and some field staff questioned this decision, saying, "Why have you put comprehension so early? It comes last on the EGRA. Shouldn't it follow fluency?" Such questions indicate that some project staff now view the "five core components" as sequential, and comprehension as the end product, rather than understanding that each of these components works in complex interaction. Indeed, some providers of technical assistance have explicitly taught country partners that there is a "correct order" to reading components. The tendency to 'save comprehension for last' and isolate it from other skills of reading may explain why projects are finding it so hard to raise comprehension scores.

Another concern was the amount of phonics instruction that students would receive (and that teachers would learn in their professional development programme). In the early phase of the project's start-up, project staff expressed the belief that the EGRA score could be the average of the scores of each subtest, represented as a percentage. (The lack of a useable composite EGRA score is another criticism of the assessment.) Along with this belief came the conviction that, if the project focused on improving basic skills such as phonics and increased that subtest score significantly, the overall percentage would rise, helping the project to be deemed "successful." While that does not seem to be the case, donors have expressed a preference to focus on phonics and phonemic awareness because they feel that those scores are the easiest and quickest to improve.

These anecdotes demonstrate the power that EGRA is having over reading pedagogy. Non-expert practitioners believe the skills, disarticulated by EGRA, must be taught to students and to teachers in the order in which they are presented in EGRA; they are failing to understand the ways in which these skills work together in the process of reading.

There are debates about how best to teach languages like Urdu. In Urdu, letters can change shape depending on their position in a word and how they are attached to proximate letters. Further, given the use of diacritics to represent short vowel sounds, it can be hard to fully separate letters in Urdu words. These differences may require different reading pedagogies. For example, one experienced Pakistani educator who is working on the project believes that a syllabic method is more appropriate than a phonics-based approach focused on individual letters. He explained that, though the letter 'b' can take four different forms, the syllable 'ba' looks the same whether it is located in the beginning, middle, or end of a word, by virtue of the way that the 'b' is connected to the 'a.' Therefore, it could be much simpler and more useful for decoding to teach a child 'ba' than 'b' + 'a'. This Pakistani educator advocated a reading pedagogy that is whole-part-whole, rather than building from letters to words. In this approach, children would learn whole words, analyse them, break them into syllables and then into letters, and then build them back into words. When they understand how the words break down in this way, he argues, they could build them back together into words. Helping students see how full words are made of syllables and in turn how those syllables are put together from individual letters may prove to be a better approach than a straight sound-symbol correspondence, phonics-based approach. As logical as this sounds, it may prove to be a difficult approach to pilot given the project's strong link to EGRA. Assessment of student learning outcomes will be done using an Urdu EGRA that mirrors the English-language EGRA. Students who are not taught individual letters would not do well on such a test.

Challenges posed by early grade reading assessment

These reflections from the field highlight concerns about the conceptualisation of reading embedded in EGRA and its suitability for multilingual locations.

The current early grade reading focus reduces literacy to a narrow, cognitive psychological model of reading, and this predefined notion of literacy promotes a deficit frame. Its use raises the question: whose model of literacy should prevail? As in the DRC experience, the "five core components" model of reading put IRC at odds with people in the Ministries of Education. Further, EGRA sometimes leads field partners to believe that they should emphasise phonics and phonemic awareness prior to and more than vocabulary and comprehension. It is unfortunate if these skills become separated because much of the literature in reading suggests the need to integrate subword, word, and comprehension work, as suggested by the Pakistani educator mentioned above. And yet such an approach might jeopardise EGRA performance, which is used to evaluate the success of interventions.

The debate over whether to emphasise phonics first or all 'core skills' simultaneously is related to a larger question: are the core components of reading (and the expectations for performance on the reading assessment) the same for learning to read in languages other than English? As the Pakistan vignette shows, in Urdu (as in Arabic), letters change their shape depending on their position in the word. How reasonable, then, is the letter-naming task? Letters also change their sound depending on diacritics: is letter sound a good test of that skill?

Further, EGRA testing in multilingual locations can inadvertently prioritise the European language over languages of wider communication. For example, in the DRC, the language policy stresses that instruction in Grades 1 and 2 is the local language; instruction then shifts to French in Grade 3. However, USAID insisted on French-medium EGRA testing, beginning in Grade 2. Such an approach conflicts with the country's language policy and ends up stressing what children cannot do rather than documenting what they can do. In Pakistan, while both languages were tested, EGRA used the same subtests, despite significant differences between the two languages; such decisions privilege a model of literacy based on English.

Finally, whose needs are being served by assessment decisions? In some instances, assessments seem designed more to provide a baseline for USAID than to provide data about the outcomes of a country's literacy approach. Further, as in Pakistan, the use of EGRA may conflict with established assessment efforts pursued by national civil society actors.

These stories, and our reflections on them, show that it can be incredibly challenging to adapt EGRA to different languages; to get appropriate curricular materials for an EGRA-guided reading intervention; and to conduct a reliable, valid, and comparable EGRA from baseline to end line.

Conclusions

This chapter argues that the reading model represented by EGRA is reductionist; it is being employed in a way that isolates, rather than integrates, different skills; it runs the risk of reifying performance on a simple task as evidence of a much larger and more complex skill; several of the tasks are questionable; and it is an imperfect fit, at best, with many of the languages in the countries where it is being employed.

It is a critical period for literacy in the field of international educational development. Millions of dollars will be invested over the next few years in early grade reading interventions and assessments. Much has been accomplished with the realignment of the international educational agenda toward reading. Ministers have been convinced of the need to focus on early grade reading. Donors have been mobilised, directing much-needed resources toward teacher training and materials preparation and distribution. Development partners are largely harmonised in their work toward this goal. These achievements are laudable. But significant problems with the prevalent model of reading, as shaped by the dominant assessment, remain. Without sufficient oversight and critical attention, the field has embraced a flawed assessment with a reductionist model of reading that does not adequately address literacy and language diversity. And yet this assessment is being used to drive policymaking and pedagogy. It is time for a serious debate about reading.

References

Abadzi, H., 2008. Efficient learning for the poor. *International Review of Education* 54, 5–6, 581–604.

Abadzi, H., Crouch, L., Echegaray, M., Pasco, C., Sampe, J., 2005. Monitoring basic skills acquisition through rapid learning assessments: a case study from Peru. *Prospects* 35, 2, 137–156.

Allington, R. (Ed.), 2002. *Big Brother and the National Reading Curriculum.* Heinemann, Portsmouth, NH.

Bender, P., 2005. Change: Mali's *Pedagogie convergente.* Paper presented at the annual conference of the Comparative and International Education Society, Palo Alto, March.

Chabbott, C., 2006. *Accelerating Early Grades Reading in High Priority EFA Countries: A Desk Review.* USAID and Equip1, Washington.

Chabbott, C., 2009. *Constructing Education for Development: International Organizations and Education for All.* Routledge, New York.

Coles, G., 2000. *Misreading Reading.* Heinemann, Portsmouth, NH.

Garan, E., 2002. *Resisting Reading Mandates.* Heinemann, Portsmouth, NH.

Goodman, K. (Ed.), 2006. *The Truth About DIBELS: What It Is – What It Does.* Heinemann, Portsmouth, NH.

Gove, A., Cvelich, P., 2010. *Early Reading: Igniting Education for All.* Research Triangle Institute, Research Triangle Park.

Gove, A., Wetterberg, A. (Eds.), 2011. *The Early Grade Reading Assessment: Applications and Interventions to Improve Basic Literacy.* RTI Press, Research Triangle Park.

Krashen, S., 2002. Defending whole language: the limits of phonics instruction and the efficacy of whole language instruction. *Reading Improvement* 39, 10, 32–42.

National Reading Panel, 2000. *Teaching Children to Read.* Report of the National Reading Panel. National Institute of Child Health and Human Development, Washington.

Research Triangle Institute, 2009. *Early Grade Reading Assessment Toolkit.* RTI, Research Triangle Park.

Riedel, B., 2007. The relation between DIBELS, reading comprehension and vocabulary in urban first-grade students. *Reading Research Quarterly* 42, 546–567.

Samuels, S., 2007. Is speed of barking at text what we mean by fluency? *Reading Research Quarterly* 42, 563–566.

Samuels, S., Farstrup, A. (Eds.), 2011. *What Research has to Say about Reading Instruction.* International Reading Association, Newark, DE.

Wagner, D., 2003. Smaller, quicker, cheaper: alternative strategies for literacy assessment in the UN Literacy Decade. *International Journal of Educational Research* 39, 293–309.

Wagner, D., 2010. Quality of education, comparability, and assessment choice in developing countries. *Compare* 40, 6, 741–760.

Wagner, D. 2011. *Smaller, Quicker, Cheaper: Improving Learning Assessments for Developing Countries.* UNESCO, Paris.

World Bank, 2002. Project performance assessment report. Brazil. Innovations in Basic Education Project (Loan 3375–BR); Second Northeast Basic Education Project (Loan 3604–BR); Third Northeast Basic Education Project (Loan 3663–BR); School Improvement Project – FUNDESCOLA I (Loan 4311–BR). Operations Evaluation Department, World Bank, Washington.

World Bank, 2006. *From Schooling Access to Learning Outcomes.* World Bank, Washington.

10

TEACHING AND LEARNING FOR ALL?

The quality imperative revisited[1]

Robin Alexander

Quality: now you see it . . .

Like its predecessors, the 2013–14 *Global Monitoring Report Teaching and Learning: Achieving Quality for All* (UNESCO 2014) – hereafter GMR 2014 – is impressive in the scale of its evidence, the progress it documents, the warnings it issues and the humanity of its endeavour.

Quality has been an EFA goal since the 2000 Dakar framework declared it to be 'at the heart of education' and a fundamental determinant of student enrolment, retention and achievement (UNESCO 2000), while, along with quality, learning featured a decade earlier in no fewer than three of the six Jomtien goals (WCEFA 1990). Yet despite these early emphases, quality in the global monitoring reports, and quality in teaching and learning in particular, have since then been surprisingly elusive. In part, this may have reflected a preoccupation with those EFA goals whose urgency has seemed the more pressing because their pathology and progress are readily computed. At least 57 million children are still out of primary school, half of them in 32 countries suffering conflict, and only 13 out of 90 countries are likely to achieve universal primary school completion by 2015. We understand why this is so. Numbers offer headlines and dramatic immediacy. 'Quality' does not.

Paradoxically, quality may also be elusive because it is ubiquitous. For instance, a consistent argument in the GMRs has been the inseparability of quality from equity because until an education system is equitable in terms of access, enrolment, gender parity, retention and completion, it can hardly be described as being of good quality, even if for some children, in some schools, the experience of learning is rewarding and high standards are achieved. We are justifiably disturbed by the finding of GMR 2014 that while the richest boys may on present trends achieve universal primary education by 2021, the poorest girls will not catch up until 2086. Quality for some is not education for all.

Indeed, quality pervades all six EFA goals. The first GMR called quality a 'composite goal', and one of the strengths of these annual reports is that though each of them has had a specific theme – gender, literacy, early childhood, governance, the marginalised, conflict, quality, inequality – each has begun by tracking progress towards all six goals as a reminder of the way they are intertwined and must be simultaneously pursued if EFA is to be achieved.[2]

But quality's very pervasiveness may have encouraged the view that it requires no further elucidation. So it becomes all the more important to examine how quality has been handled in the EFA monitoring process and how this 'composite' goal has been translated into working indicators and measures in the two GMRs – 2005 and 2014 – which have included quality in their titles and remits, for these, post hoc if not a priori, may reveal the definition we seek. Having uncovered that definition, and mindful of the pedagogical orientation of GMR 2014, we can then apply three tests:

- Does the account of quality in EFA attend to what in teaching and learning really matters?
- Are the classroom processes and outcomes that are truly transformative for our children adequately captured in the EFA goals, objectives and targets; the EFA monitoring indicators and measures; and the evidence on which EFA thinking and policy draw?
- If not, what are the implications for the UN's education mission after 2015, and if learning is to be a target, how should it be defined, indicated and assessed?

In attempting to address these questions I first return to the analysis undertaken for the UK Department for International Development (DfID) in 2007 (Alexander 2008a) during a period when I was making annual visits to India in connection with the Government of India's ambitious EFA initiative, Sarva Shiksha Abhiyan (SSA), and its predecessor, the District Primary Education Programme (DPEP). The choice of title for this chapter should now be clear. In the sense that it re-engages with quality, teaching and learning, GMR 2014 revisits GMR 2005, *The Quality Imperative* (UNESCO 2004); this first revisiting allows a second: a reassessment of my earlier concerns about how quality, teaching and learning have been handled in the GMR process as a whole.

One of those concerns was the striking neglect of pedagogy, despite the fact that pedagogy is at the very heart of education and without pedagogy discussion of educational quality makes little sense. Another was the gulf between the evidence on both quality and pedagogy cited in the EFA GMRs and the much larger body of evidence about these matters that appears in the research literature: one world but two discourses. To counter these tendencies, I shall end my paper with an example showing how the EFA movement and its post-2015 successor could increase their effective purchase on the declared priority of advancing quality in teaching and learning if they were prepared to foster a more inclusive discourse and consult a less exclusive literature.

Input, output, proxies and process

Here, briefly summarised, are the problems identified in the 2007 analysis.

First, the quest for indicators and measures of quality produced an understandable preoccupation with input and output – pupil/teacher ratio, balance of male and female teachers, balance of trained and untrained teachers, expenditure per pupil as percent of GDP, net enrolment ratio, adult literacy rate, survival rate to Grade 5 – but this was at the expense of indicators of process. Output is in part determined by process but is not synonymous with it.

Second, when attempts were made to plug the gap, the identified process elements appeared to reflect not teaching and learning as either experienced or researched but those few random aspects of classroom life that were deemed measurable, regardless of whether they had the significance that their selection implies. Hence, for example, the foregrounding of learning time, time on task and class size.

Third, the very act of isolating such aspects validated them in the eyes of those – governments, administrators, donors – who had the money and power to make them matter and set in train policies for embedding them ever more exclusively, whether or not this response was justified by the evidence. In this way, the monitoring distorted both what it monitored and the decisions and interventions to which it led. By way of illustration of the risky consequences of this approach, we might note that in Lockheed's and Verspoor's influential 1991 World Bank cost-benefit analysis of investments for improving primary education in developing countries, preservice teacher education and midday meals were rejected as 'blind alleys' (Lockheed and Verspoor 1991: 87). Today we take a very different view of the efficacy of both interventions.

Fourth, in an attempt to engage more comprehensively with process, some frameworks posited unashamedly qualitative variables such as 'high expectations', 'strong leadership', 'positive teacher attitudes', 'appropriate use of language', 'committed and motivated teachers', 'appropriate teaching and learning materials', 'meaningful assessment', 'effective management of physical assets' and the ubiquitous 'active teaching methods' and 'child-friendly environment' (Alexander 2008a: 3–6). But each of these modifiers – high, strong, positive, appropriate, committed, meaningful, effective, active, child-friendly – lacks objective meaning and is open to many interpretations, not just across cultures but also within them, while the overall selection is no less arbitrary notwithstanding its abundance of adjectives.

Fifth, in the absence of watertight measures, compensatory use was made of proxies. 'Survival rate to grade 5', as the proxy indicator of quality in the EFA Education Development Index (EDI), is a prominent example (UNESCO 2007). This approach is not confined to EFA. Many governments, and certainly the world's media, treat the performance of a sample of 15 year olds in the PISA tests at a single moment in their educational journey as a valid and reliable measure of the performance of entire education systems. Some proxy.

As a not entirely flippant aside, I find the use of 'survival' in this context bizarre as well as evidentially ambiguous. 'Survival' allows two very different takes, one of them suggesting that education is to be endured rather than enjoyed: 1) 'How good was your education?' 'Excellent: I survived to Grade 5.' 2) 'How good was your education?' 'Terrible: I survived to Grade 5 but then could take no more and left school.'

This brings me to three overarching problems, which like the tendencies summarised above seem to apply no less in 2015 than in 2007.

Quality: a mantra in need of definition

First, there remains a conspicuous lack of precision in the use of the keyword 'quality' itself. Though 'quality' is often used quasiadjectively, as in 'quality healthcare', 'quality teaching', 'quality learning' and so on, it is actually a noun. The adjectival use of 'quality' – as in 'quality education – is no more than a slogan, offering limited purchase on what quality actually entails. But even when used as a noun, 'quality' is multifaceted, for it can mean an attribute – as in 'the qualities we look for in a teacher' – or a degree of excellence, as when we say teaching is of outstanding quality, in which case 'outstanding' needs to be defined. So 'quality' – as in Teaching and Learning: quality for all – can describe, prescribe or evaluate.

In the debate about quality in EFA, this basic distinction has too often been blurred. That is to say, some have been happy to use supposed indicators of quality in teaching and learning – quality in the sense of a standard to aim for – without adequately exploring and describing those qualities or attributes of which teaching and learning are actually constituted. When we favour prescription over description, we risk producing a prospectus for quality that is arbitrary or biased. So I suggest that the task of improving the quality of teaching and learning requires closer attention to the description and analysis of quality and rather less to soundbites like 'child-friendly teaching' and 'active learning'.

Indicators and measures: not the same

The second overarching problem is a confusion between indicators and measures. The term frequently treated as interchangeable when they are not. Here I concede that I may well be minority within the EFA community (though not, I'm happy to say, outside it) for at a 2014 I don seminar of the great and good in development education, an indicator was defined ex cath as 'a precise metric from identified databases that assesses if a target is being reached', and nob thought or dared to disagree. But this definition is stipulative and context bound, and I prefe argue that if we have the luxury of two terms we should not squander the clarity and nuanc this allows by treating them as synonymous.

Thus, measures measure, indicators indicate: they do different jobs. A measure is a procedu device or unit for measuring and is irrevocably tied to quantity. An indicator is a more compl and variable clue about whether something is happening and if so to what extent. Approachii clouds indicate the imminence of rain; however, they do not guarantee it, and they certain don't measure rainfall. A noisy classroom may indicate lack of student concentration, but it do not conclusively prove it, still less measure the precise balance of student attention and inatten tion. Indeed, there are those who say that a noisy classroom indicates active learning, but that another story.

Take, as one familiar and ostensibly absolute measure of learning in school effectiveness stud ies, time on task – or what, to distinguish it from available instructional time, Hattie and Yates (2014: 37) call 'engaged time'. This is often no more than an indicator, and a less than conclusive one at that, for it depends only up to a point on objectively measured time and rather more on an inferential response to students' observable behaviour. A student who appears to be attending to the teacher or reading, and hence 'on task', may in reality be daydreaming; if not wholly off task, then (as happens to all of us) concentrating for only some of the time, apparently commit- ted and with only some of his or her available attention. Who then, from the coding categories offered by conventional classroom observation schedules, is able to calibrate the proportion of actual instructional time when in Hattie's terms the student is not only engaged but also learning?

These difficulties sustain Gage's claim that time on task is a 'psychologically empty quan- titative concept' (Gage 1978: 75). As it happens, Hattie's survey of 800 student achievement meta-analyses found time on task also to be a poor indicator of both learning and attain- ment (Hattie 2009: 184–5), for what matters is the nature of the engagement, not its quantity. Unpacking this relationship further, my own observation of teaching across cultures required me to differentiate the related measure of pace, which in UK school inspections is treated as monolithic and unproblematic, by reference to five elements:

- Organisational pace (the speed at which lesson preparations, transitions and conclusions are handled);
- Task pace (the speed at which learning tasks and their contingent activities are undertaken);
- Interactive pace (the pace of teacher–student and student–student exchanges, and contin- gent matters such as maintaining focus and the handling of cues and turns);
- Cognitive or semantic pace (the speed at which conceptual ground is covered in classroom interaction or the ratio of new material to old and of task demand to task outcome);
- Learning pace (how fast students actually learn) (Alexander 2001: 418–426).

Time, as the above study also pointed out, 'is a value, not merely a unit of measurement' (Alex- ander 2001: 425). Of course, the methodological challenge of mental/behavioural inference

is at least as old as the discipline of psychology, and time on task is just one of its manifestations. Small wonder that some have chosen to measure learning by focusing exclusively on behaviour qua behaviour. That the problem is at once methodological and conceptual is amply demonstrated in Lefstein and Snell's (2013) more recent take on the problem of pace as identified above.

Notwithstanding all this, but for reasons we know and understand, what can be measured is privileged in policy circles over what cannot. But this is a dubious and indeed pyrrhic elevation if what is measured has limited indicative power and what is important is marginalised or ignored. Some indicators can be translated into measures, some cannot, but let's talk about the full spectrum of what needs to be indicated before we start talking about measures. I accept that national education systems, and international education efforts such as EFA, entail massive expenditure and huge populations and therefore require metrics that are as precise as possible and cannot be content with high-inference indicators. But if this imperative excludes what is most important, then we have a problem.

To keep open the prospects for engaging with what really matters in teaching and learning, I believe that we should sharpen rather than blunt the distinction between indicators and measures, treating the identification of indicators as the necessary first step in the formulation of measures. If it is indeed the case that much that is essential to the quality and outcomes of learning can be indicated but not be measured, we should not arbitrarily exclude such attributes or grasp at proxies that may be conveniently measurable but barely relevant. Instead, we should leave the unmeasurable indicators in place, develop and refine them in their own terms as qualitative devices for making qualitative judgements and look for appropriate ways of using them to support our tasks of monitoring, development and improvement.

A more radical and creative discussion of EFA indicators is needed than the GMRs have so far provided; one that proceeds from the 'quality imperative' of teaching and learning as they irreducibly are, rather from numerical convenience. Hard data are not necessarily useful data.

The task I have outlined applies as much to the assessment of the learning of individual children as to the monitoring of schools and education systems. We can measure children's mathematical attainment and certain aspects of their basic literacy development. However, GMR 2014 argues, and its argument is welcome, that while the so-called basics are essential, the fractured nature of our world and the tragedies of poverty and conflict require schools to promote a global citizenship that addresses issues such as environmental sustainability and peace building – which require core transferable skills such as critical thinking, communication, cooperation, problem solving, conflict resolution, leadership and advocacy – and the promotion of core values such as tolerance, appreciation of diversity and civic responsibility (UNESCO 2014: 295).

Here we are firmly in the territory of nonmeasurable indicators. So we must find other ways to describe and assess children's learning in this vital area. A single, testable target or indicator for 'learning' across the board – as is proposed for EFA post-2015 – may not suffice, unless it can be proved that, say, numeracy correlates with tolerance, appreciation of diversity and civic responsibility. Actually, this isn't as farfetched as it may seem, for as GMR 2014 reminds us, the entire EFA effort is predicated on evidence that education, and especially literacy, reduces poverty, boosts growth, increases employment prospects, enhances health, reduces child mortality, narrows the gender gap and much else (UNESCO 2014: 144ff). Even more to the point, a British review of research on citizenship education showed that the skills in question are most effectively developed when they are embedded in the teaching process rather than merely conceived as outcomes (Deakin Crick et al. 2005), and this I also take to be the force of the references in GMR 2014 to critical thinking, communication, problem solving and so on. This,

once again, underlines the need for GMRs to engage with classroom process, for that's where citizenship starts.

Pedagogy: one thing needful

This takes me to the third overarching problem predicated on my earlier analysis. Brian Simon, the UK's most distinguished educational historian, famously asked 'Why no pedagogy in England?' (Simon 1981), and we might ask 'Why no pedagogy in the GMRs?' If pedagogy is both the act of teaching and the ideas, values, knowledge and evidence that shape and justify it, if it is what the teacher needs to know in order to make valid, effective and defensible classroom decisions (Alexander 2008b: 47), and if once access and enrolment have been achieved it is what delivers the learning outcomes towards which EFA is directed, then it should have pride of place in a report entitled "Teaching and Learning: Quality for All." But it does not.

In EFA 2002, repeated in subsequent GMRs, there is a table entitled 'an input-process-outcome framework for assessing education quality' (UNESCO 2002: 81). At least process is included; all too often it remains securely locked in its black box. But that is as far as it goes, for in this framework 'process' comprises just two elements: 'school climate' and 'teaching/learning'. The school climate indicators – high expectations, strong leadership, positive teacher attitudes, safe and gender-sensitive environments, incentives for good results, flexibility/autonomy – are preconditions or contextual factors rather than processes; and the teaching/learning indicators are confined to 'sufficient learning time', 'active teaching methods', 'integrated systems for assessment and feedback', 'appropriate class size' and 'appropriate use of language'.

Apart from the fact that these indicators display, in their use of adjectives like 'high', 'strong', 'positive', 'sufficient', 'active' and 'appropriate', the problem of prescription in the guise of description that I referred to earlier, an uncalibrated prescription at that, most of them are also about context and conditions rather than processes. Only 'active teaching methods' and 'appropriate use of language' come close, but without further explication these do not amount to much.

In fact, the striking feature of the GMRs is that they do not so much engage with pedagogy as circle around it. Like knowledge itself, pedagogy is a very deep pool. Perhaps UNESCO is afraid of falling in.

Quality and pedagogy: have the GMRs progressed?

What has changed during the GMR cycle? I should say immediately that while GMR 2005 was confined to the indicators that have been a constant since Dakar, it was an exception to some of the tendencies I've mentioned. It reviewed definitions of quality from Jomtien, Dakar, the UN Convention on the Rights of the Child and elsewhere, comparing humanist, behaviourist, critical, indigenous and adult education approaches. It also took us back to the 1996 Delors report, Learning: the treasure within, whose simple but powerful distinction between learning 'to know', 'to do', 'to live together' and 'to be' deserves to be revisited (Delors et al. 1996).

All this was timely and helpful. However, GMR 2005 then proposed a 'framework for understanding education quality' (UNESCO 2004: 36) in the hope of combining and reconciling the differences that its discussion had exposed. In fact, apart from juggling the boxes and providing a more detailed elaboration of contextual factors, and in spite of the excellent accompanying discussion of the nature of quality, the quality framework in GMR 2005 was not very different from that in GMR 2002, and its account of teaching and learning – which it revealingly

123

renamed 'inputs' rather than 'process' – was almost identical. Learning as an input? Only if you view teaching as no more than transmission.

The chronology is interesting, too. GMR 2002 offered 'a framework for assessing education quality' (UNESCO 2002: 81) while three years later, GMR 2005 gave us 'a framework for understanding education quality' (UNESCO 2004: 36). Surely it should have been the other way round, for you can't assess something without first understanding it. Does this back-to-front chronology illustrate a wider tendency in EFA monitoring, I wonder?

What happens when we fast-forward to GMR 2014? Here I can find no exploration, comparable to that provided by GMR 2005, of what educational 'quality' means. I assume that this is because it would look odd still to be debating such matters after ten reports and just one year before GMR 2015, the final report in the series. So in the assessment of progress towards EFA Goal 6, quality is characterised by the 'key indicators' of pupil/teacher ratio at the preprimary, primary and secondary stages, the continuing teacher gender imbalance and the availability of textbooks (UNESCO 2014: 84–9). To these is added a section on the need to strengthen international and regional assessments (UNESCO 2014: 89–99).

All of these are important, but are they sufficient? And where, once again, are the processes of teaching and learning that GMR 2014 itself acknowledges are so vital to the EFA effort? 'Strong national policies that make teaching and learning a high priority are essential', says the report, 'to ensure that all children in school actually obtain the skills and knowledge they are meant to acquire' (UNESCO 2014: 217). Just so. However, in the next paragraph, expectations that at last we are getting somewhere are dashed when 'teach*ing* quality' becomes 'teach*er* quality' (my italics in each case), and this unexplained but significant shift from act to agent is then consolidated in the report's detailed discussion of teacher numbers, recruitment, qualifications, subject knowledge, training, retention and governance.

The emphasis on teachers is supremely important. Without teachers there is no teaching, and without good teachers the learning potential of many children will remain untapped. The association between teacher quality and learning outcomes is both self-evident and empirically demonstrable. But what are teachers to teach and how? And on what aspects of their teaching should their training concentrate, and why? And can we answer these questions if the nature of teaching has been inadequately conceived?

GMR 2014 does engage with some of these questions. It emphasises training for pupil diversity, gender parity and children with learning difficulties. It argues the need to compensate for teachers' poor subject knowledge and the importance of tools for classroom diagnosis and assessment, especially in relation to children at risk (UNESCO 2014: 233–41). And then, in its crucial seventh and final chapter, 'Curriculum and assessment strategies that improve learning' (UNESCO 2014: 276–97), it at last enters the classroom. So 14 years after Dakar, are we there at last? Have we finally reached pedagogy?

Yes and no, but mainly no. The discussions of both curriculum and assessment are, within the limits they set themselves, useful. As I've noted, GMR 2014 departs from the exclusive preoccupation with literacy and numeracy and argues the need for a wider curriculum and transferable skills. However, it sticks to the received view, dating back to the 19th century, that literacy and numeracy are and forever should remain the sole 'basics' of education, regardless of time, location, culture or national circumstance.

In this matter, the case for literacy remains exceptionally strong as both a tool for individual empowerment and a lever for social and economic progress, and successive GMRs have convincingly documented its impact in these terms. But, heretical though some may find the thought, the case for continuing to give numeracy parity with literacy is neither proved nor even entertained; the habit of history, it seems, is sufficient justification, and because 'literacy and numeracy' has become in effect a single curriculum component, numeracy gets a free ride. Thus we are offered a curriculum in which only literacy, numeracy and citizenship are deemed 'basic'. But where, some beneficiaries of citizenship education might ask, are science or IT? And where, given the reference to transferable skills for citizenship, is the no-less-compelling evidence on transfer of learning through the arts? Questioning fixed curriculum mind-sets is surely as necessary a part of the GMR exercise as revisiting habitual assumptions about what constitutes a valid educational indicator. If the task is thought to be necessary in rich countries, why not elsewhere?

Commendation with reservation also applies to the treatment of assessment. GMR 2014 breaks new ground in EFA circles (though not elsewhere) by discussing formative as well as summative assessment, or what in the UK is called 'assessment for learning'. But here the discussion is again frustrated by the GMR's limited apprehension of pedagogy. Effective assessment for learning is more than the tools, boxes and packs that in this context GMR 2014 recommends from examples in Uganda, Liberia, South Africa, Colombia and India, which indeed their evaluations show to be effective in terms of both diagnosis and outcomes (UNESCO 2014: 288–9). More fundamentally, assessment for learning is the very stuff of which effective teaching is made: the day-to-day, minute-by-minute observations and interactions through which good teachers constantly monitor children's learning and progress, affording the feedback that will build on their understandings and probe and remedy their misunderstandings.

On this vital matter, GMR 2014, like its predecessors, has little to say. Once again, we trip over the black box or meet the timorous figures circling the deep pool of pedagogy. Curriculum prescribed but not enacted; summative assessment but not formative; input and outcome but not process.

Why no pedagogy in the Global Monitoring Reports?

If I am right that pedagogy is the missing ingredient in accounts of educational quality in these global monitoring reports, and that where pedagogic process appears its treatment is confined to random indicators, and that these tend to circle the teaching-learning process rather than engage with it, then as a prerequisite for improving matters in the post-2015 agenda we must urgently ask why this should be so. Why no pedagogy?

One answer is that when the availability and competence of teachers is a major challenge, as the GMRs show that it is, then it makes sense to focus on teachers rather than teaching; invest heavily in teacher recruitment, training and retention; and develop textbooks and classroom materials that, in 1960s US parlance, are 'teacher proof' and will enable even the minimally trained teacher to do a reasonable job. On that basis, it may be thought that there's more to be gained from providing such materials than advocating more sophisticated and interactive models of teaching, especially in the context of large classes and multigrade teaching. In these situations, textbooks and TLMs provide a predictable and reliable foundation for the teacher's work, effective even when the teacher is absent. For, as GMR 2014 reminds us, teacher absenteeism remains a major impediment to EFA (UNESCO 2014: 267).

This argument is persuasive, though we must ask whether it is right for all circumstances and all teachers and to what extent it should inform the EFA agenda after 2015. Making teaching 'teacher proof' may safeguard educational minima and compensate for teachers' poor training or erratic attendance, but it can be disempowering and, for competent and talented teachers, demeaning.

But is there another explanation for the neglect of process? I think there is, and it resides in the literature and evidence on which, since 2002, the GMRs have drawn.

A head count of the 680 or so published sources listed at the end of GMR 2014 reveals that, in a report promisingly entitled "Teaching and Learning", the titles of only 40 of the cited publications – a mere six percent – refer, directly or indirectly, to the report's claimed focus. A somewhat larger proportion deal with teacher supply, training and retention, and a much larger proportion still are macrolevel national or cross-national studies of education policies, programmes, strategies, governance, funding and outcomes (UNESCO 2014: 410–443).

That apparently skewed citation profile encourages us to dig deeper. A decade ago, a review undertaken for the US National Research Council (NRC) (2003) identified three main types of international comparative study in education. Type 1 are large-scale, policy-directed, statistical studies of educational achievement, expenditure and other matters of the kind that emanate from OECD, the World Bank and the UN. Type 2 are desk-based extrapolations from international data aimed at identifying policy options and solutions (Michael Barber's three McKinsey reports are a good example). Type 3 include the majority of studies in the published corpus of academic comparative, international and development education. These range from broadly descriptive accounts of individual education systems to the 'thick description' (Geertz 1983) of close-grained, cross-national, and cross-cultural comparative studies of school and classroom life and the forces that shape it.

Types 1, 2 and 3 add up to a literature of considerable variety and richness. However, the NRC report adds that while the majority of published comparative education studies are Type 3, and while many Type 3 studies have significant policy applications, it's the Type 1 and 2 studies that receive most of the funding, political patronage and publicity. Meanwhile, Type 3 studies have more limited funding and rarely come to the attention of policymakers or Type 2 reviewers. The NRC report judges this to be deeply unfortunate because Type 3 studies engage with education, teaching and learning as they are enacted and experienced in schools and classrooms to an extent that Type 1 and 2 studies do not and, by virtue of their methodology, cannot. This neglect of Type 3 evidence reinforces the remoteness of policymakers and the policy process from schooling as it is experienced by teachers and children, and increases the risk that high-cost and high-stakes interventions relating to teachers, teaching and learning may be misconceived or misdirected.

Following the NRC analysis, what we may have, then – not universally or inevitably but too frequently – is a six-fold problem of evidential selectivity in the corridors of power. First, the preferred evidence is top-down. It reflects the world, the preoccupations, the priorities and the experiences of policymakers rather than those of teachers and children. Second, it may privilege a supposedly international but essentially Western perspective over an indigenous one. Third, its view of school and classroom life may be generalised, coarse-grained, unnuanced, and perhaps simplistic. Fourth, its understandable pursuit of what can be measured removes from the agenda and consciousness of policymakers those vital aspects of education that quantification cannot access. Fifth, it ignores a substantial tranche of evidence of which, in the interests of competent and democratic policy making, policymakers, or at least their advisers, have a duty to be aware. Sixth, it is self-sealing and self-reinforcing. Reading UK government publications, I am constantly struck by the extent to which they refer only to other government publications. Such circularity in evidence, argument and policy is always dangerous, a fortiori in the context of global education.

It would be impolite of me to accuse GMR 2014 of these tendencies, but, given what I have said about the balance of published sources listed at the end of the report, the possibility at least deserves consideration, for GMR 2014, like all the GMRs, leans more towards Type 1 evidence than Type 3. In doing so, is it missing something important? I think it is.

Engaging with pedagogy: conceptual and empirical possibilities

I want now to show how in the elusive area of pedagogy such evidential selectivity and imbalance can be avoided and how we can then greatly enhance the debate about the quality of teaching and learning in EFA. I shall deal with the matter first conceptually then empirically.

The genealogy of the teaching-learning framework in GMR 2002, which was modified in GMR 2005 and remains influential in EFA, is clear: 1960s US process-product research transmuted into 1990s transatlantic school effectiveness research and was domesticated by international agencies like the World Bank. It atomises rather than synthesises, includes only what can be easily measured, views teaching as simple transmission and so concentrates much more on the teacher than the learner, treating culture not as an all-pervasive feature to be handled with care, sensitivity and humility but as just another variable to be factored and crunched.

I would not claim that my own alternative is impervious to critique, still less that it is the one to adopt, but at least it provides a contrast. Striving to develop a framework for the analysis of both quantitative and qualitative classroom data from five very different education systems in Europe, North America and Asia, I started with what I believed were two irreducible propositions about the nature of teaching, as it is in any context: (i) teaching, in any setting, is the act of using method x to enable students to learn y; (ii) teaching has structure and form; it is situated in, and framed by, space, time and patterns of organisation; and it is undertaken for a purpose. From these I derived a two-part framework or matrix comprising the act of teaching and the ideas that inform it.

Teaching as an act was divided into (i) the act itself, subdivided into the planned learning tasks, the activities and interactions through which tasks are mediated and the judgements by which students' needs, progress and attainment are assessed; (ii) the form by which units of teaching are bounded (usually the lesson); and (iii) the organisational, curricular, epistemic and temporal elements of its frame. Each of these was then further elaborated to support a mixture of quantitative and qualitative data analysis (Alexander 2001).

Teaching as ideas encompassed values, beliefs, theories, evidence, policies and justifications and in respect of these differentiated three levels or domains: (i) classroom (ideas relating to students, learning, teaching and curriculum that enable teaching on a day-to-day basis); (ii) system/policy (ideas about schooling, curriculum, assessment and other matters that formalise or legitimise teaching); and (iii) cultural/societal (ideas about community, culture and self that locate teaching) (Alexander 2008b: 48–9 and 180–1).

Teaching as an act identifies the cross-cultural structural invariants of teaching. This part of the framework has been shown to be not only comprehensive but also as culture-fair as any such cultural artefact can be. In 2014–15, for example, a research team at Ben Gurion University is using it to analyse Israeli pedagogy (Lefstein 2013). Teaching as ideas accesses the cultural variables that shape, breathe life and meaning into, and indeed define these invariants and thus demonstrate the extent to which (as I showed earlier) even the most securely quantifiable of them is culturally loaded.

In my own cross-cultural studies, I found that such ideas concerned not just the nature and purposes of learning, knowledge and teaching – transmission, induction, negotiation, facilitation, acceleration and so on – but even more fundamentally what I called 'primordial values' about the relationship of the individual to others and to society, which translate into culturally distinctive classroom routines and patterns of organisation. This could take us into a discussion of so-called 'Western' and 'non-Western' models of teaching for which there isn't space in this paper, except to note that to portray the cultural diversity of teaching and learning as conceived and enacted across 196 nations and thousands of cultures and subcultures as a simple choice between 'Western' and 'non-Western' is crude in the extreme. Note, too, that this dichotomy makes 'Western' the default and 'non-Western' the aberration. Edward Said (1985) would have had something to say about that.

There is no way that the inherited GMR paradigm can capture any of this. What the comparison of these frameworks also signals is another important question: are there universals in teaching and learning that apply across cultures and contexts, or is everything culturally unique? In my own work, I strenuously argue that culture and history are the keys to understanding and comparing national education systems. But I also believe from what we know about human development and education across cultures that there is a level at which pedagogic universals can be defined. My complementary frameworks for teaching as act and ideas try to capture these.

Frameworks like those I have exemplified expose the conceptual incompleteness of the input-output models in GMR 2002. Above all, the classroom interaction through which both learning and teaching are mediated is almost absent from the GMR frameworks. Let us therefore stay with interaction, mindful of the NRC's judgement that policy-directed studies lean too exclusively on Type 1 and 2 research and ignore Type 3 judgement that, in relation to the interactive heart of teaching and learning, is borne out by the bibliography of GMR 2014. Where, then, can we go to plug this gap?

There is a considerable literature on classroom interaction in general and educationally productive talk in particular, but I'll mention by way of example just two major sources that have the virtue of being comprehensive, methodologically diverse, cross-cultural, cross-national and rigorously empirical. Further, their publication dates coincide neatly with our consideration of the post-2015 agenda.

The first is a collection of research papers arising from an international conference on classroom talk that was convened in 2011 at the University of Pittsburgh, USA, under the auspices of AERA (Resnick, Asterhan and Clarke 2015). This brought together many of the world's leading researchers in the areas of pedagogy and linguistics to establish whether, after several decades of research, we have proof of the concept that high-quality classroom talk not only engages children's attention and participation – as we have known for a long time that it does – but also raises their standards of achievement in tests of literacy, numeracy and science.

The answer to that question was conclusively affirmative. There is now a critical mass of randomised control studies in different countries showing that high-quality classroom talk enhances understanding, accelerates learning and raises measured standards. This finding is also confirmed in Hattie's (2009) synthesis of 800 meta-analyses relating to student achievement in respect of interactive strategies such as reciprocal teaching, peer tutoring, student verbalisation and feedback. Such strategies, in Hattie's words, make children's learning visible to the teacher and hence amenable to appropriate diagnosis, assessment and intervention (Hattie 2009: 173–8). The quest for indicators of visible learning would be a useful exercise for the team of GMR 2015. 'Visible' and 'measurable' are not, however, synonymous.

The other study counters the claim that because the research I have cited comes from classrooms in high-income countries it cannot fairly be expected to apply in the context of education for development. This second study is a review of research on pedagogy, curriculum, teaching practices and teacher education in developing countries, which the UK government's Department for International Development (DFD) commissioned from the University of Sussex (Westbrook et al. 2013). Having trawled 489 studies from middle- and low-income countries, the Sussex team examined 54 of these in depth. While acknowledging the methodological limitations of some of the studies, the Sussex team nevertheless felt able to conclude that classroom interaction is the pedagogical key. They highlighted as feasible and proven strategies for effective teaching in these contexts inclusive and supportive communication, varied teacher questioning, informative feedback, building on student responses, student questioning and other elements of what I call dialogic teaching (Alexander 2008c).

All the studies in these important US and UK collections, which together include classroom research from high-, middle- and low-income countries, are Type 3. Being Type 3 and engaging with teaching as it happens show not just that high-quality classroom talk makes a difference but how it can be improved. But only a handful of the studies in the Sussex report, and none of those from the AERA symposium, found their way into the vast bibliographies of GMR 2005 and 2014, dominated as these were by Types 1 and 2. In the UK, meanwhile, a major research and development project capitalises on such evidence to develop, test and evaluate the capacity of talk-rich teaching strategies to close the achievement gap between some of Britain's most disadvantaged children and their more advantaged peers.

Conclusion: what is to be done?

And so we return to my initial questions:

- Does the account of quality in EFA attend to what really matters in teaching and learning?
- Are the classroom processes and outcomes that are truly transformative for our children adequately captured in the EFA goals, objectives and targets; the EFA monitoring indicators and measures; and the evidence on which EFA thinking and policy draw?
- If not, what are the implications for EFA after 2015, and if learning is to be a target, how should it be defined, indicated and assessed?

I submit that, in respect of the monitoring of quality in teaching and learning in EFA, we have a problem that is both conceptual and empirical. Neither quality nor pedagogy are adequately conceived, and some of the world's most important and relevant evidence on teaching, learning and their improvement has been ignored. Classroom interaction is the most prominent and perhaps crucial aspect of pedagogy, among several, to suffer this fate, and the example above shows that its omission is both grave and unnecessary.

How can this unsatisfactory situation be addressed?

First, education for the period post-2015 needs a radical and properly informed debate about indicators and measures in relation to the black box, or black hole, of teaching and learning, for classrooms are the true front line in the quest for educational quality. The proper sequence, surely, is not to make do with the odd measure that happens to have featured in a number of school effectiveness studies but to start with a rounded account of the educational process and the purposes it serves, then range comprehensively and eclectically across the full spectrum of relevant research and extrapolate what the evidence shows can safely be regarded as key indicators of quality, and only then proceed to the question of how those indicators that have been shown to have preeminent influence on the quality and outcomes of learning can be translated into measures. In all cases, both indicators and measures should resonate clearly with goals. It is all too common for education planners grandly to espouse goal x and then signal through what is tested that outcome y is what really matters.

Second, where an indicator has empirical provenance but cannot readily be translated into a simple measure, other ways should be found to keep it in the frame. Under no circumstances should an indicator that peer-reviewed research has shown to be critical to effective teaching and standards of learning be dropped at this stage merely because it cannot be quantified. We have to find other ways of handling it. We need a more creative and less doctrinal approach to the whole question of indicators and measures, exploiting, as I suggest above, the methodological possibilities that the vocabulary encourages. In any case, the objectivity of quantitative measures is often overstated, while there are established procedures for assuring interjudge reliability in the use of so-called subjective assessments. Again, I warn against paradigm wars.

Third, to cover the evidence as it needs to be covered, teams working on the defining and monitoring of quality in education post-2015 should become more relevantly multidisciplinary than, in the EFA context, they appear to have been thus far.

Fourth, let's accept that although much Type-3 evidence comes from and relates to high-income jurisdictions and systems, the recent DFD review of research on pedagogy, curriculum and teacher education in developing countries shows that there's now a fair Type-3 corpus from middle- and low-income contexts too. One of the post-2015 tasks, I suggest, should be to expand that corpus and make it as reliable as possible. In any case, there's sufficient evidence from cross-national studies of teaching and learning, and from Hattie-style meta-analyses of classroom research, to show that there are universals to which in any event we should attend; for example, teacher professional content knowledge (not the same as subject knowledge), the character and degree of cognitive challenges afforded by teacher-student interaction and the quality of the information conveyed in teacher-student and student-teacher feedback.

Fifth, having identified which processes matter most and having nominated them as essential indicators, we will find from Type-3 research that some of them are more amenable to measurement than may be thought. That goes especially for the teacher-student interaction that lies at the heart of teaching.

Sixth, in light of all this, we therefore need to explore targets and indicators for both learning and teaching. Learning needs a process indicator as well as an outcome one, and on the basis of what we know about the crucial conditions for learning, we might try student engagement. Similarly, if teaching has to be reduced to just one indicator, on the basis of what we know about the characteristics of effective teaching from both Hattie's meta-analysis of studies in high income countries and the 2013 DFD literature review, we might try reciprocity in teacher-student interaction. As it happens, both engagement and oral reciprocity are amenable to measurement, so mine is not a completely hopeless cause. Having said that, they are also susceptible to the same problems of behavioural inference that I discussed earlier in relation to time on task, which underlines the need for continuing caution and vigilance.

Finally, here is the double and troubling dilemma. I and others want teaching and learning as they happen and are experienced to gain the prominence in global education after 2015 that they deserve and urgently need if we are to make progress; because the modality highlights targets, indicators and metrics, that means that we need to start by exploring how far what matters in teaching and learning is amenable to this treatment. But on the basis of the reductionism we have witnessed thus far, the prospect of a single, global measure of the quality of teaching applied across all cultural and pedagogical contexts is nothing if not deeply alarming. Quite apart from the totalitarian resonance of such an idea, or the possibility – nay, probability – that the measure would be plain wrong, teaching is a quintessentially local activity; and I say this having argued above that there are observable structural invariants in teaching and learning that are encountered across cultures and systems.

This also means that while generalised process quality targets may be volunteered on the basis of what the evidence tells us makes a difference, it is only at a classroom level that they can be feasibly monitored. The trick will be to give process and the quality of process the prominence they deserve without allowing the resulting indicator(s) to tyrannise and debase what they purport to advance and improve and to find a way to add this essential local dimension to development and monitoring processes that are no less essentially about global and national development.

There are many barriers to achieving education for all, but evidence should not be one of them. Quality in teaching and learning is a global imperative. It demands a global community of discourse. At the time of going to press, a concept note from the EFA GMR team (UNESCO 2015) is somewhat self-congratulatory about the methodology of GMR 2014 and seemingly impervious to critique of the kind offered here. Nevertheless, we have to hope that UNESCO and its advisers will approach global education post-2015 with a commitment to make much more inclusive use of the abundant evidence on pedagogy that is now available in order to exert maximum impact on quality where it matters: in the classroom. Stop tiptoeing around the pool of pedagogy. Take the plunge.

Notes

1 This chapter is reproduced with permission and minor changes from Alexander (2015). An earlier version was presented as an invited keynote lecture at the Oslo conference launching the 2013/14 Education for All Global Monitoring Report on 3 February 2014. The author is grateful to the conference organisers: the Norwegian National Commission for UNESCO, Norad, the Norwegian Refugee Council and the University of Oslo.
2 The ten previous GMRs, from 2002–12, are listed on page iv of GMR 2014.

References

Alexander, R.J., 2001. *Culture and Pedagogy*. Blackwell-Wiley, Oxford.

Alexander, R.J., 2008a. *Education for All, the Quality Imperative and the Problem of Pedagogy*. CREATE Research Monograph 20, University of Sussex.

Alexander, R.J., 2008b. *Essays on Pedagogy*. Routledge, London.

Alexander, R.J., 2008c. *Towards Dialogic Teaching*. Dialogos, York.

Alexander, R.J., 2015. Teaching and learning for all? The quality imperative revisited. *International Journal of Educational Development*.

Deakin Crick, R., Taylor, M., Ritchie, S., Samuel, E., Durant, K., 2005. *A Systematic Review of the Impact of Citizenship Education on Student Learning and Achievement*. EPPI-Centre, Institute of Education, University of London.

Delors, J., Al Mufti, I., Amagi, I., Carneiro, R., Chung, F., Geremek, B., . . . Zhou, N.Z., 1996. *Learning: The Treasure Within. Report to UNESCO of the International Commission on Education for the Twenty-First Century*. UNESCO, Paris.

Gage, N., 1978. *The Psychological Basis of the Art of Teaching*. Teachers College Press, New York.

Geertz, C., 1983. *Local Knowledge: Further Essays in Interpretive Anthropology*. Basic Books, New York.

Hattie, J., 2009. *Visible Learning*. Routledge, London.

Hattie, J., Yates, G., 2014. *Visible Learning and the Science of How We Learn*. Routledge, London.

Lefstein, A., 2013. The rules of pedagogical discourse in Israel: has the time come to break them? Paper presented to the Israel Ministry of Education, October.

Lefstein, A., Snell, J., 2013. Beyond a unitary conception of pedagogic pace: quantitative measurement and ethnographic experience. *British Educational Research Journal* 39, 1, 73–106.

Lockheed, M., Verspoor, A., and Associates, 1991. *Improving Primary Education in Developing Countries*. Oxford University Press, New York.

National Research Council, 2003. *Understanding Others, Educating Ourselves*. National Academies Press, Washington.

Resnick, L., Asterhan, C., Clarke, S. (Eds.), 2015. *Socializing Intelligence through Academic Talk and Dialogue*. American Educational Research Association, Washington.

Said, E., 1985. *Orientalism*. Penguin, London.

Shulman, L.S., 1987. Knowledge and teaching: foundations of the new reform. *Harvard Educational Review* 57, 1, 1–22.

Simon, B., 1981. Why no pedagogy in England? In: Simon, B. and Taylor, W. (Eds.) *Education in the Eighties*. Batsford, London.

UNESCO, 2000. *The Dakar Framework for Action: Education for All – Meeting Our Collective Commitments*. UNESCO, Paris.

UNESCO, 2002. *Education for All: Is the World on Track? EFA Global Monitoring Report 2002*. UNESCO, Paris.

UNESCO, 2004. *Education for All: The Quality Imperative. EFA Global Monitoring Report 2005*. UNESCO, Paris.

UNESCO, 2007. Education for All Development Index (EDI). http://portal.unesco.org/education

UNESCO, 2014. *Teaching and Learning: Achieving Quality for All. EFA Global Monitoring Report 2013/14*. UNESCO, Paris.

UNESCO, 2015. Concept Note for a 2016 Report on Education, Sustainability and the Post-2015 Development Agenda, Prepared by the EFA GMR Team. http://www.unesco.org/new/fileadmin/MULTI MEDIA/HQ/ED/GMR/images/2014/2016_Concept_Note_rev2.pdf

Westbrook, J., Durrani, N., Brown, R., Orr, D., Pryor, J., Boddy, J., Salvi, F., 2013. *Pedagogy, Curriculum, Teaching Practices and Teacher Education in Developing Countries*. Education Rigorous Literature Review, DFID, London.

World Conference on Education for All, 1990. *World Declaration on Education for All and Framework for Action to Meet Basic Learning Needs*. Interagency Commission, New York.

11

LANGUAGE, EDUCATION AND DEVELOPMENT

Implications of language choice for learning

Barbara Trudell, Catherine Young and Susan Nyaga

Language and education: choices and implications

Language of instruction is an increasingly visible issue in international education today. This is especially true for primary education systems in multi-language national environments of the global South, where educational outcomes (and reading competencies in particular) are under closer scrutiny from international funding and program implementation bodies than they have been in the past.[1] Although many factors affect educational outcomes (including teacher competency, student well-being, the policy environment, and financial and infrastructural support), fluency in the language of instruction stands out as a significant predictor of learner success in both reading competencies and curriculum content (Gove and Cvelich 2011: 16; Alidou et al. 2006).

In the area of adult learning for development, language of instruction is less in the spotlight – as indeed, adult education itself is far from the center of international and national concerns about learning. Nevertheless, the role of local language in effective development is central (Djité 2008; Chumbow 2005). Good communication, clear understanding of new content and the ability to think critically about one's world are central to adult learning for development – and these features of good learning are only found when the medium of communication is one that the learner understands well.

Language choice in educational contexts also carries significant political and cultural meaning. National policy regarding language and education, and the implementation of that policy at various levels of society, reflect deeply held, and frequently contested, identity issues (Shohamy 2006; Alidou 2003; Kone 2010).

This chapter addresses three central aspects of language choice in education: the policy aspect, the cognitive and academic aspect, and the sociocultural aspect. The perspective of the chapter is generally weighted towards the social, linguistic and educational realities of nations in the global South, because the populations of these nations are the most multilingual and also the least well served in terms of education provision.

Language policy

Language policy is the means by which decision makers express their preferred language behaviors, particularly with reference to institutional uses of language. National language policy, though it is meant to apply to institutional communicative interactions generally, is seen most clearly where applied to the formal education system. In this context, language policy mandates the language(s) to be used for instruction and testing. It also determines which languages will be taught in schools, when and for how long they will be taught, by whom and how they should be taught. In the educational context, language policies are initiated primarily from above through formal government documents and are meant to be supported and implemented by teachers, materials, curricula and examinations (Shohamy 2006: 76).

In some cases national language policy directives are very detailed, specifying the languages to be used and learned, the number of hours and the methods of instruction to be employed, the specific contexts in which these languages should be used and learned, and the language tests required to demonstrate knowledge of the language. In other cases, language policy statements are much less specific. Some expressions of language policy are not at all explicit in their expectations; in these cases the real policy can be derived from textbook content, teaching practices and, especially, the testing systems (Shohamy 2006: 49).

However language policy has a less formalised aspect as well, when it is appropriated and enacted at the local level. Spolsky refers to this phenomenon, noting that "language policy exists even where it has not been made explicit or established by authority" (Spolsky 2004: 8). In fact, the local appropriation and reinvention of nationally-set language policy is quite common; such *de facto* language policy "tends to reflect the language attitudes and goals of the population of speakers, which may be either compliant or antagonistic to stated national policy goals" (Trudell and Piper 2013:1–2). And while the local siting of this policy reinvention may seem to be without influence, in fact the attitudes and priorities of headmasters, teachers and parents about language and education generally decide school language practices (ibid.). While formal policy discourse may mandate particular uses of particular languages, local language practices may regularly override that discourse (Hornberger and Johnson 2011:280).

Language ideologies and their implications for education

The formulation of language policy, whether at national or local levels, draws on the language ideologies most prevalent in the context. Language ideologies are described by McGroarty (2010: 3) as the abstract and often implicit belief systems that shape people's language attitudes and choices. These belief systems typically arise from specific historical and material contexts (Baldauf and Kaplan 2004:6).

Certain language ideologies play a significant role in the formulation of language policies in education, especially in multilingual contexts. These ideologies interact and sometimes compete; at times they even show internal inconsistency (McGroarty 2010). One ideology may shape language policy formulation at the national level, while another ideology shapes how that policy is interpreted and implemented at the regional or local level. In other cases, more than one ideology may be contributing to the interpretation and implementation of a given policy (see, for example, Johnson and Freeman 2010; Nyaga 2013).

Cobarrubias (1983) has described four broad language ideologies that have significant impact on the decisions made about language use in education. They are:

Linguistic assimilation. This ideology holds that everyone should learn and use the dominant language of the society in which they live (Wardhaugh 2009). This ideology results in language policy that gives exclusive attention to the majority language, with the aim of making immigrant groups adapt to the majority language and culture (Ruiz 1984; Durgunoğlu 1998). Monolingualism is seen as the linguistic ideal, while multilingualism is treated as an abnormal condition. The education policies arising from this ideology are subtractive in nature, supporting the exclusive use of the dominant language in the classroom.

Linguistic pluralism. This ideology recognises the legitimacy of more than one language in a society. Cobarrubias (1983: 65) views linguistic pluralism as the "co-existence of different linguistic groups and the rights to maintain and cultivate their languages on an equitable basis". This ideology lends itself to both individual and societal bi/multilingualism, resulting in language policies that support the use of both dominant and minority languages in education.

Vernacularisation. Vernacularisation is defined as "the restoration or elaboration of an indigenous language and its adoption as an official language" (Wardhaugh 1997: 358). This ideology supports language equality and intentional language maintenance, and has implications for culture maintenance as well (Durgunoğlu 1998). This ideology "envisions secure majorities and minorities in collaborative power relations" (Jeon 2003: 140). Kamwangamalu (2010) links vernacularisation with post-independence efforts to decolonise African education systems.

The educational implication of this language ideology is that both majority and minority language communities have the right to learn and to express themselves in their own languages. Such explicit acknowledgement of, and support for, learners' multilingual repertoire and competence in school also leads to the interrogation of other language ideologies being practiced in the classroom (Hélot and Ó Laoire 2011:xii).

Internationalism. This refers to "the adoption of a non-indigenous language of wider communication as an official language, or for such purposes as medium of education or trade" (Wardhaugh 1997: 358). This ideology dominates language policies in many former colonies, where the ex-colonial languages have been given official status and dominance especially in the education domain. This ideology differs from that of linguistic assimilation, in that the language given pre-eminence is not a local or national language, but rather is associated with cultures and communities outside the country. Kamwangamalu (2010) links internationalism to ideologies of development; but in fact, the educational implications of linguistic internationalism have proven to be ruinous for education systems across the global South, as entire populations of learners are subjected to a medium of instruction which they do not master (Alidou 2003; Panda and Mohanty 2009).

Jeon (2003: 131) identifies the first two ideologies (assimilation and pluralism) with language policies in the United States, while Kamwangamalu (2010: 2) identifies the second two (vernacularisation and internationalism) with language policies in the post-colonial global South. Kamwangamalu also posits an additional language ideology to those described by Cobarrubias: an ideology of *globalisation*, which privileges English specifically. Certainly the educational impact of this ideology can be seen in many curricula around the world, where the teaching of English, and the use of English as a medium of instruction, is becoming more and more common (Mazrui 2004; Pennycook 2007).

Another typology of language ideologies, this one specific to theoretical frameworks of bilingual education, is posited by García (2009: 120–121). García describes two ideologies:

- *The monoglossic* ideology assumes that learners start out as monolinguals, whether in a majority or minority language; this ideology underlies both subtractive and additive bilingual education models.
- *The heteroglossic* ideology assumes that learners may come to formal education already possessing a range of bilingual or multilingual proficiencies, rather than being monolingual in the majority or minority languages. This ideology underlies recursive and dynamic bilingual education models.

Common myths about language and education

McGroarty (2010: 4) observes that language ideologies "shape a constellation of 'common sense' beliefs about language and language use" – including the use of language in education. These beliefs surrounding the issue of language choice in education generally have little basis in fact; nevertheless, they play a significant role in shaping language policies. They include the following:

a)   That there is one and only one 'correct solution' to the choice of language(s) in education. In fact, the social, linguistic and cultural context of a given education system has enormous impact on the success of any language policy.

b)   That anyone who can speak a given language can successfully teach the language, or use it as a medium of instruction, without prior training. The reality is that, particularly for languages with a short history of existence in written form, the challenges of classroom use require specific skills including fluency in reading and writing the language.

c)   That the most effective way to build fluency in a language the learner does not speak is to maximise the time spent using that language as the medium of instruction, without building fluency in that language first and without using the learner's first language as a resource. This is one of the most pernicious myths in the entire field of language and education, even though it is solidly refuted by research on language and learning (Cummins 2005; Martin 2005; Shin 2005; Setati et al. 2002).

d)   That in multilingual societies, it is too expensive to develop materials and train teachers in a number of different languages. This myth thrives in total disregard of the evidence (see, for example, Heugh 2011). It is responsible for tremendous wastage in the education systems of multilingual nations, as evidenced in high dropout rates, low achievement and high rates of grade repetition (Bamgbose 1991).

e)   That indigenous languages are incapable of dealing with modern concepts, making the use of non-indigenous languages of instruction a practical necessity (Breton 2003: 211–12). This myth has been exploded in language after language of the global South, as corpus planning activities expand the domains of these newly-written languages (Ferguson 2006; Wardhaugh 2009).

f)   That in multilingual societies, use of a non-indigenous language as medium of instruction in formal education will reduce group conflict (Breton 2003: 209). In fact, attempting to suppress conflict this way only serves to aggravate the marginalisation of those groups whose languages are not chosen for use in the education system. Kroskrity (2004: 509) notes that when a particular language is used in the making of national or ethnic identities, the "unity" achieved actually masks the subordination of those groups that do not speak that language well.

Language policy is developed and enacted in many ways; formalised national policy, implicit national values, and local beliefs about language use all contribute to a given language policy environment. This environment in turn has a significant effect on the design and implementation of curriculum as well as actual classroom practice.

Academic and cognitive aspects of language and learning

Further to the myths associated with language policy, and focusing more specifically on the processes associated with the academic and cognitive processes of language learning, Robinson (2005) notes that

> There persists a myth in some quarters that acquiring literacy in one language reduces the chances of acquiring it satisfactorily in another: thus to acquire mother tongue

literacy may be seen as a brake on acquiring literacy in a more widely used language. A further myth, less widely held today, sees bilingualism as subtractive – learning another language reduces capacity in the one already known.

(p. 15)

Cognition studies indicate that multilingualism and the acquisition of additional languages may play a supporting role in the development of cognitive flexibility. In fact, far from being cognitively disadvantaged, multilinguals have been shown (V. Edwards 2009: 19) to have advantages over monolinguals in a variety of cognitive and metacognitive tasks. The following section outlines theoretical models and approaches supporting the viability of multilingual approaches in formal school systems and describing methodologies that can be implemented to support effective language practices in schools in multilingual contexts.

Second language acquisition and academic performance

In multilingual contexts, learners may be required to learn a new language on entry to formal education – a language that is not used, or only used in a limited manner in their home or community. This is the experience of millions of learners from multilingual contexts in Asia, Africa and other, often marginalised, communities.

Baker (2006: 169–170) cites Cummins' *common underlying proficiency* model of bilingualism and uses the Thresholds Theory, articulated by Cummins (1976) as descriptive approaches to the relationship between cognition and bilingualism. This perspective emphasises the potential of learners to function in more than one language. However, these theoretical models underline that the use of more than one language simultaneously in education will be possible only if both languages are 'well developed' (Baker 2006: 170); when one or both languages are not functioning fully, cognitive functioning and academic performance may be negatively affected. Requiring a child to learn in a second language that with which the learner is not sufficiently familiar or in which the learner has not had the opportunity to develop age-appropriate grammatical or lexical capacity will hinder academic performance (Baker 2006: 170).

Cummins (2000: 57) discusses the cognitive demand on second language learners and the nature of the support required by second language learners to succeed academically. Through study of language acquisition processes, a distinction has been developed between 'basic interpersonal communicative skills' (BICS) and 'cognitive academic language proficiency' (CALP). Children need much more time to become academically proficient in a language and gain the linguistic skills for analysis, synthesis and critical reasoning activities in the classroom environment than they would to merely become conversationally fluent. Cummins reports research that shows that conversational proficiency usually happens within two years, but five to seven years are required for academic proficiency (2000: 58). Thus, the length of time necessary to acquire academic language proficiency has significant implications for the time allocation of languages in a school curriculum – both years spent using language and time in the school day when languages are used.

In the preparation of the school curriculum for learners from multilingual situations, awareness should be developed of the knowledge and abilities that students bring to the school environment. In this context, Cummins' interprets Kozulin's analysis of 'spontaneous' and 'scientific' concepts (Cummins 2000: 60) and relates this to Vygotsky's theoretical model of sociocultural approaches to language learning. Vygotsky suggests a zone of proximal development, referring to concepts the child has already learned without a teacher from the social and physical environment, and which enable scientific concepts explained by a teacher to be processed mentally (2000: 61).

A significant study on the impact of language learning methodology – specifically the length of time that a language is used in the classroom – was conducted in the United States by researchers, Wayne Thomas and Virginia Collier (1997). The following section describes the outcome of this research and the implications of the Thomas and Collier research for the design and implementation of mother tongue-based multilingual education programmes.

Effective approaches to second language learning

Thomas and Collier (1997: 18) claim that typical studies of language minority students' academic achievement have had two drawbacks:

1)   they have been too short-term, usually covering a one to four year period. This has led to an inaccurate perception of students' long-term performance, especially when the short-term studies are conducted in the early years of school;
2)   they have focused on small test populations, resulting in data that may not be representative.

To address these two problems, the Thomas and Collier study (Thomas and Collier 1997) gathered data across all grades, with academic achievement data in the last years of high school serving as the most important measure of academic success and of the adequacy of early programme options for educating language minority students. The study also included and analysed more than 700,000 student records from 42,317 students (Thomas and Collier 1997: 30) who attended schools identified for participation in the study for more than four years.

Four major factors emerged from this study (1997: 42) that appear to be important to the success of language minority students entering the United States educational system. The researchers claimed that these factors are more powerful than other variables frequently cited in the literature as predictors of success or failure in education for language minority students. These are L1 and L2 academic development, L1 and L2 language development, L1 and L2 cognitive development, all pivoted around the sociocultural processes that are at the heart of the model of language use effectiveness. This final factor situates the pedagogical principles and curriculum design in a social context (Thomas and Collier 1997):

> Central to that student's acquisition of language are all of the surrounding social and cultural processes occurring through everyday life within the student's past, present, and future, in all contexts—home, school, community, and the broader society.
>
> (p. 42)

In the study, these predictors as described above appear to override such factors as poverty at home, a school's location in an economically depressed region or neighbourhood, or a regional context where an ethnolinguistic group has traditionally been underserved by the national schools. Thus, we see that curriculum and school experiences that consider all three of these predictors within the sociocultural context of a school which respects the cultural backgrounds of the learners are likely to produce language minority students who are successful academically in high school and in higher education. These then provide a foundation for considering appropriate design for basic education in highly multilingual contexts.

The broader context for multilingual education

In light of the clear evidence from both language acquisition theory and psycholinguistic research regarding the importance of using the language that is most familiar to the learner in basic education, it is critical to establish principled approaches to the design and development of multilingual education provision. Brisk (1998: 56–79) presents descriptions of the situational factors that indicate students, particularly language minority students, will be empowered in multilingual classrooms and impact learning outcomes. She outlines five multidimensional components that influence effectiveness, including but not exclusive to linguistic factors:

- Linguistic components (e.g., amount of language use in the community, media, technology, home)
- Cultural components (e.g., parental participation in the classroom, curriculum content and assumptions about the background knowledge of students)
- Economic components (e.g., the economic viability of the languages, career opportunities, education costs)
- Political components (e.g., the treatment of language minority speakers, attitudes to language diversity)
- Social components (e.g., the size and cohesiveness of the language community, race and gender relationships, attitudes to language and ethnic groups)

Similar to the framework above, Panda and Mohanty (2009: 295) describe the process of the development of mother tongue-based multilingual education (MTB-MLE) as more than simply bringing minority or indigenous languages into education. They suggest that the MTB-MLE curriculum should develop the first language – or home language – from supporting basic interpersonal communication to academic language proficiency (Cummins 2000: 58) thereby promoting strong multilingual competence and developing identity and collective processes that sustain the linguistic and the eco-cultural diversity of the society. Panda and Mohanty (2009) also note that MLE is:

> deeply rooted in a philosophy of critical pedagogy that seeks to actively empower the learners and their communities. If MLE is to be seen as providing a powerful model for the education of the indigenous/tribal and linguistic minority communities, it needs to replace the authoritarian, rigid, pre-ordained knowledge approach of dominant-culture-centric education by a system of critical educational experiences empowering them to become valued, equal, and responsible members of their own and the larger society outside their community and not feel estranged from it.
>
> (p. 297)

It is not only the use of the mother tongue that accounts for the difference in children's learning in situations in which Panda and Mohanty have conducted their research in Orissa, India. Panda and Mohanty (2009: 304) acknowledge the influence of Vygotsky's ethnographic and social perspectives on classroom practices on their approach to language use in the classroom. Specifically, Panda and Mohanty (2009: 304) refer to the ways in which Vygotsky describes conceptual development as "an interaction between spontaneous everyday concepts and the organised systems of concepts referred to as 'scientific' concepts."

This has implications for teaching/learning methodologies in multilingual classrooms in terms of provision of support for the development of higher order thinking skills such as synthesis, analysis and evaluation (V. Edwards 2009: 60) – skills associated with academic success (Cummins 2009: 23).

In designing teaching strategies, when a teacher starts with cognitively undemanding activities in an 'embedded' or familiar context, learners have opportunities to communicate in ways that facilitate mutual understanding. As learners experience increasingly cognitively demanding activities, the effective teacher can support the learner in developing mental schema around the concept, giving learners both the competence and the confidence to work in a 'reduced' or less familiar context (Cummins 2000: 68–69).

An enabling factor in the effectiveness of such programmes is the more careful use of learners' everyday discourses in the classroom. This involves the maintenance of, and interaction between, the 'everyday' language and understanding of the learner and a more conventional academic understanding. When children enter formal schooling, they possess their own knowledge systems, beliefs and values based on their prior experiences of their home, family, community and sociocultural identity. Individual differences in context and experience mean that these knowledge systems, beliefs and values are individualised, changing and growing in complexity as new experiences contribute to the schema the learner has constructed. This serves as a foundation on which the development of more formal knowledge clusters can be built.

When the curriculum is delivered in the language that is most familiar to the learner and the content of that curriculum reflects the experiences and knowledge that learner has brought to the formal education process, conditions are established for the learner to use the knowledge base of what they have learned in their first language to support the learning of additional languages.

Transfer and transition

Transfer is a cognitive process in language acquisition whereby knowledge acquired in one language is transferred to another language (Heugh 2009: 108). Cummins' notions of the common underlying proficiency theory (2000: 38) and threshold theory demonstrate that, although surface features of language – grammar, lexicon, phonology – may vary from language to language, they are integrated in a single thought process (Baker 2006: 330; V. Edwards 2009: 62). Thus, conceptual understanding and other cognitive skills can transfer from one language to another and do not need to be re-learned. Ball (2010) notes,

> Fluency and literacy in the mother tongue lay a cognitive and linguistic foundation for learning additional languages. When children receive formal instruction in their first language throughout primary school and then gradually transition to academic learning in the second language, they learn the second language quickly.
>
> (p. 2)

Effective transition to a second language is based on transfer of skills that support effective learning – both language skills and general academic skills – with a prerequisite of strong competence in the first language of the learner. With appropriate support from the home community, learners continue to develop their first language from birth to adolescence (Benson 2009: 69) including the use of more complex adult-like language structures. The growth of reading and writing skills contributes to the development of competencies in the first language, and a strong foundation in the first language supports cognitive academic language proficiency. This implies that, if children enter school at the age of 6 or 7, learning in first language should continue until learners are at least Grade 5 or 6 (Benson 2009: 69).

When adding a second language, the L2 should be taught orally at first while learners consolidate L1 literacy. Once children have acquired L1 literacy and strong oral L2 (Krashen 2002: 148), they can transfer skills to L2 reading and writing – since strategies such as scanning, skimming, reading for meaning, and making inferences can transfer from one language to another (Baker 2006: 330). Krashen (2002: 148) also emphasises the importance of reading for pleasure in both the first and second languages in order to build advanced reading strategies.

Transfer of reading and writing skills can also be done when two languages have different scripts or writing systems. Ovando, Collier and Combs (2003) note:

> General strategies, habits and attitudes, knowledge of text structure, rhetorical devices sensorimotor skills, visual-perceptual training, cognitive functions and many reading readiness skills transfer from L1 to L2 reading.
>
> (p. 175)

However, transfer is not unconditional and is dependent on both the context of learning and the characteristics of learning. Baker (2006: 331) outlines the following factors that may enhance or inhibit the effective transfer of skills from one language to another:

- Differences in the facilitating nature of the school, home and community environment
- Individual differences in language ability, language aptitude and language learning strategies
- Individual differences in the ability to analyse their language (metalinguistic ability)
- The interrelationship between pairs of languages (e.g., Portuguese and Spanish compared with English and Chinese)

Baker notes that reading ability in a second language is also dependent on the degree of proficiency in that second language. Children literate in their first language still need to learn the differences between the first and the second language (e.g., different sounds, vocabulary, grammatical structures), and may need explicit instruction for this.

All of these factors, particularly the last, emphasise the importance of oral language development in L2 before the introduction of literacy in L2 as well as explicit instruction in the similarities and differences between the two languages.

Thus, effective delivery of education for learners from minority ethnolinguistic communities requires that learners begin their education in languages that they understand well before transitioning to a language with which they are not familiar.

Sociocultural aspects of language, education and development

Language, society, identity and education

To the extent that the education system reproduces the culture and values of society, the question of identity is relevant to a consideration of language and education. Links between language and identity have been well addressed in the literature of linguistics and society; John Edwards (2009: 15–19) provides a useful chronology of scholarly work on the linguistic aspects of identity over the past three decades. Edwards also notes that individuals can hold multiple social identities, many of them simultaneously; those acquired earlier in life, however, tend to be more fixed than those acquired later (p. 18). It could be argued, then, that the language spoken in the home and community forms one of the earliest markers of a child's identity.

What is clear, however, is that language is an important marker of both individual and community identity. Indeed, many ethnic communities (defined as groups that share common descent and cultural belonging– J. Edwards 2009: 155) of the global South use the same word to refer to both themselves and the language of their community. Even among multilingual individuals and communities, the identification of one specific language with one's ethnicity is common. The identification of a language with a specific ethnicity seems especially prominent in environments of inter-ethnic conflict, as it is one of the more obvious markers of difference between communities.[2]

Two current paradigms of language and identity are the *language rights* paradigm and the *linguistic citizenship* paradigm (Trudell 2008). The language rights paradigm, also called the *linguistic human rights* approach, has been well articulated by Stephen May (May 2005; 2006; 2011). It is founded on several related notions:

- that language is a key marker of identity;
- that majority languages, and their speakers, hold a hegemonic political position relative to language change and language choice;
- that minority languages thus need institutional support and protection if they are to survive and thrive. This protection includes intentional and well-resourced inclusion in the formal and nonformal education systems, ideally provided by the state.

The linguistic citizenship paradigm of language and identity takes a more post-structural approach to language. In this paradigm:

- Language is a set of social practices – constructed, contingent and contested (Stroud 2001: 348; Stroud and Heugh 2004: 197).
- Language may be one marker of identity, but it is not necessarily the most important one. This is particularly true in multilingual environments, where identities can be multiple and complex. Language should thus be seen as a resource that people use as needed (Blommaert 2005).
- Language is part of a broader social and political agenda for change, sited primarily in local agency. Problems of inequality among social groups are not primarily about the relationships between languages; the issue is primarily about voice rather than language (Blommaert 2005:411).

In this paradigm, the question of language use in education systems is part of a larger debate about the role of education in either reproducing social inequality or facilitating greater agency on the part of the population being served.

It is important to note that, even with the evident differences between these models of language and identity, both of them oppose the imposition of languages through the school system which are not part of the learner's linguistic repertoire.

Global and local understandings of education and language of instruction

Issues of language, culture and society also arise in the debate on the globalisation of education and its impact on local populations. As sociologist John Meyer points out, formal education is seen as a fundamental component of the modern nation-state; adopting mass education symbolises the state's commitment to becoming a member of the "imagined community" of global society (Krücken and Drori 2009: 209). Meyer further notes that

> conventional legitimations for mass schooling insist that formal education is necessary and beneficial for economic growth, technical innovation, citizen loyalty, and

democratic institutions, among other things. Such functional justifications of schooling are rarely questioned, even though careful studies of, for example, education's effects on economic growth suggest that this functional relationship is at best weak and highly conditional.

(ibid., p. 177)

In a similar vein, Lechner and Boli (2005: 43) describe the widespread assumption that every modern state must have a formal education system – even when the resources needed to sustain it are not there and the curriculum itself does not meet the basic knowledge needs of the population. This misalignment between the expectations of this education system and the realities of the target population is often aggravated by the choice of a language with global status as the medium of instruction rather than a language that is well understood by the learners.

The formal education system is seen as central to shaping the social and cultural behaviours of young people, generating "powerful, and to some extent convergent or 'global', constructions of the 'educated person'" (Levinson and Holland 1996: 15). The institutions that deliver mass schooling encourage mastery of the knowledge and beliefs that have global (though predominantly Northern) currency and ideological grounding. When this knowledge and these beliefs coincide with what the child learns at home, as is the case in much of the global North, there are few disjunctures for the learner. However when Northern knowledge and beliefs are applied to a sociocultural and linguistic context that values other sorts of knowledge, it is usually to the detriment of children's sense of local belonging and expertise in locally valued skills – most certainly including their home languages.

Nevertheless, this Northern-generated model of education, with its attendant values and beliefs, has been uncritically adopted by "developing" nations as well. Chaudenson (2008: 173) describes a nearly-unanimous faith in universal education as a means to development, in post-independence Africa. It almost goes without saying that the languages considered acceptable for mediating this model of mass education are the high prestige international languages. Local languages are considered to have no place in mediating global culture.

In this environment, local communities in the global South are at the receiving end of an education system which ignores the knowledge, culture and language competencies that make them unique, and which more than likely does not meet the knowledge needs of their children. Assessing this system in Africa, Dei describes it as highly damaging to Africa's citizens:

> It has been an education that has for the most part failed to deeply cultivate self-esteem and pride in peoples of African descent. It was and still is a Eurocentric education, and it continues to distort, misappropriate and misinterpret African human condition and reality.

(2008: 231)

This system results in schools which are silos of foreign knowledge, language and cultural practices in the community (Trudell 2012: 370). A 2010 report from the Asian Development Bank argues that such silo-ised, exclusionary structures and processes actually "push" students out of the formal school system (Asian Development Bank 2010: 19, 36). The language choices made in these classrooms are also central to what Collins and Blot term "the disjunction between home and school" (Collins and Blot 2003: 66). Damage is done to the community as well, in the form of what Prah (1995: 65) calls a "cultural recession" in which local culture, values and language are rendered insignificant.

Yet despite these negative features, faith in this kind of education is prominent at the community level. Teachers, headmasters and parents are often vigorous promoters of a curriculum which manifestly does not serve their children well. The perceived primacy of an international language of instruction is a key feature here as well, and so local stakeholders are generally very reluctant to see local languages used as media of instruction. Bunyi (2013) notes that in Kenya,

> Both teachers and parents prefer the use of English in the mistaken belief that the earlier the children start to learn in English the more English they will learn and therefore the better they will be prepared for the KCPE [Kenya Certificate of Primary Education examination] which is in English.
>
> (p. 689)

Parents in particular have a keenly felt stake in the educational future of their children. Certainly in Africa, parents consider fluency in international languages to be crucial to the educational future of their children, as well as for success in the formal economy; they typically believe, as Bunyi notes above, that the more exposure their child gets to the international language, the more successful that child will be. Research evidence, and even informal classroom observation, clearly show that this latter belief is false; but it is nevertheless deeply embedded in parental perspectives on education (Muthwii 2002). These commonly-held parental values and beliefs about the educational world order may constitute an example of false consciousness, preventing them from recognising the unjust and ineffective nature of the educational system their children are being subjected to. Still, as is the case with most adults, theirs are rational responses to the world as they perceive it.

There is some recognition of the dubious ability of this education model to deliver the knowledge that children really need. A sort of resistant 'counter-education' can be found in pockets around the world – most visibly among the most marginalised populations, who are most cognisant of the violence being done to their children by the educational status quo. Gow (2008) describes the determination of a Colombian indigenous community to reshape their children's education system, as one aspect of an "indigenous modernity" which highlights social justice as well as cultural diversity. Anderson-Levitt (2003) argues that local resistance to, and transformation of, official models of formal education (including the accepted language policy) is widespread even in the most structured systems of Europe and the USA; examples of this subversion of official language policy in France, the United States and Israel are described by Hélot (2010), Foley (1996) and Shohamy (2010) respectively.

In addition, two of the more well-known language revitalisation efforts in recent years feature strong school-based strategies; the Maori *Kdhanga Reo* and Hawaiian *Penana Leo* immersion preschools, described by McCarty, Skutnabb-Kangas and Magga (2008: 304), recreate environments in which the indigenous language and culture are used and valued. These preschools are run by the language communities; they aim at developing strong proficiency in the indigenous language among the children, but also among the teachers and parents.

Still, such defiance of the norms and expectations of the global education model is not generally considered either feasible or desirable among national education policy makers.

Language and development

Where development takes the form of specific programs and initiatives, it tends to rely extensively on non formal learning opportunities. In this environment, language choice has a significant effect on the success, ownership and sustainability of development initiatives.

Language choice is relevant to development in several ways:

- The emphasis on human-centered development (UNDP 1990) over the past few decades has moved the discussion of development towards greater consideration of the involvement of, and impact on, the people being targeted for development. Such a move inevitably requires that the languages used by those people be taken seriously, since as Robinson (1996: 4) has observed, "wherever people are put at the centre of the development process, issues of language will always be close to the surface."

- The populations most often targeted by development efforts include rural residents, which are the populations most likely to rely on languages other than the official school language for learning and communication. The demographics and socioeconomic status of those targeted for development initiatives should influence language of instruction choices towards those that are spoken and understood by the learners.

- The very formulation of development strategies, if they are to include reference to the felt needs of the target population, must be in a language the people understand well. Dorothy Hodgson, in her work with Maasai communities of Tanzania, has noted that those who are the targets of development initiatives often hold alternative ideas about their 'development' that may clash with the dominant modernisation and economic productivity paradigms of most international donors and project implementers (Hodgson 2011: 7). If the formulation of effective, sustainable development strategies is to include those alternative ideas, the target population must be allowed to use their own language in the negotiation.

- The most economically and politically marginalised peoples tend also to be the most linguistically marginalised. May (2004: 37) has noted that it is no coincidence that the world's endangered languages are spoken by the politically least influential peoples. Relying on the 'language of power' in delivering development initiatives only entrenches this linguistic and social power imbalance, at the same time diminishing the impact of the project.

For these reasons, careful consideration of the language medium is advisable when planning and implementing learning initiatives for development.

Conclusions

In this chapter we have used the lenses of language policy, language and cognition, and sociocultural aspects of language and learning to examine some of the principal links between language, education and development – particularly from the perspective of the global South. At least three conclusions can be drawn from this analysis.

The first conclusion is related to the degree to which language policy and its implementation are open to influence. The policy environment in which language choices are made has a significant impact on curriculum design, particularly where formal education is concerned. The policy environment is, in turn, strongly influenced by the ideologies and values of decision-makers; so that national language policy decisions reflect ideologies of national-level leaders, while the appropriation of language policy in school and community contexts reflects the beliefs and values of local decision makers as they respond to national policy. The beliefs that shape language choices in education contexts may or may not align with demonstrated evidence regarding the impact of language choices.

However this cycle of beliefs-policy-response is itself open to influence, as language advocates around the world have found. Raising the awareness of decision-makers regarding the actual cultural, pedagogical and economic outcomes of language-in-education choices has allowed interrogation of existing language policy. Research and pilot education programs can demonstrate the benefits of using a language of instruction that the learner speaks, thus helping to replace or modify myths and ideologies that are not based on national or local educational realities.

The second conclusion has to do with the fact that the majority of societies in the global South today exist in a multi-language environment, even if the citizens themselves are not all multilingual. At least one of the languages in this environment is likely to be a national or international language, and it is most likely be found in the schools. For this reason, achieving effective learning outcomes depends on an understanding of the dynamics of language fluency and learning. In a multi-language society, effective and appropriate learning environments must be multilingual, which in turn implies that the knowledge that the learner brings to the classroom is taken into account in curriculum development and classroom practice. Failure to incorporate the very real pedagogical benefits of building on the learner's own language proficiency virtually guarantees on-going school failure for the learner in this environment.

The third conclusion emerges from the fact that, even though language is closely related to individual and group identity as well as to communicative competencies, the current globalised models of formal education do not accommodate learners who speak languages other than the handful of languages recognised as having international currency. Where the learning environment is not governed by formal curriculum expectations, the language chosen as medium of learning is often still determined by Northern conceptualisations of development and progress. This limited understanding of development is being challenged in some quarters, but much more attention needs to be given to alternative, locally-shaped conceptualisations of development and well-being.

Ultimately, the connections between language, education and development relate to the nature of real learning: it must take place in a language that is understood by the learner, and it must build on the learner's existing knowledge. Where these two features of learning are ignored, neither ideology nor policy is adequate to produce positive learning outcomes.

Notes

1 A range of statements from bilateral funding agencies such as USAID and DFID, as well as intergovernmental bodies such as the World Bank and the Global Partnership of Education, demonstrate a significant focus on the assessment and improvement of reading skills in recipient countries (see for example http://www.usaid.gov/what-we-do/education/improving-early-grade-reading; DFID 2010: 32–33; http://www.globalpartnership.org/focus-areas/early-grade-reading). This focus has driven an explosion of government- and NGO-implemented reading assessments and interventions in the global South.
2 In analysis of the conflict in Ukraine in early 2014, at least one major news service mapped the ethnic divisions in the country in terms of "percentage of people speaking Russian" http://edition.cnn.com/interactive/2014/02/world/ukraine-divided/?hpt=bosread (3 March 2014).

References

Alidou, H., 2003. The medium of instruction in Sub-Saharan Africa. In: Tollefson, J. and Tsui, A. (Eds.) *Medium of Instruction Policies*. Lawrence Erlbaum, Mahwah.

Alidou, H., Boly, A., Brock-Utne, B., Diallo, Y., Heugh, K. and Wolff, H., 2006. *Optimizing Learning and Education in Africa – the Language Factor*. Human Sciences Research Council, Cape Town.

Anderson-Levitt, K., 2003. A world culture of schooling? In: Anderson-Levitt, K. (Ed.) *Local Meanings, Global Schooling*. Palgrave, Basingstoke.

Asian Development Bank, 2010. *Strengthening Inclusive Education*. Asian Development Bank, Manila.

Baker, C., 2006. *Foundations of Bilingual Education and Bilingualism*. Fourth Edition. Multilingual Matters, Clevedon.

Baldauf, R., Kaplan, R., 2004. Language policy and planning in Botswana, Malawi, Mozambique and South Africa. In: Baldauf, B. and Kaplan, R. (Eds.) *Language Planning and Policy in Africa, Vol. 1.* Multilingual Matters, Clevedon.

Ball, J., 2010. *Enhancing Learning of Children from Diverse Language Backgrounds: Mother Tongue-based Bilingual or Multilingual Education in the Early Years.* UNESCO, Paris.

Bamgbose, A., 1991. *Language and the Nation.* Edinburgh University Press, Edinburgh.

Benson, C., 2009. Designing effective schooling in multilingual contexts: going beyond bilingual models. In: Mohanty, A., Panda, M., Phillipson, R. and Skuttnabb-Kangas, T. (Eds.) *Multilingual Education for Social Justice.* Orient Black Swan, New Delhi.

Blommaert, J., 2005. Situating language rights: English and Swahili in Tanzania revisited. *Journal of Sociolinguistics* 9, 3, 390–417.

Breton, R., 2003. Sub-Saharan Africa. In: Maurais, J. and Morris, M. (Eds.) *Languages in a Globalising World.* Cambridge University Press, Cambridge.

Brisk, M., 1998. *Bilingual Education.* Lawrence Erlbaum, Mahwah.

Bunyi, G., 2013. The quest for quality education: the case of curriculum innovations in Kenya. *European Journal of Training and Development* 37, 7, 678–691.

Chaudenson, R., 2008. On the futurology of linguistic development. In: Vigouroux, C. and Mufwene, S. (Eds.) *Globalization and Language Vitality.* Continuum, London.

Chumbow, B., 2005. The language question and national development in Africa. In: Mkandawire, T. (Ed.) *African Intellectuals.* CODESRIA and Zed Books, Dakar and London.

Cobarrubias, J,. 1983. Ethical issues in status planning. In: Cobarrubias, J. (Ed.) *Language Planning.* Mouton, Berlin.

Collins, J., Blot, R., 2003. *Literacy and Literacies.* Cambridge University Press, Cambridge.

Cummins, J., 1976. The influence of bilingualism on cognitive growth: a synthesis of research findings and explanatory hypotheses. Working Papers on Bilingualism, No. 9.

Cummins, J., 2000. *Language, Power, and Pedagogy.* Multilingual Matters, Clevedon.

Cummins, J., 2005. A proposal for action: strategies for recognising heritage language competence as a learning resource within mainstream classroom. *Modern Language Journal* 89, 585–592.

Cummins, J., 2009. Fundamental psychological and sociological principles underlying educational success for linguistic minority students. In: Mohanty, A., Panda, M., Phillipson, R. and Skuttnabb-Kangas, T. (Eds.) *Multilingual Education for Social Justice.* Orient Black Swan, New Delhi.

Department for International Development, 2010. *Learning for All: DfID's Educational Strategy 2010–2015.* http://consultation.dfid.gov.uk/education2010/files/2010/04/learning-for-all-strategy.pdf.

Djité, P., 2008. *The Sociolinguistics of Development in Africa.* Multilingual Matters, Clevedon.

Durgunoğlu, A., 1998. Acquiring literacy in English and Spanish in the United States. In: Durgunoğlu, A. and Verhoeven, L. (Eds.) *Literacy Development in a Multilingual Context.* Lawrence Erlbaum, London.

Edwards, J., 2009. *Language and Identity.* Cambridge University Press, Cambridge.

Edwards, V., 2009. *Learning to be Literate.* Multilingual Matters, Clevedon.

Ferguson, G., 2006. *Language Planning and Education.* Edinburgh University Press, Edinburgh.

Foley, D., 1996. The silent Indian as a cultural production. In: Levinson, B., Foley, D. and Holland, D. (Eds.) *The Cultural Production of the Educated Person.* State University of New York Press, Albany.

García, O., 2009. *Bilingual Education in the 21st Century.* Wiley-Blackwell, Oxford.

Gove, A., Cvelich, P., 2011. *Early Reading. Revised Edition.* Research Triangle Institute, Research Triangle Park.

Gow, D., 2008. *Countering Development.* Duke University Press, Durham, NC.

Hélot, C., 2010. "Tu sais bien parler Maîtresse!" Negotiating languages other than French in the primary classroom in France. In: Menken, K. and García, O. (Eds.) *Negotiating Language Policies in Schools.* Routledge, New York.

Hélot, C., Ó Laoire, M., 2011. Introduction: from language education policy to a pedagogy of the possible. In: Hélot, C and Ó Laoire, M. (Eds.) *Language Policy for the Multilingual Classroom.* Multilingual Matters, Clevedon.

Heugh, K., 2009. Literacy and bi/multilingual education in Africa. In: Mohanty, A., Panda, M., Phillipson, R. and Skuttnabb-Kangas, T. (Eds.) *Multilingual Education for Social Justice.* Orient Black Swan, New Delhi.

Heugh, K., 2011. Cost implications of the provision of mother-tongue and strong bilingual models of education in Africa. In: Ouane, A. and Glanz, C. (Eds.) *Education and Publishing in Africa.* UNESCO Institute for Lifelong Learning and the Association for the Development of Education in Africa, Hamburg and Tunis.

Hodgson, D., 2011. *Being Maasai, Becoming Indigenous.* Indiana University Press, Bloomington.

Hornberger, N., Johnson, D., 2011. The ethnography of language policy. In: McCarty, T. (Ed.) *Ethnography and Language Policy*. Routledge, New York.

Jeon, M., 2003. Searching for a comprehensive rationale for two-way immersion. In: Hornberger, N. (Ed.) *Continua of Biliteracy*. Multilingual Matters, Clevedon.

Johnson, D., Freeman, R., 2010. Appropriating language policy on the local level. In: Menken, K. and García, O. (Eds.) *Negotiating Language Policies in Schools*. Routledge, New York.

Kamwangamalu, N., 2010. Vernacularization, globalization, and language economics in non-English-speaking countries in Africa. *Language Problems and Language Planning* 34, 1, 1–23.

Kone, A., 2010. Politics of language: the struggle for power in schools in Mali and Burkina Faso. *International Education* 39, 2, 6–20.

Krashen, S., 2002. Developing academic language: early L1 reading and later L2 reading. *International Journal of the Sociology of Language* 155/156, 143–151.

Kroskrity, P., 2004. Language ideologies. In: Duranti, A. (Ed.) *A Companion to Linguistic Anthropology*. Blackwell, Malden.

Krücken, G., Drori, G. (Eds.), 2009. *World Society: The Writings of John W. Meyer*. Oxford University Press, Oxford.

Lechner, F., Boli, J. 2005. *World Culture*. Blackwell, Oxford.

Levinson, B., Holland, D. 1996. The cultural production of the educated person: An introduction. In: Levinson, B., Foley, D. and Holland, D. (Eds.) *The Cultural Production of the Educated Person*. State University of New York Press, Albany.

Martin, P., 2005. "Safe" language practices in two rural schools in Malaysia. In: Lyn, A. and Martin, P. (Eds.) *Decolonisation, Globalisation*. Multilingual Matters, Clevedon.

May, S., 2004. Rethinking linguistic human rights. In: Freeland, J. and Patrick, D. (Eds.) *Language Rights and Language Survival*. St. Jerome Publishing, Manchester.

May, S., 2005. Language rights. *Journal of Sociolinguistics* 9, 3, 319–347.

May, S., 2006. Language policy and minority rights. In: Ricento, T. (Ed.) *An Introduction to Language Policy*. Blackwell, New York.

May, S., 2011. *Language and Minority Rights*. Second Edition. Routledge, New York.

Mazrui, A., 2004. *English in Africa after the Cold War*. Multilingual Matters, Clevedon.

McCarty, T., Skutnabb-Kangas, T., Magga, O., 2008. Education for speakers of endangered languages. In: Spolsky, B. and Hult, F. (Eds.) *The Handbook of Educational Linguistics*. Blackwell, Oxford.

McGroarty, M., 2010. Language and ideologies. In: Hornberger, N. and McKay, S. (Eds.) *Sociolinguistics and Language Education*. Multilingual Matters, Clevedon.

Muthwii, M., 2002. *Language Policy and Practices in Education in Kenya and Uganda*. Phoenix, Nairobi.

Nyaga, S., 2013. Managing linguistic diversity in literacy and language development. Unpublished doctoral thesis, University of Stellenbosch.

Ovando, C., Collier, V., Combs, M., 2003. *Bilingual and ESL classrooms*. Third Edition. McGraw-Hill, Boston.

Panda, M., Mohanty, A., 2009. Language matters, so does culture. In: Mohanty, A., Panda, M., Phillipson, R. and Skuttnabb-Kangas, T. (Eds.) *Multilingual Education for Social Justice*. Orient Black Swan, New Delhi.

Pennycook, A., 2007. *Global Englishes and Transcultural Flows*. Routledge, London.

Prah, K., 1995. *African Languages for the Mass Education of Africans*. German Foundation for International Development, Bonn.

Robinson, C., 1996. *Language Use in Rural Development*. Mouton de Gruyter, Berlin.

Robinson, C., 2005. Language and literacies. Paper commissioned for Education for All Global Monitoring Report 2006: Literacy for Life. UNESCO, Paris.

Ruiz, R. 1984. Orientations in language planning. *Journal of the National Association for Bilingual Education* 8, 2, 15–34.

Setati, M., Adler, J., Reed, Y., Bapoo, A., 2002. Incomplete journeys: code-switching and other language practices in Mathematics, Science and English language classrooms in South Africa. *Language and Education* 16, 128–149.

Shin, S., 2005. *Developing in Two Languages: Korean Children in America*. Multilingual Matters, Clevedon.

Shohamy, E., 2006. *Language Policy*. Routledge, New York.

Shohamy, E., 2010. Cases of language policy resistance in Israel's centralized education system. In: Menken, K. and García, O. (Eds.) *Negotiating Language Policies in Schools*. Routledge, New York.

Spolsky, B., 2004. *Language Policy*. Cambridge University Press, Cambridge.

Stroud, C., 2001. African mother-tongue programmes and the politics of language. *Journal of Multilingual and Multicultural Development* 22, 4, 339–355.

Stroud, C., Heugh, K., 2004. Language rights and linguistic citizenship. In: Freeland, J. and Patrick, D. (Eds.) *Language Rights and Language Survival.* St. Jerome Publishing, Manchester.

Thomas, W., Collier, V. 1997. *School Effectiveness for Language Minority Students.* National Clearinghouse for Bilingual Education, George Washington University.

Trudell, B., 2008. Practice in search of a paradigm: language rights, linguistic citizenship and minority language communities in Senegal. *Current Issues in Language Planning* 9, 4, 395–412.

Trudell, B., 2012. Of gateways and gatekeepers: Language, education and mobility in francophone Africa. *International Journal of Educational Development* 32, 3, 368–375.

Trudell, B., Piper, B., 2013. Whatever the law says: language policy implementation and early-grade literacy achievement in Kenya. *Current Issues in Language Planning* 15, 1, 4–21.

United Nations Development Programme, 1990. *Human Development Report 1990*: Oxford University Press, New York.

Wardhaugh, R., 1997. *An Introduction to Sociolinguistics,* Third Edition. Blackwell Publishing, Oxford.

Wardhaugh, R., 2009. *An Introduction to Sociolinguistics,* Sixth Edition. Wiley-Blackwell, Malden.

12

THE HEYNEMAN/LOXLEY EFFECT

Three decades of debate

Stephen Heyneman

Background

While the lower performance of students from particular ethnic and income groups and geographical regions was a long-demonstrated outcome of standardised testing (Francher and Rutherford 2012; Stodolsky 1997; Ogbu 1991), the application of computers to the question was new in the 1960s. The report of James S. Coleman et al. (1966) was among the first surveys of a nationally representative population and the first to combine multiple factors into discrete categories representing those from out-of-school and within school influences.[1] Conclusions from this report were stunning because they ran counter to long-held assumptions. Gamoran and Long (2007) quote Seymour Martin Lipset as remarking to Daniel Moynihan that Coleman had found that "schools make no difference, families make the difference."

Gameron and Long note that the report has been cited in 2,700 articles, averaging approximately 55 a year since 2000. What it implied, in effect, is that efforts to close the achievement gap among students by investing in better schools would be ineffective by comparison to equalising the student backgrounds within those schools. The basic conclusion was that educational institutions could not effectively address inequalities as long as there were remaining differences in parental income, occupational prestige and educational attainment.

Many reanalyses were conducted on the data themselves. Averch et al. (1974) concluded that little efficacy could be attributed to teachers with more experience, advanced degrees or with smaller class sizes. Mosteller and Moynihan (1972) and Jencks et al. (1972) argued that resources might be ineffective because of insufficient variation across schools. But the limited effect of school resources seemed to hold up even after the order in which variables entered the regressions was varied (Hanushek and Kain 1972) and even when the size of beta coefficients was considered instead of the proportion of variance explained (Smith 1972).

Meta-analyses attempted to summarise findings across the numerous studies from the 1980s and 1990s (Hanushek 1997; Greenwald, Hedges and Laine 1996a, 1996b). The basic conclusion was that, in some instances, higher levels of resources were associated with differences in academic achievement. On the other hand, it is difficult to identify the specific school qualities that make a difference. It is reasonable to suggest that policy decisions about how resources are distributed (Nacimento 2008) or utilised within schools (Gameron and Long 2007) may be as important as simply identifying the level of resource differences across schools. Other styles and forms of analytic techniques were invented and applied to the same set of questions. Konstan-topoulos and Borman (2011) suggest that school effects are larger using the Coleman Report data when submitted to HLM techniques of analysis. Heyns argued that gain scores rather than performance at one point in time would be a superior means of calculating school effects (Heyns 1978); it was argued that school effects could be more accurately modelled not by noting what is in the schools but by treating each school as a separate and independent institution with a "fixed effect" (Rivkin, Hanushek and Kain 2005). Some of these debates spilled out into the popular press, with one scholar arguing that money invested in school quality has no effect (Hanushek 1989, 1996) while others argue that money invested in school quality has a significant effect (Greenwald, Hedges and Laine 1996a, 1996b; Hedges, Laine and Greenwald 1994).

All large scale education surveys were sometimes criticised as missing the point. The physical characteristics of the school were not the way to measure school quality; schools only provide a place where learning could take place. If one wanted to measure school quality, one would by necessity have to measure how learning occurs (Bidwell and Kasarda 1980; Barr and Dreeben 1983). This led to attention to within school processes (Gamoran and Mare 1989; Oakes 2005) and to the discovery that certain school qualities had different effects on different kinds of pupils (Summers and Wolfe 1977).

International tests of academic achievement: first results

It began as an educational experiment. In the late 1950s, Torsten Husen from the University of Stockholm was visiting friends Benjamin Bloom and C. Arnold Anderson at the University of Chicago. "Why don't we test for academic achievement internationally," he asked, "the world could be our laboratory" (Heyneman and Lykins 2008: 106). This was the origin of the International Association for the Evaluation of Educational Achievement (IEA), a nongovernmental organisation that now includes 69 countries and assists in the testing of half a dozen academic subjects – foreign languages, reading literacy, mathematics, science, civics and writing.[2]

The IEA began as a loose association of university-based personalities interested in finding solutions to pedagogical and other classroom-related problems. It sought solutions that could not be found locally and over time. Gradually, the membership expanded to include international agencies and governments, and different sources of funding from foundations and private businesses (Heyneman and Lee 2014: 38).

Beginning with the wealthier countries, the IEA now includes many middle- and even low-income countries. The IEA surveys normally include detailed assessments of each country's curriculum, textbooks and pedagogy. The surveys themselves include separate sources of information on schools, school directors, classroom teachers and students themselves. The process of designing the curriculum-based achievement tests and combining each of the sources of background information can take a decade to implement and, for some, become unaffordable. However, the need for a quicker, more easily implemented snapshot survey[3] led the member-states of the Organisation for Economic Co-operation and Development (OECD) to sponsor the design of a new achievement test based not on each nation's curriculum but on the basis of what was believed necessary for every student to be able to do. This performance-based test, called the Program for International Student Assessment (PISA), was first initiated in 2000 in 43 countries; in 2012, 65 countries participated. In addition to IEA and the OECD-sponsored studies, regional surveys have been designed for sub-Saharan Africa and Latin America, and there have been numerous national surveys. What had begun as an experiment in the 1960s over time has become an assessment requirement across much of the world. Between 1960 and 1989, there were 43 international surveys of academic achievement. Between 1990 and 1999, there were 49 regional surveys and 205 local or national surveys, and between 2000 and 2009, there were 152 international surveys, 47 regional surveys and 324 national surveys. The percentage of countries participating in at least one of these three types of academic achievement surveys includes 33% of the countries in the Europe and Central Asia region, 50% in sub-Saharan and the Arab States, 60% of the countries in East Asia and the Pacific region and 74% in the Latin America and the Caribbean region (Kamens 2013). The breadth and frequency of participation in international surveys today allows for a discussion of new and important issues such as the relationship between social cohesion and individual country performance, or the degree of in-country variation and the relationship with effective schools (Heyneman and Lee 2014).

The Heyneman/Loxley effect (H/L effect)

With the results from the first IEA surveys, it was possible for some to conclude that the "determinants of student achievement were basically the same in both developing and developed countries" (Simmons and Alexander 1978: 358). However, the evidence was not consistent. Even Simmons and Alexander admitted that home circumstances seemed to be less influential in Tunisia, Iran, Puerto Rico and Chile. They noted that student backgrounds in both primary and secondary schools "account for less variation in student performance in developing countries" (Simmons and Alexander 1978: 358). Their caveats might have been more clear had they included the early results from 18 countries summarised by Kifer (1977) or those of Bulcock, Clifton and Beebe from India (1977). In fact, escaping their notice were survey results from Uganda, Kenya, Rhodesia (among Africans), Ghana and Papua New Guinea (Heyneman 1980: 404).

Among the more startling of the studies from the 1970s was my own survey of primary schools of Uganda. A random sample of schools was personally visited in 1971 and took a year for me to collect. These schools were representative of five districts and two urban areas and constituted the first survey of primary schools in sub-Saharan Africa (Heyneman 1975). The results were released gradually, given that they seemed to be so divergent from the norm and given the fact that James Coleman was part of the dissertation committee that had to approve them.

The first findings appeared in 1976 in which it was simply pointed out that the correlations with student socioeconomic status (SES) were virtually nonexistent with respect to mathematics and general knowledge performance but were apparent with respect to English language performance. On the other hand, the association between child SES and English language performance was at about the same level (0.12) as the association between SES and nonverbal ability on the Raven's Progressive Matrices test (0.16) (Heyneman 1976: 46).

The reasons for the modest associations began to appear in 1979. Measures had been taken of a child's self-confidence. A child's self-concept is normally associated with a child's socioeconomic status (Battle and Rotter 1963; McPartland and Cummin 1958; Gordon 1971; Runciman 1969; Barber 1957) but not in Uganda. Contrary to findings from industrialised societies that had long been industrialised, no inter-relationships emerged between a Ugandan child's self-confidence and parental SES, and none appeared once controls were placed on gender and ethnicity (Heyneman 1979). This finding provided the first theory to be developed, which held that the spread of modern occupational differentiation in Uganda, with its hierarchical layers of government ministers, teachers, clerks, bus drivers, export farmers and traders, are all very recent differentiations by comparison to most societies in Western Europe and North America. It was speculated that such recent economic stratification might profoundly affect the formation of attitudes because even among the wealthiest elites, families commonly included illiterate members (Fallers 1964; Peil 1968). Unlike their occupational counterparts in Britain or North America, Ugandan bank chairmen, university professors, authors and presidents had numerous relatives who had never attended school, who were poor, and with whom they interact socially, often in the same house or compound. The experience of having respected but illiterate elders was not lost on the children of the elite. Even those at the highest levels of social differentiation tended to be an early generation that may have militated against privileged children, acquiring the feeling that top economic positions were entrenched in the hands of an elite who had passed their privilege down across generations. In this way, though differences in wealth were indeed apparent, these did not constitute the ingredients of a social class, and hence social differentiation had little impact on a child's academic performance. This is illustrated by Figure 12.1 below.

In terms of occupational attainment, in the United States the most important influence is SES (Jencks et al. 1972), but the opposite appeared to be true in Uganda. In Uganda, the most powerful predictor of occupational attainment was a child's performance in school (Currie 1977). What was startling about Ugandan school children in the early 1970s was not their low occupational expectations but the apparent irrelevance of SES to their aspirations. Ambitious children of both cabinet ministers and peasants knew three things perfectly clearly: (i) they knew that occupational success depends upon meeting the minimum educational entry requirements beyond primary school; (ii) they knew that only 10% of those who sat for the primary school leaving exam could be offered a place in a secondary school; and (iii) they knew the exam was graded by a computer, not a person. In other words, they considered it to be fair. Although in North America and Europe, examinations and standardised tests may be treated as a subtle way of restricting access of the poor to exclusive forms of training and occupational prestige, to the children in Uganda, the achievement test was one of the few universalistic sources of judgment available. While the test terrorised everyone, it did not terrorise the children of the poor any more than the children of the rich (Heyneman 1979).

But were these Ugandan findings an outlier? Were they in a category by themselves, or did their characteristics and explanations have parallels in other parts of the world? The first approach to that question was released in 1976. The Ugandan results were combined with those of the IEA test results in science that had been released three years earlier and were then combined into a single model showing the influence of SES and the effects of the school. In effect, it appeared as though there might be a pattern. The portion of the explained variation

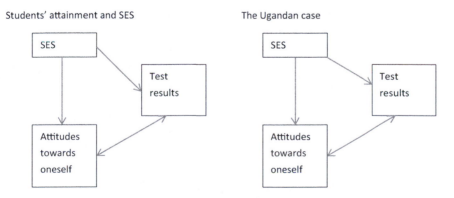

Figure 12.1 Relationship between SES, attitudes and academic performance among students characterised by social class divisions and students in Uganda in 1972

Source: Adapted from Heyneman (1979).

in achievement attributable to school effects was 31.7% in Uganda, 33.3% in India and 52.9% in Iran but only 16.4% in Scotland, 10% in Japan, 15.5% in England and 19.4% in the United States (Heyneman 1976: 208; 1977). This suggested that there might be a general rule that in low-income countries, the patterns of school performance and the statistical strength of the differences in school facilities might be higher and the strength of SES and other inherent characteristics might be lower.

Six years later my colleague, William Loxley, and I were able to test the question more systematically. First we experimented with a more accurate fit with respect to using the data on school quality. Instead of setting a minimum beta coefficient necessary for any school characteristics to enter the regression equations, we set a minimum standard for the data on school characteristics in each country separately. The strength of school characteristics was considerably enhanced as a result. These findings were released in 1982 (Heyneman and Loxley 1982). We then utilised this new method of winnowing the many school influences down to those most meaningful in each country with several new sets of surveys we collected, surveys from Egypt and Latin America. In all, we had comparable information on 29 countries. These results were released in 1983 (Heyneman and Loxley 1983a, 1983b). In essence, we found that the statistical power of school resources to influence academic achievement was considerably greater in the lower income countries and that the statistical power of SES to influence academic achievement was considerably greater in the higher income countries.

The effect of this finding was later summarised by Baker, Goesling and LeTendre:

> The Heyneman/Loxley effect (H/L effect) challenges the uniformity of what had previously been thought of as a consistent pattern across both associations, namely, a smaller association between school factors and achievement compared with a larger association between family SES and achievement. . . . Heyneman and Loxley show instead that the established pattern of larger family SES effects with smaller school effects occurs mostly in economically developed nations, while the reverse – smaller SES effects with larger school effects – occurs in less-developed nations. Specifically, in the 1970s, in nations with lower GNP per capita, school effects accounted for between student variation in achievement than did family SES.
>
> (Baker, Goesling and LeTendre 2002: 293)

As experience was gained, so were our explanations as to possible causes. One was the possibility that the findings were a statistical artefact. We tested for multicollinearity between school quality and social background, tighter selectivity of students from lower social backgrounds because of higher rates of school dropout, and lack of variation in social background. But none of these proved viable as explanations. It was noted that the economic returns to schooling were highest in the low-income countries (Psacharopoulos, Tan and Jimenez 1986; Psacharopoulos 1994); it was reasonable to think that because the opportunity for school was more scarce, its value was enhanced, and the demand for education was both high and spread more evenly across social groups. It was possible that in countries with lower incomes, the lack of primary and secondary school as a youth precludes opportunity later in life. Scarcity creates competition for school places and is well understood in both high- and low-income families. The aggregate upward mobility in low-income countries may be small, but the key may not be the aggregate upward mobility but rather the role of the school in permitting what mobility may be available. There was evidence that the influence of schooling on occupational mobility may be higher in low-income countries (Schiefelbein and Farrell 1982; Currie 1977; Fry 1983; Heyneman 1980b). To be sure, structural handicaps existed: education was not free of private cost; there was incomplete primary and secondary schooling in rural and outlying areas, and school quality varied between rich and poor, urban and rural communities (Krutikova, Rolleston and Aurino 2014) and the influence of school quality may have followed students who migrated to areas with more opportunity (Gould, Lavy and Paserman 2004). And in all societies, particularistic influences – friends, family, ethnic fraternity – would be given frequent favour in the labour market. There was no society then, nor any today, in which it can be said that occupational mobility is determined by merit alone.

The issue was not just the degree to which a society is meritocratic. Some have suggested that the difference may lie in the degree of cross-status group clarity of the importance surrounding selection and exit examinations (Bishop 1995, 1997, 1999). Instead the issue may reside in the differences in the child-rearing patterns of high- and low-status families. Substantial differences have been documented in the child-rearing patterns in high-income countries and with respect to their attitudes toward schooling (Bulcock, Clifton and Beebe 1977). Perhaps in low-income countries, there may be a higher degree of acceptance of education's functions and a more uniform aspiration among all families to utilise education for social mobility. This consensus about the importance of education may explain why the educational 'push' that children feel from their homes is not as tightly determined by the education or occupation of their parents. In low-income countries, the 'push' was certainly not equally strong from all homes, but the desire for a place in school and the pressure on students to do well on examinations might not have varied as markedly on the basis of SES; hence, the influence of SES to affect school performance may have been less in low-income countries (Heyneman and Loxley 1983a, 1983b).[4]

The H/L effect: challenges and reanalyses[5]

Challenges to these findings came quickly. In a study of secondary school students in Zimbabwe, Ridell used multilevel methods of organising the data and found that social background was more powerful than school quality in the prediction of academic achievement (Riddell 1989a, 1989b). She comments on Heyneman and Loxley by saying that:

> [O]ne is struck by their insularity and how much they are like the first wave of research in industrialised countries. There is still a preoccupation with the division of variance into school vs. home . . . the research is heavily economistic relying on production function type of approach to data that are most easily quantified, rather than the most educationally significant. . . . There are strong grounds for skepticism concerning the differences between developed and developing countries which Heyneman emphasises related to the effect of background factors on educational achievement . . . his theory remains unsubstantiated due to the extreme methodological weaknesses exposed here.
>
> (Riddell 1989a)

In the reply (Heyneman 1989), it was pointed out that criticising us for not using multilevel methods instead of ordinary least squares was like attacking Charles Lindbergh for not using radar, a technology which had not yet been invented. While multilevel methods do indeed offer a new way to organise data and Riddell's results did differ from our own, it was not necessarily the case that our data were incorrect. Nor is it the case that past research was monotheistic in terms of techniques. We used anthropological analyses to better understand the management of schools (Heyneman 1975); we used achievement gain scores as opposed to cross-sectional scores to differentiate hypothesised as opposed to real changes in learning (Heyneman and Jamison 1980); we used pupil affiliation with schools as opposed to school inputs to overcome the misspecification of school and teacher measures (Heyneman and Jamison 1980); and others at the time used time-series data, discrimination analysis and cross-tabulations to ferret out the possibilities of errors in interpretation (Schiefelbein and Farrell 1982) and path models to incorporate changes in the labour market over time (Farrell and Schiefelbein 1985). Perhaps most importantly, we tried to test the theories of school effects with experiment/control studies instead of cross-sectional surveys. In some ways, these experimental studies were superior to the multilevel analyses in that students either had the experimental input or they did not. The effect was therefore likely to be clearer and less implied. These studies suggested that the power of improved school inputs to improve school achievement was highest where school quality had previously been the lowest and in the least developed countries of the world (Heyneman, Jamison and Montenegro 1984; Jamison et al. 1981). The intervention of textbooks in the Philippines constituted an illustration. With a nationwide investment that improved the average textbook availability from 10:1 (students/book) to 2:1 (students/book), performance increased in the nation at large by one-third of a standard deviation in Grade 1 Pilipino and by almost one half of a standard deviation in Grades 1 and 2 science. The levels of achievement attained by only 50% of the student population was, one year later, achieved by 69% of the student population of eight million children. The equivalent achievement impact in the United States would have required a reduction of class size from 40 to 10 students/class (Heyneman, Jamison and Montenegro 1984: 143).

A decade later, Riddell's criticisms were reanalysed, and each proposition was retested. In 2009, Chudgar and Luschei mention that:

> [W]hile a few individual country studies have used hierarchical models to decompose variance, this approach has not been adopted systematically for multi-country data . . . and in general the models show a similar outcome in terms of countries where schools matter more or less.
>
> (Chudgar and Luschei 2009: 635 and 644)

Baker, Goesling and Le Tendre conclude that:

> HLM has not uncovered larger school effects in wealthy nations like the United States than the older ordinary least square (OLS) methods did . . . and we doubt that that HLM's use would have uncovered significantly larger school effects in wealthy nations than was reported by the 1970's OLS estimates . . . we think it unlikely that these issues invalidate the H/L effects in the 1970s data.
>
> (Baker, Goesling and LeTendre 2002: 308)

Perhaps the HLM lesson is worth reiterating. A new method, while important, is no substitute for the obvious. No academic debate, no new software, no new statistical technique that considers the relative importance or unimportance of school quality negates what is perfectly obvious to every minister of education and every parent, including those of low SES and particularly those in low-income countries. They want more and better education for their children, and they will sacrifice a great deal to keep children in school. While one may argue the relative importance of one effect versus another, such arguments are irrelevant in the world of immediate policy where the most relevant questions are how to raise the availability of school quality inputs and how to distribute them more fairly. No one seriously argues that school inputs should not be raised because academic performance is affected by the conditions of the home.

Other criticisms centred on the validity of the socioeconomic measures used in low- and middle-income countries (Theisen, Achola and Boakari 1983). However prevalent these criticisms were thirty years ago, the fact remains that measuring SES by a combination of parental education and wealth has become the standard method ever since. Moreover, the question of bias in the H/L effect because of the invalidity of the SES measures was dismissed by Baker et al. in their reanalysis. They pointed out that:

> [T]here is no evidence of such bias in the Heyneman and Loxley work. To the contrary, Heyneman and Loxley speculate on issues of more restricted variance in family background in the poorer nations but offer a number of plausible tests to indicate that their effect is not a statistical artefact of this.
>
> (Baker, Goesling and Le Tendre 2002: 309)

Other reanalyses and retests of the H/L theory have come in different categories. Some utilised regional or national data to test the degree to which home background influenced school achievement in the Philippines (Huang 2010), sub-Saharan Africa (Zumbach 2010), the Middle East and North Africa (Bouhilila 2014), Latin America and the Caribbean (Cervini 2012) and China (Xuehui, Hannum and Sargent 2007; Jiang 2006). Others have used more global data to inquire as to which school characteristics might be more significant in predicting achievement (Illie and Lietz 2010; Fuller 1987; Sandoval-Hernandez and Bosco 2010) or the degree to which learning might contribute to economic growth (Breton 2011; Fangsheng 2006; Bils and Klenow 2000; Cohn and Soto 2007; Hanushek 2006; Hanushek and Wössmann 2008, 2009, 2011; Jamison and Hanushek 2007).

However, the most systematic reanalysis of the Heyneman/Loxley effect was released by Baker Goesling and Letendre in August 2002. They were able to take advantage of the newly released results of the Third International Mathematics and Science Study (TIMSS) and hence were able to utilise data from over 36 countries, 20 of which had not previously been included in the H/L analyses.[6] Their interest was not solely concerned with the influences on learning; they were focused on whether the patterns of performance might have changed between the original results in 1983 and their results in 2002 as a result of the massive increase in access to education in the interim. Here is how they put it:

> In the time since the (H/L) findings were reported 25 years ago, the world has seen intensified political and economic investment in access to education and in organisational quality, and this intensification has ramifications for the way that educational stratification is organised in nations . . . the question is to what degree does national economic development influence the social reproductive process of schooling through human capital reproduction in schools?
>
> (Baker, Goesling and Le Tendre 2002: 292)

Essentially Baker, Goesling and Le Tendre were interested in testing two of the theories suggested in the 1983 article. The first concerned the degree to which school scarcity influences its value. They hypothesised that as schooling becomes less scarce, its value might decline, hence the pattern of performance might change. The second concerned the nature of social stratification. They hypothesised that as national economies develop they may begin to resemble each other, and this may influence the importance of SES in the prediction of academic achievement.

The findings of Baker, Goesling and Le Tendre are very important. They find very little evidence of the H/L effect in their data and conclude that the H/L effect had declined over time. They suggest that their findings:

> [D]emonstrate how the institution of family and school interact over time because of changing macro-social conditions. As formal schooling increasingly becomes the single most powerful channel for reproduction of family status, the incorporation of family as an institution into schooling as an institution also increases … this shifting HL effect indicates the dynamic, symbiotic relationship between these two institutions. … Investment in mass schooling by nation-states and multilateral agencies, backed by an ideology of providing some minimum level of school quality throughout the nation, has shifted the potential toward greater family SES effects in the social stratification process. The macro-process of mass schooling across a large part of the world may have achieved a resource threshold in the quality of schooling and be a very plausible explanation for a shifting H/L effect over time.
>
> (Baker, Goesling and Le Tendre 2002: 310)

Diminishing marginal returns?

As nations develop economically, the question of whether school effects systematically diminish has been taken up by several economists. Hanushek and Luque (2003) asked whether investments in low-income countries may have a larger effect because of the lower levels of classroom and other inputs. However, they did not find a constant change in effects. Harris (2007: 48) suggests that this might be due to the fact that they assumed constant return to scale within countries as well as between them. Harris uses a different set of functional forms to test the existence of diminishing marginal returns (DMR) but concludes, again, that no significant DMR could be found. He says:

> Using three different tests there is little evidence of DMR within countries, either for school inputs as a whole or for individual inputs such as teacher education. While the evidence is more supportive of DMR across countries, the possibility of constant returns cannot be rejected … the discussion here of the various tests for DMR in the present provides some direction about how these tests might be carried out given the influence of the Heyneman/Loxley result and related types of studies on the design of educational policies.
>
> (Harris 2007: 48)

Difference in the nations sampled?

Baker, Goesling and Le Tendre raise several important possibilities as to why the H/L effect cannot be found in 2002. One concerns the possibility that the nations that appear in their sample are wealthier than those that appeared in the original H/L sample. As they put it:

> [C]ompared with the 1994 sample of nations, the 1970s sample of nations includes more poor nations from Latin America, where educational inequality tends to be high and involve widespread private schooling for elite families.
>
> (Baker, Goesling and Le Tendre 2002: 311)

Is it possible that the H/L effect had not disappeared but was not evident 25 years later because of a change in countries from which data were collected? This is among the questions asked by Gamoran and Long. They point out that by comparison to the world average, the level of national wealth in the Baker, Goesling and Le Tendre sample (US$17,429 per capita) was 300% over the world mean whereas the level of national wealth in the Heyneman/Loxley sample (US$2,896) was about 50% over the world mean (Gameron and Long 2007: 33). Could that explain the absence of the H/L effect?

To test this question, they took the same countries that appeared in the Baker, Goesling, and Le Tendre sample and added data taken from ten countries in Latin America.[7] They then ran regressions in the same manner as Baker, Goesling and Le Tendre. But their results were quite different. With the per capita income more closely resembling the original Heyneman/Loxley sample, the portion of variation in academic achievement explained by school quality was significantly increased. While school effects in the Baker, Goesling and Le Tendre sample could account for 34.4% of the explained achievement variance, and the Heyneman/Loxley sample could explain 50.5%, school effects in their sample could explain 56.7% (Gameron and Long 2007: 33). This is summarised in Table 12.1.

Gameron and Long also retested the DMR hypothesis and found that the DMR was not constant but that there was a threshold effect. At about US$16,000 per capita, the variance that could be explained dropped from 31% to about 9%, suggesting that models utilising a threshold effect are significantly better fits. They summarised their work by saying that:

> International evidence shows that school resources do have a strong effect on academic achievement for the poorest countries. This result suggests that the Coleman report finding of a limited association between school resources and achievement once family background is controlled holds only for countries that have passed a threshold of basic resources and experience a diminishing (though non-zero) marginal return to additional school resources.
>
> (Gameron and Long 2007: 36)

The influence of inequality?

But is it only a question of economic development? Are there not other factors that might account for the continued existence of an H/L effect? After all, eight countries in the Baker, Goesling and Le Tendre sample were either from the post-Soviet Union or from Eastern and Central Europe where school systems were widely known for equality in the distribution of school resources (Heyneman 2000). Baker et al. express the concern that the lack of countries from Latin American in their sample might have affected their results. Countries in Latin America

Table 12.1 Comparison of H/L effect examples: per capita income and school effects

Sample	Per Capita Income (US$)	School Effects (% of Variance Explained)
Heyneman and Loxley	2,896	51
Baker, Goesling and Letendre	17,429	34
Gameron and Long	3,409	57

Source: Adapted from Gameron and Long 2007: 34.

are known to have problems of inequity, including in the distribution of school resources. Perhaps the limited access to data from Latin American might have depressed the measured effects of school resources (Baker, Goesling and Le Tendre 2002: 311).

The Gameron and Long sample, on the other hand, included many countries in Latin America that are known for significant inequality in the distribution of school resources. The 1994 sample, they point out, "includes more poor nations emerging from the former Soviet bloc, where there is some evidence that educational resource inequality is relative low and elite private schooling is rare" (Baker, Goesling and Le Tendre 2002: 311). Could inequality influence the degree to which school quality affects academic achievement?

The inequality hypothesis was systematically addressed by Chudgar and Luschei (2009). They wondered if:

> [G]reater inequality in school resource distribution in the original H/L sample may have strengthened the statistical power of school resources to predict achievement, thereby enhancing the H/L effect. If inequality influences the relationship between national income and the impact that schools have on achievement, then failure to consider inequality differences in country samples may lead to inaccurate conclusions.
> (Chudgar and Luschei 2009: 634)

Inequality may be evident in the distribution of school resources or in the larger distribution of personal income and wealth. If there is high inequality in wealth but low inequality in school resources, then schools may help ameliorate the lack of privilege associated with having a lower SES. On the other hand, if school resources are distributed inequitably in a country where wealth is also distributed inequitably, then the school system might be classified as having a 'privileged student bias' (Chiu and Khoo 2005; Chudgar and Luschei 2009). The question is whether either distribution affects the results of accounting for the variation in academic achievement.

Chudgar and Luschei used school fixed effects in their OLS results and total school variance in the HLM results, hence they are not able to distinguish among school systems with less equality in the distribution of individual school resources. Their results suggest that school effects tend to be stronger in low-income countries and more important in the poor countries but may be especially important in counties with high levels of income inequality. They summarise their results in this way:

> By quantifying the variance attributable to schools, we find distinct patterns indicating that schools are more important in poor countries.... Prior studies have ignored the role of income inequality. Lack of variation in access to resources should lead to relatively lower importance of school factors in more equal countries. Our analysis shows that in fact, school resources are more important in unequal countries.... Our findings argue for a consistent government role in insuring equitable and adequate schools, especially in poor and unequal regions. Focusing on low-income students in unequal regions may be a particularly high-yield strategy for directing scarce educational resources.
> (Chudgar and Luschei 2009: 651 and 653)

Student motivation?

To date, the discussion has concentrated on quantifying school inputs and school effects. Comparatively little attention has been paid to the interaction within families, the kind of interaction that might affect a student's motivation. There is a tendency to assume that interactions occur in ways parallel to middle-class homes in Europe and North America, namely that parents with more education tend to spend more time and give more attention to the cognitive development of their children. This is supported by the finding that the impact of socioeconomic status is greater with younger children who are in the home longer and may be less affected by influences from outside the home (Blossfield and Shavit 1993: 9).

Aside from knowing that parents may have completed comparatively more education, the question remains as to what constitutes the ingredients derived from families whose children perform well on tests of academic achievement. Some suggest that it might be entrepreneurialism (Wössmann et al. 2009). Others have suggested that it may have to do with family values toward schooling (Chiu 2007). Chiu and Chow (2011) suggest that the differences in family values are evidenced by the level of classroom discipline around the world. In their pioneering study, they find that classroom discipline differs systematically and that:

> [I]n poorer countries classroom discipline was higher . . . unlike academic achievement, classroom discipline does not necessarily improve as a country's economy grows. . . . Because weaker classroom discipline is evident in richer countries, this negative link opens up new avenues of research, raising the possibility that other psychological aspects of schooling (e.g., social relationships, sense of belonging at school) might be worse (or better) in richer countries.
>
> (Chiu and Chow 2011: 529)

The Heyneman/Loxley effect: a summary

In sum, we have discovered several things. Even after new tests and new methods, the pattern of socioeconomic status effects is nowhere near uniform. This is illustrated in Figure 12.2 and Table 12.2. Figure 12.2 illustrates the fact that the effect of family background in predicting math and science achievement is highly variable even within wealthy countries.

The same variability in the 'achievement gap' in reading scores based on family wealth is illustrated in Table 12.2. For instance, in Luxembourg, Portugal and Germany, the gap is greater than five times what it is in Finland and the Netherlands.

Why does the achievement gap vary even among wealthy nations where schooling is universally available? In countries where there is a high level of social cohesion, there is little variation in the desire for schooling between rich and poor families. In those environments – Korea, Japan, Canada, Netherlands, Finland – there is more classroom discipline, a lower achievement gap and higher average achievement. Not only does this occur in certain countries but also within particular subcultures (high- and low-income Jewish and Mormon families for instance). It may occur in countries that are faced with exogenous economic and social challenges (Sahlberg 2011). It may occur within countries where schooling is uniformly seen (by rich and poor alike) as being the single most important avenue of social mobility (Heyneman 1979, 1985; Furnham, Kirkcaldy and Lynn 1996).

The question at the end concerns both social background as well as school quality. In terms of social background, it may be the case that pupils have to want to learn in spite of poverty and the handicaps of the home (Bishop 2006). It is normal for impoverished children to want to learn in many parts of the world, and classrooms, even with high pupil/teacher ratios, are more peaceful. Children are uniformly ready, even anxious, to learn before the teacher even enters the classroom.

On the other hand, in those countries where classroom discipline is a major handicap to teachers and teaching, no new curriculum, no new teacher training, no new pedagogy can

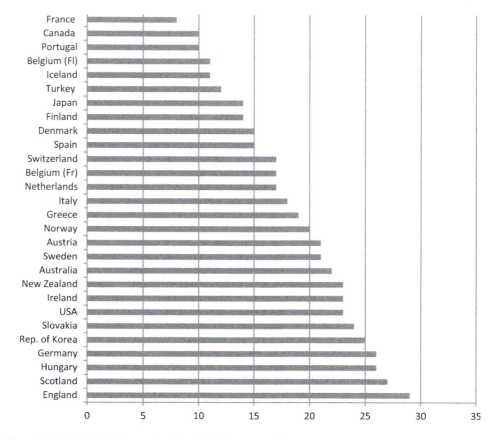

Figure 12.2 Family background effects in different countries

Notes: Coefficient estimates from a student-level regression within each country of the mean of math and science performance in the TIMSS-95 and TIMSS-Repeat international tests on books at home, which is a categorical variable with five categories. Regressions control for age, gender, family status, student born in country, mother born in country, father born in country, interactions between the three immigration variables and books, and a dummy for the second test cycle. All estimates are statistically significantly different from zero at the 1% level.

Source: Adapted from Hanushek and Wössmann 2010.

overcome a class of children who are not ready to learn. What some public and charter schools do to overcome this is to re-create a culture of initial obligations, a culture which, until recently, was universal (Heyneman 1999). They create what Edward Shils (1981) describes as a tradition, "a massive presentness" over which a minor child has no choice except to try hard.

Where there is a tradition of valuing education, a child will have no choice of wanting to attend school or trying hard in school. The source of the problem is wherever a child is allowed to have this choice. Because having a choice of attending school or trying hard in school is associated with low SES families in some high-income countries, many assume that poverty must be the cause of the gap in achievement. However problematic poverty may be, it is not the cause of lower achievement among the poor. The cause of lower achievement among the poor is the comparative disregard for those who have sacrificed to make it possible for them to be educated. This includes a disregard for both the 'elders' in their own families as well as the general public.

Table 12.2 Differences in reading scores by family wealth in PISA 2007

Luxembourg	8
Portugal	6.7
Germany	5.2
France	4.5
Spain	3.1
Belgium	3
Austria	2.6
UK	2.6
Sweden	2.4
Denmark	2.3
Italy	2.1
Greece	2
Ireland	1.7
Finland	0.9
Netherlands	0.2

Source: Adapted from Gorard and Smith 2004.

Where cultures require every child to desire schooling, there is a lower achievement gap. The question is whether what pertains in those societies can be re-created elsewhere. I think it can.

About school effects we also have learned a great deal. The fact is that school quality varies considerably from one country to another, and the difference is roughly associated with GNP/capita (Heyneman 2004). But we have also learned that we should not hold schools or school teachers responsible for only a small fraction of their professional responsibilities. Since the beginning, the purpose of public schooling has been to create well-balanced adults with a variety of lifelong interests who act as responsible citizens (Heyneman 1999; 2000, 2005). It may be more difficult to quantify, but this makes its assessment no less important to emphasize. Some have called for an emphasis on subjects other than mathematics, science and reading. These might include civics education, foreign languages and technical skills. A broader approach might include noncognitive skills, attitudes of self-worth, or social responsibility (Hanushek and Wössmann 2010: 54).

What we know is that these large-scale tests of academic achievement will be more common in the future; they will include cities and states as well as nations; they will include tests over time, tests with experiment and control groups, tests that emphasize problem solving as well as information retrieval. But regardless of how important these new arenas become, they will not eliminate the importance of schools and school effects. After three decades of debate, that issue is settled.

Notes

1 A similar report was issued in the United Kingdom at about the same time with parallel conclusions (Central Advisory Council for Education 1967; Kogan 1987).
2 See http://www.iea.nl/
3 The impetus for a new test originally came from Britain, whose minister of education could not wait a decade for the necessary achievement results on which his government depended.
4 What did James Coleman say about the H/L effect? This is described in Heyneman (1997).
5 According to Google Scholar, the original article (Heyneman and Loxley 1983b) has been cited 777 times with about 25 new citations appearing/year.

6 Latvia, Lithuania, Romania, the Russian Federation, Slovakia, the Czech Republic, Slovenia, Korea, Greece, Portugal, Spain, Iceland, Ireland, Cyprus, Austria, Denmark, Hong Kong, Singapore, Switzerland and Kuwait.

7 Honduras, Bolivia, Dominican Republic, Paraguay, Columbia, Brazil, Venezuela, Chile, Mexico and Argentina.

References

Averch, H., Carroll, S., Donaldson, D., Kiesling, H., Pincus, J., 1974. *How Effective Is Schooling?* Educational Technological Publications, Englewood Cliffs.

Baker, D., Goesling, B., Letendre, G., 2002. Socioeconomic status, school quality, and national economic development: a cross-national analysis of the 'Heyneman-Loxley Effect' on mathematics and science achievement. *Comparative Education Review* 46, 3, 291–312.

Barber, B., 1957. *Social Stratification.* Harcourt, Brace and Company, New York.

Barr, R., Dreeben, C., 1983. *How Schools Work.* University of Chicago Press, Chicago.

Battle, E., Rotter, J., 1963. Children's feelings of personal control as related to social class and ethnic group. *Journal of Personality* 31, 482–90.

Bidwell, C., Kasarda, J., 1980. Conceptualizing and measuring the effects of school and schooling. *American Journal of Education* 88, 4, 401–30.

Bils, M., Klenow, P., 2000. Does schooling cause growth? *American Economic Review* 90, 5, 1160–83.

Bishop, J., 1995. The impact of curriculum-based external examinations on school priorities and student learning. *International Journal of Education Research* 23, 8, 653–752.

Bishop, J., 1997. The effect of national standards and curriculum-based examinations on achievement. *American Economic Review* 87, 2, 260–64.

Bishop, J., 1999. Are national exit examinations important for educational efficiency? *Swedish Economic Policy Review* 6, 2, 349–98.

Bishop, J., 2006. Drinking from the fountain of knowledge: student incentive to study and learn: externalities, information problems, and peer pressure. In: Hanushek, E. and Welch, F. (Eds.) *Handbook on the Economics of Education.* North Holland, Amsterdam.

Blossfield, H., Shavit, Y., 1993. Persisting barriers. In: Shavit, Y. and Blossfield, H. (Eds.) *Persistent Inequality.* Westview, Boulder.

Bouhilila, D., 2014. The quality of secondary education in the Middle East and North Africa: essays using TIMSS 2007 Data. PhD Dissertation, University of Tunis.

Breton, T., 2011. The quality vs. the quantity of schooling: what drives economic growth? *Economics of Education Review* 30, 765–73.

Bulcock, J., Clifton, R., Beebe, M., 1977. *A Language Resource Model of Science Achievement Comparison Between 14-year olds in England and India.* Institute for the Study of International Problems in Education, University of Stockholm.

Central Advisory Council for Education, 1967. *Children and Their Primary Schools.* Her Majesty's Stationery Office, London.

Cervini, R., 2012. The school effect in some Latin American countries (in Spanish). *Education Policy Analysis Archives* 20.

Chiu, M.-M., 2007. Families, economies, cultures and science achievement in 41 countries: country, school and student level analyses. *Journal of Family Psychology* 21, 510–19.

Chiu, M.-M., Chow, B.-W., 2011. Classroom discipline across 41 countries: school, economic and cultural differences. *Journal of Cross Cultural Psychology* 42, 3, 516–33.

Chiu, M.-M., Khoo, L., 2005. Effects of resources, inequality and privilege bias on achievement: country, school and student level analysis. *American Education Research Journal* 42, 4, 575–603.

Chudgar, A., Luschei, T., 2009. National income, income inequality, and the importance of schools. *American Education Research Journal* 46, 3, 626–58.

Cohn, D., Soto, M., 2007. Growth and human capital: good data, good results. *Journal of Economic Growth* 12, 1, 51–76.

Coleman, J., Campbell, E., Hobson, C., McPartland, J., Mood, A., Weinfield, F., York, R., 1966. *The Equality of Educational Opportunity.* U.S. Government Printing Office, Washington.

Currie, J., 1977. The occupational attainment process in Uganda: effects of family background and academic achievement on occupational status among Ugandan secondary school graduates. *Comparative Education Review* 21, 14–28.

Fallers, L., 1964. The modernisation of social stratification. In: Fallers, L. (Ed.) *The King's Men*. Oxford University Press, Oxford.

Fangsheng, J., 2006. Student learning and national economic development: a re-examination of Heyneman-Loxley effect using TIMSS 1999 and 2003 data. *Education Policy Forum* August, 161–76.

Farrell, J., Schiefelbein, E., 1985. Education and status attainment in Chile: a comparative challenge to the Wisconsin model of status attainment. *Comparative Education Review* 29 November, 490–506.

Francher, R., Rutherford, A., 2012. *Pioneers of Psychology*. WW Norton and Company, New York.

Fry, G., 1983. Empirical indicators of educational equity and equality: a Thai case study. *Social Indicators Research* 12, 2, 199–215.

Fuller, B., 1987. What school factors raise achievement in the Third World? *Review of Educational Research* 57, 3, 255–92.

Furnham, A., Kirkcaldy, B., Lynn, R., 1996. Attitudinal correlates of national wealth. *Personality and Individual Differences* 21, 3, 345–53.

Gamoran, A., Long, D., 2007. The equality of opportunity: a 40 year retrospective. In: Teese, R., Lamb, S. and Duru-Bellat, M. (Eds.) *International Studies in Educational Inequality: Theory and Policy*. Springer, New York.

Gamoran, A., Mare, R., 1989. Secondary school tracking and educational inequality: compensation, reinforcement, or neutrality? *American Journal of Sociology* 94, 3, 1146–83.

Gorard, S., Smith, E., 2004. What is underachievement at school? *School Leadership and Management* 24, 2, 205–25.

Gordon, C., 1971. *Looking Ahead: Self-Conceptions, Race and Family as Determinants of Adolescent Orientation to Achievement*. American Sociological Association Rose Monograph Series, Washington.

Gould, E., Lavy, V., Paserman, M., 2004. Immigrating to opportunity: estimating the effect of school quality using a natural experiment on Ethiopians in Israel. *The Quarterly Journal of Economics* 119, 2, 489–526.

Greenwald, R., Hedges, L., Laine, R., 1996a. The effect of school resources on student achievement. *Review of Education Research* 66, 361–96.

Greenwald, R., Hedges, L., Laine, R., 1996b. Interpreting research on school resources and student achievement: a rejoinder to Hanushek. *Review of Education Research* 66, 411–16.

Hanushek, E., 1989. The impact of differential expenditures on school performance. *Educational Researcher* 18, 45–51.

Hanushek, E., 1996. A more complete picture of school resource policies. *Review of Educational Research* 66, 367–409.

Hanushek, E., 1997. Assessing the effects of school resources on student performance: an update. *Educational Evaluation and Policy Analysis* 19, 141–64.

Hanushek, E., 2006. Alternative school policies and the benefits of general cognitive skills. *Economics of Education Review* 25, 447–62.

Hanushek, E., Kain, J., 1972. On the value of equality of educational opportunity as a guide to public policy. In: Mosteller, F. and Moynihan, D. (Eds.) *On Equality of Educational Opportunity*. Vintage, New York.

Hanushek, E., Luque, J.A., 2003. Efficiency and equity in schools around the world. *Economics of Education Review* 22, 481–502.

Hanushek, E., Wössmann, L., 2008. The role of cognitive skills in economic development. *Journal of Economic Literature* 46, 3, 607–68.

Hanushek, E., Wössmann, L., 2009. Do better schools lead to more growth? Cognitive skills, economic outcomes, and causation. National Bureau of Economic Research Working Paper No. 14633, Washington.

Hanushek, E., Wössmann, L., 2010. The economics of international differences in educational achievement. National Bureau of Economic Research Working Paper No. 15949, Washington.

Hanushek, E., Wössmann, L., 2011. The economics of international differences in education achievement. In: Hanushek, E., Machin, S. and Wössmann, L. (Eds.) *Handbook in Economics*. Volume 3. North Holland, Amsterdam.

Harris, D., 2007. Diminishing marginal returns and the production of education. *Education Economics* 15, 1, 31–53.

Hedges, L.V., Laine, R., Greenwald, R., 1994. Does money matter: a meta-analysis of studies of the effects of differential school inputs on student outcomes. *Educational Researcher* 23, 5–14.

Heyneman, S.P., 1975. *Influences on Academic Achievement in Uganda: A Coleman Report from a Non-Industrialized Society*. PhD Dissertation, University of Chicago.

Heyneman, S.P., 1976. A brief note on the relationship between socioeconomic status and test performance among Ugandan primary school children. *Comparative Education Review* 20, 1, 481–502.

Heyneman, S.P., 1977. Influences on academic achievement: a comparison of results from Uganda and more industrial societies. *Sociology of Education* 11, 2, 245–59.

Heyneman, S.P., 1979. Why impoverished children do well in Ugandan schools. *Comparative Education* 15, 2, 175–85.

Heyneman, S.P., 1980. Differences between developed and developing countries: comment on Simmons and Alexander's determinants of school achievement. *Economic Development and Cultural Change* 28, 2, 403–6.

Heyneman, S.P., 1985. Diversifying secondary school curricula in developing countries: an implementation history and some policy options. *International Journal of Educational Development* 5, 283–88.

Heyneman, S.P., 1989. Multilevel methods for analyzing school effects in developing countries. *Comparative Education Review*, 33, 4, 498–504.

Heyneman, S.P., 1997. Jim Coleman: a personal story. *Educational Researcher* 26, 1, 28–30.

Heyneman, S.P., 1999. American education: a view from the outside. *International Journal of Leadership in Education* 2, 1, 31–41.

Heyneman, S.P., 2000. From the party/state to multi-ethnic democracy: education and social cohesion in the Europe and Central Asia region. *Educational Evaluation and Policy Analysis* 21, 4, 173–91.

Heyneman, S.P., 2004. International education quality. *Economics of Education Review* 23, 441–52.

Heyneman, S.P., 2005. Student background and school achievement: what is the right question? *American Journal of Education* 112, 1, 1–9.

Heyneman, S.P., Jamison, D., 1980. Student learning in Uganda: textbook availability and other determinants. *Comparative Education Review* 24, 2, 108–18.

Heyneman, S.P., Jamison, D., Montenegro, X., 1984. Textbooks in the Philippines: evaluation of the pedagogical impact of a nationwide investment. *Education Evaluation and Policy Analysis* 6, Summer, 139–50.

Heyneman, S.P., Lee, B., 2014. The impact of international studies of academic achievement on policy and research. In: Rutkowski, L., von Davier, M. and Rutkowski, D. (Eds.) *Handbook of International Large Scale Assessment: Background, Technical Issues, and Methods of Data Analysis.* CRC Press, London.

Heyneman, S.P., Loxley, W., 1982. Influences on academic achievement across high- and low-income countries: a re-analysis of IEA data. *Sociology of Education* 55, 1, 13–21.

Heyneman, S.P., Loxley, W., 1983a. The distribution of primary school quality within high- and low-income countries. *Comparative Education Review* 27, 1, 108–18.

Heyneman, S.P., Loxley, W., 1983b. The effect of primary school quality on academic achievement across 29 high- and low-income countries. *American Journal of Sociology* 88, 6, 1162–94.

Heyneman, S.P., Lykins, C. 2008. The evolution of comparative and international education statistics. In: Ladd, H.F. and Fiske, E.B. (Eds.) *Handbook of Research in Education Finance and Policy.* Routledge, New York.

Heyns, B., 1978. *Summer Learning and the Effects of Schooling.* Academic Press, New York.

Huang, F.-L., 2010. The role of socio-economic status and school quality in the Philippines: revisiting the Heyneman-Loxley effect. *International Journal of Educational Development* 30, 3, 268–96.

Illie, S., Lietz, P., 2010. School quality and student achievement in 21 European countries: the Heyneman-Loxley effect re-visited. In: *Issues and Methodologies in Large-Scale Assessments.* Volume 3. IEA-ETS Research Institute, Princeton, New Jersey.

Jamison, D., Hanushek, E., 2007. The effects of education quality on income growth and mortality decline. *Economics of Education Review* 26, 772–89.

Jamison, D., Searle, B., Galda, K., Heyneman, S.P., 1981. Improving elementary mathematics education in Nicaragua: an experimental study of the impact of textbooks and radio on achievement. *Journal of Educational Psychology* 73, 556–67.

Jencks, C., Smith, M., Acland, H., Bane, M., Cohen, D., Gintis, H., Heyns, B., Michelson, S., 1972. *Inequality: A Reassessment of the Effect of Family and Schooling in America.* Basic, New York.

Jiang, F., 2006. Student learning and national economic development: a re-examination of the Heyneman/Loxley effect using TIMSS 1999 and 2003 data. *Education Policy Forum* August, 161–76.

Kamens, D., 2013. Globalization and the emergence of an audit culture: PISA and the search for 'best practice' and magic bullets. In: Meyer, H.-D. and Benavot, A. (Eds.) *PISA Power and Policy.* Symposium, Oxford.

Kifer, E., 1977. A cross-cultural study of the impact of home environment variables on academic achievement and affective traits. Paper presented at the annual meeting of the American Education Research Association, New York, April.

Kogan, M., 1987. The Plowden Report twenty years on. *Oxford Review of Education* 13, 13–21.

Konstantopoulos, S., Borman, G.D., 2011. Family background and school effects on student achievement: a multilevel analysis of the Coleman data. *Teachers College Record* 113, 1, 97–132.

Krutikova, S., Rolleston, C., Aurino, E., 2014. How much difference does school make and for whom? A two country study of the impact of school quality on educational attainment. In: Bourdillon, M. and Boyden, J. (Eds.) *Growing Up in Poverty: Findings from Young Lives*. Palgrave Macmillan, Basingstoke.

McPartland, T., Cummin, J., 1958. Self-conception, social class and mental health. *Human Organization* 17, 24–30.

Mosteller, F., Moynihan, D., 1972. A path-breaking report further studies of the Coleman Report. In: Mosteller, F. and Moynihan, D. (Eds.) *On Equality of Educational Opportunity*. Vintage, New York.

Nascimento, P., 2008. School resources and student achievement: worldwide findings and methodological issues. *Educate* March, 19–30.

Oakes, J., 2005. *Keeping Track: How Schools Structure Inequality*. Yale University Press, New Haven.

Ogbu, J., 1991. Minority coping responses and school experience. *Journal of Psychohistory* 18, 4, 433–56.

Peil, M., 1968. Aspirations and social structure. *Africa* 31, 71–79.

Psacharopoulos, G., 1994. Returns to investment in education: a global update. *World Development* 22, 9, 1325–1343.

Psacharopoulos, G., Tan, J.P., Jimenez, E., 1986. Financing education in developing countries: an exploration of policy options. World Bank, Washington.

Riddell, A., 1989a. A multilevel analysis of school effectiveness in Zimbabwe: a challenge to prevailing theories and methodology. *Comparative Education Review* 33, 4, 481–97.

Riddell, A., 1989b. Response to Heyneman. *Comparative Education Review* 33, 4, 505–6.

Rivkin, S., Hanushek, E., Kain, J., 2005. Teachers, schools and academic achievement. *Econometrica* 73, 417–58.

Runciman, W., 1969. Relative deprivation – attitudes to class and status inequality in England. In: Heller, C. (Ed.) *Structural Social Inequality: A Reader in Comparative Social Stratification*. Macmillan, Basingstoke.

Sahlberg, P., 2011. *Finnish Lessons*. Teachers College Press, New York.

Sandoval-Hernandez, A., Bosco, E., 2010. The relationship between national development and the effects of school and student characteristics on education achievement: a cross national comparison. Paper presented at the annual meeting of the International Association for the Evaluation of Educational Achievement, Bangkok, August.

Schiefelbein, E., Farrell, J., 1982. *Eight Years of Their Lives*. International Development Research Center, Ottawa.

Shils, E., 1981. *Tradition*. University of Chicago Press, Chicago.

Simmons, J., Alexander, L., 1978. The determinants of school achievement in developing countries: a review of research. *Economic Development and Cultural Change* 26, January, 341–58.

Smith, M., 1972. Equality of educational opportunity: the basic findings reconsidered. In: Mosteller, F. and Moynihan, D.P. (Eds.) *On Equality of Educational Opportunity*. Vintage, New York.

Stodolsky, S., 1997. *The Subject Matters: Classroom Activity in Math and Social Studies*. University of Chicago Press, Chicago.

Summers, A., Wolfe, B., 1977. Do schools make a difference? *American Economic Review* 67, 639–52.

Theisen, G., Achola, P., Boakari, F., 1983. The underachievement of cross-national studies of achievement. *Comparative Education Review* 27, 1, 46–68.

Wosessmann, L., Ludemann, E., Schuetz, G., West, M., 2009. *School Accountability, Autonomy, and Choice Around the World*. Edward Elgar, Cheltenham.

Xuehui, A., Hannum, E., Sargent, T., 2007. Teaching quality and student outcomes: academic achievement and educational engagement in rural Northwest China. *China: An International Journal* 5, 2, 309–34.

Zumbach, D., 2010. *The Heyneman-Loxley Effect in Sub-Saharan Africa: School Quality, Socio-Economic Status and National Economic Development (in German)*. Center for Comparative and International Studies, University of Zurich.

13

NUTRITION IN INTERNATIONAL EDUCATION AND DEVELOPMENT DEBATES

The impact of school feeding[1]

Lesley Drake, Carmen Burbano and Donald Bundy

Education, health and nutrition interventions

The reciprocal relationship between education, health and nutrition has been recognized for many years: improvements in education are linked to improvements in health, and improvements in health are linked to improvements in learning (Vince-Whitman et al. 2001; Simeon 1998; Semba et al. 2008; Bundy 2011). These relationships have become starker with the success of Education for All efforts, which have been very successful in increasing access to school but less effective in enhancing learning outcomes. Part of the challenge now is that the poorest children and those least likely to access education are also those who suffer most from ill health and hunger and are less able to learn as a result. While traditionally the health sector utilised the school as a platform to deliver interventions that improve health outcomes, there is now increased recognition of the importance of improving educational outcomes with health interventions, particularly school feeding. Providing a meal at school can act as a magnet to get children, especially girls, into the classroom, and continuing provision of daily school meals can keep children in school, which supports achievement of their educational goals.

School feeding programmes support families in securing education for their children, especially girls who are often differentially excluded. If combined with school health interventions such as fortification, supplementation, deworming and/or nutrition education, school meals can further contribute to a child's readiness to learn and their ability to participate in their own educational process. Thus, school feeding promotes the development of human capital by influencing education and health. This in turn helps to break the intergenerational cycle of hunger and poverty (Alderman and Bundy 2011). For example, the odds of having a stunted child decreased by about four to five percent for every additional year of formal education achieved by mothers (Semba et al. 2008).

It is for this reason that at the High Level Meeting of Education for All in Addis Ababa in February 2010, participants urged, "Education For All Partners [should] intensify efforts to support initiatives targeted at the most marginalised, such as cash transfers, school health and school feeding, scholarships and gender-specific-interventions" (Bundy et al. 2013). Furthermore, school health and nutrition interventions have been recognised in addressing the Millennium Development Goals of universal basic education and gender equality in educational access. In order to achieve these goals, it is essential that even the poorest children, who suffer most from ill health and hunger, are able to attend school and learn while there (Bundy 2011).

The role of school feeding in supporting the Education for All efforts is further emphasised through internationally agreed frameworks such as the FRESH (Focusing Resources on Effective School Health) framework. FRESH was launched at the World Education Forum in Dakar, Senegal, in 2000 by the United Nations Educational, Scientific and Cultural Organisation; the World Health Organisation (WHO); the United Nations Children's Fund (UNICEF); the World Bank; the United Nations World Food Programme (WFP); The Partnership for Child Development (PCD) and other partners and was included as a component of the effort to achieve Education for All (UNESCO 2000). The FRESH framework specifically highlights the importance of implementing four elements together in all schools: effective school health and nutrition policies; a safe and sanitary school environment with potable water; skills-based health education; and school-based health and nutrition services, such as school feeding and deworming. Importantly, this consensus framework was a clear policy statement that good health and nutrition were prerequisites for good education, and the adoption of the framework by the participating countries was followed by a progressive increase in the quality and quantity of school health and school feeding programmes: when the FRESH framework was launched in Dakar in 2000 only four percent of sub-Saharan African countries had school health and nutrition policies that covered all four areas defined in the framework; but following the High Level Meeting of Education for All in Addis Ababa in 2010, this was reported to have risen to 100 percent, although the quality and coverage varied between programmes (Bundy et al. 2013).

School feeding programmes are both more expensive and more complex than school health programmes but potentially provide multiple benefits beyond education outcomes, including nutrition and social safety nets (Alderman and Bundy 2011). Perhaps for these reasons, adoption of school feeding programmes in Africa has been slower than for school health programmes. An important step-up in the quality and quantity of programmes followed the joint publication by WFP and the World Bank Group on Rethinking School Feeding (Bundy et al. 2009), which summarised the evidence that school health and school feeding programmes have multiple benefits: they constitute a mechanism to reach the most vulnerable, provide income support to families through the provision of food, contribute to learning by increasing children's access to education, and maintain children's nutritional status and overall health. School feeding programmes therefore act as a safety net in the short term to children and their families and constitute an attractive long-term social protection investment (Drake et al. 2014). If combined with local purchase of food, school feeding programmes can also help to stimulate local economies and benefit smallholder farmers, increasing their access to markets and their livelihoods. However, the causal interaction is not simple, so school feeding programmes require careful design and high standards to be effective.

Current state of school feeding

The publication *State of School Feeding Worldwide 2013* (WFP 2013) provides the first global picture of school feeding and shows that school feeding is now present in almost every country in the world, with approximately 368 million schoolchildren, about one out of every five, receiving a meal at school every day. Following its publication, there has been sustained demand from high- and low-income countries for evidence-based guidance in this area. The publication showed that there are marked differences between programmes in high-, middle- and low-income countries, which indicate that the income level of a country is associated with both the size and the level of consolidation of the school feeding programmes into national policy (WFP 2013).

In high-income and upper-middle-income countries, school feeding has been around for a long time, often dating back to the middle of the twentieth century, and it is an established industry to improve education as only one of its outcomes (Nelson and Joao 2013; Nelson 2013; Bundy et al. 2013). However, there is a renewed interest in school feeding in many high-income countries due in part to the need to address issues with overweight children and obesity and the need for a growing understanding of the wider role that food can play in health, academic achievement and health inequalities. New evidence (Waters et al. 2011) suggests that well-designed school health and school feeding programmes can usefully contribute to the pre- vention of obesity – one of the few interventions shown prospectively to do so. In many coun- tries, new standards have been introduced that aim to limit total energy in meals and improve the nutritional balance of foods offered (WFP 2013).

In these countries, free school meals are generally integrated within social protection pro- grammes that are targeted to individual children on the basis of vulnerability and means-based indicators. Children not considered at risk normally pay for the meal, though often at subsi- dised cost (Bundy et al. 2009). Programmes in high- and upper-middle-income countries are generally more established than programmes in low-income countries and have consolidated regulatory frameworks and stronger institutionalisation. For example, these countries often have mechanisms for recovering costs from better-off families and using this income to support the cost of feeding those from vulnerable backgrounds (Gelli and Daryanani 2013; WFP 2013). Also, as countries become wealthier, costs for school feeding constitute a much smaller relative pro- portion of the investment in education, typically around 10 to 20 percent (Bundy et al. 2011).

While there are large variations in the scale and coverage of school feeding programmes, the most extensive coverage exists in high- and middle-income countries, as most countries that can afford to provide food for their schoolchildren do so (Nelson and Joao 2013; Nelson 2013). However, where the need is greatest in terms of hunger, poverty and poor social indicators, the programmes tend to be the smallest, often targeted to the most food-insecure regions. An estimated 49 percent of schoolchildren in middle-income countries receive free school meals, compared to 18 percent in low-income countries (WFP 2013).

In low-income countries, programmes have a tendency to be limited in geographical scope, reflecting the availability of resources. Programmes have traditionally been targeted on the basis of food insecurity, and today there is also a growing trend to target areas with the greatest educational need. Some school feeding programmes combine onsite feeding with take-home rations to vulnerable children, such as girls in areas with large gender inequality in education and social contexts or vulnerable children in the context of HIV (human immunodeficiency virus). Take-home rations can be more finely targeted, can give higher value transfers, and have lower administrative costs yet apparently result in increases in enrolment on a similar scale to in-school meal programmes. Thus, from a social protection point of view, and depending on context, they may be preferred to in-school meal programmes. Take-home rations are considered particularly appropriate when providing support to orphans and vulnerable children (Fiszbein et al. 2009). However, take-home rations may not contribute so directly to improved cognition and learning outcomes when compared to school meals targeted at individual children.

School feeding programmes in low-income countries have less consolidation in national policy frameworks than in high-income countries and usually have not introduced the ele- ment of cost recovery. Furthermore, they can exhibit exceptionally large variation in cost, with opportunities for cost containment (Gelli and Daryanani 2013; Bundy et al. 2013). Benchmark estimates suggest that school feeding per child should represent some 10 to 15 percent of the cost of primary education for that child, based on data across a wide range of gross domestic products per capita (Bundy et al. 2009). Many low-income countries have achieved a similar cost ratio, but there are some remarkable exceptions where school feeding can be twice the per capita cost of education – a clearly unsustainable situation and one that is often a result of inappropriate external influences on investment. This suggests a role for development partners in supporting low-income countries through a transition towards programme frameworks that are more effective and sustainable (WFP 2013).

Furthermore, in low-income countries, school feeding programmes often rely on external funding and implementation (WFP 2013). About 83 percent of school feeding expenditures in low-income countries originates from donors, compared to five percent in middle-income countries. In high-income countries, expenditures originate almost exclusively from national budgets. However, poor countries tend to transition from externally supported projects to nationally owned programmes. The main preconditions for the transition to sustainable national school feeding programmes are mainstreaming school feeding into national policies and plans, especially education sector plans; identifying national sources of financing; and expanding national implementation capacity (Bundy et al. 2009).

An analysis of school feeding costs has shown that national governments in low-income countries are increasing their investments in school feeding, showing a rise of 12 percent in 4 years, from 6 percent in 2008 to 18 percent in 2012 (WFP 2013). As the wealth of countries increases, the cost of school feeding compared to the cost of education decreases, which results in school feeding becoming relatively more affordable. School feeding costs, on average, 68 percent of education costs in low-income countries, 24 percent of education costs in lower-middle-income countries and 11 percent of education costs in upper-middle-income countries (Gelli and Daryanani 2013; WFP 2013).

A recent compilation of 14 country case studies of actual national programmes (Drake et al. 2014) shows the variety of approaches that have proven effective and clearly demonstrates that there is no 'one size fits all' for school feeding programmes. Different approaches can even coexist within the same country, for example, where programme implementation is owned by decentralised institutions or where external agencies are complementing the national programme. Programmes have evolved and adjusted over time, often quite rapidly, demonstrating school feeding to be a dynamic intervention area where learning and adaptation are ongoing (Drake et al. 2014).

School feeding and nutritional outcomes

School feeding programmes, when designed with a nutritional objective, can enhance children's nutritional and health status, contributing to educational achievement, productivity and other outcomes over the lifecycle. When properly designed, school meals can provide at least 30 to 45 percent of the international recommended daily allowances of energy and micronutrients established by the FAO/WHO/UNU for schoolchildren. In particular, school feeding can play an important role in addressing deficiencies in micronutrients that are critical for children's cognitive development. While the prevalence of these deficiencies vary across regions and countries, the most critical in low-income countries are iron, vitamin A and iodine. Increasing iron intake to meet international recommended levels in particular has been a priority in order to reduce anemia, of which the adverse impacts on cognition and learning are well-established (Gratham-McGregor and Ani 2001; McCann and Ames 2007).

School feeding programmes typically take one of two approaches to help children meet recommended daily intakes of micronutrients. In some countries, programmes include multifortified foods (i.e., adding micronutrients such as iron or vitamin A to foods at the processing stage to enhance their nutritional value) or micronutrient powders (MNPs). Sachets of MNPs include an assortment of vitamins and minerals in powder form that can be sprinkled on cooked meals and enhance their micronutrient value. For example, in Uganda, the provision of both school meals and take-home rations that were fortified to meet daily requirements for iron and other micronutrients was associated with declines in anemia prevalence (Adelman et al. 2008). In South Africa, a randomised, controlled trial of fortified biscuits with children aged 6 to 11 years showed increased levels of vitamin A, iodine and serum ferritin and lower prevalence of anemia (van Stuijvenberg et al. 1999).[2] In Kenya, a randomised, controlled trial with children aged three to eight years showed improved indicators of iron status from iron-fortified whole maize flour (Andang'o et al. 2007). While including fortified foods in school feeding programmes presents some logistical challenges, it can be cost-effective.

In the short term, school feeding programmes can provide multifortified foods or MNPs in order to meet a nutrition objective. As a longer-term strategy, however, efforts can be undertaken to substitute multifortified foods and MNPs with micronutrient-rich, diverse foods including fresh fruits and vegetables, meat and dairy products. The Ghana School Feeding Programme (GSFP), which was launched in 2005, is an example of a programme that seeks to provide meals with diverse, locally available foods. The box below presents an overview of the GSFP. Less evidence has been generated on the impact of diversified school meals on nutrition and education outcomes, although several studies from Kenya suggest that diversifying meals by inclusion of animal source foods can lead to improved cognition for children (Neumann et al. 2003; Whaley et al. 2003).

Box 13.1. The Ghana School Feeding Programme

School enrolment and attendance

The Government of Ghana promoted access to free universal basic education as enshrined in the 1992 Constitution of Ghana. However, in 2011/12 the primary gross enrolment ratio was 96.5, and projections suggested that it may not reach the target of 107 in 2015. Primary completion rates are rising but at slightly below the rate required to remain to ensure a 100 percent completion rate by 2015. The completion rate for girls remains three percentage points lower than for boys, but the gender gap is narrowing. In terms of quality education, the National Education Assessment of English and Maths at P3 and P6 level shows a higher proficiency in English than Maths. The Ministry of Education concedes that quality improvements are not occurring at the levels expected.

The school feeding programme

The history of school feeding programmes in Ghana dates back to the 1950s when pupils of several Catholic primary and middle schools were given take-home rations of food aid. The objective, as in many cases, was to improve the nutritional status of schoolchildren and increase school enrolment and retention. Over time, WFP and Catholic Relief Services became two leading agencies providing programmes on school feeding in the country, focusing on the North due to its high incidence of poverty and food insecurity.

In response to the New Partnership for Africa's Development (NEPAD) recommendation to adopt the Home Grown School Feeding (HGSF) concept, the Government of Ghana launched a nationally owned HGSF programme: the Ghana School Feeding Programme (GSFP). This was piloted in 10 primary schools in 2005. Schoolchildren are provided with a cooked midday meal. A typical ration breakdown consists of 150 grams of cereal (rice or maize) with 40 grams of legumes (beans or peas) and 10 grams of vegetable oil per child per day. This provides slightly above the 30 percent recommended dietary allowance (approximately 760 kilocalories). In 2013, the cost per child per day was 0.50 Ghana Cedis (approximately US$0.23). The GSFP is expected to have reached 1,739,357 schoolchildren in 5,000 primary schools for the school year 2013/14 (Gandah 2014).

The GSFP was designed as a strategy to increase domestic food production, household incomes and food security in deprived communities (Government of Ghana 2006). Coordination and implementation are undertaken by the GSFP National Secretariat, with programme oversight provided by the Ministry of Local Government and Rural Development.

Source: Adapted from Drake et al. 2014.

The transition to school meals that incorporate diverse, locally available foods raises a number of challenges, namely how to combine foods into meals in order to meet international recommendations while meeting budget constraints. A web-based menu planning tool has been developed to address these two concerns in order to promote the transition. With this tool, programme implementers can design menus using locally available ingredients and view the nutrient value and cost of the menu per child. Quantities of ingredients can be adjusted, and foods can be added or removed in order to increase nutrient value or reduce costs.

More research is needed on the benefits of school feeding on the health and nutritional status of preschool children and adolescents, particularly girls. These benefits can be generated through spillover effects or in the use of school feeding as a platform to deliver other interventions. For example, in Uganda, the school feeding programme had spillover benefits for the preschool siblings of schoolchildren who were the primary beneficiaries of the programme (Adelman et al. 2008). School feeding can in some contexts provide a platform to meet the specific nutritional needs of adolescent girls through provision of meals with folic acid or higher levels of iron.

Linking with local agriculture

Transitioning from external aid to nationally owned programmes in many cases requires food to be sourced through alternative mechanisms. Locally sourced food, through many context-specific school feeding models, has been used by many countries in the transition to nationally owned programmes. As school feeding programmes run for a fixed number of days a year (on average 180) and normally have a predetermined food basket, they provide the opportunity to benefit smallholder farmers and producers by generating a stable, structured, and predictable demand through the school food basket, thereby building the market and the enabling systems around it (Gelli et al. 2010). Thus, school feeding programmes that purchase from smallholder farmers have the potential to increase household income and reduce food insecurity. Locally purchased food can also potentially help increase the dietary diversity of children by including fresh, perishable foods such as fruits, vegetables or animal protein and reducing the amount of processed foods in the basket.

The structured demand from the school feeding market can provide the incentive for small-holder farmers to invest in quantity and quality of production. It is these same farmers who will be able to send their children to school, where they will receive a nutritious school meal and where they will increase their educational attainment and their ability to contribute as active cit-izens within their community. In addition, as programmes expand and become nationally owned and part of the national policy framework, the size and stability of the demand will also increase. This increased market security could encourage increased inputs into productivity-enhancing technologies and practices that will improve local agricultural production for smallholder farm-ers, many of whom are women. This in turn will have broader impacts on the local economy. Jobs and profits may be created not only for farmers but for those involved in the transportation, processing and preparation of food along the school-feeding value chain. Off-farm investment may in turn further stimulate productivity and agricultural employment, producing a 'virtuous cycle' benefitting long-term food security and improving welfare in rural households (Sumberg and Sabates-Wheeler 2011). Therefore, money is invested into the economic base while at the same time the next generation of farmers are becoming better equipped and informed. The evidence on the impact on smallholder farmers is being strengthened through a number of impact evaluations currently underway. These potential economic benefits from agriculture are additional to the education, nutrition and social protection benefits and could contribute very significantly to the overall cost-effectiveness of school feeding programmes.

Box 13.2. The O'Meals Programme, Osun State, Nigeria

The Osun Elementary School Feeding and Health Programme (O'Meals) is a leading example of an effective HGSF programme providing hot, fresh and nutritious meals using ingredients procured from local smallholder farmers. With over 252,000 school children being fed a nutritiously balanced hot meal every school day, and employment generated for caterers, farmers and traders, the pro-gramme has grown significantly since its redesign in April 2012.

Within a month of the programme launch, school enrolment increased by approximately 25 percent. The O'Meals programme promotes and boosts income-generation opportunities, par-ticularly for women. To date, the programme has economically empowered over 3,000 previously unemployed women by hiring them as food vendors to serve nutritious meals to pupils during the school term.

The Osun State Government with the Ministry of Agriculture and Food Security in collabo-ration with the private sector has invested N253 million (US$1.5 million) to implement the Osun Fisheries Out-Growers Production Scheme (OFOPS). This scheme helps to improve the livelihood of 2,000 fish out-growers for mass fish production in Osun State. Each week, these fish out-growers produce approximately five metric tonnes of fish for the O'Meals programme. In tandem with this, 100 factory workers are involved in the fish processing. In the first three months of the project, OFOPS generated a profit of N2.5 million (US$15,330).

The Osun Broilers Out-Growers Production Scheme (OBOPS) initiative seeks to boost the chicken production in Osun State to enable it to supply 15,000 chickens and 252,000 eggs required every week by the O'Meals programme. Similar to the fisheries model, the OBOPS programme contracts out the growing of chickens to a network of over 2,000 smallholder farmers by supplying them with 3.1 million day-old chicks, leading to the production of 4.4 million kilograms of broiler meat valued at N1.7 million for the O'Meals programme.

The Osun State Government designed the Cocoyam Rebirth Programme with the joint aims of promoting the nutritional benefits of cocoyam (rich in vitamin B6, magnesium iron and protein) and improving the income of cocoyam farmers. Over 1,000 cocoyam farmers have been trained in modern methods of cultivating cocoyam, and Osun State has provided funding for planting materials and fertilisers.

The Osun Youth Empowerment Scheme (O-YES) was designed by the Osun State Government to engage and include youth in the economic opportunities created by the O'Meals programme. Over 300 O-YES youth have received training and loans of N100,000 (US$623,000) to act as cocoyam intermediaries between the cocoyam farmers and food vendors.

Source: Adapted from PCD 2014.

School feeding and obesity

In high- and middle-income countries, and increasingly in the wealthier regions of low-income countries, the epidemic of overweight, obesity and type 2 diabetes is a matter of growing concern (Nelson and Joao 2013; Nelson 2013; Rito et al. 2013). The increasing global prevalence of noncommunicable diseases in low- and middle-income countries is attributed to the nutrition transition, in which traditional diets are replaced by Western diets characterised by consumption of energy-dense, processed foods (Popkin and Gordon-Larsen 2004). The diet of children and adolescents has been causally implicated in this epidemic, and the potential role of school feeding programmes has attracted scrutiny in this context.

A recent Cochrane Review examined the effects of obesity on behaviour change, physical activity and the wider obesogenic environment and concluded that there was evidence that some child obesity prevention programmes resulted in reduced body mass index (BMI) (Waters et al. 2011). This was particularly effective for programmes aimed at children who are in the primary school system (aged 6 to 12 years). A broad range of components were employed in these studies, and the authors concluded it was difficult to disentangle which aspects contributed most (see also Kristjansson et al. 2007). Overall, the recent study concludes that school-based interventions that influence the school curriculum, provided support to teachers and improved the nutritional quality of school food were effective in reducing BMI. Importantly, there was no evidence to suggest any adverse effect of the school feeding interventions. The school meal studies are among the very few prospective studies that have demonstrated effective interventions to reduce obesity; nevertheless, there remains a need for further robust studies with long-term follow-up and cost-effective analysis.

These studies suggest that school feeding programmes do not contribute to obesity and that if properly designed can serve as effective preventive measures (see also Pearce, Wood and Nelson 2013; Rito et al. 2013; Harrison et al. 2011). Some policy conclusions from these studies are: the need to encourage healthy diets by imposing taxes on unhealthy food and subsidising locally grown healthy food; the establishment of healthier school meal programmes (which may have the added benefit of improving school attendance); and the institutionalisation of school-based programmes to promote healthy lifestyles.

Linking with broader school health and nutrition programmes

Health and nutrition interventions that are part of cross-sectoral policies and programmes can help reinforce the benefits of school feeding programmes in terms of nutrition and education and should be strongly promoted. The framework for FRESH specifically highlights the importance of implementing four core elements together in all schools: effective school health and nutrition policies; a safe and sanitary school environment; skills-based health education and health and nutrition interventions, such as school feeding and deworming (UNESCO 2000). Since this inclusion of school health in the strategic thinking of the World Education Forum, some of the school-based options for addressing health and nutrition conditions have been implemented by an increasing number of low-income countries as part of a systematic approach to school health and nutrition (Vince-Whitman et al. 2001; Bundy 2011).

Evidence suggests that the integration of deworming into school feeding programmes has the potential to augment educational benefits. Deworming has significant impacts on school participation; a large, randomised, controlled trial in Kenya found that treatment increased school participation by seven percent, amounting to a 25 percent decline in total absence (Miguel and Kremer 2004). An earlier comprehensive review of studies found that schoolchildren infected with worms performed poorly in tests of cognitive function (Watkins and Pollitt 1997). Results from additional randomised, controlled trials show that those heavily infected with worms showed improvements in cognitive function after deworming treatment (Nokes et al. 1992; Grigorenko et al. 2006).

Children benefit disproportionally from deworming because infection with common roundworms and bilharzia tends to be most prevalent and intense in children of school age (Bundy 2005). While it is difficult to detect changes in growth in schoolchildren because growth has slowed down at that age, there is evidence of some catch-up growth through school meals documented in systemic reviews (Kristjansson et al. 2007). There is also evidence of significant reduction in anemia with deworming (Gulani et al. 2007; Brooker, Hotez and Bundy 2008). Because worm infections affect some 500 million schoolchildren, deworming can make an additional nutritional contribution if included in a school feeding package. Programmatic evidence showed that deworming through schools is safe, cheap, and remarkably cost-effective (J-PAL 2005; Bleakley 2007). Intervention studies have also found that children with poor nutritional status benefit the most from deworming (Simeon, Grantham-McGregor and Wong 1995).

Iron deficiency anemia is also linked with poor cognitive abilities in children (Grantham-McGregor and Ani 2001). Experimental studies with school-age children have shown that iron supplementation improves performance on memory, visual/motor coordination and concentration tests as well as on school exams (Soemantri, Pollitt and Kim 1985; Seshadri and Gopaldas 1989). Even though the improvements were large (approximately 0.5 standard deviations in some cases), the appropriateness of delivering iron supplements along with deworming should be considered because there is an interrelationship between schistosomes, hookworms, anemia and vitamin A. In KwaZulu-Natal, South Africa, the impact of multiple micronutrient fortification, including iron, iodine and beta-carotene (a precursor to vitamin A), was studied. Children who received fortified biscuits for 43 weeks demonstrated improved short-term memory compared with children in the control group (van Stuijvenberg et al. 1999). More research is needed on multiple micronutrient fortification as performance on other tests was mixed, though both supplementation and fortification are very low-cost interventions (Bundy et al. 2009).

Additional complementary interventions, such as water treatment, hygiene and sanitary interventions have been shown to improve child health outcomes inclusive of absenteeism, infections, knowledge, attitudes, and practices and adoption of point-of-use water treatment

(Joshi and Amadi 2013). However, implemented alongside school feeding and neglected tropical disease (NTD) control programmes, the benefits are multiplied through a more comprehensive NTD control package and, in turn, greater nutritional benefits attained through the school feeding programme.

The interventions mentioned above may not be relevant everywhere but in many communities and countries using schools to promote good health and avoid hunger may make a crucial contribution to Education for All (Bundy 2011).

Partnerships

By 2009, the global community began to understand the broader benefits of school feeding in response to the 2008 food, fuel and financial crises and developed an evolved understanding of school feeding as a social safety net contributing to national social protection and development goals, including learning and educational achievement.

This new vision for school feeding has been strengthened by several partnerships at global, regional and country levels and the development of new consensus tools.

At the *global* level, the FRESH partnership drove forward the move for multisectoral collaboration in school health and nutrition. One tripartite partnership created in 2009 among WFP, the World Bank and PCD has focused on improving the quality of programmes in low-income countries by applying a more rigorous, evidence-based approach to school feeding and providing coordinated support to the countries that are in the process of transitioning to national ownership. The joint research agenda, established in 2009, has strengthened the knowledge base and led to the development of practical tools and guidance as well as publications such as *Rethinking School Feeding* (Bundy et al. 2009), the *State of School Feeding Worldwide 2013* (WFP 2013) and this chapter, amongst others. The tripartite partnership has also been central in moving forward the Systems Approach for Better Education Results (SABER) tool for systematic policy analysis of school health and school feeding interventions. Led by the World Bank education sector, SABER was developed in partnership with WFP, PCD, UNICEF and other partners and has been used in more than 20 countries in Africa. The SABER approach is intended to assist countries as they work towards a transition to more sustainable programmes (WFP 2013).

Recently, partners such as the Government of Brazil (through the WFP Centre for Excellence Against Hunger), FAO and the Global Partnership for Education have also been instrumental in strengthening support to countries. There is growing recognition that country-to-country support – in the form of south-south collaboration and other types of collaboration – is important and that development partners have a role to play in facilitating these connections. Moving forward, other partners, such as Russia and China, will continue to shape and influence global thinking and practice on school feeding: the Russian Federation has reintroduced school feeding and is working with its neighbours to support similar interventions, while school feeding in China is a key element of the US$5 billion per year national strategy to support the development of poor children. The Global Partnership for Education was established in 2002 as a 'global compact' between low-income and donor countries and has provided a clear mechanism for coordination among multilateral agencies, donor countries, the private sector, NGOs and countries to allocate resources according to national priorities in education. In recent years, it has provided approximately US$30 million in financing for school feeding (WFP 2013).

At the *regional* level, the clearest formal efforts have been established in the coordination mechanisms between partners and countries. For example, in 2003, African Governments included locally sourced school feeding programmes in the Comprehensive Africa Agriculture Development Programme (CAADP), a programme of NEPAD. That same year, NEPAD, in collaboration with WFP and the Millennium Hunger Task Force, launched a pilot Home Grown School Feeding and Health Programme designed to link school feeding to agricultural development through the purchase and use of locally and domestically produced food (NEPAD 2003). Strategic leadership from NEPAD guided governments in sub-Saharan Africa to include HGSF as a key intervention within CAADP. The resulting framework for national school feeding implementation through locally sourced foods has been further strengthened through subregional school health and nutrition Networks, consisting of members officially appointed by the different ministers of education. These Networks, based within Regional Economic Communities (e.g., the Economic Community of West African States and the East African Community), provide a platform for sharing good practice and operational experience in school health and nutrition and have proven key to building capacity and developing consensus on good practice in the Africa subregions. Similar school health and nutrition Networks exist in Southeast Asia (the Southeast Asian Ministers of Education Organisation) and Latin America (LA-RAE).

At the *country* level, effective coordination of partners is often achieved when partner activities are framed within national policies and resulting action plans. However, in many countries school feeding features in more than one sectoral plan and is discussed by several partner groups, leading to a lack of coordination, confusion and inefficiencies. Despite these challenges, there are many examples where governments, technical partners and donors have achieved results through successful partnerships (WFP 2013).

The Bill and Melinda Gates Foundation has supported local agricultural production and its link to school feeding through its portfolio of grants in the 'structured demand' area – a cluster of organisations supporting the connection between smallholder farmer production and demand-based programmes such as school feeding. Focused primarily in Africa, each organisation has a role to play along the supply chain. The Alliance for a Green Revolution in Africa, for example, supports the supply by financing the provision of inputs, credit and training; WFP's project 'Purchase for Progress' works on market access; and PCD and the Dutch NGO, the Netherlands Development Organisation, provides support for school feeding looking at issues related to procurement, governance and research. In total, the Gates Foundation has invested almost half a billion dollars in support of structured demand platforms, including school feeding.

While these partnerships have been formed at the global level, the greatest successes are being seen in-country – where structured demand learning groups are coordinating activities in line with government strategies and plans that include all partners.

Conclusions

The paradigm shift for both education and the health sectors in recognising the importance of health and nutrition on attaining education outcomes marks an increased recognition of the child being central to learning and that excellent education services alone will not achieve learning goals if children are sick, tired and hungry. It also marks a new focus by the health sector on how the improved health and nutrition of a child affects cognition, learning and education outcomes. There are additional complexities, however, since the school-based health and nutrition interventions, such as school meals, can also play an important role as social safety net programmes that help ensure that the poorest children, especially girls, have access to education.

These linkages between the health and nutrition of a child and educational outcomes, along with cognition and learning, have become evident and reinforced both by the global community and national governments. Multisectoral partnerships at all levels (global, regional and in-country) have been critical in supporting the creation of an enabling environment where comprehensive health, nutrition and education programmes can effectively address the needs of children.

Simultaneously, country governments are investing in nutrition and health interventions that have broader educational (as well as agricultural, social and economic) benefits. School feeding is a perfect example of this, where global investment has now reached over US$50 billion per year, feeding over 368 million children (WFP 2013); however, there are still considerable variations in the scale and coverage of national programmes.

Investment in school feeding by low-income countries, while more recent, is growing. Many of these governments are increasing investment because of an increased recognition of the multisectoral benefits from the programmes, particularly when the school feeding programmes link with local agricultural production. However, while the documented benefits of school feeding on nutrition indicators are well understood in practice, countries have struggled to reach the high standards that are needed, particularly with regards to guaranteeing minimum requirements of energy and reaching the micronutrient standards.

One impediment to the adoption and expansion of school feeding programmes has been the perception that this is a high-cost intervention in terms of education outcomes alone. An important shift in perspective has followed the recognition that there are multiple benefits from the programmes: not only for education but also potentially for health, nutrition, social protection and the development of rural agricultural economies. The cost-effectiveness of the programmes can change markedly when the returns across the fiscal space are considered together.

When addressing the nutrition and hunger of schoolchildren, based on country context and need, there are three intervention approaches that many national school feeding programmes seek to combine: interventions that address nutrition secondarily through health improvement, such as deworming; interventions that address specific and direct nutrient input, such as micronutrient supplementation; and finally interventions that seek to provide more or better food, such as school meals.

There is compelling evidence that all three of these intervention approaches, depending on the country context and need, are effective in improving education outcomes, both in terms of learning and access. For example, the effects are often most apparent for children with the worst indicators initially, especially for girls, and there have also been concerns that feeding schoolchildren would contribute to the obesity epidemic in some settings, but evidence from trials suggests the reverse – that appropriate school health curricula and improved nutritional quality of school food are among the few interventions that actually contribute to obesity prevention. However, this also echoes the importance of programmes responding to the nutritional challenges of populations in different settings.

Tools, technical support and multisectoral partnerships at all levels (global, regional and country) are increasingly available and strongly needed to enable governments to make informed decisions about programme design, menu design and complementary school health programmes.

Almost all countries have in place a school health and school feeding programme. The priority now is to ensure that these health and nutrition interventions effectively impact the development and education outcomes of children.

Notes

1 The authors were supported in the writing and coordination of this chapter by Brie McMahon, who provided technical input, and Carmen Aldinger, who collated the evidence. Additional support was provided by Daniel Mumuni, Josephine Kiamba and Charlotte Broyd. This chapter was internally edited by Anastasia Said.
2 The ferritin blood test measures the level of ferritin, which is a protein that stores iron, in the body. Low levels of ferritin indicate iron deficiency, which may lead to anemia.

References

Adelman, S., Alderman, H., Gilligan, D.O., Konde-Lule J., 2008. *The Impact of Alternative Food for Education Programs on Learning Achievement and Cognitive Development in Northern Uganda.* IFPRI, Washington.

Alderman, H., Bundy, D.A.P., 2011. School feeding programmes and development: are we framing the question correctly? *World Bank Research Observer* 27, 2, 204–221.

Andang'o, P.E.A., Osendarp, S.J.M., Ayah, R., West, C.E., Mwaniki, D.L., Wolf, C.A.D., Kraaijenhagen, R., Kok, F.J., Verhoef, H., 2007. Efficacy of iron-fortified whole maize flour on iron status of schoolchildren in Kenya: a randomized controlled trial. *Lancet* 369, 9575, 1799–1806.

Bleakley, H., 2007. Disease and development: evidence from hookworm eradication in the American South. *Quarterly Journal of Economics* 122, 1, 73–117.

Brooker, S., Hotez, P.J., Bundy, D.A.P., 2008. Hookworm-related anaemia among pregnant women: a systematic review. *PLoS Neglected Tropical Diseases* 2, 9, e291.

Bundy, D.A.P., 2005. School health and nutrition: policy and programs. *Food and Nutrition Bulletin* 26, 2 (Suppl 2), S186–192.

Bundy, D.A.P., 2011. *Rethinking School Health: A Key Component of Education for All.* World Bank, Washington.

Bundy, D.A.P., Burbano, C., Gelli, A., Risley, C., Neeser, K., 2011. On the transition to sustainability: an analysis of the costs of school feeding compared to the costs of primary education. *Food Nutrition Bulletin* 32, 3, 201–205.

Bundy, D.A.P., Burbano, C., Grosh, M., Gelli, A., Jukes, M.C.H., Drake, L.J., 2009. *Rethinking School Feeding: Social Safety Nets, Child Development, and the Education Sector.* World Bank, Washington.

Bundy, D.A.P., Drake, L.J., Burbano, C., 2013. School food, politics and child health. *Public Health and Nutrition* 16, 6, 1012–1019.

Drake, L.J.; Bundy, D.A.P., Burbano, C. et al., 2014. *Sourcebook on School Feeding.* PCD, London.

Fiszbein, A., Schady, N., Ferreira, F.H.G., Grosh, M., Kelleher, N., Olinto, P., Skoufias, E., 2009. *Conditional Cash Transfers: Reducing Present and Future Poverty.* World Bank, Washington.

Gandah, E.A., 2014. Personal communication (Ministry of Education Officer of the GSFP) via text to Getrude Ananse-Baiden, 27th June.

Gelli, A., Cavallero, A., Minervini, L., Mirabile, M., Molinas, L., Regnault de la Mothe, M., 2010. New benchmarks for costs and cost-efficiency for food provisions in schools in food insecure areas. *Food and Nutrition Bulletin* 32, 4, 324–332.

Gelli, A., Daryanani, R., 2013. Are school food programs in low-income settings sustainable? Insights on the costs of school feeding compared to investments in primary education. *Food and Nutrition Bulletin* 34, 3, 310–317.

Government of Ghana, 2006. *Ghana School Feeding Programme Document 2006–2010.* Ministry of Local Government and Rural Development, Accra.

Grantham-McGregor, S.M., Ani, C., 2001. A review of studies on the effect of iron deficiency on cognitive development in children. *Journal of Nutrition* 131, 2, 649S-668S.

Grigorenko, E.L., Sternberg, R.J., Jukes, M.C.H., Alcock, K., Lambo, J., Ngorosho, D., Nokes, C., Bundy, D.A.P., 2006. Effects of antiparasitic treatment on dynamically and statically tested cognitive skills over time. *Journal of Applied Developmental Psychology* 27, 6, 499–526.

Gulani, A., Nagpal, C., Osmond, C., Sachdev, H.P.S., 2007. Effect of administration of intestinal anthelminthic drugs on haemoglobin: systematic review of randomized controlled trials. *British Medical Journal* 334, 7603, 1095.

Harrison, F., Jennings, A., Jones, A., Welch, A., van Sluijs, E., Griffin, S., Cassidy, A., 2011. Food and drink consumption at school lunchtime: the impact of lunch type and contribution to overall intake in British 9–10-year old children. *Public Health Nutrition* 16, 6, 1132–1139.

HGSF, 2014. Menu Planner. PCD, London. http://www.hgsf-global.org/en/bank/menu-planner

Joshi, A., Amadi, C., 2013. Impact of water, sanitation, and hygiene interventions on improving health outcomes among school children. *Journal of Environmental and Public Health* 2013. doi:10.1155/2013/984626.

J-PAL (Abdul Latif Jameel Poverty Action Lab), 2005. Education: meeting the Millennium Development Goals. *Fighting Poverty: What Works?* 1.

Kristjansson, E.A., Robinson, V., Petticrew, M., MacDonald, B., Krasevec, J., Janzen, L., Greenhalgh, T., Wells, G., MacGowan, J., Farmer, A., Shea, B.J., Mayhew, A., Tugwell, P., 2007. School feeding for improving the physical and psychosocial health of disadvantaged elementary school children. *The Cochrane Database of Systematic Reviews* 1, CD004676.

McCann, J.C., Ames, B., 2007. An overview of evidence for a causal relation between iron deficiency during development and deficits in cognitive or behavioral function. *American Journal of Clinical Nutrition* 85, 4, 931–945.

Miguel, E., Kremer, M., 2004. Worms: identifying impacts on education and health in the presence of treatment externalities. *Econometrica* 72, 1, 159–217.

Nelson, M., 2013. School food cost–benefits: England. *Public Health Nutrition* 16, 6, 1006–1011.

Nelson, M., Joao B., 2013. School food research: building the evidence base for policy. *Public Health Nutrition* 16, 6, 958–967.

NEPAD, 2003. *The NEPAD Home Grown School Feeding Programme: A Concept.* NEPAD, Johannesburg.

Neumann, C., Bwibo, N., Murphy, S., Sigman, M., Whaley, S., Allen, L., Guthrie, D., Weiss, R., Demment, M., 2003. Animal source foods improve dietary quality, micronutrient status, growth and cognitive function in Kenyan school children: background, study design and baseline findings. *Journal of Nutrition* 11, 3491S–3949S.

Nokes, C., Grantham-McGregor, S.M., Sawyer, A.W., Cooper, E.S., Robinson, B.A., Bundy, D.A.P., 1992. Moderate to heavy infections of *Trichuris trichiura* affect cognitive function in Jamaican school children. *Parasitology* 104, 3, 539–547.

PCD, 2014. *O'Meals: Why It's More than Just Lunch.* PCD, London.

Pearce, J., Wood, L., Nelson, M., 2013. Lunchtime food and nutrient intakes of secondary-school pupils; a comparison of school lunches and packed lunches following the introduction of mandatory food-based standards for school lunch. *Public Health Nutrition* 16, 6, 1126–1131.

Popkin, B., Gordon-Larsen, P., 2004. The nutrition transition: worldwide obesity dynamics and their determinants. *International Journal of Obesity* 28, S2–S9.

Rito, A.I., Carvalhoa, M.A., Ramosa, C., Breda, J., 2013. Program Obesity Zero (POZ): a community-based intervention to address overweight primary-school children from five Portuguese municipalities. *Public Health Nutrition* 16, 6, 1043–1051.

Semba, R.D., de Pee, S., Sun, K., Sari, M., Akhter, N., Bloem, M.W., 2008. Effect of parental formal education on risk of child stunting in Indonesia and Bangladesh: a cross-sectional study. *Lancet* 371, 9609, 322–328.

Seshadri, S., Gopaldas, T., 1989. Impact of iron supplementation on cognitive functions in preschool and school-aged children: the Indian experience. *American Journal of Clinical Nutrition* 50, 3 Suppl, S675-S684.

Simeon, D.T., 1998. School feeding in Jamaica: a review of its evaluation. *American Journal of Clinical Nutrition* 67, 4, 790S-794S.

Simeon, D.T., Grantham-McGregor, S.M., Wong, M.S., 1995. Trichuris trichiura infection and cognition in children: results of a randomized clinical trial. *Parasitology* 110, 4, 457–464.

Soemantri, A.G., Pollitt, E., Kim, I., 1985. Iron deficiency anaemia and educational achievement. *American Journal of Clinical Nutrition* 42, 6, 1221–1228.

Sumberg, J., Sabates-Wheeler, R., 2011. Linking agricultural development to school feeding in sub-Saharan Africa: theoretical perspectives. *Food Policy* 36, 3, 341–349.

UNESCO, 2000. *The Dakar Framework for Action.* UNESCO, Paris.

Van Stuijvenberg, M.E., Kvalsvig, J.D., Faber, M., Kruger, M., Kenoyer, D.G., Benade, A.J.S., 1999. Effect of iron-, iodine-, and beta-carotene-fortified biscuits on the micronutrient status of primary school children: a randomized controlled trial. *American Journal of Clinical Nutrition* 69, 3, 497–503.

Vince-Whitman C., Aldinger C., Levinger B., Birdthistle, I., 2001. *Education for All 2000 Assessment: Thematic Studies: School Health and Nutrition.* UNESCO, Paris.

Waters, E., de Silva-Sanigorski, A., Hall, B.J., Brown, T., Campbell, K.J., Gao, Y., Armstrong, R., Prosser, L., Summerbell, D.C., 2011. Interventions for preventing obesity in children. *The Cochrane Database of Systematic Reviews* 12, CD001871.

Watkins, W.E., Pollitt, E., 1997. "Stupidity or worms": do intestinal worms impair mental performance? *Psychological Bulletin* 121, 2, 171–191.

Whaley, S., Sigman, M., Neumann, C., Bwibo, N., Guthrie, D., Weiss, R., Alber, S., Murphy, S., 2003. The impact of dietary intervention on the cognitive development of Kenyan school children. *Journal of Nutrition* 11, Suppl 2, 3965S-3971S.

WFP, 2013. *State of School Feeding Worldwide 2013.* WFP, Rome.

14

DOES EDUCATIONAL EXCLUSION EXPLAIN HEALTH DIFFERENTIALS AMONG CHILDREN?

An empirical analysis of children in Ethiopia using Young Lives data

Ricardo Sabates, Mariachiara Di Cesare and Barry Reilly

Introduction

Millions of children in less developed countries suffer from ill health and malnutrition. A recent report by UNICEF (2013) suggests that stunting, or low height for age, affects 165 million children under five, which represents 25% of children in this age category globally. Ill health and malnutrition trap children in a vicious developmental cycle, as the damage to a child's physical and cognitive development, especially during the first two years of life, is largely irreversible and carries major consequences for future educational success (Dewey and Begum 2011; Grantham-McGregor et al. 2007; Pridmore 2007). For instance, recent research with well-nourished six year olds from medium to high socioeconomic backgrounds reported a significant positive relationship between iron and folate intake and both total and nonverbal IQ (Arija et al. 2006). Deficiencies in iron and zinc have been associated with the impairment of neuropsychologic function and retardation of growth and development (Sandstead 2000). Other research suggests that sufficient B vitamin intake early in life is also important for the development of the central nervous system and thus later cognition (Bryan et al. 2004).

Notwithstanding the consequences of poor health and malnutrition for children's education, which include educational exclusion, lower daily attendance, and less efficient learning in school, there are also strong arguments to sustain the health benefits of education. Education can endow children with psychosocial instruments for adopting healthier behaviours, means for accessing health services and knowledge for understanding health information (Cutler and Lleras-Muney 2006). Education can also enrich children's personal resources such as self-esteem, self-efficacy, resilience and confidence, which are important mechanisms by which health benefits are generated (Bandura 1991; CSDH 2008). Children also increase their personal relations through education, and this yields important gains in terms of support received, changes in behaviour and general social integration, which are important determinants of health (Hammond 2003, 2004).

In comparison to the large body of research that links poor health to educational achievement in children (Glewwe and Miguel 2008), we know little about the effects of children's educational exclusion on their own health. We attempt to fill this void by examining how educational exclusion relates to health during childhood using longitudinal data from the Young Lives Study in Ethiopia. We focus on Ethiopia due to the significant proportion of children who suffer from malnutrition in that country, estimated at 44% of children under five years being stunted according to UNICEF (2013), and the substantial variation in educational access and exclusion. In particular, the gross enrolment rate in primary schools is around 75%, with completion rates for primary schooling reported at only 44% (UIS 2014). Our paper investigates the following central question: is educational exclusion responsible for disparities in health outcomes and, if so, how important is its contribution?

In order to conduct our investigation, we adopt a meaningful framework for educational exclusion developed by the Consortium for Research on Educational Access, Transitions and Equity (Lewin 2007). The *Zones of Exclusion Framework* differentiates between children who have never enrolled in school, those who dropped out, those enrolled with low attendance or low achievement, and those enrolled but with an age not appropriate for their grade compared to those who are age appropriate, attending schooling and achieving appropriate grades (Lewin 2007). This framework views educational access as a complex dimension incorporating not only progression and success but also dropout and achievement levels within the school system. The framework makes explicit the term for silent exclusion, which refers to children who are in education but who are not attending regularly, not performing and ultimately not learning.

Children in different zones of educational exclusion have the potential to acquire health benefits from their differential exposures to education. At the greatest level of educational exclusion, children who have never attended school should not receive any health benefits from education. Children who have dropped out of school retain the potential to gain some health benefits from their previous educational exposure. Children who are in silent exclusion, that is attending school irregularly, not learning and not progressing, may generate a limited amount of health benefit from their current education. Finally, children who are in education, attending regularly, learning and progressing have the greatest potential to benefit from their educational experience. Therefore, it is anticipated that a health gap will be observed for children with differential exposures to education of the types outlined above.

Differences in health status for children are not exclusively determined by education. It is well known that the child health gap is largely determined by circumstances during early childhood, including poor health and malnutrition, and by environmental factors that are strongly influenced by poverty and deprivation (Case, Fertig and Paxson 2005). Therefore, the key point of our research is to analyse if the observed average differences in health outcomes among children is a result of their differential exposure to education once we condition out the impact of differences in early childhood health, children's own characteristics and their exposure to poverty. In doing so, we measure whether the impact of previous health, children's characteristics and poverty on later health outcomes differ according to a child's degree of educational exclusion. To the best of our knowledge, there has been no study decomposing the child health gap in this way and focusing on the importance of educational exclusion when quantifying this gap.

Methods

Data and sample

Data for this paper are drawn from the Young Lives Longitudinal Study (YL), a 15-year study of childhood poverty in four developing countries including Ethiopia (Boyden 2006). The first round of data collection for YL occurred in 2002, with the second in 2007. The questionnaires were applied to two different cohorts of children in Ethiopia. The youngest cohort contained children aged between six and 17 months of age in 2002, hence they were born around the turn of the millennium. The oldest cohort comprised children aged seven to eight years of age in 2002. Our research exploits data from the first two rounds (2002 and 2007) and for the older cohort exclusively.

The way in which the Young Lives team selected children for the longitudinal study was based on a 'sentinel site surveillance' approach (Wilson, Huttly and Fenn 2006). Under this selection process, 20 of the poorest geographical areas were selected for the study, and 100 children within each area were selected. Children had to satisfy the age requirement to be part of the cohort for the Young Lives study. The geographical sites were selected based on poverty indicators, while children within each site were randomly selected (Wilson, Huttly and Fenn 2006). The sample as a whole is not nationally representative, but children living in selected households are representative of children from that cohort living within their geographical sites. The attrition rate for the oldest cohort between the first and the second round was 1.9%, which is negligible for a longitudinal study. Although this attrition rate is small, previous studies have confirmed that there is no bias in the sample according to the nutritional status and educational attainments of the children that remain in the Young Lives study in both rounds of interviews (Sanchez 2009; Outes-Leon and Dercon 2008). For the purpose of our study, taking into account children for whom we have complete information on the variables of interest, the useable sample size comprised 940 children (51% boys and 49% girls).

Definition of educational exclusion

In this paper, we adapt the framework of educational exclusion developed by Lewin (2007) for the Consortium for Research on Educational Access, Transitions and Equity (CREATE). According to the CREATE framework, there are six zones of educational exclusion. The first is for children who have never been enrolled in school, not even in any form of preschool education. This form of educational exclusion is experienced by the most marginalised and deprived children in low-income and fragile countries, for example children of nomadic families, ethnically marginalised groups, and those living in extreme poverty (Lewin 2009). The second form of educational exclusion is experienced by children who attend some form of primary education but drop out without completion. Precursors to dropping out include repetition, low achievement, poor teaching, degraded facilities, very large classes, household poverty, child labour and poor health and nutrition (Hunt 2008; Lewin and Sabates 2012; Sabates, Hossein and Lewin 2013). The third zone of educational exclusion includes children who are attending primary school but who are at risk of dropping out since they are over-age, underperforming or missing a significant proportion of lessons. Lewin (2007) defines this group as silent exclusion because children remain formally enrolled in school but their attendance is sporadic, their achievement is below what is specified by the curriculum, and they tend to be discriminated against on the basis of their race, ethnicity gender or culture.

The fourth zone of educational exclusion includes children who complete the primary school cycle but who fail to make the transition into secondary school. Barriers to secondary school education include both the unavailability of infrastructure as well as inaccessibility due to the prohibitive costs of education for children of poor families. The fifth zone of educational exclusion comprises children who enrolled into secondary school but failed to complete the cycle. The reasons for dropping out of secondary school in this case include poor performance, affordability and loss of interest (Lewin 2008). The last zone of exclusion is experienced by children enrolled in secondary school but whose attendance is sporadic and their performance below the level determined by the curriculum. These are also children in silent exclusion from secondary schooling (Lewin 2007). Meaningful access is defined by CREATE as when children complete a full cycle of primary and secondary education and achieve the required level of learning, skills and competences.

We operationalise the CREATE framework for educational exclusion using the Young Lives data for children at age 12–13 in Table 14.1 as follows. Using the question "Has the child ever been to school?" we identified children completely excluded from education, those in the first zone of educational exclusion. We identified 34.2% of boys and 31.2% of girls in this zone of

Table 14.1 Operationalisation of zone of exclusion (12–13 years)

Zone	Ever attended school	Currently attending school	Child is currently enrolled	Missed school (1 week)	Level of achievement[a]	Grade[b]	Boys %	Girls %	
0	No	X	X	X	X	X	34.2	31.2	Never enrolled
1	X	No	X	X	X	X	2.6	2.1	Dropped out
2	X	X	Yes	Yes	Low	Yes	42.1	47.1	Low achievers, on time, missed school
	X	X	Yes	Yes	High	Yes			High achievers, on time, missed school
	X	X	Yes	No	Low	Yes			Low achievers, on time, attending regularly
	X	X	Yes	Yes	Low	No			Low achievers, not on time, missed school
	X	X	Yes	Yes	High	No			High achievers, not on time, missed school
	X	X	Yes	No	Low	No			Low achievers, not on time, attending regularly
	X	X	Yes	No	High	No			High achievers, not on time, attending regularly
3	X	X	Yes	No	High	Yes	21.1	19.6	High achievers, on time, attending regularly

[a] Low and High achievement are defined according to the results in the PPVT test and mathematical test (high is defined if both test scores were over the average score for the sample).
[b] Not in time is defined if the child was currently attending Grade 4 or a lower school grade. Children who are 10 years of age should be enrolled in Grade 4.
Proportion based on 479 boys and 461 girls in the sample.

exclusion. Then, using the question "Is the child currently attending school?" we identified children in the second zone of exclusion, defined by those who have dropped out of primary school (2.6% and 2.1% of boys and girls, respectively). It is important to highlight that in Ethiopia compulsory primary education starts at age seven and the primary school cycle lasts six years. Hence, for the sample of children of the Young Lives data, we do not expect these children to have made the transition into secondary school by the time the second round of data were collected. For the third zone of educational exclusion, we used information on attendance, school performance, and number of overage children to identify silent exclusion. More specifically, to measure school performance, we used two tests administrated to the Young Lives children (old cohort) during Round 2: the Peabody Picture Vocabulary Test (PPVT), able to measure the vocabulary acquisition in people aged 2.5 years old and more, and the mathematics achievement test, aimed to measure basic numeric skills needed by any person within a society (Cueto, Leon and Guerrero 2009). Children who have missed the whole week of school prior to the survey, those who were performing below the average for the PPVT and the mathematics test, and those who were overage for their grade were considered to be in silent exclusion. A significant proportion of children were identified as in silent exclusion (42.1% and 47.1% of boys and girls, respectively). Meaningful access was defined for children who did not miss the week of school prior to the survey, were achieving above the average in both PPVT and mathematics tests, and were in the correct grade for their age (21.1% and 19.6% of boys and girls, respectively).

Health gap: height for age

The health outcome considered is malnutrition at age 12–13 years. We used height for age z-score, constructed according to the WHO's child growth standards, as a proxy measure of early nutritional status (Wisniewski 2010). Despite the fact that height for age has been widely used as an indicator of a child's health status (Stevens et al. 2012), the variable does not capture diseases or disabilities, which are important for learning. For example, poor vision has no effect on height but has a strong impact on how children perform in school (Glewwe 2005).

Figure 14.1 shows the height for age for children in the sample according to the four zones of educational exclusion identified earlier. There is a clear gradient in malnutrition according to educational exclusion. Children in the worst zone of exclusion 1 (never enrolled in school) have the worst average height for age z-score (-1.96). Children in zone of exclusion 2, dropouts from primary school, have an average height for age z-score of -1.57. Children in silent exclusion exhibit an average height for age of -1.20; finally, children with meaningful access report an average height for age of -0.87. The average health gap between zones of exclusion 1 and 2 is 0.39 of a standard deviation in the height for age z-score; the average health gap between zone of exclusion 2 and silent exclusion is 0.37 of a standard deviation; and the average health gap between silent exclusion and meaningful access is 0.33 of a standard deviation in the height for age z-score.

Background factors

We include a number of background factors known to influence educational exclusion and nutritional outcomes in order to provide an unbiased estimate of the average treatment effects to be discussed in more detail later. One of the key factors in estimating health differences at age 12 is previous health in childhood. Given that the Young Lives data follow the same children over time, we have information on the nutritional status of children at age eight. Therefore, we

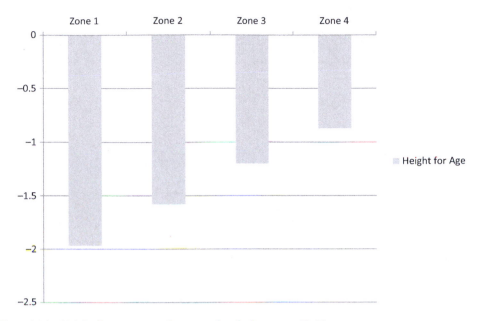

Figure 14.1 Height for age *z*-score by zone of exclusion at age 12–13 years

include the height for age *z*-score at age eight as a measure of prior nutritional status. We also include an indicator from the question "Has the child ever had a serious illness or injury where you really thought they might die?" to condition out health risks in life. A second important predictor of educational exclusion and current health status is poverty (Aber et al. 1997). We constructed a household wealth index using information on a number of factors related to the quality of housing, consumption of goods and the use of services. The household wealth index is based on three components: housing quality, consumer durable and services, and its value was standardised and centred at zero. Parental socioeconomic background also affects a child's health and access to education (DiCesare, Sabates and Lewin 2013). We hypothesised that the inclusion of parental education, both father and mother, would partially control for any confounding bias associated with the socioeconomic background of the child. Other variables included in the analysis relate to the child's personal attributes, such as gender, household size and whether the child undertook paid work in the year prior to the survey. Descriptive statistics for these variables are contained in Table 14.2.

Average decomposition analysis

In order to investigate the average gap in health outcomes attributable to children's educational exclusion, we use a technique popularised by Blinder (1973) and Oaxaca (1973). This technique enables us to decompose the average health gap between two groups of children located in different zones of exclusion into two components (Jann 2008; O'Donnell et al. 2007). The first component is the part of the gap that can be explained by the average differences in the characteristics of the children (for example, differences in their previous health status or differences in their socioeconomic characteristics). The second part of the gap is commonly known as the unexplained component but in the evaluation literature is routinely interpreted, under certain assumptions, as the average treatment effect on the treated (ATT).

Table 14.2 Descriptive statistics for background variables, mean and standard deviation

Variable	Mean	Std. dev.
Height for age *z*-score (7–8 y) (standardised score)	−1.45	1.29
Sex (% female)	0.49	0.50
Household size (#)	6.50	2.06
Child has ever had risk of dying (%)	0.31	0.46
Wealth Index (standardised score)	0.16	0.12
Paid work in the last 12 months (%)	0.07	0.26
Father education (≥ 6 y) (%)	0.48	0.50
Mother education (≥6 y) (%)	0.31	0.46

We provide some notation to explain how the average health gap can be decomposed into these two components. Assume that we have children in two groups of educational exclusion according to the CREATE framework (zone 1 and zone 2). For each group of children, we also have a measure of health status. In the current paper, this measure is height for age *z*-score (**HforA**). For each group of children, we also observe a number of background indicators (defined as **X**); in particular, we have a measurement of malnutrition measured at age eight, previous poverty status, parental background and family size. Height for age *z*-scores can be estimated separately for each group of children in the different zones of exclusion using linear regression models of the following form:

$$\mathbf{HforA}_1 = \mathbf{X}_1 \text{¢} \mathbf{b}_1 + \mathbf{e}_1 \tag{1}$$

$$\mathbf{HforA}_2 = \mathbf{X}_2 \text{¢} \mathbf{b}_2 + \mathbf{e}_2 \tag{2}$$

where the subscripts 1 and 2 refer to children in zones of exclusion 1 (never enrolled) and zone of exclusion 2 (dropout from primary school), respectively. The matrix of background characteristics is denoted by **X**, while the vector of unknown parameters to be estimated by Ordinary Least Square (OLS) are contained in the **β** vector. The error terms are expressed as **e** and are assumed to satisfy the standard set of assumptions for the purposes of OLS estimation.

An important property of the OLS procedure is that the regression line (or regression plane) passes through the means of the data. Using this property, we could then rewrite the above mean expressions for (1) and (2) as:

$$\overline{\mathbf{HforA}_1} = \overline{\mathbf{X}_1}' \hat{\boldsymbol{\beta}}_1 \tag{3}$$

$$\overline{\mathbf{HforA}_2} = \overline{\mathbf{X}_2}' \hat{\boldsymbol{\beta}}_2 \tag{4}$$

where the bars denote the mean values and the circumflexes the OLS estimates. Since we are interested in the average health gap, which is the difference in average health outcomes between the two groups of children, we can express the average health gap as the difference between equations (3) and equation (4). After some manipulation, the average health gap can then be re-expressed as:

$$\overline{\mathbf{HforA}_1} - \overline{\mathbf{HforA}_2} = [\overline{\mathbf{X}_1} - \overline{\mathbf{X}_2}]' \hat{\boldsymbol{\beta}}_1 + \overline{\mathbf{X}_2}' [\hat{\boldsymbol{\beta}}_1 - \hat{\boldsymbol{\beta}}_2] \tag{5}$$

where the first component on the right-hand side of equation (5) is the part of the average health gap between the two groups of children attributable to the difference in the characteristics between the two groups evaluated at the estimated coefficients for children in the worst zone of educational exclusion (i.e., children in zone 1). This is generally known as the composition effect. The second component on the right-hand side is part of the average difference in health outcomes attributable to differences in the estimated parameters weighted by the average characteristics of children who are in the second zone of educational exclusion (zone 2). Under assumptions outlined in Fortin, Lemieux and Firpo (2010), this second term is equivalent to the average treatment of the treated (ATT) effect commonly used in the programme evaluation literature but is more commonly known as the treatment effect. Therefore, this latter component may be interpreted in the current context as reflecting the average impact of the treatment associated with improved educational access on those subject to this treatment.

Estimation

The first step in the implementation of the Oaxaca-Blinder decomposition of the average health gap is to define the group of children in educational exclusion that are comparable to each other in order to recover the ATT. Given the fact that educational exclusion is not a random event, but children face educational exclusion due to a number of circumstances, it is not possible to compare children who are highly excluded with those who enjoy meaningful educational access. Therefore, we use the CREATE zones of exclusion to identify the following comparison groups. First, children who have never been enrolled in education will be compared against children who dropped out of education. Here the idea is that children who dropped out of school have only benefitted marginally from the educational experience, and children who dropped out of school are likely to also encounter socioeconomic problems similar to those who have never been to school. The second comparison group is children who are in silent exclusion, and these are compared to children who drop out of school. The main assumption here is that children in silent exclusion experienced additional schooling compared to the children who have already dropped out. However, the fact that there are overage children for the grade, nonattendance and low performance render these children vulnerable to dropping out. Finally, we compare children with meaningful access to those who are in silent exclusion. In this case, we have two groups of children who are at school, but one group is attending and performing according to their adequate age-in-grade while the other faces some risk of dropping out. For each of these groups, we will estimate the average health gap, the proportion of the average health gap due to differences in background characteristics (composition) and the proportion due to the treatment (i.e., ATT).

We further investigate children who are in silent exclusion and differentiate between those who are missing school, those who are low achievers and those who are overage for their grade. Each of these groups of children are compared with those who have meaningful access to education. The main aim of this analysis is to gain further insights into the factors that drive silent exclusion and that are also known to be precursors of dropping out (Hunt 2008; Lewin and Sabates 2012). For each of the groups, we estimate the total average health gap and the proportion of the average gap due to composition and treatment effects.

Results

We implement the Oaxaca-Blinder decomposition of the gap in nutritional status at age 12–13 according to the different levels of educational exclusion experienced by children. The estimates include controls for the background factors discussed earlier. The results are reported in Table 14.3. For the first set of results, we compare children who have never been to school

Table 14.3 Decomposition of the gap in average height for age *z*-score between children with different zones of exclusion

	Zone 2 vs 1	*Zone 3 vs 2*	*Access vs zone 3*
Avg. predicted health higher exclusion	−1.968 (0.07)★★	−1.578 (0.22)★★	−1.209 (0.06)★★
Avg. predicted health lower exclusion	−1.578 (0.20)★★	−1.209 (0.06)★★	−0.863 (0.09)★★
Health gap	−0.390 (0.20)★	−0.369 (0.21)★	−0.345 (0.10)★★
– due to composition	−0.404 (0.16)★★	−0.306 (0.17)★★	−0.236 (0.07)★★
– due to unexplained/ATT	0.014 (0.22)	−0.063 (0.22)	−0.110 (0.08)

Source: Young Lives Data.

Notes: Standard errors in parenthesis. Asterisks (★★,★) indicate statistical significance at 1% and 5% levels, respectively.

(zone 1) with those who have dropped out (zone 2). The average height for age *z*-score for children in the highest zone of exclusion, those in zone 1, is −1.97, and the height for age *z*-score for those who dropped out, zone 2, is −1.58. The health gap between these groups is −0.39 of standard deviation in the average height for age *z*-score. The decomposition shows that more than 100% of the health gap between these two groups is explained by differences in the average value of the background factors between children who have never been to school and those who have dropped out. There is only a very small and insignificant proportion of the health gap that remains unexplained, which is the part attributable to the educational treatment. Figure 14.2 provides a graphical representation of the percentage of the decomposition that is attributable to the composition and the treatment components. For the difference between children who have never been to school and those who dropped out, the composition part explains 104% of the gap and the treatment accounts for −4% of the gap.

We now compare children who are in silent exclusion (zone 3) against those who dropped out (zone 2). We find a health gap in nutritional status of −0.37 of a standard deviation in the height for age *z*-score (Table 14.3). The greater portion of the health gap is explained by differences in the average value of the background factors between those children who have dropped out and those in silent exclusion (83% as shown in Figure 14.2). However, the proportion of the gap that could be attributable to education is now 17%. Finally, comparing children with meaningful access to those in silent exclusion (zone 3), a health gap in nutritional status of −0.35 of a standard deviation in height for age *z*-score is detected (Table 14.3). Interestingly, 63% of the gap is explained by differences in the average value of the background factors between children in silent exclusion and those with meaningful access (Figure 14.2). Importantly, the role of education treatment increases, since now the part of the average health gap that is attributable to the treatment is about one-third.

One of the interesting results is that the potential impact of education on health outcomes for children increases as children experience meaningful access to education. To further investigate the issue of silent exclusion, we used information on overage children, school attendance and performance as different groups for the decomposition of the health gap. In our sample, for children in silent exclusion, 199 were overage for their grade, 78 were missing school during the week prior to the survey and 326 had low school performance (below the average for the cohort). Each of these groups of children will be compared to the 199 children with meaningful access to decompose the average health gap. The results are contained in Table 14.4.

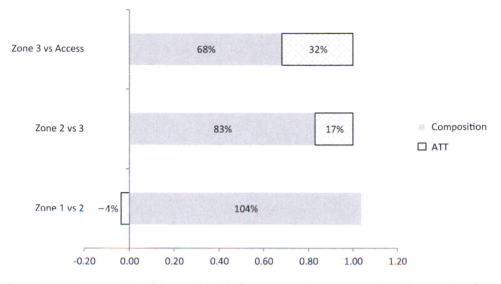

Figure 14.2 Decomposition of the gap in height for age *z*-score in percentages for different zones of exclusion

Table 14.4 Decomposition of the gap in average height for age *z*-score between children with different precursors of silent exclusion

	Access vs silent exclusion (overage)	Access vs silent exclusion (missing school)	Access vs silent exclusion (low performance)
Avg. predicted health higher exclusion	−1.348 (0.09)★★	−1.147 (0.14)★★	−1.171 (0.06)★★
Avg. predicted health lower exclusion	−0.863 (0,09)★★	−0.863 (0.09)★★	−0.863 (0.09)★★
Health gap	−0.485 (0.12)★★	−0.283 (0.16)★★	−0.307 (0.10)★★
– due to composition	−0.331 (0.10)★★	−0.158 (0.12)	−0.221 (0.08)★★
– due to unexplained/ATT	−0.154 (0.12)	−0.125 (0.16)	−0.086 (0.09)

Source: Young Lives Data.

Notes: Standard errors in parenthesis. Asterisks (★★,★) indicate statistical significance at 1% and 5% levels, respectively.

The largest health gap between children in silent exclusion and those with meaningful access was for children who were overage. The difference between the average predicted height for age *z*-score for children with meaningful access and those who were overage was −0.48 of standard deviation (Table 14.4). The second largest health gap was between children who were low performers and those with meaningful access (−0.30 of a standard deviation), and the smallest difference was between children who reported missing one week of school prior to the survey and those with meaningful access (−0.28 of standard deviation). Figure 14.3 reveals how this health gap is decomposed into composition and treatment effects. For children who have low performance in school, only 28% of the health gap could be attributable to the impact of education when compared to children with meaningful access. Over 70% remains explained by differences

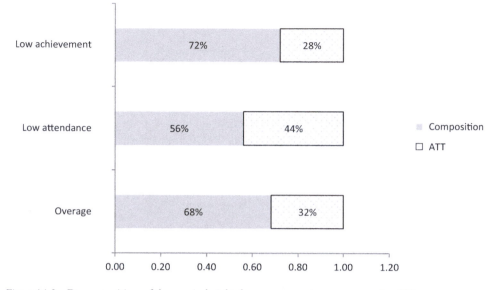

Figure 14.3 Decomposition of the gap in height for age *z*-score in percentages for different precursors of silent exclusion

in the average value of the background characteristics between these children. A higher proportion of the average health gap could be explained by the treatment for children who are overage for their grade (32%). Interestingly, for children who are missing school, we find that 44% of the health gap could be attributable to differences in educational treatment.

Discussion

Educational exclusion has important short- and long-term consequences on an individual's life, among which health is extremely important. A number of studies have been undertaken to investigate the dual relationship between education and health (see Grossman 2005 for a review). These studies have found that in the dual relationship between education and health, health status in infancy impacts a child's cognitive development (Mendez and Adair 1999), delays primary school enrolment (Glewwe and Jacoby 1995), increases education wastage (Pollitt 1984) and affects the overall school performance of children (Pollitt 1990; Pridmore 2007). In addition, on the education to health relationship, education promotes healthier behaviours and improves access to information as well as usage of health facilities, thus improving overall health (Currie and Moretti 2002; Cutler and Lleras-Muney 2006).

This paper raised a simple question: how important is the contribution of educational exclusion for average disparities in health outcomes among children in Ethiopia? To answer this question, we relied on the Young Lives longitudinal data, the CREATE framework for educational exclusion and the Oaxaca-Blinder decomposition to investigate the proportion of the average health gap that could be attributable to educational treatment. Our first key result shows that a higher proportion of the health gap could be attributable to treatment as educational inclusion improves. In support of this conclusion, our results reveal that children who had dropped out from education potentially did not gain anything from the educational experience to be able to gain health benefits when compared with children who have never been to school. Therefore, school dropout continues to be a waste of resources (Hunt 2008). Children who were in silent exclusion benefited from the learning experience, and as such a small proportion of the health gap (17%) could be attributable to the educational treatment. Interestingly, when comparing the health gap between children in silent exclusion and those with meaningful access, we found that up to 32% of the gap could be attributable to the educational treatment. Unfortunately, the vast majority of children in Ethiopia continue to suffer some form of educational exclusion, thus limiting the potential to realise the health benefits of education.

Our second key result suggests that of the three mechanisms that drive silent exclusion, over-age children in school drive the large health gap, but irregular school attendance is the largest loss for the potential benefits of education. Inappropriate age-in-grade continues to persist in many low-income countries, with more than 30% of children being overage in a large number of these countries (Lewin and Sabates 2012). Overage enrolment arises due to late enrolment during the first grade of compulsory primary schooling and deteriorates with grade repetition, and it is fuelled by poverty and deprivation (Sabates et al. 2010). Our estimates support the large health differences between children who are overage in school compared with children who have achieved meaningful access. Still, the health benefits of education can only be quantified if children attend school regularly. Our second set of results revealed that up to 44% of the health gap could be attributable to education when we compare children with irregular school attendance and those with meaningful access. Perhaps we highlight what is obvious, but not attending school (and not catching up at home) provides larger loses in terms of health benefits than attending school and not performing well or attending school as an old child for the grade enrolled.

There are also some limitations from our study worth highlighting. First, the treatment component of the Oaxaca-Blinder decomposition clearly depends on the explanatory variables included in the model. The inclusion of the nutritional status at age 7–8 years as an explanatory variable for the nutritional status at a 12–13 years drastically reduced the treatment component. This result suggests that we must be extremely cautious when interpreting this component. Second, our treatment effects are estimated to be statistically insignificant at a conventional level. Although this suggests that most of the differences observed are driven by differences in characteristics, the size of the point estimate in the average treatment effect increases drastically, indicating the potential that educational health benefits increase as educational exclusion decreases. This is the argument that is highlighted in this paper. Third, the nutritional status measured through the height for age z-score is a stock measure of malnutrition and indicates slow physical growth from birth. Current nutritional status is strictly correlated to previous nutritional height for age z-score levels. Fourth, our empirical approach is not experimental and does not provide a robust causal inference framework. Therefore, additional research is needed to establish the causal relationship between access to education and health. Fifth, results from Young Lives cannot be generalised at the country level; the sample is not designed to be representative of the population but representative of those living in poverty. Therefore, the observed relationships between educational exclusion and health found for the case of Ethiopia may exist in other similar contexts (poor areas within low-income countries). Notwithstanding these limitations, our results still highlight the relevance of meaningful access to education as an important factor for enhancing health opportunities among children and thus reducing health inequalities.

References

Aber, J.L., Bennett, N.G., Conley, D.C., Li, J., 1997. The effects of poverty on child health and development. *Annual Review of Public Health* 18, 463–483.

Arija,V., Esparo, G., Fernandez-Ballart, J., Murphy, M.M., Biarnes, E., Canals, J., 2006. Nutritional status and performance in test of verbal and non-verbal intelligence in 6 year old children. *Intelligence* 34, 141–149.

Bandura, A., 1991. Self-efficacy mechanism in physiological activation and health-promoting behavior. In: Madden IV, J. (Ed.) *Neurobiology of Learning, Emotion and Affect*. Raven, New York.

Blinder, A.S., 1973. Wage discrimination: reduced form and structural estimates. *Journal of Human Resources* 8, 436–455.

Boyden, J., 2006. Young Lives Project: Conceptual Framework. Project Document. http://www.younglives.org.uk/publications/project-documents

Bryan, J., Osendarp, S., Hughes, D., Calvaresi, E., Baghurst, K., van Klinken, J., 2004. Nutrients for cognitive development in school-aged children. *Nutrition Review* 62, 8, 295–306.

Case, A., Fertig, A., Paxson, C., 2005. The lasting impact of childhood health and circumstance. *Journal of Health Economics* 24, 2, 365–389.

Commission on the Social Determinants of Health, 2008. *Closing the Gap in a Generation. Health Equity Through Action on the Social Determinants of Health*. WHO, Geneva.

Cueto, S.J., Leon, G., Guerrero, I.M., 2009. Psychometric characteristics of cognitive development and achievement instruments in Round 2 of Young Lives. Young Lives Technical Note No. 15, University of Oxford.

Currie, J., Moretti, E., 2002. Mother's education and the intergenerational transmission of human capital: evidence from college openings and longitudinal data. NBER Working Paper 9360, National Bureau of Economic Research, Cambridge, MA.

Cutler, D.M., Lleras-Muney, A., 2006. Education and health: evaluating theories and evidence. NBER Working Paper 12352, National Bureau of Economic Research, Cambridge, MA.

Dewey, K.G., Begum, K., 2011. Long-term consequences of stunting in early life. *Maternal and Child Nutrition* 7, 5–18.

DiCesare, M., Sabates, R., Lewin, K., 2013. A double prevention: how maternal education can affect maternal mental health, child health and child cognitive development. *Longitudinal and Life Course Studies International Journal* 4, 3, 166–179.

Fortin, N., Lemieux, T., Firpo, S., 2010. Decomposition methods in economics. NBER Working Paper 16045, National Bureau of Economic Research, Cambridge, MA.

Glewwe, P., Jacoby, H.G., 1995. An economic analysis of delayed primary school enrolment in a low income country: the role of early childhood nutrition. *The Review of Economics and Statistics* 77, 1, 156–169.

Glewwe, P., 2005. The impact of child health and nutrition on education in developing countries: theory, econometric issues, and recent empirical evidence. *Food Nutrition Bulletin* 26, 2 (Suppl 2), S235–S250.

Glewwe, P., Miguel, E.A., 2008. The impact of child health and nutrition on education in less developed countries. In: Schultz, T.P. and Strauss, J.A. (Eds.) *Handbook of Development Economics*. Elsevier, Oxford.

Grantham-McGregor, S., Cheung, Y.-B., Cueto, S., Glewwe, P., Richter, L., Strupp, B., 2007. Developmental potential in the first 5 years for children in developing countries. *Lancet* 369, 9555, 65.

Grossman, M., 2005. Education and nonmarket outcomes. NBER Working Paper 11852, National Bureau of Economic Research, Cambridge, MA.

Hammond, C., 2003. How education makes us healthy. *London Review of Education* 1, 1, 61–78.

Hammond, C., 2004. Impacts of life-long learning upon emotional resilience, psychological and mental health: fieldwork evidence. *Oxford Review of Education* 30, 4, 551–568.

Hunt, F., 2008. Dropping out from school: a cross country review of literature. CREATE Pathways to Access, Research Monograph No. 16, University of Sussex.

Jann, B., 2008. The Blinder–Oaxaca decomposition for linear regression models. *The Stata Journal* 8, 4, 453–479.

Lewin, K., 2007. Improving access, equity and transitions in education: creating a research agenda. CREATE Pathways to access, Research Monograph No.1, University of Sussex.

Lewin, K., 2008. Strategies for sustainable financing of secondary education in Africa. World Bank Working Paper No. 136, Africa Human Development Series, World Bank, Washington.

Lewin, K., 2009. Access to education in sub-Saharan Africa: patterns, problems and possibilities. *Comparative Education* 45, 2, 151–174.

Lewin, K., Sabates, R., 2012. Who gets what? Is improved access to basic education pro-poor in SSA? *International Journal of Educational Development* 32, 4, 517–528.

Mendez, M.A., Adair, L.S., 1999. Severity and timing of stunting in the first two years of life affect performance on cognitive tests in late childhood. *Journal of Nutrition* 129, 1555–1562.

Oaxaca, R., 1973. Male-female wage differentials in urban labor markets. *International Economic Review* 14, 693–709.

O'Donnell, O., van Doorsaler, E., Wagstaff, A., Lindelow, M., 2007. Analyzing health equity using household survey data. A guide to techniques and their implementation. WBI Learning Resources Series, World Bank, Washington.

Outes-Leon, I., Dercon, S., 2008. Survey attrition and attrition bias in Young Lives. Young Lives Technical Note No. 5, University of Oxford.

Pollitt, E., 1984. *Nutrition and Educational Achievement. Nutrition and Education Series.* Issue 9. UNESCO, Paris.

Pollitt, E., 1990. *Malnutrition and Infection in the Classroom.* UNESCO, Paris.

Pridmore, P., 2007. Impact of health on education access and achievement: a cross-national review of the research evidence. CREATE Pathways to Access, Research Monograph No.2, University of Sussex.

Sabates, R., Akyeampong, K., Westbrook, J., Hunt, F., 2010. School drop out: patterns, causes, changes and policies. Background Paper for the UNESCO GMR, UNESCO, Paris.

Sabates, R., Hossein, A., Lewin, K., 2013. School drop out in Bangladesh: insights using panel data. *International Journal of Educational Development* 33, 3, 225–232.

Sanchez, A., 2009. Early nutrition and cognitive achievement in pre-school children in Peru. Young Lives Working Paper 57, University of Oxford.

Sandstead, H.H., 2000. Causes of iron and zinc deficiencies and their effects on the brain. *Journal of Nutrition* 130, 347S–349S.

Stevens, G., Finucane, M., Paciorek, C., Flaxman, S., White, R., Donner, A., Ezzati, M., 2012. Trends in mild, moderate, and severe stunting and underweight, and progress towards MDG 1 in 141 developing countries. *Lancet* 380, 9844, 824–834.

UNESCO Institute for Statistics, 2014. Indicators for Education and Development. http://www.uis.unesco.org/datacentre/pages/default.aspx?SPSLanguage=EN

UNICEF, 2013. *Improving Child Nutrition.* UNICEF, New York.

Wilson, I., Huttly, S.R.A., Fenn, B., 2006. A case study of sample design for longitudinal research: Young Lives. *International Journal of Social Research Methodology* 9, 5, 351–365.

Wisniewski, S.L.W., 2010. Child nutrition, health problems, and school achievement in Sri Lanka. *World Development* 38, 3, 315–332.

15

SPACES FOR 21ST-CENTURY LEARNING

Ola Uduku

A school is two students sitting under a tree

(unattributed saying)

Introduction

The formal delivery of education in the 21st century has been transformed radically from its 19th-century origins. The focus on the ways in which children learn is becoming critical to how education provision is structured in different educational contexts across the world. Exemplar 21st century schools are now tasked with an expanded range of roles in the postmillennium goal era. It is no longer enough to simply be able to record good enrolment rates at different educational stages. UNESCO and other international education bodies now require indicators of educational attainment through functional literacy indicators and test attainment results, including PISA and other international benchmarks.

Aside from these more quality-oriented attainment indicators, the classroom and school have once again become important in our contextualisation and assessment of appropriate and successful contemporary educational delivery. In the late 1970s and 1980s, the classroom and the school estate went out of fashion as funding was channelled to staff education and learning resources. Today the classroom, now the 'learning space', and the school, 'community hub', are central to student-based learning and constructively aligned learning.

How has this become the new 'norm' for education across the world, and how do schools in drastically varying circumstances in the 'North' and the 'emerging world' respond to this shift of focus? Described here is the contextual background to this evolution of contemporary expectations of school usage and space. Also, with the use of case studies and current school design trends, exemplar school design successes and failures are presented. Finally, an attempted forecast of future educational design for the mid-21st century is discussed, considering evidence of current educational space resource and technology trends.

Up until the early 20th century, education was primarily provided to the public by the church and other charitable organisations. The school classroom as a separate physical entity from ecclesiastical or purely charitable institutions emerged from the Industrial Revolution, where the formalisation of education was legislated, which signified the beginning of 'mass education' (Saint 1987; Dudek 2000a; Harwood 2010).

The church and later the philanthropic state brought about the establishing of 'church' and 'state' schools. In the UK, the emergence of the Board School system from the mid-19th century formalised the school room with standardised furniture, classroom sizes, and design layouts (Seaborne and Lowe 1971; Saint 1987).

In the case of both the UK and France, this system was exported wholesale to the colonies, where the elite could send their children to copies of schools to be found in metropoles of France and England in which the European curriculum was taught in surroundings mimicking those to be found of schools in Europe. Indeed, at the most elite end, the schools were regulated to the same standards as in Paris and London. Similar systems were exported by the Germans to German West Africa and its other concessions, and by other colonising powers.[1]

Post–World War 2

The support for, and sponsoring of, world education has been and remains the main objective for UNESCO. Thus, in the 1950s to 1960s, the UNESCO school building division was active in setting up school design standards and, in some countries, sending 'specialists' to build schools throughout the emerging world (de Raedt 2014). In the 'West' and elsewhere, the organisation also went on to set international design 'norms and standards' for schools. As the UK, and to a lesser extent the USA, already had clear classroom and school design standards, the agencies involved with school design in both countries helped support the development of the UNESCO school building programme. Moreover, UNESCO expertise, in the form of technical experts, though drawn from a number of countries, had significant representation from both countries and also France (de Raedt 2014).

Associated with the work of UNESCO in advocating international standards for school design, mainly based on UK/US research, was financial aid by means of loans from bilateral sources and from the International Development Agency (IDA), the precursor to the World Bank (Uduku 1992; de Raedt 2014). Thus, Nigeria, for example, was able to negotiate an IDA-UNESCO supported loan for demonstration schools to be built throughout the country (to UNESCO consultant standards) in the 1960s (Uduku 1992, 2013).

At the same time, USAID built comprehensive high schools at Aiyetoro (Western Nigeria) and Port Harcourt (Southeastern Nigeria) with support from Harvard and UCLA, respectively. Unlike the UNESCO projects, the funding, design, construction and initial staffing of these schools was entirely American (Uduku 1992). Elsewhere in the emerging world, school provision and design ranged from the 'aid-assisted' to 'full-aid construction and donation' approaches, the latter model being more typical.

Islamic education, via the historic 'madrasa' system, remained in place in much of Asia and North Africa, linked to local mosques and religious tutors. The madrasa layout was similar to the basic prewar classroom, although this might be indoors or outdoors depending on location and climate. Aside from its exclusion of girls in its formal educational structures, it appears that Lugard's governorship of Northern Nigeria felt that the Islamic system was as organised and advanced as the church school system in the UK.[2] Thus, it could successfully leave Islamic education in place and discourage missionary influence and proselytisation in the region. More traditional educational systems in parts of the emerging world survived but not within the formalised structure of the UNESCO educational mandate. These include the coming-of-age ritual ceremonies in Africa and spaces for learning and induction required of many initiation systems (Precourt 1975; Marah 2006).

The North's formalised systems of education, and the prewar model of schools, remained in place up until the late 1950s (Saint 1987; McCulloch 2005.[3] However, from then on, education theorists increasingly challenged historic educational practices focused on students being given knowledge to 'learn'. The child-focused or student-centred learning practice, which is central to contemporary educational practice, had direct effects on the classroom or, as it became called, 'learning space'. With the office architectural styles of the day, the open plan classroom evolved, and early-years learning in the developed world in particular became more child centred and activity based. This led to the demise of the traditional classroom, with its ordered seating, and the rise of the flexible classroom or learning space, with moveable child-scaled furniture and soft furnishings for use in the classroom setting (Dudek 2000a, 2000b).

Figure 15.1 International 'aid' to schools in the South cartoon critique

Source: Editorial cartoon RLM, *Mimar* 31 March 1989, 4.
Photo Credit: Aga Khan Trust for Culture, Geneva.

For older students, learning could now be 'project-based', with less focus on traditional, subject-based learning. This again meant the classroom space transformed to allow grouped tables to work on project tasks but included necessary desks that might be rearranged to recreate the more 'traditional' learning environment. A genre of newly designed schools, which took into account this significant transition in learning styles, emerged in Europe and the USA from the late 1950s (Dudek 2000b; Hille 2011).

In the emerging world, the high point for educational developments in school design was the 1960s, when major school building projects took place in Africa (Ghana and Nigeria had new schools and upgrading programmes for missionary schools) and Southeast Asia (Le Roux 2004; Uduku 2006). The oil crises and economic upheaval from the early 1970s up until the late 1980s resulted in the near collapse of emerging economies and the resorting to Structural Adjustment Programmes by the international financial institutions, which effectively underwrote much of the economic debt of countries such as Ghana. The effect on education was directly felt, as the World Bank's emphasis focused on capacity building of personnel (teachers and administrators/parent groups) and not on school infrastructure or classrooms (World Bank 1986).

In Southern Africa, despite the heinous apartheid education system, the standards and norms for schools did derive from UNESCO and Building Research Establishment standards to produce neotraditional 1950s schools in the UK mode up until the end of the apartheid era.[4] In Nigeria and Ghana, school design remained linked directly to colonial and more recent UNESCO/World Bank design standards. Southeast Asia also benefited from the creation of the School Building Research Office in Bangkok in the 1960s (Uduku 1992; de Raedt 2014).

Latin American school design also benefited from the post-World War Two international educational standards set by UNESCO. Furthermore, its proximity to the USA also had an effect on its educational systems, school design and delivery. Also of influence was the political slant of many Latin American states, including the Caribbean island of Cuba, in which more 'revolutionary' educational systems such as the *Escuela Nueva* system were introduced. Characterised by its emphasis on multigrade schooling, peer-to-peer learning and the involvement of the local community in education, spatially the classroom broke with the traditional 1950s 'children listen

Figure 15.2   Escuela Nueva
Photo Credit: Esteban Cadena, Francisco Suarez y Pascual Gangotena and Al Borde Architects 2009.

and teacher talk' layout and instead had large, multiclass spaces for activities such as the library area, group activity space, etc. and thus was more akin to the student-based learning methods influencing school design in the 'North' (Psacharopoulos, Rojas and Velez 1992).

The mid-1990s to early 2000s

Since the end of the 20th century, most countries in the North, including the UK, have had to invest significantly in building new schools and upgrading school buildings that had had little renovation or attention since the postwar school building boom of the 1950s. This has both been in recognition of the fact that in urban areas, where most citizens now live, school-age populations have increased significantly and the pressure on the existing school stock has made the provision of increased school places imperative. Also it was acknowledged that many of the post-World War Two schools had been built using early prefabrication systems. These schools have suffered significant deterioration, and many had become unfit for purpose well before the end of the 20th century (DfES 2003).

In the UK, the Schools for the Future Programme, initiated by the then Labour Government, resulted in a few exemplar schools that responded to the new teaching theories around education being a community activity and learning hub as well as flexible classroom spaces, St Luke's Infant and Primary School being one of these.[5] A significant number, however, ended up being built with no architectural supervision to lower contract delivery standards, and their legacy may be less significant.

In the emerging world, the mid-1990s heralded the end of the structural adjustment era. Theories related to child-centred learning did ultimately trickle down to school planning and design. Education became less nationalised and more decentralised to the regional level (Uduku

Figure 15.3   St Luke's Infant and Junior School, Wolverhampton, England
Photo Credit: Architype Architects 2010.

Figure 15.4   Kontonase Secondary School, Kumasi, Ghana
Photo Credit: Ola Uduku 2007.

2010). Furthermore, neoliberal reforms encouraged the development of private schools of all levels of funding. Thus, the aftermath of the structural adjustment era resulted in an uneven school landscape of often poorly funded state schools and a range of private schools of various funding means and expertise (World Bank 1986).

Despite this, the UNESCO international school design standards and norms remain the basis for school design standards and inspection in the emerging world and are the basis for Western schools as well. However, whilst new educational theory has ensured that schools in the West and those with higher levels of funding elsewhere, normally in the private sector, have been able to develop more contemporary, learning psychology-based interpretations and design responses to the standard school norms, most schools in the emerging world and in poorer parts of the West remain focused on the historic post-World War Two model where the 'teacher teaches – students listen' traditional classroom design form.

2001–2010

With the United Nations' declaration of the Millennium Development Goals in 2000 and the further realignment of geo politics after the 9/11 bombing, the global goal to achieve access to basic education for all was reinforced and backed by major international organisations, including the World Bank, UNESCO and bilateral donors. Child-based learning, flexible classrooms and schools as a community resource have also re-entered the vocabulary of school provision, as has 'educational facilities management' or school building programmes.[6] Examples of international schools with elements of child-based learning or more radical *escuela neuva*-focused designs have been recorded in architectural journals, fora and some educational development texts. The destruction of the Iron Curtain and the globalisation of education has further spread ideas of contemporary education and new learning space design across the world.

From 2008 to date, however, the realignment of the global financial markets has inevitably had an effect on investment in education, particularly capital infrastructure such as school buildings. In the North, in the UK for example, there was a cut in funding for the upgrading of school infrastructure (Curtis 2010).

In the emerging world, the economic downturn has had less national effect on school investment as, despite the global situation, local economies have continued to grow. However, at a global level, more strategic areas of investment, such as technology in classrooms, has had less funding, and this in turn has slowed investment and development of ICT in education.

The context for school design history over the post-World War Two years has been dominated by global policies and trends dictated by international bodies, the most influential of those being the World Bank and UNESCO. Increased access to education remains the main policy goal of all organisations as, despite various programmes including Education for All, the Millennium Development Goals and others, a significant proportion of school-age children remain out of school, and those in school are functionally illiterate at school completion (UNESCO 1990, 2014).

The interest and investment in educational facilities provision, incorporating school design programmes, has fluctuated in parallel with economic strength and growth. Often, as in the UK case, capital funding for school building projects is cut as the economy enters a downturn. However, there has been near-total acknowledgement amongst education practitioners of the need to develop the learning space to respond to contemporary educational needs and practice in which student-centred learning is promoted, as is the flexible use of the classroom for varied group and single-function activities. Exemplar schools from the emerging world and the North that demonstrate this design response to new learning space requirements and also the link of learning and the classroom to local communities abound in contemporary and to a lesser extent in academic writing (e.g., Dudek 2000b; Hille 2011).

Schools of the 21st century

School building programmes today share many of the historic issues of the past; particularly there remains limited provision and poor access to schools and education in the most vulnerable communities. This section explores what future possibilities present themselves for contemporary learning and teaching practice, utilising the technologies and media to support existing and create new learning spaces that are now available globally.

Education researchers and commentators have investigated and discussed various ways in which education can be better integrated within local communities, engaging with contemporary education and sociological discourses focused on flexibility of learning, inclusivity of learners and widening access to all. As discussed earlier, the flexible classroom concept has been developed and embedded into school design since the 1980s, as has the idea of the school being a community resource, with areas of shared access such as libraries and ICT-technology learning areas (Criticos and Thurlow 1987).

More radical ideas have also been explored, such as the programme-based learning approach, doing away with the classroom altogether (Chicago public schools strategy) or having learning centred around the teenage body clock (UCL-London strategy) (Stepien and Gallagher 1993). Whilst there has also been a 'back to the traditional' trend amongst some – i.e., doing away with technology in classrooms and returning to more traditional modes of learning – future trends point to the increased incorporation and use of digital technologies for learning and as part of the future development of the 21st-century learning environment. The last section explores this further.

ICT and learning

As Prensky (2001) has noted, today's youth are now digital natives; their facility and ability to not only communicate but exist in the digital world opens up channels of educational development. The ubiquity and relative low cost of mobile telephone technology suggests that this medium has the most potential in future education expansion.

There have already been a number of digital education initiatives such as the USA-originated, but now wound down, one laptop per child programme, which achieved some penetration in Latin America, Africa and Asia.[7] India and China have also been successful in creating bespoke online learning programmes, which are reliant on access to power and functioning desktop computers (Carr-Chellman 2004; Moore and Kearsley 2011).

A number of externally mediated programmes aimed at giving access to learning to the disadvantaged in the emerging world have ranged from the donation of old computer equipment to schools to the 'upcycling' of old computers to the donation of new computers and ICT facilities (within purpose-built classrooms, technology centres or, in some cases, as container classrooms).[8]

In the developed world, much of this digital provision and access has been provided through the creation of more flexible school campuses and also by the upgrade and design of new libraries that now function as learning centres, giving access to digital learning to all local users, such as the 'Idea Store' libraries in London (Idea Store 2009).

The main issues with this traditional approach to ICT provision and learning in education is the cost and infrastructure required to enable students to engage with online learning. With adequate capital investment – and ongoing investments in upgrading, local technical support and staff support – this approach has proven to be successful, as is evidenced in some Indian cities and parts of urban South Africa (see Bélissent 2010). For poorer, more rural, and hard-to-access areas, this traditional ICT hardware provision approach is impossible, due both to the aforementioned cost limitations and also the paucity of fixed communication networks.

Models of digital learning using mobile phones as the main medium for learning are being developed and reported on. Being linked to a wider ecology of open-access information sources and cloud-based Wi-Fi networks, possibly transmitted from central community buildings, means that access to and the use of this form of digital learning can be affordable, community located and flexible to access.

Interestingly, this 'mobile learning' model has relevance in both learning 'worlds'; in the emerging world, this might be obvious due to the relatively low-tech, low-maintenance and low-cost approach. In developed countries, its ability to enable flexibility of learning – and also, in its ideal form, be less tied to the scarce resource of good schools, teachers and equipment – makes it attractive to struggling locations and neighbourhoods. The approach also is particularly suited to rural neighbourhoods in more remote parts of the world, where regular communications infrastructure is nonexistent or limited.

Test projects already exist that have begun to explore the possibilities of this approach. At present, these may seem aspirational, but as technology is set to continue to follow Moore's law[9] and the ubiquity of the smart phone grows in new markets, manufacturers are pursing in the emerging world. Furthermore, as with the music industry, access to open-access books, particularly learning materials, could be the disruptive technology that changes both the marketing model for learning or, more precisely, learning media (traditional textbooks and paper-based content) and also its consumption – from the traditional regulated school environment to the flexibility and accessibility of one's personal handheld mobile phone device (Pyramid Research 2010).

This scenario is likely to be a game changer for the conceptualisation and delivery of education worldwide, much like the spread and coverage of the mobile telephone. More importantly, this will have a direct influence on the ways in which learners engage with information. This in turn will challenge how 21st-century learning spaces are conceived and designed.

How will learning evolve to respond to the incorporation of e-content on a pervasive scale? In certain situations where delivering traditional classroom-taught education is difficult, such as in war or natural disaster zones, the potential for near 100% e-education scenarios delivered via mobile devices becomes plausible. In such cases, the learning space might be secondary to ensuring there is a space able to provide a safe shelter to learners from outside danger with only limited or mediated contact to a teacher-facilitator.

The flexibility of learning, currently being 'trialled' now via the UCL schools experiment, could become the mainstream or norm as the economic reality of children's lives in poorer emerging countries is recognised or the needs of 'out-of-school' and 'excluded' children elsewhere are met via more consistent levels of educational delivery tailored to the student or student group and not to a dated conventional norm.

The accessibility of learning material online and the already-discussed ubiquity of mobile phones and today's communications media have successfully shrunk major barriers to learning; however, the organisational and logistical skills that are still crucial to ensuring the future places and spaces for new forms of e-learning remain lacking and will need to be supported in challenging environments, particularly – but not only – in the emerging world. This will be critical if we are to succeed in delivering the required range of 21st-century places as transformational learning spaces.

Challenges to new school design and pedagogy

The key challenges to delivering the contemporary infrastructure required for learning in the 21st-century classroom therefore are much more diffuse than in the century past.

Learning spaces, like classrooms of the past, are still going to be the most important requirement. In the developed and emerging world alike, children need quiet, accessible, physical places where they can learn. For those with limited wherewithal and resources throughout the world, particularly the poor, the traditional classroom is either nonexistent or hard to get to. In the emerging world, the physical classroom has yet to be built in remote areas, whilst in the developed world, where the physical classroom exists, its integration into contemporary learning technologies and connection with the community, through 'out-of-school-hours' access or as part of a community learning 'hub', is often limited.

In the emerging world particularly, there remains the critical need to have teachers and educators better skilled to engage with new learning technologies in the classroom. Teaching quality remains a problem across the world; however, access to teaching material to supplement this in the contemporary classroom for students is particularly difficult in emerging countries where the infrastructure is weak or not in place. The 'hole in the wall' and Ethiopian experiments, allowing students to adopt peer-to-peer learning strategies with computers, suggests that teachers supported to supervise learning with such technologies could make a significant difference to childhood learning in remote locations in the emerging world.[10]

Current views support the future spread of reduced-cost smartphone usage in the emerging world as being the likely vehicle for future supported learning models, the new generation of such devices being considerably cheaper and therefore accessible enough for teachers and learners alike to use (Economist 2011, 2014; Ebenezer and Omane-Antwi 2014). The emergence of packaged learning, such as the success of MOOCs in tertiary education, is also likely to have a qualified impact on learning material distribution support and access at primary and intermediate education levels.[11]

The need for these alternative forms of access to learning as discussed is not only an emerging world issue; for disenfranchised communities in the North, schools are sometimes poorly supported and also have a lacking infrastructure in place, meaning the supported self-learning approach is a resource.

The traditional teacher-centred classroom learning model, however, remains successful when well resourced, as seen in countries in Southeast Asia such as Singapore and Hong Kong, as demonstrated in current PISA scores (www.oecd.org/pisa). However, this is often

Figure 15.5 ICT classroom prototype illustration – daytime
Photo Credit: Shaun McLeod et al. 2013. ESALA Project Office, Edinburgh University.

Figure 15.6   ICT classroom prototype illustration – nighttime
Photo Credit: Shaun McLeod et al. 2013. ESALA Project Office, Edinburgh University.

counterbalanced with the more relaxed Scandinavian and liberal constructive learning models popular elsewhere in the developed world.

All learning needs space to take place; the future technologies discussed are ubiquitous and small enough not to need more space but instead allow for the better integration of different spaces for learning. A recently completed design project demonstrated how learning spaces for challenging areas can be created from a standard shipping container (Uduku 2013), whilst new flexible classroom architecture is being created for location-specific learning spaces globally.

Conclusions

> Public schools were not only created in the interests of industrialism – they were created in the image of industrialism. In many ways, they reflect the factory culture they were designed to support.
>
> (Robinson 2010: 9)

The design and delivery of classrooms and schools in the second decade of the 21st century has changed very little from the previous century. Whilst there remains the universal goal to have the resources and wherewithal to have all children educated, today the means to achieve this is more contested than had been the case in the post-World War Two era when the ambition first emerged. There are now a range of different educational ethos and strategies by which to achieve this end: from the traditional to the liberal; with or without the use of contemporary technologies and forms of supported learning; and driven by different interests – political, sociological or economic.

For the emerging world, there remains the real challenge to get large sections of the child population into education, who by means of remoteness or sheer numbers in rapidly urbanising areas either do not have the learning spaces, the teaching support, or both in which to learn. Traditional modes of provision have so far been unable to meet this continuing need, and new methods of incorporating digital learning technologies are still rare or only found in unique case study projects.

What seems clear is that the future learning space will need to be hybrid, flexible and accessible to a range of different learners and environments. As the world's failure to achieve the Millennium Development Goals set out for access to basic education has shown, the traditional model, predicated on the building of more classrooms and schools, and the education of more teachers will not solve the existing education challenges.

Twenty-first century learning can, and already has begun to, take on a more flexible approach, acknowledging new technologies and the reconceptualisation of learning as an integrated process taking place in a range of different spaces and places. The classroom may indeed be everywhere, but there still needs to be an understood 'frame' in which actual learning take place spatially and temporally, where and when the learner absorbs the information and the support that is available. The 21st-century learning space needs to be designed to these terms as well as its socioeconomic and contextual parameters if it is to deliver places that ensure learners thrive.

As Ischinger (2011) argues:

> Education facilities are the theatre, the stage and the backdrop for learning at all levels from pre-primary to higher education and beyond. Educators everywhere are encouraging their students to explore more individualized learning and active engagement with learning within and beyond the classroom. As our approaches to teaching and learning evolve so too must our learning environments . . . [but] these buildings do not need to be technologically complex to be outstanding. They do need to be flexible and enable teachers to adapt their environments to suit their educational goals.

Notes

1 Literature on the comparative history of nonmetropolitan national education systems is less plentiful. However, Brock and Alexiadou (2013), Arnove and Torres (2012) and McCulloch (2005) all have made contributions to this literature.

2 For more on Lugard, Perham (1961) remains the main source, and see Uduku (1994) for the analysis of an educational institution in Wusasa, Northern Nigeria.

3 Exceptions to this included the child-centred ethos of the Montessori schools and less formalised learning systems in place in schools such as the Steiner schools in Germany (Dudek 2000a, 2000b).

4 The South African equivalent of the Building Research Institute published its own design guide for schools, distinguishing the needs of 'native' students from whites but essentially suggesting all school design remained within the inherited colonial British standards; see for example Van Straaten, Richards and Lotz (1967).

5 Design for learning spaces, Woolner (2010).

6 See Woolner (2010): there are on average more than 30 articles per month in the *Architects Journal* on schools from the Building Schools for the Future 1990s era to date; also see Middlewood and Parker (2005).

7 The OLPC website, http://one.laptop.org/, is no longer active.

8 For the ethics of computer donations see Iles (2004). For upcycling see http://www.bbc.co.uk/news/technology-27346567;Samsung container school:http://www.samsungvillage.com/blog/2011/10/27/samsungblog-solar-powered-internet-school-provides-new-opportunities-for-students-in-africa/; Learning Planet computer classroom: http://www.blogs.hss.ed.ac.uk/after-development/2014/02/10/ict-classroom-project/

9 Moore's law suggests that the number of transistors or circuit boards doubles every year, which partly explains the rapid speed in the development of computing and mobile telephony.

10 See Mitra (2005) and http://www.technologyreview.com/news/506466/given-tablets-but-no-teachers-
    ethiopian-children-teach-themselves/
11 Whilst there is much hype about MOOCs, others are more cautious about their long-term effects, as
    their use is relatively recent and the data is yet to be fully analysed; see for example: Liyanagunawardena,
    Williams and Adams (2013).

References

Arnove, R., Torres, C., 2012. *The Dialectic of the Global and the Local*. Rowman and Littlefield, Lanham.
Bélissent, J., 2010. Getting Clever about Smart Cities. http://193.40.244.77/iot/wp-content/uploads/
    2014/02/getting_clever_about_smart_cities_new_opportunities.pdf
Biggs, J., 1991. Approaches to learning in secondary and tertiary students in Hong Kong: some comparative
    studies. *Educational Research Journal* 6, 27–39.
Brock, C., Alexiadou, N., 2013. *Education Around the World*. Bloomsbury, London.
Carr-Chellman, A. (Ed.), 2004. *Global Perspectives on E-Learning: Rhetoric and Reality*. Sage, Thousand Oaks.
Criticos, C., Thurlow, M., 1987. *The Design of Learning Spaces*. Durban Media Resources Centre, School of
    Education, University of Natal.
Curtis, P., 2010. School buildings programme scrapped in latest round of cuts. *Guardian*, 5th July.
De Raedt, K., 2014. Between "true believers" and operational experts: UNESCO architects and school
    building in post-colonial Africa. *Journal of Architecture* 19, 1, 19–42.
DfES, 2003. Building schools for the future. DfES/0134/2003, Nottingham.
Dudek, M., 2000a. *The Architecture of Schools*. Routledge, London.
Dudek M., 2000b. *Kindergarten Architecture*. Spon, London.
Ebenezer, E., Omane-Antwi, K., 2014. Massification of Tertiary Education Sector in Ghana and Imple-
    mentation of "M-Learning": Case Study of Pentecost University College. http://globalbizresearch.org/
    Singapore_Conference/pdf/pdf/S491.pdf
Harwood E., 2010. *England's Schools: History, Architecture and Adaptation*. English Heritage, London.
Hille, T., 2011. *Modern Schools, a Century of Design for Education*. Wiley, London.
Idea Store, 2009. Idea Store Strategy 2009. http://www.ideastore.co.uk/public/documents/PDF/IdeaStow
    StrategyAppxICAB290709.pdf
Iles, A., 2004. Mapping environmental justice in technology flows. *Global Environmental Politics* 4, 4, 76–107.
Ischinger B., 2011. Foreword. In OECD (Eds.) *Designing for Education Compendium of Exemplary Facilities*.
    OECD, Paris.
Le Roux, H., 2004. The post-colonial architecture of Ghana and Nigeria. *Architectural History* 47, 361–392.
Liyanagunawardena, T., Williams, S., Adams, A., 2013. The impact and reach of MOOCs: a developing
    countries' perspective. *eLearning Papers* 33, 1–8.
Marah, J., 2006. The virtues and challenges in traditional African education. *Journal of Pan African Studies* 1,
    4, 15–24.
McCulloch, G., 2005. *The RoutledgeFalmer Reader in the History of Education*. Routledge, London.
Middlewood, D., Parker, R., 2005. *Leading and Managing Extended Schools*. Sage, Thousand Oaks.
Mitra, S., 2005. Self organising systems for mass computer literacy: findings from the "hole in the wall"
    experiments. *International Journal of Development Issues* 4, 1, 71–81.
Moore, M., Kearsley, G., 2011. *Distance Education*. Cengage Learning, Boston.
Perham M., 1961. *Native Administration in Nigeria*. Oxford University Press, Oxford.
Precourt, W., 1975. Initiation ceremonies and secret societies as educational institutions. In Brislin, R.,
    Bochner, S. and Lonner, W. (Eds.) *Cross-Cultural Perspectives on Learning*. Sage, Beverly Hills.
Prensky, M., 2001. Digital natives, digital immigrants. *On the Horizon* 9, 5, 1–13.
Psacharopoulos, G., Rojas, C., Velez, E., 1992. Achievement evaluation of Colombia's Escuela Nueva: is
    multigrade the answer? Working Paper 896, Technical Department, Latin American and Caribbean
    Region, World Bank, Washington.
Pyramid Research Services, 2010. The Impact of Mobile Services in Nigeria: How Mobile technologies
    Are Transforming Economic and Social Activities: Case Study: Longman Nigeria Introduces Mobile
    Reading to Nigeria. http://www.pyramidresearch.com/documents/IMPACTofMobileServicesIn
    NIGERIA.pdf
Robinson, K., 2010. *Finding your Element*. Penguin, London.
Saint, A., 1987. *Towards a Social Architecture: The Role of School Buildings in Post-War Britain*. Yale University
    Press, Yale.

Seaborne, M., Lowe, R., 1971. *The English School: Its Architecture and Organisation*. Routledge and Kegan Paul, London.

Stepien, W., Gallagher, S., 1993. Problem based learning, as authentic as it gets. *Educational Leadership* 50, 7, 25–28.

The Economist, 2014. A Tablet a Day: Using Technology for Education in Nigeria. http://www.economist.com/blogs/baobab/2014/07/using-technology-education-nigeria?fsrc=nlw | newe | 7–07–2014 | 5356cb88899249e1ccc53228 | UK

The Economist, 2011. Mobile telecoms in Africa: digital revolution. www.economist.com/node/18529875.

Uduku, O., 1992. An Analysis of Factors Affecting the Design of Secondary Schools in Nigeria. PhD Thesis, University of Cambridge.

Uduku, O., 1994. Wusasa, where the future acknowledges the past. *Habitat International* 18, 4, 67–79.

Uduku, O., 2006. Modernist architecture and "the tropical" in West Africa: the tropical architecture movement in West Africa, 1948–1970. *Habitat International* 30, 3, 396–411.

Uduku, O., 2010. Designing schools as development hubs for learning. Final project report for EdQual project, University of Bristol.

Uduku, O., 2013. The UNESCO-IDA school building programme in Africa: the Nigerian "Unity Schools". School is Another Place Conference, London, June.

UNESCO, 1990. Background Document, World Conference on Education for All 5–8 March, 1980, Jomtien. http://unesdoc.unesco.org/images/0009/000975/097552e.pdf

UNESCO, 2014. *Teaching and Learning: achieving quality for all. EFA Global Monitoring Report 2013/14*. UNESCO, Paris.

Van Straaten, J.F., Richards, S.J., and Lotz, F.J., 1967. *Ventilation and Thermal Considerations in School Building Design*. CSIR, Pretoria.

Woolner, P., 2010. *The Design of Learning Spaces*. Bloomsbury, London.

World Bank, 1986. *The Financing of Education in Developing Countries*. World Bank, Washington.

16

INCLUSIVE EDUCATION AND INTERNATIONAL DEVELOPMENT

Multilateral orthodoxies and emerging alternatives

Guy Le Fanu

Introduction

In recent years, inclusive education has become the subject of extensive global debate and discussion. Over 160 volumes containing the phrase "inclusive education" (most published in the last 10 years) are listed in the library catalogue of the Institute of Education in London. Several international journals are now exclusively devoted to the subject, and inclusive education is regularly selected as the theme for national and international conferences. Outside the academy, the promotion of inclusive education has provided the rationale for numerous international development programmes and the focus for international agreements such as the *Salamanca Statement* (WCSNE 1994) and *Dakar Framework for Action* (WEF 2000).

Inclusive education is a contested concept with a complex history. Barton (1997) believes inclusive education is a set of beliefs, values, and associated practices that has emerged as a result of struggles by disadvantaged people in particular contexts to transform education systems so they serve the interests of all, rather than interests of elites. Bines and Lei (2011) believe inclusive education has emerged from global human rights discourse, although they note that inclusive education is increasingly associated with international target setting (such as the Millennium Development Goals) in which human rights frameworks are "implicit" rather than "explicit" (p. 421). By contrast, Vislie (2003) and Singal (2006) express concern that education policymakers in some countries have narrowly equated inclusive education with the provision of special educational support for students with disabilities in mainstream schools, rather than with the promotion of Education for All and the transformation of education systems. However, despite these differences of interpretation, two emerging areas of consensus can be identified in inclusive education discourse. First, it is widely agreed that inclusive education is concerned with universalising access – in other words, with ensuring that all young people (irrespective of their socioeconomic background, gender, ethnicity, or any other factors) have access to education from early childhood onwards. Second, it is agreed that inclusive education is concerned with universalising quality – in other words, with ensuring all young people receive education of good quality that meets their various and collective educational needs.

This chapter discusses conceptualisations of inclusive education in the policy documents of three multilateral development agencies – UNESCO (United Nations Educational, Scientific and Cultural Organisation), UNICEF (United Nations Children's Fund), and the World Bank. These conceptualisations not only reflect various strands of global thinking about education but inform this thinking, as these organisations enjoy considerable global prestige, whilst the World Bank also has considerable financial resources at its disposal (Jones 2005). These conceptualisations are critiqued in the light of a substantial body of research evidence, and the chapter ends by discussing the implications of the findings for the policies and practices of the international development community in the field of inclusive education.

Conceptualisations of inclusive education among the multilaterals

In this section of the chapter, I discuss the conceptualisations of inclusive education in the policy documents of the aforementioned multilaterals. The term 'policy documents' refers to the literature produced by these agencies that identifies: their goals; the strategies these agencies and their partners will adopt in order to achieve these goals; and the rationales for the selection of these goals and strategies. First, the 'theories of inclusive education provision' are examined, i.e., the theories about the forms inclusive education should take. Second, the 'theories of educational change' are examined, i.e., the theories about how inclusive education will be achieved. The author is aware of the dangers of taking the policy documents of development agencies at face value, as sometimes this literature is designed to appease individuals and interest groups inside and outside the organisation, as much as to identify goals and associated strategies. Furthermore, goals and/or strategies are sometimes quietly 'shelved' by these agencies when obstacles to these goals/strategies emerge, e.g., the agencies are unable to access necessary funding and/or contexts of implementation prove unexpectedly challenging. However, the policy documents of international development agencies are not mere tissues of language. Once certain statements of intent are made by these organisations, it can be difficult for them to 'back down', particularly when they are subject to external scrutiny by the media and the research community. In addition, these documents are often developed through extensive processes of internal discussion and therefore possess considerable organisational 'buy in'.

UNESCO's policy guidelines on inclusion in education

UNESCO is formally the lead United Nations agency for education, although in practice it has been eclipsed by UNICEF and the World Bank in recent years (Jones 2005). UNESCO's *Policy Guidelines on Inclusion in Education* (2009) describes how senior policymakers in developing countries – particularly Ministries of Education – can promote inclusive education. The guidelines imply that UNESCO will support this process through advocacy and the provision of technical assistance – i.e., by persuading and assisting policymakers to implement these guidelines.

For UNESCO, inclusive education is:

> [A] process of addressing and responding to the diversity of needs of all children, youth, and adults through increased participation in learning, cultures, and communities, and reducing exclusion within and from education. It involves changes in content, approaches, structures and strategies, with a common vision that covers all children of the appropriate age range and a conviction that it is the responsibility of the regular school system to educate all children.
>
> (UNESCO 2009: 8–9)

UNESCO therefore acknowledges the diversity of students' educational needs, the complexity of educational processes, and the need to change these educational processes when they fail to meet students' requirements.

In order to achieve the above, UNESCO believes that Ministries of Education – working in association with the international development community and civil society – should develop and implement comprehensive policies, affecting all aspects of education. In order to "support the policy cycle" (UNESCO 2009: 22) (i.e., ensure the above policies are evidence based, implemented effectively, and amended in the light of emerging realities), these ministries must also improve their data-collection systems, draw up appropriate legal frameworks, establish monitoring and evaluation mechanisms, and develop assessment approaches that are flexible and nonstigmatising. The guidelines therefore assume that governments in developing countries have a certain amount of capacity in the fields of both policymaking and implementation. The guidelines also assume that this type of education reform will command popular support as inclusive education has an "educational justification", as it improves the lives of all children, a "social justification", as it promotes equity and social cohesion, and an "economic justification", as it is more cost-effective to educate all children in regular schools than have an expensive, multi-tiered system based on selection and segregation (UNESCO 2009: 8–9). Inclusive education is also cost-effective as it can be implemented relatively inexpensively through strategies such as: "multi-grade, multi-age and multi-ability classrooms", "initial literacy in mother tongues", "training of trainer models for professional development", "peer teaching", and "converting special schools into resource centres" (p. 11).[1]

UNICEF's Child Friendly Schools Manual

In its substantial and comprehensive *Child Friendly Schools Manual* – 244 pages in length and drawing on evidence from the 56 countries in which child-friendly schools (CFS) models have been implemented – UNICEF describes how schools can become more inclusive.

Like UNESCO's guidelines, the manual sees inclusive education as a multifaceted process, observing: "CFS models embrace a concept of quality that goes well beyond pedagogic excellence and performance outcomes" (UNICEF 2009: 18). However, UNICEF's conceptualisation of inclusive education is even broader than UNESCO's, encompassing health and nutrition as well as education-related matters. Furthermore, while stressing that CFS can take different forms in different contexts, the manual identifies broad areas of concern that schools need to address (e.g., location, design, and construction), specific issues of concerns within these areas of concern (for instance, 21 aspects of school design are identified in Table 3.1 on pages 64–65 of the manual), and specific ways in which these concerns can be met – for instance, Diagram 2A on page 73 depicts the footing for a timber post. There is therefore a tension in the UNICEF document between its focus on context sensitivity and its somewhat prescriptive approach. In terms of teaching and learning, the manual – like UNESCO's guidelines – prescribes "child-centred, interactive methodologies (which) make learning enjoyable and exciting to students and improve their retention, participation and performance" (p. 18), although the manual also acknowledges that transmission-based approaches to teaching and learning may have some validity in certain contexts (e.g., traditional societies in which the wisdom of village-elders is highly valued) and for certain purposes (e.g., the transfer of simple information and skills). The manual also rejects narrowly parochial approaches to education, stating "schools should not simply be a means of learning about local reality (but) also the gateways to the legacy of human endeavours and possibilities" (p. 62).

While UNESCO's guidelines envisage senior policymakers as the primary agents of change, the CFS manual anticipates local stakeholders will adopt this role – although, at a later stage in the education reform process, UNICEF expects governments are expected to play a significant role in 'scaling up' the child-friendly provision. The manual therefore expects school heads and classroom teachers to form "broad-based alliances" with "communities, local governments, civil society and the private sector" (UNICEF 2009: 113) in order to identify ways in which their schools can become more inclusive, with local education authorities and teacher-training colleges providing additional catalytic inputs (for instance, by providing high quality learning resources and continuing professional development for teachers). Whilst the reform process should be informed by local knowledge, the manual stresses that the reform process should be directed to the realisation of the *United Nations Convention on the Rights of the Child* (UNCRC; Office of the High Commission for Human Rights [OHCHR], 1989) – a document that identifies the diverse educational and education-related entitlements of children and the related role and responsibilities of various stakeholders, particularly parents, schools, and governments. Like UNESCO's guidelines, UNICEF's CFS manual claims that the change process will develop its own internal momentum as "important synergies are generated by linking elements of the child-friendly schools model" (UNICEF 2009: p. 34). For instance, if schools are well designed (e.g., classrooms are spacious, well furnished, and adequately soundproofed), then it will be easier for teachers to adopt child-centred pedagogies (e.g., encourage group-based, participatory learning). Furthermore, the manual posits that UNCRC provides a useful set of guiding principles to which stakeholders can refer when establishing child-friendly schools.

World Bank's Learning for All

In *Learning for All* (World Bank 2011), the World Bank outlines its ten-year strategy for promoting global educational development.

While *Learning for All* does not mention the phrase 'inclusive education', the World Bank's strategy is broadly inclusive. First, the strategy reaffirms the Bank's commitment to achieving universal access to education. Second, the strategy stresses the importance of educational quality, noting "quality needs to be the focus of education investments, with learning gains as a metric of quality" (World Bank 2011: 4). Third, the document recognises that education systems should particularly focus on meeting the needs of marginalised groups, namely "girls, people with disabilities, and ethno-linguistic minorities" (p. 5). However, unlike UNICEF's *Child Friendly Schools Manual*, *Learning for All* does not attempt to identify the diverse, complex, and evolving educational needs of young people and, in the light of this, specify the various forms inclusive provision should take. Rather, inclusive education is defined principally in terms of its ends: an economically productive population, enjoying "better health (and) reduced fertility", possessed of "an enhanced ability to adopt new technologies and/or cope with economic shocks", and engaged in "civic participation, and . . . environmental friendly behaviour" (p. 13). In its lack of concern for the needs of the whole child, *Learning for All* therefore lacks inclusiveness.

In order to promote universal access to education of good quality, *Learning for All* says that education systems need to be able to "transform . . . resources efficiently and effectively into learning outcomes" (World Bank 2011: 29). This in turn is only possible when these systems have the capacity "to formulate policy, set standards, implement quality assurance, assess student performance, manage human and financial resources, and engage in intergovernmental and external partnerships" (p. 29). This in turn will only happen if certain "mechanisms" are in place to "support clear and aligned function, authority, and responsibility with accountability within the system" (p. 32). In other words, education systems need to be carefully designed, intricately constructed, and subjected to close and continual scrutiny. In order to boost the performance of schools, it is also argued that education authorities should provide schools with targets, and incentives to achieve these targets, while simultaneously giving schools the freedom to decide how they should achieve these targets and parents the freedom to send their children to the best-performing schools in their localities (a process that could involve parents receiving vouchers to cover the costs of private education).

The World Bank believes it can assist Ministries of Education around the world to develop the capacities to design and operate effective and efficient education systems through providing them with high-quality technical assistance. In order to ensure this assistance is appropriate and relevant, the Bank "will develop a high-quality knowledge base on education reform" through deploying "new tools for system assessment and benchmarking (which) will provide detailed analysis of country capacities in a wide array of education policy domains" (World Bank 2011: 7). This knowledge base will be made widely available, thus promoting educational discussion within and between countries. The World Bank's knowledge-focused strategy reflects what I will term a 'context-transcendent' theory of knowledge. This theory assumes that reliable, accurate, meaningful, and useful educational data can be collected from countries, irrespective of local contexts; that these data can be stored in data-systems and easily retrieved from these systems; that these data are relatively straightforward, as well as reliable and accurate, and therefore that these data can be internationally compared and contrasted, irrespective of their source of origin; that these data can be understood by a wide variety of audiences, or at least their significance clearly communicated to a variety of audiences; and that these data can provide the basis for evidence-based educational decision making.

Comparing, contrasting, and contextualising the multilaterals' conceptualisations

Policy Guidelines (UNESCO 2009) and *Child Friendly Schools Manual* (UNICEF 2009) state that inclusive education must be sufficiently holistic to meet the diverse needs of learners, although UNICEF's understanding of what this involves is broader than UNESCO's. By contrast, *Learning for All* (World Bank 2011), while recognising the importance of educational quality, does not provide a comprehensive definition or detailed description of educational quality, either in terms of educational processes or educational outcomes. Both the UNESCO and World Bank documents assume that national governments will play a central role in initiating and directing educational change – although the World Bank wants local education providers to be granted significant levels of autonomy during the change process. However, while the World Bank stresses the need for governments to develop sophisticated systems and frameworks in order to manage this change process, UNESCO (while adopting a similarly technocratic approach) wants governments to ensure that inclusive educational principles are translated into inclusive educational practice. In short, UNESCO's approach is more values driven than the World Bank's approach, which is more concerned with boosting the effectiveness and efficiency of education systems. In contrast to the World Bank and UNESCO, the UNICEF document emphasises the leading role that schools and communities should play in planning and achieving inclusive education, although UNICEF also believes governments should also play a key role in supporting and scaling-up education reform. As the UNESCO and World Bank documents envisage education reform as a centrally orchestrated process, the two documents imply that it is the primary responsibility of UNESCO and the World Bank to engage with national governments. By contrast, the UNICEF document implies UNICEF will, at least initially, devote considerable resources to assisting local stakeholders to set up and run small-scale pilot projects.

The different conceptualisations of inclusive education of the three agencies can be placed in various discursive contexts. According to Jones (2005), the policies of UNESCO and UNICEF have been shaped by child-rights discourse – in particular the multidimensional depiction of these rights in *United Nations Convention on the Rights of the Child* (1989). By contrast, Menashy (2013: 751) believes the educational philosophy of the World Bank reflects the influence of 'human capital theory', which views education "as valuable only as it increases a human being's economic input based on his or her productivity". Neoliberalism's influence can be detected in the World Bank's enthusiasm for encouraging competition between education providers and providing choice for 'education consumers', coupled with the organisation's positive attitude towards low-fee private schools (p. 751). In addition, it can be posited that the system-centred approach of both UNESCO and the World Bank is informed by Western managerialism – a theory that assumes "all aspects of organisational life . . . should be controlled" (Hoyle and Wallace 2005: 68).

The conceptualisations of the three agencies can also be placed in institutional contexts. UNICEF's belief that schools should provide multiple services reflects the organisation's long-running commitment to promoting comprehensive child-welfare services, encompassing heath, child nutrition, and social inclusion, as well as education (Jones 2005). UNICEF's focus on the local and specific reflects the organisation's "long-standing tradition of small, if innovative and catalytic work" (Jones 2005: 164). UNESCO's somewhat formulaic and 'top-down' approach to educational development can be attributed to the organisation's detachment from development realities – the result of poorly funded programme offices, overly centralised decision-making processes, diminishing technical expertise, and other factors (Benavot 2011). The World Bank's 'economistic' approach to educational development reflects the fact that the Bank is essentially "a borrowing and lending financial institution" (Jones 2005: 94) that is "predominantly and disproportionately staffed by economists" (Menashy 2013: 758).

Conceptualisations of inclusive education in the research literature

The evidence base

Having discussed the conceptualisations of inclusive education of the three multilateral agencies, I now assess the validity of these conceptualisations in the light of a considerable body of research evidence – namely, 100 country-specific studies published in the *International Journal of Educational Development* (IJED) between 2011 and 2014. These studies discuss the extent to which education provision in individual countries (or occasionally small groups of countries) is inclusive, the reasons for the inclusiveness/noninclusiveness of this provision, and the attempts by various stakeholders to improve this situation. Thirty-six of the papers are qualitative case studies providing probing, densely textured analyses of particular educational situations; 34 are quantitative analyses identifying trends across broad educational terrains; 16 employ 'mixed methods' approaches; and 14 are exploratory studies, drawing on various sources, to generate hypotheses about educational realities. The vast majority of the studies focus on 'developing countries' – either countries classified as having medium levels of human development (50 of the studies) or low levels of human development (42 of the studies) in United Nations Development Programme's *Human Development Index* (UNDP 2013).

IJED was chosen as a source of papers because of its global reputation, its specific focus on educational development, and its nonideological editorial stance. Studies from the years 2011 and 2014 were selected to ensure that the material was as 'up to date' as possible. However, while the studies examine education provision from different angles in 37 countries, there are certain 'lacunae' within the research evidence – a subject that is discussed at the end of this section.

Conceptualisations of inclusive education provision in the research evidence

A number of interview-based studies convey the views of young people about their education. These studies are particularly valuable as young people's perceptions of inclusive education have an authenticity often lacking in the sometimes rather abstract formulations of educationalists. In Vietnam, Phelps et al. (2014) found that primary school students particularly appreciated being able to socialise with their friends; being treated with respect by their teachers; studying relevant and useful subjects; and attending clean, well-maintained schools with adequate toilet facilities. In rural China, Chung and Mason (2012) interviewed an 11-year-old boy and his mother and teachers and found he had dropped out of school because his school had failed to accommodate his intellectual interests, offer individualised support, and provide a distraction-free learning environment. In Peru, Ames (2012) – having interviewed two young children and their parents and teachers – concluded the children were struggling in school because their schools failed to value, or even acknowledge, their indigenous linguistic and cultural identities. Ames also found that both children had already been subjected to corporal punishment, even though they were only six years old. More positively, Lattimer and Kelly (2013) found that secondary students in Kenya enjoyed participating in an oral history project because they were able to take control of their own learning and carry out research in their own communities. Collectively, these studies, and others (see, for instance, Ananga 2011; Jere, 2012; Kim et al. 2012; Trudell 2012), indicate that students enjoy studying in safe, attractive, supportive, orderly, and sociable learning environments in which they have access to relevant, meaningful, varied, and structured curricula, which are both accessible and challenging.

Barriers to inclusive education according to the research evidence

While an increasing proportion of young people in developing countries are now enrolled in education programmes, significant numbers of young people still remain out of education, either because they have never enrolled in education or because they have 'dropped out' (Lewin and Sabates 2011). Even those enrolled in education programmes may only attend infrequently. The various barriers to educational access are discussed in the studies. Several of the studies note that education remains unaffordable for many families, even when education is theoretically free, as there are supplementary costs (such as the purchase of school uniforms), indirect costs (such as the cost of transport to and from school), and opportunity costs (such as the inability of young people enrolled in education to take up certain employment opportunities) (Zuze and Leibbrandt 2011; Hartwig 2013; Agrawal 2014). Even when education is affordable, family and community members sceptical or even hostile towards education may discourage, or even prevent, young people participating in education. Girls and young women in particular may be subjected to such pressure and intimidation (Warrington and Kiragu 2012; Unterhalter, Heslop and Mamedu 2013). Alternatively, socioeconomically disadvantaged families may be unable to provide young people with the various types of support – e.g., adequate nutrition or home conditions conducive for study – that promote students' retention in education (Abuya, Onsomu and Moore 2012; Le Fanu 2013). Complex enrolment procedures – particularly for people who have migrated from rural areas to cities (Tsujita 2013) and for immigrants (Buckland 2011) – may also deter young people from attending education institutions. There may also be a lack of educational options in certain regions – not only in rural areas with widely dispersed populations (Chung and Mason 2012) but also in urban areas where education authorities have failed to build sufficient schools to accommodate rapidly rising school-age populations (Cameron 2011). While the private sector has significantly increased the educational supply in many countries – particularly India – poor parents are generally unable to afford such provisions, even when school fees are relatively low (Bangay and Latham 2013).

Even if young people are enrolled in schools and colleges, they often receive a substandard education – another problem widely discussed in the studies. This problem is often associated with rapidly increasing enrolments in already overstretched education systems, leading (for instance) to increased class sizes, which in turn present significant pedagogical challenges (Zuze and Leibbrandt 2011; Sua 2012; Hartwig 2013). Thus, progress towards the first objective of inclusive education – universal access to education – can ironically hinder progress towards the second objective – education provision of good quality. However, the difficulties experienced by education systems in this respect are not just the result of 'student factors' but rather the interaction between 'student factors' and 'resource factors' such as: poorly maintained, poorly designed educational environments; insufficient teaching and learning resources, often of poor quality; and an inadequately trained, poorly remunerated, demoralised, and sometimes grossly unprofessional education workforce (Hammett and Staehili 2011; Zuze and Leibbrandt 2011; Davidson and Hobbs 2013). In some cases, the poor performance of teachers is associated with another 'resource-factor' – the inability and/or unwillingness of senior management to provide instructional leadership of good quality (Meade 2012; Hallinger and Lee 2013). School systems are also often antithetical to teaching and learning of good quality. Several of the studies highlight the damage caused when inappropriate curricula (systems for transferring, generating, and organising knowledge) are taught in schools. Sometimes these curricula are so narrow and irrelevant that they fail to engage and stimulate students (Bajaj 2012; Sua 2012), while, at other times, they are so broad and ambitious that teachers are only able to deliver 'watered-down' or selective versions of them (Peng et al. 2014; Zuze and Leibbrandt 2011). A number of studies also highlight the negative effects on schools of ill-considered language-of-instruction policies and associated practices. For instance, students may be taught in unfamiliar languages (rather than their mother tongues) and as result become confused, demoralised, and demotivated (Posel and Casale 2011; Graham 2013); or, alternatively, teachers may inexpertly attempt bilingual communication, with the result that students both fail to learn properly through their first language and fail to acquire proficiency in another language (Garrouste 2011). The studies also express concern about other problematic school-based practices such as grade retention, which demoralises 'failing' students (Chen et al. 2010); multigrade teaching, which places considerable demands on teachers (Chung and Mason 2012); and examination-centred teaching and learning (Le Fanu 2013). Another subject of concern is the disengagement of communities from schools in some locales, with the result that communities are unwilling to provide schools with necessary types and levels of support – a process observed in the highlands of Lesotho (Urwick 2011).

It should be noted that the above sets of 'exclusion factors' ('student factors', 'resource factors', 'system factors', and 'community factors') are closely linked. These sets of factors not only coexist but are symbiotic – for instance, disintegrating school infrastructure may demoralise school stakeholders, resulting in further neglect and abuse of this infrastructure. Similarly, rigid curricula can ossify already overly teacher-centred pedagogical practices.

Poor educational quality in developing countries is placed in various contexts in the studies. First, it is placed in geographic-demographic contexts, as discussed earlier: the difficulties governments face in providing education services to rapidly rising school-age populations in urban areas and to widely dispersed, sometimes diminishing populations in rural areas. Second, it is placed in the sociocultural context of (often long-standing and deep-rooted) hostility, contempt, and/or indifference towards certain sectors of the population – for instance, girls and young women (Warrington and Kiragu 2012; Unterhalter, Heslop and Mamedu 2013) and ethno-linguistic minorities (Ames 2012; Pherali and Garratt 2014).[2] Third, it is placed in the context of growing social-economic inequality, which means (for instance) disadvantaged young people often receive a substandard education because government education programmes in their locality are under-resourced and private education is prohibitively expensive (Cameron 2011; Woodhead, Frost and James 2013). Fourth, it is placed in governance contexts – specifically, the failure of governments around the world to provide the necessary inputs to schools (Zuze and Leibbrandt 2011; Hartwig 2013), to provide schools with clusters of support and supervision (Lynch et al. 2011; Meade 2012), to develop a substantial cadre of motivated and knowledgeable teachers (and thereafter provide these teachers with continuing professional development of good quality (Hardman, Abd-Kadir and Tibuhyinda 2012; Akyeampong et al. 2013), and the failure of governments to practise socially responsible, evidence-based decision making (Buckland 2011; Foulds 2013; Kucita et al. 2013). Fifth, it is placed in international development contexts – the sometimes negative influence of international agencies on domestic policymaking, particularly in low-income countries dependent on aid (Tabulawa 2011; Tikly 2011; Le Fanu 2013). Sixth, it is placed in historical contexts – the continuing, distortive influence of colonialism on education systems[3] and more country-specific historical events, such as the aftershocks of the Khmer Rouge regime on educational governance in Cambodia (Kim 2011). Like the aforementioned 'exclusion-factors', these 'contexts of exclusion' not only coexist but are symbiotic. For instance, the caste system in Nepal both generates and is sustained by inequalities of wealth and power (Pherali and Garratt 2014); and the inability of the Ministry of Education in Guatemala to provide the necessary support and supervision for rural schools is not only the result of government incapacity but the distant and sometimes hard-to-access location of these schools (Meade 2012).

Opportunities for inclusive education according to the research evidence

In this section, I briefly summarise five case studies of largely successful/partly successful attempts to promote inclusive education in developing countries, as described in the country-specific studies. The underlying messages of these case studies in terms of the promotion of inclusive education are also identified.

In rural Bangladesh, preprimary children were taught a "comprehensive, stimulating (and) challenging mathematics programme" (Opel et al. 2012: 108), which addressed "skills such as numbers, measurement, shapes, patterns, and space" (p. 104). At the end of the programme, it was found that the children had doubled their scores on almost all the tests, while the scores of the 'control group' had only slightly increased. The cost of developing the materials for the course (which were designed to be used in pairs or small groups) was only US$4 per child, and whilst the teachers required 95 hours of training in total, the authors believe this training would not be necessary if the underlying principles of the programme were incorporated in preservice and in-service training courses.

In rural Malawi, a programme was trialled in 20 rural primary schools to support the learning of children affected by HIV and AIDS, a number of whom had been orphaned (Jere 2012). The programme established various "circles of support" for these children (p. 758), with various stakeholders being assigned various responsibilities. For instance, 'class buddies' were selected to support the children in the classroom, and youth volunteers were appointed to set up afterschool clubs for these students and their buddies. At the end of the programme, it was found that dropout rates for the intervention group were far lower than those for the control group. Several head teachers and classroom teachers also observed increased social solidarity in their schools.

In India, thousands of children from socioeconomically disadvantaged backgrounds are enrolled in *Gyan Shala*, an alternative, nongovernment education programme (Bangay and Latham 2013). The programme is methodically organised. For instance, a manual has been developed that identifies what needs to be covered in a step-by-step basis during the school day, and learning is structured so the teachers provide some individualised support for all students during the course of the day. The programme is also designed to be equitable in terms of timetable, location, and cost. Teaching and learning is carried out in the first languages of students. Various comparative studies have established the effectiveness of the *Gyan Shala* approach in boosting students' learning. Dropout rates in these schools are also relatively low.

In Vietnam, the government developed 'Fundamental School Quality Level (FSQL) minimum standards', which defined "the minimum institutional capacity, instructional materials and teacher support, physical infrastructure, and school-community linkages required to maintain a healthy and productive learning environment" (Attfield and Vu 2013: 78). Data were then collected from the whole country to identify those schools "with an FSQL deficit" (p. 78). Those schools then received a "package of interventions" (p. 78) designed to ensure they met these standards. While "the impact of FSQL minimum standards is still not conclusively proven", the authors believe "initial evidence does point to improved scores linked to some interventions" (p. 81).

In China, the national government has promoted early childhood education and care (ECEC) in areas where there was previously little or no provision, particularly rural areas (Hu and Roberts 2013). This has involved strengthening the role of local government in managing and funding kindergartens (*Youreyuan*). A study was carried out of three rural, government-owned, privately run *Youreyuan*, which found that ECEC was now affordable to local people as a result of the new fee structures established by the government. The study also noted that local government was not only overseeing ECEC provision but increasingly able to monitor and regulate this provision. The author therefore concluded that the foundations for "structural quality" (p. 323) were now in place.

The above studies, to different extents and in different ways, reveal the diverse capacities of diverse actors and agencies to support inclusive education in development contexts. The Malawi study shows how various members of the school community can collectively support the education of vulnerable children. The Bangladesh study shows how the nonstate sector – in the form of BRAC, a large, national, nongovernmental organisation – can promote improved teaching and learning through developing an innovative mathematics programme for preprimary students. The India study shows how the nonstate sector can pioneer education provision outside government structures, which is both equitable and of good quality. Both the Vietnamese and Chinese case studies describe how subnational government contributed to the implementation of national initiatives. These studies also illustrate the growing capacities of some national governments to implement ambitious, system-wide educational initiatives (see also Jaramillo 2012). Finally, the studies show how the international development community in its various manifestations can contribute to, rather than impede, educational development (see also Davidson and Hobbs 2013). For instance, the programme in Malawi was funded by the Department for International Development (DFID) in the United Kingdom, with technical assistance not only being provided by a national research institute but universities in other sub-Saharan African countries and in the United Kingdom and United States. The data system employed in Vietnam was developed by World Bank and DFID, and, according to another study, funding for the under-resourced primary schools was provided by a consortium of donors to the tune of US$160 million (Carr-Hill 2011).

The studies also show the validity of employing certain strategies in the field of educational development. The Malawi study shows the value of using existing resources in communities and schools – in this case, the expertise and commitment of local stakeholders. The Malawi, Bangladesh, and India studies show the importance of designing carefully considered, multifaceted interventions that are sensitive to local realities. The studies also show the value of piloting certain approaches and then assessing and, if necessary, refining these approaches in the light of programme evidence before attempting 'scale-up'. The Vietnam study shows the potential benefits of collecting and analysing large quantities of data when designing and implementing large-scale interventions. The China study shows the need for education reform to be pragmatic – as the government-owned, privately run model of ECEC provision promoted by the government, whilst imperfect, was considered the most feasible, given existing resource constraints.

However, while the interventions discussed in this section are encouraging, even inspiring, they also reveal the significance of the obstacles to inclusive education. In Malawi, a number of children supported by the programme still struggled to attend school regularly. Furthermore, stakeholders expressed concern that only 15 children per school were supported by the programme, as there were substantially more children suffering significant levels of deprivation. This study therefore revealed the depth and scale of disadvantage in a particular development context and the inability of small-scale interventions, however thoughtfully designed, to resolve this problem. In India, the future of *Gyan Shala* is not assured, as it receives limited and uncertain funding from the government and cannot fully recoup its remaining expenses through cost-recovery measures. The study therefore indicates the precariousness of many development initiatives supported by the nonstate sector. In China, the authors expressed concern about the lack of "process quality" (Hu and Roberts 2013: 323) in the rural *Youeryuan* as a result of the lack of trained, experienced teachers; the shortage of equipment and materials; and the cost-cutting, profit-focused orientations of the directors of the *Youeryuan*. This study therefore illustrates the challenges governments face in endeavouring to increase educational access while simultaneously improving educational quality. In Vietnam, Carr-Hill (2011) found that, despite significant investments in under-resourced primary schools, the academic performance of the students in these schools actually declined relative to the performance of students in other schools – a phenomenon that the author attributes to increasing economic inequality in the country. The Vietnam case study therefore illustrates that even significant, targeted investments in education systems cannot always compensate for broader, structurally based patterns of social and economic change.

Gaps in the research evidence

While the studies are insightful about the various aspects of inclusive education, there are significant gaps in the research evidence, despite the size and scope of the evidence base.

First, the studies are not globally representative, suggesting that national research cultures are particularly weak in certain parts of the world and also that certain locales are less accessible and/or less attractive to international researchers than others. For instance, while 24 of the studies discuss East African countries and 16 Southern African countries, only seven of the studies cover West African countries and none Central African countries.[4] As education systems in these understudied regions/countries tend to be particularly fragile, these education systems deserve much greater attention from the research community. Second, certain important topics are not adequately covered by the studies. For instance, only four of the studies discuss at length the interactions between national governments and the international development community (Tabulawa 2011; Tikly 2011; Jaramillo 2012; Le Fanu 2013), and none of the studies scrutinises the workings of Ministries of Education at national, district, and/or local levels. Certain phases of education are also largely unconsidered, as only two of the studies focus on preprimary education provision (Opel et al. 2012; Hu and Roberts 2013) and only two on universities (Wang 2011; Bernardo and Baranovich 2014).

It is particularly concerning that the educational situation for young people with disabilities is only discussed in two studies (Lynch et al. 2011; Kocačević and Maćešić-Petrović 2012), as these individuals are particularly likely to be excluded from education or receive substandard education provision (Le Fanu 2014). High-quality ethnographic research (much of it published in the journal *Disability and Society*) has identified the barriers preventing young people with disabilities accessing education systems in developing countries. However, very little research has assessed the quality of the provision offered to the increasing numbers of young people enrolled in mainstream education systems, and very little research has discussed how this provision can be improved. Researchers also need to investigate both complementary forms of education support for children with disabilities, such as home and community-based education provision, and alternative forms of provision, such as special schooling and integrated education (a sort of 'halfway house' between special schooling and 'full mainstreaming'). Although educationalists have expressed often justified concern about the harmful effects of these alternative forms of provision (Bines and Lei 2011), educationalists should at least be prepared to consider the possibility that these forms of provision (as long as they are of good quality) may best meet the fundamental educational needs of some students in some circumstances – for instance, the need of profoundly deaf children to learn in sign language-rich environments (particularly when audiology services are not available or ineffective) and the need for blind children to receive the sustained and intensive support that will enable them to develop specific skill sets, such as Braille literacy. In this respect, these alternative forms of provision may therefore be more 'inclusive' than full mainstreaming. Furthermore, these alternative forms of provision may represent 'pathways to inclusion' if they help children to develop the various capacities that will enable them to transit successfully to mainstream education (see Le Fanu 2014 for further discussion).

Conclusion: reconsidering inclusive education in international development

This chapter has discussed the conceptualisations of inclusive education in policy documents produced by three multilateral agencies – UNESCO, UNICEF, and the World Bank. Drawing upon a considerable body of research evidence (100 country-specific studies), the chapter has also described stakeholder perceptions of inclusive education and barriers to/opportunities for the promotion of inclusive education in low-income countries. In the light of this evidence, how valid are the conceptualisations of the three agencies?

Both the UNICEF and UNESCO documents define inclusive education holistically as a process that meets the multiple, evolving, and inter-related needs of young people, including the need of young people to take control of their own learning as much as possible. (Disappointingly, the World Bank document does not define inclusive education in any depth or detail.) However, in a number of the country-specific studies, young people expressed their desire for relatively unsophisticated education forms of educational provision that met certain fundamental needs – for instance, the need to study relevant and interesting subjects, to be treated with respect by their teachers, and to be taught in their mother tongues (See Abuya et al. 2012; Chung and Mason 2012; Phelps et al. 2014). As these desires are relatively modest, it can be argued that they not only reflect stakeholder expectations but stakeholder requirements in many developing countries. When interviewed, the young people also tended to depict themselves as relatively passive participants in the learning process – as absorbers rather than generators of knowledge. These self-perceptions can in turn be attributed to the socially, culturally, and religiously conservative backgrounds of these individuals, as noted above. It can therefore be argued that UNICEF's and UNESCO's conceptualisations of inclusive education, while valuable, are not sufficiently attuned to local realities in developing countries. However, both UNICEF and UNESCO would counterargue that it is their role to promote an enlarged vision of educational opportunity, rather than be constrained by local context. It is also noticeable that in several of the studies, students enthusiastically participated in active learning, despite their lack of previous classroom exposure to this type of learning (See Kim et al. 2012; Opel et al. 2012; Lattimer and Kelly 2013).

In order for inclusive education is to be achieved in developing countries, UNICEF believes that schools and communities should be encouraged to set up small-scale demonstration projects. If successful, these projects can then be replicated in neighbouring schools and communities or even scaled-up nationally by Ministries of Education. According to UNICEF, these sorts of initiatives are valuable because they are 'owned' by local stakeholders who are therefore committed to their successful realisation. These initiatives are also informed by local knowledge and thus sensitive to local realities. Furthermore, these interventions can easily be modified in the light of emerging realities because they are 'works in progress', rather than ambitious, carefully planned, intricately structured, large-scale programmes. As discussed in the previous section, a number of the studies confirm the value of UNICEF's approach to educational development as they describe successful grassroots-based initiatives that have significantly improved educational access and quality. However, as also earlier discussed, the studies also describe significant obstacles to the promotion of inclusive education in developing countries. Even if these obstacles do not destabilise small-scale educational experiments, they can prevent the 'scale-up' of these experiments to other areas of the country. Rather than seeking to transform schools so they become 'child friendly' in multiple respects, UNICEF should therefore consider adopting more incremental and selective approaches in challenging development contexts. For instance, it is infeasible for UNICEF (and indeed UNESCO) to expect teachers to adopt 'learner-centred' pedagogies if they are unable (as well as unwilling) to do so. Rather, teachers should be provided with the various levels and types of support to modify their existing 'teacher-centred' pedagogies so these pedagogies become more attuned to the needs of students. Ironically, such a context-sensitive approach to education reform would not only be more appropriate in many development situations but more closely aligned with the context-sensitive rhetoric of *Child Friendly Schools Manual* (UNICEF 2009; see Schweisfurth 2011 for a discussion of this). Wherever possible, school-based initiatives should also be preceded and accompanied – as well as succeeded – by broader systemic reform in order for these initiatives to be sustainable.

Unlike the UNICEF document, the UNESCO document expects Ministries of Education to initiate transformative educational change through developing the complex policy frameworks and operating systems that (UNESCO believes) are necessary for the promotion of inclusive education. However, the studies indicate that many Ministries of Education in developing countries lack the capacity to carry out these ambitious tasks, as these organisations are struggling to provide schools and colleges with basic support and oversight. The UNESCO document also largely neglects the 'demand side' of education, even though the studies show social attitudes and practices are often significant obstacles to inclusive education. Rather than expecting struggling Ministries of Education to carry out tasks beyond their scope, UNESCO should therefore assist these organisations to steadily develop their capacities to improve educational access and quality. UNESCO should also identify feasible strategies for involving communities in education-reform processes. However, in order to perform these roles effectively, UNESCO will need to engage with development realities in all their complexity rather than stand on the sidelines.

The World Bank strategy places similarly unrealistic demands on Ministries of Education across the world. It also posits that educational opportunities for disadvantaged young people will increase and improve as a result of the expansion of the private sector in developing countries, as this phenomenon will both stimulate educational competition and increase educational supply. However, although several of the studies describe how local stakeholders have succeeded in establishing 'pro-poor' education programmes outside the state sector, other studies conclude that private schools have increased, rather than reduced, the inequality of educational opportunity in various development contexts. In addition, the World Bank recommends that Ministries of Education should provide parents with school performance data so parents can select the best schools for their children. Again, the studies indicate that this strategy is likely to prove inappropriate in certain development contexts. For instance, will governments always be able to effectively collect and disseminate these data? And how much sense does it make to talk of educational choice when educational options are so limited for so many people in developing countries?

Central to the World Bank's strategy is its knowledge-based approach to educational development. This approach is particularly concerned with the collection of context-transcendent 'top-line' education data that enable comparisons to be made within and between countries. However, while some of the studies indicate these data can be invaluable for policymakers and implementers (assuming these data can be effectively collected across wide geographical areas), many of the studies also show that educational interventions must be informed by the context-specific knowledge of local stakeholders if they are to be sensitive to local realities and thus both effective and sustainable. It is hard to collect, store, analyse, and disseminate context-specific knowledge, and these processes are fraught with ethical dilemmas as well as technical challenges. However, in order to both practise and promote effective educational development, the World Bank needs to develop a knowledge-management strategy that recognises the significance of context-specific knowledge (see McGrath and King 2004 for a discussion of this).

In summary, this chapter has shown that, while there are formidable barriers to the promotion of inclusive education in developing countries, international development agencies can significantly contribute to improving educational access and quality for young people. However, in order to do this, these agencies must question development orthodoxies, engage with development realities, and form 'two-way' development partnerships. Researchers in both the North and the South also have an obligation to widen the scope of their operations in order to broaden the evidence base for educational development. In particular, they must be more ready and willing to carry out research in the most challenging development contexts among the most marginalised groups.

Notes

1 For a more detailed discussion of UNESCO's approaches towards inclusive education, see Le Fanu (2013).
2 None of the studies discusses social attitudes and practices towards people with disabilities in any detail. However, the subject is addressed later in this chapter.
3 This is exemplified in the use of 'prestigious' European languages as languages of instruction in sub-Saharan African countries, although they are not the first languages of most students (Posel and Casale 2011; Trudell 2012).
4 Furthermore, none of the studies discusses North Africa, only one the Middle East and only one Oceania.

References

Abuya, B.A., Onsomu, E.O., Moore, D., 2012. Educational challenges and diminishing family safety net faced by high-school girls in a slum residence, Nairobi, Kenya. *International Journal of Educational Development* 32, 81–91.

Agrawal, T., 2014. Educational inequality in rural India. *International Journal of Educational Development* 34, 11–19.

Akyeampong, K., Lussier, K., Pryor, J., Westbrook, J., 2013. Improving teaching and learning of basic maths and reading in Africa: Does teacher preparation count? *International Journal of Educational Development* 33, 272–282.

Ames, P., 2012. Language, culture and identity in the transition to primary school: Challenges to indigenous children's rights to education in Peru. *International Journal of Educational Development* 32, 454–462.

Ananga, E.D., 2011. Typology of school dropout: The dimensions and dynamics of dropout in Ghana. *International Journal of Educational Development* 31, 374–381.

Attfield, I., Vu, B.T., 2013. A rising tide of primary school standards – The role of data systems in improving equitable access for all to quality education in Vietnam. *International Journal of Educational Development* 33, 74–87.

Bajaj, M., 2012. From "time pass" to transformative force: School-based human rights education in Tamil Nadu, India. *International Journal of Educational Development* 32, 72–80.

Bangay, C., Latham, M., 2013. Are we asking the right questions? Moving beyond the state vs non-state providers debate: Reflections and a case study from India. *International Journal of Educational Development* 33, 244–252.

Barton, L. 1997. Inclusive education: romantic, subversive or realistic? *International Journal of Inclusive Education* 1, 3, 231–242.

Benavot, A., 2011. "Imagining a transformed UNESCO with learning at its core." *International Journal of Educational Development* 31, 558–561.

Bernardo, M.A.C., Baranovich, D.-L., 2014. Higher education in the heart of armed conflict: The pivotal role of student affairs. *International Journal of Educational Development* 35, 78–85.

Bines, H., Lei, P., 2011. Disability and education: The longest road to inclusion. *International Journal of Educational Development* 31, 419–424.

Buckland, S., 2011. From policy to practice: The challenges to educational access for non-nationals in South Africa. *International Journal of Educational Development* 31, 367–373.

Cameron, S., 2011. Whether, and where to enrol? Choosing a primary school in the slums of urban Dhaka, Bangladesh. *International Journal of Educational Development* 31, 357–366.

Carr-Hill, R., 2011. A large scale donor attempt to improve educational status of the poor and household income distribution: The experience of PEDC in Vietnam. *International Journal of Educational Development* 31, 251–261.

Chen, X., Liu, C., Zhang, S., Shi, Y., Rozelle, S., 2010. Does taking one step back get you two steps forward? Grade retention and school performance in poor areas in rural China. *International Journal of Educational Development* 30, 544–559.

Chung, C., Mason, M., 2012. Why do primary school students drop out in poor, rural China? A portrait sketched in a mountain village. *International Journal of Educational Development* 32, 537–545.

Davidson, M., Hobbs, J., 2013. Delivering reading intervention to the poorest children: The case of Liberia and EGRA-Plus, a primary-grade reading assessment and intervention. *International Journal of Educational Development* 33, 283–293.

Foulds, K., 2013. The continua of identities in postcolonial curricula: Kenyan students' perceptions of gender in school textbooks. *International Journal of Educational Development* 33, 165–174.

Garrouste, C., 2011. Explaining learning gaps in Namibia: The role of language proficiency. *International Journal of Educational Development* 31, 223–233.

Graham, B., 2013. Creating cycles of writing and reading in a resource-poor school community in Kenya: Could one literacy event lead to ongoing literacy practices? *International Journal of Educational Development* 33, 294–301.

Hallinger, P., Lee, M., 2013. Exploring principal capacity to lead reform of teaching and learning quality in Thailand. *International Journal of Educational Development* 33, 305–315.

Hammett, D., Staehili, L.A., 2011. Respect and responsibility: Teaching citizenship in South African high schools. *International Journal of Educational Development* 31, 269–276.

Hardman, F., Abd-Kadir, J., Tibuhyinda, A., 2012. Reforming teacher education in Tanzania. *International Journal of Educational Development* 32, 826–834.

Hartwig, K.A., 2013. Using a social justice framework to assess educational quality in Tanzanian schools. *International Journal of Educational Development* 33, 487–496.

Hoyle, E., and Wallace, M., 2005. *Educational Leadership: Ambiguity, Professionals and Managerialism.* Sage Publications, London.

Hu, B.Y., Roberts, S.K., 2013. A qualitative study of the current transformation to rural village early childhood in China: Retrospect and prospect. *International Journal of Educational Development* 33, 316–324.

Jaramillo, M., 2012. The changing role of international cooperation in developing countries (as they develop): A case study of skills development policies in Peru. *International Journal of Educational Development* 32, 22–30.

Jere, C.M., 2012. Improving educational access of vulnerable HIV prevalence communities of Malawi: The potential of open and flexible learning strategies. *International Journal of Educational Development* 32, 756–763.

Jones, P., 2005. *The United Nations and Education: Multilateralism, Development and Globalisation.* Routledge-Falmer, Abingdon.

Kim, C.Y., 2011. Child labour, education policy and governance in Cambodia. *International Journal of Educational Development* 31, 496–504.

Kim, P., Buckner, E., Kim, H., Makany, T., Taleja, N., Parikh, V., 2012. A comparative analysis of a game-based learning model in low-socioeconomic communities in India. *International Journal of Educational Development* 32, 329–340.

Kocačević, J., Maćešić-Petrović, D., 2012. Inclusive education – Empirical experience from Serbia. *International Journal of Educational Development* 32, 463–470.

Kucita, P., Kivunja, C., Maxwell, T.W., Kuyini, B., 2013. Bhutanese stakeholders' perceptions about multi-grade teaching as a strategy for achieving quality primary universal education. *International Journal of Educational Development* 33, 206–212.

Lattimer, H., Kelly, M., 2013. Engaging Kenyan secondary students in an Oral History Project: Education as emancipation. *International Journal of Educational Development* 33, 476–486.

Le Fanu, G., 2013. The inclusion of inclusive education in international development: Lessons from Papua New Guinea. *International Journal of Educational Development* 33, 139–148.

Le Fanu, G., 2014. International development, disability, and education: towards a capabilities-focused discourse and praxis. *International Journal of Educational Development* 38, 69–79.

Lewin, K.M., Sabates, R., 2011. Who gets what? Is improved access to basic education pro-poor in Sub-Saharan Africa? *International Journal of Educational Development* 32, 517–528.

Lynch, P., McCall, S., Douglas, G., McLinden, M., Mogesa, B., Mwaura, M., Muga, J., Njoroge, M., 2011. Inclusive educational practices in Kenya: Evidencing practices of itinerant teachers who work with children with visual impairments in local mainstream schools. *International Journal of Educational Development* 31, 478–488.

McGrath, S., King, K., 2004. Knowledge-based aid: A four agency comparative study. *International Journal of Educational Development* 24, 2, 167–181.

Meade, A., 2012. A mixed-methods analysis of achievement disparities in Guatemalan primary schools. *International Journal of Educational Development* 32, 575–589.

Menashy, F., 2013. Interrogating an omission: The absence of a rights-based approach to education in World Bank policy discourse. *Discourse: Studies in the Cultural Politics of Education* 34, 5, 749–764.

OHCHR, 1989. *United Nations Convention on the Rights of the Child.* Author, Geneva.

Opel, A., Zaman, S.S., Khanom, F., Aboud, F.E., 2012. Evaluation of a mathematics program for pre-primary children in rural Bangladesh. *International Journal of Educational Development* 32, 104–110.

Peng, W.J., McNess, E., Thomas, S., Wu, X.R., Zhang, C., Li, J.Z., Tian, H.S., 2014. Emerging perceptions of teacher quality and teacher development in China. *International Journal of Educational Development* 34, 77–89.

Phelps, R., Graham, A., Tuyet, N.H.T., Geeves, R., 2014. Exploring Vietnamese children's experiences of, and views on, learning at primary school in rural and remote communities. *International Journal of Educational Development* 36, 33–43.

Pherali, T., Garratt, D., 2014. Post-conflict identity crisis in Nepal: Implications for educational reforms. *International Journal of Educational Development* 34, 42–50.

Posel. D., Casale, D., 2011. Language proficiency and language policy in South Africa: Findings from new data. *International Journal of Educational Development* 31, 449–457.

Schweisfurth, M., 2011. Learner-centred education in developing country contexts: From solution to problem? *International Journal of Educational Development* 31, 425–432.

Singal, N., 2006. Inclusive education in India: international concept, national interpretation. *International Journal of Inclusive Education* 53, 3, 351–369.

Sua, T.Y., 2012. Democratization of secondary education in Malaysia: Emerging problems and challenges of educational reform. *International Journal of Educational Development* 32, 53–64.

Tabulawa, R., 2011. The rise and attenuation of the basic education programme (BEP) in Botswana: A global-local dialectic approach. *International Journal of Educational Development* 31, 433–442.

Tikly, L., 2011. A roadblock to social justice? An analysis and critique of the South African education roadmap. *International Journal of Educational Development* 31, 86–94.

Trudell, B., 2012. Of gateways and gatekeepers: Language, education and mobility in francophone Africa. *International Journal of Educational Development* 37, 368–375.

Tsujita, Y., 2013. Factors that prevent children from gaining access to schooling: A study of Delhi slum households. *International Journal of Educational Development* 33, 348–357.

UNDP, 2013. *Human Development Report 2013. The Rise of the South: Human Progress in a Diverse World.* UNDP, New York.

UNESCO, 2009. *Policy Guidelines on Inclusion in Education.* UNESCO, Paris.

UNICEF, 2009. *Child Friendly Schools Manual.* UNICEF, New York.

Unterhalter, E., Heslop, J., Mamedu, A., 2013. Girls claiming education rights: Reflections on distribution, empowerment and gender justice in Northern Tanzania and Northern Nigeria. *International Journal of Educational Development* 33, 566–575.

Urwick, J., 2011. "Free primary education" in Lesotho and the disadvantages of the highlands. *International Journal of Educational Development* 31, 234–243.

Vislie, L., 2003. From integration to inclusion: focusing global trends and changes in western European societies. *European Journal of Special Needs Education* 18, 1, 17–35.

Wang, L., 2011. Social exclusion and inequality in higher education in China: A capability perspective. *International Journal of Educational Development* 31, 277–286.

Warrington, M., Kiragu, S., 2012. "It makes more sense to educate a boy": Girls "against the odds" in Kajiado, Kenya. *International Journal of Educational Development* 32, 301–309.

Woodhead, M., Frost, M., James, Z., 2013. Does growth in private schooling contribute to Education for All? Evidence from a longitudinal, two cohort study in Andhra Pradesh, India. *International Journal of Educational Development* 33, 65–73.

World Bank, 2011. *Learning for All: Investing in People's Knowledge and Skills to Promote Development. World Bank Group Education Strategy.* Author, Washington.

World Conference on Special Needs Education, 1994. *The Salamanca Statement on Special Needs Education Access and Quality.* UNESCO, Paris.

World Education Forum, 2000. *Dakar Framework for Action.* UNESCO, Paris.

Zuze, T.L., Leibbrandt, M., 2011. Free education and social inequality in Ugandan primary schools: A step backwards or a step in the right direction? *International Journal of Educational Development* 31, 169–178.

17

LOW-COST PRIVATE SCHOOLS

What we need to know, do know, and their relevance for education and development

James Tooley

Introduction

It is now widely accepted that low-cost private schools exist in large numbers across developing countries, serving a majority of children in poor urban settings and a significant minority in rural areas. From tentative initial thoughts on the sector (Tooley 2000a, 2000b, 2000c), there is now a burgeoning literature on low-cost private schools, including several major books (e.g., Srivastava and Walford 2007; Srivastava 2013; Macpherson, Robertson and Walford 2014; Dixon 2013; Dixon and Tooley 2009). However, the literature reveals a hugely polarised debate about the *significance* of low-cost private schools.

Why the controversy? I have used the phrase "de facto privatisation" to describe the low-cost private school movement (Tooley and Dixon 2006); this phrase is now in wide circulation (e.g., CEDAW 2014; Rolleston and Adefeso-Olateju 2014). But this term carries huge significance: privatisation is the assigning of businesses or services to private rather than state control or ownership. It is normally considered a *top-down* approach (governments 'denationalise' particular industries, e.g., railways or steel). "De facto privatisation", on the other hand, is a "bottom-up" privatisation, where *the people themselves*, not the state – indeed, often against the wishes of the state – are engaged in reassigning education to private rather than state control and ownership. So the controversy seems engendered by the realisation that the people themselves are embracing an alternative solution to the delivery of education to that which has been the accepted wisdom since around 1948 (with the Universal Declaration of Human Rights). There is a lot at stake if the people themselves appear to be rejecting 65 years of development consensus.

My reading of the literature suggests a categorisation of three main positions that stake out this controversy concerning the relevance of low-cost private schools to development:

1. Low-cost private schools are largely irrelevant to the promotion of Education for All; endorsing parental choices for them is positively harmful to the goal of promoting universal and free public[1] education (e.g., Lewin 2007).
2. Parental choices for low-cost private schools have to be tolerated, given the parlous state of public education; their continued patronage should inspire us to our main goal of getting the public education sector in order (e.g., Härmä 2013).

3.   Parental choices for low-cost private schools and the parlous state of public education should make us think differently about the potential role of public and private sectors in education for development; private education itself can offer a route to providing educational opportunities for all (e.g., Dixon 2013).

That is, low-cost private schools are either irrelevant, a temporary solution, or a potentially permanent alternative. This chapter asks what evidence we would need to know in order to be able to adjudicate between these positions before outlining what we do in fact know. The conclusion also addresses some fundamental issues. First I define my terms.

What are low-cost private schools?

Private schools are familiar enough: they are defined as schools that are owned and managed independently of government, usually under government regulations, and that charge user fees. *Low-cost* private schools are those that have *a low cost of delivery* – all the costs of inputs are low, reflected in low fees charged to parents. (This is why I prefer *low-cost* rather than the alternative sometimes used, *low-fee* private schools: even high-cost private schools can charge low fees if they are subsidised. The subject of interest, however, is schools with a low cost of delivery.[2]) There is no one type of low-cost private school – as we shall see, they have emerged in settings across continents. When I first encountered them in poor areas of Hyderabad, I could identify three types, which I've seen replicated across settings since: first, some had started as a nursery by a woman, typically with her own and neighbours' children. Once the children had reached primary-school age, parents had persuaded the woman to continue with their children, and so a school had emerged, from class I upwards. Another type had started typically by a young man as a 'tuition' class 'cramming' for school-leaving examinations. The students would point out that they learnt more in his tuition class than they did in school, so why not stay with him full-time? So a school emerged, this time from Class X downwards. A third type would feature men or women, sometimes a couple, who, presumably seeing the success of existing private schools in their locality, started one themselves. Buildings varied enormously, and their finesse would reflect the relative conditions of the communities they served. Some would be in a converted house, perhaps the very home where the school had been started, others in converted buildings that had been created for other purposes, a shop, a factory, an office; finally others were in purpose-built schools, often growing organically as more rooms, floors, or side-buildings were added to accommodate increased demand. I've seen low-cost private schools built on stilts in the dark waters of the Lagos lagoon, perched on the edge of villages in the mountains of Gansu province, China, or crowded in amongst the wooden shacks in Nairobi slums, Kenya. A key feature of all low-cost private schools is that they typically employ teachers from the communities themselves, so teachers have no 'social distance' from the children they teach; schools are typically large employers of unemployed youth (especially in Africa) or in India, young women who are encouraged to do any other work (Tooley 2009 gives more flavour of the low-cost private school sector across the developing world).

'Nonprofit' private schools, run by churches, mosques, charities, or NGOs, can be distinguished from 'for profit', those run by proprietors, partnerships, or companies. The second category does not necessarily make large or even any surpluses. But if any surpluses are made, then these are available to the person/partnership/company to use as they want, including reinvesting in the school and/or for personal use. (In India, where for profit education is currently illegal, a third category could be useful: 'de facto' for profit private schools, ostensibly run by a nonprofit trust or society, but in effect run by an individual or partnership.)

Finally, how low is 'low-cost'? A recent literature review, noting the difficulties in definition, settled on schools engaged in "delivery of education to poorer sections of society", which were clearly "non-elite private schools" (Day Ashley et al. 2014:1 and 5). I have suggested a more exact definition (e.g., Tooley 2013a; Tooley and Longfield 2014a, 2014b), which I hope will gain traction. This works backwards from poor families' incomes to estimate what they could afford to spend on private schooling. Using the internationally accepted $1.25 and $2 per person per day poverty lines (at 2005 exchange rates and purchasing power parity), we first calculate, for a specific country/region, the total annual income for an average-sized family. We then take some percentage of that total annual income and specify that this is the maximum amount that can be spent on schooling (I used 10%, inspired by discussion in Lewin, 2007. But the figure can be adjusted higher or lower as more is known about what families can afford). Finally, we divide that 'maximum amount' by the average number of school-aged children in a family. This gives us the maximum annual per child schooling costs, in other words, maximum fees affordable in private schools. For the $1.25 poverty line calculation, we specify this as 'lowest cost', while the $2 poverty line gives 'low cost' private schools. (For instance, the study in the slums of Monrovia, Liberia, found 78 % of for profit private schools were 'lowest cost'. Looking at all areas of Sierra Leone (Western Area), i.e., not just the poorest, found 66 % of 'for profit' private schools were lowest cost and 15 % low cost (Tooley and Longfield 2014a, 2014b).

What do we need to know?

What would we need to know about low-cost private schools in order to be able to adjudicate between the three major positions concerning their relevance outlined above? Given the sharply polarised nature of the debate, it may be useful to think about this in a general way at first, before putting this in the context of low-cost private schools. Let me try this thought experiment:

Suppose a phenomenon is identified as having emerged, without outside assistance, in poor areas of a developing country that one or more commentators say seems to be a *major solution* to an *important development issue*. Let's call this phenomenon X. In what follows, we could think of it as being a cure for diarrhoea or malaria, a new way of creating affordable homes, or of growing nutritious food, anything that satisfies being "a *major solution* to an *important development issue*".

What should be the reaction? I suggest that those concerned about finding major solutions to important development issues should be concerned with finding answers to the following 10 propositions. If evidence could be found positively supporting all 10 propositions, then it would seem positively negligent of international agencies, philanthropists, academics, etc., not to take this phenomenon seriously.

1. Generalisability: Is X generalisable beyond the communities where it was first identified? We would take this phenomenon seriously if it could be shown that *it was already serving several different communities,* say poor communities in more than one city. If we found it in rural communities as well as urban in that country, even better, and if in more than one country, better still. It would be especially significant if it is serving large numbers of the poor, rather than only a handful. Our Gold Standard might be if we found that, acting on their own, communities on different continents, e.g., Africa, South Asia, Latin America, had also found and were using X.
2. Quality: Is the phenomenon X better than other alternatives? In particular if government is also involved in attempts to solve the same problem, is the proposed alternative better than government provision? It would be probably unrealistic to require that X *already* delivers quality comparable to leading international standards – for this phenomenon has emerged

229

from poor communities themselves, without access to the R&D resources that have led to international standards. Instead, our Gold Standard would be that the quality is better than alternatives; this in itself would be remarkable given that this innovation has emerged without any of the advantages and resources of government or international agencies. This would suggest, of course, that if additional resources were available to this phenomenon, its quality could be improved even further.

3. Equity – Affordability: Is the phenomenon X affordable to the poor and poorest? Again it would seem unreasonable to expect that it should be affordable by *all* of the poor *already*. Instead, it would count in its favour if many in different types of poor communities were clearly able to afford it. Ways of reaching *all* of the poor through X would then be a separate matter for the sector itself, international agencies, philanthropists, governments, etc. Finally, we would also be interested if X was as or more affordable than other options, including those provided by government. Again, we wouldn't here assume that X should be the same cost to families as heavily subsidised government provision (otherwise what would the government subsidies be for?); rather we would assume it could be competitive with this.

4. Equity – Geography: Is X geographically available to different types of poor communities? If we found X was already being used by, say, lowest caste groups (in India), lowest quintile of income/wealth groups, poorest religious groups, etc. and reaching rural as well as urban communities, then this would make X appear very desirable. Again, we wouldn't need to show that it was reaching *all of the poor* now, for the reasons given above. What we're particularly concerned with here is that X is not discriminatory against ethnic, religious, caste, or other disadvantaged groups. Moreover, if X could be shown to reduce differences between the most disadvantaged groups and others in society, relative to alternatives, including government, then this would also count in its favour.

5. Equity – Gender: Does the phenomenon discriminate against girls?[3] If there are cultural or socioeconomic barriers to girls using X, then it might be unrealistic to expect X to *already* reach equal numbers of girls and boys. However, we'd reasonably expect that, where these cultural or socioeconomic barriers are lower, then we do approach or even exceed gender parity. Finally, we might also be interested in whether or not X was able to narrow gender gaps better than alternatives, including government.

6. Financial – sustainability: Is supply of the phenomenon financially sustainable? Obviously financial data would be preferable, but in their absence one key indicator might be the length of time that suppliers are in the market. Another might be the numbers of participants already in the market, for if we found huge numbers then it would seem unlikely such supply was not financially sustainable.

7. Financial – cost-effectiveness: Is the supply of the phenomenon as cost-effective as alternatives, including government alternatives? This is not such an important criterion because it is implicit that financial sustainability tempered with the poor's ability to pay will lead to a cost-effective approach. Nonetheless, X would be expected to be at least as cost-effective as any government alternative.

8. Choice – Desired option for the poor: Is the phenomenon actually desired by the poor? If it's used by many, then we need to know that they have chosen it because it is what they want. The Gold Standard here would be if it was found to be the most preferred option of the poor, more preferred than other alternatives, including government provision.

9. Choice – Poor able to make informed choices: Can the poor make informed choices about X? Are the poor able to understand what X is giving them, whether through technical knowledge about X or through proxy measures?

10. Accountability: Is the delivery of X accountable to the poor? That is, is it responsive to their needs and desires and able to deliver what is required when and where and at the price that is required?

These 10 propositions seem to be the areas that would be of most concern to those interested in finding major solutions to important development problems.

Let's return from our thought experiment. If we substitute 'low cost private schools' for the phenomenon X above, then we have 10 propositions that would need to be satisfied if those interested in development were to take this area seriously. If all of them are satisfied, then low-cost private schools would need to be taken very seriously indeed as a solution to the problem of delivery of educational opportunities to the poor.

Now, usefully these 10 propositions neatly overlap with the first 12 'assumptions' of a recent literature review commissioned by the British aid agency, Department for International Development (DFID). This review was in response to the controversy about low-cost private schools, commissioned in order to establish what is known and what needs to be known about the area to inform policy decisions (Day Ashley et al. 2014). (The commissioned report also has assumptions 13 to 17, which are all about government capacity [e.g., "government regulation/subsidies improves the quality, equity, sustainability" of low-cost private schools]. I suggest these assumptions are not relevant to the discussion to decide the significance of low-cost private schools to development; discussion of government capacity should come only after we've decided on the importance of the sector.)

What do we know?

In this section, I summarise the evidence about each of the 10 propositions above concerning low-cost private schools. To avoid any misgivings about potential bias, in this section I restrict myself only to the evidence base used by Day Ashley et al. in addressing their first 12 'assumptions'. This is done even though their restriction on publications from the past five years (p. 4) seemed to exclude all research conducted by pioneers in this area and even though some recent major sources seem to be missing. However, I felt it important in a topic as controversial as this to explore the significance of low-cost private schools from the same research territory as that set out by this DFID-sponsored review.

Generalisability

Low-cost private schools exist across the developing world. They satisfy the Gold Standard (as above) of being found in urban and rural areas, in different parts of the same country, in different countries, and across continents. This is so much taken for granted now that it doesn't even appear as a proposition in Day Ashley et al.; it is only implicit. But I believe it is hugely significant and needs reinforcing: low-cost private schools as a phenomenon are ubiquitous, across communities, countries, and continents. In the literature in Day Ashley et al., focused only on DFID 'priority countries', they are found in India, Pakistan, Bangladesh, Nepal, Nigeria, Kenya, Tanzania, Ghana, South Africa, Malawi, and Jamaica. Other research has shown them in South-East Asia (Tooley 2009), and there are also studies from Latin America. Moreover, within the countries researched, a large majority of urban children are using low-cost private schools – for example, 70% of pre- and primary children are in private schools in Lagos, Nigeria, according to Härmä and Adefisayo (2013: 129), while across India, it is reported that 28% of rural children nationally are in private school, rising to 50% in certain states (Day Ashley et al. 2014: 23).

Quality

The evidence shows that low-cost private schools are of higher quality, in terms of educational outcomes and teacher commitment, than government school. Low-cost private schools have met the desired Gold Standard. It doesn't mean to say that they already satisfy international standards, which would seem unrealistic given that international standards have been acquired with large expenditure of R&D by governments and agencies. But although low-cost private schools have emerged without any of the resources of government or international agencies behind them, they are already achieving better results than government schools. If R&D resources were available, then their quality could clearly be improved even further.

The first hypothesis of Day Ashley et al., "Private schools are better quality than state schools", leads to two "testable assumptions" that are well-supported by the literature. First, "pupils attending private schools achieve better learning outcomes than state school pupils". Here, excellent studies from India including Desai et al. (2008) and French and Kingdon (2010) show "positive private school achievement advantage based on standardised test scores" even after controlling for observable and unobservable household factors (Day Ashley et al. 2014: 15). Other rigorous studies find similar effects from other settings, including in Africa (p. 16).

Notwithstanding this superior performance of private schools, the authors note "*overall learning levels of children in rural areas in many countries remain worryingly low*, whether at private or public schools" (p. 18). As already noted, it would be odd to expect an initiative that has wholly emerged from poor communities themselves to be already offering an education of international standards.

Evidence also strongly supports the second assumption, that "teaching in private schools is better than in state schools" (p. 14). Teaching is better "in terms of more teacher presence and teaching activity, and teaching approaches that are more likely to lead to improved outcomes" (p. 19). This is positively supported by 12 out of the 14 studies reviewed.

Equity – affordability

The evidence shows that low-cost private schools are affordable to the poor. They are used by significant numbers of the poor and poorest communities extending to caste, income/wealth, and rural and urban. This is not to say that they are necessarily affordable by *all* of the poor or poorest *now*, an unrealistic expectation of an initiative that has emerged from within poor communities themselves. Moreover, the cost of sending a child to low-cost private schools is sometimes very competitive against government options – some evidence even suggests it could be a cheaper option to parents than government schools.

Here (and for each of the 'equity' propositions) I part company with Day Ashley et al. While their assumption is "The poor and poorest are able to pay private school fees" (p. 27), in places they seem to have interpreted this to mean 'all of the poor' and 'all of the poorest'; with this unrealistic assumption, their evidence leads them to an overall 'neutral' conclusion. I suggest on the contrary that their evidence in fact positively supports their assumption (and my proposition) because they show private schools being used by significant proportions of the poor, including even *the poorest*.

For instance, Härmä (2011) "finds that despite a vast majority of parents indicating a *preference* for private schools over poor quality government alternatives, *only 41 percent* of the children in the sample were actually attending private schools" (Day Ashley et al. 2014: 28). Someone determined to find the glass half empty might take that as negative evidence against private education. I suggest that two out of five children going to private schools in very poor, remote villages in one of India's poorest states is instead evidence indicating the affordability of private education.

But are they the poor*est*? Härmä and Rose (2012) is reported as finding "that only 10 percent of children from the poorest quintile were accessing private schools in their study area in India (compared to 70 percent of the richest quintile)" (Day Ashley et al. 2014: 28). However, Härmä had created bespoke wealth and income quintiles for the villages researched. In very poor villages in remote Uttar Pradesh, itself a poor Indian state, one might assume that *everyone* or nearly everyone is poor. Indeed, that is the case. Investigating income quintiles for India as a whole shows that all but one, the richest of Härmä's quintiles, is either poor or very poor by Indian standards. Her bottom *two quintiles* are *very poor* by Indian standards, while her third and fourth *relatively* wealthy quintiles are in fact *poor* by Indian standards. So, yes, it is true that in these very poor villages, only 10% of the lowest quintile accesses private schools. But we should not ignore the 30% of the second lowest, nearly 50% of the middle quintile, and nearly 60% of the fourth quintile who are also using private schools. (Härmä and Rose 2012: 251). These are *all poor* by Indian standards, and the first two categories are the *poorest*; large proportions of each are currently able to afford low-cost private schools.

What about the second assumption of Day Ashley et al., "Private schools are as affordable to users as state schools"? Unless one believed that 100% of government subsidies were always wasted, this target seems set unfairly high. A more realistic target might ask whether the overall cost of sending a child to private school is competitively priced against sending to a government school. Here the evidence suggests a more positive conclusion in favour of private schools.

For instance, elsewhere (Tooley 2013b) I've investigated Akaguri's (2013) Ghanaian evidence and suggested that it was not the most useful way of answering the general question about low-cost private school affordability because he did not compare like with like. For example, because children using private schools currently spend more on food or transport, say, than those using government schools does not mean that a child currently using a government school would have to pay more on these items if he/she transferred to private school. Using instead like-for-like assumptions, I show that the cost of sending a child to government school could vary between 79% and 87% of the cost of sending a child to a private school. It is more for the private schools but not so much more that it might not be as affordable to many poor parents as government school.

Moreover, in Ghana, private schools are also typically open for longer hours than public; taking this into account, the cost of sending a child to a low-cost private school, using Akaguri's evidence, could work out *less* on an hourly basis than sending a child to a government school (the hourly rate at government school could be between 119% and 130% of the hourly rate at private school). Private schools can sometimes work out as more affordable to poor parents.

Equity – geography

Research evidence shows that low-cost private schools are geographically accessible to the poor and to the poorest. Low-cost private schools also appear better to narrow achievement gaps for disadvantaged groups than government schools. Finally, low-cost private schools are not discriminatory; where they don't serve *all* of a poor community, this is not because of any discrimination on the part of school owners.

It is not always clear how Day Ashley et al. (2014: 22) interpret their assumption: "Private schools geographically reach the poor". For instance, they count as "neutral" evidence showing private schools emerging in poor parts of rural India, Pakistan, and South Africa because, they observe, it is not clear that they "generally serve the poorest" in these places. But the fact that they are in these poor communities at all should be taken as *positive* evidence of private schools' geographical reach.

Indeed, not only are the private schools reaching poor areas, but they are serving increasingly large numbers of children: for instance, from 25% of children in 2005, private schools are now serving 50% of rural primary-age children in Uttar Pradesh, "denoting a furious rate of growth of private school enrolment in rural north India" (Day Ashley et al.: 23, footnote 12). Moreover, Nishimura and Yamano (2013) report a nearly fivefold increase in the number of private schools between 2002 and 2005 in rural Kenya.

Supporting further aspects of our proposition, Pal and Kingdon (2010: 19) show that where there is greater enrolment in private schools, children from disadvantaged groups in India (SC/ST: Scheduled Castes and Scheduled Tribes) have significantly higher literacy levels than where private enrolment is lower: "there are some large literacy gains to be had from private school growth even among SC/ST children, especially among 10–14 year olds". Finally, in my proposition I am also concerned about discrimination against disadvantaged groups. One study that addresses this issue is Härmä (2011: 353), which explicitly finds that where groups are missing from private schools, this "was not due to discrimination on the part of LFP school operators", since they "must compete for all possible 'clients'".

Equity – gender

The evidence suggests that low-cost private schools do not discriminate against girls. In places where there are cultural or socioeconomic barriers to girls using low-cost private schools, they attend them in significant proportions. Moreover, where these cultural or socioeconomic barriers are lower, then low-cost private schools *already* arrive at or even exceed gender parity. Finally, low-cost private schools seem to have a positive impact on narrowing gender achievement gaps.

Day Ashley et al. explore evidence for their assumption, "Private schools are equally accessed by boys and girls". This time the assumption *as written* appears unrealistic. Private schools alone are unlikely to be able to challenge entrenched cultural or socioeconomic barriers against girls. However, the evidence in the sources collated by Day Ashley et al. shows that even this strong assumption, of gender parity now, is supported by much of the evidence adduced.

For instance, Srivastava (2008) and Andrabi et al. (2008) are reported as showing private schools are equal or better for girls in terms of enrolment: The first "finds an equal likelihood of sending girls and boys to [low-cost private schools] among the households studied in Lucknow, India", while the second finds "the presence of private schools is strongly associated with female enrolment in rural Pakistan: the share of female enrolment in private schools is 3–5 percentage points higher than in government schools" (Day Ashley et al. 2014: 25).

Next, Pal (2010: 19, footnote 17), using data from the 1999 Probe Report study in five Indian states, reports that "a larger proportion of ever-enrolled girls (19.6% as opposed to 15.6% of boys) go to private schools"; it is true that a larger proportion of boys than girls is "ever-enrolled" (60% boys compared to 40% girls): "If however we consider the proportion of total boys and girls going to private schools, the proportion is very similar (around 11% for both boys and girls)." Again, positive evidence even for the strong assumption that "private schools are *equally* accessed by boys and girls".

Similarly, Hartwig's (2013: 494) study in rural Tanzania compares public and private at secondary school level. Hartwig reports, "Our secondary school enrolment figures *for mixed gender schools* suggest that girls still do not have equal access to boys' (emphasis added); however, the vast majority of mixed gender schools are public. In the public mixed gender schools, there *are* more boys than girls (44% girls). However, in the private schools, which are mostly single gender, there are 77% girls (see Hartwig 2013, Table 2). So whereas public secondary schools are biased against girls, private schools are dramatically biased *in favour of girls*, more evidence in favour of the strong assumption of gender parity.

Moreover, Maitra, Pal and Sharma (2011) provide evidence of differences in gender parity within countries: while there were statistically significant differences in gender enrolment in North Indian states, the report says this was not true for Gujarat (Western India) and Kerala and Tamil Nadu (Southern India). For these states, "there is no evidence that girls are less likely to be enrolled in private schools relative to boys, irrespective of whether the girls belong to single gender or mixed gender households." (Maitra, Pal and Sharma 2011: 17). In fact, looking in detail at Maitra, Pal and Sharma (2011), it is clear that in *nine* out of the 14 states researched, neither the "GIRL" variable, nor any of the other combined variable measures they examine are significant. That is, there is no evidence of gender inequality in private schools in states as diverse as Orissa, Jammu and Kashmir, Tamil Nadu, Gujarat, and Kerala (Maitra, Pal and Sharma 2011: Table 9).

The study gives reasons why there might be these disparities between states, pointing amongst other things to lower economic development in some northern states (Maitra, Pal and Sharma 2011: 17–8), suggesting that gender parity in private schools could arrive even in these states as India's development continues. Again, very positive evidence for gender parity *now* (in certain states) and the possibility of gender parity elsewhere in the future, as development progresses.

Finally, Pal and Kingdon (2010: 14) provide evidence on the impact of private schools in closing the gender gap in achievement: "higher private school share is associated with significantly higher literacy for all age groups while it is associated with significantly lower gender gap in literacy . . . among 10–14 year old children".[4] Moreover, this study benefits from disaggregating data about India as a whole to look at different regions. Again what it finds is striking. In South India, there is an even more pronounced narrowing of the gender gap: "while private school share remains insignificant to determine both literacy and gender gap among 10–19 year olds in the northern districts, both these effects are significant in the southern districts" (Pal and Kingdon 2010: 17).

In short, the evidence suggests that low-cost private schools are already an important player in closing the gender gap: in terms of enrolment, they've already succeeded in doing this in parts of India and rural Africa. They also narrow the gender gap in terms of achievement.

Financial – sustainability

The available evidence shows that low-cost private schools are financially sustainable: in the absence of financial data in the literature, one proxy for this is the length of time private schools are in the market.

Many studies in Day Ashley et al.'s sample show that private schools have remarkable longevity, particularly given the huge expansion of the sector in recent years: Tooley et al. (2008: 454) showed, for private schools in the slums of Kenya, that the mean age of schools was seven years in 2003. Nishimura and Yamano (2013), researching private school growth in rural Kenya, report a more or less identical figure: private schools were on average 7.2 years old, even though there was huge expansion after 2003.[5]

Moreover, Andrabi et al. (2008: 335), again in the context of extremely rapid expansion of private schooling, find that the median age of a private school in 2000 was four years, even though over one fifth of the schools had opened in the last two years. Finally, Härmä and

Adefisayo (2013: 133) show that one quarter of the private schools in Lagos, again in a time of rapid expansion, was 13 years old or more.

This is all circumstantial evidence of private schools' financial sustainability. But even stronger circumstantial evidence can surely be found by reflecting on the huge numbers of private schools present in the market. ASER data from rural India (2013), for instance, show that half of India's villages have access to a private school, suggesting nearly 300,000 low-cost private schools serving India's villages alone. Similarly Härmä and Adefisayo (2013: 133) report over 12,000 private schools in Lagos State alone, with around three quarters likely to be *low-cost* (as unapproved). So many entrepreneurs from poor communities are not likely to be in this market unless they know schools are financially sustainable.

Financial – cost-effectiveness

The cost of education delivery "is lower in private schools than in state schools" (Day Ashley et al. 2014: 25). The reason for private schools' greater cost-effectiveness is the lower teacher salaries in private than government schools. This could either be seen as providing 'employment where it would otherwise not exist' or, possibly 'exploitative', an area that could warrant "further investigation" (p. 26).

Choice – desired option for the poor

Private schools are preferred by the poor. When asked for their preferences, Härmä (2011: 353) found the "vast majority of parents indicating a preference for private schools over poor quality government alternatives". Härmä reports that there is a *"near universal preference for private schools"* (p. 353, emphasis in the original), with "94.4 percent of sample parents" preferring private over government school. Indeed, in her large-scale household survey, "the majority of families (84 percent) view government schools negatively and LFPs positively (77 percent)" (p. 353).

Choice – poor able to make informed choices

The poor make informed choices about low-cost private schools and use a variety of proxy measures to make judgements about quality. Day Ashley et al. (2014: 30) report a "majority of studies . . . indicate that perceived quality of education is a priority for users when choosing between schools, and that private schools are often perceived to be of higher quality than government ones". Moreover, they find positive support for "Users make informed choices about the quality of education" (p. 31), where "informed choice implies users have adequate information on the performance of schools to be able to judge them. Informal sources including networks of parents were found to play a significant but often under-recognised role in informing users in their choice of school" (p. 31).

Accountability

Finally, low-cost private schools are accountable to the poor. The literature shows how private schools are accountable, *by definition*, because parents pay fees and have the right to 'exit', keeping private school owners on their toes: for instance, evidence from South Africa shows that "parents felt *payment of fees made private schools more accountable to parents*" (Day Ashley et al. 2014: 34, citing Schirmer 2010). Similarly, from Bangladesh, "Sommers (2013) attributes fewer teacher absences and more teaching time to [private schools'] awareness of dependence on tuition fees" (Day Ashley et al. 2014). Finally, experimental evidence from rural Punjab, Pakistan, is taken as showing that "the potential (veiled) threat of parents exercising choice is what matters", making private schools "alert to signals about users' preferences" (Day Ashley et al. 2014, citing Andrabi et al. 2008).

In summary, confining myself only to the studies identified by DFID's commissioned literature review (Day Ashley et al. 2014), I have shown that low-cost private schools satisfy all 10 of the features that are required to be a serious solution to the major development challenge of delivering quality education for all. (For further details concerning the DFID-sponsored study, see Tooley and Longfield 2015.)

Discussion and conclusion

From being an area in which no one was interested, low-cost private schools have emerged as an important area for research. The debate around them is polarised, however, with three positions definable within research and research-based advocacy: that low-cost private schools are irrelevant to discussions of education for all; that they must be seen as a temporary solution, until public schools are sorted out; or that they themselves are a major and potentially permanent part of any solution to the problem of delivering education to the poor and poorest.

This topic is controversial; to try to consider the area afresh, I suggested thinking in more general terms about what might be demanded of any phenomenon that was seen as a potential solution to major development problems. I came up with 10 propositions, covering areas such as generalisability, quality, equity (in three forms, affordability, geographical reach, and gender), financial sustainability, cost-effectiveness, choice, and accountability.

Putting these back into the context of education, I suggested that if these 10 propositions were satisfied, then this would provide a very strong case for embracing low-cost private schools as a solution to the problem of delivering education to the poor and poorest. More development work would still need to be done – in helping low-cost private schools extend their reach to be able to serve *all* of the poorest, for instance, or finding ways of reaching gender parity in environments where there were sociocultural impediments. And more research may still be needed – to find out the best ways of assisting private schools in extending their reach and further improving their quality, for instance. But if these 10 propositions are satisfied, there could be no question that private schools should be a major part of the solution.

Usefully, a major literature review has recently been published, commissioned by DFID precisely in order to find the state of knowledge on low-cost private schools and so help with policy discussion around them. Even more usefully, our 10 propositions covered virtually the same ground as the first 12 propositions of this DFID report (Day Ashley et al. 2014). In order to avoid any doubts about a biased reading of the literature in this controversial area, I decided to use only the studies included in Day Ashley et al. as my evidence base.

Using those studies as evidence, it is clear that all 10 of our propositions are supported. Low-cost private schools are a *generalisable* solution, occurring across rural and urban areas of disparate countries across continents. They provide higher *quality* education than government schools, in terms of pupil achievement and teaching quality. They satisfy our *equity* criteria, being affordable already to many of the poor and poorest and geographically available to them (allowing a range of players, philanthropists, governments, international agencies, and companies, and the schools themselves, to work to further extend that access). They are also, perhaps surprisingly given the way data are often presented, not only accessible to girls but in many places already showing gender parity.

Finally, low-cost private schools are cost-effective, providing education at a lower cost than government schools, financially sustainable and the likely preferred choice of the poor, who are able to make informed choices about what is on offer. They are also accountable to the poor, responsive to their needs and demands.

I return to the three possible reactions to low-cost private schools (irrelevance, a temporary expedient, or a permanent solution). I suggest that the first position is untenable, given the wealth of evidence showing the nature and extent of the low-cost private school sector. Adjudicating between the second and third options is harder because it could be argued that further fundamental dimensions need to be brought in when we're discussing education and the role of government, over and above the 10 propositions above.

In an earlier summary of the DFID-funded research, Mcloughlin (2013: 4) points to some of these fundamental issues: "Some commentators are opposed *in principle* to the delivery of education" (emphasis added) through private education because *first*, education is "typically regarded as an "imperfect public good" that produces both individual and collective benefits" (p. 4). *Second*, "*education is a right* and should be universal and free at the point of use". *Third*, "In practice, government schooling remains the only education option available to the vast majority of economically disadvantaged or vulnerable households in poor countries".

I have discussed each of these arguments at length elsewhere (Tooley 2008, 2009), and there is not space to go into detail here. Briefly, in reverse order, it's simply not true that government schools are 'the only education option available' to the most disadvantaged. The evidence outlined above shows that significant minorities of the most disadvantaged are *already* using private schools. If there was a will, even *all* disadvantaged children could access private schools, for instance, through targeted vouchers, cash transfers, innovative ways of allowing school payment, and growing prosperity as nations develop (which can be helped or impeded by the international community). Government schooling only remains the only option if we decide that it has to be. It seems odd doing so in the face of all the evidence outlined above.

Second, on human rights, the second Millennium Development Goal (MDG) committed governments to "ensure that, by 2015, children everywhere . . . will be able to complete a full course of primary schooling". It doesn't mention *free* schooling, although the "education for all" (EFA) goal of the Dakar Framework for Action does. However, if we look at the *motivations* behind EFA, we can see that its intent is not incompatible with private fee-paying education. UNESCO helpfully published an expanded commentary on EFA, where it notes "Every government has the responsibility to provide *free*, quality basic education, *so that no child will be denied access because of an inability to pay*." But if targeted vouchers, cash transfers, and other methods ensure no child *will* be denied access *to private schools* 'because of an inability to pay', then this surely would satisfy the intention behind the EFA goal. Moreover, it is frequently observed that governments are *not* meeting their responsibilities to provide "quality basic education" for all. Embracing private schools could be one way of circumventing this lack of commitment or delivery.

Finally, on public goods: the basic idea is that there are social benefits to be had from people being educated. If a parent educates his child, this child, so the theory goes, will contribute to society by being healthier, fairer, more democratic, and so on. But these *public* benefits, it is claimed, are not reflected in the market price of education, so there will be "market failure".

It seems odd discussing this in the abstract, because now we have enormously powerful evidence, some adduced above, that in fact shows that poor parents *are* willing to spend on education and so produce the desired social benefits. That is, the perceived *private* benefits of schooling are enough to make them pay for education; with parents thus paying, society at large can obtain the social benefits that arise from individual parents' decisions.

If convincing arguments can be made along the lines of these sketches, then I suggest this could also lead to an adjudication between the second and third positions (low cost private schools are a temporary solution, or a potentially permanent one) in favour of the third. The evidence shows low-cost private schooling satisfies what we should be looking for as a solution to the developmental problem of meeting the educational needs of the poor. It has to be accepted at least as a temporary solution but perhaps also as something more permanent, a solution created by the people themselves through their *de facto* privatisation.

Notes

1 'Public' education is, in its international usage, used to denote 'government' provision, rather than the idiosyncratic British and South Asian usage.
2 There is no good name for the sector. Microfinance benefitted from having a snappy name. It would do a good service if someone could come up with one here. Entries on a postcard....
3 Or women, if X is aimed at adults.
4 Pal and Kingdon (2010: 14) report that the 10–14-year-old age group are those "who naturally benefitted more from the recent trend of private school growth around the country".
5 The evidence is from 2005.

References

Akaguri, L., 2013. Fee-free public or low-fee private basic education in rural Ghana: how does the cost influence the choice of the poor? *Compare* 44, 2, 140–161.

Andrabi, T., Das J., Khwaja, A.I., 2008. A dime a day: the possibilities and limits of private schooling in Pakistan. *Comparative Education Review* 52, 329–355.

ASER India, 2013. *Annual Status of Education Report (Rural) 2012.* ASER Centre, New Delhi.

CEDAW, 2014. Privatization and its Impact on the Right to Education of Women and Girls. United Nations Committee on the Elimination of Discrimination against Women (CEDAW), Written Submission, 27 June 2014.

Day Ashley, L., Mcloughlin, C., Aslam, M., Engel, J., Wales, J., Rawal, S., Batley, R., Kingdon, G., Nicolai, S., Rose, P., 2014. *The Role and Impact of Private Schools in Developing Countries.* Department for International Development, London.

Desai, S., Dubey, A., Vanneman, R., Banerji, R., 2008. *Private Schooling in India: A New Educational Landscape.* University of Maryland.

Dixon, P., 2013. *International Aid and Private Schools for the Poor: Smiles, Miracles and Markets.* Edward Elgar, Cheltenham.

French, R., Kingdon, G., 2010. *The Relative Effectiveness of Private and Government Schools in Rural India: Evidence from ASER Data.* University of London Institute of Education.

Härmä, J., 2011. Low cost private schooling in India: is it pro poor and equitable? *International Journal of Educational Development* 31, 4, 350–356.

Härmä, J., 2013. Access or quality? Why do families living in slums choose low-cost private schools in Lagos, Nigeria? *Oxford Review of Education* 39, 4, 548–566.

Härmä, J., Adefisayo, F., 2013. Scaling up: challenges facing low-fee private schools in the slums of Lagos, Nigeria. In: Srivastava, P. (Ed.) *Low-fee Private Schooling: Aggravating Equity or Mitigating Disadvantage?* Symposium, Oxford.

Härmä, J., Rose, P., 2012. Is low-fee private primary schooling affordable for the poor? Evidence from rural India. In: Robertson, R. and Mundy, K. (Eds.) *Public-Private Partnerships in Education: New Actors and Modes of Governance in a Globalizing World.* Edward Elgar, Cheltenham.

Hartwig, K.A., 2013. Using a social justice framework to assess educational quality in Tanzanian schools. *International Journal of Educational Development* 33, 5, 487–496.

Lewin, K., 2007. *The Limits to Growth of Non-Government Private Schooling in Sub Saharan Africa.* CREATE Pathways to Access Research Monograph No. 5, University of Sussex.

Macpherson, I., Robertson, S., Walford, G. (Eds.), 2014. *Education, Privatization and Social Justice.* Symposium, Oxford.

Maitra, P., Pal, S., Sharma, A., 2011. *Reforms, Growth and Persistence of Gender Gap: Recent Evidence from Private School Enrolment in India.* Institute for the Study of Labor, Bonn.

Mcloughlin, C., 2013. *Low-Cost Private Schools: Evidence, Approaches and Emerging Issues.* EPS-Peaks, London.

Nishimura, M., & Yamano, T., 2013. Emerging private education in Africa: determinants of school choice in rural Kenya. *World Development 43*, 266–275.

Pal, S., 2010. Public infrastructure, location of private schools and primary school attainment in an emerging economy. *Economics of Education Review* 29, 5, 783–794.

Pal., S., Kingdon, G., 2010. *Can Private School Growth Foster Universal Literacy? Panel Evidence from Indian Districts.* Institute for the Study of Labor, Bonn.

Rolleston, C., Adefeso-Olateju, M., 2014. De facto privatization of basic education in Africa: a market response to government failure? A comparative study of the cases of Ghana and Nigeria. In: Macpherson, I., Robertson, S. and Walford, G. (Eds.) *Education, Privatization and Social Justice.* Symposium, Oxford.

Schirmer, S., 2010. *Hidden Assets: South Africa's Low-fee Private Schools.* Centre for Development and Enterprise, Johannesburg.

Sommers, C., 2013. *Primary Education in Rural Bangladesh: Degrees of Access, Choice, and Participation of the Poorest.* CREATE Pathways to Access Research Monograph No. 75, University of Sussex.

Srivastava, P., 2008. School choice in India: disadvantaged groups and low-fee private schools. In: Forsey, M., Davies, S. and Walford, G. (Eds.) *The Globalisation of School Choice?* Symposium, Oxford.

Srivastava, P. (Ed.), 2013. *Low-fee Private Schooling: Aggravating Equity or Mitigating Disadvantage?* Symposium, Oxford.

Srivastava, P., Walford, G. (Eds.), 2007. *Private Schooling in Less Economically Developed Countries: Asian and African Perspectives.* Symposium, Oxford.

Tooley, J., 2000a. Private Education: The Poor's Best Chance? *UNESCO Courier.* http://www.unesco.org/courier/2000_11/uk/doss22.htm

Tooley, J., 2000b. Private schools for the poor. *Economic Affairs* 20, 2, 60.

Tooley, J., 2000c. *Reclaiming Education.* Continuum, London.

Tooley, J., 2008. *E.G. West: Economic Liberalism and the Role of Government in Education.* Continuum, New York and London.

Tooley, J., 2009. *The Beautiful Tree: A Personal Journey into How the World's Poorest People Are Educating Themselves.* Penguin, New Delhi.

Tooley, J., 2013a. Challenging educational injustices: "grassroots" privatisation in South Asia and Sub-Saharan Africa. *Oxford Review of Education* 39, 4, 446–463.

Tooley, J., 2013b. *School Choice in Lagos State.* DFID, Lagos.

Tooley, J., Dixon, P., 2006. "*De facto*" privatisation of education and the poor: implications of a study from sub-Saharan Africa and India. *Compare* 36, 4, 443–462.

Tooley, J., Dixon, P., Stanfield, J., 2008. Impact of free primary education in Kenya: a case study of private schools in Kibera. *Educational Management Administration and Leadership* 36, 4, 449–469.

Tooley, J., Longfield, D., 2014a. *Private Education in Low-Income Areas of Monrovia: School and Household Surveys.* EG West Centre, Newcastle and Development Initiatives Liberia, Inc.

Tooley, J., Longfield, D., 2014b. *Private Primary Education in Western Area, Sierra Leone.* EG West Centre, Newcastle University and People's Educational Association.

Tooley, J., Longfield, D., 2015. *The Role and Impact of Private Schools in Developing Countries: A Response to the DFID-Commissioned "Rigorous Literature Review".* London: Pearson.

SECTION 3

Beyond schools

Adult, vocational and higher education for development

18

THE IMPORTANCE OF EARLY CHILDHOOD FOR EDUCATION AND DEVELOPMENT

Emiliana Vegas and Analía Jaimovich

Introduction

In recent years, scientific research on how the brain develops has provided convincing evidence that the early years are a critical time in an individual's life. It is during these years that the brain develops at the fastest rate in our lifetimes, providing (or not) essential abilities that influence wide-ranging important skills, including, among others, our capacity to learn and analyse problems, speak multiple languages, develop musical ability, have better physical health, and effectively cope with stress and other emotions during adulthood (Shonkoff and Phillips 2000).

Complementing the scientific evidence on the role of brain development in the early years, social scientists have rigorously evaluated the impact of various interventions in early childhood on outcomes later in life. These evaluations have yielded convincing evidence that investing in early childhood development (ECD) is one of the best decisions a society can make. In an influential paper, Carneiro and Heckman (2003) put forth that the rates of return to investments in early childhood are substantially higher than rates of return to investments later in life (see Figure 18.1).[1]

Indeed, Nobel Laureate Economist James Heckman argues that the impact of early investment is not only important for productivity but also for equity. From his and his coauthors' analyses of the evidence of many long-term studies on early childhood interventions, he draws four important conclusions: (1) inequality in the experiences that young children have result in inequality in (cognitive and socioemotional) abilities, academic achievement, health status, the probability of having a job, and earnings; (2) cognitive and socioemotional (such as perseverance, sociability, self-control) skills matter for these lifelong outcomes; (3) effective interventions in ECD can mitigate or even reverse genetic, parental, and environmental disadvantages; and (4) focusing investments on disadvantaged children from birth to age five can substantially contribute to reduce inequality in later outcomes (Heckman 2011).

While there is rich evidence on the need for investing in the early years in a comprehensive set of areas, including cash transfers, nutrition, and healthcare as well as education, in this paper we focus specifically on investments in early childhood care and education. In the next section, we summarise the international evidence on the impacts of early childhood interventions on long-term outcomes. Then, we present an overview of the status of early childhood development in developing countries before describing access to ECD services in developing countries.

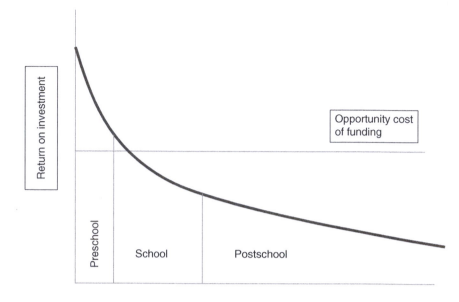

Figure 18.1   Lifetime returns to investments in human capital
Source: Adapted from Carneiro and Heckman 2003.

We then review the evidence on the impact of ECD programmes from developing countries. Last, we discuss some of the challenges of scaling up ECD services in developing countries.

Evidence on the impacts of early childhood investments on long-term outcomes

Researchers have capitalised on a series of longitudinal studies that have followed individuals from early childhood through adulthood. These studies have provided rigorous evidence of the enormous impact that early childhood investments have on long-term outcomes. Perhaps the most influential study involves the High/Scope Perry Preschool programme in the United States, a high-quality preschool programme that was offered to children aged three and four who were born in poor households. The programme included a randomised control trial and followed individuals for over 24 years. The study found that attending a high-quality preschool programme led to short-term gains in cognitive ability (as measured by IQ), greater success in school (as evidenced by higher test scores in middle school, reduced participation in special education programmes, higher grade point average in high school, improved on-time high school graduation rates), and higher economic productivity and contributions to society in adulthood (as evidenced by higher earnings, increased rates of home ownership, reduced participation rates in social services, and reduced rates of participation in criminal activities) (Barnett 2011; Schweinhart 2001).

Similar results were found in the Abecedarian study in North Carolina, US, a randomised experiment designed to evaluate the impact of a full-time, year-round childcare programme for children aged four months through five years that followed individuals through age 21. Similarly to the High/Scope Perry Preschool programme study, this experiment found an impact of programme participation on short- and long-term gains in cognitive ability (as measured by IQ), greater success in school (as measured by improved test scores in reading and math, reduced repetition rates in primary school, and reduced participation in special education programmes), and improved health in adulthood (Barnett 2011; Campbell et al. 2001; Campbell et al. 2002; McLaughlin et al. 2007).

ECD interventions in developing countries have also shown long-term impacts. In Jamaica, an intervention subject of much rigorous research provided nutritional supplements and/or psychosocial stimulation during two years to low-income, stunted children aged 9–24 months. Follow-up studies show that stunted children who received psychosocial stimulation had sustained cognitive and educational benefits by the time they reached the age of 17–18 years, and their average earnings were 28 to 60 percent higher than the control group, catching up to the earnings of a matched nonstunted comparison group (Gertler et al. 2013).

These longitudinal studies have provided convincing evidence that interventions in early childhood can effectively reduce gaps in income and individual well-being later in life. These impacts also translate into widespread and long-lasting social benefits, as the most disadvantaged children who access high-quality early care and education programmes benefit the most, leading to higher productivity rates, lower crime rates, and greater equity.

State of early childhood development in developing countries

UNICEF (2010) estimates that about 92 percent of children live in low- and middle-income countries. Of these children, 25 percent live in poverty, 30 percent are stunted, seven percent will die before reaching the age of five, 68 percent will not receive early childhood education, and 17 percent will never enrol in primary school. These figures, in turn, mask great disparities across and within regions. This section provides an overview of the state of ECD in developing countries, providing information on key indicators on the situation of young children and how they have evolved over time.

Adequate nutrition, especially from conception to age two, and early childhood stimulation in the first five years of a child's life play a critical role in the process of brain formation and development (Nelson, de Hahn and Thomas 2006; World Bank 2006). Children growing up in poverty are often exposed to multiple and cumulative risks, which range from nutritional deficiencies to lack of stimulation and greater risk of not attending school, among many others. The number of people living in extreme poverty around the world has declined over the past three decades, but there are great differences across countries: while the number of extremely poor individuals has declined in middle- and high-income countries, it has increased in low-income countries. In 2010, there were roughly 400 million children estimated to be living in extreme poverty. More than one third of the extremely poor individuals are children under the age of 13, and half of the children in low-income countries live in extreme poverty (World Bank 2013).

Child mortality is often used as a barometer of child well-being in general, as it is the result of a variety of factors that affect the living conditions of children and their families. The overall under-five mortality rate has decreased from 90 children per 1,000 live births in 1990 to 48 in 2012 (UNICEF 2014a). While the decrease in mortality rates is a common trend across regions, there are still great disparities in the prevalence of the phenomenon. Sub-Saharan Africa has the highest rates (at 98 children per 1,000 live births) followed by South Asia (60), Middle East and North Africa (30), East Asia and Pacific (20), and Latin America and the Caribbean (19). In turn, regional estimates hide large disparities within regions: countries like Angola, Chad, Sierra Leone, and Somalia still have under-five mortality rates above 150 children per 1,000 live births (UNICEF 2014a). In addition, while there has been a decrease in overall mortality rates, disparities within countries may have widened. In 18 out of 26 developing countries that experienced a decrease of at least 10 percent in child mortality rates, inequality between the lowest and highest income quintile either increased or stayed the same. Moreover, in 10 of these 18 countries, inequality in under-five mortality increased by 10 percent or more. Under-five mortality rates are higher for boys than for girls, among rural populations, among children of less educated mothers, and among minority population groups (UNICEF 2010).

In two recent reviews of the effect of nutritional conditions on early childhood development, Walker et al. (2007, 2011) conclude that stunting, iron deficiency, iodine deficiency, and low birth weight are among the risks on which there is stronger evidence of negative developmental outcomes. Stunting (defined as a height for age less than two standard deviations below the norms developed by the World Health Organisation) is one of the indicators most commonly used as a proxy for child nutritional status in developing countries. While improvements in nutrition have led to an overall 37 percent drop in stunting rates since 1990, the prevalence of stunting is still high in developing countries. Countries like Afghanistan, Ethiopia, Guatemala, and Bangladesh, for example, have stunting rates higher than 40 percent (UNICEF 2014a). Stunting rates are much higher in rural than in urban areas: children in rural areas have a 50 percent higher chance of being stunted than children living in urban households (UNICEF 2010). It is estimated that in all countries, over twice as many children from the poorest quintile are stunted as compared to children from the highest quintile (Engle, Nirmala and Petrovic 2013).

Compared to the measures of physical well-being, measures of the cognitive and socioemotional status of children are less widespread, and comparisons across regions are harder to achieve given the lack of data. Some studies have attempted to document cognitive development in early childhood in developing countries. These studies (Paxson and Schady 2007; Macours, Schady and Vakis 2012; Macours and Vakis 2010; Fernald et al. 2011; Fernald et al. 2012; Nadeau, Martinez and Filmer 2011; López Boo 2013; Schady et al. 2014) provide an approximation to the state of early childhood cognitive development in Ecuador, Nicaragua, Peru, Chile, Colombia, Madagascar, Cambodia, Mozambique, Ethiopia, India, Indonesia, Senegal, and Vietnam. Overall, findings from these studies show that:

1. There are important differences in early language and cognitive development between children in richer and poorer households before they even enter school. For example, the documented language development gaps between richer and poorer households at young

Table 18.1 The state of ECD in developing countries. Selected indicators.

	Under-5 mortality rate (‰)	Infant mortality rate (under 1) (‰)	Neonatal mortality rate (‰)	Moderate and severe stunting (%)	Moderate and severe wasting (%)	Moderate and severe overweight (%)
Sub-Saharan Africa	98	64	32	38	9	6
Eastern and Southern Africa	77	51	28	39	7	5
West and Central Africa	118	76	37	37	11	6
Middle East and North Africa	30	24	15	18	8	11
South Asia	60	47	32	38	16	4
East Asia and Pacific	20	17	11	12	4	5
Latin America and Caribbean	19	16	10	11	1	7
CEE/CIS	19	16	9	11	1	15
Least developed countries	85	58	30	37	10	5
World	48	35	21	25	8	7

Source: UNICEF 2014.

ages were as high as 1.3 standard deviations in Peru (López Boo 2013) and 1.2 standard deviations in urban Colombia and rural Ecuador (Schady et al. 2014).

2.   These differences tend to persist even after children begin primary schooling. In Ecuador, for example, differences between wealthier and less wealthy children at 12–13 years of age, when children are of an age where they would be completing elementary school, were very similar to those found at 5–6 years of age (Schady et al. 2014). López Boo also found that disparities found at age five persist into the early school years across all four countries studied (India, Peru, Ethiopia, Vietnam).

3.   Socioeconomic gradients in cognitive development appear even at very low levels of economic development, as Nadeau et al.'s (2011) study shows for Cambodia and Mozambique, where they found socioeconomic gradients in cognitive development even in rather homogeneous samples of mostly poor children.

4.   Socioeconomic gradients in cognitive development may actually *increase* as children grow older (Schady 2011; Fernald et al. 2011; Fernald et al. 2012; Rubio-Codina et al. 2013).

Early childhood cognitive development has been associated with the level of stimulation that children receive at home. Data from the Multiple Indicator Cluster Survey developed by UNICEF (MICS3 and MICS4, 2005–2012) allow for a comparative approximation to this issue with nationally representative household data from a sample of developing countries. The data show vast disparities among and within countries in indicators such as learning materials at home (children's books and toys), children left in inadequate care, and adult support for learning. For example, the MICS measures the percentage of children 36–59 months old with whom an adult has recently engaged in activities such as reading books; telling stories; singing songs; playing with the child; taking the child outside the home; and spending time naming, counting, or drawing things. The data show differences larger than 30 percentage points between the richest and the poorest 20 percent of children in countries like Yemen, Vietnam, Tajikistan, Sierra Leone, Myanmar, Ghana, and Bangladesh. Similarly, there are differences as large as 24 percentage points between the richest and the poorest quintiles in the percentage of children 0–59 months old left in inadequate care; that is, in the care of another child younger than 10 years. Socioeconomic differences are equally stark in the percentage of children 0–59 months old who have three or more children's books at home: of the 37 countries surveyed for this indicator, 22 had differences between the poorest and the richest households that were greater than 20 percentage points. In some countries (Belize, Guyana, Suriname, Macedonia), the differences were greater than 50 percentage points.

While comparative data on ECD is still relatively scarce, particularly with regard to cognitive and socioemotional development, there are a few efforts underway that aim to improve the knowledge base on child outcomes in developing countries. Of note are the new modules introduced in round 4 of the MICS, which aim to provide comparative data on an early childhood development index including literacy–numeracy, physical, socioemotional, and learning domains and the PRIDI project for Latin America.[2]

Access to early childhood development services in developing countries

Obtaining a global perspective on access to and quality of ECD services is difficult due to a lack of comparable data across countries. Few data exist on children's participation in early childhood care and education (ECCE) centres for children 0–3 years old. When data are reported for children older than three years, it is often difficult to distinguish among ages and types of services. In addition, when analysing access to ECCE services, it is necessary to distinguish between the availability of services and the actual use families and children make of such services. This is particularly important in the case of younger children, as families may decide not to send their children to ECCE centres for cultural or other reasons, even when these services are available (Mateo-Diaz and Rodriguez-Chamussy 2014). There are no comparative data on the actual availability of service provisions to cover potential demand for ECCE. In this section, we describe trends in access to early childhood development services, with a focus on centre-based ECCE programmes. We rely on household survey data when available, as these data provide a clearer picture of the actual take-up individuals make of ECCE services, regardless of whether such take-up depends on availability of services, cultural norms, or other reasons.

Data on ECCE participation for children younger than three years is scarce, as not all household surveys include a childcare question for younger children, and administrative data for this age group is lacking in several countries. Mateo-Diaz and Rodriguez-Chamussy (2014) provide an approximation to this issue using household survey data in a sample of 10 Latin American countries. Their analysis shows that participation of 0–3 year olds in ECCE centres is still extremely low, even in countries that have high participation rates, comparatively, in the group of three and four year-olds. In Uruguay, for example, 75 percent of three and four year olds attend some sort of ECCE centre, whereas only 26 percent of children 0–3 do so (Figure 18.2).

The most recent rounds of MICS (rounds 3 and 4, 2005–2012) provide comparable and nationally representative information on children's participation in ECCE programmes for a sample of developing countries. MICS measures the percentage of children three to five years old who are attending an early childhood education programme, whether public or private, including preschool and community-based child care programmes. The data show that attendance varies greatly across countries, from one percent in Afghanistan to 98 percent in the Democratic People's Republic of Korea (UNICEF 2014b). Large overall attendance rates for the whole age group can mask large

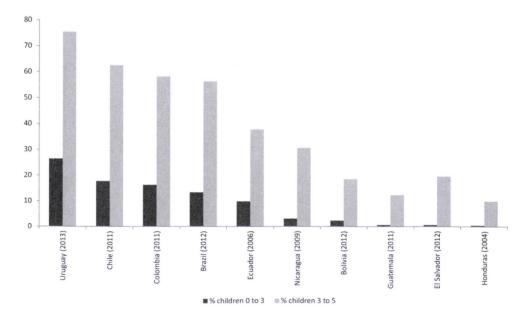

Figure 18.2 Share of children attending formal childcare or early education centres

Notes: a) Year in parenthesis indicates the year of the survey. Data comes from household surveys that included a childcare use question. b) Age range "0 to 3" includes children from 0 to 2 years and 11 months; age range "3 to 5" includes children from 3 to 4 years and 11 months.

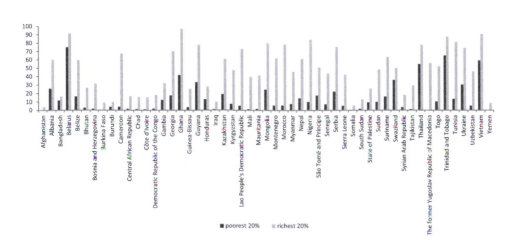

Figure 18.3   Percentage of 3 and 4 year olds attending ECCE services by income quintile

Source: Author's calculations, UNICEF global databases (2014), based on DHS, MICS (2005–2012), and other nationally representative surveys.

income inequalities. In 44 out of 49 countries for which there are available data on income ine-quality, the attendance rate of the richest 20 percent of children is *at least two times* that of the poor-est 20 percent (own calculations based on UNICEF 2014b). The difference in attendance between the poorest and the richest 20 percent of 3–4 year-olds can be as large as 33, 19, 6, and 4 times in Mali, Bosnia-Herzegovina, Myanmar, and Suriname, just to provide a few examples (Figure 18.3).

The extreme wealth disparities described in the case of the 3–4 year olds are greatly reduced once children begin primary school. A comparison of the wealth disparities in attendance rates among 3–4 year olds vs. net attendance rate in primary school in the same group of develop-ing countries participating in the latest rounds of MICS (2005–2012) shows that while in 44 out of 49 countries the attendance rate of the richest quintile is *at least two times* that of the poorest in the case of 3–4 year olds, there are only seven countries for which this is the case in primary school attendance, most of them in sub-Saharan Africa (own calculations based on UNICEF 2014a) (Figure 18.4). Alderman and Vegas (2011) find a similar pattern of differences between preschool and primary school enrolment using data from administrative records. It is important to note, however, that these data mask great income disparities in progression during primary school, as children who live in rural areas, are from poor families, or have mothers with no education are more likely to drop out of school than other children. In addition, overall survival rates to the last grade of primary school are still much lower in developing countries than in the developed world (59 percent in low-income countries as compared to 94 percent in high-income countries). In the majority of countries in sub-Saharan Africa, for example, less than two thirds of pupils reach the last grade of primary school (UNESCO 2014).

Higher access to ECCE services may not necessarily result in reduced disparities in devel-opmental outcomes among the rich and the poor. Araujo et al. (2013) and Mateo-Diaz and Rodriguez-Chamussy (2014) look into structural variables of ECCE services in Latin America, such as child-to-adult ratios and qualifications of staff. They conclude that often it is doubtful that the current structure of ECCE services may be conducive to a high quality of experiences for children. A few studies have attempted to provide an approximation to the nature of expe-riences and interactions in ECCE services, finding that quality is lacking.[3] Araujo (2015) finds that quality levels in ECCE centres in Ecuador and Peru catering for low-income children

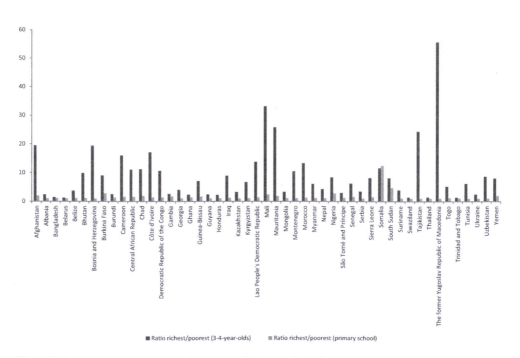

Figure 18.4 Inequality in ECCE and primary school attendance between first and last income quintile

Source: Author's calculations, UNICEF global databases, 2014, based on DHS, MICS, and other nationally representative surveys.

(CIBV and Cuna Más, respectively, targeting children 0–6 and 0–3 years old respectively) are dismal. Using ITERS and CLASS, Araujo finds that in general the median scores are below what is considered minimum acceptable quality by international standards. Verdisco and Perez Alfaro (2010) and Campos et al. (2011) also find low quality levels using ITERS and ECERS in crèches (0–3 year olds) and preschools (4–6 year olds) in Brazil, which in addition vary greatly by locality. Similar low quality levels have been reported for NGO-managed preschools in Bangladesh (Aboud and Hossain 2011).

Evidence from early childhood development programmes developing countries: what works?

In a meta-analysis of 56 studies reporting the effects of 30 interventions in 23 countries in Europe, Asia, Africa, and Central and South America, Nores and Barnett (2010) describe the effects of different types of interventions in a range of outcomes including cognition, behaviour, health, and schooling. Comparing across types of interventions, they observe that interventions that have an educational or stimulation component (as compared to nutrition-only interventions and cash transfers) evidence the highest effect sizes on cognitive, behavioural, and schooling outcomes.

This section summarises recent causal research on the effects of ECD programmes and policies in developing countries, prioritising studies that analyse the effects of interventions that include a stimulation or educational component. The analysis focuses on research that allows identifying the causal effects of ECD interventions on short- and long-term outcomes and describes the main characteristics of these programmes in order to provide insights on what works. The analysis is organised by type of intervention, covering home visiting and parenting support interventions, early childhood care programmes, preschool programmes, and conditional cash transfers.

Home visiting and parenting support programmes

Parenting education and support programmes are often delivered through home visits, community groups, or as part of regular health clinic visits by the families. These programmes aim to promote specific parent-to-child interactions to improve responsiveness in feeding infants and young children, improve attachment, and encourage support for learning through activities like book reading and play. Some of these programmes focus mostly on the parents, that is, on trying to change parental behaviour through the provision of information. Other programmes combine information with modelling of successful practices at home and direct interaction between programme staff and children. In addition, many of these programmes combine early stimulation with nutritional components.

Studies have found substantial positive effects of these programmes both on parental knowledge and practices and on child development. Regarding the former, several home visiting and parent training programmes have shown effects on parental knowledge (Al-Hassan and Lansford 2011; Hamadani et al. 2006; Powell 2004; Powell et al. 2004; Rahman et al. 2008), as well as on their practices, mainly on the level of stimulation they provide to their children at home (Aboud 2007; Peairson et al. 2008; Powell et al. 2004; Sharma and Nagar 2009; Walker et al. 2004; Morris et al. 2012). Regarding the latter, studies have found positive effects of home visiting and parenting support interventions on language and cognitive development (Aboud and Akhter 2011; Bentley et al. 2010; Jin et al. 2007; Klein and Rye 2004; Janssens and Rosemberg 2011; Grantham-McGregor et al. 1987; Nahar et al. 2009; Powell 2004) as well as long-term educational and earning trajectories (Gertler et al. 2014; Grantham-McGregor et al. 1997; Kagitcibasi, Sunar, and Bekman 2001; Kagitcibasi et al. 2009).

In a recent review of ECD programme effects, Engle et al. (2011) found that effect sizes were larger for interventions that included both parent and child programmes, rather than parent-only interventions. Effects of solely information-based, parent-only interventions were small. In contrast, more effective programmes provided opportunities for active parental behaviour change, including guided parenting practice with children, coaching, role play, feedback, and videotaped interactions. The frequency of contact has also been found to be related to programme effectiveness (Walker 2011). Most interventions showing positive effects rely on a frequency of visits of two to four times per month. Powell and Grantham-McGregor (1989) formally evaluated the impact of visit frequency on the benefits achieved, concluding that a minimum of fortnightly visits was necessary, and that weekly visits had even larger effect sizes. Other important structural aspects shared by successful home visiting and parenting support programmes are having systematic training methods for programme staff, a clear and evidence-based curriculum (Engle et al. 2011), and clear supervision structures with adequately trained professional staff (Walker 2011).

Centre- and community-based care

Home visiting and parenting support programmes aim to affect children's experiences at home. In contrast, centre- and community-based care services provide an opportunity for parents to leave their children in the care of other adults in an institutional setting. Centre- and community-based care programmes vary in the extent to which they engage local communities for the provision of services, the extent to which they offer formal preprimary schooling experiences, the ages of the children that attend the services, the qualifications of programme staff, quality control mechanisms, and the nature of child-to-adult interactions. As a result, research on this type of settings encompasses a myriad of interventions that make comparisons difficult. In this section, we discuss community-based interventions that provide childcare to young children, as well as more formal institutional settings that provide care and education for children before they enter preschool.

Centre-based care programmes have been found to have a positive effect on female labour participation (Mateo-Diaz and Rodriguez-Chamussy 2013). Results on children's cognitive and psychosocial outcomes, however, are mixed. A number of studies have found positive effects of attending child care centres on cognitive and psychosocial development (Armecin et al. 2006; Attanasio and Vera-Hernandez 2004; Behrman, Cheng and Todd 2004; Bernal et al. 2009), on nutritional status (Ruel et al. 2002), and in longer-term educational outcomes (Bernal et al. 2009). In some of these studies, impacts were greater for older children and for longer programme exposure (Behrman, Cheng and Todd 2004; Bernal and Fernandez 2013). In contrast, studies analysing the *Estancias Infantiles* programme in Mexico (Angeles et al. 2011) and the FODI childcare centres in Ecuador (Rosero and Oosterbeek 2011; Rosero 2012) found no positive, and even negative, effects on child cognitive and motor development. Along these lines, Bucarey, Ugarte and Urzua (2014) find no effects of attendance to early childhood education and care centres in Chile prior to preschool in student academic performance in primary school.

Among the programmes that showed positive effects are the *Proyecto Integral de Desarrollo Infantil* (PIDI) in Bolivia (Behrman, Cheng and Todd 2004) and the *Hogares Comunitarios de Bienestar* in Colombia (Bernal and Fernandez 2013; Bernal et al. 2009). Both programmes provide care for young children up to age six through community mothers. Groups of up to 15 children are cared for by three adults (in Bolivia) or by one community mother and one assistant (in Colombia). Both programmes provide a combination of nutrition and stimulation interventions. In both cases, caregivers received specific training; in the case of Colombia, community mothers were supervised by staff form the *Instituto Colombiano de Bienestar Familiar, ICBF*. However, both programmes rely on low-educated community members to serve as caregivers, with high turnover rates and relatively low salaries, and the quality of service has been considered low (Bernal et al. 2009).

The Children's Development Fund (FODI) in Ecuador is an early childhood development programme targeted to poor families. FODI supports two types of programmes: home visits and child care centres. In the child care centres modality, services are subsidised by FODI and run by nonprofit organisations providing daycare eight hours per day, five days a week throughout the entire year, together with nutrition and educational activities. A trained teacher is assigned to a group of eight to 10 children to follow a curriculum designed by FODI. An average centre serves 45 children in the age range of zero to six years. In their evaluation of the programme, Rosero and Oosterbeek (2011) and Rosero (2012) found positive developmental effects for the home visiting modality and zero or negative impacts of childcare centres in cognitive and motor development and nutritional status. The authors attribute this difference to possible differences in quality and frequency of adult–child interactions.

This description highlights the need to better understand what happens inside the centre in centre-based programmes. Structural differences (child-to-adult ratio, qualifications of programme staff, number of hours children spend in the centre, presence of a curriculum, supervision structures, among others) may mask great differences in the quality of child-adult interactions. As mentioned earlier in the Access section, when adult-child interactions are taken into account, centre-based care programmes in developing countries seem to exhibit extremely low quality levels. Hard-to-observe differences in the quality of interactions may be at the basis of the mixed developmental outcomes of centre- and community-based child care programmes.

Preschool programmes

As compared to centre- and community-based child care programmes, preschool programmes seem to result in larger effect sizes on short- and long-term cognitive and schooling outcomes (Engle et al. 2011). Preschool services vary by country and may be offered by public or private providers. These programmes share the commonality of having a specified curriculum, learning materials, paid and trained teaching staff, and a fixed classroom site.

A number of studies have addressed the question of whether attending preschool brings about specific outcomes. Berlinski, Galiani and Manacorda (2008) and Berlinski, Galiani and Gertler (2009), for example, have estimated the effects of preprimary education on subsequent school performance in Argentina and Uruguay. In both cases, they found a positive effect of preschool attendance on subsequent educational performance, either in test scores and behavioural measures during primary school (Argentina) or school attendance (Uruguay). Similarly, Urzúa and Veramendi (2011) found that children who attended preschool programmes in Chile had significantly higher scores on a Spanish IQ test than those who did not. Mwaura, Sylva and Malmberg (2008) and Aboud, Hossain and O'Gara (2008) found similar positive effects of preschool attendance for Bangladesh, Kenya, Uganda, and Zanzibar.

Thus, attending preschool seems to matter for cognitive outcomes and subsequent educational performance. However, not all preschool seems to matter the same. Aboud and Hossain (2011) look into changes in the quality of a preprimary education programme implemented by an NGO in Bangladesh. The programme was designed for five year olds in the year before entering first grade. It operated six days a week for three hours a day and catered to children from poor and very poor rural families. Class sizes were generally 20–25 students per teacher. The quality of the programme was initially low (as measured by ECERS). Play was often not free, materials were in short supply and not rotated, nonplaytime entailed whole-group activities where a group response was often required, and there was little informal talk between teachers and individual children. The programme underwent significant improvement over a period of four years. Students who experienced the improved preschool programme attained more competencies, particularly in math, than the earlier samples of graduates who had been exposed to a lower quality programme. They also sustained their advantage into second grade. Other studies found similar results: children who attended improved or higher quality preschools had greater levels of cognitive development than those who did not in Vietnam (Watanabe et al. 2005), Turkey (Kagitcibasi, Sunar and Bekman 2001), and East Africa (Kenya, Uganda, and Zanzibar) (Malmberg, Mwaura and Sylva 2011). Recent studies have analysed deeper what makes for a quality preschool experience. Araujo et al. (2014) randomised an entering cohort of approximately 15,000 preschool children in Ecuador to teachers within schools. They found substantial teacher effects: increases in teacher quality resulted in higher test scores in language, math, and executive functions. Teacher behaviours were strongly associated with better learning outcomes: one third of the within-school, cross-teacher differences in learning outcomes can be accounted for by differences in teaching practices as measured by the Classroom Assessment Scoring System (CLASS).

Conditional cash transfers

As discussed earlier, poverty is a major cause of low child development. To address this issue, conditional cash transfer programmes aim to improve early childhood development through poverty alleviation. Many conditional cash transfer programmes provide financial benefits conditional on mandatory attendance to regular health checkups, nutrition supplements, and school attendance.

Based on a review of international evidence on CCTs, Fiszbein and Schady (2009) find that while research on the effects of CCTs on the *use* of education and health services shows significant, and sometimes even large, effects on school enrolment and attendance, evidence is much less conclusive when it comes to developmental outcomes, particularly for early childhood. CCTs appear to have reduced the incidence of stunting only in some countries and only among some populations and resulted in modest improvements in cognitive development among very young children. However, they had no discernible effect on learning outcomes by school-aged children who benefited from these programmes.

Specifically, a few studies have analysed the effects of cash transfer programmes on cognitive development in Ecuador (Paxson and Schady 2010; Fernald and Hidrobo 2011), Nicaragua (Macours, Schady and Vakis 2012), and Mexico (Fernald, Gertler and Neufeld 2008, 2010). Programme effects on cognitive outcomes and language development are positive but small. in terms of programme design, while conditional cash transfer programmes' conditions do promote that children have access to a (depending on the programme) more or less comprehensive set of interventions, most of these programmes lack a component specifically focused on early stimulation, which may explain the relatively small programme effects on cognitive development.

Scaling up ECDs: a development challenge

Despite the growing consensus that ECD interventions can have important effects on both short- and long-term outcomes, data from developing countries show that access to ECD services is still limited and extremely unequal, particularly for infants and toddlers. There are several reasons that conspire against the expansion of quality ECD services, including knowledge gaps, the difficulty of establishing sustainable mechanisms to ensure programme and systemic quality, and the political economy around the financing of ECD programmes and services.

As we reviewed in this chapter, research on ECD interventions suggests that there are significant gains that could ensue from expanding ECD services in the developing world. However, evidence on the relative cost-effectiveness of alternative interventions is still scarce. As Behrman and Urzúa (2013) argue, an economic justification must depend on the comparison of benefits and costs of each ECD programme. However, the knowledge base on ECD services and programmes still relies on relatively few studies, usually with a small scale of operation and limited outcome indicators and programme information. Moreover, many programmes have different components, and thus attributing impact to specific interventions is made difficult. Evidence on costs is even scarcer, and it often prioritises public expenditures over private ones, which are known to be particularly important in the case of ECD.

Moreover, as the previous section suggests, there is encouraging evidence supporting the view that it is *quality ECD programmes* – and not just *any* ECD programme – that bring about desirable outcomes. Despite the fact that available research can suggest certain elements that can be used as leverage to improve ECD programmes and services, much more research is needed to better identify the most convenient match between specific contexts and delivery modes (centre-, family-, or community-based interventions), delivery agents (community health workers, parents, teachers), and the frequency and duration of interventions. In addition, the jury is still out regarding the relative benefit of comprehensive programmes (that combine, for example, nutrition and early stimulation) vs. specific ones, as well as universal vs. targeted programmes.

An additional difficulty regarding quality of ECD programmes pertains not just to *individual* programme quality but to how to ensure the development of quality ECD *systems* (Kagan and Kauerz 2012). Recent research has analysed systemic aspects of ECD provision in developing countries (Chile, Colombia, Brazil, Trinidad and Tobago, Guatemala, Peru, Cambodia, Lao, and

Kenya), finding that institutional arrangements to ensure good quality levels are still extremely weak (Rebello Britto et al. 2014; Kagan et al. 2015). Moreover, there is a growing trend towards the implementation of comprehensive ECD policies that require complex coordination between previously "siloed" sectors such as health, education, and social protection, among others. Such developments bring additional complexity to the already daunting task of ensuring adequate, timely, and coordinated high quality programmes and services for ECD.

Finally, developing countries often face strong fiscal constraints and political economy considerations that limit their possibilities of taking to scale ECD services. The scaling up of ECD services in many developing countries may require shifting resources away from other existing services, something not many governments may be willing to embrace. In addition, often populations that stand to gain the most from ECD interventions lack the necessary empowerment to demand expansion of access to services and improvements in quality (Vegas and Santibañez 2010).

Notes

1 A large body of analyses has consistently found that returns to schooling are highest at the lower levels of schooling compared to secondary and tertiary levels (see Montenegro and Patrinos 2014 for a review of the evidence). More recent analyses (Montenegro and Patrinos 2014) presenting new and comparable estimates of the private returns to schooling using data from 139 economies with a total of 819 harmonised household surveys find that returns to tertiary education are highest, although returns to primary school are still substantial. This study does not include returns to preprimary education.
2 PRIDI is the Spanish acronym for "Regional Programme for ECD Indicators".
3 Most of these studies use measures like ITERS (Infant-Toddler Environment Rating Scale), ECERS (Early Childhood Environment Rating Scale), and CLASS (Classroom Assessment Scoring System). These measures aim to describe the context and nature of interactions in which children engage. The ITERS and ECERS scales are observational scales that gather data along seven main dimensions: physical space and equipment, care routines, speaking and communication, activities, interaction, programming, and parents and childcare team. CLASS looks into emotional and behavioural support (positive or negative climate, teacher sensitivity, regard for children's perspectives) as well as instructional support (behaviour guidance, facilitation of learning and development, quality of feedback, language modelling).

References

Aboud, F.E., 2007. Evaluation of an early childhood parenting programme in rural Bangladesh. *Journal of Health Population and Nutrition* 25, 3–13.

Aboud, F., Akhter, S., 2011. A cluster-randomized evaluation of a responsive stimulation and feeding intervention in Bangladesh. *Pediatrics* 127, 1191–97.

Aboud, F.E., Hossain, K., O'Gara, C., 2008. The Succeed Project: challenging early school failure in Bangladesh. *Research in Comparative International Education* 3, 295–307.

Aboud, F.E., Hossain, K., 2011. The impact of preprimary school on primary school achievement in Bangladesh. *Early Childhood Research Quarterly* 26, 2, 237–46.

Alderman, H., Vegas, E., 2011. The convergence of equity and efficiency in ECD programs. In: Alderman, H. (Ed.) *No Small Matter: The Impact of Poverty, Shocks, and Human Capital Investments in Early Childhood Development*. World Bank, Washington.

Al-Hassan, S., Lansford, J., 2011. Evaluation of the Better Parenting Program in Jordan. *Early Childhood Development and Care* 181, 587–98.

Ángeles, G., Gadsen, P., Galiani, S., Gertler, P., Herrera, A., Kariger, P., Seira, E., 2011. *Evaluación de Impacto del Programa Estancia Infantiles para Apoyar a Madres Trabajadoras. Informe Final de la Evaluación de Impacto*. Instituto Nacional de Salud Pública, México.

Araujo, M.C., 2015. Center-based care. In: Berlinski, S. and Schady, N. (Eds.) *Development in the Americas: The Early Years*. Inter-American Development Bank, Washington.

Araujo, M.C., Carneiro, P., Cruz-Aguayo, Y., Schady, N., 2014. *A Helping Hand? Teacher Quality and Learning Outcomes in Kindergarten*. Unpublished manuscript.

Araujo, M.C., López Boo, F., Puyana, J.M., 2013. *Overview of Early Childhood Development Services in Latin America and the Caribbean.* Inter-American Development Bank, Washington.

Armecin, G., Behrman, J.R., Duazo, P., Ghuman, S., Gultiano, S., King, E., Lee, N., 2006. *Early Childhood Development Through an Integrated Program: Evidence from the Philippines.* World Bank Policy Research Working Paper 3922, World Bank, Washington.

Attanasio, O., Vera-Hernandez, M., 2004. *Medium and Long Run Effects of Nutrition and Child Care: Evaluation of a Community Nursery Programme in Rural Colombia.* EWP04/06, Centre for the Evaluation of Development Policies, Institute for Fiscal Studies, London.

Barnett, W.S., 2011. Effectiveness of early educational intervention. *Science* 333, 975–78.

Behrman, J., Cheng, Y., Todd, P., 2004. Evaluating preschool programs when length of exposure to the program varies: a nonparametric approach. *Review of Economics and Statistics* 86, 108–32.

Behrman, J., Urzúa, S., 2013. Economic perspectives on some important dimensions of early childhood development in developing countries. In: Britto, P., Engle, P. and Super, C. (Eds.) *Handbook of Early Childhood Development Research and its Impacts on Global Policy.* Oxford University Press, New York.

Bentley, M., Vazir, S., Engle, P., Balakrishna, N., Johnson, S., Creed, H., Griffiths, P., Fernandez Rao, S., 2010. A home-based educational intervention to caregivers in south India to improve complementary feeding and responsive feeding, and psychosocial stimulation increases dietary intake, growth and development of infants. *FASEB Journal* 24, 564.14.

Berlinski, S., Galiani, S., Gertler, P., 2009. The effect of pre-primary education on primary school performance. *Journal of Public Economics* 93, 1–2, 219–34.

Berlinski, S., Galiani, S., Manacorda, M., 2008. Giving children a better start: preschool attendance and school-age profiles. *Journal of Public Economics* 92, 5–6, 1416–40.

Bernal, R., Fernandez, C., 2013. Subsidized childcare and child development in Colombia: effects of Hogares Comunitarios de Bienestar as a function of timing and length of exposure. *Social Sciences and Medicine* 97, 241–9.

Bernal, R., Fernandez, C., Flores Nieto, C.E., Gaviria, A., Ocampo, P.R., Samper, B., Sanchez, F., 2009. *Evaluation of the Early Childhood Program Hogares Comunitarios de Bienestar in Colombia.* Centro de Estudios sobre Desarrollo Económico, Universidad de los Andes, Bogotá.

Bucarey, A., Ugarte, G., Urzúa, S., 2014. *El Efecto de la Educación Preescolar en Chile.* Unpublished manuscript.

Campbell, F.A., Pungello, E.P., Miller-Johnson, S., Burchinal, M., Ramey, C.T., 2001. The development of cognitive and academic abilities: growth curves from an early childhood educational experiment. *Developmental Psychology* 37, 231–42.

Campbell, F.A., Ramey, C.T., Pungello, E.P., Sparling, J., Miller-Johnson, S., 2002. Early childhood education: young adult outcomes from the Abecedarian Project. *Applied Developmental Science* 6, 42–57.

Campos, M., Esposito, Y., Bhering, E., Gimenes, N., Abuchaim, B., 2011. Quality of early education: a study in six Brazilian state capitals. *Cadernos de Pesquisa* 41, 142, 20–54.

Carneiro, P., Heckman, J., 2003. *Human Capital Policy.* NBER Working Paper 9495, National Bureau of Economic Research, Cambridge, MA.

Engle, P., Fernald, L., Alderman, H., Behrman, J., O'Gara, C., Yousafzai, A., Cabral de Mello, M., Hidrobo, M., Ulkuer, N., Ertem, I., Iltus, S., 2011. Strategies for reducing inequalities and improving developmental outcomes for young children in low and middle income countries. *Lancet* 378, 9799, 1339–53.

Engle, P., Nirmala, R., Petrovic, O., 2013. Situational analysis of young children in a changing world. In: Britto, P., Engle, P. and Super, C. (Eds.) *Handbook of Early Childhood Development Research and its Impacts on Global Policy.* Oxford University Press, New York.

Fernald, L., Gertler, P., Neufeld, L., 2008. Role of cash in conditional cash transfer programmes for child health, growth, and development: an analysis of Mexico's *Oportunidades. Lancet* 371, 828–37.

Fernald, L., Gertler, P., Neufeld, L., 2010. Ten-year impact of *Oportunidades* – Mexico's conditional cash transfer programme-on child growth, cognition, language, and behavior. *Lancet* 374, 1997–2005.

Fernald, L., Hidrobo, M., 2011. Ecuador's cash transfer program (*Bono de Desarrollo Humano*) and child development in infants and toddlers: a randomized effectiveness trial. *Social Science and Medicine* 72, 9, 1437–46.

Fernald, L., Kariger, P., Hidrobo, M., Gertler, P., 2012. Socioeconomic gradients in child development in very young children: evidence from India, Indonesia, Peru, and Senegal. *Proceedings of the National Academy of Science* 109, 2, 17273–80.

Fernald, L., Weber, A., Galasso, E., Ratsifandrihamanana, L., 2011. Socioeconomic gradients and child development in a very low income population: evidence from Madagascar. *Developmental Science* 14, 4, 832–47.

Fiszbein, A., Schady, N., 2009. *Conditional Cash Transfers. Reducing Present and Future Poverty.* World Bank, Washington.

Gertler, P., Heckman, J., Pinto, R., Zanolini, A., Vermeersch, C., Walker, S., Chang, S., Grantham-McGregor, S., 2014. Labor market returns to an early childhood stimulation intervention in Jamaica. *Science* 344, 6187, 998–1001.

Gertler, P.J., Pinto, R., Zanolini, A., Vermeersch, C., Walker, S., Chang, S., Grantham-McGregor, S., 2013. *Labor Market Returns to Early Childhood Stimulation: A 20 Year Follow-up to the Jamaican Study.* CEGA Working Paper 027, University of California at Berkeley.

Grantham-McGregor, S., Schofield, W., Powell, C., 1987. Development of severely malnourished children who received psychosocial stimulation: six-year follow-up. *Pediatrics* 79, 247–54.

Grantham-McGregor, S., Walker, S., Chang, S., Powell, C., 1997. Effects of early childhood supplementation with and without stimulation on later development in stunted Jamaican children. *American Journal of Clinical Nutrition* 6, 2, 247–53.

Hamadani, J.D., Huda, S.N., Khatun, F., Grantham-McGregor, S., 2006. Psychosocial stimulation improves the development of undernourished children in rural Bangladesh. *Journal of Nutrition* 136, 2645–52.

Heckman, J., 2011. The economics of inequality. The value of early childhood education *American Educator* 35, 1, 31–47.

Janssens, W., Rosemberg, C., 2011. *The Impact of a Home-Visiting Early Childhood Intervention in the Caribbean on Cognitive and Socio-Emotional Child Development.* Amsterdam Institute for International Development, Amsterdam.

Jin, X., Sun, Y., Jiang, F., Ma, J., Morgan, C., Shen, X., 2007. "Care for Development" intervention in rural China: a prospective follow-up study. *Journal of Developmental and Behavioral Pediatrics* 28, 213–18.

Kagan, S.L., Araujo, M.C., Cruz-Aguayo, Y., Jaimovich, A., 2015. The institutional architecture of early childhood development policies and programs in Latin America and the Caribbean. In: Berlinski, S. and Schady, N. (Eds.) *Development in the Americas: The Early Years.* Inter-American Development Bank, Washington.

Kagan, S.L., Kaurez, K. (Eds.), 2012. *Early Childhood Systems. Transforming Early Learning.* Teachers College Press, New York.

Kagitcibasi, C., Sunar, D., Bekman, S., 2001. Long-term effects of early intervention: Turkish low-income mothers and children. *Applied Developmental Psychology* 22, 333–61.

Kagitcibasi, C., Sunar, D., Bekman, S., Baydar, N., Cemalcilar, Z., 2009. Continuing effects of early enrichment in adult life: the Turkish Early Enrichment Project 22 years later. *Journal of Applied Developmental Psychology* 30, 764–79.

Klein, P., Rye, H., 2004. Interaction-oriented early intervention in Ethiopia: the MISC approach. *Infants and Young Children* 17, 340–54.

López Boo, F., 2013. *Intercontinental Evidence on Socioeconomic Status and Early Childhood Cognitive Skills: Is Latin America Different?* IADB Working Paper Series 435, Inter-American Development Bank, Washington.

Macours, K., Schady, N., Vakis, R., 2012. Cash transfers, behavioral changes, and cognitive development in early childhood: evidence from a randomized experiment. *American Economic Journal: Applied Economics* 4, 2, 247–73.

Macours, K., Vakis, R., 2010. Seasonal migration and early childhood development. *World Development* 38, 6, 857–69.

Malmberg, L.E., Mwaura, P., Sylva, K., 2011. Effects of a preschool intervention on cognitive development among East-African preschool children: a flexibly time-coded growth model. *Early Childhood Research* 26, 124–33.

Mateo-Diaz, M., Rodriguez-Chamussy, L., 2013. *Childcare and Women's Labor Participation: Evidence for Latin America and the Caribbean.* IDB Technical Note 586, Inter-American Development Bank, Washington.

Mateo-Diaz, M., Rodriguez-Chamussy, L., 2014. *Working Parents and Childcare. A Policy Review for Latin America and the Caribbean.* Inter-American Development Bank, Washington.

McLaughlin, A.E., Campbell, F.C., Pungello, E.P., Skinner, M., 2007. Depressive symptoms in young adults: The influences of the early home environment and early educational childcare. *Child Development* 78, 3, 746–56.

Montenegro, C., Patrinos, H., 2014. *Comparable Estimates of Returns to Schooling Around the World.* World Bank Policy Research Working Paper 7020, World Bank, Washington.

Morris, J., Jones, L., Berrino, A., Jordans, M.J.D., Okema, L., Crow, C., 2012. Does combining infant stimulation with emergency feeding improve psychosocial outcomes for displaced mothers and babies? A controlled evaluation from northern Uganda. *American Journal of Orthopsychiatry* 82, 349–57.

Mwaura, P., Sylva, K., Malmberg, L., 2008. Evaluating the madrasa preschool programme in east Africa: a quasi-experimental study. *International Journal of Early Years Education* 16, 237–55.

Nadeau, S., Martinez, S., Filmer, D., 2011. Cognitive development among young children in low-income countries. In: Alderman, H. (Ed.) *No Small Matter: The Impact of Poverty, Shocks, and Human Capital Investments in Early Childhood Development*. World Bank, Washington.

Nahar, B., Hamadani, J.D., Ahmed, T., Tofail, F., Rahman, A., Huda, S.N., Grantham-McGregor, S., 2009. Effects of psychosocial stimulation on growth and development of severely malnourished children in a nutrition unit in Bangladesh. *European Journal of Clinical Nutrition* 63, 725–31.

Nelson, C.A., de Haan, M., Thomas, K., 2006. *Neuroscience and Cognitive Development: The Role of Experience and the Developing Brain.* John Wiley, New York.

Nores, M., Barnett, S., 2010. Benefits of early childhood interventions across the world: (under) investing in the very young. *Economics of Education Review* 29, 271–82.

Paxson, C., Schady, N., 2007. Cognitive development among young children in Ecuador: the roles of wealth, health, and parenting. *Journal of Human Resources* 42, 1, 49–84.

Paxson, C., Schady, N., 2010. Does money matter? The effects of cash transfers on child health and development in rural Ecuador. *Economic Development and Cultural Change* 59, 1, 187–29.

Peairson, S., Berghout Austin, A.M., Nielsen de Aquino, C., Urbieta de Burro, E., 2008. Cognitive development and home environment of rural Paraguayan infants and toddlers participating in Pastoral del Niño, an early child development program. *Journal of Research in Childhood Education* 22, 343–62.

Powell, C., 2004. *An Evaluation of the Roving Caregivers Programme of the Rural Family Support Organization, May Pen, Clarendon, Jamaica.* UNICEF, Kingston.

Powell, C., Grantham-McGregor, S., 1989. Home visiting of varying frequency and child development. *Pediatrics* 84, 157–64.

Powell, C., Baker-Henningham, H., Walker, S., Gernay, J., Grantham-McGregor, S., 2004. Feasibility of integrating early stimulation into primary care for undernourished Jamaican children: cluster randomized controlled trial. *British Medical Journal* 329, 89–92.

Rahman, A., Iqbal, Z., Roberts, C., Husain, N., 2008. Cluster randomized trial of a parent-based intervention to support early development of children in a low-income country. *Child: Care, Health and Development* 35, 56–62.

Rebello Britto, P., Yoshikawa, H., van Ravens, J., Ponguta, L., Reyes, M., Oh, S., Dimaya, R., Nieto, A.M., Seder, R., 2014. Strengthening systems for integrated early childhood development services: a cross-national analysis of governance. *Annals of the New York Academy of Science* 1308, 245–55.

Rosero, J., 2012. *On the Effectiveness of Child Care Centers in Promoting Child Development in Ecuador.* Tinbergen Institute Discussion Paper TI 2012–075/3, Tinbergen Institute, Amsterdam.

Rosero, J., Oosterbeek, H., 2011. *Trade-Offs between Different Early Childhood Interventions: Evidence from Ecuador.* Tinbergen Institute Discussion Paper TI 2011–102/3, Tinbergen Institute, Amsterdam.

Rubio-Codina, M., Attanasio, O., Meghir, C., Varela, N., Grantham-McGregor, S., 2013. *The Socio-Economic Gradient of Child Development: Cross-Sectional Evidence from Children 6–42 Months in Bogota.* IADB Working Paper Series 527. Inter-American Development Bank, Washington.

Ruel, M.T., de la Brière, B., Hallman, K., Quisumbing, A.R., Coj, N., 2002. *Does Subsidized Childcare Help Poor Working Women in Urban Areas? Evaluation of a Government-Sponsored Program in Guatemala City.* IFPRI, Washington.

Schady, N., 2011. Parental education, vocabulary, and cognitive development in early childhood: longitudinal evidence from Ecuador. *American Journal of Public Health* 101, 12, 2299–307.

Schady, N., Behrman, J., Araujo, C., Azuero, R., Bernal, R., Bravo, D., López-Boo, F., Macours, K., Marshall, D., Paxson, C., Vakis, R., 2014. *Wealth Gradients in Early Childhood Cognitive Development in Five Latin American Countries.* IADB Working Paper Series 482, Inter-American Development Bank, Washington.

Schweinhart, L.J., 2001. How the High/Scope Perry preschool study has influenced public policy. Paper prepared for the Third International, Inter-disciplinary Evidence-Based Policies and Indicator Systems Conference, CEM Centre, University of Durham.

Sharma, S., Nagar, S., 2009. Influence of home environment on psychomotor development of infants in Kangra district of Himachal Pradesh. *Journal of Social Science* 21, 225–29.

Shonkoff, J.P., Phillips, D.A. (Eds.), 2000. *From Neurons to Neighborhoods: The Science of Early Childhood Development.* National Academies Press, Washington.

UNESCO, 2014. *EFA Global Monitoring Report.* UNESCO, Paris.

UNICEF, 2010. *Progress for Children: Achieving the MDGs with Equity.* UNICEF, New York.

UNICEF, 2014a. *State of the World Children.* UNICEF, New York.

UNICEF, 2014b. UNICEF Global Databases, Based on DHS, MICS and Other Nationally Representative Surveys. http://www.childinfo.org/mics4_surveys.html

Urzúa, S., Veramendi, G., 2011. *The Impact of Out-of-Home Childcare Centers on Early Childhood Development.* IADB Working Paper Series 240, Inter-American Development Bank, Washington.

Vegas, E., Santibañez, L., 2010. *The Promise of Early Childhood Development in Latin America and the Caribbean.* World Bank, Washington.

Verdisco, A., Perez Alfaro, M., 2010. *Measuring Education Quality in Brazil.* Briefly Noted Series, Inter-American Development Bank, Washington.

Walker, S., 2011. Promoting equity through early child development interventions for children from birth through three years of age. In: Alderman, H. (Ed.) *No Small Matter: The Impact of Poverty, Shocks, and Human Capital Investments in Early Childhood Development.* World Bank, Washington.

Walker, S., Chang, S., Powell, C., Grantham-McGregor, S., 2004. Psychosocial intervention improves the development of term low-birth- weight infants. *Journal of Nutrition* 134, 6, 1417–23.

Walker S., Wachs, T., Gardner J., Lozoff, B., Wasserman, G., Pollitt, E., Carter, J., 2007. Child development: risk factors for adverse outcomes in developing countries. *Lancet* 369, 145–57.

Walker, S., Wachs, T., Grantham-McGregor, S., Black, M., Nelson, C., Huffman, L., Baker-Henningham, H., Chang, S., Hamadani, J., Lozoff, E., Meeks Gardner, J., Powell, C., Rahman, A., Richter, L., 2011. Inequality in early childhood: risk and protective factors for early child development. *Lancet* 378, 1325–38.

Watanabe, K., Flores, R., Fujiwara, J., Tran, L.T.H., 2005. Early childhood development interventions and cognitive development of young children in rural Vietnam. *Journal of Nutrition* 135, 1918–25.

World Bank, 2006. *Repositioning Nutrition as Central to Development: A Strategy for Large-Scale Action.*

World Bank, 2013. *The State of the Poor.* World Bank, Washington.

19

"115 MILLION GIRLS …"

Informal learning and education, an emerging field

Alan Rogers[1]

"Today, all over the world, 115 million girls are doing no learning" because they are not in school or are in inadequate schools. These are the opening words of a video issued to promote the latest UNESCO Education for All *Global Monitoring Report* 2013/14 (GMR 2014). It is almost impossible for such a statement to be made within a discussion of formal education in Western educational contexts, for in that field there has been growing interest in informal learning, all that learning that goes on *outside* of formal educational establishments (schools and colleges), and in its relationships with education, both formal and nonformal. That it is possible in the field of education in international development for this very large and important field of learning to be demeaned or denied remains puzzling, especially when some other sectors of development do take informal learning seriously. It is when talking about schooling in international development that the learning that these 115 million girls and others are doing in their everyday life in family and community is very often dismissed or ignored.

Informal learning

It is important to identify what we are discussing, as "there is a tendency to treat education and learning as synonymous concepts" (Duke 2001: 502) and this leads to "the persisting confusion of education with learning" (Jarvis 1990: 203). The term 'informal learning' is often used to mean 'informal education', flexible learning programmes outside formal educational institutions, such as e-learning, open and distance education as well as active teaching–learning methods in the classroom (see, for example, Cofer 2000; for informal education, see Jeffs and Smith 1990; Childs and Greenfield 1977; Bekerman et al. 2006). The 'informal learning' of this paper is not informal (or nonformal) education; it is not planned learning. It is all that unplanned, everyday learning from life's experience that every person does, a natural, continuous but unintentional and very largely unconscious process. Learning is like breathing, something we all do without thinking about it except occasionally. "Among the most basic of human activities, learning is as crucial as breathing. Learning is the process … by which we internalise the external world and through which we construct our experiences of that world" (Jarvis, Holford and Griffin 1998: vii). In this sense, learning is *ubiquitous* in every arena of life, not just in specific places (school, adult class or workplace, etc.); it is *universal*, everyone does it, there are no 'nonlearners'; and it is

260

continuous – lifelong and everyday – not confined to specific times and events. It is simply a part of living (for a more detailed review of informal learning, see Rogers 2014a).

Informal learning and education in western discourses

An interest in informal learning in relation to education in Western societies is not, of course, new, but it has increased recently for a number of reasons. First, in reaction to a number of perceived failures of education systems, informal learning is thought to be able to help to improve the effectiveness of formal and nonformal learning – education and training, schooling in all its various forms (e.g., DIUS 2009). Second, informal learning is recognised as the source of many antisocial tendencies and practices such as learning drugs, gangs, domestic violence, radicalisation, racial and gender prejudice, etc. (Patterson, DeBaryshe and Ramsey 1993) that can be addressed by formal learning. And third it is widely recognised (e.g., Cross 1981; Merriam, Cafarella and Baumgartner 2006) that learners come into learning programmes with what have been called 'funds of knowledge' (Gonzales, Moll and Amanti 2005; Hogg 2012) and 'banks of skills', most of which have been learned informally through experience. These need to be taken into account if we are to achieve effective learning in school or other learning programmes.

Studies of this informal learning show that it is larger and more influential than formal learning (attempts to quantify the difference between the two can be made only in the most general of terms since, unlike formal learning, informal learning is largely unconscious and cannot be measured in any detail).

> If all learning were to be represented by an iceberg, then the section above the surface of the water would be sufficient to cover formal learning, but the submerged two thirds of the structure would be needed to convey the much greater importance of informal learning.
>
> (Coffield 2000: 1; see Schugurensky 2000)

It is informal learning in the main that creates the values and belief systems, the preunderstanding, the frames of meaning, the social imaginaries, the assumptions of normality that learners bring to any formal or nonformal learning situation. It establishes aspirations and expectations and the level of confidence essential to tackling any tasks, including new learning (Rogers 2014a).

Formal and informal learning are perhaps best seen not as discrete categories but "as attributes present in all circumstances of learning" (Colley, Hodgkinson and Malcolm 2003: 1). Thus there are elements of formality in much informal learning, and unconscious informal learning is taking place within formal learning programmes:

> Inevitably, embedded in the knowledge, information and skills being passed on are certain values, norms and biases which reflect the dominant views and beliefs of those who have constructed the curriculum and the learning materials.
>
> (Leach 2003: 102)

> As children learn to read and write, they are learning to engage with the culture and with specialised cultural practices . . . learning about being black, girls, working-class, even poor, *in this culture.*
>
> (Miller 1990: 159, original emphasis)

However, although at times inextricably mixed, informal learning and formal/nonformal learning can still be distinguished, in that, unlike formal and nonformal learning, informal learning is unintentional, unplanned and very largely unconscious.

Three aspects of the relationship between informal learning and formal learning seem to stand out in Western discussions. First, much of the interest centres on *socialisation*, especially of young people, "the process by which infants acquire the skills necessary to perform as a functioning member of their society – the most influential learning process one can experience" (Billingham 2007: 336). While some see socialisation as confined to childhood, for others it is a "lifelong process of inheriting and disseminating norms, customs and ideologies" (Clausen 1968: 5).

Second, there is growing concern about *home-school links*, the relationship between what is learned informally outside of school and what is learned formally in school or nonformal learning programme. All learners bring to all learning programmes tacit funds of knowledge (Moll and Gonzales 2004) and banks of skills that have been learned unconsciously from family and community (see, e.g., Street, Baker and Toulmin 2005). They bring their own frames of meaning developed socially over the years without being conscious of these, their own sense of the normal. Third, especially in the area of workplace learning (human resource development) (Bell and Dale 1999; Garrick 1998) but also in further education, attention is given to finding ways to give recognition to the students/trainees' funds of knowledge and banks of skills built up through experience, in the *assessment of prior learning* (APL) (e.g., Merrifield, McIntyre and Osaigbovo 2000; Day 2002; Pokorny 2013). The importance of this informal, unconscious, unplanned, unintended learning for educational programmes, formal and nonformal, is widely acknowledged in discussions of education in Western contexts.[2]

Informal learning in the context of education in developing societies

But in the context of international aid to education, informal learning is not only less frequently discussed; at times, it seems to be actively dismissed. The UNESCO statement about 115 million girls who "are doing no learning" because they are not in (adequate) schools cited above is only one such example. Calls for people to 'participate in learning', thus 'widening participation in learning', and for 'learning to learn' are all predicated on the assumption that some people are learning and some are not. The importance given to getting children into school, any school, expresses a belief that 'learning' only takes place in schools or in nonformal education and training; that what they are learning in their daily lives is not of value; and that without participation in formal or nonformal learning programmes, young people and adults lack learning. Assertions in training-of-trainers programmes in developing countries that adults who have had no schooling have not been socialised and "cannot judge between right and wrong" are not uncommon. The everyday learning that all persons, young and old, unschooled as well as schooled, do is demeaned or denied by many aid agencies and educational planners.

But these '115 million girls' are, of course, learning a great deal outside of school. Like their Western counterparts, they are building up tacit funds of knowledge and banks of skills, and the knowledge and skills they are building up are very important to them for negotiating life. They are also, of course, learning many other things – poverty and power (both its potential and its limits); they may learn parenthood and property. Not all they learn will be correct, and not all will be socially desirable; some will learn prejudice and drugs, many are learning violence. But since the Education for All programme came to focus exclusively on schools within a deficit discourse (see *Convergence* 2004), there appears to be little awareness of this informal learning in the context of educational planning and practice in developing societies.[3]

But the ignoring of the informal learning of these '115 million girls' (and of course others) cannot be justified, for this everyday learning is even more important in such contexts than in Western contexts. Large numbers of children and even larger numbers of adults are not and have not been in school at all – and yet they have learned a great deal from experience and from their sociocultural context, and they are all continuing to learn throughout their lives without educational assistance. For example, young people and adults are learning to use new technologies for their own purposes – mobile phones to acquire information, digital calculators to indicate prices and to record sales (Jacobson 2012; Erstad and Sefton-Green 2013; UIL 2014).[4] There is increasing awareness that different "epistemologies of the South" exist (the best recent study is by Santos 2014): many adult educators have found themselves working with participants "who, while unschooled, routinely drew on a complex, even sophisticated, body of local knowledge based on their collective life experiences" (Nirantar 2007: 4). Informal learning in these contexts needs to be studied, not simply because of its relationship to the education and training provided by governments and nongovernmental agencies but in its own right – seeking to understand how and what nonschooled (and also schooled) persons, young and old, are learning through their everyday experiences, both socially useful and antisocial learning.

It may be argued that the long-standing concern for 'indigenous knowledge' in several development sectors is an indication of an interest in informal learning (Breidlid 2013; see also Brock-Utne 1994; Kincheloe and Semali 1999). This is to some extent true. But there is a distinction between the funds of knowledge built up by informal learning and 'indigenous knowledge' (or 'knowledges'). Definitions of 'indigenous knowledge' are, of course, contested, but they are usually seen in terms of 'local' knowledge set in opposition to 'global' or 'Western' knowledge, as 'traditional' as against 'modern', or as 'subjugated and marginalised' as contrasted with mainstream and dominant (Morgan 2005; Kincheloe 2008; King and Aikman 2012). But, although indigenous knowledge in any of these senses is *part* of funds of knowledge, the funds of knowledge developed informally through experience are wider than 'indigenous knowledge'. They include elements drawn from global, Western, modern and dominant knowledges as well as local and traditional elements. For example, the skills of using mobile phones and knowledge of European football matches – all learned informally – are now part of the funds of knowledge of many youth and adults throughout Asia and Africa, but they cannot be called in any meaningful way 'indigenous knowledge'. Unlike some concepts of indigenous knowledges, the funds of knowledge built up by informal learning by everyone, including the unschooled, are constantly changing and growing, a swirling cloud of knowing drawn from many different sources, modern and traditional, local and global, mainstream and marginal, but the knower will very largely be unconscious of this, although using such tacit knowledges in the course of their daily lives.

Case studies of informal learning and education

The significance of informal learning is, however, being taken seriously in a number of sectors of international development assistance. Three examples – literacy, skills development and citizenship – can be taken to illustrate some of the ways in which informal learning and different forms of education and training in developmental contexts interact.

Informal learning and literacy

Those who work in what have been called the New Literacy Studies (Street 1993: 1–21) have taken seriously the informal learning that nonschooled and nonliterate persons have done and continue to engage in (Rogers 2008). Unschooled and nonliterate youth and adults have learned, and are learning, from their own experience many things in relation to literacy. The importance of this informal and largely unconscious learning in relation to literacy focuses on four main areas:

Literacy strategies

First, almost all nonliterate adults have "developed their own strategies" to engage with the literacies they require for their everyday activities (Ewing, 2003, cited in Papen 2005: 139). Some of these engagements will be through mediation or proximal literacy, getting someone to help them (Kalman, 1999; Mace 2002; Iversen and Palmer-Jones 2009), through coconstruction (Blommaert 2007), or they will find other ways of managing travel situations or interacting with bureaucracies (Kell 2009). It is through informal learning that they learn "to adapt . . . to the requirements of new technologies, or . . . to navigate the literacy environment of unfamiliar institutional settings" (Papen 2005: 24). They engage in their required literacy practices in their own way.

Informal literacy skills

Some indeed have learned through informal means enough literacy skills to manage parts of their lives. Research has shown that significant numbers of nonschooled youth and adults have, through informal learning, come to "possess a range of informally acquired literacy and numeracy skills" (Papen 2005: 131).

> [M]ost children and adults are not 'illiterate' when they start school . . . they already have a great deal of experience of leading literate lives in their homes and communities. Most come to education with 'funds of knowledge' in terms of the literacy practices in their everyday lives.
>
> (Ivanic 2009: 102–3)

The nonliterate plumber who offers to provide a receipt; the rickshaw driver who has learned to read and understand words like 'school', 'clinic' and 'hospital' because he takes passengers to these locations frequently; the shopkeeper who keeps a record of sales, stock and credit on scraps of paper have all learned such skills informally – and they are not unusual (Rogers and Street 2012; Nabi, Rogers and Street 2009; see also Maddox 2001; Uddin 2006). These 'hidden literacies' are increasingly being recognised as important, for they can form the basis of new literacy learning, both in terms of confidence and a sense of relevance of the new learning. Ignoring or demeaning such funds of knowledge will almost certainly demotivate many from learning, leading to an increase in their sense of marginalisation. Many students bring their own informally acquired skills with them to the formal and nonformal learning programme.

The meaning of literacy

But, as Nabi, Rogers and Street's work (2009) and other studies have shown, many nonliterate adults engaged in such everyday reading and writing activities do not see the informal writings they are making as 'literacy': "He did not really view what he did in his daily life as using literacy; to his mind, literacy meant learning, and learning took place in a classroom" (Fowler and Mace 2005: 32). Through informal learning, nonschooled youth and adults have developed what is known as a 'pre-understanding' of literacy (Rogers 2014a) – what literacy is and what it is not in their particular context, who literacy is for and who is excluded from that literate world – and they tend to assume that there is only one normally accepted and unproblematic meaning of the word. Fieldwork in Africa shows that some people do not see the texts they send on their mobiles as being 'literacy' – "this is not literacy" or "this is not *your* literacy". They still feel themselves to be 'illiterate' (Rogers and Street 2012). To develop the skills of the 'real' literacy, the literacy of the elites, they have learned that they need to attend adult literacy classes.

Where literacy is normal and not normal

And finally, they have learned unconsciously from their literate environment to distinguish between those contexts in which 'literacy' practices are enacted and those where literacy is "not normal". For example, the woman in Bangladesh who kept a written record of the transactions of the women's credit and savings group of which she was a member but not of her own livelihood activities because, as she said, "it is not normal" in her context for accounts to be kept for personal activities; and the woman in Egypt who, although taught in an adult literacy class to keep accounts, did not do so for her own income-generation activities, again, as she said, "because it is not normal" to do so such activities in her context (Rogers 2008; Rogers and Street 2012) – these represent many others. It is through informal learning rather than formal learning that practices based on assumptions of normality are developed and applied to life's situations.

Thus these 115 million girls and all unschooled youth and adults are learning informally and unconsciously through their everyday experience of life a great deal about literacy and their relationship to it. This informal learning profoundly affects the meanings, expectations and intentions, the knowledge, skills and practices that participants bring to their literacy learning programme, and these in turn will profoundly affect the learning outcomes. It is therefore important that such unconscious learning should be understood and built into the planning and processes of education, formal and nonformal, not dismissed.

Informal learning and vocational education and training

A second example of the way in which informal learning impacts on education and training can be found in the field of skills development. An understanding of the nature and outcomes of informal learning has major implications for programmes of skills development, whether in functional literacy programmes, formal government-provided TVET, work-place training or in informal skills development programmes provided by commercial agencies and NGOs (Akoojee 2012; Allais 2012; GMR 2012).

The basis of most skills training is a perceived 'skills deficit' – a lack of skills on the part of the trainee. The aim is to provide what is missing from both the individual and the national workforce, in terms of 'hard' skills (technical training) and the so-called soft or people skills (communicative skills, thinking skills and problem solving, team work, information management, entrepreneur skill, ethics, professionalism, leadership skills, etc.) (Jain 2009). But studies of work-related learning in industrialised societies have again shown that workers have developed through experience large funds of knowledge and banks of skills of which they are largely unconscious and which they may even deny (Marsick and Volpe 1999; Moll and Gonzales 2004; Gonzales, Moll and Amanti 2005).

This is also true in development contexts where some providers of formal and nonformal skills development programmes are becoming increasingly aware of the funds of knowledge and banks of skills participants bring with them. One example is the DDR (Disarmament, Demobilisation and Reintegration) programmes in several postconflict arenas. Providers of education and skill training programmes for demobilised fighters in different arenas such as Afghanistan, Sierra Leone and South Sudan (Brooks 2006; Molloy 2007; Paulson 2009; Smith-Ellison 2014) are discovering that trainees bring with them "relevant experiential knowledge and skills which need to be incorporated into . . . trainings" (Afghan National Association for Adult Education 2008, cited in Rogers 2014b). Many of the skills they bring are soft skills – planning, decision making, problem analysis; some have considerable (oral) communication and leadership skills, initiative and persistence. They also bring large funds of knowledge and 'hard' skills such as the use of technology and vehicle maintenance, learned informally through experience or nonformally in military training programmes. In many cases, they do not recognise these in themselves, or if they do, they do not see them as relevant to the new skills they are learning; they construct themselves as unskilled. What in practice many of them lack – and are conscious they lack – are the formal 'schooled' skills of literacy, written numeracy[5] and study skills (Rogers 2014b).

The same is true of trainees in other skills development programmes. They, too, have substantial funds of knowledge and banks of skills, all learned through the informal (and unaccredited) ways of learning that most societies have developed. Crafts like weaving and carpentry are often learned from a practising craftsman or woman (Lave 1977; Johanson and Adams 2004). It is important that we do not see the forms of localised training in vocational and other skills such as traditional apprenticeships as entirely informal (unconscious) learning: a number of studies (Lancy 1975, 2012; Studstill 1979) have pointed out that these bear many of the characteristics of intentional, agentic learning.

But in addition to such informal learning opportunities provided by the society in which the trainees are located, many skills, both traditional and modern, have been and are being developed through the less conscious forms of experiential learning. There are many routes to skills development, and everyday community-based learning is one of the more important routes (Lugalla 1994). Thus again, these 115 million girls and other unschooled youth and adults will have learned and will be learning, informally and unconsciously, useful occupational and life-related skills through their everyday experience of life. Instead of a 'skills deficit', the tacit funds of knowledge and banks of skills the trainees bring with them, all learned informally, can be built upon in the implementation of programmes of TVET and skills development.

Thus informal learning is increasingly being recognised by those concerned with making provision for the perceived national 'skills deficit'. One way in which this increased interest is expressed is through the widespread development and use of national qualifications frameworks to try to accredit this informal learning. But because the informal learning is very varied, this is often accompanied by increasingly detailed lists of competences that soon become a requirement. Thus recognition often comes to incur obligations. In Afghanistan, for example, a newly developed National Qualifications Framework being created with international assistance is accompanied by a National Occupational Skills Schedule that is very elaborate: a stonemason's assistant now requires skills running into 60 pages (Rogers 2014b). The obstacles, problems and costs of this adaptation of informal to formal are considerably underestimated. Converting the unconscious processes of informal learning into conscious formal or nonformal training programmes in an attempt to control and regulate the informal is probably not the best way to take account of the informal.

But that does not mean this informal learning can be ignored; unless the trainees appreciate what they already know and what they already can do, they will often lack the confidence to develop new knowledge and skills. And the existing sets of values and meanings and especially the practices they follow, all learned through informal learning, will influence and in some cases hinder the acquisition of new values, new meanings and new practices. The prior (informal) learning of each participant in skills development programmes is a vital element in the planning of new programmes – despite the difficulties in discovering what the trainees bring with them.

Informal learning and citizenship education

A third area that reveals much about informal learning is that of education for citizenship. Dewey's (1916) concept of education for democracy has reappeared today in the form of "the development of active citizenship", currently at the head of the agenda of many educational policymakers (e.g., Global Campaign for Education statement on International Benchmarks 2005; see Arthur, Davies and Hahn 2008). "We see a key purpose of lifelong learning as democratic citizenship" (*Mumbai Statement* 2000: 266). Behind this lies Giddens' assumption that 'democracy' is the most important concept in the world of today and that 'democracy' needs to be learned formally: "The act of taking part in deciding how society is to be governed is fundamentally a learned activity . . . citizenship [is] one of the fundamental roles to be learned and performed by men and women" (Welton 2002: 16–17).

This is sometimes taken to imply that unschooled or inadequately schooled persons do not learn citizenship. There is a view that there is:

> [A] democratic deficit that must be reduced through culture and citizenship education. . . . [Citizenship education] is the main instrument for [maintaining] the democratic project . . . [since] individuals [do not] spontaneously grasp the principles of democratic life and develop attitudes and behaviour patterns aligned with these principles.
>
> (Korsgaard, Walters and Andersen 2002: 11–12)

Such beliefs imply that citizenship needs to be taught to the untaught: they must be provided with "opportunities to learn active citizenship" (Holst 2002), "to learn free elections, freedom of the press, and the rights of the individuals to express themselves freely, the institutionalisation of opposition to government, the participation of all people in framing and making decisions that affect them" (Medel-Anonuevo 2002: 115–116). From such freedoms, the unschooled are often thought to be excluded; they 'must be brought in' into a Western form of citizenship that is highly normative, 'democratic citizenship', 'active citizenship' (Prakash and Esteva 1998). Such an approach assumes that there is only one form of democracy, that "the principles of democratic life" are universal and uncontested, and that this is the only citizenship that needs to be taught.

But alternatives have been and are being explored, not least in Latin America and South Africa. There is growing awareness of the fact that the lack of confidence in the political arena and the sense of alienation have been internalised, learned informally – "learned helplessness" in the face of the forces of society, learned deprivation (Mayo 2005: 35). It is possible to view 'exclusion' as a construct created by the educated and powerful elites and passed to and internalised by others who have been designated as 'excluded' – all by a process of osmosis, by informal learning.

But 'learned exclusion' from the dominant concepts of citizenship does not mean that many of the less formally educated do not have alternative perceptions and practices of citizenship built up through their life's experience (Dean 2004; see Prakash and Esteva 1998). There is some evidence that, as Stromquist (1997: 210, citing other studies) points out, through a continuous process of exercising of citizenship, people do form for themselves principles of democratic life and develop attitudes and behaviour patterns aligned with their own perceptions of these principles. And the imaginaries of citizenship they develop through informal learning in their daily round may not be the same as those being taught: "Empirical research on citizenship indicates different conceptions within and between different countries." As Dean (2004: 3–4) indicates, each person and each culture constructs and expresses in practice their conception of political and social life – learning through practice. These alternative conceptions and practices are not less valid than those being taught to them. "The context (the person, the institution, the country, the setting) determines the content of . . . citizenship" (UIE 2005: 18).

And it is not just a question of alternative constructions of citizenship but also alternative practices of citizenship. Some of these practices of citizenship are gendered. Thus "women's role in the home [can be seen] as active citizenship" (Jackson 2002: 8). "Women tend to be engaged in community-level demands for the improvement of infrastructure and services . . . more localised and involving a small number of constituents" (Stromquist n.d.: 7). Similarly, many nonschooled have developed their own "critical conscience" (Stromquist 1997: 191) and find ways of engaging in activities tending towards their own goals. Studies of social media reveal people (especially among the younger generations) who are felt by the dominant groups to be alienated from existing political processes, developing their own forms of engagement, their own networks and social identity, and promoting their own values by waging virtual campaigns (Banaji and Buckingham 2013).

> Young people's competence in using media, their ability to produce, understand and interact with the multiplicity of both new and old media formats and technologies have been instrumental in the manifestation of social processes of change.
>
> (Youth 2009)

And such uses of social media have been learned informally.

Thus once again, these 115 million girls and all those not in schools are learning informally and unconsciously much about citizenship – what citizenship means in their culture, who has the power and who does not, whether and in what circles they can get their voices heard, even if only locally. All those engaged in citizenship education need to explore and engage with these tacit alternative perceptions and practices of citizenship learned through informal learning outside of any educational programme, rather than ignore them and impose their own assumptions of normality on the participants.

Informal learning and other sectors of education

Something of the same can be seen in other educational and training sectors in development. The impact of informal learning on agricultural extension is being explored in some detail. Farmers have for many years been seen as having learned farming practices informally from elders, peers and the community, from the market, etc.; these largely tacit funds of knowledge and banks of skills are increasingly being taken seriously by extension workers (see Robinson-Pant this volume). Similarly, environmental education and education for sustainability are looking at local practices and understandings that have been developed over many years through informal learning (e.g., Palmer and Neal 1994; Pavlova 2013). Again, existing knowledge is being taken seriously in some areas of health extension, though judging by some of the most recent material available on health extension in development contexts (WHO 2006a; Teklehaimanot and Teklehaimanot 2013), there is less awareness of the funds of knowledge and banks of skills participants in these programmes bring; extension here is still mainly a supply-and-deliver model, technical, medical instructions from the top down. Where an awareness of indigenous knowledge exists, it tends to focus on local remedies and practices not generally known but which might be useful, such as traditional healers. But there are health extension programmes that seek to adopt "a collaborative model for knowledge development, transfer and exchange between the community and the [extension staff]"; "most . . . learning about health and SDOH [social determinants of health] occurs outside the formal academic sphere" (including extension). The greatest teacher of health, as of other substance, is the community (English and Mayo 2012: 201; see also Wisconsin 2008; Hogg 2005; Jayne 1999; Golding 2011). Programmes of nutrition and welfare sometimes start with what the participants already know, do and have access to, including the tacit funds of knowledge and banks of skills learned informally; these are often tapped into through storytelling (WHO 2006b; see Sanders et al. 2008). "The underlying premise of most of these processes is the value it places on experience, of truly believing the people in the community know what is best for them" (English and Mayo 2012: 201).

It is therefore somewhat strange that it is in education in development, with its focus on schools and classes, that informal learning is almost completely ignored or demeaned, that statements like '115 million girls are doing no learning' can be made. Few health workers, agricultural extension workers, or skills developers would make such a statement, for they are at least to some extent aware of the everyday learning that goes on in the community.

An examination of the nature of informal learning reveals something of the importance of informal learning for schooling. This importance arises in part from the *products* of informal learning – the students' preunderstanding, the funds of knowledge and the banks of skills, the frames of meaning, the values and assumptions we have seen have been developed over time and influence the learning outcomes from educational inputs. But the importance also springs from the *processes* of informal learning, the 'ways of learning' through which such funds of knowledge and banks of skills, such values and assumptions were developed.

The processes of informal learning

This raises the question, *how* does informal learning come about? There appear to be three main characteristics of informal learning that are relevant to this discussion – it is social, it is individual and it is experiential.

Social processes of informal learning

Informal learning is social in that most comes from interaction with others – especially with family, with other practitioners (peer learning, including work colleagues) and with the wider community. Every society develops its own (often unseen) methods of the transfer of knowledge and development of skills from one generation to another. Youth are inducted into their community roles through community learning (usually but not always informal). While recognised 'apprenticeships' are a key feature in many situations (Grierson 1995), craftsmen and women learn much about their craft informally through the sharing of knowledge and the stimulation and encouragement of other members of their extended families, of other practitioners, of market traders and suppliers of materials, and, more remotely, of writers about their craft. The commonality of learning through knowledge exchange and through participation in community practices by the emulation (more than imitation) of significant others[6] suggests that those educators and development agencies who encourage the growth of small-group activities (group work in class and self-help credit and savings groups in development projects, for example) will be both building on and strengthening the strategies of informal learning.

Individual learning

But informal learning is at the same time *individual*. The dual nature of learning is widely rec-ognised: "learning is both a socialisation process and the inner-driven construction of one-self" (Belanger 2011: 93). "While it is the individual who learns, learning always happens in a social context and is socially constructed within the normative demands and values of different cul-tures" (Livingstone 2010: 73).

The primary means of the individual element in learning would seem to be critical reflection (Moon 2007; Mezirow 1990). The relationship between critical reflection and schooling is not clear. Many adults who have been to school have developed little in the way of the capabilities and aptitudes for critical reflection, while many of the unschooled possess both. But the encour-agement of the practice of critical reflection, the making of conscious and the self-challenging of the unconscious assumptions and existing meaning frames that are the fruits of informal learning, would seem to be a valuable feature of both educational and developmental inter-ventions (Fook and Gardner 2007). Getting the best possible balance between individual and collaborative learning activities, especially in education (schooling), is not easy.

Learning from experience

Third, informal learning is *experiential*. Critical reflection is largely on experience, and this expe-rience is of two kinds. On the one hand, it is often unintended – accidental or incidental learning, learning through the daily round of life as experienced. This experience, like learning, is at one and the same time both individual and social – common happenings yet interpreted uniquely. At the same time, learning by experience can be intended; self-directed; or auto-didactic through trial and error, discovery learning, experimentation and practice. It is in this way that banks of skills are exercised and enhanced. The fact that informal learning is both reactive, unintended, and also deliberative, intentional (Eraut 2000: 115; Livingstone 2010:165), suggests that those educational programmes that encourage active learning methods (practice-based learning, see Gherardi and Strati 2012) and those development interventions that are more fully participatory (Nelson and Wright 1995) will build on the existing informal learning and at the same time bring about yet more learning in a continuous, lifelong process of learning.

Conclusion

We can then conclude that our 115 million girls and the many others who are not in (adequate) schools are learning from others, from their own critical reflection and from their individualised experience throughout their lives. They are learning about their relationships with the schooled skills of literacy and numeracy; they are learning occupational and life skills; and they are learn-ing their assigned place in the political structures of their society. It is this informal, unconscious learning that makes them who they are.

It is important that the argument of this paper is clear. It is not an argument in favour of giving greater attention to nonformal education than is currently given under the Education for All programme (that is a quite different argument and needs to continue to be made). Rather, it is an argument that efforts to help developing countries to develop national systems of schooling of quality will be undermined if we deny the informal learning the potential students are already doing (unconsciously) outside of school – in the homes, in the community, in their religious activities, in the occupational activities of themselves and those close to them. An understanding of the natural processes of informal learning in which all persons, schooled and nonschooled, engage is necessary for both effective educational planning and effective teaching-learning. For informal everyday learning from the immediate cultural context through social interactions, whether direct or mediated by technology, creates in everyone tacit funds of knowledge and banks of skills. It forms the learners' dispositions, self-horizons, aspirations, expectations and above all the confidence to learn. It develops preunderstanding, meaning frames, the lens through which we see the world, the horizons that determine what we see and what we do not see. And such attributes, learned informally and held unconsciously, determine the responses of the participants to the learning programmes in schools or nonformal education, both for youth and adults – for informal learning is deep with strong emotional attachments.

Two dimensions need further exploration. First, *research* into informal learning is required – not just into the knowledge and skills that have been built up and are held unconsciously but also into the processes by which they have been developed. Because this learning is unconscious, these processes are difficult to research: asking the participants how they learn, although a necessary part of the research process, would clearly be inadequate in itself. "The focus of ... surveys of adult informal learning is necessarily on self-reported learning that ignores the depths of everyday tacit learning" (Livingstone and Scholtz 2010: 16; see also von Krogh, Ichijo and Nonaka 2000; Greenfield 1984). Conducting surveys of participation in learning programmes will not reveal the full extent of informal learning, especially the deep and invisible part of the iceberg; for this, ethnographic approaches are necessary (Bryman 2004; Nirantar 2007; Atkinson and Hammersley 2011). "We need to examine learning across a range of time and place scales to understand it better, however difficult this may be as an empirical challenge" (Sefton-Green and Erstad 2013: 5).

Second, more effective programmes of *training* of those who teach (teachers in school, trainers, facilitators and extension workers in adult learning programmes and workplace training) in ways of discovering the knowledge and skills, meanings and values, and the learning preferences that learning programme participants bring with them are needed. For without an understanding of the fruits of informal learning, much of the teachers' efforts will be nullified. The prior learning the learners bring, although unconscious, will determine the nature and extent of the new learning attained. The achievement of the millennium educational goals depends on informal learning. Those 115 million girls *are* learning – and *what* they are learning and *how* they are learning will determine what and how they learn when they get into good quality schools.

Notes

1 I am very grateful to Professors Anna Robinson-Pant and Simon McGrath for comments on an early draft of this paper, but they are not responsible for the views expressed.

2 The main field in which informal learning is discussed in relation to schools in Western contexts appears to be in science; e.g., Martin 2004; see Wellcome Review of Informal Science Learning 2011, Center for Informal Learning and Schools (CILS) (http://cils.exploratorium.edu/), etc.

3 It is important to recognise that the words 'informal learning' used by some international aid agencies refer to informal *education*, i.e., planned learning programmes, not to the unconscious, unintentional 'informal learning': for examples, see several recent publications by IIEP such as Werquin 2007 and UNESCO's *Guidelines for the Recognition, Validation and Accreditation of the Outcomes of Non-formal and Informal Learning*, UIL 2012. This is a vital distinction.

4 It is likely that the informal learning associated with religion will come more sharply into focus in development policy discussions; for one study where religion is a significant factor, see Jeffrey, Jeffery and Jeffery 2008.

5 Such trainees frequently possess considerable numeracy skills in the form of mental calculation, but they lack the written forms of calculation that enable them to do more, and more complex, calculations.

6 It is worth noting that in engaging with 'communities of practice', learners share in *some* of the community practices. There is a diversity of practices in every CoP, and learners engage only with some practitioners and some practices. It is easy but dangerous to essentialise communities of practice.

References

Akoojee, S., 2012. Skills for inclusive growth in South Africa: promising tides amidst perilous waters. *International Journal of Educational Development* 32, 5, 674–685.

Allais, S., 2012. Will skills save us? Rethinking the relationships between vocational education, skills development policies and social policy in South Africa. *International Journal of Educational Development* 32, 5, 632–642.

Arthur, J., Davies, I., Hahn, C. (Eds.), 2008. *Handbook of Education for Citizenship and Democracy.* Sage, London.

Atkinson, P., Hammersley, M., 2011. Ethnography and participant observation. In: Denzin, N.K. and Lincoln, Y.S. (Eds.) *Handbook of Qualitative Research.* Sage, London.

Banaji, S., Buckingham, D., 2013. *The Civic Web: Young People, the Internet, and Civic Participation.* The John D. and Catherine T. MacArthur Foundation Series on Digital Media and Learning, MIT Press, Cambridge, MA.

Bekerman, Z., Burbules, N.C., Silberman Keller, D., 2006. *Learning in Places.* Wiley, Oxford.

Belanger, P., 2011. *Theories in Adult Learning and Education.* Barbara Budrich, Opladen.

Bell, J., Dale, M., 1999. *Informal Learning in the Workplace.* Department for Education and Employment, Research Report No. 134. Department for Education and Employment, London.

Billingham, M., 2007. Sociological perspectives. In: Stretch, B. and Whitehouse, M. (Eds.) *Health and Social Care Book 1.* Heinemann, Oxford.

Blommaert, J., 2007. Writing as a problem: African grassroots writing, economies of literacy, and globalization. *Language in Society* 33, 643–671.

Breidlid, A., 2013. *Education, Indigenous Knowledges and Development in the Global South.* Routledge, London.

Brock-Utne, B. (Ed.), 1994. *Indigenous Forms of Learning in Africa.* Oslo Institute of Education Research, Oslo.

Brooks, A., 2006. *Disarmament, Demobilisation and Reintegration of Children Associated with the Fighting Forces.* UNICEF, New York.

Bryman, A., 2004. Ethnography and participant observation. In: Bryman, A. (Ed.) *Social Research Methods.* Second Edition. Oxford University Press, Oxford.

Childs, C.P., Greenfield, P.M., 1977. Informal modes of learning and teaching. In: Warren, N. (Ed.) *Advances in Cross-Cultural Psychology.* Academic Press, London.

Clausen, J.A. (Ed.), 1968. *Socialization and Society.* Little, Brown and Company, Boston.

Cofer, D., 2000. *Informal Workplace Learning.* Practice Application Brief No 10, U.S. Department of Education, Clearinghouse on Adult, Career, and Vocational Education.

Coffield, F. (Ed.), 2000. *The Necessity of Informal Learning.* Policy Press, Bristol.

Colley, H., Hodgkinson, P., Malcolm, J., 2003. *Informality and Formality in Learning.* University of Leeds.

Convergence, 2004. Special Issue, Education for All: putting adults back in the frame. *Convergence* 37, 3.

Cross, P., 1981. *Adults as Learners.* Jossey-Bass, San Francisco.

Day, M., 2002. *Assessment of Prior Learning: A Practitioner's Guide.* Nelson Thornes, Cheltenham.

Dean, B.L., 2004. Pakistani perceptions of "citizenship" and their implications for democratic citizenship education. In: Mundel, K. and Schugurensky, D. (Eds.) *Lifelong Citizenship Learning: Participatory Democracy and Social Change.* Volume 1. OISE, Toronto.

Dewey, J., 1916. *Democracy and Education: An Introduction to the Philosophy of Education.* Free Press, New York.

DIUS, 2009. *The Learning Revolution: Adult Informal Learning.* Department of Industry, Universities and Skills, London.

Duke, C., 2001. Lifelong learning and tertiary education: the learning university. In: Aspin, D., Chapman, J., Hatton, M. and Sawano, Y. (Eds.) *International Handbook of Lifelong Learning.* Kluwer, Dordrecht.

English, L.M., Mayo, P., 2012. *Learning with Adults.* Sense, Rotterdam.

Eraut, M., 2000. Non-formal learning, implicit learning and tacit knowledge in professional work. *British Journal of Educational Psychology* 70, 1, 113–136.

Erstad, O., Sefton-Green, J. (Eds.), 2013. *Identity, Community and Learning Lives in the Digital Age.* Cambridge University Press, Cambridge.

Ewing, G., 2003. The New Literacy Studies: a point of contact between literacy research and literacy work. *Literacies* 1, 15–21.

Fook, J., Gardner, F., 2007. *Practising Critical Reflection.* Open University Press, Buckingham.

Fowler, E., Mace, J. (Ed.), 2005. *Outside the Classroom: Researching Literacy with Adult Learners.* NIACE, Leicester.

Garrick, J., 1998. *Informal Learning in the Workplace.* Routledge, London.

GCE Benchmarks, 2005. *Writing the Wrongs: International Benchmarks for Adult Literacy.* ActionAid, London.

Gherardi, S., Strati, A., 2012. *Learning and Knowing in Practice-Based Studies.* Edward Elgar, Cheltenham.

GMR, 2012. *Global Monitoring Report 2012: Youth and Skills.* UNESCO, Paris.

GMR, 2014. *Global Monitoring Report 2014: Teaching and Learning.* UNESCO, Paris.

Golding, B., 2011. Men's Informal learning and wellbeing beyond the workplace. In: Jackson, S. (Ed.) *Innovations in Lifelong Learning: Critical Perspectives on Diversity, Participation and Vocational Learning.* Routledge, London.

Gonzales, N., Moll, L.C., and Amanti, K., 2005. *Funds of Knowledge: Theorizing Practices in Households and Classrooms.* Lawrence Erlbaum, New Jersey.

Greenfield, P., 1984. Theory of teacher in the learning activities of everyday life. In: Rogoff, B. and Lave, J. (Eds.) *Everyday Cognition.* Harvard University Press, Cambridge, MA.

Grierson, J.P., 1995. Using traditional apprenticeships for self-employment. *Development and Cooperation* 6, 21–22.

Hogg, A., 2005. Finding a curriculum that works under trees: literacy and health education for adolescent girls in rural Malawi. *Development in Practice* 15, 5, 655–667.

Hogg, L., 2012. Funds of knowledge: an examination of theoretical frameworks. *New Zealand Annual Review of Education* 21, 47–76.

Holst, J., 2002. *Social Movements, Civil Society and Radical Adult Education.* Bergin and Garvey, London.

Ivanic, R., 2009. Bringing literacy studies into research on learning across the curriculum. In: Baynham, M. and Prinsloo, M. (Eds.), 2009. *The Future of Literacy Studies.* Palgrave Macmillan, Basingstoke.

Iversen, V., Palmer-Jones, R., 2009. Literacy sharing, assortative mating or what? Labour market advantages and proximate illiteracy revisited. In Basu, K., Maddox, B. and Robinson-Pant, A. (Eds.) *Interdisciplinary Approaches to Literacy and Development.* Routledge, London.

Jackson, S., 2002. Widening participation for women in lifelong learning and citizenship. *Widening Participation and Lifelong Learning* 4, 1, 5–13.

Jacobson, E., 2012. *Adult Basic Education in the Age of New Literacies.* Peter Lang, Bern.

Jain, V., 2009. Importance of Soft Skills Development in Education. http://schoolofeducators.com/2009/02/importance-of-soft-skills-development-in-education/

Jarvis, P., 1990. *An International Dictionary of Adult and Continuing Education.* Routledge, London.

Jarvis, P., Holford, J., Griffin, C., 1998. *The Theory and Practice of Learning.* Kogan Page, London.

Jayne, S., 1999. The effect of education on health. In: Wagner, D., Venezky, R. and Street, B. (Eds.) *Literacy: An International Handbook.* Westview Press, Boulder.

Jeffrey, C., Jeffery, P., Jeffery, R., 2008. *Degrees Without Freedom: Education, Masculinities and Unemployment in North India.* Stanford University Press, Stanford.

Jeffs, T., Smith, M., 1990. *Using Informal Education.* Open University Press, Milton Keynes.

Johanson, R., Adams, A., 2004. *Skills Development in Sub-Saharan Africa.* World Bank, Washington.

Kalman, J., 1999. *Writing on the Plaza: The Mediated Literacy Practice Among Scribes and Clients in Mexico City.* Hampton Press, Cresskill.

Kell, C., 2009. Literacy practices, text/s and meaning making across time and space. In: Baynham, M. and Prinsloo, M. (Eds.) *The Future of Literacy Studies.* Palgrave Macmillan, Basingstoke.

Kincheloe, J.L., 2008. *Critical Pedagogy Primer.* Peter Lang, New York.

Kincheloe, J.L., Semali, L.M. (Eds.), 1999. *What is Indigenous Knowledge? Voices from the Academy.* Falmer, New York.

King, L., Aikman, S., 2012. Indigenous knowledges and education. *Compare* 42, 5, 673–681.

Korsgaard, O., Walters, S., Andersen, R. (Eds.), 2002. *Learning for Democratic Citizenship.* University of Western Cape, Cape Town.

Lancy, D.F., 1975. The social organization of learning: initiation rituals and public schools. *Human Organization* 34, 457–468.

Lancy, D.F., 2012. Apprenticeship: a survey and analysis of the ethnographic record. *Society for the Anthropology of Work Review* 33, 2, 113–126.

Lave, J., 1977. Cognitive consequences of traditional apprenticeship training in West Africa. *Anthropology and Education Quarterly* 8, 177–180.

Leach, F., 2003. *Practising Gender Analysis in Education.* Oxfam, Oxford.

Livingstone, D. (Ed.), 2010. *Lifelong Learning in Paid and Unpaid Work*. Routledge, London.

Livingstone, D., Scholtz, A., 2010. Work and learning in the computer era: basic survey findings. In: Livingstone, D. (Ed.) *Lifelong Learning in Paid and Unpaid Work*. Routledge, London.

Lugalla, J., 1994. Survival tactics and informal learning strategies during the period of structural adjustments: the Tanzanian experience. *AALAE Journal* 8, 1, 12–25.

Mace, J., 2002. *The Give and Take of Writing: Scribes, Literacy and Everyday Life*. NIACE, Leicester.

Maddox, B., 2001. Literacy and the market: the uses of literacy and numeracy among the peasantry of north-west Bangladesh. In: Street, B. (Ed.) *Literacy and Development: Ethnographic Perspectives*. Routledge, London.

Marsick, V.J., Volpe, M. (Eds.), 1999. *Informal Learning on the Job*. Berrett-Koehler, San Francisco.

Martin, L.M.W., 2004. An emerging research framework for studying informal learning and schools. *Science Education* 88, 71–82.

Mayo, M., 2005. *Global Citizens: Social Movements and the Challenge of Globalization*. Zed, London.

Medel-Anonuevo, C., 2002. Lifelong learning and citizenship: possibilities for strengthening democracy in the 21st century. In: Korsgaard, O., Walters, S. and Andersen, R. (Eds.) *Learning for Democratic Citizenship*. University of Western Cape, Cape Town.

Merriam, S.B., Caffarella, R.S., Baumgartner, L.M., 2006. *Learning in Adulthood: A Comprehensive Guide*. Third Edition. Jossey-Bass, San Francisco.

Merrifield, J., McIntyre, D., Osaigbovo, R., 2000. *Mapping APEL: Accreditation of Prior Experiential Learning in Higher Education*. Learning from Experience Trust, London.

Mezirow, J. (Ed.), 1990. *Fostering Critical Reflection in Adulthood*. Jossey-Bass, San Francisco.

Miller, J., 1990. *Seductions: Studies in Reading and Culture*. Virago, London.

Moll, L.C., González, N., 2004. Engaging life: a funds of knowledge approach to multicultural education. In Banks, J. and McGee Banks, C. (Eds.) *Handbook of Research on Multicultural Education*. Second Edition. Jossey-Bass, San Francisco.

Molloy, D., 2007. DDR in Sierra Leone, 1999–2004, the Lessons Learned and the Pitfalls of DDR in Liberia 2003–9. http://www.academia.edu/672798/DDR_in_Sierra_Leone_1999-2004_the_Lessons_Learned_and_the_Pitfalls_of_DDR_in_Liberia_2003–2009

Moon, J., 2007. *Critical Thinking*. Taylor and Francis, London.

Morgan, W.J., 2005. Local knowledge and globalization: are they compatible? In: Cullingford, C. and Gunn, S. (Eds,) *Globalization, Education and Cultural Shock*. Ashgate, London.

Mumbai Statement on Lifelong Learning, Active Citizenship and the Reform of Higher Education, 2000. UNESCO. http://www.unesco.org/education/uie/pdf/mumbstat.pdf

Nabi, R., Rogers, A., Street, B., 2009. Hidden Literacies. http://www.balid.org.uk/wp-content/uploads/2012/12/HiddenLiteracies_all_02.pdf

National Report on the Situation of Adult Learning and Education, 2008. Prepared for CONFINTEA VI by Afghan National Association for Adult Education. http://www.unesco.org/fileadmin/MULTIMEDIA/INSTITUTES/UIL/confintea/pf/National_Reports/Asia%20-%20Pacific/Afghanistan.pdf

Nelson, N., Wright, S. (Eds.), 1995. *Power and Participatory Development*. Intermediate Technology Publications, London.

Nirantar, 2007. Exploring the Everyday. http://www.nirantar.net/index.php/page/view/88

Palmer, J., Neal, P., 1994. *The Handbook of Environmental Education*. Routledge, London.

Papen, U., 2005. *Adult Literacy as Social Practice: More than Skills*. Routledge, London.

Patterson, G.R., DeBaryshe, B., Ramsey, E., 1993. A developmental perspective on antisocial behavior. In Gauvain, M. and Cole, M. (Eds.) *Readings in the Development of Children*. Second Edition. Freeman, New York.

Paulson, J., 2009. TVET and community re-integration in Sierra Leone's DDR process. In: Maclean, R. and Wilson, D. (Eds.) *International Handbook of Education for the Changing World of Work*. Springer, Dordrecht.

Pavlova, M., 2013. Towards using transformative education as a benchmark for clarifying differences and similarities between environmental education and education for sustainable development. *Environmental Education Research* 19, 5, 656–672.

Pokorny, H., 2013. Portfolios and meaning-making in the assessment of prior learning. *International Journal of Lifelong Education* 32, 4, 518–534.

Prakash, M.S., Esteva, G., 1998. *Escaping Education: Living as Learning Within Grassroots Cultures*. Peter Lang, New York.

Rogers, A., 2008. Informal learning and literacy. In: Street, B. and Hornberger, N. (Eds.) *Encyclopedia of Language and Education*. Second Edition. Springer, Dordrecht.

Rogers, A., 2014a. *The Base of the Iceberg. Informal Learning and its Impact on Formal and Non-formal Learning.* Barbara Budrich Publishers, Opladen.

Rogers, A., 2014b. *TVET, Skills Development and Literacy.* CARE Working Paper, University of East Anglia.

Rogers, A., Street, B., 2012. *Adult Literacy in Development: Stories from the Field.* NIACE, Leicester.

Sanders, D., Stern, R., Struthers, P., Ngulube, T.J., Onya, H., 2008. What is needed for health promotion in Africa: Band-Aid, Live Aid or real change? *Critical Public Health* 18, 4, 509–519.

Santos, B. de S., 2014. *Epistemologies of the South: Justice Against Epistemicide.* Paradigm, Boulder.

Schugurensky, D., 2000. The Forms of Informal Learning: Towards a Conceptualization of the Field. https://tspace.library.utoronto.ca/bitstream/1807/2733/2/19formsofinformal.pdf

Sefton-Green, J., Erstad, O., 2013. Identity, community and learning lives in the digital age. In: Erstad, O. and Sefton-Green, J. (Eds.) *Identity, Community and Learning Lives in the Digital Age.* Cambridge University Press, Cambridge.

Smith-Ellison, C., 2014. The role of education in peacebuilding: an analysis of five change theories in Sierra Leone. *Compare* 44, 2, 186–207.

Street, B.V. (Ed.), 1993. *Cross-Cultural Approaches to Literacy.* Cambridge University Press, Cambridge.

Street, B., Baker, D.A., Tomlin, A., 2005. *Navigating Numeracies: Numeracy Practices at Home and at School.* Kluwer/Springer, Dordrecht.

Stromquist, N., 1997. *Literacy for Citizenship: Gender and Grassroots Dynamics in Brazil.* SUNY, Albany.

Stromquist, N., n.d. Women's rights to adult education as a means to citizenship. Unpublished paper.

Studstill, J.D., 1979. Education in a Luba secret society. *Anthropology and Education Quarterly* 10, 67–79.

Teklehaimanot, H.D., Teklehaimanot, A., 2013. Human Resource Development for a Community-Based Health Extension Program: A Case Study from Ethiopia. http://www.human-resources-health.com/content/11/1/39

Uddin, M.A., 2006. Perceptions, Motivations, Learning and Uses of Literacies in Relation to Livelihoods: A case study of two Bangladeshi villages. Unpublished PhD thesis, University of Nottingham.

UIE, 2005. *Why Literacy in Europe.* UIE, Hamburg.

UIL, 2012. *UNESCO's Guidelines for the Recognition, Validation and Accreditation of the Outcomes of Non-formal and Informal Learning.* UIL, Hamburg.

UIL, 2014. Reading in the Mobile Era: A Study of Mobile Reading in Developing Countries. http://unesdoc.unesco.org/images/0022/002274/227436e.pdf

Von Krogh, G., Ichijo, K., Nonaka, I., 2000. *Enabling Knowledge Creation.* Oxford University Press, Oxford.

Wellcome Trust, 2011. *Review of Informal Science Learning.* Wellcome Trust, London.

Welton, M., 2002. Perspectives in citizenship in the age of information. In: Korsgaard, O., Walters, S. and Andersen, R. (Eds.) *Learning for Democratic Citizenship.* University of Western Cape, Cape Town.

Werquin, P., 2007. *Recognising Nonformal and Informal Learning: Outcomes, Policies and Practices.* OECD, Paris.

WHO, 2006a. Ethiopia's Human Resources for Health Programme. http://www.who.int/workforcealliance/knowledge/case_studies/Ethiopia.pdf

WHO, 2006b. Health Impact Assessment: international best practices principles. http://www.iaia.org/modx/assets/files/SP5.pdf

Wisconsin, 2008. Community Engagement Health Extension Program. http://videos.med.wisc.edu/files/NancyD_HeallthExtension.pdf

Youth, 2009. *Engaging with the World: Media, Communication and Social Change.* The International Clearinghouse on Children, Youth and Media's Yearbook, UNESCO, Paris.

20

VOCATIONAL EDUCATION AND TRAINING FOR HUMAN DEVELOPMENT

Simon McGrath and Lesley Powell

Introduction

Vocational education and training (VET) almost slipped off the development agenda after 2000. Excluded from the Millennium Development Goals and marginalised in the Education for All debate, the dominant policy and research view of VET was that it was largely a waste of time. Yet, the current decade has seen VET staging something of a comeback. As we approach the launch of the post-2015 development goals, VET is clearly represented in various proposals for subgoals; UNESCO convened a World Conference on the subject in 2012 and is working on a new Revised Recommendation – its key standard-setting tool – whilst a range of international reports have emerged on skills from organisations such as McKinsey and the OECD, as well as the Global Monitoring Report on Youth and Skills. These global policies come against a backdrop of national commitments in developed and developing contexts to diversify and expand VET.

Given our personal involvement in VET policy, implementation, evaluation and research over the past 20 years, we welcome this revisiting of VET. However, it also highlights a massive challenge for the field in its lack of an adequate theory of vocational education and training for development (cf. McGrath 2012). Whilst those 20 years have seen the rise of human development accounts, VET has not progressed in its account of why it matters and what it is for.

Without a new account, we are concerned that VET is likely to fail in its role of contributing to development and that its current rise is simply a prelude to a more dramatic fall. However, there are signs of potential promise, and this is what where we shall focus. In this chapter, we will explore an emerging literature (Wheelahan and Moodie 2011; Dif-Pradalier, Rosenstein and Bonvin 2012; López-Fogués 2012; McGrath 2012; Powell 2012; Tikly 2013; Powell 2014; Powell and McGrath 2014), which has begun to build a human development and capability account of VET. Though very new, this literature is finding purchase in policy discussions, such as in UNESCO and in South Africa, in settings where there is a broader acceptance of the need for an overall human development vision.

What we will do in this chapter first is to offer a brief critical reading of the orthodoxy. The nature of orthodoxies is that they have many defenders, and our intention is to motivate for a paradigm shift not for a minor revision of the established account. From this, we will proceed to sketch out a human development alternative. Space, and the large existing literature, means that we will not provide a detailed account of the varied human development accounts but, rather, we will proceed via a quick overall introduction to a discussion of the capability approach as the principal source of inspiration for the approach we are taking. We will then consider what it is that a capability approach offers that is useful for VET on theoretical, policy and practical grounds. This includes a reappraisal of the purpose of VET that insists on the primacy of human flourishing; an ethical stance that stresses agency, student voice and deep democracy; a commitment to social justice; and a strong and more positive focus on institutions as central to VET delivery.

We also will include some reflections on the limitations of the capability approach as a way of developing a new VET theory and some of the ways in which we and others are seeking to draw on other approaches to address this. We will acknowledge that other critiques (liberal and post-Marxist) also exist and briefly address what is distinctive about the human development response. We will conclude by pointing to some of the possibilities and challenges that still lie ahead in trying to develop this approach more fully.

Critiquing the current VET orthodoxy

The orthodoxy can be summarised as follows. It is grounded in human capital theory, which sees VET in an instrumental mode, purely in terms of its contribution to economic performance. This includes what Anderson (2009) describes as its two key productivist assumptions:

1. Training leads to productivity (which) leads to economic growth (training for growth);
2. Skills lead to employability (which) lead to jobs (skills for work).

This leads to a critique of VET as inefficient and ineffective at delivering the 'appropriate' and 'relevant' skills required by the labour market, particularly in its public forms. This generates three further steps, not all of which have been advanced in all contexts but which can be taken together as the ideal form. First, despite growing unemployment in many contexts, a decline in quality work and increasingly complex pathways into work, there is a celebration of the skills market as part of a wider theoretico-ideological argument that markets are efficient and effective. Second, as the political costs of abandoning public provision are too high, at least in the medium term, and with increasing political pressure for opportunities to access post-secondary education and training, there is a reform agenda for VET systems and institutions based on the introduction of a new public management toolkit. Third, and spreading beyond VET, is an attempt to repurpose all education as having the goal of enhancing employability and enhancing the national workforce.

The most visible effect of the orthodoxy in the past decade has been the policy travel of a "VET toolkit" (McGrath 2012) centred on:

- Systemic (and increasingly sectoral) governance reforms – shifting power away from bureaucracy and towards employers so as to make VET more relevant and responsive.
- Qualifications frameworks – through making qualifications more transparent to all stakeholders, vertical and horizontal movement of learners is improved as well as the wider accreditation of informal and nonformal learning.
- Quality assurance systems – building new accreditation and inspection regimes with an ultimate aim of ensuring that VET providers internalise notions of quality and continuous improvement.
- New funding mechanisms – signalling a shift towards funding based on outcomes that is institutionally neutral, thus allowing private providers to access state funding.

- Managed autonomy for public providers – introducing new governance structures that give a larger voice to stakeholders (especially industry) and greater autonomy for providers to be the locus of decision making. Yet, at the same time, making institutions more aligned to national policies through funding, reporting and inspection and institutional evaluation regimes (adapted from McGrath 2012: 625).

Our starting point for a critique is to note that the orthodoxy is much more one of policies and practices than it is of explicit theory. The vast majority of work done on VET in developing country contexts has been donor- or state-funded and has been empirical work aimed at evaluating policy implementation rather than directed at theory generation. This is largely true even in the most developed Southern VET research traditions (cf. Powell 2013; Powell and McGrath 2014 on South Africa). Whilst this is ultimately drawn from neoclassical economics, this has been largely implicit, and it has not generated any significant theoretical advances.

Rather than a paradigm being developed strongly through a combination of theory and evidence, the current orthodoxy is better seen as the travelling of a fragile policy. Key elements of the VET toolkit have been transmitted internationally by national agencies (such as the Scottish and South African Qualifications Authorities and the British Council) that are themselves disciplined to export their services as part of public management reforms, whilst coming from systems that are not sites of best practice but rather of systemic crisis, according to their own policy literatures. Thus, the policy is doubly fragile in its weak grounding in realities in the exporting countries and in its trafficking by organisations that often themselves have been subject to drastic budgetary and staffing cuts (cf. McGrath 2010 for discussion of this in the South African context).

The new public management approach described above has been subjected to wider critiques, including within education (e.g., Ball 2003, 2009). These have often focused on its power to discipline learners, staff and institutions in ways that are seen as invidious. However, the approach can also be critiqued from an international and comparative education perspective as fatally flawed due to the impossibility of successful policy transfer to settings that are radically different from that at home, even setting aside the points above regarding successes at home. As well as downplaying context, the orthodox approach fails to regard people as complex agents and neglects the promotion of agency. Moreover, the new public management approach underestimates the complexity of situations and assumes institutional and systemic change are predictable and linear.

Elsewhere, we have also developed Anderson's productivist critique (McGrath 2012; Powell 2012; Powell and McGrath 2014). We argue that the vision of life contained in the approach is dismally narrow in its reduction of everything to economics. Moreover, its atomistic individualism is doubly pernicious in denying the existence of society, whilst blaming rather than empowering the individual and pathologising millions as undeserving poor who have failed in their duty to be citizen-consumers. These individuals are rendered voiceless as there is no need to debate what the purpose of VET is: it is simply to promote employability and productivity.

Alongside this is the contested notion of skills that underpins the orthodoxy. In this view, skills are understood as neutral and universal rather than as contested social and political constructions. The "VET toolkit", together with this simplistic view of skills, has resulted in a narrow understanding of skills as tasks (Allais 2012) that has served to drive learning in VET closer to the "concreteness of the world" and away from the "context of thought" (Gamble 2013).

Moreover, the orthodoxy is problematic in its account of work. Implicitly, it is grounded in a neoclassical view of work as disutility that has been subjected to long-standing critiques from a variety of positions (cf. Marx 1844 [2007]; Leo XIII 1891) that argue that work should be seen as an integral part of human self-actualisation. Its productivism is also fundamentally masculinist in its devaluing of work in what feminist economists have termed "the other economy . . . concerned with the direct production and maintenance of human beings as an end in itself." (Donath 2000: 115). Moreover, it largely skirts the issue of decent work, which must be central to any development agenda that seeks to make a real difference to the lives of the poor (Sehnbruch 2008).

Finally, from the vantage point of development theory, the orthodox account appears incredible, ignoring as it does critiques of the neoclassical account of development and the rise of alternative accounts, including human development, human rights and human security approaches.

The human development alternative: the capability approach

At the core of human development approaches is that the purpose of development is human flourishing (Sen 1999). One prominent attempt to define human development has been in the UNDP *Human Development Reports*. The twentieth anniversary report summed this up thus:

> Human development is the expansion of people's freedoms to live long, healthy and creative lives; to advance other goals they have reason to value; and to engage actively in shaping development equitably and sustainably on a shared planet. People are both the beneficiaries and drivers of human development, as individuals and in groups.
>
> Thus stated, human development has three components:
>
> * Wellbeing: expanding people's real freedoms – so that people can flourish.
> * Empowerment and agency: enabling people and groups to act – to drive valuable outcomes.
> * Justice: expanding equity, sustaining outcomes over time and respecting human rights and other goals of society.
>
> (UNDP 2010: 23)

In this view, economic development is a means to an end and, indeed, is not an unquestioned good as it may sometimes run counter to broader human development (Sen 1999). In the same way, human capital is not replaced as a theory about education and development but is transcended by the broader purpose of human development, which certainly includes the agency of human beings in relation to their productivity, but is broader than this in that the focus is on the freedom and agency that human beings have to live flourishing lives (Sen 1975).

The capability approach offers three key concepts (capabilities, functionings and freedom) that offer crucial lenses for this paper. Capabilities comprise "what a person is able to do or be" and represent "the opportunity to achieve valuable combinations of human functionings" (Sen 2005: 153) and the freedom to elect from these. They are the set of real opportunities from which an individual can choose in order to achieve a life that they value. Functionings, on the other hand, represent what a person actually does, the life that a person actually lives and a person's wellbeing (or illbeing) achievements.

Bonvin and Farvaque (2003), drawing on Sen (1993), clarify the distinction between capabilities and functionings and between agency and well-being:

Thus, individual well-being consists of both well-being freedom (capabilities) and well-being achievement (functionings), i.e., both opportunities from which a person has to select (capabilities) and those that have been achieved (functionings). This distinction highlights the importance

Table 20.1 Four possible informational bases of judgement in justice

	Achievement	*Freedom to achieve*
Promotion of individual well-being	Well-being achievement	Well-being freedom
Pursuit of individual agency goals	Agency achievement	Agency freedom

Source: Adapted from Bonvin and Farvaque 2003: 3.

of human freedom with Sen's focus being on individuals' choices and opportunities rather than only on their actual achievements. Freedom and the ability to choose from a range of capabilities are seen as intrinsically important to a person's well-being as "acting freely" and "being able to choose are . . . directly conducive to wellbeing" (Sen 1992: 50).

The approach further distinguishes between two overlapping aspects of freedom: the opportunity aspect (capabilities), which is concerned with the opportunities available to people to achieve functionings, and the process aspect of freedom, which is concerned with the agency and the processes of choice involved (Sen 1985). The process aspect of freedom, or a person's agency achievement, refers to the goals or personal projects an individual has reason to value, even if these are not directly connected to his or her own personal interest, whilst agency freedom refers to those goals or personal projects that "are constitutive of one's wellbeing" (Sen 1992: 57).

Education is typically seen as a basic capability, but it also takes on a greater significance. It is a "fertile functioning" (Wolff and De Shalit 2007) that permits and promotes the development of other capabilities and functionings, such as the capability to work and the capability to learn. As we argue elsewhere, it also builds a "capacity to aspire" that is essential if capabilities are to be realised:

> The capacity to aspire provides an ethical horizon within which more concrete capabilities can be given meaning, substance and sustainability. Conversely, the exercise and nurture of these capabilities verifies and authorises the capacity to aspire and moves it away from wishful thinking to thoughtful wishing. Freedom, the anchoring good in Sen's approach to capabilities and development, has no lasting meaning apart from a collective, dense, and supple horizon of hopes and wants. Absent such a horizon, freedom descends to choice, rational or otherwise, informed or not.
>
> (Appadurai 2004: 82)

This is particularly important for, as Appadurai argues, poverty tends to result in "more brittle horizon of aspirations" (Appadurai 2004: 69) for individuals and communities so that they cannot imagine, let alone achieve, what might be possible in other circumstances.

The purpose of VET

All of this is useful in starting to sketch out an account of VET for human development. The first step it legitimates is a questioning of the purpose of VET that goes beyond the instrumental accounts of the orthodoxy. Drèze and Sen (2002) see the importance of education and training as threefold. First, there is instrumental importance in developing basic literacy and numeracy and providing the knowledge and skills necessary to access economic opportunities. Second, education has intrinsic value as an achievement in its own right for human fulfilment. Third, it plays a distributive role in enabling individuals to engage with and transform their lives, their communities and their world (Drèze and Sen 2002).

Initial research on VET and human development suggest that many learners do not have an instrumental and productivist worldview (López-Fogués 2012; Powell 2012, 2014). Rather, their accounts of their needs and expectations from VET privilege a broader human development perspective. These authors see VET as playing a key role in empowering learners to imagine a better future: a building of their "capacity to aspire" in Appadurai's terms (Powell 2012). Thus, the process of learning to become a fuller person is core to this approach (Nussbaum 2000). In this it shows continuity with the Deweyian liberal tradition (Leßmann 2009) of VET philosophy as well as UNESCO's broader approach to education as represented in the Faure and Delors Reports. Like those reports, it sees this process of learning to be inherently lifelong and lifewide.

A human development perspective on VET rejects the implicit underpinning assumptions of the VET-for-economic-development orthodoxy that work is a disutility, suffered only for the income it generates. While sharing the position of the orthodoxy that VET fundamentally is about work, it is radically subversive of the meaning that the orthodoxy attaches to this assertion. Rather, in the capability approach, work is not only about being productive and earning an income but also about the value that it adds to the quality of human life through the identity and self-respect that being engaged in something worthwhile bring to the individual (Sen 1975). The capability to work is part of being human and a means to becoming a more flourishing person and community member (Bonvin and Farvaque 2006), with the emphasis being on 'quality work' that expands freedoms and well-being (Sehnbruch 2008).

The human development approach is sensitive to the argument from feminist economists, and others, that work needs to be seen more broadly. It agrees with Power (2004: 3) on the need for the "incorporation of caring and unpaid labour as fundamental economic activities; [and the] use of wellbeing as a measure of economic success". Work can and should be seen in terms of its contribution to human development. It is not a 'necessary evil' but a potentially great good. Work is social, reproductive and intergenerational in its nature and effects. It makes us more fully human. In this view, VET should be concerned about developing the person more than the worker.

In this view, skills are understood in its broadest sense as allowing humans to be, rather than in the narrow human capital sense where the focus is on training people to do. They are defined in relation to the context (including the workplace, the family and the community) and targeted not just towards economic development but also social, cultural and political development (Tikly 2013).

The human development approach to VET has the potential to open up the black box of the human capital approach, which is largely silent about processes of vocational teaching and learning (Tikly 2013). Instead, it insists that what goes on in education matters hugely and often more so than the immediate and narrow instrumental outcomes and outputs that are supposedly the focus (Wheelahan and Moodie 2011). How teaching, learning and becoming interact is complex and contingent but is fertile of possibility and always greater than what is planned.

At the policy level, the approach stresses that the policy discussion needs to start from a careful discussion of purpose, rather than taking this for granted. This requires reconnecting VET policy debates to overall national policy debates, many of which now reflect broader notions of human flourishing and well-being, and to national social imaginaries.

Public participation – the capability for voice

This leads to an insistence that the answer to how the three broad goals mapped out by Drèze and Sen are weighted in educational provision cannot be generated from consultations with experts or business representatives but must take heed of the voices of all relevant stakeholders. It argues that the purpose of VET, like development, is not only about "what is decided" but, at least equally importantly, about "how it is decided" and "who decides" (Apsan-Frediani, Boni and Gasper 2014: 3).

It insists that a more radical approach of listening to stakeholders is required than is the current emergent practice of greater employer involvement in policy discussions. This cannot simply be through some simplistic process of consensus building but must take account of a series of critiques of how consensus is formed. These would include Young's critique of the common good, Appadurai's worries about poverty's negative effects on aspirations, Sen's concerns regarding adaptive preferences, and the new political economy of skills' insistence on the historically constructed and contingent nature of national skills paradigms. Indeed, the VET-for-human-development approach stresses the importance of locally grounded readings of the processes, structures and discourses of inequality and injustice. It follows writers such as Crocker (2008) and Mehrotra (2008) in calling for a deep democracy regarding development priorities. Wheelehan and Moodie (2011) apply this to VET in the workplace by linking skills, agency and workplace democracy in ways that parallel the long Marxist tradition in this area (cf. Elster 1986).

Agentic engagement

The capability approach also speaks to policy through its insistence on agency. Alkire (2002) holds that approaching development from a capability perspective demands that recipients are understood as agents of change rather than as beneficiaries. For Sen, the voices of the poor matter greatly – first, because prioritisations need to be subject to public dialogue at all appropriate levels and, second, because enhancing empowerment and self-determination is seen as central to the developmental project. A social justice perspective clearly shapes the emerging VET and human development perspective, as we shall explore below.

Whilst acknowledging the importance of agency, those writing about a human development approach to VET are very conscious of the dangers of overstressing agency and of downplaying the importance of power and structure. Indeed, whilst Sen has been criticised for a weakness in this regard, this appears to be more a product of his methodological toolkit rather than his ethical stance, which is profoundly committed to social justice. Nonetheless, the early writings on VET for human development have sought to augment the capability approach with a set of theoretical approaches that are stronger on issues of power, inequality and structure.

Powell (2014) uses the work of Archer (2003) to engage with the interplay of agency and structure at the micro level. This allows analysis of the structural constraints and possibilities that affect the lives of learners while at the same time acknowledging students' agentic moves and responses. Others have begun an attempt to move the debate to the macro level. López-Fogués draws on Young's work on oppression as the necessary counterbalance to Sen's account of freedom. For Young, oppression is to be understood as "the advantages and disadvantages experienced by some people, not because of a tyrannical power of coercion, but by the practices of a well-intentioned liberal society" (Young 1990: 74). In capabilities language, these are experiential constraints that limit the agency freedom of the individual to conceive of and pursue desired functionings and achieve capabilities. López-Fogués takes Young's "five faces of oppression": exploitation, marginalisation, powerlessness, cultural imperialism and violence, and shows how these can be applied to the context of VET in Spain. McGrath's work is rooted in the new political economy of skills, with its post-Marxist concerns with the way in which national skills systems evolve as part of wider systems of accumulation (cf. Crouch, Finegold and Sako 1999;

Brown, Green and Lauder 2001; McGrath et al. 2004). This approach emphasises the point that VET must be understood as a complex process that has local, national and international dimensions and that is profoundly influenced by cultural, economic, political, social and technological factors.

All of these attempts to build beyond the core of the capability approach to a macro account of VET and human development highlight the challenges that structural factors pose for what appears to be a highly agential approach (cf. Deneulin, Nebel and Sagovsky 2006 for a response within the capability tradition). They also raise important questions about the notion of consensus building. Young directly attacks the notion of a 'common good', seeing it as inevitably shaped by power and always in need of contestation, whilst the new political economy of skills tells a story of national systems of VET that have emerged through long historical processes of conflict and compromise. Neither approach sees a process of aggregating individual capabilities as simple (cf. Alkire 2002).

Challenging homogenising stereotyping

The capability approach refuses the current policy thrust towards narrow initial VET for youth and of labelling young people as NEETs (not in employment, education and training). The tendency to homogenise VET students within a deficit framework defined by what they are held to lack from the perspective of more powerful others is challenged by the capability approach's focus on inequality and injustice. Here, and through the distinction between capabilities and functionings, the capability approach highlights differences in students' abilities to convert skills into employment (Robeyns 2005; Walker and Unterhalter 2010), seeing this as located crucially in wider economic and societal contexts (De Jaeghere and Baxter 2014). Through its emphasis on the adaptive preferences of persons (Sen 1985), it helps to understand the identities of students and how these shape and define the actions that they take. Here the VET-for-human-development account is strongly influenced by comparative education insistences that context matters (Crossley and Jarvis 2001) and by comparativist concerns with travelling policies as noted above.

Equally, insofar as the critique of VET as 'second chance' and/or 'second choice' is correct (and Powell [2014] strongly argues against this), there is a moral obligation to focus very clearly on why this is so. This must not simply be about blaming the learner or taking inequality as a given, as is implicit in the orthodox approach. Rather, it necessitates dealing seriously with multidimensional poverty and capability deprivation and what can be done to maximise the range of capabilities and the probability of achieved valued functionings. A narrow, economistic view of development is far too limited to generate an adequate understanding of the role VET institutions can play in poverty alleviation, unemployment reduction and well-being enhancement.

Institutional transformation

Whilst much of the focus on capability in education has been at the level of either the individual or on overall philosophy, a clear ambition of a capability perspective is the transformation of educational policies and institutions leading to a focus on the institutional level (e.g., Alkire 2008; Walker 2008). Walker and McLean (2013), for example, in their work on pro-poor professionalism in South Africa, develop the notion of a capable institution. Powell and McGrath (2014) stress the potential value of using a capability lens to recast the process of evaluating VET institutions.

The human development approach to VET is less concerned with institutional form than with the complex needs of individuals over their lives, both horizontally and vertically. Nonetheless, institutions remain important, and the work of Powell (2012, 2014) has strong implications for public providers. As with the policy level, a reimagining of institutional purpose is called for in the VET-for-human-development paradigm. Powell suggests that VET institutions are not simply about equipping learners for immediate employability. Rather, learners also look to them to support the achievement of "satisfying work in workplaces where they will be respected and where they can make a contribution" (Powell 2014: 289). Moreover, VET institutions can also help reinforce individuals' capacity for lifelong learning, enable them to contribute more effectively to their families and communities, and support the further development of the "creative and social aspects of their lives" (Powell 2014: 289).

Evaluation

Evaluation research is central to the current VET toolkit. Drawing on the South African example, Powell (2013) argues that evaluation is crucial to the project of making VET institutions more effective and accountable. However, conventional evaluations of VET are limited to measures of participation; institutional efficiency and effectiveness; graduate employment; and employer and student satisfaction, which remain locked in the assumptions of the VET toolkit, the human capital approach and their wider theoretical underpinnings. As such, they are incapable of answering what Bonvin and Farvaque stress is the central social policy question to be asked of institutions: "Do they really improve [people's] prospects in terms of capabilities?" (Bonvin and Farvaque 2006: 3). The VET-for-human-development position is that the purpose of VET is to improve the lives of students, so this must form the central purpose of the institution and the core of what should be evaluated. If people are the ends rather than the means of development, then the goal of evaluation is to assess whether an intervention (such as a VET programme or institution) has served to expand or contract human freedoms. Institutional effectiveness (like economic development) is recast as a means to human flourishing and demoted from the central focus of evaluation (Powell and McGrath 2014).

By distinguishing between capabilities and functionings, the focus of evaluation is shifted from an emphasis on resources and income to a focus on opportunities and freedoms:

> Rather than aiming to equalise the income of an elderly farmer and a young student, for example, policy makers should aim to equalise the capability that each has to enjoy valuable activities and states of being.
>
> (Alkire 2008: 4)

Thus, a capabilities perspective shifts the questions of VET institutional evaluation towards the following:

- Do these institutions serve to expand or to constrict the capabilities, the functionings and the agency freedom of VET learners?
- Which dimensions of institutional functioning enable individuals to expand the capabilities that they have reason to value and which serve to limit and constrict the expansion of capabilities and functionings?
- Which capabilities and functionings matter to students and are these being met by institutional arrangements, institutional cultures and by the pedagogic approach of VET?

In all of this, the institution is conceived of as both an organisation with its own agency and purpose and a site of complex interaction, cooperation and contestation over purposes, processes and outcomes. Evaluation has to be owned and self-managed, not imposed as part of a regime of surveillance and performativity.

Final thoughts

The development of a coherent theoretical and methodological approach on VET and human development is still underway. As with the neoclassic orthodoxy (Chang 2014), there is little within the capability approach to draw upon regarding the centrality of work to human life and social organisation and how this may be changing under the impact of globalisation (Bartelheimer, Leßmann and Matiaske 2012; Leßmann 2012). Bonvin and colleagues have developed the notion of a capability to work and have explored the relationship between employability and capabilities but have only recently begun to link this to VET (Dif-Pradalier, Rosenstein and Bonvin 2012). From a different angle, McGrath has begun to explore this challenge from a VET perspective through a drawing on Marxist, Catholic and feminist approaches to work as human development (McGrath 2012). However, more effort is required to develop a strong human development account linking VET and work.

Many of those who have started writing in this area, like ourselves, come with a history of engaging with earlier VET literatures. For our own part, we have been particularly influenced by the more structuralist tradition of the new political economy of skills. Much of that approach still seems salient, and we draw upon it still. However, we believe that drawing also on the capability approach helps balance this in terms of both agency and voice, particularly at the level of learners and teachers. We have also shared common ground with the liberal-vocational tradition with its questioning of the narrowness of the employability agenda (e.g., Winch 2000, 2002; Lewis 2009) and an insistence on a moral purpose and value for VET. However, we believe that the approach taken in this chapter brings benefits in its focus on the points of transformation in the lives of individuals and the works of institutions at which human flourishing may be promoted and, hence, in its evaluative as well as normative impulse.

However, the VET-for-human-development approach is still very new, and what little empirical work that has emerged has been very small scale. It is also apparent that there is still more work to be done on developing a multilevel account of VET and human development. Various theoretical resources have been deployed to build a more sociopolitically credible account of skills, work and development than exists in the core texts of the capability approach. Nonetheless, as yet, there is not an integrated account but rather the bolting together of different elements.

A major methodological challenge, which is also of considerable practical and policy importance, is that of proceeding from individual identifications of capabilities and functionings to some form of aggregation that could prove useful as the basis for talking about learners' collective capabilities/functionings or those of communities or nations. This is particularly important as capability writers frequently invoke collectives in their arguments for social justice (Deneulin and McGregor 2010; Griewald and Rauschmayer 2013).

What work has been done has focused on the impact that structure has on the capability of individuals. Ibrahim (2011), for example, applies the notion of "collective capabilities" to refer to the bundle of functionings that an individual obtains by virtue of participation in a particular community or collective. Smith and Seward (2009) argue that individual capabilities emerge from and must be analysed as being a combination of individual and structural factors. Despite these contributions, there is very little work in the capability approach that moves beyond a discussion of the structural impacts on individual well-being. Deneulin and McGregor suggest that one way of doing this would be to expand the capability approach from a focus on "living well" to a focus on "living well together" (2010: 503). Insisting on the collective element of the capability approach is vital, without losing sight of its core focus on improving individuals' lives.

This chapter sketches out the possibilities of using a capability approach to address VET evaluation, and we have developed this further in Powell and McGrath (2014) as the starting point of an ongoing research project. However, one of the tests of this new approach will be its ability to engage with and support the transformation of institutional practices. Otherwise, it will be simply another academic account. This would run counter to the whole capability project.

Finally, at the level of institutional and national policies, it is important to note that part of the seductive attractiveness of the present toolkit, like all toolkits, is that it offers quick and easy solutions to complex challenges. Whilst the possibility of generating universal capabilities and functionings and resultant best practices should be shunned (Alkire 2002; Robeyns 2005), there is nonetheless the need to develop some tools and options than can make the lives of those seeking to shift towards a human development approach to VET easier (cf. Alkire 2008).

We believe that such an endeavour is worth embarking upon both because of the theoretical and practical failings of the current orthodoxy and because of the rich potential for a new approach to VET. Such an approach would be better aligned to the growing realisation that human development is more important than economic development. It would be grounded in an ethical stance stressing agency, student voice and deep democracy, as well as a commitment to social justice. It would acknowledge that work is a source of individual and collective value and that its breadth transcends traditional masculinist and modernist notions of a job. It would build from an acceptance that vocational education and training is not simply about the immediate employability of youth but is about empowering the growth of young and old alike not just as workers but as whole human beings, family members, community actors and citizens. Adapting Deneulin and McGregor: it is about working and living well together.

References

Alkire, S., 2002. *Valuing Freedoms*. Oxford University Press, New York.

Alkire, S., 2008. Using the capability approach: prospective and evaluative analyses. In: Comim, F., Qizilbash, M. and Alkire, S. (Eds.) *The Capability Approach: Concepts, Measures and Applications*. Cambridge University Press, Cambridge.

Allais, S., 2012. Will skills save us? Rethinking the relationships between vocational education, skills development policies, and social policy in South Africa. *International Journal of Educational Development* 32, 5, 632–642.

Anderson, D., 2009. Productivism and ecologism: changing dis/courses in TVET. In: Fien, J., Maclean, R. and Park, M.-G. (Eds.) *Work, Learning and Sustainable Development*. Springer, Dordrecht.

Appadurai, A., 2004. The capacity to aspire. In: Rao, V. and Walton, M. (Eds.) *Culture and Public Action*. Stanford University Press, Stanford.

Apsan-Frediani, A., Boni, A., Gasper, D., 2014. Approaching development projects from a human development and capability perspective. *Journal of Human Development and Capabilities* 15, 1, 1–12.

Archer, M., 2003. *Structure, Agency and the Internal Conversation*. Cambridge University Press, Cambridge.

Ball, S., 2003. The teacher's soul and the terrors of performativity. *Journal of Education Policy* 18, 2, 215–228.

Ball, S., 2009. Privatising education, privatising education policy, privatising educational research. *Journal of Education Policy* 24, 1, 83–99.

Bartelheimer, P., Leßmann, O., Matiaske, W., 2012. The capability approach: a new perspective for labor market and welfare policies? *Management Revue* 23, 2, 91–97.

Bonvin, J.-M., Farvaque, N., 2003. Employability and capability. In: *Proceedings of the Third Conference on the Capability Approach*. University of Pavia.

Bonvin, J.-M., Farvaque, N., 2006. Promoting capability for work. In: Deneulin, S., Nebel, M. and Sagovsky, N. (Eds.) *Transforming Unjust Structures: The Capability Approach*. Springer, Dordrecht.

Brown, P., Green, A., Lauder, H., 2001. *High Skills*. Oxford University Press, Oxford.

Chang, H.-J., 2014. *Economics: The User's Guide*. Pelican, London.

Crocker, D., 2008. *Ethics of Global Development*. Cambridge University Press, Cambridge.

Crossley, M., Jarvis, P., 2001. Context matters. *Comparative Education* 37, 4, 405–408.

Crouch, C., Finegold, D., Sako, M., 1999. *Are Skills the Answer?* Oxford University Press, Oxford.

De Jaeghere, J., Baxter, A., 2014. Entrepreneurship education for youth in sub-Saharan Africa. *Progress in Development Studies* 14, 1, 61–76.

Deneulin, S., McGregor, J., 2010. The capability approach and the politics of a social conception of wellbeing. *European Journal of Social Theory* 13, 4, 501–519.

Deneulin, S., Nebel, M., Sagovsky, N., 2006. Transforming unjust structures: the capability approach. In: Deneulin, S., Nebel, M. and Sagovsky, N. (Eds.) *Transforming Unjust Structures: The Capability Approach*. Springer, Dordrecht.

Dif-Pradalier, M., Rosenstein, E., Bonvin, J.-M., 2012. Vocational training as an integration opportunity for struggling young adults? A Swiss case study. *Social Work & Society* 10, 1.

Donath, S., 2000. The other economy: a suggestion for a distinctively feminist economics. *Feminist Economics* 6, 1, 115–123.

Drèze, J., Sen. A., 2002. *India: Development and Participation*. Oxford University Press, Oxford.

Elster, J., 1986. Self-realisation in work and politics: the Marxist conception of the good life. *Social Philosophy and Policy* 3, 91–126.

Gamble, J., 2013. Why improved formal teaching and learning are important in technical and vocational education and training (TVET). In: *Revisiting Global Trends in TVET*. UNESCO-UNEVOC, Bonn.

Griewald, Y., Rauschmayer, F., 2013. *Exploring a Nature-Related Conflict from a Capability Perspective*. Helmholtz-Zentrum für Umweltforschung, Leipzig.

Ibrahim, S., 2011. From individual to collective capabilities. *Journal of Human Development* 7, 3, 397–416.

Leo XIII, 1891. Rerum Novarum. http://www.vatican.va/holy_father/leo_xiii/encyclicals/documents/hf_lxiii_enc_15051891_rerum-novarum_sen.html

Leßmann, O., 2009. Capability and learning to choose. *Studies in Philosophy and Education* 28, 5, 449–460.

Leßmann, O., 2012. Applying the capability approach empirically: an overview with special attention to labor. *Management Revue* 23, 2, 98–118.

Lewis, T., 2009. Towards reclaiming the high ground in the discourse on vocationalism in developing countries. *International Journal of Educational Development* 29, 6, 558–564.

López-Fogués, A., 2012. Theorising further education through a capability lens: vulnerability and freedoms. Jubilee Working Papers, School of Education, University of Nottingham.

Marx, K., [1844] 2007. *Economic and Philosophic Manuscripts of 1844*. Dover, Mineola.

McGrath, S., 2010. Beyond aid effectiveness: the development of the South African further education and training college sector, 1994–2009. *International Journal of Educational Development* 30, 5, 525–534.

McGrath, S., 2012. Vocational education and training for development. *International Journal of Educational Development* 32, 5, 623–631.

McGrath, S., Badroodien, A., Kraak, A., Unwin, L. (Eds.), 2004. *Shifting Understandings of Skills in South Africa*. HSRC Press, Cape Town.

Mehrotra, S., 2008. Democracy, decentralisation and access to basic services. In: Comim, F., Qizilbash, M. and Alkire, S. (Eds.) *The Capability Approach: Concepts, Measures and Applications*. Cambridge University Press, Cambridge.

Nussbaum, M., 2000. *Women and Human Development*. Cambridge University Press, Cambridge.

Powell, L., 2012. Reimagining the purpose of VET: expanding the capability to aspire in South African further education and training students. *International Journal of Educational Development* 32, 5, 643–653.

Powell, L., 2013. A critical assessment of research on South African further education and training colleges. *Southern African Review of Education* 19, 1, 59–81.

Powell, L., 2014. Reimagining the Purpose of Vocational Education and Training: The Perspectives of Further Education and Training College Students in South Africa. Unpublished PhD thesis, University of Nottingham.

Powell, L., McGrath, S., 2014. Exploring the value of the capability approach for vocational education and training evaluation: reflections from South Africa. *International Development Policy* 5, 126–148.

Power, M., 2004. Social provisioning as a starting point for feminist economics. *Feminist Economics* 10, 3, 3–19.

Robeyns, I., 2005. The capability approach: a theoretical survey. *Journal of Human Development* 6, 1, 93–117.

Sehnbruch, K., 2008. From the quantity to the quality of employment. In: Comim, F., Qizilbash, M. and Alkire, S. (Eds.) *The Capability Approach: Concepts, Measures and Applications*. Cambridge University Press, Cambridge.

Sen, A., 1975. *Employment, Technology and Development*. International Labour Organisation, Geneva.

Sen, A., 1985. Wellbeing, agency and freedom. The Dewey Lectures 1984. *Journal of Philosophy* 82, 4, 169–221.

Sen, A., 1992. *Inequality Reexamined*. Oxford University Press, Oxford.

Sen, A., 1993. Capability and well-being. In: Nussbaum, M. and Sen, A. (Eds.) *The Quality of Life*. Clarendon Press, Oxford.

Sen, A., 1999. *Development as Freedom*. Oxford University Press, Oxford.

Sen, A., 2005. Human Rights and Capabilities. *Journal of Human Development* 6, 2, 151–166.

Smith, M., Seward, C., 2009. The relational ontology of Amartya Sen's capability approach. *Journal of Human Development and Capabilities* 10, 2, 213–235.

Tikly, L., 2013. Reconceptualising TVET and development: a human capability and social justice approach. In: *Revisiting Global Trends in TVET*. UNESCO-UNEVOC, Bonn.

UNDP, 2010. *Human Development Report 2010*. Oxford University Press, New York.

Walker, M., 2008. A human capabilities framework for evaluating student learning. *Teaching in Higher Education* 13, 4, 477–487.

Walker, M., McLean, M., 2013. *Professional Education, Capabilities and Contributions to the Public Good*. Routledge, London.

Walker, M., Unterhalter, E., 2010. *Amartya Sen's Capability Approach and Social Justice in Education*. Palgrave Macmillan, United Kingdom.

Wheelahan, L., Moodie, G., 2011. *Rethinking Skills in Vocational Education and Training: From Competencies to Capabilities*. New South Wales Board of Vocational Education and Training, Darlinghurst.

Winch, C., 2000. *Education, Work and Social Capital*. Routledge, London.

Winch, C., 2002. Work, well-being and vocational education. *Journal of Applied Philosophy* 19, 3, 261–271.

Wolff, J., De Shalit, A., 2007. *Disadvantage*. Oxford University Press, Oxford.

Young, I., 1990. *Justice and the Politics of Difference*. Princeton University Press, Princeton.

21

THE IMPACT OF HIGHER EDUCATION ON DEVELOPMENT

Tristan McCowan and Rebecca Schendel

Describing the university as an 'ivory tower' has become something of a cliché. The idea that the university is, or is in danger of becoming, isolated from the world, endlessly gazing at its own intellectual navel and disregarding the wishes and needs of the broader society, provides a constant backdrop to contemporary policy discussions of higher education. Historically, it is for the most part true that the 'membrane' of the university was fairly impermeable in both directions: the knowledge generated and transmitted within the university drew little on the outside world and concerned itself little with applying itself to the outside world's problems.

In the contemporary world, this kind of impermeability is no longer possible. The expansion of higher education systems across all regions has brought new socioeconomic groups into the university, with a greater diversity of cultures, levels of academic grounding and expectations. The now preeminent role of the university degree as a sorting mechanism for employment has placed increasing pressure on universities to form professionals and workers for the job market. The costs of university expansion have also led to intensified pressures from governments for a justification of state funding, a justification that is usually framed in terms of direct and measurable social and economic impact. In some cases, there have also been social justice-oriented moves by universities to engage more fully with marginalised communities outside their gates.

These processes have been supplemented by broader attention to 'impact' in policy and society. Policy choices according to this logic must be made on the basis of evidence, rather than 'ideology', and therefore any interventions in the social realm should have their impact gauged in a similar way to, say, medical interventions. Despite concerns about the inevitably ideological nature of evidence, and about the extent to which social phenomena lend themselves to this kind of evaluation, this approach has had a significant influence over all forms of policy, including that relating to international development. Investments by bilateral aid agencies must be justified to taxpayers on the basis of their impact and those by NGOs to their donors. This trend has been accompanied by a parallel movement within education away from assessing quality in terms of inputs (school buildings, teacher qualifications, etc.) to outputs (principally learning achievement gauged through standardised tests). The confluence of these trends has led to the new emphasis on measuring and understanding the influence of higher education on development.

Concerns about the impact of higher education are common to all countries. In part, this attention stems from the squeeze on public budgets and the need to justify the allocation of taxpayers' money. The concerns also derive from the tremendously high expectations placed on the university to solve some of the most complex and pressing challenges of our age, including global warming, an expanding global population and emerging epidemics. In the impoverished countries of the Global South, this pressure to demonstrate impact is understandably greater. In such contexts, public funds are even more stretched, the challenges of the broader society more acute, and concentration of privilege in the hands of the few often more extreme.

This chapter provides an overview of existing knowledge about the impact of higher education on development in lower income contexts by drawing on the results of a large-scale literature review recently completed for the UK Department for International Development (Oketch, McCowan and Schendel 2014). As in that study, this chapter will adhere to a broad conception of tertiary education, including universities but also nonuniversity institutions such as polytechnics, specialist faculties, teacher education colleges, medical schools and business schools. This definition does not include short-duration vocational education and training nor broader forms of adult education. The term 'impact' is here employed in an expansive sense to include different forms of influence on society, in contrast to the more restricted use of the term in impact evaluations. The higher education research literature includes very few studies that attempt to investigate impact following the principles of impact evaluation, largely because of the difficulty of identifying an appropriate counterfactual. Furthermore, as will be explored below, the kinds of impact that higher education may have on society are multifaceted, and there are disagreements about what can be seen to constitute 'impact' in the first place. The term 'development' is also used in its broadest sense, encompassing economic growth and infrastructural improvement, as well as a range of personal, social, political and cultural ends.

The chapter highlights a range of empirical studies that show these effects in low- and lower-middle-income countries. However, it also exposes a critical lack of research and evidence in many of these areas. A number of the benefits of higher education may be known intuitively to those working or studying in universities, but the lack of systematic documentation limits the extent to which arguments can be made to shape policy and aid flows. There are important implications of this lack of evidence in the context of debates over the post-2015 development agenda. While there is increasing acknowledgement by development agencies of the crucial role of higher education, the strength of evidence amassed has not as yet been sufficient to overcome residual assumptions that higher education is either irrelevant to development or restricted to benefiting a privileged elite. The evidence that does exist, however, provides crucial support for the argument that universities can positively impact society in multiple ways, some of which are little recognised or insufficiently valued in the contemporary context.

Historical antecedents

Before engaging with the detail of the current body of evidence, it is useful to acknowledge the long history of university engagement with society, across a broad range of cultural contexts. While the conceptualisation of universities as being engines of economic growth is a relatively new phenomenon, largely supported by the rise of the so-called knowledge economy, the idea of higher education as a public good has a much more entrenched history, although the nature of university engagement with the public has shifted over time.

Early models of higher education in lower-income countries were highly elitist, as they were restricted to a small percentage of the population and focused on training future leaders of church and state. However, despite the inequitable nature of such models, the *function* provided by such institutions – that of training leaders – was considered to be a public good. In many lower-income contexts, this notion manifested itself in the provision of government-funded scholarships for those able to gain admission to higher education (Schendel and McCowan 2015).

These early models were heavily criticised in the late 1960s and early 1970s for being both reliant on former colonial powers and out of touch with local populations. Following independence, public universities in many newly independent states were modelled on universities in the *metropole* (Lulat 2005). However, as debates around limited economic development in low-income contexts spawned new ideas around dependency and underdevelopment (Rist 2008), this replication of Western models came under attack. As nationalist leaders increasingly advocated for 'self-reliance' and autonomy from Western control, higher education institutions were encouraged to adopt policies of 'indigenisation', in which expatriate faculty were replaced by local staff and new curricula were proposed, focusing on local languages and cultural traditions (Ajayi et al. 1996; Lee 2006). This era shifted understandings of higher education's contribution to society by expanding beyond the traditional notion of leadership development to incorporate higher education's role as preserver and defender of – and advocate for – local traditions and values.

Critiques of the elitist nature of higher education also encouraged new models of university engagement with society in so-called developing contexts. In 1918, the Cordoba reforms in Argentina advocated for an increased engagement between public universities and society, leading to a revitalisation of the public university across Latin America. Similar reforms took hold across Africa in the 1970s, following the Association of African Universities' call for universities to become more 'developmental' by focusing research efforts on pressing development needs and engaging more constructively with their surrounding communities (Yesufu and AAU 1973).

Since the 1980s, however, the idea of higher education as a public good has declined in prominence across the world. The twin influences of economic globalisation – which has increased pressure on nation-states to enhance their economic competitiveness – and the neoliberal policies of international organisations such as the World Bank – which have framed higher education as a private benefit, rather than a public good – have fundamentally changed the nature of university engagement with society. Increasingly, universities need to generate income from their engagement with society, and the corresponding contribution they make is largely through economic pathways, by producing employable graduates, developing research to support the productivity of industries and engaging more directly with the private sector. In this conceptualisation of university engagement, the economic benefits of higher education are privileged over the noneconomic (Lebeau 2008; Marginson 2011; Naidoo 2003; Slaughter and Leslie 1997; Unterhalter and Carpentier 2010).

Pathways to impact

Against this backdrop, the review aimed to expand our contemporary understanding of the ways in which higher education contributes to society by investigating evidence of both economic and noneconomic impacts. Such an examination of impact requires a consideration of three important questions: who or what is being impacted? What kind of impact is it? And by what means does that impact come about?

In terms of the first point, universities can have an impact on a range of different individuals, groups or institutions. The primary constituency is, of course, the students – those undertaking formal courses within a university, whether at an undergraduate or graduate level. However, there are also a number of other constituencies that the university may impact, including the government and other organisations that commission research and consultancy, and local communities surrounding institutions with which they may engage in different ways. More broadly, some of the functions of the university can be seen to influence everyone in society, albeit in an indirect way.

The potential impacts are equally diverse. The benefits discussed most commonly in the public discourse are of an economic nature – either directly through salary increases or indirectly through national economic growth. Yet there are a number of potential noneconomic benefits, including improvements in health and well-being, political participation and democratisation, environmental protection and so forth.

Finally, the means through which impact is achieved are multiple. These means are best understood through what are sometimes termed the three 'pillars' of the university: teaching, research and service. The third of these pillars refers to the range of services provided directly by universities to external communities. These can include conducting consultancy work for governments and businesses; providing short courses for adults; allowing local communities to use university facilities; running university-affiliated hospitals, schools and sports facilities; and so forth. These activities are alternatively known as 'community engagement', 'public service', 'extension' or 'third stream' activities.

All three of these pillars can bring impact on development in different ways, as can be seen in the framework developed by Oketch, McCowan and Schendel (2014) in Figure 21.1.

In the diagram, the three pillars can be seen in the column marked 'tertiary education'. The boxes to the left of the central column depict a range of input factors that affect the ways that institutions are organised, the composition of their student and staff bodies and their level of resources. In this framework, we have conceptualised the primary outcomes of tertiary education in terms of five categories: earnings, productivity and efficiency, technological transfer,

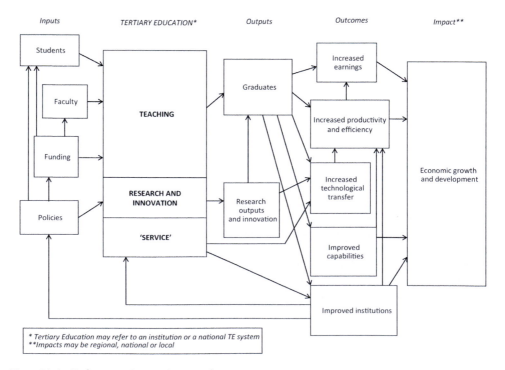

Figure 21.1 Pathways to impact framework

Source: Oketch, McCowan and Schendel 2014.

capabilities and institutions. For the teaching and research pathways, the outputs of tertiary education that lead to such outcomes are graduates and research outputs. Service activities are assumed to affect outcomes directly. These outcomes may be considered valuable in their own right, but they are also assumed to have an instrumental function in relation to a broader notion of 'development'.

These pathways draw on a number of theories from economic and political theory. Most prominent of these is human capital theory (e.g., Becker 1965; Schultz 1961), which asserts that investments in education (as well as associated areas such as health) will enhance the productivity of workers and thereby lead to an increase in individual earnings, with a consequent positive impact on economic growth. From the 1980s, endogenous growth theory (Lucas 1988; Romer 1986) began to supplement this conceptualisation of human capital by acknowledging the importance of spillover effects of knowledge between individuals and society. Much like human capital theory, endogenous growth theory assumes that the increased knowledge and skills generated through education can contribute to increased productivity of individuals (and, in the aggregate, the broader economy) through the uptake and development of technology and other innovation. However, from this perspective, the uptake of innovation is seen to have a multiplier effect, as it increases the productivity of everybody in society, not only those with education. McMahon (2009; McMahon and Oketch 2013) extended this idea to suggest the notion of 'endogenous development', which acknowledges that, in addition to the market benefits, there are positive *nonmarket* benefits that derive from education (e.g., democratisation, rule of law, health and well-being, smaller family size, etc.). These externalities increase individual productivity in the labour market, thereby enhancing the economy, but they also increase the productivity of nonlabour time, thereby contributing positively to individual life chances.

The dominance of economistic understandings of the benefits of education has been challenged by the concepts of capabilities and human development, emerging from the work of Amartya Sen (1992, 1999, 2009) and others (Boni and Walker 2013; Nussbaum 1997; Walker 2006; Unterhalter 2003). From this perspective, development is understood as the maximisation of freedoms for all in a society, in which individuals have the capability to do and be what they have reason to value. This vision allows for a much broader recognition of the benefits of higher education: one that will be adopted in the discussion of empirical research below.

Some of the benefits of higher education encapsulated in the framework are *private* – i.e., they are restricted to individuals or organisations engaging directly with the institution. The most obvious beneficiaries of private benefits are students, but others can also gain private benefit from higher education (e.g., companies commissioning research). These are the benefits that have received the greatest attention in recent years, in part at least because they are more readily observable and easier to measure (particularly salary increases). However, the framework also includes a range of significant *public* benefits. These include the indirect influence of the attributes acquired by graduates (e.g., the positive influence of a doctor or a teacher on their patients and pupils); the broader social benefits accrued by advances in research and scholarship not restricted by licensing; the important role played by universities as guardians and promoters of cultural heritage; and the space that higher education provides for critical reflection on government, policy, and society and revitalisation of political thought and action.

The framework above represents a map of the *potential* pathways through which higher education can impact on development. However, it is important to emphasise that the question of whether such impact actually occurs, and in which ways, is dependent on contextual factors. Movement along the pathways can be constrained by a number of barriers including: inadequate enrolment rates and/or quality of primary and secondary levels of education; a low quality teaching and learning environment within institutions; limitations on academic freedom; and a range of factors in the external environment, including the existence of employment opportunities. It is clear that a number of these barriers exist in resource-starved contexts. Lack of evidence of impact is, therefore, likely to be the result of such limiting factors, rather than an indication that higher education cannot have a positive impact on development in such contexts.

The evidence base

Despite the very large body of literature on higher education in lower-income contexts, there are relatively few studies that provide any empirical evidence of impact. Many publications provide descriptions of a system, analyses of policy, or normative assessments of the current state of affairs, without documenting their impact. In addition, there are a number of studies that assess intermediate outcomes of an intervention within an institution, without assessing the impact on the broader society. For example, Smith (2010) explores how a training programme, delivered at a distance by a UK-based institution, has improved the teaching capacity of lecturers at two vocational colleges in Zambia, without assessing how such changes may have impacted local innovation or productivity, while Dagenais, Binh and Currie (2010) outline how a collaboration between Vietnamese and Canadian universities enhanced the gender sensitivity of research outputs in agriculture, forestry and the social sciences, without investigating how such changes may have resulted in broader changes in environmental protection.

Although nearly 7,000 studies were initially identified through a detailed database search, Oketch, McCowan and Schendel (2014) found only 99 studies demonstrating impact in low- and lower-middle-income countries. The preponderance of the empirical evidence relates to the economic impact of tertiary education. This tendency is partly due to the focus on economic engagement, outlined earlier in the chapter, and the subsequent value placed on indicators such as earnings and economic growth. There are also methodological reasons: many of the non-economic benefits of higher education are difficult to gauge, particularly through quantitative analysis. However, pioneering work in this regard has been carried out by McMahon (1999, 2003, 2009), who has assessed the returns to education in relation to a range of market and nonmarket benefits (e.g., reduced infant mortality, democratisation, lower crime rates, environmental protection and increased levels of community volunteering). Beyond the intrinsic value of nonmarket benefits, McMahon shows that they feed back into economic growth, as much as doubling the direct economic impact, thereby highlighting the important interaction between economic and noneconomic benefits. Such quantitative advances combine with a long history of qualitative analysis of the ways in which higher education can impact individuals and societies.

This section provides an overview of the research evidence synthesised in the review. The evidence presented here has been organised into four broad categories relating to impact on economic growth, inequalities, institutions and individual capabilities – although acknowledging the significant interaction between the four. In the space available, it has not been possible to adequately contextualise the individual studies nor explore any specific countries in detail: a full understanding of the nature of, and conditions affecting, higher education impact would require this kind of in-depth engagement.

Driving economic growth

The most extensive body of evidence relating to the impact of higher education considers impact on individual earnings. As might be expected, studies from across the Global South show that graduates of higher education tend to earn higher incomes in comparison to people with lower levels of education. These findings are consistent for sub-Saharan Africa (e.g., Al-Samarrai and Bennell 2007; Gyimah-Brempong, Paddison and Mitiku 2006; Rolleston and Oketch 2008); South Asia (e.g., Abbas and Foreman-Peck 2008; Afzal 2011; Azam 2010); Southeast Asia (e.g., Doan and Stevens 2011; Glewwe, Gragnolati and Zaman 2002; Schady 2003) and the Pacific Islands (Born, McMaster and De Jong 2008).

As discussed above, human capital theory assumes that higher earnings correspond to greater worker productivity. Consequently, these findings can be understood as an indication that the knowledge, skills and other attributes acquired by graduates enhance their productivity, thereby helping to drive economic growth. Indeed, there is some evidence that this may be the case. Some of the studies identified through the review attempt to isolate productivity from wages in order to directly assess the impact of higher education on increased productivity. In reference to African contexts, Bloom, Canning and Chan (2006) suggest that higher education raises the rate of technological convergence in Africa, while Teal (2011) demonstrates that higher education raises productivity within the public sector. Abbas and Foreman-Peck (2008) have found similar evidence relating to the public sector in Pakistan.

However, it is debatable if higher earnings are always representative of increased productivity. This assumption is violated when employee salaries are determined by other means, such as patronage, or when graduates work for industries in which wages are regulated (e.g., the public sector). As both conditions are typical of many of the contexts considered in the review, the evidence around impact on increased earnings may not reflect a similar impact on economic growth. In fact, the evidence of economic impact at the macro level is less conclusive than the micro-level evidence. There are various studies that show the impact of the expansion of higher education systems on economic growth: for example, in Cameroon (Fonkeng and Ntembe 2009), Sri Lanka (Ganegodage and Rambaldi 2011), Pakistan (Stengos and Aurangzeb 2008) and the Philippines (Ramos et al. 2012). However, other studies have shown positive impact in some regions and not others (see McMahon 2009). This discrepancy can at least partly be explained by the limiting factors outlined earlier in the chapter. In two regional studies, one focused on Asia (di Gropello, Tandon, and Yusuf 2012) and one on Latin America (de Ferranti et al. 2003), correlations can be drawn between low levels of investment in research and low levels of economic growth, a finding that suggests that limited research activities within universities may be restricting the economic impact of tertiary education. Although there is evidence that universities can positively contribute to the productivity of local industries (e.g., Ca 2006; Collins 2012), a finding echoed in another recent review of the literature on higher education in the African context (Pillay 2011), it is harder to identify such impact at the national level. Studies in contexts as diverse as Vietnam, Guatemala and Ethiopia (Ca 2006; Loening 2005; Gondo and Dafuleya 2010) point to a similar reason for this lack of impact: limited interaction between institutions and local industries appears to prevent the possibility of technological transfer in many lower-income contexts.

Evidence is also mixed when it comes to comparing the relative impact of investments in primary, secondary and higher levels of education on economic development. This is a question of considerable interest to development agencies, given the ever present challenge of determining funding priorities between the different levels. As regards individual earnings, earlier studies (e.g., Psacharopoulos 1994; Psacharopoulos, Velez and Patrinos 1994; Psacharopoulos and Patrinos 2004) showed a concave relationship between investment and income in low-income contexts (i.e., returns were found to be greater for lower levels of education than higher levels). However, more recent studies (e.g., Teal 2011 and Schultz 2004) have shown the contrary (i.e., that the relationship is convex). This change over time is likely to be due to the expansion of access to primary and secondary education, which has created a surplus of jobseekers with lower levels of education. At the macro level, some studies (e.g., Keller 2006; McMahon 1999,

2003) show greater impact of primary and secondary levels on economic growth, while others (e.g., Gyimah-Brempong, Paddison and Mitiku 2006) show a greater effect of higher education.

One reason for the apparent discrepancy within the available body of evidence relates to the fact that macro-level relationships between higher education and economic outcomes are harder to demonstrate than micro-level relationships. One limitation is the lack of adequate macro-level enrolment and labour market data in many low income contexts. Another is the methodological difficulties caused by the time lag between higher education and any potentially attributable impact. In some cases, for example, it is hard to assert definitively that economic growth has been the result of the expansion of higher education, rather than the cause (Teal 2011).[1] However, methodological advances have been made in this domain, and research that has attempted to address the issue of time lag in its design has shown positive impact on economic growth.[2] Such advances in statistical modelling suggest that there may be more macro-level evidence in future years.

Influence on socioeconomic inequalities

The relationship between higher education and inequalities in the broader society is complex and varies markedly depending on the funding and access arrangements in place in specific contexts. Keller (2006) uses her findings as the basis for an argument against public investment in higher education in low-income countries, suggesting that such investment disproportionately benefits the wealthy and cannot be justified given the high levels of illiteracy. It is certainly the case that the direct benefits of higher education remain restricted to the few in many low-income countries. In such circumstances, higher education can play a role in exacerbating societal inequality, as it can help elites to entrench their existing privilege by enabling further economic opportunities and positions of political influence for themselves and their offspring. However, the history of investment in higher education in low-income contexts suggests that any consideration of further reductions in public subsidy to higher education must be met with caution. Years of limited investment in higher education has led to a crisis of quality at many higher education institutions; further reductions in funding would carry inevitable implications for the potential of higher education institutions to contribute to development. Mechanisms for ensuring equitable access to higher education help to address this problem (Meyer et al. 2013; McMahon and Oketch 2013), but, unfortunately, current trends are likely to have the opposite effect. The move towards 'cost sharing' in public institutions and the expansion of fee-charging private institutions can exacerbate, rather than address, this problem in many contexts.

The macro-level relationship between higher education and poverty reduction is not very well understood, as existing studies present contradictory evidence (Nsowah-Nuamah, Teal and Awoonor-Williams 2012; Tilak 2010). Indeed, the phenomenon of highly restricted access alluded to above might appear to militate against any significant impact on poverty reduction. Yet a focus purely on individual earnings accruing from tertiary-level diplomas misses many of the knock-on benefits to society that can positively influence both economic growth and poverty reduction. Poverty reduction can also be influenced by the training of professionals in key areas, through research and through community engagement. These public benefits of higher education will be explored further in the sections below.

Forming professionals and strengthening institutions

Strong institutions, whether in the sense of organisations such as the judiciary and parliament or in the broader sense of social norms, are central to both economic and human development.

In most societies, these institutions are the primary mechanism through which welfare and participation of the population are achieved. Economists (e.g., Acemoglu, Johnson and Robinson 2005; North 1990) have also asserted their centrality to economic growth.

The most obvious way in which universities strengthen institutions is through educating the professionals who work within them. The early European universities were closely linked with the formation of professionals in specific areas (the clergy, doctors, lawyers and so forth), and this function continues to this day, with a vastly expanded selection of courses, now including teaching, nursing and business. The quality of teacher education, needless to say, is central to the quality of primary and secondary education, and thereby all of the knock-on benefits of those levels are also pertinent. Lack of investment in universities makes it extremely difficult to provide basic welfare services for the population, including education and health, or to provide an efficient and accountable civil service and local administration.

A number of studies also demonstrate the positive impact of higher education on political institutions. The cross-national studies conducted by McMahon (1999, 2003) and Keller (2006) show the link between higher education and improvements in the rule of law and the existence of political rights. In relation to Africa, Gyimah-Brempong (2010) shows the impact on political stability, while links between higher education and the strengthening of legislative bodies are identified in Mattes and Mozaffar (2011). Higher education is also seen to be conducive to the formation of positive attitudes and social norms, for example on attitudes towards democracy in Pakistan (Shafiq 2010) and lower tolerance for corruption in Nepal (Truex 2011). Ehrhardt-Martinez (1998), in a study of 51 developing countries, also shows a link between higher education and slowing rates of deforestation through the influence of awareness raising and social activism, as well as technological development.

However, a less positive portrayal of the impact of higher education is provided by Urdal (2006), who shows that higher education expansion is associated with increasing risk of terrorism around the world. This finding can, nevertheless, be explained by the lack of jobs available for graduates in these contexts and the consequent frustrations that accompany such barriers in the enabling environment.

Enhancing capabilities

Improvements in institutions are not sufficient for development if a population remains incapable of or obstructed from taking up the opportunities enabled by them. A final category of impact concerns the extent to which individuals are empowered through higher education to exercise their capabilities in a number of areas.

The first way in which higher education can affect individual capabilities is, of course, through individual income. As discussed earlier, there is clear evidence that enrolment in higher education is likely to increase an individual's earnings. This effect may be because the knowledge and skills acquired in university have a positive impact on graduate productivity, but it may also be for other reasons, such as exposure to enhanced social networks that may aid access to valuable employment. Regardless of the reason for the link between higher education and earnings, the connection is clear in the literature, with inevitable implications for the expansion of individual capabilities throughout the life course.

Evidence of expansion of noneconomic capabilities also exists in a number of areas, including health and nutrition, political participation and women's empowerment. In relation to the political sphere, the democratic institutions outlined above are only effective if there exists an active and critical citizenry willing and able to exert their influence over them. Final-year students in Kenya, South Africa and Tanzania were found by Luescher-Mamashela et al. (2011) to have greater levels of political awareness and participation than those with lower levels of education.[3] There are also clear benefits of higher education for health, shown in a range of studies: higher education has been found to have a positive effect on psychological well-being in India (Agrawal et al. 2011) and Nigeria (Akinyemi 2012), lower fertility in Sudan (Ahmed 2010), and nutrition in East Timor (Raghbendra and Dang 2012) – each of these cases has been gauged through the association of university-level study with these positive outcomes in the lives of individual graduates. Cross-national studies have also observed a positive relationship between higher education and life expectancy (Tilak 2003, 2010; Gyimah-Brempong 2010).

Finally, a number of studies show an empowerment effect for women in contexts of significant gender inequality, with greater freedoms and voice in relation to social and marital relations observed in Eritrea (Müller 2004), Pakistan (Malik and Courtney 2011) and India (Singh, Thind and Jaswal 2006). However, studies in Ghana (DeRose, Dodoo and Patil 2002) and Kenya (Dalal 2008) show that such effects of higher education, while significant, are not enough to counteract deeply entrenched norms about control over reproductive decisions and responsibilities for childcare. More positively, Gyimah-Brempong (2010) found that, across the African region, the expansion of tertiary education systems is linked to higher proportions of female parliamentarians.

Conclusions and implications

The evidence outlined in this chapter supports many of the pathways to impact depicted in Figure 21.1. Higher education has a clear impact on both economic and noneconomic individual capabilities. The macro-level effects are harder to isolate, but there is persuasive, if limited, evidence of impact on the strengthening of formal institutions, informal social norms and attitudes, and overall economic growth.

Evidence of the impact of higher education on development is of clear interest to policymakers and development agencies, in terms of both justifying existing expenditure and orienting future investments, because such evidence can potentially influence decision making about whether or not to invest in higher education. It can also guide decisions about what form specific interventions and reforms should take (i.e., whether it is better to fund scholarship programmes, institutional partnerships, ICT infrastructure, etc.). However, the evidence on this latter question is very thin. Most of the studies that provide empirical assessment of impact analyse relationships between higher education enrolment and a particular outcome. Studies, therefore, tend to consider whether individuals have studied at the higher education level (or, in national studies, the proportion of the population that has done so). In terms of the logic of the framework in Figure 21.1, such studies gauge the movement from the 'output' boxes to the 'outcomes' boxes. These studies do not give us much of an indication of which factors within the tertiary education stage (or the input stage) might be influential: i.e., whether public or private institutions are more effective in developing research with economic and social impact, whether distance or face-to-face provision makes a difference to human capital enhancement, or how institutional governance affects community engagement.

Readers of research on this topic, therefore, need to piece together evidence relating to the impact of 'inputs' on the functioning of higher education (e.g., the ways in which pedagogical approaches in universities may be influenced by funding decisions) with evidence relating higher education outputs to development outcomes. This task is made more difficult by the significant gaps in the available literature. There is an overall lack of studies gauging impact on society, particularly in terms of noneconomic benefits, and there is very little that considers the impact of research and service. All of these areas warrant significantly more attention in the empirical literature.

At the same time, while acknowledging the importance of evidence, it is important to guard against fetishisation: the fact that there may currently be little or no evidence for a particular phenomenon does not mean we should dismiss it, and indeed there may be areas in which it will never be possible to obtain satisfactory evidence. Higher education can produce profound changes in people's understanding of the world, their relationships with others and their ability to pursue flourishing lives, and it may not always be possible to gauge these impacts fully.

Higher education is without doubt a key component of development. It is a public good, enabling opportunities for higher learning; allowing for the maintenance and development of intellectual and cultural traditions; and providing a space for scholarship, enquiry and innovation. It is also essential for economic prosperity; it enhances high-level knowledge and skills in its graduates and provides the basic and applied research that help to fuel innovation. It also yields a range of noneconomic benefits for graduates and others in society. Higher education's relevance to development has been largely underestimated, so the increased attention being paid to universities in the development discourse is a welcome development. However, this shift does not imply that funding for primary and secondary levels should be reduced. The interdependence of all levels of the education system is such that success can only be achieved by healthy and effective investment across the sector. Furthermore, the potential of universities can only be realised in conducive institutional and external environments, ones that allow academic freedom for research and scholarship, offer a broad and intellectually challenging curriculum, and ensure that access to university is not restricted to traditional or newly formed elites. With these supportive conditions, higher education can be truly transformative, responding to contemporary challenges and helping to forge prosperous, innovative and just societies.

Notes

1 Without doubt, there is influence both ways, given the considerable public and private expense of university study.
2 See Tilak's 2003 and 2010 studies focusing globally and on Asia.
3 Although in a further study by Mattes and Mughogho (2009), it was not possible to distinguish higher education from high school graduates in these respects.

References

Abbas, Q., Foreman-Peck, J., 2008. The Mincer human capital model in Pakistan: implications for education policy. *South Asia Economic Journal* 9, 2, 435–462.

Acemoglu, D., Johnson, S., Robinson A., 2005. Institutions as fundamental cause of long-run growth. In: Aghion, P. and Durlanf, S. (Eds.) *Handbook of Economic Growth*. North Holland, Amsterdam.

Afzal, M., 2011. Microeconometric analysis of private returns to education and determinants of earnings. *Pakistan Economic and Social Review* 49, 1, 39–68.

Agrawal, J., Murthy, P., Philip, M., Mehrotra, S., Thennarasu, K., John, J., Girish, N., Thippeswamy, V., Isaac, M., 2011. Socio-demographic correlates of subjective well-being in urban India. *Social Indicators Research* 101, 3, 419–434.

Ahmed, H., 2010. Non-market returns to women education in Sudan: case of fertility. *Journal of Comparative Family Studies* 41, 5, 783–798.

Ajayi, J., Goma, L., Johnson, G., 1996. *The African Experience with Higher Education*. Association of African Universities, Accra.

Akinyemi, A., 2012. Assessment of the influence of socio-economic status on aging males' symptoms in Ijesaland, south-western Nigeria. *Journal of Men's Health* 9, 1, 51–57.

Al-Samarrai, S., Bennell, P., 2007. Where has all the education gone in Sub-Saharan Africa? Employment and other outcomes among secondary school and university leavers. *Journal of Development Studies* 43, 7, 1270–1300.

Azam, M., 2010. India's increasing skill premium: role of demand and supply. *B E Journal of Economic Analysis and Policy* 10, 1, 1–28.

Becker, G., 1965. A theory of the allocation of time. *Economic Journal* 75, 299, 493–517.

Bloom, D., Canning, D., Chan, K., 2006. *Higher Education and Economic Development in Africa*. World Bank, Washington.

Boni, A., Walker, M., 2013. *Human Development and Capabilities: Re-imagining the University of the Twenty-First Century*. Routledge, London.

Born, J., McMaster, J., De Jong, A., 2008. Return on investment in graduate management education in the South Pacific. *International Journal of Management in Education* 2, 3, 340–355.

Ca, T., 2006. *Universities as drivers of the urban economies in Asia: The case of Vietnam*. World Bank Policy Research Working Paper 3949, Washington.

Collins, C.S., 2012. Land-grant extension as a global endeavor: connecting knowledge and international development. *The Review of Higher Education* 36, 1, 91–124.

Dagenais, H., Binh, D., Currie, D., 2010. Enhancing capacities to engender research for sustainable development in Vietnam, 1999–2009. *Gender Technology and Development* 14, 1, 89–101.

Dalal, K., 2008. *Causes and Consequences of Violence Against Child Labour and Women in Developing Countries*. Karolinska Institutet, Stockholm.

De Ferranti, D., Perry, G., Gill, I., Guasch, J., Maloney, W., Sanchez-Paramo, C., Schady, N., 2003. *Closing the Gap in Education and Technology*. World Bank, Washington.

DeRose, L., Dodoo, F., Patil, V., 2002. Fertility desires and perceptions of power in reproductive conflict in Ghana. *Gender and Society* 16, 1, 53–73.

Di Gropello, E., Tandon, P., Yusuf, S., 2012. *Putting Higher Education to Work*. World Bank, Washington.

Doan, T., Stevens, P., 2011. Labor market returns to higher education in Vietnam. *Economics – the Open Access Open-Assessment E-Journal* 5: 1–21.

Ehrhardt-Martinez, K., 1998. Social determinants of deforestation in developing countries: a cross-national study. *Social Forces* 77, 2, 567–586.

Fonkeng, G., Ntembe, A., 2009. Higher education and economic development in Africa: the case of Cameroon. *Educational Research and Review* 4, 5, 231–246.

Ganegodage, K., Rambaldi, A., 2011. The impact of education investment on Sri Lankan economic growth. *Economics of Education Review* 30, 6, 1491–1502.

Glewwe, P., Gragnolati, M., Zaman, H., 2002. Who gained from Vietnam's boom in the 1990s? *Economic Development and Cultural Change* 50, 4, 773–792.

Gondo, T., Dafuleya, G., 2010. Technical vocational education and training for micro-enterprise development in Ethiopia: a solution or part of the problem? *Industry and Higher Education* 24, 5, 381–392.

Gyimah-Brempong, K., 2010. Education and economic development in Africa. Paper presented at the 4th African Economic Conference, Tunis, October.

Gyimah-Brempong, K., Paddison, O., Mitiku, W., 2006. Higher education and economic growth in Africa. *Journal of Development Studies* 42, 3, 509–529.

Keller, K., 2006. Investment in primary, secondary, and higher education and the effects on economic growth. *Contemporary Economic Policy* 24, 1, 18–34.

Lebeau, Y., 2008, Universities and social transformation in sub-Saharan Africa: global rhetoric and local contradictions. *Compare* 38, 2, 139–153.

Lee, M., 2006. Higher education in Southeast Asia in the era of globalization. In: Forest, J. and Altbach, P. (Eds.) *International Handbook of Higher Education*. Springer, Dordrecht.

Loening, J., 2005. *Effects of Primary, Secondary and Tertiary Education on Economic Growth: Evidence from Guatemala*. World Bank, Washington.

Lucas, R., 1988. On the mechanics of economic development. *Journal of Monetary Economics* 22, 1, 3–42.

Luescher-Mamashela, T., Kiiru, S., Mattes, R., Mwollo-ntallima, A., Ng'ethe, N., Romo, M., 2011. *The University in Africa and Democratic Citizenship: Hothouse or Training Ground?* Centre for Higher Education Transformation, Cape Town.

Lulat, Y., 2005. *A History of African Higher Education from Antiquity to the Present*. Praeger, London.

Malik, S., Courtney, K., 2011. Higher education and women's empowerment in Pakistan. *Gender and Education* 23, 1, 29–45.

Marginson, S., 2011. Higher education and public good. *Higher Education Quarterly* 65, 4, 411–433.

Mattes, R., Mozaffar, S., 2011. *Education, Legislations and Legislators in Africa.* Centre for Higher Education Transformation, Cape Town.

Mattes, R., Mughogho, D., 2009. *The limited impacts of formal education on democratic citizenship in Africa.* Afrobarometer Working Paper No. 109.

McMahon, W., 1999. *Education and Development: Measuring the Social Benefits.* Oxford University Press, Oxford.

McMahon, W., 2003. Investment criteria and financing education for economic development. In: Tilak, J. (Ed.) *Education, Society and Development.* AHP Publishing, New Delhi.

McMahon, W., 2009. *Higher Learning, Greater Good.* Johns Hopkins University Press, Baltimore.

McMahon, W., Oketch, M., 2013. Education's effects on individual life chances and on development: an overview. *British Journal of Educational Studies* 61, 1, 79–107.

Meyer, H.-D., St. John, E., Chankseliani, M., Uribe, L., 2013. The crisis of higher education access: a crisis of justice. In: Meyer, H.-D., St. John, E., Chankseliani, M. and Uribe, L. (Eds.) *Fairness in Access to Higher Education in a Global Perspective.* Sense, Rotterdam.

Müller, T., 2004. "Now I am free": education and human resource development in Eritrea. *Compare* 34, 2, 215–229.

Naidoo, R., 2003. Repositioning higher education as a global commodity: opportunities and challenges for future sociology of education work. *British Journal of Sociology of Education* 24, 2, 249–259.

North, D., 1990. *Institutions, Institutional Change and Economic Performance.* Cambridge University Press, New York.

Nsowah-Nuamah, N., Teal, F., Awoonor-Williams, M., 2012. Jobs, skills and incomes in Ghana: how was poverty halved? *Comparative Education* 48, 2, 231–248.

Nussbaum, M., 1997. *Cultivating Humanity.* Harvard University Press, Cambridge, MA.

Oketch, M., McCowan, T., Schendel, R., 2014. *The Impact of Tertiary Education on Development: A Rigorous Literature Review.* Department for International Development, London.

Pillay, P., 2011. *Higher Education and Economic Development: Literature Review.* Centre for Higher Education Transformation, Cape Town.

Psacharopoulos, G., 1994. Returns to investment in education: a global update. *World Development* 22, 9, 1325–1343.

Psacharopoulos, G., Patrinos, H., 2004. Returns to investment in education: a further update. *Education Economics* 12, 2, 111–134.

Psacharopoulos, G., Velez, E., Patrinos, H., 1994. Education and earnings in Paraguay. *Economics of Education Review* 13, 4, 321–327.

Raghbendra, J., Dang, T., 2012. Education and the vulnerability to food inadequacy in Timor-Leste. *Oxford Development Studies* 4, 3, 341–357.

Ramos, C., Estudillo, J., Sawada, Y., Otsuka, K., 2012. Transformation of the rural economy in the Philippines, 1988–2006. *Journal of Development Studies* 48, 11, 1629–1648.

Rist, G., 2008. *The History of Development.* Third Edition. Zed, London.

Rolleston, C., Oketch, M., 2008. Educational expansion in Ghana: economic assumptions and expectations. *International Journal of Educational Development* 28, 3, 320–339.

Romer, P., 1986. Increasing returns and long-run growth. *Journal of Political Economy* 94, 5, 1002–1037.

Schady, N., 2003. Convexity and sheepskin effects in the human capital earnings function: recent evidence for Filipino men. *Oxford Bulletin of Economics and Statistics* 65, 2, 171–196.

Schendel, R., McCowan, T., 2015. Higher education and development: critical issues and debates. In: McCowan, T. and Unterhalter, E. (Eds.) *Education and International Development: An Introduction.* Bloomsbury, London.

Schultz, T.W., 1961. Investment in human capital. *American Economic Review* 51, 1, 1–17.

Schultz, T.P., 2004. Social value of research and technical skills: does it justify investment in higher education for development? *Journal of Higher Education in Africa* 2, 1, 92–134.

Sen, A., 1992. *Inequality Reexamined.* Clarendon Press, Oxford.

Sen, A., 1999. *Development as Freedom.* Knopf, New York.

Sen, A., 2009. *The Idea of Justice.* Allen Lane, London.

Shafiq, M., 2010. Do education and income affect support for democracy in Muslim countries? Evidence from the "Pew Global Attitudes Project". *Economics of Education Review* 29, 3, 461–469.

Singh, R., Thind, S., Jaswal, S., 2006. Assessment of marital adjustment among couples with respect to women's educational level and employment status. *Anthropologist* 8, 4, 259–266.

Slaughter, S., Leslie, L., 1997. *Academic Capitalism.* Johns Hopkins Press, Baltimore.

Smith, C., 2010. "Distance learning" or "learning at a distance"? Case study of an education initiative to deliver an in-service bachelors degree in Zambia. *Innovations in Education and Teaching International* 47, 2, 223–233.

Stengos, T., Aurangzeb, A., 2008. An empirical investigation of the relationship between education and growth in Pakistan. *International Economic Journal* 22, 3, 345–359.

Teal, F., 2011. Higher education and economic development in Africa: a review of channels and interactions. *Journal of African Economies* 20, AERC Supplement 3, iii50-iii79.

Tilak, J., 2003. Higher education and development in Asia. *Journal of Educational Planning and Administration* 17, 2, 151–173.

Tilak, J., 2010. Higher education, poverty and development. *Higher Education Review* 42, 2, 23–45.

Truex, R., 2011. Corruption, attitudes, and education: Survey evidence from Nepal. *World Development* 39, 7, 1133–1142.

Unterhalter E., 2003. The capabilities approach and gendered education. An examination of South African complexities. *Theory and Research in Education* 1, 1, 7–22.

Unterhalter, E., Carpentier, V. (Eds.), 2010. *Global Inequalities and Higher Education*. Palgrave Macmillan, Basingstoke.

Urdal, H., 2006. A clash of generations? Youth bulges and political violence. *International Studies Quarterly* 50, 3, 607–629.

Walker, M., 2006. *Higher Education Pedagogies: A Capabilities Approach*. Society for Research in Higher Education, Maidenhead.

Yesufu, T., 1973. *Creating the African University*. Association of African Universities, Ibadan.

22

ECONOMIC GLOBALISATION, SKILL FORMATION AND DEVELOPMENT

Hugh Lauder and Phillip Brown

Introduction

In this chapter, we review the dominant approach to education and economic development as represented by human capital theory. We find it to be wholly inadequate in guiding policy with respect to the relationship of education to economic development. We then turn to a recent, more sophisticated account of the relationship between education and economic development, 'capabilities, productive transformation and development' (Nübler 2014, 2015). While this account is a significant advance over human capital theory, it does not take into account the role of transnational companies and global value chains (GVCs). What is missing from these accounts is an understanding of global capitalism and its implications for theorising the relationship between education and economic development.

Human capital theory in the development literature

Human capital theory makes a series of inferences about the relationship between education, productivity and income. The insight of the early human capital theorists was that a significant element of economic growth that had, hitherto, been unexplained could be accounted for by education (Schultz 1961). With the rise of technology, it was assumed that more educated workers were needed to service the economy. These educated workers were considered more productive than those with only basic education because they could put their knowledge to good use in servicing and developing technology. It was further assumed that employers would, over time, always choose educated workers because they would raise productivity and hence profits.

Human capital theory was developed within neoclassical economics, which employed the idea that as more educated workers came into the labour market, so a new equilibrium would be established, whereby educated workers would receive higher returns for their productive potential. In essence, this account rests on the idea of a constant upward adjustment of equilibria as employers reap the benefits of greater productivity and reward their educated workers accordingly. It is precisely the promise of greater reward that is believed to drive individuals to invest in themselves through education, based on the neoclassical view that students act according to the tenets of *Homo economicus*.

In his presidential address, Schultz (1961) indicated the importance of human capital theory for economic development. Schultz's ideas sparked considerable policy interests and empirical research that provided the foundation for the World Bank's education for development policies from the 1980s to the present day.

The World Bank had shown little interest in education for the rise of human capital theory because it was not seen as important to economic development. Gradually, an interest emerged in relation to technical and vocational education and then in relation to primary education. In 1981, the Bank appointed George Psacharopoulos as Head of the Education Department's Research Unit, and his analysis of rate of returns to different levels of education in developing countries proved highly influential. What is also significant is that, by then, human capital theory was wrapped in the wider assumptions of the Washington Consensus. Williamson (1990) summarises the economic policies "that Washington urges on the rest of the world" as "prudent macroeconomic policies, outward orientation, and free-market capitalism". This included opening countries to 'free trade'; privatisation of state assets; user-pays policies, especially in tertiary education; and state deregulation. The reason this list of policies is so significant is because the Washington Consensus tried to get developing countries to mimic the conditions of the competitive markets of orthodox economics. It was not the first, nor the last attempt, as we shall see, to assume that the closer economies approximated to the strictures of neoclassical economics, the more efficient and productive they would be.

It would be true to say that these policies ended in failure, and there have been no shortage of critics that have pointed out the flaws in this strategy at the time and subsequently (Chang 2007). For countries forced to conform to the Washington consensus to qualify for World Bank loans, these policies were the equivalent of being visited by a natural disaster. So why did the World Bank pursue these policies? A short answer is that it suited political elites in the United States and in other developed countries to have developing economies open to trade. But there are further theoretical reasons that can be given.

The highly mechanistic assumptions about human behaviour, rationality and markets that the orthodox approach makes were seen as a way of identifying the universal laws of economics (Becker 1992). When initially conceived, it was thought that while this form of economics would articulate universal laws, deviations could be explained by other disciplines, such as sociology, psychology and anthropology, where their explanations of these deviations would be a first step in building an economy that was indeed approximated to the orthodox model (Clarke 1982). This is one way of interpreting the policies of the Washington consensus. There are, of course, intractable problems with this approach, as we know that there are many 'varieties of capitalism'; German capitalism is very different from American or Swedish capitalism (Hall and Soskice 2001). Each country has specific institutions that have their 'own history' and different ways of doing things, giving rise to vested interests and path dependencies. But human capital theory makes no reference to institutions, as it assumes a universe of rational egoists and market responses. The reason why institutions have been left out of the account is that they can only be understood as specific to particular countries – their culture and histories. An analysis of institutions would confound the orthodox aim of producing universal laws by making economic claims specific to particular contexts.

Fundamental problems with the human capital theory approach can be illustrated by drawing on the work of Hanushek and Wössmann (2007), two of the leading contemporary proponents of human capital theory, whose work is embraced by the World Bank. In their widely disseminated paper for the World Bank, Hanushek and Wössmann (2007) seek to establish that the 'quality' of education can make a significant difference to a nation's notional future GDP. In particular, they make the claim that the quality of education, as measured by international tests such as PISA and TIMSS, can have a significant influence on future GDP. They calculate that if the educational reforms they recommend were implemented, GDP would rise in developing countries by 5 percent. In a later article (Hanushek, Wössmann and Zhang 2011), they make more extravagant dollar estimates as to how much can be gained by improving education.

While there are many criticisms that can be made of their methodology, our focus is on the theory that drives it. There are several points to be made. The most general is that whether these returns are achieved will depend upon the industrial development path taken. If, for example, we compare the current fates of Ireland and South Korea, we find radically different growth rates based on quite different models of skill formation and economic development (Kim 2000; Field 2002). This suggests that the relationships between the state, private enterprise and education systems are crucial to understanding the different outcomes of countries such as South Korea and Ireland. Critics such as Ha-Joon Chang (2002) have pointed out that the pathways to development taken in East Asia departed radically from the Washington Consensus formula, including education. Chang focuses on the political economy of development that takes into account the way corporate and state institutions were constructed to promote development.

Human capital theory has no account of economic development because of its static equilibrium model of the labour market. Furthermore, the assumption made by Hanushek and Wössmann is that educational institutions and cultures have no impact on the way students are taught and socialised and, consequently, on how their educational experience may impact on innovation and the application of knowledge and skills in the labour market. Yet, we know that different schooling systems approach questions of knowledge, pedagogy and learning quite differently; this appears to impact on the capacity for innovation and the application of skill. It is for this reason that many countries in East Asia, despite frequently topping the various international educational test-league tables, worry about their lack of creativity (Lauder et al. 2012). At the same time, it is also clear that success in tests like PISA does not mean that students are more likely to conform to the behavioural profiles of corporate 'talent' in TNCs. This appears to be a problem that Singapore, as one of the best PISA performers, is confronting (Brown, Lauder and Sung 2015).

Finally, human capital theory, as exemplified by Hanushek and Wössmann (2007), appears to take little account of the global economy. They work with a very limited measure of openness to trade that tells us nothing of the effects of economic globalisation on specific economies. Their strategy of using inductive reasoning to extrapolate from past trends to the future will no longer hold, as the world has changed fundamentally.

This discussion of human capital theory suggests that in order to develop a fuller understanding of the relationship between education and economic development, we need an institutional analysis of the education-labour market relationship in specific contexts that takes into account the effects of economic globalisation. Without these elements, human capital theory has no basis for guiding policy.

Capabilities, productive transformation and development

One of the most sophisticated accounts that does embrace institutions is 'capabilities, productive transformation and development' (Nübler 2014, 2015) at the International Labour Organisation. Given its level of sophistication in comparison to the work of Hanushek and Wössmann, it is worth examining in some detail.

The author's account involves developing a conceptual framework of social capabilities that can be fruitfully applied to empirical data and to case-study countries. The reason for this focus is, as Nübler (2015: 53) argues: "Differences in social capabilities explain why countries, even with similar factor endowments, demonstrate very different performance in catching up and development." From this starting point, she develops a dynamic account of "catching up". There are two elements in this process: productive capacities and social capabilities. The former concerns "the technologies applied in the economy and its existing productive portfolio" (p. 57). This productive capacity is determined by "capital, the technology embodied in equipment and processes, human capital and infrastructure" (p. 57). In contrast, social capabilities define:

> [T]he ability of the economy to shift into the production of goods and services which are not yet produced in the country, and the ability to adopt advanced technologies which have not been adopted before.
>
> (p. 57)

Nübler (2014) explains that catching up:

> [I]s expressed in structural change patterns that help countries achieve development objectives and aspirations of their societies, in rapid and sustained processes of catching up.
>
> (p. 144)

This is contrasted with mainstream economics where "catching up" is defined in terms of productivity increases and GDP growth rates; along with evolutionary economic perspectives it sees in terms of technological catching up, by emphasising product space and structural change perspectives. Key to this analysis and what contributes to its novelty is the view that two countries with the same factor endowments, including technology, may differ substantially in their social capabilities and hence prospects for development.

There are two dimensions to social capabilities that are linked to productive capacity. Firstly, Nübler (2015) develops the concept of option space – that is, the feasible set of products and technologies that a country may develop. Secondly, social capabilities reflect the ability and competencies to take advantage of these options (p. 58). These competencies are understood as operating at the institutional level and are required within firms, by governments and in the wider economy to take advantage of feasible option spaces (p. 61). Interestingly, the argument for such social capabilities is supported by recent economic history of the industrial revolution by showing that the material basis of productive capacity, by itself, cannot explain the transformation of economies in the industrial revolution (Perez 2002).

A further refinement to this account concerns the role of knowledge innovation that, in its various manifestations (e.g., scientific knowledge, tacit knowledge, cultural knowledge, and in techno-economic knowledge systems), is seen as central to social capability. It is how this knowledge is developed, disseminated and applied that is crucial to the capabilities that are necessary to exploit option spaces. These forms of knowledge extend beyond the scientific and technological to those necessary for institution building. A final piece in this theoretical architecture is the notion of a knowledge community, which is defined as distinct knowledge sets that can be combined in various ways for the production of different products. This enables a rich characterisation and explanation for why firms can shift from one product to another and from one sector to another. In doing so, the role of tacit knowledge as part of their institutional culture assumes importance.

It is worth giving a brief description of how this theory is put to use with respect to education because it utilises most of the key concepts outlined above. Nübler provides an analysis of the relationship of educational levels and the distribution of education levels that in turn create key elements of the option spaces available for productive transformation. She shows that, in contrast to human capital theory, simply looking at educational outcomes will not explain industrial transformation because it is also necessary to examine the relationship between what she calls educational structures, where the distribution of education assumes importance in the development, in particular, of manufacturing. What she hypothesises is that when educational structures are taken into account, this defines the limits and possibilities for industrial development and transformation. For example, Malaysia, Taiwan and South Korea have had strong middle-range qualifications with a significant proportion of students completing secondary education, which has enabled industrial development and transformation. In contrast, Brazil has a missing middle, which helps to explain why it has a few sophisticated industries, like aerospace, alongside a large proportion of low-skill industries. In effect, Brazil cannot exploit the range of option spaces available to, for example, Taiwan for industrial development because it does not have a significant group of intermediately skilled workers. This means that neither overseas nor indigenous investors will seek to develop such industries, leaving a highly unbalanced form of development.

The reasons why this is a more sophisticated study of the economics of development should now be clear. It does not assume that there is a more or less direct connection between education and economic development, as implied by Hanushek and Wössmann (2007; Hanushek, Wössmann and Zhang 2011). It does not assume that open markets and free trade are necessary or even desirable because the Asian economies used as case studies in her research did not conform to a free-market model; rather, they focus on the social capabilities required to engineer productive capacities and transformations. This is a long way from the Washington Consensus, and her work opens the way for industrial policy interventions at different institutional levels and in different contexts.

However, there are several factors concerning economic development that have not been considered in Nübler's account. The most significant gaps in this theory are as follows: first, fundamental changes in the structuring of the global economy are not adequately theorised; second, fundamental changes in the global structuring of manufacturing and services, particularly with respect to automation, have also not been fully considered; and third, the account of knowledge innovation, and in particular the role of tacit knowledge, is problematic. Therefore, what is required is a theory that takes into account the strengths of the theory of capabilities, productive transformation and development but that also takes into account fundamental changes in the global economy. Indeed, Nübler's account fails to overcome the limitations of methodological nationalism: that is, the unit of analysis is national development with global economic developments having, at best, a peripheral role.

We now turn to addressing these issues through an account of the way the global economy is making the possibility of national development far more difficult. However, it is intended that such an account will enable the development of educational, labour market and industrial policies that have a chance of success.

Fundamental changes in the structuring of the global economy: two waves of globalisation

When examining the role of economic globalisation, two 'waves' of development can be identified in the organisation of global value chains (Brown, Lauder and Sung 2014).

During the first wave of contemporary globalisation, beginning in the 1970s, corporate value chains were limited to low-skilled, low-paid work, with most high-value-added activities remaining in close proximity to the head office. The multinational companies (MNCs) at the time began to experiment with back-office services, as well as manufacturing, in low-cost countries such as India, Mexico and Singapore, but these developments remained piecemeal. HR strategies and talent management were organised within national contexts as access to intermediate- and high-skilled workers and were primarily supplied through local or national training systems and 'closed' job markets.

Some developing economies understood the opportunities and were well positioned to take advantage of this phase of globalisation. For example, the Singapore government gained early mover advantage in recognising the economic potential of attracting foreign direct investment at a time when Western and Japanese companies were looking to reduce manufacturing costs and respond to growing potential in emerging Asian markets. Through an extensive education and training strategy, the Singapore government sought to upgrade the skills of the workforce, working closely with companies to move in the direction of more skilled jobs, exemplified by its push into higher-value manufacturing in the electronics sector. Through building what Sung (2006) called the "developmental worker" model of economic development, it was largely successful in 'matching' the supply of young workers with anticipated demand in key sectors of the economy based on technical and engineering skills.

As we can see from the discussion above, the global economy has entered accounts of the education-economy relationship in terms of foreign direct investment (FDI). There has been a linear model in which foreign direct investment enabled, in principle, workers to move up the value chain, creating better jobs, which, when combined with the skills required to undertake those jobs, led to higher productivity. The attraction of FDI from transnational corporations lay in the view that their efficiency would lead to better jobs and higher productivity. This has certainly been the case in countries like Singapore (Brown, Lauder and Sung 2014) as it developed.

The second wave of globalisation gave TNCs much greater control over their sourcing options further up the value chain. Many aspects of production, design and research are now located wherever skills are available and the costs and other advantages benefit companies most. It includes a widespread use of offshoring beyond back-office jobs, commonly found in the first wave of globalisation. It also initiated an ongoing process of companies integrating key aspects of human resource management on a global basis, challenging preconceived notions derived from past experience within Western economies.

If the first wave is characterised by the offshoring of low-skilled, low-value work, the second wave is defined by a step-change in scale and scope as TNCs move toward the regional and global integration of value chains. This is facilitated by new technologies that do not respect the distinction between 'high' and 'low' skilled work or between British, Chinese, Indonesian and American workers.

These enterprises developed greater capacity to move across established borders and boundaries. It is this shift from national to international skill webs that distinguish the multinational companies (MNCs) of the past from the transnational companies (TNCs) of the future.

Two major factors in the global extension of value chains have been the 'inside-out' model of production and the use of new technology, which have enabled both the communications

Corporate FDI → Progression up value chain → Higher skilled work → Increased productivity → Improved wages → National growth with shared prosperity

Figure 22.1   Linear model: corporate inward investment and national skill formation strategy
Source: Adapted from Brown, Lauder and Sung 2014.

necessary to control GVCs and a significant increase in automation that has moved up the occupational hierarchy.

When we look at how TNCs now locate their productive units, it is clear that they are operating an 'inside out' model that combines world-class infrastructure in terms of communication and production systems – within a context where the first and third world share the same postcode – with a supply of educated labour that can be now be found across the emerging economies (Brown, Lauder and Ashton 2011). This poses fundamental problems for national development. It means that within national borders, there can be pockets of affluence; this then raises the question of how such FDI can be utilised to bring wider benefits to a developing country (Wade 2010). Indeed, in some developing countries, the rich have more in common with their counterparts in developed economies that they do with their compatriots (Palma 2011). In other words, the idea of developing nations 'catching up' is problematic because it is based on a linear model of development (see Figure 22.1). This is why industrial policy that can spread the benefits of FDI is so important.

The digital means of controlling global supply chains

Given that TNCs can now set up production facilities for both tradable goods and services virtually anywhere, if the infrastructure and education levels are obtained, then the fundamental problem confronted by governments is how to lock into GVCs for the purposes of job creation and skills upgrading when they are often globally dispersed and potential suppliers are numerous. For example, Rolls Royce has 8,000 supplier companies. However, the "internet of things" (Porter and Heppelmann 2014) that combines an elaborate system of physical, smart and connected components that feed data in real time from any supplier, production facility or sales outlet to a central information point, known as a digital control tower, now enables TNCs to control the flow of goods and services globally.

The full implications of the second wave of globalisation cannot be understood without taking into account the rise of digital Taylorism. This is analogous to the introduction of mechanical Taylorism characterised by the Fordist production line, where the knowledge of craft workers was captured by management, codified and re-engineered in the shape of the moving assembly line (Brown, Lauder and Ashton 2011: 65). In the twenty-first century, digital Taylorism involves translating knowledge work into working knowledge through the extraction, codification and digitalisation of knowledge into software prescripts and templates that can be transmitted and manipulated by others, regardless of location. The result is the standardisation of functions and jobs, including an increasing proportion of technical, managerial and professional roles that raise fundamental questions about the future of 'knowledge' work. Consequently, employers are not always looking for employees who possess academic knowledge or analytical skills but rather the flexibility to enable them to fit into clearly defined roles that are simplified and codified to enable 'plug-and-play,' even for highly qualified employees.

Automation, tacit knowledge and manufacturing

Some forms of manufacturing, e.g., textiles, are less amenable to automation than others. However, in light of the emphasis that has been put on middle-range qualifications and manufacturing development by the capabilities, productive transformation and development model, the question of automation looms large because it is precisely for these middle-range qualifications that automation is most threatening. Indeed, it is now threatening postsecondary degree holders. China has seen a decline of workers in the manufacturing sector precisely for this reason.

Corporate FDI $\longrightarrow$ Dispersed value chain* $\longrightarrow$ Job segmentation with some better jobs
$\longrightarrow$ Increased income disparities $\longrightarrow$ National growth without shared prosperity

Figure 22.2 Differentiated model: corporate supply chains and national skill formation strategy

Source: Adapted from Brown, Lauder and Sung 2014.

* It is dispersed horizontally (spatial division of labour) and vertically (occupational hierarchy). Horizontally, this is done through price competition across national borders. Vertically, this is done through the segmentation both within and between occupations, often aided by new technologies, different employment contracts, etc.

As such, there is a clear view that technology is now more likely to be skill replacing than skill biased (Brynjolfsson and MacAfee 2011). The threat is not to the possibility of developing manufacturing or indeed manufacturing transformations but that it will not lead to significant job creation. A similar point can be made with respect to the service sector because so much of it is now being automated. Korea stands out as a paradigm example of how high levels of education are required by consumers to manipulate new technologies alongside high levels of graduate underemployment, leading to an attempt to construct mid-range software designer jobs.

In turn, this raises fundamental questions about the role of tacit knowledge in the workplace. Nübler is not alone in assuming that there are limits to standardisation given the importance of tacit knowledge. However, we see increasing examples of how TNCs seem to be able to codify tacit knowledge. The clearest examples are in automation but also in outsourcing (often related) and in crowdsourcing for projects and in R&D value chains. It seems that Polanyi's idea is being reversed; rather than knowledge shifting from the conscious to the unconscious, it is rapidly going in the other direction. While tacit knowledge may remain central to some work contexts, especially those where corporate talent are given 'permission to think' or in leading-edge research, it is clear that there is far more potential for firms to translate knowledge work into working knowledge than is commonly understood (Head 2014).

When taken together, this second wave of globalisation makes economic development more complex and a shared prosperity difficult to achieve. Our argument is that an adequate theory of education and development needs to take account of the differentiated model of corporate supply chains and national skill formation (See Figure 22.2).

Conclusion: toward a political economy of industrial policy

This chapter rejects the human capital assumption that there is a more or less automatic correlation between raising educational standards and economic growth that will benefit nations. While Nübler offers a more plausible account of education and development, we have outlined a number of limitations, including the need to take account of the second wave of globalisation. We've shown that the 'pick-n'-mix' approach of TNCs as to where they locate their supply chains mean that we are more likely to see pockets of well-rewarded workers, rather than a more uniform increase in education and economic standards. Hence, we are more likely to see a greater stratification of income not restricted to developing economies.

In conclusion, this analysis challenges the assumption that further investments in education or merely attracting FDI is enough to trigger economic development, although, as Wade (2010) has noted, FDI was not always put to good use. It may seem that when confronted with the power of TNCs, nations are in a weak position in terms of steering economic development that benefits all citizens. We would argue that it is precisely at this historical juncture that nation-states become more – not less – important. And it is in this context that some of the insights of capabilities and transformation approach are very helpful. It is the case that TNCs employ some 25 percent of the global labour force directly; their influence on economies will be consequently wider. However, while it may be that nation-states can capture some of the spillover effects from TNC investment, they need to be located within a broader strategy of economic development. There are many options available, but judicious choices need to be made as to when states intervene and how (Stiglitz and Lin 2013).

At this point, the role of education enters in two ways: first, industrial policies can only be successfully developed if there is a sufficient cadre of well-trained policymakers working with sophisticated intelligence systems to enable appropriate industrial policy choices to be made. It should be emphasised that just as there are market failures, so there will be industrial policy failures. Second, Nübler's concept of social capability remains important. This is because nations can be more fleet of foot if they have a broadly educated workforce, although the role of intermediately skilled workers remains uncertain. Nevertheless, it is on balance better to have a significant group of overqualified workers who have the possibility of contributing to both intermediately and lower-skilled work than a small elite of highly skilled workers and a mass of poorly educated workers locked into a future of low-skilled work or unemployment. Often speed is of the essence in capitalising on opportunities, and a workforce without the requisite skills will not be able to take advantage of emerging opportunities. It does not mean that having social capability will translate into 'catching up,' but it allows for that possibility, as the respective 'take-off' of both Ireland and South Korea had in common a reserve army of highly educated labour.

That said, we should also acknowledge that expertise in industrial policy takes a long time to accumulate and that there is no guarantee of its success. It is, however, in the present wave of economic globalisation, the only game in town.

References

Becker, G., 1992. Prize Lecture: The Economic Way of Looking at Life. http://www.nobelprize.org/nobel_prizes/economic-sciences/laureates/1992/becker-lecture.html

Brown, P., Lauder, H., Ashton, D., 2011. *The Global Auction*. Oxford University Press, New York

Brown, P., Lauder, H., Sung, J., 2014. *Global Value Chains and the Future of High Skills: Evidence from Singapore and Implications for the UK*. Institute for Adult Learning, Singapore.

Brown, P., Lauder, H., Sung, J., 2015. Higher education, corporate talent and the stratification of knowledge work in the global labour market. In: van Zanten, A., Ball, S. and Darchy-Koechlin, B. (Eds.) *World Yearbook of Education* 2015. Routledge, London.

Brynjolfsson, E., McAfee, A., 2011. *Race Against the Machine*. Digital Frontier Press, e-book.

Chang, H-J., 2002. *Kicking Away the Ladder*. Anthem, London.

Chang, H-J., 2007. *Bad Samaritans*. Random House, London.

Clarke, S., 1982. *Marx, Marginalism and Modern Sociology*. Macmillan, London.

Fields, B., 2002. The Accidental Tiger: An Exploration of the Irish Economic Disposition During the Belated Golden Age of Development. PhD Thesis, University of Leicester.

Hall, P., Soskice, D. (Eds.), 2001. *Varieties of Capitalism: The Institutional Foundations of Comparative Advantage*. Oxford University Press, Oxford.

Hanushek, E., Wössmann, L., 2007. The role of education quality in economic growth. World Bank Policy Research Working Paper No. 4122, World Bank, Washington.

Hanushek, E., Wössmann, L., Zhang, L., 2011. General education, vocational education, and labour market outcomes over the life cycle. National Bureau of Economic Research Working Paper 17504, Cambridge, MA.

Head, S., 2014. *Mindless: Why Smarter Machines Are Making Dumber Humans*. Basic, New York.

Kim, L., 2000. Korea's national innovation system in transition. In: Kim, L. and Nelson, R. (Eds.) *Technology Learning and Innovation: Experiences of Newly Industrialised Economies*. Cambridge University Press, Cambridge.

Lauder, H., Young, M., Daniels, H., Balarin, M., Lowe, J., 2012. Introduction. In: Lauder, H., Young, M., Daniels, H., Balarin, M. and Lowe, J. (Eds.) *Educating for the Knowledge Economy: Critical Perspectives.* Routledge, London.

Nübler, I., 2014. A theory of capabilities for productive transformation. In: Salazar-Xirinches, J.M., Nübler, I. and Kozul-Wright, R. (Eds.) *Transforming Economies: Making Industrial Policy Work for Growth, Jobs and Development.* ILO, Geneva.

Nübler, I., 2015. *Capabilities, Productive Transformation and Development: A New Perspective on Industrial Policies.* ILO, Geneva.

Palma, J., 2011. Homogeneous middles vs. heterogeneous tails, and the end of the inverted U: it's all about the share of the rich. *Development and Change* 42, 1, 87–153.

Perez, C., 2002. *Technological Revolutions and Financial Capital: The Dynamics of Bubbles and Golden Ages.* Edward Elgar, London.

Porter, M., Heppelmann, J., 2014. How smart, connected products are transforming competition. *Harvard Business Review* November, 65–88.

Schultz, T., 1961. Investment in human capital. *American Economic Review* 51, 1, 1–17.

Stiglitz, J., Lin, J. (Eds.), 2013. *The Industrial Policy Revolution I: The Role of Government Beyond Ideology.* Palgrave Macmillan, New York.

Sung, J., 2006. *Explaining the Economic Success of Singapore: The Developmental Worker as the Missing Link.* Edward Elgar, London.

Wade, R., 2010. After the crisis: industrial policy and the developmental state in low income countries. *Global Policy* 1, 2, 150–161.

Williamson, J., 1990. What Washington means by policy reform. In: Williamson, J. (Ed.) *Latin American Adjustment. How Much Has Happened?* Institute for International Economics, Washington.

23

UNIVERSITIES AS A PUBLIC GOOD

Melanie Walker

At a recent debate among South African universities (*Monday Paper*, 17 March 2014, University of Cape Town) on the role of universities in social transformation (and by implication the public good), the Vice-Chancellor of the University of Cape Town (UCT) argued that universities do not just lead public debate around moral behaviour and conflict resolution through rational debate. They are also a unique space where students are exposed to 'the other' – and come to grips with their misconceptions around this otherness:

> They come to a university campus which is very diverse, and they are confronted with this diversity, with people from different backgrounds, different social classes, different languages, different religions. . . . I think one of the most powerful things you do at university is to educate people about tolerance, about reconciliation, and to reduce the fear of the unknown. In the post-apartheid society, what can be more important than that?

Prins Nevhutalu, Vice-Chancellor of the Cape Peninsula University of Technology, argued that universities should guard against merely producing students that exacerbated present social inequalities:

> South Africa has one of the world's largest Gini coefficients. Do universities produce students who are going to exacerbate these divisions between the very rich and the very poor? For example, if our students become MDs of companies, how do they treat their workers? What kind of graduates do we produce so that we can be part of a changed society?

Responding to perceptions that universities conduct esoteric research, UCT Vice-Chancellor Price noted that one would be hard-pressed to find research at local universities that did not add value to society, either immediately or as a foundation for future endeavours. Such concerns seem to inflect towards aligning university teaching and research with the public good.

Nor are such concerns specific only to public good concerns in global South countries. For example, Derek Bok (2013) highlights a 2012 survey among first-year university students in the United States in which 88% cited getting a better job as an important reason for attending college. But, he says, among the outcomes they considered essential or very important, 45.6% cited "developing a meaningful philosophy of life", and many listed such goals as community leadership, promoting racial understanding, and involvement in environmental programmes. Bok concludes that the survey suggests that what people want most is the satisfaction that comes from a full and meaningful life, which includes adequate income but also human relationships, acts of kindness, absorbing interests, and the chance to live in an ethical and democratic society. He notes that economic stagnation and lack of opportunity are problems but so are low voting rates; civic apathy; disregard for ethical standards; and indifference to art, music, literature, and ideas. It is, he says, the responsibility of educators in universities to help students live satisfying, responsible lives.

Can universities then make contributions to the public good as these commentators seem to suggest? This in turn raises questions of what kind of universities; for what kind of public good development; and how this might play out both as internal to universities as equity in access, participation and student achievement, and broader contributions to social development by engaged universities and graduate professionals equipped with knowledge, skills, and public good values. Nixon (2011) argues that the public good can reside both in individuals working inside and in graduates outside the academy, as well as in the ethos and democratic mission of the university itself. In higher education, individuals and institutions together produce goods of wide public benefit such as informed citizens, health professionals, business people, and so on, transcending narrower self-interest. 'Public good' then captures, as Leibowitz (2012) suggests, the idea that a university as a whole leans consistently towards the collective values, practices, and policies of social justice and inclusion both within the institution and in its external dealings. This notion of the public good then both faces inward to equity and outwards to inclusive development contributions, and both dimensions are likely to be interwoven and mutually reinforcing; in developing one, we develop the other.

For example, a combined inward and outward approach might ask how universities educate and train graduate professionals so that they develop knowledge and values (internal goods) that will enable them to work for human well-being and quality of life and to be effective leaders in reducing inequalities (external good) as a public good contribution. Graduates who work as health, legal, planning, engineering, and educational professionals with people living vulnerable and precarious lives could foster voice, justice, and less inequality (Walker and McLean 2013). Nussbaum (2004: 337) also underlines the case for the significance of university education for gender equality in that university-educated women "are far more likely to be able to influence debates at a national level as well as have access to the more influential and higher paying jobs". In the argument made by Nussbaum (2004) and Walker and McLean (2013), inclusive public-good development cannot be effectively tackled without also paying attention to universities. Moreover, it seems not unreasonable to suggest that university goals should be part of the fair distribution of benefits, including improving the lives and well-being of the poor and vulnerable in society.

However, it is also the case that foregrounding universities and the public good faces considerable challenges, not least of which is to develop a new language that challenges that of the market and managerialism. The argument has to be made in a context in which neoliberal ideas now profoundly influences and indeed, constitutes, university policy. This leads commentators such as Naidoo (2010) to argue that market mechanisms and new managerialism have led to the growing and relatively unmediated influence of economic pressures and the prioritisation of economic capital in the field of university policy in order to enhance national economic competitiveness within a global knowledge-driven economy. It then becomes progressively harder to sustain public values that support a social contribution such as informed citizens as well as the individual benefits of education, together with the rationale for public investment in education and advancing public purposes. As UNESCO points out, public-good university education is "easily neglected in the rush for income and prestige" (2009: 21). Even an activity as apparently virtuous as community engagement is commodified and credited as another form of capital to be acquired by mostly middle-class students rather than valued as a public good, while even well-meaning service learning strategies still confront pressures to identify the costs and benefits of such activities. A new policy orthodoxy for developing countries now advanced by the World Bank is similarly primarily instrumental in its growing demand for human capital – a well-educated workforce to drive economic growth (Singh 2010). However, it must also be said that individual economic opportunities are critical: professionals without jobs cannot use their knowledge and skills to contribute to society. Unemployed graduates are will not be socially mobile and are likely to be unsatisfied with their lives: a graduate without job prospects is a wasted national resource in any developing country.

Nonetheless, neoliberal policies cannot be entirely reproduced in the discursive practices of universities and in the consciousness of people who work in them. In the everyday lives of students and academics, the picture is more complex. While it might be that the public-good benefits of universities have become fainter in many countries, they have also not been obliterated, as the earlier commentaries from Price, Bok, and others suggest. Moreover, recently there has been robust critique of the state of higher education (for example, Holmwood 2011; Nussbaum 2010). It is also the case that expansive conceptualisations of the purpose of university education are available. For example, Habermas (1989: 118) outlines four functions of the university: the generation of technically exploitable knowledge for producing wealth and services; the academic preparation of public service professionals; the transmission, interpretation, and development of cultural knowledge; and 'the enlightenment of the political public sphere'. Castells (2001) also draws attention to universities as a critical source of equalisation of chances and democratisation of society. He identifies for universities the function of the production and consolidation of values, drawing attention to the importance in a fast-changing, precarious world of a few "solid" (for which we can read public) values. Lobera and Escrigas (2009) cite a Delphi study of 214 experts (higher education specialists, vice-chancellors and other university employees, policymakers, and members of civil society involved in development work) from 80 countries of whom the majority agreed that universities should play an active role in human and social development. Finally, Calhoun (2006) reminds us that universities offer tremendous public benefits, not only in the field of science and technology but also in contributions from the social sciences and humanities to debates on how to live well. He urges more and better thinking about how universities can be truly public and how this debate can be pursued reflexively within universities and on national and international levels.

The public good as 'human development'

If we accept that there is a case to be made for universities as and for the public good, even if from the margins, the next step is how we conceptualise this public good. I propose a human development approach to the public good and universities' contributions for its potential in addressing global and national development agendas and offering an interdisciplinary, multidimensional, reflexive, and justice-enhancing approach. Haq (1999) explains that the key purpose of development (and hence of the public good) is to enlarge people's choices to lead good lives. He argues that we often value achievements that do not show up in income or growth figures, such as access to knowledge, better nutrition, and health services; more secure livelihoods; security against crime and physical violence; satisfying leisure hours; political and cultural freedoms;

and participation in community activities. The objective of development, Haq proposes, should then be to create an enabling environment for people to enjoy long, healthy, and creative lives.

The core dimensions of human development include: 1) empowerment, understood as the expansion of capabilities or valuable freedoms to choose valued functionings (beings and doings or ways of life) (Sen 1999; Nussbaum 2000); 2) equality and nondiscrimination in access to and distribution of economic and social opportunities as conditions for expanding capabilities; and 3) security and sustainability of people's valued achievements and freedoms. Furthermore, the well-being of each and every person as the objective of development should be the outcome. People should have the agency freedom to pursue and achieve goals they value and to participate meaningfully in decisions that affect their lives and well-being. University education would form people's capabilities – their freedoms to be and to do and to achieve well-being and agency – and universities would contribute individually and systemically to human development in society: empowerment, equalities, security, and well-being.

The public good in this approach is about more than developing human capital to get a job and to contribute to a country's economic growth. Education is important in a richer way; it has instrumental and intrinsic value and transformative potential (e.g., greater gender equality). Education is also valuable for its democratic contributions; it can teach us to reason and deliberate with others – critically and in an informed way. Education has interpersonal effects in opening up opportunities for others, e.g., younger brothers or sisters or people in the communities of which we are a part. From a social perspective, education can have empowerment and distributive effects, e.g., disadvantaged groups can increase their ability to resist inequalities and get a fairer deal in and through education. Crucially, having a good education affects the development and expansion of other capabilities so that an education capability expands other important human freedoms. As 'public-good' university educators, we would ask more demanding questions than human capital does. What are people actually able to do and be? What opportunities do they have to attend a university, to participate, to change and develop their knowledge, to experience cooperative relationships, to form their values, to get rewarding jobs, to have good lives, to participate in their communities, and to contribute to society? What broader contribution does the university make to the economy and society? A human development and capabilities perspective requires, as Nussbaum (2011) explains, that we ask how we build a society that values capabilities and functionings for all. While neoliberal discourses might be dominant, there is nonetheless an emergent discourse at the margins of university education around human development and capabilities (Boni and Walker 2013). This is supported by UNESCO's (2003) affirmation of universities as a vital component of cultural, social, and political development; of endogenous capacity building; the consolidation of human rights; sustainable development; democracy; and peace, in a context of justice.

Furthermore, human development draws our attention to the broader location of education and grounds it in an alternative economics that acknowledges the role of human capital but subsumes it within more expansive concerns. Integration into economic life matters if people are to possess a sense of belonging in society by participating in income generation and securing remunerative employment. That said, income alone cannot capture the full range of contributions to a state of well-being in a person's life. A strong economy ought to be a means to good lives, but, as Sen (1999) has reminded us, we cannot evaluate resources as an end; rather, we need rich and full information about how resources are being realised in actual human lives, activities, and achievements.

Universities oriented to the public good would then work to infuse their core functions of teaching, research, and community service with the principles drawn from human development and operationalised as the development of human capabilities inside and outside the university.

They would acknowledge that university education generates both private and public benefits, but from a human development perspective, these benefits need to be in balance. Access to and success in higher education for students from less-privileged backgrounds and for women – thanks to the expansion of access that has accompanied globalisation and knowledge economy drivers – represents real and positive changes in lives and family circumstances but does not yet go far enough. Access and participation need further attention so that the outward face of public good commitments is mirrored in inwards equity commitments. We can argue that universities have played and will continue to play a significant role in distributing fairer opportunities and attainments, even as they simultaneously advance the interests of elites in society. Nonetheless, elites may make choices to contribute to social change, as research by De Swaan et al. (2000) argues.

Possibilities exist in complicated tension and leave open spaces in which universities might choose contributions to public-good development. For example, the public dimensions of universities in Africa are dealt with by Sall et al. (2003). They discuss African universities in civil society, explaining that while they may have reproductive effects, they also have the potential as part of the public sphere to hold the state and business accountable and provide critical discussion and direction on changes in society. Importantly, they note that universities produce most of the people employed at the higher echelons of the public and private sector, including, we might add, professions in law, engineering, and so forth. The university is then both a participant in changing social processes and affected by processes of change and transformation. Moreover, the social significance of university expansion lies in graduate social mobility and integration into the labour market, both critical for the transformation roles and functions of universities. Crucially, the choices and experiences of young people in higher education in Africa will themselves be critical to whether it fulfils a reproductive role for privilege and private advantages only or also encompasses a transformative role for well-being across society.

Public-good contributions by universities

Producing knowledge

I turn now to considering the significance of the knowledge contributions of universities that uniquely conserve, disseminate, and advance scholarly knowledge through teaching and research and why this matters for understanding and advancing the public good of universities.

The knowledge that researchers produce and graduates acquire is a singular public good. The economist Paul A. Samuelson (1954: 387) is usually credited as the first to develop a theory of "public goods", which he defined in opposition to private goods as "[goods] which all enjoy in common in the sense that each individual's consumption of such a good leads to no subtractions from any other individual's consumption of that good". This is the property that has become known as "non-rivalrous": for example, a poem can be read by many people without reducing the consumption of that good by others. In addition, public goods possess a second property called "non-excludability", that is, it is impossible to exclude any individuals from consuming the good. Relevant to an ethical stance on the part of universities is that knowledge, as Stiglitz (2003) suggests, is a public good because it retains its value. For example, a mathematical theorem can be used over and over again across the globe or a book read by millions across the world without diminishing in value. But in current times, university-produced knowledge can be excludable through intellectual property rights, patents, commercial distribution, the selection of students, and so on and is then not equitably distributed. Further, as Calhoun (2006) points out, while knowledge (when it made freely available) is not used up by sharing, it can be collected in the form of credentials based on access to the same knowledge, thereby transforming it into a private good. If credentials are too widely shared, they diminish in professional and financial value. The issue then is how or if the credentialed elite use their knowledge to contribute to the wider good, as citizens participating in the public sphere. Thus we cannot entirely separate knowledge as a public good from public values and the role the university might have in their formation.

There is a further way in which university knowledge is significant for the public good. Here I draw on Wally Morrow's (2009) insightful essay on the functions of higher [university] education. He argues that there is a muddying of aims and the empirical development impact of higher education. His concern is that higher education cannot contribute to society and especially to the modernising project of particular relevance to developing countries if it loses it capacity "to constitute the domain of higher knowledge" (p. 129) through well-meaning attempts to control and direct higher education in a particular direction. This, he argues, "is never good news for a society, especially one on the track towards modernisation" (p. 129). The distinctive knowledge project of higher education is not the same as everyday, common-sense knowledge; it is not readily accessible and is acquired "through an extensive and systematic process of guided learning" (p. 116). It is, he argues, qualitatively different; in other words. it is not just more knowledge – adding more to primary or more to secondary. Higher knowledge is 'prized' in modern societies in that it constitutes a "potent source of innovation and development" (p. 117) and hence new ideas, new thinking; it encourages doubt, not certainty, imagination, and critical thinking. To have this higher knowledge (whether of physics, mathematics, history, or philosophy) is to understand the grammar of the practice of mathematics, for example, an understanding that enables "the capacity to generate new routines" (p. 120). Such knowledge then is potentially potent for innovation and growth. Nor should this knowledge be misunderstood as private good; it is (or ought to be) fundamentally a public good of general benefit to society.

Without the kind of expertise and the experts produced in universities, we are, Morrow argues, "unlikely to be able to overcome the challenges with which we are confronted" (p. 123). The academic disciplines in his view, while not to be treated with "uncritical reverence", do nonetheless "provide the springboard from which to leap into the future" (p. 131). For example, in South Africa scientific research is the forerunner for developing new and innovative technologies that can in turn be applied in disadvantaged areas, such as the Cofimbava School Project in the Eastern Cape Province, which is testing tablets, wireless, and energy solutions. But a purely production paradigm of knowledge will not do for Morrow; it is not a product or a commodity. If this distinctive knowledge project of higher education is undermined or misunderstood, it will also, he argues, paradoxically damage the training function of universities. Morrow points out that the value of professional training is in its relationship to higher knowledge. He explains:

> Because of its setting within institutions where research and higher knowledge are acknowledged as vital, professional training can be embedded in a wider humanistic endeavour. It is the flexibility and openness to new ideas that universities at their best engender that should characterise professional knowledge – a far cry from the mechanical application of learning skills that will then be mechanically applied. Professional knowledge is thus closely linked to higher knowledge.
>
> (2009: 136)

Thus the public good of the professional education and training function requires a foundation in scholarly knowledge and expertise.

Reinforcing Morrow's (2009) case for the distinctiveness of higher knowledge, Hall (2007: 3) reminds us that universities are key sites for producing knowledge, writing that, "the academic obsession with evidence, argument, peer review, publication and refutations are the essence of knowledge creation". Using the significant example of understanding poverty and its causes in South Africa, this calls, Hall says, for complex and specialist intellectual skills, including sophisticated research methods and the argument that most robustly and rigorously explains the problem. Importantly, then, universities "are specialised sites where knowledge is formed and reformed on the merits of theory and evidence, rather than according to the emergencies of immediate and short term interests" (p. 5).

Knowledge exchanges

My second example takes on the issue of exchanging university knowledge with wider publics as a key public-good arena. The relevant question concerns how the distinctive knowledge outlined by Morrow above is circulated and made more equally accessible. Marginson (2006: 10) argues that universities have neglected dialogical exchanges, even though they now have "impressive technologies and discursive resources for conversations at a previously impossible scale", such as via mobile phone and computer technology, which reach most parts of the world. The larger goal, he suggests, is to deploy the communicative resources of the university not simply to advance money and hierarchies of power. To do this would require valuing university contributions to public debate and policy formation and to a "socially communicative faculty". He explains:

> For example, the public university could position itself as the medium for translating expert science into popular forms. This would reduce the expert/democratic tensions in disciplinary knowledges – with internal as well as external democratic dividends – and provide a practical grounding for socially responsible science. It also offers a more attractive rationale for public support than the notion of a self-referencing city of the intellect.
>
> (2006: 10)

The communication and transfer of university-produced knowledge then becomes a public-good contribution. Even though some of the current knowledge transfer debates in higher education are reductive and instrumental, focusing on unidirectional knowledge transfer for economic development and growth, transfer is not necessarily oriented only or mainly to instrumental economic ends nor always unidirectional. For example, Graham et al. (2006) propose an expansive view of knowledge transfer that, "encompasses the processes of both knowledge creation and knowledge application" (p. 22). The process is neither linear nor uncomplicated but involves ideas, meanings, contexts, histories, experts, and communities.

However, this is not uncontested in higher education circles, as debates in South Africa demonstrate. Martin Hall (2009) has written about "new knowledge and the university", taking as his starting point disputes over access by forensic archaeologists at the University of Cape Town to skeletons from a recently discovered burial ground in the city. He challenges approaches that "insist on disciplinarity and the continued exclusion of the profane world from the academy" (p. 69) of the knowledges that thrive outside the university. What counts as legitimate knowledge is to be decided from inside the university, a place apart, an inner community of scientists who produce the rational consensus. Yet, as Hall points out, we have examples of rather spectacular failure on the part of university experts to predict, explain or find solutions, or convince those outside the university about tremendous global problems. What is pertinent here is his unpicking of university claims, made by those opposing the exhumation and examination of the human remains (what Hall calls the Science Discourse), about the alleged 'shameful' ignorance of biology. Yet, as Hall points out, those opposing the exhumation (in the discourse he calls this Memory Work) were far from ignorant but were able to, and in the case of the making of the District Six Museum[1] already had, employ methodologies for collecting, interpreting, and synthesing a range of data sources across the academy and communities that, Hall says, are as 'disciplined' as anything Science offers. Hall concludes that "if such engagements were to align the interest of science with those of the memory community, the creation of new knowledge could be enhanced considerably" (2009: 75). These discourses need not be in conflict but could produce vibrant, mutually rewarding hybrid forms of knowledge.

Hall provides a further striking example in another paper (Hall 2007) in which he recounts the work of a small company called Stitch Wise, which makes backfilled bags instead of wooden props to support underground tunnels in mines, thereby both addressing safety and, by employing disabled miners in doing the machine work, providing employment for paraplegic miners. Hall explains that Stitch Wise's success (they supply over 50% of the South African market) depends on integrating common-sense knowledge of underground mining conditions with specialised materials science and engineering. He describes (2007: 12) how the process of dialogic knowledge creation proceeded from "an initial hunch" that the backfilled bags could be refined, through development based on an underground testing site, but also from the observations and "rich" conversations with those who held tacit knowledge about the extreme environment of deep underground mine shafts. Such discussion, "shared experience, collecting stories, trying out ideas and abandoning dead ends" and Stitch Wise's practical knowledge assets were integral to the application of the abstract materials science knowledge held by research scientists. Their access to the deep levels mine was an asset that allowed "the further refinement of codified knowledge through practical application". The dialogic and iterative theory-practice development was completed when Stitch Wise formally rewrote the recognised standards and safety conditions for backfilled bags in the underground mining sector – "a formal codification of the various strands of tacit knowledge".

The point is that engagement outside the realm of the academy need not compromise academic scholarship or advanced codified knowledge nor diminish, reduce, or even replace the work of experts in the academy. Or it need not do so. Hall (2007: 3) is clear that universities are still relevant as key sites for producing knowledge, writing that, "the academic obsession with evidence, argument, peer review, publication and refutations are the essence of knowledge creation". Using the significant example of understanding poverty and its causes in South Africa, this calls, Hall says, for complex and specialist intellectual skills, including sophisticated research methods and the argument that most robustly and rigorously explains the problem. Importantly, then, universities "are specialised sites where knowledge is formed and reformed on the merits of theory and evidence, rather than according to the emergencies of immediate and short term interests" (2007: 5).

How might we foster such public-good dialogues? Linda Alcoff (2002) proposes a way of understanding the public obligations of scholarship. Alcoff notes that in only some countries is public intellectual work undertaken at the expense of an academic career or public work devalued in the academy because it is seen as lacking rigour and challenge and often regarded therefore as compromised (rather as Hall's Science Discourse above claims). She suggests instead the idea of a publicly engaged intellectual "who spends a significant portion of his or her time engaged with the non-academic public" (Alcoff 2002: 524). She proposes three ways of conceptualising such a public intellectual. The first is that of "permanent critic" of social problems, but what is to be done or changed is not proposed. This can be disempowering. For example, there are necessary and trenchant critiques of neoliberalism by sociologists of education, but they also leave us nowhere to go in terms of what to do to bring about change. The second is that of "populariser", somebody who translates academic ideas for wider publics but at the risk of simplifying complex ideas. Nonetheless, the aim is valuable, she says. Alcoff's third position is that of "public theorist", the researcher who recognises that theory building is not located solely in the academy but in and through wider public arenas where ideas can be tested dialogically to produce better, more rigorous knowledge. Such "public theorising" is democratic in intent and practice. Alcoff (2002) therefore advocates "doing theory in public" and "publicly engaged work". She writes:

> Publicly engaged work is actually one of the best sites from which to engage in at least certain kinds of intellectual work, not because one is merely applying and testing theory developed in the academy to the public domain nor because one can simply gather raw data from which to build theory, but rather because the public domain is sometimes the best or the only place in which to alter one's thoughts. . . . and thus to engage in intellectual work.
>
> (Alcoff 2002: 533)

The public domain is then a place for reciprocity, conversations, debates, and mutual respect Similarly, Calhoun (2007) similarly argues for the role of public intellectual, "someone still bold enough to put his or her knowledge to use in analysing the world around us, in language that most of us can understand, and with an eye to effecting practical improvements" (p. 12). Confrontation between different perspectives inside but also outside the academy, he argues, advances social science. Burawoy (2009), too, proposes "reflexive science", which deploys multiple dialogues to reach explanations of empirical phenomena, and engaging multiple perspectives from diverse groups of stakeholders.

We could do, for example, with informed public debate about the moral limits of markets or about inequalities and poverty and their impact at macro, meso, and micro levels of higher education. Moreover, the dialogue that ensues is itself constitutive of development (Sen 2009). Sen makes the case for the crucial importance of public reasoning and rational scrutiny to democratic life, arguing that "When we try to determine how justice can be advanced, there is a basic need for public reasoning, involving arguments coming from different quarters and divergent perspectives" (2009: 392). Sen does not argue for complete agreements on every issue but rather "reasoned scrutiny" (p. 401). It is then up to us as a community of higher researchers to think through how his broadly framed emphasis on public reasoning and open impartiality would work in our specific situation and in a context of higher education's contributions to equity, justice, and democratic life. As both Marginson (2006) and Alcoff (2002) point out, universities need to explicitly value their own and in doing so may sustain a more robust warrant for the place and role of universities in difficult times in which funding is increasingly being clawed back from public universities.

Professional education

A third key arena of knowledge-based intervention is professional education. Professionals acquire university-produced knowledge and can be carriers for the transfer and use of such knowledge in the form of public service. As Nixon (2011: 26) suggests, higher education can educate people "who are not only efficient and effective in their use of acquired knowledge, but who can use that knowledge to make complex choices regarding the rights uses and application of that knowledge" – for the public good. Higher education trains people for positions of responsibility – their decisions can have a positive or negative impact on people, communities, and society:

> Higher education can be focused on training professionals or on educating citizens who will interchange value with society through the exercise of their professional responsibilities. This second approach implies the education of citizens knowledgeable about the human and social condition, with ethical awareness and civic commitment.
>
> (GUNI 2008: 11)

Seeing university education and research as educating people to be able to contribute to the common welfare connects the singular public good of higher education to the notion of plural public goods. It means further to understand the obligations to others conferred by the advantage of having a university education. For Sen (2009), if we have the effective power to improve lives (as many graduates do, for example, as doctors, lawyers, and teachers), we also have the obligation to act to do so. Graduates as "other-regarding" agents take on obligations to develop the capabilities of all citizens, asking what they should do to help each other in defending or promoting freedoms. The good of others is not a constraint on their own good but integral to it. Professional education is then one area that shapes the relationship between the integrity of professional life and the health of civic cultures and where an other-regarding social consciousness and public values might be fostered. By doing particular kinds of educational things, universities educate particular kinds of professionals as both professionals and citizens; the "particular kinds of things" ought to be to educate 'public-good professionals' (Walker and McLean 2013) who act responsibly towards others. However, for graduate professionals to work to expand the capabilities of those living in poverty, they need themselves to develop as transformative agents, having professional capabilities that enable them to choose to act in this way. To do this, they need exposure to professional education programmes in departments in which curriculum, pedagogy, and assessment foster the appropriate knowledge, understanding, and professional ways of being.

To regard professional education as a public-good contribution by universities is to conceptualise professionals educated to provide a good quality public service for their societies and to be supported in doing so by public policy and funding. Societies need professionals educated with the knowledge, awareness, and social values for operationalising inclusive public services contributing thereby to the formation of a public culture that places human dignity and the alleviation of remediable injustices at its core. It requires universities' engagement with the moral-political urgencies of poverty, human security, environmental sustainability, and fair access to technology. "Public-good professional capabilities" (Walker and McLean 2013) constitute the 'space' for thinking about 1) the public good; 2) public good professional education; and (3) university transformation. Professional capabilities produce the opportunity structures to enable people to choose professional lives they value and to choose the public good if this is what they value. Universities have a crucial role to play as a space to facilitate the critical conditions that enable the formation of a professional consciousness and knowledge oriented to making the lives of people living in conditions of poverty better.

Concluding thoughts

The GUNI collective describes the public good as relating "directly to the roles that academic institutions can play in society ... a public commitment to the general interests of the society of which they form part" (GUNI 2008: 8). I have argued for a human development and capabilities perspective and the underpinning public values of inclusion, participation, sustainability, and justice that the approach supports and have considered in particular the knowledge contributions of universities as a public good, as resources for community dialogues and development, and as a basis for professional education. I have not gone into detail about teaching as a key area for the public good, as I have discussed this elsewhere (Walker and Boni 2013).

Nonetheless, the production and exchange of knowledge is also being reshaped in the face of increasing calls for what is described as 'impact' in the UK, that is, calls to how publicly funded research (knowledge production) makes a direct economic and social contribution, although it is not spelled out in what direction this contribution ought to be; in other words, impact is non-normative. Thus, in theory, an economic impact could be in the direction of redistribution or in the direction of consolidating private benefits. This does leave the concept open to reinterpretations in a human development direction. Here Brewer (2013: 151) is especially helpful in the argument he makes for the normative public value of social science (which includes the field of education studies) for its role in nurturing "a moral sentiment" and "shared responsibility for the future of humankind", directed to understanding and ameliorating unfair social conditions. He argues that social science develops and disseminates public values (trust, empathy, social solidarity, and so on) that support the betterment of society. If social science is understood as a public good, a normative interpretation of knowledge impacts should flow from this so that we are directed not to any old impact but impact that advances the public good and the policies and actions that support this. Without such an approach, impact, as Brewer explains, "is a deeper and deeper hole leading nowhere", whereas a normative public value argument "leads social science to engagement with our humanitarian future" (p. 157).

As Brewer also notes, this requires a different kind of social science. Moreover, public goods and the public good cannot be provided through market mechanisms or individual efforts only (important though the latter may be); they require public action, agency, and a different stance on the part of academics and students to fight for what is valuable about universities and their public-good contributions when so many policymakers are wilfully obtuse in their dealings with universities. The question is, are we in universities up to the challenge of advancing higher education for the public good and claiming a public good normative space for 'impact'? Whose public good do we have in mind? Do we care enough to find ways to act for the public good, whether locally, nationally, or internationally, when "globalising forces are channeling the voices of the world's citizens into ever narrower spaces" (Taylor 2008: xxv)? The challenge is considerable, but not impossible, to articulate a robust truth about universities and the public good.

Note

1 District Six in Cape Town was originally established as a socially mixed community of freed slaves, merchants, artisans, labourers and immigrants, with close geographical links to the city and the port. In 1966, it was declared a white area under the apartheid Group Areas Act of 1950; by 1982, the life of the community was over. 60,000 people were forcibly removed to outlying areas known as the Cape Flats, and their houses in District Six were flattened by bulldozers. The District Six Museum, established in December 1994, works with the memories of these experiences and with the history of forced removals more generally. See http://districtsix.co.za

References

Alcoff, L., 2002. Does the public intellectual have intellectual integrity? *Metaphilosophy* 33, 5, 521–534.
Bok, D., 2013. Higher Education Misconceived. http://www.project-syndicate.org/commentary/derek-bok-on-policymakers—misconceptions-of-the-role-of-higher-learning#uq4WaCcADpKpuw34.99

Boni, A., Walker, M. (Eds.), 2013. *Human Development and Capabilities. Reimagining the University of the Twenty-First Century.* Routledge, London.

Brewer, J., 2013. *The Public Value of the Social Sciences.* Bloomsbury, London.

Burawoy, M., 2009. *The Extended Case Method.* University of California Press, Berkeley.

Calhoun C., 2006. The university and the public good. *Thesis Eleven* 84, 7–43.

Calhoun, C., 2007. Social Science for Public Knowledge. Social Science Research Council. http://www.ssrc.org/publications/view/49173559-675F-DE11-BD80-001CC477E>

Castells, M., 2001. Universities as dynamic systems of contradictory functions. In: Muller, J., Cloete, N. and Badat, S. (Eds.) *Challenges of Globalisation. South African Debates with Manuel Castells.* HSRC, Pretoria.

De Swaan, A., Manor, J., Øyen, E., Reis, E.P., 2000. Elite perceptions of the poor: reflections for a comparative research project. *Current Sociology* 4, 1, 43–54.

Graham, I.D., Logan, J., Harrison, M.B., Straus, S.E., Tetroe, J., Caswell, W., Robinson, N., 2006. Lost in knowledge translation: time for a map. *Journal of Continuing Education in the Health Professions* 26, 13–24.

GUNI (Eds.), 2008. *Higher Education in the World.* Palgrave Macmillan, New York.

Habermas, J., 1989. *The Structural Transformation of the Public Sphere.* Polity, Cambridge.

Hall, M., 2007. Poverty, inequality and the university: poorest of the poor. Paper presented to Institute for the Humanities, University of Michigan, February.

Hall, M., 2009. New knowledge and the university. *Anthropology Southern Africa* 32, 1/2, 69–76.

Haq, Ul M., 1999. *Reflections on Human Development.* Second Edition. Oxford University Press, Delhi.

Holmwood, J. (Ed.), 2011. *A Manifesto for the Public University.* Bloomsbury Academic, London.

Leibowitz, B. (Ed.), 2012. *Higher Education and the Public Good.* SUNMedia, Stellenbosch.

Lobera, J., Scrigas, C., 2009. New dynamics for social responsibility. In: GUNI (Eds.) *Higher Education at a Time of Transformation.* Palgrave Macmillan, Basingstoke.

Marginson, S., 2006. Putting "public" back into the public university. *Thesis Eleven* 84, 44–59.

Morrow, W., 2009. *Bounds of Democracy: Epistemological Access in Higher Education.* HSRC Press, Pretoria.

Naidoo, R., 2010. Global learning in a neoliberal age: implications for development. In: Unterhalter, E. and Carpentier, V. (Eds.) *Whose Interests Are We Serving? Global Inequalities and Higher Education.* Palgrave, New York.

Nixon, J., 2011. *Higher Education and the Public Good.* Continuum, London.

Nussbaum, M., 2000. *Women and Human Development.* Cambridge University Press, Cambridge.

Nussbaum, M., 2004. Women's education: a global challenge. *Signs* 29, 2, 325–355.

Nussbaum, M., 2010. *Not for Profit.* Princeton University Press, Princeton.

Nussbaum, M., 2011. *Creating Capabilities. The Human Development Approach.* Belknap Press, Cambridge, MA.

Sall, E., Lebeau, Y., Kassimir, R., 2003. The public dimensions of the university in Africa. *Journal of Higher Education in Africa* 1, 1, 126–148.

Samuelson, P.A., 1954. The pure theory of public expenditure. *The Review of Economics and Statistics* 36, 4, 387–389.

Sen, A., 1999. *Development as Freedom.* Oxford University Press, Oxford.

Sen, A., 2009. *The Idea of Justice.* Allen Lane, London.

Singh, M., 2010. Re-orienting internationalisation in African higher education. *Globalisation, Societies and Education* 8, 2, 269–282.

Stiglitz, J.E., 2003. Knowledge as a global public good. In: Kaul, I., Grunberg, I. and Stern, M. (Eds.) *Global Public Goods: International Cooperation in the 21st Century.* Oxford University Press, Oxford.

Taylor, P., 2008. Introduction. In: GUNI (Eds.) *Higher Education in the World.* Palgrave Macmillan, New York.

UNESCO, 2003. *General Report by Mr Jacques Proulx, the Meeting of Higher Education Partners.* UNESCO, Paris, June.

UNESCO, 2009. *Trends in Global Higher Education: Tracking an Academic Revolution.* UNESCO, Paris.

Walker, M., Boni, S., 2013. Higher education and human development: towards the public and social good. In: Boni, A. and Walker, M. (Eds.) *Human Development and Capabilities. Reimagining the University of the Twenty-First Century.* Routledge, London.

Walker, M., McLean, M., 2013. *Professional Education, Capabilities and the Public Good.* Routledge, London.

24

MEANING, RATIONALES AND TENSIONS IN THE INTERNATIONALISATION OF HIGHER EDUCATION[1]

Jane Knight

The international dimension of higher education has been active for centuries through academic cooperation among universities and the mobility of scholars and knowledge around the world. The fact that 'universe' is the root concept for university is clear evidence of its internationality. But the priorities and strategies of internationalisation have twisted and turned over the years in response to the environment in which it operates. There is little doubt that the current age of globalisation has had a profound impact on higher education and especially the process of internationalisation.

As we progress into the 21st century, the international dimension of higher education is becoming increasingly important and at the same time more complex. The changing dynamics of internationalisation are contributing to the current state of turmoil in the higher education sector (Knight 2008a). During the last decade, there have been new actors, new rationales, new programs, new regulations, and new developments in international higher education. Internationalisation has become a formidable force for change, as the following developments and initiatives in higher education demonstrate:

- Development of new international networks and consortia
- The growing numbers of students, professors and researchers participating in academic mobility schemes
- Increases in the number of courses, programmes and qualifications that focus on comparative and international themes
- More emphasis placed on developing international/intercultural and global competencies
- Stronger interest in international themes and collaborative research
- A growing number of academic programmes delivered across borders
- Decreasing interest in international cooperation
- More interest and concern with international and regional rankings of universities
- An increase in campus-based extracurricular activities with an international or multicultural component
- Increased attention given to recruiting fee-paying foreign students

- Rising numbers of joint and double degree programmes
- Growth in the number and types of for-profit, cross-border education providers
- Expansion of partnerships, franchises and branch campuses
- Creation of international education hubs, education cities and gateways
- Establishment of new national, regional and international organisations focused on international education
- Greater attention being given to regionalisation through alignment and recognition of national education systems and policies.

As internationalisation adapts to meet new challenges, it is important to examine the key concepts; the driving rationales at individual, institutional, national and regional levels; and the current tensions that inform, shape and challenge the internationalisation process.

The confusion and complexity of 'internationalisation'

Internationalisation is a term that means different things to different people. While it is encouraging to see the increased use and attention being given to the term, there is a great deal of confusion about what internationalisation means.

For some people, it means a series of international activities such as academic mobility for students and teachers; international networks, partnerships and projects; new international academic programmes; and research initiatives. For others, it means delivering education to other countries through new types of arrangements such as branch campuses or franchises using a variety of face-to-face and distance techniques like MOOCs. To many, it means including an international, intercultural and/or global dimension into the curriculum and teaching-learning process. Still others see internationalisation as a means to improve to recruit the best and brightest international students and scholars. International development projects have traditionally been perceived as part of internationalisation, but more recently it seems that 'status building' has become as or even more important than 'capacity building'. The development of education hubs, zones, hotspots, education cities and knowledge villages is also being attributed to the internationalisation process. Finally, internationalisation is being linked more and more to national geopolitical interests and for some countries is seen as an instrument of soft power rather than a form of diplomacy to further international engagement.

Clearly, internationalisation is interpreted and used to describe a vast array of issues, strategies and new developments around the world, yet there is concern that internationalisation is becoming a catchall concept for anything that is related to the international dimension of higher education. Perhaps the elasticity of the concept may have stretched too far when internationalisation is described or interpreted as international league tables (Knight 2012). The current obsession by higher education institutions around the world about their global standing and brand is a sign of the times. Definitely, there is an appetite for international and regional rankings of institutions, but one needs to question whether this is part of the internationalisation process or part of an international marketing and public relations campaign – two very different approaches.

In addition to questions about definition, other important issues are being raised about internationalisation. What is the purpose of internationalisation? What are the expected benefits or outcomes? What are the values that underpin it? What are the positive consequences, unintended results and negative implications? What is the past, current and future role of international higher education and international development? Are there new risks attached to internationalisation? How are institutions and policymakers responding to the competing interests within the domain of internationalisation? How are governments and NGOs addressing the issue and moving forward? Are for-profit and nonprofit internationalisation strategies compatible? Does internationalisation have a role in brain drain, homogenisation/ hybridisation of culture, or international labor mobility? Clearly, there are important issues and questions to address. As the internationalisation agenda changes, these questions and tensions require close scrutiny.

Defining internationalisation

'Internationalisation' as a term is not new, nor is the debate over its meaning. Internationalisation has been used for years in political science and government, but its popularity in the education sector has really soared only since the early 1980s. Prior to this time, 'international education' and 'international cooperation' were favoured terms and still are in some countries. In the 1990s, discussions on terminology centred on differentiating 'international education' from such overlapping terms as 'comparative education,' 'global education,' and 'multicultural education.' But today, more than two decades later, the relationships and nuances of meaning among 'cross-border,' 'transnational,' 'borderless' and 'international' modes of education are more common and cause much confusion.

The purpose in trying to develop a clear and somewhat comprehensive definition for internationalisation is to help clarify the confusion and misunderstanding that currently exists.

The challenge in defining internationalisation is the need for it to be generic enough to apply to many different countries, cultures and education systems. This is no easy task. While it is not necessarily the intention, or even appropriate, to develop a universal definition, it is imperative that there is a common understanding in a broad range of contexts and for comparative purposes across countries and regions of the world. With this in mind, it is important to ensure that a definition does not specify the rationales, benefits, outcomes, actors, activities and stakeholders of internationalisation, as they vary enormously across nations and also from institution to institution. Higher education needs to be alert to the negative implications of internationalisation becoming an instrument of standardisation by carefully defining rationales, strategies and major actors. What is critical is that the international dimension relates to all aspects of education and the role that it plays in society. A universally used working definition of internationalisation is "the process of integrating an international, intercultural or global dimension into the purpose, functions or delivery of higher education" (Knight 2004: 9). While it is already a decade old, it remains relevant as it does not identify the complex array of rationales, strategies or actors involved in the internationalisation process, thus respecting local context and priorities around the world.

This definition of internationalisation is intentionally neutral, although no matter what definition is used, politicians and higher education leaders often use internationalisation as a politicised instrument. Many would argue that the process of internationalisation should be described in terms of promoting cooperation and solidarity among nations, improving quality and relevance of higher education, or contributing to the advancement of research on international issues. While these are noble intentions and internationalisation can contribute to these goals, a definition needs to be objective enough that it can be used to describe a phenomenon that is, in fact, universal but has different purposes and outcomes, depending on the actor or stakeholder and the country/regional context.

A significant development in the conceptualisation of internationalisation in the last five years has been the introduction of the terms 'internationalisation at home' and 'cross-border education'. Campus-based strategies are most often referred to as internationalisation 'at home', and off-campus initiatives are called 'crossborder education'. As a result of the heightened emphasis on international academic mobility, institutions have developed the 'at home' concept to give greater prominence to campus-based elements such as the intercultural and international dimension in the teaching-learning process, research, extracurricular activities, relationships with local cultural and ethnic community groups, and the integration of foreign students and scholars into campus life and activities. The internationalisation process consists of these two separate but closely linked and interdependent pillars (Knight 2008a). Thus cross-border education has significant implications for campus-based internationalisation and vice versa.

Cross-border education implies mobility, but it is no longer just the students who are moving. While students and scholars constitute the first generation of education mobility, academic programs, institutions, alternative providers and policies are also crossing borders. In fact, there has been an exponential growth in branch campuses, twinning programmes and double/joint degree programmes in the last two decades. More recently, the third generation of academic mobility has emerged with the development of education hubs, zones and cities. The purpose of Table 24.1 is to summarise the highlights of the three generations. Worth noting is that these generations are not mutually exclusive.

Table 24.1 Three generations of cross-border education

Cross-border education	Primary focus	Description
First generation	**People mobility – students and faculty** Movement of students to foreign country for education purposes. Movement of faculty for teaching, research and other academic purposes	Full degree program or for short-term study research, field work, internships exchange programs faculty sabbaticals
Second generation	**Program and provider mobility** Movement of programs or institutions/companies across jurisdictional borders for delivery of education	*Program mobility* Twinning Franchised Articulated/Validated Joint/Double Award Online/Distance/MOOCs *Provider mobility* *Branch Campus* *Virtual University* *Merger/Acquisition* *Independent Institutions* *Cofounded Institutions*
Third generation	**Education hubs** Countries attract foreign students, researchers, workers, programs, providers, R&D companies for education, training, knowledge production, innovation purposes	*Student hub* – students, program, providers move to foreign country for education purposes *Talent hub* – students, workers move to foreign country for education and training and employment purposes *Knowledge/Innovation hub* – education researchers, scholars, HEIs, R&D centres move to foreign country to produce knowledge and innovation

Rationales driving internationalisation

The necessity of having clear, articulated rationales for internationalisation cannot be overstated. Rationales are the driving force for why an institution, country, or region (or any other actor) want to address and invest in internationalisation. Rationales are reflected in the policies and programs that are developed and eventually implemented. Rationales dictate the kind of benefits or expected outcomes. Without a clear set of rationales – accompanied by a set of objectives or policy statements, an implementation plan, and a monitoring/evaluation system – the process of internationalisation is often an ad hoc, reactive and fragmented response to the overwhelming number of new international opportunities available.

The motivations and realities driving internationalisation are undergoing fundamental changes (Altbach and Knight 2007). Traditionally, rationales have been presented in four groups: social/cultural, political, academic and economic (Knight and de Wit 1999). This provides a useful macro view, but, as internationalisation becomes widespread and complex, a more nuanced set of motives is necessary. Furthermore, it is important to distinguish between rationales at different levels of actors/stakeholders, especially individual, institutional, national and regional levels. Table 24.2 juxtaposes the four categories of rationales first defined in the late 1990s with those most prominent as of 2014 according to four levels of actors/stakeholders.

There is ample evidence to show that the increasing diversity of rationales, strategies and actors involved in the internationalisation process has introduced new complexities and tensions

Table 24.2 Change in rationales driving internationalisation

Four categories of rationales (1999)	*Levels of rationales (2015)*
Academic	**Individual level**
International dimension to research and teaching	Develop worldview
Extension of academic horizon	Enhance career
Institution building	Intercultural understanding and skills
Profile and status	Knowledge of national/international issues
Enhancement of quality	Develop international network
International academic standards	**Institutional level**
Economic	International branding and profile
Revenue generation	Student and staff development
Competitiveness	Strategic alliances
Labour market	Knowledge production
Financial incentives	Income generation
Political	**National level**
Foreign policy	Human resources/skill development
National security	Increased access to higher education
Technical assistance	Commercial trade
Peace and mutual understanding	Nation building
National identity	Social cultural development
Regional identity	Diplomacy and soft power
Social	**Regional level**
National cultural identity	Alignment of national systems
Intercultural understanding	Regional identity
Citizenship development	Geo-political alliances
Social and community development	Regional competitiveness

in the higher education sector and beyond to other sectors such as international relations, immigration, industry, labour, science and technology. The following section identifies and examines these ongoing and emerging tensions and categorises them into three main groups. The categories are not mutually exclusive but help to illustrate that tensions impact institutions and the higher education sector itself, as well as countries/ regions. These tensions are what shape and transform the very essence of higher education, in both positive and negative ways.

Tensions in the internationalisation of higher education

Institutional/individual level tensions

Status and profile: world rankings of higher education institutions

There is no question that international and regional rankings of universities have become more popular and problematic in the last five years (Hazelkorn 2011; Horn et al. 2007). The heated debate about their validity, reliability and value continues. But at the same time, university presidents appear to use them to structure priorities, declaring in their strategic plans that a measurable outcome of internationalisation will be the achievement of a higher rank in one or more of the global league tables. Some institutions perceive internationalisation as a means to gain a worldwide profile and prestige. The intense competition for world rankings would have been impossible to imagine a mere 20 years ago, when international collaboration among universities, through academic exchanges and development cooperation projects, was the norm. Of course, these types of activities still take place, but the factors influencing internationalisation are becoming increasingly complex, and the process is becoming increasingly competitive. Is international cooperation and exchange becoming overshadowed by competition for status, bright students, talented faculty, research grants, and membership in networks? The answer is probably yes, especially for those universities already placed in the top 25 percent of their national league tables or the two international ranking systems developed by Shanghai Jiao Tong University and Times Higher Education. Asia is one region of the world that takes competitiveness and rankings very seriously (Mok 2007). National programmes, such the 211 and 985 projects in China or the Brain Korea 21, aim to help their best research universities improve their international rankings (Kim and Nam 2007; Liu 2007).

The concept of 'world-class universities' is a subject of intense scrutiny (Altbach and Balan 2007), but 'world-class' is still in the eye of the beholder, in spite of all the attention being given to rankings. National, regional, international and discipline/profession-specific rankings allow self-appointed ranking bodies, whether they be magazines, consumer guides, universities, newspapers or private companies, to make judgments about the 'prestige' of universities and other institutions of higher learning. But in spite of rhetoric about the 'hollowness' of the ranking game, the competition among institutions hoping to be ranked as 'world-class' is increasing, not diminishing.

Student access

Does internationalisation through cross-border education programme and provider mobility help countries satisfy the growing demand for higher and continuing education? Many would answer yes and that increased access for students is a driving motivation for all forms of cross-border education (Wilkins and Huisman 2010). But the critical issue of equity of access and whether it will be available only to those who can afford it or have the language skills (primarily

English) prevails. No precise data exists on the rate of participation of students in cross-border programmes at the national or international levels. Only a handful of countries around the world collect reliable data on enrolments in cross-border education programmes, although this situation is improving. Thus, there is inconclusive evidence as to whether cross-border education in the form of programme and provider mobility is a successful and sustainable way to increase access to higher education for the general cohort of students wanting higher education.

Capacity building through cross-border education

It is clear that cross-border education can be considered a double-edged sword. On the one hand, it can increase access for local students and in many cases regional students. On the other hand, by importing foreign programmes and providers, one can question the relevancy of the curriculum to local context and needs. More importantly, it often does not help domestic higher education institutions and faculty to design and offer the programmes themselves. Critics of cross-border education believe that relying on foreign expertise to prepare and teach courses for local populations introduces tensions related to dependency, sometimes neocolonisation, and also sustainability.

The critical role of intercultural competence for academic staff and students

One of the key factors involved in the success and sustainability of international education and research partnerships is effective and respectful communication and shared decision making. While this may be obvious, it is not always evident in the relationship. Many reasons account for this. The motivations driving the education partnership are not always academic in nature and, second, the intercultural competence of academics is often limited. This is a particular challenge with senior professors and scholars who believe that knowledge of the discipline and research area is the number one priority and that 'science' is an international language, thereby diminishing the importance of what is perceived to be the soft skill of intercultural competence. This is an ongoing risk and challenge in international education partnerships.

In terms of the design and delivery of collaborative education programmes, the situation of intercultural competence is more critical and complex. There are multiple challenges involved in designing appropriate curriculum, but a more fundamental factor is the intercultural dimension of teaching/learning in multicultural situations. Not only do you have faculty coming from different cultural, linguistic and disciplinary backgrounds; the same is true for the students. To complicate matters further, the language of instruction is often not the native tongue of the instructors or learners. Thus, the role of intercultural awareness and competence is as important in the teaching/learning process as the recognition of cultural norms and practices in the design of curriculum. While there is increasing awareness of the intercultural realities and challenges in education partnerships, the importance attached to this issue and the professional development opportunities available for staff to improve their intercultural competence are unfortunately limited.

Double and joint degrees – twice the benefit or double counting?

Improvement in the quality of research, the teaching-learning process, and curriculum has long been heralded as a positive outcome of international collaboration. Through exchange of good practice, shared curricular reform, close research cooperation, and mobility of professors/students, there is much to be gained through internationalisation. Recently, joint programmes have been established between institutions in different countries, leading to double or multiple degrees, and in some cases to joint degrees, although the latter face steeper legal constraints (EUA 2004). Joint programmes are intended to provide a rich international and comparative academic experience for students and to improve their opportunities for employment (Kuder and Obst 2009), but questionable adaptations and unintended consequences have also resulted. For instance, in some cases, double degrees can be nothing more than double counting one set of course credits. In some cases, participating institutions have conferred two or even three credentials (one from each participating institution) for little more than the work load required for one degree.

While it may be very attractive for students to have two degrees from two institutions in two different countries, some might describe the situation as academic fraud if course requirements for two full degrees are not completed or if differentiated learning outcomes are not achieved (Knight 2008c). It is important to add that there are many excellent and innovative joint and double degree programmes being offered, especially by European institutions, given the priority these programmes have in the Bologna process. However, one of the unanticipated consequences has been the misuse or abuse of this new internationalisation initiative. In cases where these programmes span two or more jurisdictions, more work on the quality assurance and credential recognition is necessary because these programmes can be exempt from national regulations.

Higher education system or sector level

Internationalisation and the knowledge economy

There is no question that universities play a central role in the new knowledge enterprise. Countries hoping to become regional education hubs or to develop education cities see private education providers and branch campuses of foreign universities as key partners. While these initiatives include first-generation cross-border strategies like branch campuses and franchised programmes, they also include projects of another magnitude, such as colocating a critical mass of foreign universities with private companies, research and development enterprises, and science and technology parks to collectively support and develop new knowledge industries. The emergence of education hubs and cities is concrete proof that higher education is gaining more importance and influence as an economic and political actor in the burgeoning knowledge era – but at what cost?

International education cities and hubs represent new territory for the higher education sector. That being said, it is important to recognise that the higher education sector is not always the sponsor of these new education initiatives. In many cases, branch campuses of foreign institutions are seen as tenants in huge, multifaceted complexes just like any other commercial enterprise. Economic development boards, tourism authorities, science and technology parks, and multinational investment companies see higher education institutions and providers as key players in the preparation of future knowledge workers and the production of new knowledge. No matter how distasteful many academics will find the treatment of education as a commodity, the development of these hubs and education cities are positive proof that education is seen as a commodity to be used for developing the required human capital to gain a competitive advantage in the knowledge economy.

Cultural diversity or homogenisation?

Debates on the impact of new forms of international academic mobility on cultural diversity often provoke strong positions and sentiments. Some take a positive view of the ways that modern information and communication technologies and the movement of people, ideas and culture across national boundaries promote the fusion and hybridisation of culture. Others contend that these same forces are eroding national cultural identities and leading to cultural homogenisation and tensions, most often in the form of Westernisation.

These arguments have often centred on education and its traditional role as a vehicle of acculturation, at times focusing on the specifics of curriculum content, language of instruction (particularly the increase in English) and the teaching-learning process in international education. Research has long focused on the impact of historic forms of colonisation on education, but the place of internationalisation in contemporary processes of cultural change has not been sufficiently studied.

Internationalisation of higher education was originally conceived in terms of exchange and sharing of ideas, cultures, knowledge and values. Formalised academic relations between countries were normally expressed in bilateral cultural and scientific agreements. Today, the agreements often must take trade, economic, and political factors into account, representing a significant shift from the original idea of academic exchange. Thus, there are two factors at play here: one is the potential for cultural homogenisation, which may be perceived as threatening, and the second is the weakening of the cultural exchange component of internationalisation in favour relationships based more on economic and political concerns.

Commodification and commercialisation: for-profit internationalisation

The General Agreement on Trade in Services (GATS) has been a wake-up call for higher education around the world. Higher education has traditionally been seen as a 'public good' and a 'social responsibility' (Knight 2008b). But with the advent of this new international trade agreement, higher education has become a tradable commodity or, more precisely in GATS terms, an internationally tradable service. Many see GATS as presenting new opportunities and benefits while others see it as introducing new risks. Others question why the trade sector needs to impose regulations at all; the education sector has been using its own agreements and conventions for decades.

At the heart of the debate for many educators is the impact of increased commercial cross-border education on the purpose, role and values of higher education. The growth in new commercial and private providers, the commodification of education and the implications of new trade-policy frameworks have stimulated serious reflection on the role, social commitment and funding of public higher education institutions in society. Universities have traditionally combined teaching, research and service as they seek to evolve and contribute to national development. Is this combination still valid, or can these roles be disaggregated and rendered by different providers?

Finally, how will commercialisation change the incentives for institutions to internationalise? Currently, one of the leading rationales at the institutional level for internationalisation is that it makes graduates more internationally knowledgeable and interculturally skilled and prepares them to live and work in more culturally diverse communities. Institutions must ask how an increased emphasis on the 'buying and selling' of education across borders will affect the nature and priority given to academic, social and cultural rationales of nonprofit international education activities (Altbach and Knight 2007).

Is the quality of new cross-border education being assured?

A decade ago, the Singapore Ministry of Trade and Industry estimated that the higher education sector is a $2.2 trillion market (MTI 2003). Furthermore, it is forecasted that by 2025 the demand for international education will grow to 7.2 million students – a quantum leap from 1.2 million students in 2000 (Bohm et al. 2002). These staggering figures illustrate the magnitude of the interest in international education. Some, but certainly not all, of this demand will be met by student mobility. Consequently, the number of new providers, such as commercial companies and nongovernmental entities, that deliver programmes to students in their home countries is accelerating at an unprecedented rate. It is no longer just students, faculty, researchers who are internationally mobile; academic degree/diploma programmes are being delivered across borders, and branch campuses are being established in developing and developed countries around the world. While these new developments are intended to increase access to higher education and meet the appetite for foreign credentials, there are serious issues related to the quality of the academic offer, the integrity of the new types of providers and the recognition of credentials (Vincent-Lancrin 2004).

In the last decade, increased importance has been given to quality assurance at the institutional and national levels. New regional quality networks have also been established. The primary task of these groups has been quality recognition and assurance of domestic higher education provision by public and private higher education institutions. However, the increase in cross-border education by institutions and new private commercial providers has introduced a new challenge (and gap) in the field of quality assurance. Historically, national quality assurance agencies have generally not focused their efforts on assessing the quality of imported and exported programmes. The question now facing the field of quality assurance is how to deal with the increase in cross-border education, delivered both by traditional higher education institutions and also by new private commercial and noninstitutional providers who have not historically been addressed by nationally based quality assurance projects.

Recognition of qualifications

Increased academic mobility raises the issue of credential recognition to a more prominent place in international education policy. The credibility of higher education programmes and qualifications is extremely important for students, their employers, the public at large and for the academic community itself. It is critical that the qualifications awarded by cross-border providers are legitimate and will be recognised for employment or further studies both at home and abroad. To establish a credential review and assessment agency is still a challenge facing many countries of the world, especially in developing countries.

The internationalisation and commercialisation of accreditation

The increased awareness of the need for quality assurance and/or accreditation has led to several new developments in accreditation, which have had both positive and negative aspects. Before discussing these developments, it is important to acknowledge the efforts of many countries to establish criteria and procedures for quality assurance recognition systems and approving accreditors. At the same time, it is necessary to recognise the increase in self-appointed and rather self-serving accreditors, as well as accreditation mills that sell 'bogus' accreditation labels.

As higher education becomes increasingly subject to market forces, the profile and reputation of a given institution or provider are more and more important. Institutions are making major investments in marketing and branding campaigns in order to gain name recognition and increase enrolments. Accreditation is part of the overall campaign and assures prospective students that the programmes are of high standing. The desire for accreditation status is leading to the commercialisation of quality assurance and accreditation, as programmes and providers strive to gain as many accreditation 'stars' as possible in order to increase competitiveness and perceived international legitimacy. Prospective students are challenged to distinguish between bona fide and rogue accreditors, especially when neither the cross-border provider nor the accreditor is nationally based or recognised as part of a national higher education system.

At the same time, networks of institutions and new organisations have appointed themselves as accreditors of their members. These are positive developments when seen through the lens of trying to improve the quality of their academic programmes. But there is concern that they are not totally objective in their assessments and may be more interested in generating income than improving quality. While this can apply to both cross-border and domestic programmes, it is particularly worrisome for cross-border programs, as attention to national policy objectives and cultural orientation is often neglected by foreign accreditors.

The growth of foreign degree mills (selling 'parchment-only' degrees), accreditation mills (selling bogus accreditations for programs or institutions) and rogue for-profit providers (not recognised by national authorities) is a reality of which students, parents, employers and the academic community now need to aware (Garrett 2005).

Who would have guessed two decades ago that international education would be struggling to deal with fake degrees and accreditations, that academic credentials would sometimes be earned but not recognised, and that nonregulated 'fly-by-night' institutions would be blights on the international education scene? Of course, one must also acknowledge innovative developments by bona fide new providers and traditional universities who are delivering high-quality programs and legitimate degrees through new types of arrangements and partnerships (franchise, twinning, double degree and branch campus to name a few). The perpetual tension of balancing cost, quality and access bring into question the potential benefits and risks of cross-border education.

National and regional level

Human, social and cultural development

The potential of higher education's contribution to national development remains underdeveloped and often misunderstood. In today's globalised world, which prioritises economic growth through liberalised trade and competitive market strategies, much emphasis has been placed on higher education's ability to produce graduates to serve the labour market and produce new knowledge for the knowledge economy. While these are important contributions, the role and responsibilities of higher education to address human development and social, cultural, health, environmental and governance issues should not be neglected. New knowledge produced and applied to these areas of development is crucial and should not be ignored in favour of knowledge for economic and competitiveness purposes only.

The brain train

Twenty-five years ago, we could not have anticipated that international academic mobility for students, scholars and professors would have the potential to grow into a highly competitive, international recruitment business. Today, several countries such as Australia, the UK, and Germany are investing in major marketing campaigns to attract the best and brightest talent to study and work in their institutions. The need to meet the heavy demand from government and private industry for human resources to achieve innovation and research agendas is a major driver (Agarwal et al. 2007). The original goal of helping students from developing countries move to another country to complete a degree and return home is fading fast as nations compete for retaining brain power.

While 'brain drain' and 'brain gain' are well-known concepts, research is showing a more complex picture. International students and researchers are increasingly interested in earning multiple degrees in multiple countries, before perhaps returning to their home countries after eight to 12 years of international study and work experience. Hence, the emergence of the term 'brain train'. These various 'brain circulation' concepts present benefits, risks and new challenges for both sending and receiving countries, but the term tends to whitewash the potential negative consequences for countries that lost significant numbers of qualified people. The concept of 'brain chain' is perhaps more appropriate. It captures the movement of brains but acknowledges that those countries at the bottom of the brain chain are net losers and suffer from the exodus of a talented workforce. Higher education is becoming a more important actor in policymaking and is now working in closer collaboration with immigration, industry and the science and technology sectors to build an integrated strategy for attracting and retaining knowledge workers.

Education hubs – a fad, a brand, an innovation?

Education hubs represent the third generation of cross-border activities emerging onto the landscape of our more globalised world. The term 'education hub' is being used by countries who are trying to position themselves as centres for student recruitment, education and training, and in some cases research and innovation. Education hubs, at the country, zone or city levels, are full of lofty expectations and fraught with potential challenges. They can be seen as instruments of modernisation, competitiveness, knowledge economy, soft power and other benefits. But are education hubs sustainable? Are the required plans, policies and investments in place? Is there a critical mass of local and international actors working together and committed for the long term? Or is the term education hub a new label for international student recruitment plans and campaigns? Is the notion of education hub just a fad, more rhetoric than reality, more of a public relations campaign to gain profile and status (Knight 2014a)?

International higher education and the MDGs

The relationship between higher education, the international dimension and MDGs is linked to the broader debates around higher education and development. A basic premise is that higher education in general, and its international dimension in particular, can play a central role in strengthening and sustaining the overall social, human, cultural and economic growth of developing countries, particularly with respect to advancing progress towards achieving the Millennium Development Goals (MDGs). Developing countries face diverse challenges, and higher education institutions have always been depended upon to provide solutions through research that has practical applications and relevance for social, health, economic, environment, education and other key areas. Second, higher education is considered to be an effective way to develop human resource capacity through formal, informal and nonformal education and training programmes. Third, higher education can partner with governmental and nongovernmental bodies, locally and internationally, to develop necessary policies and programmes as well as mobilise resources to address the challenges posed by the MDGs (Sehoole and Knight 2013). To date, the direct contribution of higher education's international dimensions to meeting the MDGs has been limited and not reached full potential. Is it a matter of priorities? Has economic development overshadowed and usurped higher education's social responsibility? Can economic, social and human development be framed as mutually reinforcing goals?

International education as a tool for diplomacy or soft power

Soft power is on the lips of scholars, policymakers and education leaders alike. Developed by Joseph Nye about a decade ago, the concept is popularly understood as the ability to influence others and achieve national self-interest(s) through attraction and persuasion rather than through coercion, military force or economic sanctions – commonly known as hard power (Nye 2004).

International higher education has been drawn to this new concept of soft power like bees to honey. Witness the number of references to it in conferences, academic journals, blogs and media articles in the last five years. Many hail it as a fundamental premise of today's international education engagement. Some treat it like a modern branding campaign using culture and media to win over foreign publics, especially students. Others interpret it as a form of neocolonisation. And there are those who see attraction and persuasion as a way to build trust because trust can pay dividends in terms of economic and geopolitical benefits. In short, the role and use of soft power is interpreted in a myriad of ways. But a common motivation is to achieve self-interests through attraction, whether the benefits be political, economic, reputation or overall competitiveness. After all, the basic notion of power is about gaining some kind of dominance, whether it uses soft, hard or smart means. This reality raises hard questions. Are the primary goals of international higher education to serve self-interests and gain dominance, or is international education an instrument of diplomacy to further bilateral and multilateral engagement and collaboration (Knight 2014b)?

Looking to the future

This discussion has shown without a shadow of a doubt that internationalisation has come of age. No longer is it an ad hoc or marginalised part of the higher education landscape. University strategic plans, national policy statements, regionalisation initiatives, international declarations and academic articles all indicate the centrality of internationalisation in the world of higher education.

But, it is prudent to take a close look at the policies, plans and priorities of the key actors, such as universities, government ministries, national/regional/international academic associations and international government agencies. These documents reveal that internationalisation of education and research is closely linked with economic and innovation competitiveness, the great brain race, the quest for world status and soft power. Economic and political rationales are increasingly the key drivers for national policies related to the international higher education, while academic and social/cultural motivations appear to be decreasing in importance.

Recent national and worldwide surveys of university internationalisation priorities and rationales show that establishing an international profile or global standing is seen to be more important that reaching international standards of excellence or improving quality. Capacity building through international cooperation and development is being replaced by status-building projects to gain world-class recognition. International student mobility is now big business and becoming more closely aligned to recruitment of brains for national science and technology agendas. Some private and public education institutions are lowering academic standards and transforming into visa factories in response to immigration priorities and revenue generation imperatives. More international academic projects and partnerships are becoming commercialised and profit driven, as are international accreditation services. Diploma mills and rogue providers are selling bogus qualifications and causing havoc for international qualification recognition. Awarding two degrees from institutions located in different countries based on the workload for one degree is being promoted through some rather dubious double degree programmes. And all of this is in the name of internationalisation?

Who could have forecasted that internationalisation would transform from what has been traditionally considered a process based on values of cooperation, partnership, exchange, mutual benefits and capacity building to one that is increasingly characterised by competition, commercialisation, self-interest and status building? At the same time, there are countless examples of positive internationalisation initiatives that illustrate how internationalisation at home, cross-border education, and collaborative scholarship contribute to the development of individuals, institutions, nations and the world at large.

It may behove us to look back at the last 20 or 30 years of internationalisation and ask ourselves some questions. Has international higher education lived up to our expectations and its potential? What have been the values that have guided it through the information and communication revolution, the unprecedented mobility of people, ideas and technology; the clash of cultures; and the periods of economic booms and busts? What have we learned from the past that will guide us into the future? What are the core principles and values underpinning internationalisation of higher education that in 10 or 20 years from now will make us look back and be proud of the track record and contribution that international higher education has made to the more interdependent world we live in, the next generation of citizens, and the bottom billion people living in poverty?

Note

1 This paper updates and adapts Knight (2009).

References

Agarwal, P., Said, M., Sehoole C., Sirozie, M., de Wit, H., 2007. The dynamics of international student circulation in a global context. In: Altbach, P. and McGill Peterson, P. (Eds.) *Higher Education in the New Century: Global Challenges and Innovative Ideas.* Sense, Rotterdam.

Altbach, P., Balan, J. (Eds.), 2007. *World Class Worldwide: Transforming Research Universities in Asia and Latin America.* Johns Hopkins University Press, Baltimore.

Altbach, P., Knight, J., 2007. The internationalisation of higher education: motivations and realities. *Journal of Studies in International Education* 11, 3–4, 290–305.

Bohm A., Davis, D., Meares, D., Pearce, D., 2002. *The Global Student Mobility 2025 Report: Forecasts of the Global Demand for International Education.* IDP, Canberra.

European University Association, 2004. *Developing Joint Masters Programmes for Europe.* EUA, Brussels.

Garrett, R., 2005. Fraudulent, Sub-Standard, Ambiguous: The Alternative Borderless Higher Education. Briefing Note, July 2005 of the Observatory on Borderless Higher Education, London.

Hazelkorn, E., 2011. *Rankings and the Reshaping of Higher Education: The Battle for World Class Excellence.* Palgrave Macmillan, Basingstoke.

Horn, A., Hendel, D., Fry, G., 2007. Ranking the international dimension of top research universities in the United States. *Journal of Studies in International Education* 11, 3–4, 330–358.

Kim, K.S., Nam, S., 2007. The making of a world-class university at the periphery: Seoul National University. In: Altbach, P. and Balan, J. (Eds.) *World Class Worldwide: Transforming Research Universities in Asia and Latin America.* Johns Hopkins University Press, Baltimore.

Knight, J., 2004. Internationalisation remodeled: rationales, strategies and approaches. *Journal of Studies in International Education* 8, 1, 5–31.

Knight, J., 2008a. *Higher Education in Turmoil: The Changing World of Internationalisation.* Sense, Rotterdam.

Knight, J., 2008b. The role of crossborder education in the debate on education as a public good and private commodity. *Journal of Asian Public Policy* 1, 2, 174–188.

Knight, J., 2008c. *Double and Joint Degrees: Vexing Questions and Issues.* OBHE, London.

Knight, J., 2009. New developments and unintended consequences: whither thou goest, internationalization? In: Bhandari, R. and Laughlin, S. (Eds.) *Higher Education on the Move: New Developments in Global Mobility.* Institute for International Education, New York.

Knight, J., 2012. Concepts, rationales, and interpretive frameworks in the internationalisation of Higher Education. In: Deardoff, D., De Wit, H. and Heyl, J. (Eds.) *Handbook of International Higher Education.* Sage, Thousand Oaks.

Knight, J., 2014a. *International Education Hubs: Student, Talent, Knowledge/Innovation Models.* Springer, Dordrecht.

Knight, J., 2014b. The limits of soft power in higher education. *University World News,* 31 January 2014.

Knight, J., de Wit, H., 1999. *Quality and Internationalisation in Higher Education.* Programme on Institutional Management in Higher Education, OECD, Paris.

Kuder, M., Obst, D., 2009. *Joint and Double Degree Programs in the Transatlantic Context – A Survey Report.* Institute of International Education, Freie Universität, Berlin.

Liu, N., 2007. Research universities in China: differentiation, classification and future world-class status. In: Altbach, P. and Balan, J. (Eds.) *World Class Worldwide: Transforming Research Universities in Asia and Latin America.* Johns Hopkins University Press, Baltimore.

Ministry of Trade and Industry, 2003. Growing Our Economy. Singapore Government. http://app.mti.gov.sg/data/pages/507/doc/DSE_recommend.pdf

Mok, K.-H., 2007. Questing for internationalization of universities in Asia: critical reflections. *Journal of Studies in International Education* 11, 3–4, 433–454.

Nye, J.S., 2004. Soft power: the means to success in world politics. Public Affairs, New York.

Sehoole, C., Knight, J., 2013. *Internationalizing African Higher Education: Towards the MDGs.* Sense, Rotterdam.

Vincent-Lancrin, S., 2004. Implications of recent developments for access and equity, coast and funding, quality and capacity building. In: OECD (Eds.) *Internationalisation and Trade in Higher Education.* CERI, OECD, Paris.

Wilkins, S., Huisman, J., 2010. Student recruitment at international branch campuses: can they compete in the global market? *Journal of Studies in International Education* 15, 3, 299–316.

25

TRENDS, ISSUES AND CHALLENGES IN INTERNATIONALISATION OF HIGHER EDUCATION

Where have we come from and where are we going?

Hans de Wit and Fiona Hunter

Introduction

The international dimension in higher education is moving from margin to centre and assumes a more comprehensive rather than fragmented approach. This relatively new phenomenon has only become apparent since the beginning of the 21st century, but its roots lie in several manifestations of increased international orientations from the previous century, in particular in the period following the Second World War until the end of the Cold War.

In order to understand the current trends and issues in internationalisation of higher education, it is relevant to summarise first the historical international dimensions in higher education before examining the implications of globalisation on higher education and its international dimensions and the way in which cooperation and competition develop new and, at times, contradictory forms that can lead to unintended consequences, myths and misconceptions.

After having described the broader evolution of internationalisation in the context of globalisation, we will address two trends in the two key components of internationalisation: internationalisation abroad – mobility of students (degree and credit) and of programmes, projects and institutions (cross-border education); and internationalisation at home – curriculum, teaching and learning, learning outcomes and global citizenship. We will conclude with an examination of the challenges that universities face in defining a clear pathway for internationalisation as a higher education response to the current environment.

International dimensions over the past centuries

Universities have always had some form of international dimension, either in the concept of universal knowledge and related research or in the movement of students and scholars. Altbach

(1998: 347) identifies the university as the one institution that has always been global, while Kerr (1994: 6) states that universities "by nature of their commitment to advancing universal knowledge" are essentially international institutions, although "living, increasingly, in a world of nation-states that have designs on them."

Middle ages to 18th century

Many publications on the internationalisation of higher education refer back to the days of the Middle Ages and the period up to the end of the 18th century. At that time, in addition to religious pilgrims,

> [P]ilgrims or travellers (*peregrini*) of another kind were also a familiar sight on the roads of Europe. These were the university students and professors. Their pilgrimage (*peregrinatio*) was not to Christ's or a saint's tomb, but to a university city where they hoped to find learning, friends, and leisure.
>
> (de Ridder-Symoens 1992: 280)

Although academic pilgrimage started long before the 12th century, it became a common phenomenon at that time. As de Wit and Merkx (2012) observe, de Ridder-Symoens (1992) describes the impact of the mobility of students and scholars on higher education and society in that period in a way that reminds us of many of the arguments that are used to promote mobility today. De Ridder-Symoens states:

> The use of Latin as a common language, and of a uniform programme of study and system of examinations, enabled itinerant students to continue their studies in one "*stadium*" after another, and ensured recognition of their degrees throughout Christendom. Besides their academic knowledge they took home with them a host of new experiences, ideas, opinions, and political principles am views.
>
> (1992: 302–303)

Reading this, it comes as no surprise that the European Commission chose the name of Erasmus, one of the best-known wandering scholars of that period, for its most important mobility programme.

Because nations did not yet exist as political units, we can speak of a medieval "European space", defined by this common religious credence and uniform academic language, programme of study and system of examinations (Neave 1997: 6). This medieval European education space, while limited and scattered in comparison to present mass higher education, is relevant to the current debate on the development of a new European Higher Education Area. One expression is the gradual growth of the English language as the common academic language today, resembling the role of Latin, and in a later period also French, albeit more moderately. However, only a superficial resemblance and reference between the two periods is possible because of the very different social, cultural, political and economic circumstances.

Moreover, according to Scott (1998), we cannot call this notion of the university as an international institution anything more than a myth or symbolic expression, while Neave describes it as "a pleasant legend untroubled by the slightest relevance, save to the romantically inclined" (Neave 1997: 1). These historical references to the university as an essentially international institution ignore the fact that most universities originated in the 18th and 19th centuries with a clear national orientation and function (de Wit 2002: 3–18). De Wit and Merkx (2012: 44) note that "with the emergence of the nation-state, universities became de-Europeanised and nationalised". In several countries, study abroad was prohibited, and the universal language of instruction, Latin, was replaced by local languages. Scott (1998: 123) states that "paradoxically perhaps, before it became an international institution the university had first to become a national institution – just as internationalisation presupposes the existence of nation states". However, de Wit and Merkx (2012: 44–47) note that in the 18th and 19th centuries, there were three characteristics of higher education that could still be called *international*: dissemination of research, individual mobility of students and scholars and export of higher education systems. In that period according to Kerr (1994), Altbach (1998) and Scott (1998), "the focus of higher education was more directed to developing a national identity and serving national needs and less to amassing universal knowledge" (de Wit and Merkx 2012: 47).

The two World Wars

The period between the two world wars saw greater attention paid to international cooperation and exchange in higher education. The creation of organisations such as the *Institute of International Education* (IIE) in 1919 in the United States, the *Deutscher Akademischer Austauschdienst* (DAAD) in Germany in 1925, and the *British Council* in the UK in 1934 are illustrations of political initiatives to stimulate peace and mutual understanding under the umbrella of the *League of Nations*. This trend received further impetus after the Second World War, although first and foremost in the United States and primarily by the *Fulbright Programme*, given that Europe was still recovering from the devastation of two wars and concentrating its efforts on reconstruction.

US higher education and its position in the global higher education environment changed almost overnight following the Second World War, as described by Goodwin and Nacht (1991: 4–5): "From a cultural colony the nation was changed, at least in its own eyes, into the metropolis: from the periphery it moved triumphantly to the centre". And, as de Wit and Merkx (2012: 49) state, although peace and mutual understanding continued to be the declared driving rationale, "national security and foreign policy were the real forces behind its expansion, and with it came government funding and regulations." This was also stimulated by fierce competition between the United States and the Soviet Union with respect to North-South academic exchanges. Holzner and Greenwood (1995: 39) speak in that respect "of a chess game between the superpowers".

The Cold War was the principal rationale in the internationalisation of higher education in that period. It explains the dominance of national security and foreign policy as driving forces that stimulated area studies and foreign language programmes and provided increased attention to technical assistance and capacity building in developing countries.

1950s to today

Europe in the period 1950–1970 did not develop an active international higher education policy. Baron (1993: 50) describes the period as a "benevolent laissez-faire" open-door policy to foreign students and Chandler (1989: viii) as a passive policy of "humanitarianism and internationalism". But in the 1980s, a shift became apparent. As de Wit and Merkx (2012) describe:

> [T]he strengthening of the European Community and the rise of Japan as an economic world power challenged U.S. dominance, not only in the political and economic arenas but also in research and teaching. . . . In terms of internationalisation during this period, the international dimension of higher education began to move from the incidental

and individual into organised activities, projects, and programmes, based on political rationales and driven more by national governments than by higher education itself.

(pp. 52–53)

They agree with Kerr (1994: 50) who wrote that: "it has been to the advantage of nation-states to support the expansion of higher education and its internationalisation within and beyond their borders". It is in this period that internationalisation emerges as a process and strategy. Until then, it had not been recognised as such and the more common terms used were – and to a certain extent still are – 'international education' or terms related to specific activities such as study abroad, exchanges, academic mobility, multicultural education, area studies, etc. (de Wit 2013a: 18).[1]

In the 1990s, building on the initiatives by the European Commission of the 1980s such as ERASMUS and the Research Framework programmes, in which driving rationales were competitiveness with the United States and Japan and development of a European identity, we can observe a shift to purely economic rationales for internationalisation. Although after September 11, 2001, a renewed focus has since emerged on political rationales related to the war on terrorism, advocating the need to understand better Islamic culture and their languages, the principal driving force for internationalisation has now become economic. Income generation through recruitment of international students, global competition for talented students and scholars for the knowledge economy, increasing global professional competencies and employability of graduates, national demand for higher education through degree mobility and cross-border delivery of education, and capacity building through higher education are the diverse ways in which the economic rationale has changed and refocused the internationalisation of higher education in the past decade.

Globalisation and internationalisation

Scott (1998, 2005), Altbach (2006), van Vught, van der Wende and Westerheijden (2002), Knight (2008), Maringe and Foskett (2010), Jones and de Wit (2012) and Varghese (2013), among others, address the complex relationship between globalisation and internationalisation of higher education. According to Scott (2005: 14) "the distinction between internationalisation and globalisation, although suggestive, cannot be regarded as categorical. They overlap, and are intertwined, in all kinds of ways." Cantwell and Maldonado-Maldonado (2009: 304) speak of the distinction between "globalisation of higher education" and "internationalisation of higher education" as a common distinction in higher education but also one that is challenged by researchers and perceived as "theoretically unsatisfying".

Even though different interpretations are given by these and other authors, we can say that globalisation is a social, economic and political process to which higher education responds and in which it is also an actor. Internationalisation is the way in which higher education responds and acts. Knight (2008) states that:

> [G]lobalisation is the process that is increasing the flow of people, culture, ideas, values, knowledge, technology, and economy across borders, resulting in a more interconnected and interdependent world. . . . Education is one of the sectors impacted by globalisation.

(pp. x–xi)

Her definition of internationalisation as "the process of integrating an international, intercultural or global dimension into the purpose, functions or delivery of post-secondary education" is one that is widely accepted.

The broad interpretation of internationalisation under the impetus of globalisation, the shifting emphasis in rationales from social and political to economic, the move from cooperation to competition and the inclusion of new dimensions such as cross-border delivery of higher education have stimulated the emergence of different components, rationales and perceptions in an attempt to grasp better the different, sometimes even conflicting, dimensions of internationalisation.

In reaction to increased commercialisation in higher education and its international dimensions, some authors call for more attention to social cohesion and to the public role of higher education as an alternative force to the growing emphasis on competition, markets and entrepreneurialism in higher education. Naidoo and Jamieson (2005), for instance, state:

> The forces unleashed on higher education in the present context have propelled universities to function less as institutions with social, cultural and indeed intellectual objectives and more as producers of commodities that can be sold in the international marketplace.
>
> (p. 39)

Other authors describe the risk of the increased competitive dimension of international higher education for developing countries. Lesley Wilson (2013), Secretary General of the European Universities Association (EUA), observes:

> As the global pressure to develop knowledge societies accelerates, there is a risk that the gap between the developed and the developing countries will continue to widen. Brain drain, the large scale emigration of highly-skilled human capital, is a major concern to society at large, and for the higher education and research community. In spite of attempts to promote 'brain circulation', it will surely remain a major concern in the decades to come.
>
> (p. 33)

Jegede (2012) even goes so far to speak of the potential emergence of "slave trade in education". Mohamedbhai (2012) refers to the African case:

> Internationalisation is not new to African higher education. Indeed, it was through internationalisation that most African universities were created and developed. The majority of them were patterned on universities in countries of which they were former colonies. Most of their faculty were trained in universities in the North; the institutions with which they had the largest number of exchange programmes were located in the North, the curricula and programme structures of their degrees were similar to those in Northern universities, and all the institutions used a European language for instruction. Whether these universities were appropriate to Africa's social and economic development at the time is debatable. They were alienated from the rural areas where the majority of the population lived and where the development challenges were greatest. It has been argued that this was one of the reasons for the eventual decline of many African universities in the decades that followed.
>
> (p. 19)

It is perhaps then not surprising that, as Egron-Polak notes, there is increasing awareness of the risks internationalisation may bring:

> [B]rain-drain, cultural homogenisation, competition among higher education institutions as well as increased commercialisation continues to be attributed as possible

consequences of higher education internationalisation. They are seen by some as the risks of internationalisation, by others as collateral damage of the process.

(Egron-Polak 2012: 15)

Knight (2008) has written about other unintended consequences of internationalisation and (2011) about myths of internationalization, whilst de Wit (2011) addresses misconceptions of internationalisation. In the IAU Action Plan, *Affirmative Values for Internationalisation of Higher Education* (IAU 2012), attention is given to the risks and challenges of higher education alongside the benefits of internationalisation. In these critical assessments of the development of internationalisation, four points emerge: an overly quantitative approach; an almost exclusive focus on mobility for the sake of mobility alone; the lack of outcomes and impact assessment; and the notion of internationalisation as a goal in itself rather than a means to enhance the purpose, functions and delivery of higher education.

The "globalisation of internationalisation", as it is called by Jones and de Wit (2012), is a manifestation of the increasing importance of higher education in emerging and developing countries and regions. The sector in these countries is shifting from a reactive and 'Western' copied and dominated system into a more proactive sector of public and private universities that challenges 'Western' dominance and its way of internationalisation. An illustration is the fact that emerging economies are developing their own strategies and programmes for study abroad, such as the Science without Borders programme in Brazil, or for attracting international students, such as the targets set by several Asian countries for recruitment of international students. We also see more cases of intraregional cooperation and exchange between developing countries.

It is important that these new approaches to internationalisation should not be dominated by the traditional hegemony of 'Western' concepts and strategies but rather find the space to develop an autonomous and refreshing approach for emerging and developing countries and regions. Two aspects are central in that process: increased regional and South-South cooperation, and more attention to strategies that build on the social responsibility and civic engagement role of higher education in these regions.

Internationalisation: abroad and at home

Knight (2008) states that the following two components are evolving: (a) *internationalisation at home*: activities that help students develop international understanding and intercultural skills (curriculum oriented) and that prepare students to be active in a much more globalised world; and (b) *internationalisation abroad*: all forms of education across borders, including circulation of students, faculty, scholars, and programmes. It should be said, however, that these two components are closely intertwined.

In addition to this division into two components, Jones and de Wit (2012) make reference to other researchers who create alternative divisions in order to understand the complex evolution of internationalisation in higher education: between cooperation and competition (van der Wende 2001), between institutional and student-focused internationalisation (Jones and Brown 2007, Jones 2010), between internationalisation ideologies ("instrumentalism", "idealism", and "educationalism") (Stier 2010), and between "internationalisation of the curriculum" and "internationalisation at home" (Beelen 2007). Another division is between intercultural, international and global competences (Deardorff 2006).

A comprehensive approach to internationalisation, including abroad and at home, is provided in the Communication *European Higher Education in the World*, in which the European Commission (2013) is striving for a comprehensive internationalisation with three key pillars: promoting the international mobility of students and staff; promoting internationalisation at home and digital learning; and strengthening strategic cooperation, partnerships and capacity building. The inclusion of internationalisation at home is a recognition of the increasing importance of the large proportion of nonmobile students and staff and their needs for intercultural and international competences.

In order to explore further the recent developments in internationalisation, we will use Knight's division into components of internationalisation abroad and at home.

Internationalisation abroad

In recent decades, international students have become an important social and economic factor for higher education institutions, governments, cities and a range of other organisations connected to the "business of higher education". We can distinguish two main types of mobility of students: credit mobility undertaken as part of the home degree and degree mobility in which a student studies abroad for a whole degree (bachelor, master and/or PhD). Although much attention is focused on degree mobility, credit mobility is also an important dimension of internationalisation, for instance in programmes such as ERASMUS in Europe, the study abroad programmes in American higher education and recently in the Science without Borders programme in Brazil. A third more recent development is the mobility of programmes, projects and even institutions, referred to as transnational or cross-border education.

Degree mobility

The first decade of the 21st century has seen the number of globally mobile students almost double from 2.1 million in 2000 to 4.1 million in 2010, growing at an average annual rate of 7.2% (OECD 2012). It is forecast that the number will further increase to over 7 million in the next 10 years. These figures are based predominantly on degree mobility.

> Europe is the preferred destination for students studying outside their country, with 41% of all international students. North America has 21% of all international students. Nevertheless, the fastest growing regions of destination are Latin America and the Caribbean, Oceania and Asia, mirroring the internationalisation of universities in an increasing set of countries.
>
> (OECD 2012: 361)

The pace, directions, and outcomes of international student mobility are significantly influenced by a complex interplay of multiple push and pull variables: mutual understanding (political, social and cultural factors), revenue earning (economic factor), skill migration (economic factor) and capacity building (educational factors).[2] While some variables hinder mobility, many more enable it to grow constantly.

In the last decade, the dominance of three English-speaking destinations has remained relatively steady (OECD 2012). In 2000, 39% of globally mobile students were enrolled either in the United States (23%), UK (11%), or Australia (5%). This aggregate share declined slightly to 37% in 2010, with the United States hosting 17%, UK 13%, and Australia 7%. The other two nations in the top five are Germany and France, but they differ in several ways from the other three; first of all by language, which is not English, the dominant language in education currently; second by their tuition fees, which are much lower than in the other three countries; and in the case of

France by the background of their students, more related to their historical ties and cultural and linguistic area of influence.

In the UK and Australia, the rationale for international student recruitment shifted in the 1980s from attracting diverse talent to seeking additional revenue sources. More recently, other countries such as the United States, Canada, the Netherlands, Denmark, and Sweden are now following the same approach. As a result, universities are increasingly becoming over-reliant on a few select countries (typically China and India), which not only compromises in-class and on-campus diversity but also creates potential financial risks. These issues highlight the importance of identifying and cultivating new source countries for recruiting international students (Choudaha and Kono 2012).

At the same time, an increasing number of universities around the world have moved from teaching in their own language to teaching in English in order to attract international students. In general, as the OECD (2011: 323) observes: "countries whose language is widely spoken and read such as English, French, German, Russian and Spanish, are therefore leading destinations of foreign students, both in absolute and relative terms". However, it would be too easy to state that language is the sole solution for attracting international students.

The issue of teaching in English has become a serious academic quality concern for all universities, whatever the local language. A more diverse faculty and student population in the classroom demands that universities address these academic issues. Teaching in English is not synonymous with internationalisation but is only one of several instruments available. Universities that choose to use such an instrument also need to address the related quality concerns and think more strategically about when, where, how and why they should transfer programmes from being taught in the local language into English (or any other language) (de Wit 2011).

It is also important to look at how mobility is related to disciplines and the need for skilled migrants. According to the OECD (2012), all countries show higher incoming student mobility relative to total enrolments in advanced research programmes:

> This may be due to the attractiveness of advanced research programmes in these countries, or to a preference for recruiting international students at higher levels of education because of their potential contribution to domestic research and development, or in anticipation of recruiting these students as highly qualified immigrants.
>
> (p. 368)

In the United States, nearly one in five international students is currently enrolled at the doctoral level (IIE 2012), but, at the same time, recent growth in enrolment is being driven by students from China and Saudi Arabia at the bachelor level (Choudaha and Kono 2012). As for the areas of study, there seems to be a dominance of social sciences, business and law, followed by humanities, while there is a stronger need for enrolment in engineering and sciences.

Currently, an important driver is the global competition for top talents in the knowledge economy. We observe related demographic and economic factors on a global scale. Northern America, Europe, Australia and Japan face a demographic challenge. For the OECD, "over the next couple of decades nothing will impact on (member) economies more profoundly than demographic trends, and chief among them, ageing" (Cotis, in Hawthorne 2012: 420).

The knowledge economies of the OECD member countries require highly skilled people who, due to ageing but also due to less interest of their own youth in the hard sciences, will not be available in sufficient numbers, hence skilled immigrants are needed to fill the gaps. A recent report entitled *The World at Work: Jobs, Pay, and Skills for 3.5 Billion People* speaks of a "mismatch between jobs and graduates" (McKinsey 2012). The study claims that although there is global unemployment for 75 million young people, 39% of the employers indicate they have difficulties filling vacancies for skilled labour.

The pattern of low skilled immigration from the so-called South to the North of the past century has been replaced by a need for highly skilled migrants. At the same time, the emerging societies in Asia, Africa and Latin America also need more skilled labour to develop their economies, which is leading to global competition for top talent. Several countries over the past decades have made it more attractive for highly skilled people to come and work, while at the same time restricting immigration of lower-skilled people (Sykes 2012: 9).

Countries increasingly understand that immigration of skilled people is not always effective, and for that reason "international students have come into the spotlight as an attractive group of prospective skilled immigrants" (Sykes 2012: 8). Whereas in the past, these countries would have had an open mind to the reception of international students in general and even subsidised their education, one can observe a shift in several countries towards a more controlled immigration of fee-paying international students and measures to increase their stay rate. The Netherlands, Denmark and Sweden are examples of such policies. Over the past decade, they have introduced full-cost fees for non-EU students and at the same time developed scholarship schemes to selectively target talent and create opportunities to stay after graduation.

The percentage of international students who stay after their graduation in the country of study, the so-called stay-rate, is on average 25% for OECD-countries (Sykes 2012: 10–11), where the regional and local alumni retention rate in general is 60% for all graduates and 70% for master and doctoral graduates.[3] Besides languages, levels and areas of studies, there are other push and pull factors that play a role. Costs of study, both tuition fees and costs of living, are another factor. As tuition fees in the United States and the UK increase and several European countries introduce full-cost fees for non-EU students, students and their families are more likely to take tuition fees in combination with costs of living into consideration.[4]

Last but not least, reputation, as expressed in rankings by area of study, institution and higher education system, is increasingly becoming a pull factor. The higher the position of universities in the rankings, the more attractive that institution becomes for talented international scholars and students; the more international talents a university has, the higher its position in the league tables.

Credit mobility

The analysis on international student mobility above has focused primarily on what is called degree mobility: students that study in another country for their bachelor, master or PhD. Study abroad as part of the home degree (credit mobility) is in absolute numbers and in social, political and economic impact less a factor than degree mobility. However, its importance in Europe should not be neglected, in particular in the regional, national and institutional policies, but also in the presence and impact of these students in European institutions and cities.

If we compare study abroad numbers for the home degree in Europe and even the United States to other parts of the world, there is still significant difference. In countries such as Australia and Canada, the numbers are comparable to the United States. In Japan, this is far less the case, even though the Japanese government recently initiated plans to stimulate study abroad. In Latin America, Asia and Africa, study abroad is still relatively absent. We know little about the impact of study abroad on employability, skilled migration and degree mobility, but it is generally assumed that there is an impact; in that sense, study abroad can be seen as a major push factor in stimulating degree mobility and skilled migration in that region of the world.

In the United States, only 1.4% of the total student population spends some time abroad, predominantly white (81%) undergraduate (nearly 89%) students, with Europe (55%) still being the most popular destination and only 4% of students going for a whole academic year (De Wit, Ferencz and Rumbley 2012: 3). Although the participation and location of study abroad over the past decade has increased both in absolute numbers and diversity, and although it is more strongly emphasised in both national and institutional policy statements, the percentages stay very low, and the length of the international experience is shrinking.

In Europe in 2012, the 25th anniversary of the European Commission flagship programme ERASMUS was celebrated amid fears of becoming a victim of its own success due to increased numbers and reduced funding. In 1987, 3,244 students spent a part of their ERASMUS study in another member country. Three million students have followed their example in the past 25 years, and the number of countries has grown from 11 to 33, including non-EU member states such as Croatia, Iceland, Lichtenstein, Norway, Turkey and Switzerland. The budget of the programme for the period 2007–2013 was €3.1 billion.

The new ERASMUS+ programme, in which all education programmes at all levels are combined and offered to countries both within and beyond the EU, has an increased overall budget for the period 2014–2020 of €14.7 billion, compared to €10.5 billion for the period 2007–2013. Most of the budget, 63%, goes to Action 1, learning mobility of individuals, and will include both the old ERASMUS credit mobility and exchange of students and staff but also scholarships for joint master degrees, and a new scheme for master student loans. Twenty-eight percent of the budget will go to Action 2, cooperation for innovation and the exchange of good practices, and is focused on strategic partnerships, including those between higher education institutions and enterprises. Action 3 (4.2% of the budget) will be oriented to innovative policy development in higher education (Wilkie 2014: 10–13). In times of budget constraints and political tensions on European integration, this is an indication of the importance of internationalisation in European higher education.

Looking back over the years of ERASMUS, we can see that the impact of the programme has gone beyond numbers of mobile students to fostering internationalisation and the reform of higher education. The ERASMUS programme paved the way for the reform of European higher education under the Bologna Process, has been a pilot for its credit system ECTS, and was an initiator for the opening up to countries in Central and Eastern Europe to EU-membership, as it still is today for current aspiring candidate members. It also inspired cooperation between Europe and the rest of the world and – unfortunately still with little success – similar initiatives in other regions.

The programme has stimulated both national governments and institutions of higher education to develop European and international strategies.[5] Accompanying these success stories, however, is also an increased concern about the focus on numbers and percentages, which detracts from the need to concentrate on the content and the quality of the international experience.

Cross-border delivery

There is also increasingly the option of studying at a foreign university in one's own country or region, making cross-border delivery of higher education an alternative option for degree mobility. Varghese (2013) identifies three phases in the globalisation of higher education: first, the surge in cross-border student flow (degree mobility); second, the development of education hubs and branch campuses; and third, programme mobility, revolutionised by the massification of online courses.

Although the number of branch campuses and franchise operations by foreign universities is increasing, its impact is still limited both in numbers and origin of providers (primarily the English-speaking world) and recipients (primarily the emerging and developing world). A study by the British Council and DAAD (2014) on transnational education (2014 Executive Summary) states that this dimension of internationalisation in higher education "has accelerated in recent years to such an extent that it now constitutes a significant component of higher education systems in a number of developing countries."

The study concludes that transnational education reaches a different profile of students who are often older and seeking to combine work and study. This is confirmed by Wilkins and Balakrishnan (2012), who state that growth in enrolment numbers at branch campuses is not affecting enrolments at the home campuses. They also state that a degree from a Western university can provide greater opportunity on the labour market in the country where the branch campus operates.

The fact that costs are higher at the branch campus compared to study at a home institution but remain lower compared to degree mobility is a choice factor, although nearly half of the students in transnational education state that they have included study abroad as part of their study. For the receiving countries, increased access and improvement of the overall quality of education are the benefits, although there have also been issues around quality of education at branch campuses in some countries. However Wilkins and Balakrishnan (2012) point out that it should not be automatically assumed that these institutions, typically for profit, cannot achieve high standards and that while some may fail, others serve their student populations well. Offshore activities present high risks to the higher education institutions involved, and there can be many reasons for failure (Fielden 2013).

There is also a significant growth in cross-border activity in Europe. According to Bischof (2014), a study for the European Commission identified 253 instances of branch campuses, franchising, and validation activities in the European Union, with English-speaking countries as the main providers.[6] This picture is confirmed by other studies. The impact in particular in countries such as the UK and Australia is significant, as it is in some receiving countries. 20% of students enrolled for a first academic degree in the UK are at a British campus or at a foreign institution that has franchised a British degree (Altbach 2012). More than one in four of Australia's international students study not in Australia but in offshore transnational programmes.

Franchising arrangements with no direct involvement of the awarding institution are described by Altbach (2012) as the "macdonaldisation of higher education". He alerts to the danger of substandard quality and questions why franchising does not opt for the higher end of the education segment.

Varghese (2013) and others consider the recent development of Massive Open Online Courses (MOOCs) as an alternative option for international students to access higher education at no or low costs, although its impact is still unclear. It is also possible that it might stimulate the interest for degree study abroad rather than becoming an alternative.

In summary, internationalisation abroad patterns are an outcome of a complex interplay of external and internal and push and pull variables. These include variables like 9/11, the global financial crisis, demographic factors and the development of the global knowledge economy. The growth of international student mobility is not coming to an end yet and will be dominated by current major sending and receiving countries for several years to come.

However, at the same time, we will see a gradual diversification in both sending and receiving countries, with global competition for students becoming more dominant and large sending countries such as China, India, South Korea, Singapore, Malaysia, South Africa, Russia and Brazil also becoming receiving countries. There will also be an increase in the mobility of programmes, projects and institutions as an alternative to the mobility of students. And although degree mobility is predominantly funded from private sources, we see an increase in national scholarship schemes both at the sending (the Becas Chile programme for instance) and at the receiving end (scholarship programmes to attract top talents, such as in Denmark and Sweden). These scholarship programmes are mainly at the graduate level and in the STEM fields (Engberg et al. 2014, Perna et al. 2014), but there are also large scholarship schemes for credit mobility, such as ERASMUS+ in the European Union and Science without Borders in Brazil, that are more evenly spread across the disciplines and between undergraduate and graduate level.

Internationalisation at home

Internationalisation at home is the other side of the internationalisation coin. It focuses on the curriculum, teaching and learning and learning outcomes. This division into an 'abroad' and 'at home' component is not new in itself. We can already see this divide after the Second World War when multicultural education became a common theme for all levels of education, promoted by international organisations such as UNESCO and considered separately from mobility.

Nevertheless, the main focus in higher education in the past decades has been on degree and credit mobility of students. In 1999 in Europe, a counter-reaction emerged to this dominant focus on mobility with the foundation of the 'Internationalisation at Home' movement. Similar developments took place in Australia and the UK, where 'internationalisation of the curriculum' is the term more currently used, and in the United States, where 'internationalising the campus' and more recently 'comprehensive internationalisation' are the approaches taken. What they have in common is their reaction to the fact that internationalisation abroad reaches only a limited number of students who are able and/or willing to study abroad. With reference to the 1990's ERASMUS target of 10% for student mobility, internationalisation at home focuses on the 'other 90%'.

Beelen (2012) describes internationalisation at home as a set of instruments and activities 'at home' that focus on developing international and intercultural competences in all students. Leask defines an internationalised curriculum as one that "purposefully develops all students' international and intercultural perspectives as global professionals and citizens" (Leask 2009). Hudzik (2011: 6) describes comprehensive internationalisation as

> [A] commitment, confirmed through action, to infuse international and comparative perspectives throughout the teaching, research, and service missions of higher education. It shapes institutional ethos and values and touches the entire higher education enterprise. It is essential that it be embraced by institutional leadership, governance, faculty, students, and all academic service and support units.[7]

The inclusion and assessment of intercultural and international competences referred to by Leask is an essential part of internationalisation at home. Deardorff and Jones (2012), in their overview of intercultural competences, state that its importance is increasingly recognised by the higher education sector, but many questions still have to be answered. On the assessment of intercultural competences, Deardorff and van Gaalen (2012) point to the importance of moving from output to outcomes assessment and give several examples of the relationship between outcomes assessment and internationalisation.[8]

Virtual exchange, virtual mobility or collaborative online international learning are recent terms emerging as part of internationalisation at home. They reflect the increasing link between ICT, social media and internationalisation. Although MOOCs are the most debated form of impact of ICT on higher education, there are many other forms that are being developed and used that are more focused on cooperation and exchange between students and academic staff (de Wit 2013b).

Global citizenship

Global citizenship is also a term that is increasingly used in international education to address the alternative, noncommercial and curriculum-oriented approach to internationalisation, and many universities are in the process of integrating the concept into their internationalisation efforts.

The term is being used increasingly to define the main outcome of international education: to educate graduates who will be able to live and work in the global society. "The notion of global citizenship has become part of the internationalisation discourse in higher education around the world . . . and is increasingly the focus of doctoral research and scholarly work" (Deardorff and Jones 2012: 295).

Jorgenson and Schultz (2012) note that:

> [I]t is evident that global citizenship is far from a uniform idea and, in fact, is a much contested term. There is a general consensus, however, that higher education institutions have a role to play in preparing citizens who are informed and able to participate in our complex globalised and globalising world. Post-secondary institutions join other social institutions in working toward understanding their role in addressing social, economic, and political issues of our times.
>
> (p. 1)

Two components, the social and professional, are seen as key aspects of living and working in a global society; while the social may have dominated so far, the professional aspect (employability) has been moving more to the forefront recently. As Deardorff (2009: 206) states: "One can observe a shift in the definition of global citizenship as a concept built on a triad of knowledge, understanding, and action to one that is built on a triad of knowledge, skills, and economic competitiveness."

Clifford and Montgomery (2014: 29) take an ideological and moral stand on global citizenship and question what they call "the increasingly reductionist employability agenda". According to their thinking "the concept of global citizenship fits uneasily within current capitalist societies and requires a review of the goal of higher education" (p. 43). This is also what Chao (2014) looks for when he states that "the role of developing people as global citizens mindful of their individual actions and the repercussions of their actions is becoming more necessary in an increasingly competitive, interdependent and unpredictable world" and calls for a fourth mission of the university, peace building.

Although global citizenship is a highly contested and multifaceted term, three key dimensions seem to be commonly accepted: social responsibility, global competence and civic engagement, according to Morais and Ogden (2011: 449) who state that "Global citizenship is understood as a multidimensional construct that hinges on the interrelated dimensions of social responsibility, global competence, and global civic engagement."

Institutional capacity for response

Internationalisation may be seen as a key response to the competitive pressures of the new higher education environment, but which internationalisation, which balance of activities and approaches, which stakeholders, and so on are complex questions that do not lead to easy answers. What is apparent, however, is that the answers can no longer be found through ad hoc opportunistic solutions.

As internationalisation moves from the margin to the centre of institutional, national and international attention, the need for greater systematisation of activities becomes paramount, and as universities seek, or struggle, to make sense of internationalisation, they also seek to engage in more strategic behaviour as a means to achieve their international goals. Alongside the many understandings and rationales for internationalisation, we can also observe a very broad range of strategic ability across institutions, even within the same national context.

Strategic planning in higher education has been defined as "positioning, defining or discovering the institution's niche and seeking to be the best in what it can do" (Hayward and Ncayiyana 2003: 1), and if internationalisation is understood as a means to enhance mission, it has a key role to play in enabling an institution to perform well in its environment. However, there is no "one size fits all" approach, and every university must develop a model that is in line with its own profile, capacity and ambition and within the opportunities and constraints of its particular national framework.

Implementing a more strategic approach while developing a more coherent international dimension in an increasingly competitive and uncertain environment often takes universities into unchartered waters. For many, it is not a free choice but an inevitable one; they find themselves operating in less than ideal circumstances. Many strategies for internationalisation are introduced on a trial-and-error basis with varying degrees of success. Nolan and Hunter (2012) point out that every successfully internationalised university succeeds in its own particular way, while universities that fail to internationalise tend to do so in remarkably similar ways. This implies that there are fundamental factors, elements and conditions that promote or discourage internationalisation efforts.

If the "which" implies making choices, the "how" is enacting internationalisation. Choices around internationalisation inevitably depend on factors such as age, academic configuration, location, reputation and availability of resources, but it is also acknowledged that institutions can change through agency and the power of imagination (Marginson 2007). This may well be a key differentiator in levels of international ambition. Ultimately, an internationalisation strategy is about change and adaptation, going deep and broad into the academic and organisational activities to the very heart of the institution, and sense of identity can become a powerful resource in making an uncommon effort. It can enable universities to identify opportunity and exploit it to institutional advantage.[9]

As internationalisation becomes central to mission and strategy, it can be seen both as an institutional effort and a force for innovation. It enables universities to think beyond their usual ways of operation to create institutional energy to make internationalisation an essential component of their identity.

Facing future challenges

De Wit (2002: 109–116) describes the development in the meanings and definitions of the terms 'international education' and 'internationalisation of higher education', illustrating the different perceptions behind their use and meaning. While the discourse seems to suggest a move towards a process-oriented, comprehensive internationalisation, as outlined by Hudzik (2011), a largely activity-oriented or even instrumental approach towards internationalisation still seems to be predominant.

Brandenburg and de Wit (2011) give a critical reflection on the state of internationalisation and the need for innovation and change. Major myths and misconceptions about what internationalisation actually means can be the result (Knight 2011; de Wit 2011). The International Association of Universities (IAU) in 2012 started a process of rethinking internationalisation and established an action plan based on it: *Affirming Academic Values in Internationalisation of Higher Education: A Call for Action* (IAU 2012).

De Wit (2013a: 215–216) gives eight reasons for the need to rethink internationalisation:

1. The discourse of internationalisation does not always match reality in that, for too many universities, internationalisation means merely a collection of fragmented and unrelated activities, rather than a comprehensive process.
2. The further development of globalisation, the increasing commodification of higher education and of the notion of a global knowledge society and economy has resulted in a new range of forms, providers and products and new, sometimes conflicting dimensions, views and elements in the discourse of internationalisation.
3. The international higher education context is rapidly changing. 'Internationalisation', like 'international education', was until recently predominantly a Western phenomenon in which the developing countries only played a reactive role. Now the emerging economies and the higher education community in other parts of the world are altering the landscape of internationalisation. This shift from a Western, neocolonial concept, as 'internationalisation' is perceived by several educators, means incorporating other emerging views. Jones and de Wit (2012) call this trend the 'globalisation of internationalisation'.
4. The discourse on internationalisation is often dominated by a small group of stakeholders: higher education leaders, governments and international bodies. Other stakeholders, such as employers – and in particular the faculty and the student voice – are heard far less often, with the result that the discourse is insufficiently influenced by those who should benefit from its implementation (see Jones 2010).
5. Too much of the discourse is oriented towards national and institutional levels with little attention for programmes themselves. Research, the curriculum, and the teaching and learning process, which should be at the core of internationalisation, as expressed by movements such as 'Internationalisation at Home', often receive little attention (see Aerden et al. 2013).
6. Internationalisation is evaluated too often in quantitative terms through numbers, or input and output, instead of a qualitative, outcome-based approach on the impact of internationalisation initiatives.
7. To date, there has been insufficient attention to norms, values and the ethics of internationalisation practice. With some notable exceptions (e.g., McKenzie et al. 2003), the approach has been too pragmatically oriented towards reaching targets without a debate on the potential risks and ethical consequences.
8. The increased awareness that the notion of 'internationalisation' is not only a question of the relations between nations but even more to the relations between cultures and between the global and the local.

De Wit adds: "The overarching reason is that we consider internationalisation of higher education too much as a goal in itself instead of as a means to an end", with the end being "to enhance the quality of education and research" (de Wit 2013a: 25).

Green, Marmolejo and Egron-Polak (2012: 453) state that there is much that cannot be foreseen or predicted about the future of internationalisation of higher education. According to these authors, globalisation is a fact of life, and its impact on higher education will continue to be profound, with demographic and economic trends as well as technology having an impact, but how they will impact is less clear.

Internationalisation may occur as a result of external isomorphic pressures:

> [B]ut those pressures, their content, reach and pervasiveness are heavily conditioned by the way the organisations and organisational actors receive, select, make sense of, interpret, combine, reconstruct, use, in a word, translate them in the face of their organisational, cultural and knowledge context of action and purposes.
>
> (Vaira 2004: 495)

The ability to respond to these pressures will depend significantly on historical legacy and how historically developed practices and identities enable regions, countries and institutions to interpret them and develop appropriate strategies for change (Krücken 2003).

In conclusion

In this chapter, we have provided an overview of the development of internationalisation in higher education. The picture we have described is that the landscape of international higher education is changing at an ever-increasing rate. From a de-Europeanised and nationalised higher education system in the 18th and 19th century, the international dimensions in higher education took on new forms and shapes in the 20th century and are changing again in the 21st century as internationalisation becomes mainstream and a comprehensive part of higher education. The increasing importance of knowledge in the globalised economy implies that not only research but also teaching and learning cross borders and create new forms of cooperation and competition. Globally, the focus on mobility (internationalisation abroad) is shifting to a mixture of mobility and curriculum, teaching and learning and learning outcomes (internationalisation at home).

We would like to suggest that an inclusive internationalisation where abroad and at home, cooperation and competition, virtual and physical, North and South, global citizenship and professional competence become more intertwined and interpreted according to local context is the current imperative of higher education to play its role in the global market place.

Notes

1 Also Taylor (2010) observes that internationalisation was hardly recognised as such within higher education.
2 For an overview of push and pull variables, see Agarwal et al. (2008: 241).
3 Hawthorne (2008, 2010, 2012) and OECD (2011) warn that an increase of the stay rate is not a guaranteed solution for the needs of the national economies, either in quantitative and qualitative terms, but still governments make increasingly more efforts to stimulate the stay rate of top talent.
4 See a study by HSBC (2013) for a comparative analysis of study costs.
5 For a more detailed analysis of international credit mobility in Europe and the United States, see for instance de Wit et al. (2012).
6 The complete study is to be found at http://ec.europa.eu/education/highereducation/doc/studies/bor ders_en.pdf. For an overview and analysis of cross-border education, see also Lawton and Katsomitros (2012) and Knight (2014).
7 For a more detailed analysis of internationalisation of the curriculum, see Leask (2001, 2009) and Brewer and Leask (2012).
8 For an overview of the dimensions of intercultural competence, see Deardorff (2009). For the assessment of internationalisation, see also de Wit (2009).
9 See also the concept of the internationalisation circle developed by Knight (1994: 12) and adapted by de Wit (2002: 136), identifying the nine different stages in an internationalisation strategy: analysis of context, awareness, commitment, planning, operationalisation, implementation, review and reinforcement, keeping in mind also the integration effect: the impact on research, teaching and learning, and the service function.

References

Aerden, A., de Decker, F., Divis, J., Frederiks, M., de Wit, H., 2013. Assessing the internationalisation of degree programmes: experiences from a Dutch-Flemish pilot certifying internationalisation. *Compare* 43, 1, 56–78.

Agarwal, P., Elmahdy Said, M., Sehoole, M., Sirozi, M., de Wit, H., 2008. The dynamics of international student mobility in a global context: summary, conclusions, and recommendations. In De Wit, H., Agarwal, P., Elmahdy Said, M., Sehoole, M. and Sirozi, M. (Eds.) *The Dynamics of International Student Circulation in a Global Context*. Sense, Rotterdam.

Altbach, P., 1998. Comparative perspectives in higher education for the twenty-first century. *Higher Education Policy* 11, 347–356.

Altbach, P., 2006. Globalization and the university: realities in an unequal world. In: Altbach, P. and Forest, J. (Eds.) *International Handbook of Higher Education*. Springer, Dordrecht.

Altbach, P., 2012. Franchising: the McDonaldization of higher education. *International Higher Education* 66, 7–8.

Baron, B., 1993. The politics of academic mobility in Western Europe. *Higher Education Policy* 6, 3, 50–54.

Beelen, J. (Ed.), 2007. *Implementing Internationalisation at Home*. European Association for International Education, Amsterdam.

Beelen, J., 2012. The long wait: researching the implementation of internationalisation at home. In: Beelen, J. and de Wit, H. (Eds.) *Internationalisation Revisited: New Dimensions in the Internationalisation of Higher Education*. CAREM, Amsterdam University of Applied Sciences, Amsterdam.

Bischof, L., 2014. Franchising, validation and branch campuses in the European Union. *International Higher Education* 74, 16–17.

Brandenburg, U., de Wit, H., 2011. The end of internationalization. *International Higher Education* 62, 15–16.

Brewer, E., Leask, B., 2012. Internationalization of the curriculum. In: Deardorff, D., de Wit, H., Heyl, J. and Adams, T. (Eds.) *The SAGE Handbook of International Higher Education*. Sage, Thousand Oaks.

British Council, DAAD, 2014. Impacts of Transnational Education on Host Countries. www.britishcouncil.org/education/ihe

Cantwell, B., Maldonado-Maldonado, A., 2009. Four stories: confronting contemporary ideas about globalisation and internationalisation in higher education. *Globalisation, Societies and Education* 7, 3, 289–306.

Chandler, A., 1989. Obligation or opportunity: foreign student policy in six major receiving countries. IIE Research Report No. 18, Institute for International Education, New York.

Chao, R.Y., 2014. Peace-building: the university's fourth mission. *University World News* 322.

Choudaha, R., Kono, Y., 2012. Beyond more of the same: the top four emerging markets for international student recruitment. *World Education News and Reviews.*

Clifford, V., Montgomery C., 2014. Challenging conceptions of Western higher education and promoting graduates as global citizens. *Higher Education Quarterly* 68, 1, 28–45.

Deardorff, D., 2006. Identification and assessment of intercultural competence as a student outcome of internationalization. *Journal of Studies in International Education* 10, 3, 241–266.

Deardorff, D. (Ed.), 2009. *The SAGE Handbook of Intercultural Competence*. Sage, Thousand Oaks.

Deardorff, D., Jones, E., 2012. Intercultural competence: an emerging focus in international higher education. In: Deardorff, D., de Wit, H., Heyl, J. and Adams, T. (Eds.) *The SAGE Handbook of International Higher Education*. Sage, Thousand Oaks.

Deardorff, D., van Gaalen, A., 2012. Outcomes assessment in the internationalization of higher education. In: Deardorff, D., de Wit, H., Heyl, J. and Adams, T. (Eds.) *The SAGE Handbook of International Higher Education*. Sage, Thousand Oaks.

de Ridder-Symoens, H., 1992. Mobility. In: de Ridder-Symoens, H. (Ed.) *A History of the University in Europe: Volume I. Universities in the Middle Age*. Cambridge University Press, Cambridge.

de Wit, H., 2002. *Internationalization of Higher Education in the United States of America and Europe: A Historical, Comparative, and Conceptual Analysis*. Greenwood Press, Westwood.

de Wit, H. (Ed.), 2009. Measuring success in internationalisation of higher education: how do we measure what we do? EAIE Occasional Paper No. 22, European Association for International Education, Amsterdam.

de Wit, H., 2011. Internationalization misconceptions. *International Higher Education* 64: 6–7.

de Wit, H., 2013a. Internationalization of higher education, an introduction on the why, how and what. In: de Wit, H. (Ed.) *An Introduction to Higher Education Internationalization*. Università Cattolica University Press Vita e Pensiero, Milan.

de Wit, H., 2013b. COIL: virtual mobility without commercialisation. *University World News* 274.

de Wit, H., Ferencz, I., Rumbley, L., 2012. International student mobility: European and US perspectives. *Perspectives: Policy and Practice in Higher Education* 17, 1, 17–23.

de Wit, H., Merkx, G., 2012. The history of internationalisation of higher education. In: Deardorff, D., de Wit, H., Heyl, J. and Adams, T. (Eds.) *The SAGE Handbook of International Higher Education.* Sage, Thousand Oaks.

Egron-Polak, E., 2012. Internationalization of higher education: an introduction. *IAU Horizons* 17, 3, 15.

Engberg, D., Glover G., Rumbley L., Altbach, P., 2014. *Rationale for Sponsoring International Study.* British Council and DAAD, London and Bonn.

European Commission, 2013. *European Higher Education in the World.* European Commission, Brussels.

Fielden, J., 2013. Financial aspects of offshore activities. *International Higher Education* 72, 10–12.

Goodwin, C., Nacht, M., 1991. *Missing the Boat: The Failure to Internationalize American Higher Education.* Cambridge University Press, Cambridge.

Green, M., Marmolejo, F., Egron-Polak, E., 2012. The internationalization of higher education: future perspectives. In: Deardorff, D., de Wit, H., Heyl, J. and Adams, T. (Eds.) *The SAGE Handbook of International Higher Education.* Sage, Thousand Oaks.

Hawthorne, L., 2008. *The Impact of Economic Selection Policy on Labour Market Outcomes for Degree-Qualified Migrants in Canada and Australia.* Institute for Research Policy, Ottawa, Canada.

Hawthorne, L., 2010. How valuable is "two-step migration"? Labour market outcomes for international student migrants to Australia. *Asia Pacific Migration Journal* 19, 1, 5–36.

Hawthorne, L., 2012. Designer immigrants? International students and two-step migration. In: Deardorff, D., de Wit, H., Heyl, J. and Adams, T. (Eds.) *The SAGE Handbook of International Higher Education.* Sage, Thousand Oaks.

Hayward, F., Ncayiyana, D., 2003. *Strategic Planning: A Guide for Higher Education Institutions.* Centre for Higher Education Transformation, Cape Town.

Holzner, B., Greenwood, D., 1995. The institutional policy contexts for international higher education in the United States of America. In: de Wit, H. (Ed.) *Strategies for Internationalisation of Higher Education. A Comparative Study of Australia, Canada, Europe and the United States of America.* European Association for International Education (in cooperation with IMHE/OECD and AIEA), Amsterdam.

HSBC, 2013. Study costs most in Australia. *HSBC News and Insight.*

Hudzik, J., 2011. *Comprehensive Internationalization.* NAFSA, Washington.

Institute for International Education, 2012. *Open Doors 2012.* Institute for International Education, New York.

International Association of Universities (IAU). 2012. *Affirming Academic Values in Internationalization of Higher Education: A Call for Action.* International Association of Universities, Paris.

Jegede, O., 2012. African leader wants end to "slave trade" in education. *Times Higher Education*, March 1st.

Jones, E. (Ed.), 2010. *Internationalisation and the Student Voice: Higher Education Perspectives.* Routledge, London.

Jones, E., Brown, S. (Eds.), 2007. *Internationalising Higher Education London.* Routledge, London.

Jones, E., de Wit, H., 2012. Globalization of internationalization: thematic and regional reflections on a traditional concept. *AUDEM* 3, 35–54.

Jorgenson, S., Shultz, L., 2012. Global citizenship education (GCE) in post-secondary institutions: what is protected and what is hidden under the umbrella of GCE? *Journal of Global Citizenship and Equity Education* 2, 1, 1–21.

Kerr, C., 1994. *Higher Education Cannot Escape History.* State University of New York Press, Albany.

Knight, J., 1994. Internationalization: Elements and Checkpoints. CBIE Research Paper No. 7, Canadian Bureau for International Education, Ottawa.

Knight, J., 2008. *Higher Education in Turmoil. The Changing World of Internationalization.* Sense, Rotterdam.

Knight, J., 2011. Five myths about internationalization. *International Higher Education* 64, 14–15.

Knight, J. (Ed.), 2014. *International Education Hubs.* Springer, Dordrecht.

Krücken, G., 2003. Learning the "new, new thing": on the role of path dependency in university structures. *Higher Education* 46, 315–339.

Lawton, W., Katsomitros, A., 2012. *International Branch Campuses: Data and Developments.* Observatory on Borderless Higher Education, London.

Leask, B., 2001. Bridging the gap: internationalising university curricula. *Journal of Studies in International Education* 5, 2, 100–115.

Leask, B., 2009. Using formal and informal curricula to improve interactions between home and international students. *Journal of Studies in International Education* 13, 2, 205–221.

Marginson, S., 2007. In: Enders, J. and Jongbloed, B. (Eds.) *Public-Private Dynamics in Higher Education: Expectations, Developments and Outcomes.* Transcript Verlag, Bielefeld.

Maringe, F., Foskett, N. (Eds.), 2010. *Globalization and Internationalization in Higher Education. Theoretical, Strategic and Management Perspectives.* Continuum, London.

McKenzie A., Bourn D., Evans S., Brown M., et al., 2003. *Global Perspectives in Higher Education*, London: Development Education Association.

McKinsey, 2012. *The World at Work: Jobs, Pay, and Skills for 3.5 Billion People.* McKinsey, New York.

Mohamedbhai, G., 2012. Internationalization in African higher education: a different approach? *IAU Horizons* 17, 3, 19–20.

Morais, D., Ogden, A., 2011. Initial development and validation of the global citizenship scale. *Journal of Studies in International Education* 15, 5, 445–466.

Naidoo R., Jamieson I., 2005. Knowledge in the marketplace: the global commodification of teaching and learning in higher education. In: Ninnes, P. and Hellsten, M. (Eds.) *Internationalizing Higher Education: Critical Explorations of Pedagogy and Policy.* Springer, Dordrecht.

Neave, G., 1997. The European dimension in higher education: an historical analysis. Background document for the conference on The Relationship between Higher Education and the Nation-State, Enschede.

Nolan, R., Hunter, F., 2012. Institutional strategies and programs: learning from experiences of change. In: Deardorff, D., de Wit, H., Heyl, J. and Adams, T. (Eds.) *The SAGE Handbook of International Higher Education.* Sage, Thousand Oaks.

OECD, 2011. *Education at a Glance 2011.* OECD, Paris.

OECD, 2012. *Education at a Glance 2012.* OECD, Paris.

Perna, L., Orosz, K., Gopaul, B., Jumakulov, Z., Adil Ashirbekoc, A., Kishkentayeva, M., 2014. Promoting human capital development: a typology of international scholarship programmes in higher education. *Educational Researcher* 43, 2, 63–73.

Scott, P., 1998. Globalization and the university. In: Scott, P. (Ed.) *The Globalization of Higher Education.* Open University Press, Buckingham.

Scott, P., 2005. The global dimension: internationalizing higher education. In: Kehm, B. and de Wit, H. (Eds.). *European Responses to the Global Perspective.* European Association for International Education, Amsterdam.

Stier, J., 2010. International education: trends, ideologies and alternative pedagogical approaches. *Globalisation, Societies and Education* 8, 3, 339–349.

Sykes, B., 2012. *Mobile Talent? The Staying Intentions of International Students in Five EU Countries.* Sachverständigenrat deutscher Stiftungen für Integration und Migration, Berlin.

Taylor, J., 2010. The response of governments and universities to globalization and internationalization in higher education. In: Maringe, F. and Foskett, N. (Eds.) 2010. *Globalization and Internationalization in Higher Education. Theoretical, Strategic and Management Perspectives.* Continuum, London.

Vaira, M., 2004. Globalisation and higher education organizational change: a framework for analysis. *Higher Education* 48, 4, 483–510.

Van der Wende, M., 2001. Internationalisation policies: about new trends and contrasting paradigms. *Higher Education Policy* 14, 3, 249–259.

Van Vught, F., van der Wende, M., Westerheijden, D., 2002. Globalization and internationalization. Policy agendas compared. In: Enders, J. and Fulton, O. (Eds.) *Higher Education in a Globalizing World.* Kluwer, Dordrecht.

Varghese, N., 2013. Globalization and higher education: changing trends in cross border education. *Analysis Reports in International Education* 5, 1, 7–20.

Wilkie, G., 2014. ERASMUS+ Going Global. *FORUM* Spring, 10–13.

Wilkins, S., Balakrishnan, M., 2012. How well are international branch campuses serving students? *International Higher Education* 66, 3–5.

Wilson, L., 2013. The internationalisation of higher education and research: European policies and institutional strategies. In: de Wit, H., Hunter, F., Johnson, L. and van Liempd, H.-G. (Eds.) *Possible Futures: The Next 25 Years of the Internationalisation of Higher Education.* European Association for International Education, Amsterdam.

26

TRANSNATIONAL FLOWS OF STUDENTS

In whose interest? For whose benefits?

Qing Gu and Michele Schweisfurth

Introduction

Student mobility is not a new phenomenon. Historical accounts of scholar exchanges and intercultural education can be traced back to 272 BC (Ward, Bochner and Furnham 2001). However, in modern times, the concepts, forms, focus and drivers of the internationalisation agenda have changed profoundly over time, from aid in the 1970s, cooperation and exchange in the 1980s to trade by the end of the 20th century (de Wit 2008). By the end of the first decade of the 21st century, the competition for international students has intensified on a global scale (de Wit 2008; OECD 2008) and the study destinations for international mobile students have become increasingly diversified (UNESCO 2009). The latest report from OECD (2014) shows that over the last three decades, the population of mobile international students has risen from 0.8 million worldwide in 1975 to 4.5 million in 2012, representing a more than fivefold increase. However, it is the last decade that has seen the most rapid proliferation of international students worldwide. According to the statistics from UNESCO (2013), the number of students enrolled in educational institutions outside of their country of origin increased from 1.3 million in 1999 to 4.3 million in 2011, representing an increase of almost 70%. In response to the global expansion of internationalisation, since 2003 the International Association of Universities (IAU) has conducted four global surveys (2003, 2005, 2010, 2014) in more than 130 countries in every world region, and the results consistently show that student mobility is among the highest priority internationalisation activities within institutions. With regard to the destinations of student mobility, China, the Republic of Korea and New Zealand have emerged as new popular host countries, whilst some traditional 'hot spots' (e.g., the United States and Australia) have seen their favourable shares of the world's mobile students decline (UNESCO 2009; OECD 2014). The general pattern, significantly and increasingly, is student movement from lower-income to higher-income countries.

Internationalisation has not been a value-free phenomenon since its first emergence (Gu and Schweisfurth 2011). The historical and current migration of skills and academic talent is closely associated with the flows of economic, social and cultural capital. Inequalities in terms of individual access to international opportunities and benefits are inherent in the phenomenon and have remained intact. For example, the 3rd IAU Global Survey (2010) reported that irrespective of the persistent increase in international student mobility, studying abroad activities remain reserved for a select few. Results of their latest 4th Global Survey (2014) reaffirm the concern that the exponential growth in the world population of mobile students only represents a fraction of the individuals in higher education who have the financial resources to expand their horizons through the study-abroad experience. In the case of China, for example, despite the fact that it sends the highest absolute numbers of students abroad, less than 2 percent of tertiary students from the country have contributed to the global statistics on student mobility (UNESCO 2009). They represent two groups of elites in the society: the socioeconomic elite (e.g., mostly self-funded students) and the educated elite (e.g., students funded by scholarships) (Wang and Miao 2013).

It is perhaps, then, not surprising that as the transnational flows of mobile students are predicted to continue to proliferate (Böhm et al. 2004; Advisory Panel on Canada's International Education Strategy 2012; International Education Advisory Council 2013; British Council 2012, 2013, 2014), international student mobility (or flows) has also become a popular topic of study. Scholars from different disciplinary backgrounds, driven by their own respective methodological and ideological concerns, have, collectively, provided a wealth of evidence depicting the lives of international students and the personal, institutional and societal factors that are perceived to have influenced the quality of their study-abroad experiences. Researchers in psychology, for example, have primarily focussed upon stress levels and coping strategies and the quality of the support mechanisms that are available to promote (or inhibit) individual students' intercultural adaptation, intra- and interpersonal interactions and psychological well-being (Ward and Kennedy 1993; Cushner and Karim 2004; Zhang and Goodson 2011; Suspitsyna 2013; Glass and Westmont 2014). Such a focus is reflected in their conceptualisation of students' study-abroad experiences, which are defined as "a significant transitional event that brings with it a considerable amount of accompanying stress, involving both confrontation and adaptation to unfamiliar physical and psychological experiences and changes" (Cushner and Karim 2004: 292). Whilst these studies are valuable as a means of identifying key issues in intercultural education, most are predominantly quantitative and "objectivistic in nature" (Gudykunst 2005: 25) and often fail to consider the role of human agency in the management by international students of their overseas learning experiences or to elaborate on the complexity of international students' identity negotiations and sense making in the cultural, social and educational worlds to which they are exposed.

The educational literature, in contrast, has provided detailed accounts of international students' struggles, challenges and achievements in different educational and sociocultural environments (e.g., Montgomery and McDowell 2009; Sherry, Thomas and Chui 2010; Guo and Chase 2011) and the essential qualities required to achieve personal changes and expansion over time (e.g., Murphy-Lejeune 2003; Gu and Maley 2008; Gu 2009). The bulk of this body of research tends to be driven by practice-oriented concerns and thus has attracted growing criticism for its lack of theorisation (Gudykunst 2005). In addition, neither the psychological nor the educational literature engages directly with the political economy of student flows and the development issues and imbalances that arise from them.

Geographers' research on mobile students tends to be grounded in theories of migration, sociology and/or socioeconomics. This body of migration research tends to be qualitative and, in many cases, small scale in nature. However, it has provided important evidence on the ways in which biographical, sociocultural and socioeconomic factors influence the geographical (im) mobility of students (e.g., Findlay and King 2010; Carlson 2013; Geddie 2013; Waters and Leung 2013a) and how mobile students' access to transnational education – whether it was through family migration (e.g., Waters 2007) or studying in off-shore programmes in their home country (e.g., Sin 2013; Waters and Leung 2013b) – can be converted to social and cultural capital that fosters their social and economic advantage, class reproduction and employment and social mobility (e.g., Brooks, Waters and Pimlott-Wilson 2012). It has also provided useful analyses of the embedded inequalities in flows of knowledge, pedagogical practice and discrimination (e.g., Madge, Raghuram and Noxolo 2014).

The purpose of this chapter is to bring together evidence on issues related to international student mobility and provide a synthesis of key discussions within scholarship that are critical to understanding the motivation, challenges and benefits of study-abroad experiences to individual students' personal transformations and employability. It will locate the analysis within the wider question about *development*, questioning the underlying values and principles that drive many higher education institutions and governments to expand their continued appetite for international students and the possible benefits as well as risks for both universities and societies. The chapter will conclude with a critical response to a question that may be fundamental to understanding the meaning and consequences of transnational flows of international students: What are the benefits of global student mobility, and to whom?

While we focus primarily on the experiences and outcomes of individual mobile students, and patterns across these, not least due to the nature of our own body of research in this area, the sheer scale of mobility along with its cumulative transformative potential raises questions about its contribution to development. The relatively neglected link between individual and aggregated student mobility and broader issues of development deserve attention. The general patterns of flow – from South to North or East to West – generate a range of significant outcomes, intended or unintended. On the one hand, these include 'brain drain' or 'brain circulation', as study abroad precipitates longer or permanent migration of skilled workers and critical thinkers. On the other hand, individuals transformed by study abroad bring new skills, attitudes, expectations and social and political agendas into their home environment if or when they do return. These issues are situated in a context of competing priorities for development investment, particularly as the Millennium Development Goal era comes to a close and new agendas emerge for all phases of education.

Transnational connections, competences and identities: what matters to the students

Over the last decade, research on the experiences of international students has shifted, quite rightly, from a *deficit* approach that tends to see students as the primary cause of their struggle, stress and failure to a *transformative* approach that focuses on processes of learning and development and the human agency and support that influence these.

The deficit approach

The research literature from a deficit perspective is criticised for having focused far too much upon the deterministic role of culture in international students' experiences (Jones 2005; Gu and Schweisfurth 2006; Grimshaw 2007; Schweisfurth and Gu 2009; Signorini, Wiesemes and Murphy 2009). The level of difference in cultural norms, values and behaviour patterns between the host country and the international students' country of origin tends to be perceived as *the* factor that has contributed to the struggles and challenges that many students experience while studying abroad. There are at least four limitations in such conceptualisation.

First and foremost, the international student population is not a homogeneous group. However, despite their diverse cultural, social and linguistic backgrounds, international students are too often uncritically regarded as "an undifferentiated block" (Jones 2005: 341). 'The' Chinese (or Asian) learner (e.g., Watkins and Biggs 1996; Watkins and Biggs 2001) is probably one of the most frequently researched student groups in the educational literature, but it is a phrase that paints too simplistic a picture of their often fragmented, differentiated and complex individual and collective study-abroad experiences. Given the heterogeneity of the student group, it can be argued that the tendency to use cultural models alone to identify and remedy the challenges that international students experience should be treated with caution.

Second, the deterministic notion of culture tends to work on a deficit model and problematise international students in that they perform less well academically and require more institutional support (Morrison et al. 2005). In the case of Chinese students, for example, despite the empirical evidence that suggests that Chinese students are also cognitively able and highly motivated learners (e.g., Biggs 1996), Chineseness has been defined in terms of deviation from Western norms (Chang 2000), implying that they are significantly different from Western learners and thus less adequate in a Western learning environment (Jones 2005). In their research that compared academic achievement levels of UK-domiciled undergraduate students with non-UK domiciled undergraduate students, Morrison et al. (2005) found that the performance of Chinese students did not differ significantly from that of UK students. This observation was "a surprise" because it did not support the expectation that "students domiciled in China – who are generally considered to face significant problems in adapting to linguistic, cultural and educational differences in the UK – would do worse than UK-domiciled students" (Morrison et al. 2005: 335).

Third, the deterministic notion of culture also fails to take into account the role of individual agency and resilience in managing setbacks and challenges in adverse circumstances. These qualities are individualised and may vary greatly even within a mono-cultural group. Gu and Schweisfurth (2006) carried out a mixed method comparative pilot study on Chinese learners' experiences in the UK and in British Council's language teacher education projects in China and found that in addition to culture, factors such as the identities and motivations of the learners and the power relationships between them and their teachers were also significant issues in the strategic adaptations made by Chinese students. Moreover, an excessive emphasis upon the impact of cultural models tends to overlook the "maturing process" (Murphy-Lejeune 2003: 113) that many international students experience while studying abroad. They are found to go through two types of transition whilst studying abroad: 1) maturation and human development and 2) intercultural adaptation (Gu, Schweisfurth and Day 2010). These transitional experiences interactively influence the nature and process of their change and development in a different educational environment and a different culture and society over time.

Finally, culture is itself a fluid and dynamic construct. It is even more so when the world has entered the third phase of globalisation in which knowledge, information, skills, values, cultures and systems have been able to interact on the "flat-world platform" more easily and more seamlessly than ever before (Friedman 2005). The sheer rapidity of change and its accumulated effects have altered the character of work and many features of contemporary living in a fundamental way (Held et al. 1999; Coolahan 2002; Little and Green 2009). A fixed and static view to compare cultural models in such an increasingly globalised world may, therefore, be of limited and dubious value. Culture evolves and 'the' international learner transforms within the changing cultures.

Thus, important though it may be, culture is not the only determinant of teaching and learning practices, preferences and experiences. All too easily, teachers and learners may fall into the trap of cultural stereotyping. However, it is clear that other factors are at least as influential: the backgrounds and aspirations of learners, their specific motivation for learning, the settings in which the interactions take place, and the nature of the relationship between teachers and learners. In particular, the cultural blinkers may screen out the importance of the individual personality and professional identity or orientation of learners. Moreover, a rigid view of cultural essentialism will, unfortunately, fail to capture a profound change process of maturation that many international students learn to manage over time.

The transformative approach: managing transitions

The transformative approach acknowledges the wide range of struggles and challenges that many international students may have encountered whilst studying abroad but focuses more on how they learn to become problem solvers and how they feel socially, culturally and intellectually competent over time. Rather than continuing to focus upon psychological, education and culture shock and its associated frustrations and struggles, this approach reconceptualises the deficit problems of stress and struggles as a positive need for change and development. The great news is that there has been growing and ample evidence in education, psychology and geography over the last decade that shows that, irrespective of the challenges embedded in the academic, institutional and social conditions and irrespective of the variations in international students' backgrounds, there are more common patterns of challenges, change and development than differences. These developments often impact permanently on the individual (as our research on Chinese students has shown; Gu and Schweisfurth 2015) and cumulatively they potentially have transformative implications for wider social developments, although evidence of these is largely anecdotal or speculative at this stage.

First, for many international students, the nature of their study-abroad experiences develops from essentially a *cross*-cultural experience to an *inter*-cultural experience. Cross-cultural experience and intercultural experience tend to be used interchangeably in the literature. Although they are not mutually exclusive, they embrace different focuses. The notion of cross-cultural experience inherently stresses boundary crossing, differences and diversity; intercultural experience, on the other hand, "encompasses both domestic and international contexts and implies cultures interacting" (Landreman 2003, cited in King and Baxter Magolda 2005: 572). Although individuals may experience both cross- and inter-cultural experiences simultaneously when they are exposed to different cultural environments and in encounters with different people, the tensions caused by their attempts to manage cultural differences tend to be more overwhelming in the initial phase of their studies. As they adapt to the new environment, they may gradually notice that they have, either consciously or subconsciously, become 'one of them'. However, as some writers note (Berger and Luckman 1966; Paulston 1992; Byram 2003), certain aspects of cultural beliefs and values may be beyond modification or 'integration' and will never be completely abandoned for others. Thus, individuals may develop "proficiency in self-expression and in fulfilling their various social needs" in the host culture (Kim 2005: 391), whilst continuing to experience a sense of boundary or 'otherness' when confronted with conflicting values and beliefs. In other words, although sense of belonging and alienation coexist, as international students initially fear and then appreciate new ways of learning in their studies and new ways of functioning in the host society, they act as agents of their own success and create a coherent trajectory out of the fragmentations and contradictions. This can be seen in their improved linguistic competence, increased self-confidence, greater involvement in class activities and a strong sense of independence in learning. Thus, by the end of their studies, it is unlikely that culture will continue to function as "a source of conflict", as Hofstede announces on his website (http://www.geert-hofstede.com), or a source of stress and struggle. Rather, different fabrics of the host culture of learning and teaching will have been absorbed, integrated and personalised by individual students to take on different forms that enable them to perform in their studies and fuel them with strength, confidence and power. Evidence as such led Gu, Schweisfurth and Day to argue that "the cross-cultural is not only within the intercultural: it is within themselves" (2010: 20).

Related to the above is the second common pattern that *international students' intercultural learning experiences are both transitional and transformational and necessitate identity change.* Students who spend a period of time outside their own national systems experience opportunities to act as participant observers of their home system and the host system. In theory, the natural juxtaposition of these experiences should help individual students to better understand their own and the host's education systems. However, evidence from Schweisfurth and her colleagues' research (Schweisfurth 2012) has led her to question the validity and depth of these understandings. Whilst it may be true that the day-to-day lived experience of the internationalisation of higher education does not necessarily make individual students experts of their host culture or system, such experience challenges their values and behaviour and can take on "the shape of a personal expansion, an opening of one's potential universe" (Murphy-Lejeune 2003: 113).

Our research on international students over the last decade supports Murphy-Lejeune's observation. Evidence consistently shows that for most (home and international) students, going to university is a further step on a journey of self-discovery in which they assess themselves and experience themselves being assessed by others in a range of personal, social and academic settings. Those who do well demonstrate a sense of agency and are able to learn and develop new skills and qualities that enable them to survive and flourish. For international students, because some challenges that they face may be "exclusive to them (as opposed to native students)" (Furnham and Bochner 1986, cited in Furnham 2004: 17), the processes of change and adaption to new norms of social behaviour, languages and academic pedagogies can be doubly difficult and complex on a number of personal, social and emotional levels. Establishing a 'locus of self' in such circumstances is likely to require a different order of change competence, awareness and resilience. In this process, "identity is constructed in transactions at and across the boundary" (Jenkins 2004: 22). Jenkins asserts that during these transactions, "a balance is struck between (internal) group identification and (external) categorisation by others" (2004: 22). To achieve such balance, the social actor is constantly engaged in a process of identity negotiations in terms of how they perceive themselves and how they would like to be perceived by others each time when they cross the boundary. Evidence from our research points to three types of inter-related transition: students' own maturing process, their improved intercultural understanding and competence, and their intellectual development. The process of identity change is, therefore, interwoven with the growth of their *maturity, interculturality* and *intellectuality*.

The third common pattern is that *upon return home, study-abroad experience is perceived by many as an opportunity that enhances their career and employment prospects.* As yet, the experiences of returnees and the ways in which their overseas studies impact on their identity and professional and personal lives have been an underdeveloped area in the literature. Earlier research on international students' homecoming experiences also had a strong 'deficit' focus, emphasising returnees' emotional and psychological difficulties of "readjusting, re-acculturating, and re-assimilating into one's own home environment after living in a different culture for a significant period of time" (Gaw 2000: 83–84; see also Butcher 2002; Christofi and Thompson 2007). However, more recent research evidence on international graduates appears to convey rather contrasting messages. Whilst acknowledging the variations in individual returnees' experiences, it tends to see returnees as having accumulated transnational "assets" (Levy, Peiperl and Bouquet 2013) and report the values that their professional and social networks and their cosmopolitan skills and competences can bring to themselves and the society (e.g., McGrath, Stock and Butcher 2007; Han 2013; Zweig and Wang 2013; Zweig and Yang 2014). This may be because, at least in part, the contemporary, unprecedented information and communications technology revolution has transformed the quantity and quality of the global flows of knowledge and skills (e.g., Coolahan 2002; Little and Green 2009); the transnational experiences of mobile students and graduates on the "flat-world platform" (Friedman 2005: 11) are thus qualitatively distinct.

The research commissioned by the UK Department for Business, Innovation and Skills (Mellors-Bourne et al. 2013) on the values and benefits of studying in the UK, for example, identified:

> [T]angible personal benefits for international graduates in relation to career progression and/or change, their position in society and especially their personal growth, not least the development of extensive networks of social, and potential future professional, contacts. As higher-performing and more highly skilled employees they introduce benefits to their employers and economies, in their home or chosen country. There they can bring impacts in education, capacity building and societal development, which will increase with time as they become more influential.
>
> (Mellors-Bourne et al. 2013: xiii)

Our research on the experiences of 652 Chinese students who returned home upon completion of their degrees in UK universities over the last 25+ years (Gu and Schweisfurth 2015) offers additional, detailed qualitative and quantitative evidence on the ways in which study-abroad experiences may contribute to the employment qualities and opportunities of international graduates. For the large majority of the Chinese returnees in our research, such experiences were avenues of diverse social networks that reinforce a complex cosmopolitan identity and awareness. They were also avenues of transnational(ised) new competences, skills and worldview, which were increasingly valued by the students themselves upon return home. Irrespective of differences in their demographics and backgrounds, their journeys of studying abroad and returning home were perceived by most as dynamic and interconnected transnational experiences facilitating new ways of seeing themselves, their networks and prospects. These new connections, competences and identities enabled them to view and live life with a new sense of self at "home" and, as a result, function in ways that continued to distinguish themselves from those around them over time. Taken together, we argue that the patterns of migration found in these students is a reminder that:

> [M]igration can be transient and that when researching over cultural boundaries class-based habitus theories have limited capacity to explain how transmigrant individuals from diverse socioeconomic and class backgrounds have experienced similar struggles and transitions during their study-abroad periods....
>
> For most international students, study abroad is for a fixed period, to an environment designed (at least in part) to accommodate them, and for a particular set of purposes different from the motivations of migrant labour. All of these have implications for the nature of their network affiliations, for the long-term application of the skills, knowledge and attitudes they have acquired, and for their identities as Chinese and cosmopolitan citizens. This study has shown that both the original and new identities are sustainable over time, with the support of diverse networks.
>
> (Gu and Schweisfurth 2015)

The cumulative impact of these flows not only point to a new kind of networked and competent individual – they also raise questions about whether traditional understandings of development, such as human capital for national economic growth, bear scrutiny in the context of transnationalism.

Sustaining transnational flows of international students: wider benefits and impact in whose interest?

The changing landscape of the internationalisation of higher education is driven by a range of dynamic social, cultural, economic and political forces. However, the most constant and profound driver of internationalisation continues to be globalisation, and much has been written about the complex relationships between the two (Teichler 2004; Knight 2008; Altbach, Reisberg and Rumbley 2009; Foskett and Maringe 2010; de Wit 2011). For example, Altbach and Knight (2007) argue that globalisation is:

> [T]he economic, political, and societal forces pushing 21st century higher education toward greater international involvement. . . .
>
> Globalisation and internationalisation are related but not the same thing. Globalisation is the context of economic and academic trends that are part of the reality of the 21st century. Internationalisation includes the policies and practices undertaken by academic systems and institutions – and even individuals – to cope with the global academic environment.

> (p. 290)

Internationalisation, therefore, is "changing the world of higher education, and globalisation is changing the world of internationalisation'" (Knight 2008: 1).

Understanding the connections between globalisation and internationalisation and especially the political, sociocultural, academic and economic drivers of the international mobility of students and higher education programmes is critical in understanding a simple reality that *internationalisation is unequal*. The significant increase in East–West and South–North student mobility (Seddoh 2001; OECD 2007, 2014; Uvalic-Trumbic, Daniel and West 2007; UNESCO 2009, 2013) has major implications for the generation of economic and social capital in the host nations. The total value of American education exports was $14.5 billion in 2007, compared to $12 billion in 2004 (NAFSA 2006, 2007). Profit making and the drive for geo-political and commercial advantage have remained a key motive for many internationalisation projects (Altbach and Knight 2007; Scott 2011). Moreover, knowledge production, utilisation and distribution have been dominated by the powerful universities and academic systems at the centre (Altbach 2006). Associated with this is the migration of academic talent, which in many ways has been pulled towards developed countries. While the specific costs and potential benefits to developing countries are less well documented, the internationalisation of higher education in some respects reinforces the centre-periphery tensions (Altbach, Reisberg and Rumbley 2009).

The significant increase in East–West and South–North student mobility and the skewed expansion of internationalised higher education are most likely to witness a continued increase in the scale of the international migration of skills in the world of work. Since the 1990s, migration flows of highly skilled workers have also expanded dramatically (OECD 2008). Many students have remained in the country in which they study. In the United States, the average stay rate for Chinese doctorate recipients skyrocketed to 96 percent from 65 percent between 1992 and 2001 and from 72 percent to 85 percent for Indians. OECD (2008) data show that of the 113 countries for which information is available, 27 have expatriation rates of their tertiary educated people to the OECD area of over 20 percent, including nine countries where the rate is over 50 percent.

In addition, thanks to the continuing advancement of science and technology, the mobility of people and skills has already made possible for everyone – including those who travel and those who do not – to consume cultural products and knowledge and ideas that are globally produced and distributed and, through this, transformed the nature of work and social life in the wider world (Rizvi 2008). Rizvi (2008), in agreement with Appadurai (1996), argues that global imagination:

> [N]ow plays a crucial role in how people engage with their everyday activities, consider their options and make decisions within the new configuration of social relations that are no longer confined to local communities but potentially span, either directly or indirectly, national boundaries.
>
> (2008: 18–19)

The trend of skills mobility is likely to see continued proliferation in the "flattening and shrinking" world (Friedman 2005: 11), driven by unevenly distributed economic, political and ideological forces, as well as the forces of cultural (and local) diversity and forces of global interconnectivity.

Knight (2006) provided a useful distinction between national- and institutional-level rationales for expanding internationalisation and the competition for global mobile students. The key drivers, which are of particular importance at the national level, include human resources development, strategic alliances, income generation/commercial trade, nation and institution building and social/cultural development and mutual understanding. At the institutional level, key driving forces of internationalisation are international branding and profile, quality enhancement/international standards, alternative income generation, student and staff development, networks and strategic alliances, and knowledge production (Knight 2006: 216).

Coming into the second decade of the 21st century, some policy movements in the UK and Australia suggest an emerging ideologically driven rationale for internationalisation at the national level. Governments in both countries have imposed changes to visa criteria and skilled migration rules despite warnings from the higher education sector. In Britain, international students contribute 10–30 percent of most universities' total income (UKCISA 2010) and approximately £12.5 billion per year to the UK national economy (British Council 2008). In addition, they offer UK business-enhanced opportunities (British Council 2010). However, despite the economic recession, funding cuts and these financial incentives, the UK coalition government is committed to deliver its immigration pledges, and actions have been taken to cap the number of skilled workers from outside the European Economic Area (BBC 2010) and also reduce international student visa numbers by 230,000 over the next five years (Guardian 2011). In Australia, the Department of Immigration and Citizenship's tough new immigration rules send "an unmistakable signal" to the higher education industry that it 'needs to set its marketing around selling an education that is valuable back in the country of origin' (THE 28th July 2011). This signal has successfully depressed the prospects of recruitment, and the number of applications from international students fell dramatically in 2011 (THE 11th August 2011).

It is then perhaps not surprising that such an ideologically driven approach to immigration policies is under increasing criticism because it is, at least in part, in conflicting interest to most higher education institutions' internationalisation agendas to increase their international profiles, develop their academic extension, secure their financial health, and also gain a competitive edge in the global competition for talent.

Conclusions

Internationalisation is the most revolutionary development of higher education in the 21st century (Seddoh 2001). The scope and complexity of this phenomenon have expanded and deepened at an unprecedented pace over the past decade, fuelled by the process of economic, social and cultural globalisation and localisation (Rizvi 2008). The benefits to universities of internationalising are academic and cultural as well as financial. These are the rewards that demand a transformative approach to internationalisation (Bartell 2003; Turner and Robson 2008). This orientation is internally driven, partnership-focused, and cooperative in process (Turner and Robson 2008). It is also a far more challenging prospect for institutions than the symbolic, market-oriented approach, but it offers sustainable benefits, and not just for international students.

As the global education competition has become more intense, securing high-quality learning experiences of international students in receiving institutions holds one key to success. Given the complexities of the phenomenon of internationalisation, its development has been inextricably intertwined with new challenges over time. One much debated challenge confronting higher education institutions is the offering of pedagogically and culturally responsive and appropriate curricular to a student population that is increasingly massified and diversified. Related with this challenge is a growing need for well-defined quality assurance, accountability and qualifications frameworks that can be understood and shared across borders and cultures (Altbach, Reisberg and Rumbley 2009) and that ensure that the broadening and deepening of cross-border education provision is systematic and sustained. Finally, at a time when no one knows how deep the economic crisis will become or how long higher education will have to suffer from significant cutbacks (Altbach, Reisberg and Rumbley 2009), the role of the academic profession and university administrations in providing a high-quality learning experience for all international mobile students – both abroad and at home – will remain a pressing challenge now and in the times to come within the moral framework of transformative internationalisation.

From the perspectives of low- and middle-income countries, the asymmetries of the internationalisation phenomenon generally and student flows specifically raise a number of questions going forward to the post-2015 development agenda. In the light of the benefits and costs of student mobility, how should governments in the global South and development agencies respond to it? Debates are ongoing as to whether mobility should be a priority for targeted support and funding, through scholarships for example, and if so, under what conditions. As the strong emphasis on basic education of the past two decades creates new demand for higher levels of education, and as understandings of development shift in emerging contexts of transnationalism and securitisation, the role of student mobility demands further attention by researchers and policymakers alike.

References

Advisory Panel on Canada's International Education Strategy, 2012. *International Education: A Key Driver of Canada's Future Prosperity*. Foreign Affairs, Trade and Development Canada, Ottawa.

Altbach, P., 2006. Globalisation and the university: realities in an unequal world. In: Forest, J. and Altbach, P. (Eds.) *International Handbook of Higher Education*. Springer, Dordrecht.

Altbach, P., Knight, J., 2007. The internationalisation of higher education: motivations and realities. *Journal of Studies in International Education* 11, 3–4, 290–305.

Altbach, P., Reisberg, L., Rumbley, L., 2009. *Trends in Global Higher Education: Tracking an Academic Revolution*. A Report Prepared for the UNESCO 2009 World Conference on Higher Education: Executive Summary. UNESCO, Paris.

Appadurai, A., 1996. *Modernity at Large: Cultural Dimensions of Globalisation*. University of Minnesota Press, Minneapolis and London.

Bartell, M., 2003. Internationalization of universities: a university culture-based framework. *Higher Education* 45, 43–70.

BBC, 2010, 23 November. UK Government Agrees on Skilled Migration Gap. http://www.bbc.co.uk/news/uk-politics-11816979

Berger, P., Luckmann, T., 1966. *The Social Construction of Reality*. Penguin, Harmondsworth.

Biggs, J., 1996. Western misperceptions of the Confucian-heritage learning culture. In: Watkins, D. and Biggs, J. (Eds.) *The Chinese Learner: Cultural, Psychological and Contextual Influences*. CERC and ACER, Hong Kong.

Böhm, A., Follari, M., Hewett, A., Jones, S., Kemp, N., Meares, D., Pearce, D., Cauter, K., 2004. *Vision 2020: Forecasting International Student Mobility: A UK Perspective*. British Council, London.

British Council, 2008, 24 April. International Student of the Year. http://www.britishcouncil.org/new/press-office/press-releases/international-student-of-the-year-20080424/

British Council, 2010. *A Guide for Employers Recruiting International Students and Graduates*. British Council, London.

British Council, 2012. *Shape of Things to Come: Higher Education Global Trends and Emerging Opportunities to 2020*. British Council, London.

British Council, 2013. *The Future of the World's Mobile Students to 2024*. British Council, London.

British Council, 2014. *Postgraduate student mobility trends to 2024*. British Council, London.

Brooks, R., Waters, J., Pimlott-Wilson, H., 2012. International education and the employability of UK students. *British Educational Research Journal* 38, 2, 281–298.

Butcher, A., 2002. A grief observed: grief experiences of East Asian international students returning to their countries of origin. *Journal of Studies in International Education* 6, 4, 354–368.

Byram, M., 2003. On being "bicultural" and "intercultural". In: Alred, G., Byram, M. and Fleming, M. (Eds.) *Intercultural Experience and Education*. Multilingual Matters, Clevedon.

Carlson, S., 2013. Becoming a mobile student – a processual perspective on German degree student mobility. *Population, Space and Place* 19, 168–180.

Chang, W.-C., 2000. In search of the Chinese in all the wrong places! *Journal of Psychology in Chinese Societies* 1, 1, 125–142.

Christofi, V., Thompson, C., 2007. You cannot go home again: a phenomenological investigation of returning to the sojourn country after studying abroad. *Journal of Counselling and Development* 85, 1, 53–63.

Coolahan, J., 2002. Teacher education and the teaching career in an era of lifelong learning. OECD Education Working Papers No. 2, OECD, Paris.

Cushner, K., Karim, A., 2004. Study abroad at the university level. In: Landis, D., Bennett, J., and Bennet, M. (Eds.) *Handbook of Intercultural Training*. Third Edition. Sage, Thousand Oaks.

de Wit, H., 2008. Changing Trends in the Internationalisation of Higher Education. http://www.cshe.unimelb.edu.au/research/seminarpapers/deWitPres061008.pdf

de Wit, H., 2011. Trends, issues and challenges in internationalisation of higher education. Centre for Applied Research on Economics and Management, Hogeschool van Amsterdam, Amsterdam.

Findlay, A., King, R., 2010. Motivations and experiences of UK students studying abroad. BIS Research Paper No. 8, Department for Business, Innovation and Skills, London.

Foskett, N., Maringe, F., 2010. Internationalisation of HE: a prospective view to 2025. In: Maringe, F. and Foskett, N. (Eds.) *Globalisation and Internationalisation of HE: Theoretical, Strategic and Management Perspectives*. Continuum, London.

Friedman, T., 2005. *The World is Flat*. Penguin, London.

Furnham, A., 2004. Foreign students education and culture shock. *Psychologist* 17, 1, 16–19.

Furnham, A., Bochner, S., 1986. *Culture Shock*. Methuen, London.

Gaw, K., 2000. Reverse culture shock in students returning from overseas. *International Journal of Intercultural Relations* 24, 1, 83–104.

Geddie, K., 2013. The transnational ties that bind. *Population, Space and Place* 19, 196–208.

Glass, C., Westmont, C., 2014. Comparative effects of belongingness on the academic success and cross-cultural interactions of domestic and international students. *International Journal of Intercultural Relations* 38, 106–119.

Grimshaw, T., 2007. Problematizing the construct of "the Chinese learner": insights from ethnographic research. *Educational Studies* 33, 3, 299–311.

Gu, Q., 2009. Maturity and interculturality: Chinese students' experiences in UK higher education. *European Journal of Education* 44, 1, 37–52.

Gu, Q., Maley, A., 2008. Changing places: a study of Chinese students in the UK. *Language and Intercultural Communication* 8, 4, 224–245.

Gu, Q., Schweisfurth, M., 2006. Who adapts? Beyond cultural models of "the" Chinese learner. *Language, Culture and Curriculum* 19, 1, 74–89.

Gu, Q., Schweisfurth, M., 2011. Editorial: re-thinking university internationalisation: towards transformative change. Special Issue of *Teachers and Teaching: Theory and Practice* 17, 6, 611–617.

Gu, Q., Schweisfurth, M., 2015. Transnational connections, competences and identities: Experiences of Chinese international students after their return "home". *British Educational Research Journal* (in press).

Gu, Q., Schweisfurth, M., Day, C., 2010. Learning and growing in a "foreign" context: intercultural experiences of international students. *Compare* 40, 1, 7–23.

Guardian, 2011, 12 June. Foreign Student Visa Numbers to Be Cut by 230,000 over Five Years. http://www.guardian.co.uk/uk/2011/jun/13/foreign-student-visa-numbers-cut

Gudykunst, W. (Ed.), 2005. *Theorizing about Intercultural Communication*. Sage, Thousand Oaks.

Guo, S., Chase, M., 2011. Internationalisation of higher education: integrating international students into Canadian academic environment. *Teaching in Higher Education* 16, 3, 305–318.

Han, D., 2013. Returnees and their political impact: evidence from returned students and trainees from the Soviet Union in China, 1950–1966. *Journal of Contemporary China* 22, 84, 1106–1123.

Held, D., McGrew, A., Goldblatt, D., Parraton, J., 1999. *Global Transformation: Politics, Economics and Culture*. Stanford University Press, Palo Alto.

International Association of Universities, 2003. *Internationalisation of Higher Education. Practices and Priorities: 2003 IAU Survey Report*. IAU, Paris.

International Association of Universities, 2005. *Internationalisation of Higher Education: New Directions, New Challenges*. IAU, Paris.

International Association of Universities, 2010. *Internationalisation of Higher Education: Global Trends, Regional Perspectives*. IAU, Paris.

International Association of Universities, 2014. *Internationalisation of Higher Education: Growing Expectations, Fundamental Values*. IAU, Paris.

International Education Advisory Council, 2013. *Australia–Educating Globally*. Commonwealth of Australia, Canberra.

Jenkins, R., 2004. *Social Identity*. Second Edition. Routledge, Abingdon.

Jones, A., 2005. Culture and context: critical thinking and student learning in introductory macroeconomics. *Studies in Higher Education* 30, 3, 339–354.

Kim, Y.-Y., 2005. Adapting to a new culture: an integrative communication theory. In: Gudykunst, W. (Ed.) *Theorizing about Intercultural Communication*. Sage, Thousand Oaks.

King, P., Baxter Magolda, M., 2005. A developmental model of intercultural maturity. *Journal of College Student Development* 46, 6, 571–592.

Knight, J., 2006. Internationalisation: concepts, complexities and challenges. In: Forest, J. and Altbach, P. (Eds.) *International Handbook of Higher Education*. Springer, Dordrecht.

Knight, J., 2008. *Higher Education in Turmoil. The Changing World of Internationalization*. Sense, Rotterdam.

Landreman, L., 2003. A multidimensional model of intercultural consciousness: A reconceptualization of multicultural competence. Paper presented at the Annual Meeting of the Association for the Study of Higher Education, Portland, November.

Levy, O., Peiperl, M., Bouquet, C., 2013. Transnational social capital: A conceptualization and research instrument. *International Journal of Cross Cultural Management* 13, 3, 319–338.

Little, A., Green, A., 2009. Successful globalisation, education and sustainable development. *International Journal of Educational Development* 29, 166–174.

Madge, C., Raghuram, P., Noxolo, P., 2014. Conceptualizing international education: From international student to international study. *Progress in Human Geography*. doi:10.1177/0309132514526442

McGrath, T., Stock, P., Butcher, A., 2007. *Friends and allies: The impacts of returning Asian students on New Zealand-Asia relationship*. Asia–New Zealand Foundation Outlook Paper 05, Wellington.

Mellors-Bourne, R., Humphrey, C., Kemp, N., Woodfield, S., 2014. *The Wider Benefits of International Higher Education in the UK*. Department for Business, Innovation and Skills, London.

Montgomery, C., McDowell, L., 2009. Social networks and international student experience: an international community of practice? *Journal of Studies in International Education* 13, 4, 455–466.

Morrison, J., Merrick, B., Higgs, S., Le Métais, J., 2005. Researching the performance of international students in the UK. *Studies in Higher Education* 30, 3, 327–337.

Murphy-Lejeune, E., 2003 An experience of interculturality: student travellers abroad. In: Alred, G., Byram, M. and Fleming, M. (Eds.) *Intercultural Experience and Education*. Multilingual Matters, Clevedon.

NAFSA, 2006. Public Policy. http://www.nafsa.org/public_policy.sec/international_education_1/the_economic_benefits

NAFSA, 2007. Public Policy. http://www.nafsa.org/public_policy.sec/international_education_1/eis_2007

OECD (with the World Bank), 2007. *Cross-border Tertiary Education: A Way towards Capacity Development*. OECD, Paris.

OECD, 2008. Policy brief: cross-border higher education and development. OECD, Paris.

OECD, 2014. *Education at a Glance 2014*. OECD, Paris.

Paulston, C., 1992. Biculturalism: some reflections and speculations. In: Paulston, C. (Ed.) *Sociolinguistic Perspectives on Bilingual Education*. Multilingual Matters, Clevedon.

Rizvi, F., 2008. Epistemic virtues and cosmopolitan learning. *Australian Educational Researcher* 35, 1, 17–35.

Schweisfurth, M., 2012. Are sojourners natural comparativists? critical perspectives on the learning experiences of international students. *Research in Comparative and International Education* 7, 1, 81–89.

Schweisfurth, M., Gu, Q., 2009. Exploring the experiences of international students in UK higher education: possibilities and limits of interculturality in university life. *Intercultural Education* 20, 5, 463–473.

Scott, P., 2011, 6 June. Universities are all "internationalising" now. *The Guardian*. http://www.guardian.co.uk/education/2011/jun/07/universities-global-ambitions-internationalising/print

Seddoh, F., 2001. Internationalisation of higher education: what for, how and at what cost? *International Association of Universities Newsletter* 7, 3, 1–3.

Sherry, M., Thomas, P., Chui, W.-H., 2010. International students: a vulnerable student population. *Higher Education* 60, 33–46.

Signorini, P., Wiesemes, R., Murphy, R., 2009. Developing alternative frameworks for exploring intercultural learning: a critique of Hofstede's cultural difference model. *Teaching in Higher Education* 14, 3, 253–264.

Sin, L.-I., 2013. Cultural capital and distinction: aspiration of the "other" foreign student. *British Journal of Sociology of Education* 34, 5–6, 848–867.

Suspitsyna, T., 2013. Socialisation as sensemaking: a semiotic analysis of international graduate students' narratives in the USA. *Studies in Higher Education* 38, 9, 1351–1364.

Teichler, U., 2004. The changing debate on internationalisation in higher education. *Higher Education* 48, 1, 5–26.

Times Higher Education (THE), 2011, 28 July. Degree Path to Migration Narrows. http://www.timeshighereducation.co.uk/story.asp?storyCode=416930andsectioncode=26

Times Higher Education (THE), 2011, 11 August. Visa Application Sink Down Under. http://www.timeshighereducation.co.uk/story.asp?storyCode=417078andsectioncode=26

Turner, Y., Robson, S., 2008. *Internationalising the University*. Continuum, London.

UKCISA, 2010. *International Students in the UK: Facts, Figures and Fiction*. UKCISA, London.

UNESCO, 2009. *Global Education Digest 2009*. UNESCO, Paris.

UNESCO, 2013. *The International Mobility of Students in Asia and the Pacific*. UNESCO, Paris and Bangkok.

Uvalić-Trumbić, S., Daniel, J., West, P., 2007. The role of international online courses in the worldwide provision of education. Paper presented at European Association of Distance Teaching Universities 20th Anniversary Conference, Lisbon, September.

Wang, H.-Y., Miao, L., 2013. *Annual Report on the Development of Chinese Students Studying Abroad*. Social Sciences Academic Press (China), Beijing.

Ward, C., Bochner, S., Furnham, A., 2001. *The Psychology of Culture Shock*. Second Edition. Routledge, Hove.

Ward, C., Kennedy, A., 1993. Where's the "culture" in cross-cultural transition: comparative studies of sojourner adjustment. *Journal of Cross-Cultural Psychology* 24, 2, 221–249.

Waters, J., 2007. "Roundabout routes and sanctuary schools": the role of situated educational practices and habitus in the creation of transnational professionals. *Global Networks* 7, 4, 477–497.

Waters, J., Leung, M., 2013a. Immobile transnationalism? *Urban Studies* 50, 3, 606–620.

Waters, J., Leung, M., 2013b. A colourful university life? *Population, Space and Place* 19, 155–167.

Watkins, D., Biggs, J. (Eds.), 1996. *The Chinese Learner: Cultural, Psychological and Contextual Influences*. CERC and ACER, Hong Kong.

Watkins, D., Biggs, J. (Eds.), 2001. *Teaching the Chinese Learner: Psychological and Pedagogical Perspectives.* CERC, Hong Kong.

Zhang, J., Goodson, P., 2011. Acculturation and psychosocial adjustment of Chinese students: examining mediation and moderation effects. *International Journal of Intercultural Relations* 35, 614–627.

Zweig, D., Wang, H., 2013. Can China bring back the best? The Communist Party organizes China's search for talent. *China Quarterly* 215, 590–615.

Zweig, D., Yang, F., 2014. Overseas students, returnees, and the diffusion of international norms into post-Mao China. *International Studies Review* 16, 2, 252–263.

SECTION 4

International cooperation in education and development

27

THE HISTORY AND FUTURE OF INTERNATIONAL COOPERATION IN EDUCATION[1]

Kenneth King

Introduction

The history of aid or cooperation is inseparably intertwined with the offer of 'development' and its relations with education, skills, technical assistance and capacity building. Similarly, the future of aid or cooperation in the mid-2010s seems to be linked to wider debates about the next development agenda, which will have been settled by September 2015. The actors in these exchanges have altered a great deal over the lengthy period being reviewed, with former recipients of aid becoming donors and completely new donors emerging. Equally, the modalities of assistance have changed a great deal. There have been mood swings from euphoria to pessimism about aid's role in helping countries to reach the global targets. A good number of the serious accounts of aid to education have actually been supported by development agencies.

Western traditions of mission

The dominant tradition in aid for education for several hundred years was that of Christian mission. Though there were many different denominations of Christianity, almost all of them regarded knowledge of the Bible and particularly of the four gospels of the New Testament to be essential to understanding the faith. Hence, literacy was critical to mission. But for sustainability, there was a requirement for local teachers and pastors to be created, and thus there arose the need for secondary education, teacher training and seminaries. In other faiths that depended on reading essential texts, such as Islam, schooling was also vital. But Koranic schools remained very much more closely tied to the teaching of the Koran than the schools of Christian missionaries to the Old and New testaments. There have been other notable examples of the spread of religious faiths, such as that of Buddhism to China, but these did not generalise into missionary movements.

These Christian missionary initiatives were a global phenomenon, but they were facilitated by empire and by those European nations that dominated Africa, Asia, the Caribbean and the Pacific. Though missionaries regarded themselves as very different from their countrymen associated with empire and with trade, many also recognised that their offer of Christianity was in many ways supported by commerce and by the 'civilising mission' of empire (Livingstone 1858).

The literacy and numeracy skills acquired in the mission schools proved attractive – indeed essential – for the tens of thousands of clerks needed for the colonial administrations. With the colonies running in the languages of the metropolis, there were soon Christian colleges in the Indian subcontinent, and these appeared even in areas such as China where there was no formal empire. The same was true of Catholic universities in Latin America, both before and after its independence from Spain and Portugal.

If mission schools had remained focused on the catechisms of Christianity, as the Koranic schools had focused on the Koran, the links between mission schools and secular jobs would not have become so quickly obvious. Globally, missions proved a challenge to traditional religions and local cultures, even though they were responsible for providing literacy (and the Bible) in local languages for the first time in many parts of the world, especially in sub-Saharan Africa (Achebe 1958).

The formalisation of mission was linked to the formalisation of colonial rule; hence, missions had to work with the new government departments of education and had to provide inspection and some uniformity of curriculum. Quality became important and, across sub-Saharan Africa, from South Africa to the Gold Coast and to Kenya Colony, there arose great schools and colleges with famous names, such as Alliance High School, Achimota College and Fourah Bay College.

Some of the key issues that arose during the missionary period had some resonance with later periods of international cooperation. Amongst these would be the tension between the curricula of the metropolis and those adapted for the colonial mission schools, the attractiveness of academic curricula and those associated with technical and vocational education, the dependence on international staff versus local leadership, and financial dependency on the headquarters of the mission versus domestic funding (King 1971).

The growth of bilateral and multilateral cooperation agencies

The start of development cooperation is often linked to President Truman's Inaugural in 1949 (Rist 1997). One of the key elements in that address was the offer of technical knowledge to the developing world and, with that, the notion of technical assistance and capacity building. During the same period from 1948, and conscious of the perceived threat from the Soviet Union, the United States promoted the Marshall Plan for the rebuilding of European nations after the war. Like the parallel support to Japan, this massive aid effort was not principally educational but economic. The recipients of such aid had had compulsory education for some 70 years. Nevertheless, these economic development initiatives did lead to very large offers of scholarship aid in the United States, much of this associated with the new international reach of US foundations, such as Rockefeller, Ford and Carnegie. The Soviet Union also offered large numbers of scholarships at this time.

The United Nations emerged towards the end of the Second World War; associated with that was the birth of UNESCO. At the beginning of the 1960s, UNESCO had already organised a series of regional conferences that illustrated one enduring dimension of international aid – the setting of regional (and later global) targets for different levels of education. Equally, the Bretton Woods organisations had developed towards the end of the war, but it was not until the early 1960s that the World Bank funded its first educational project.

In the early 1960s, bilateral aid agencies were established. These were no longer linked only to countries that had had colonies but included countries such as those in the Nordic region, as well as Switzerland, Austria and Canada. It should also be noted that South Korea, China, India and Japan also began their bilateral aid programmes at this time. Such aid, in the case of the first three, could be termed South-South cooperation (SSC), as it was aid between countries that still regarded themselves as developing their economies. This notion of SSC has its origins in the Non-Aligned Movement (NAM) of 1961, which positioned leading developing countries such as India, Indonesia, Yugoslavia and Egypt outside the competing Eastern and Western blocs. It is worth recognising also that the offer of international co-operation was frequently associated with the need to build the donor country's own understanding of the nations they were aiding. Hence, there was the development of area studies and development studies in many countries from the 1960s. Parallels can be seen today, within SSC, in which China's increasing aid to Africa, for example, has led to the dramatic growth of African studies within China.

A key dimension of international cooperation to education has always been support from civil society organisations. Nongovernmental organisations (NGOs), such as Oxfam, began their work in Europe during the Second World War and extended to developing countries in the early 1950s. The same was true of Save the Children, which started in the USA by serving the poor of that country, then moved to the poor children in Europe, and on to the children of the developing world in the 1950s.

Education in parallel with development shifts

While it is difficult to generalise across the several different actors in educational cooperation – bilaterals, multilaterals, NGOs and foundations – there was still a tendency for there to be patterns in the support of educational aid that paralleled what was happening to development thinking and development debates more generally.

Education for national development

Thus, the era of education for national development took place after the achievement of independence when countries were seeking to pursue rapid economic development. Whether in India, Zambia or Nigeria, there were education commissions that looked across the whole of the education sector. But they paid particular attention to the development of what was called 'high level manpower', which, in many newly independent countries, was in very short supply. This implied the rapid development of both secondary academic and technical education, as well as many different levels of tertiary education, including teacher training, polytechnic and university. In the field of vocational training, the International Labour Organisation (ILO) developed a whole series of national industrial and vocational training institutions across developing countries. Local staffing for these institutions, both academic and technical, was insufficient in many countries, and there was a massive outpouring of staff from Europe, North America, but also to a lesser extent from Asia, in order to provide the first generation of teachers for these new institutions. In this form, technical assistance from the North was critical to rapid institutional development.

This huge demand led in 1958 to the origin of the Voluntary Service Overseas (VSOs) from the UK, to the Peace Corps from USA in 1961, and to the Japanese Overseas Cooperation Volunteers (JOCVs) in 1965, amongst several other volunteer organisations. The majority of these volunteers staffed the new education institutions across Asia, Africa and Latin America. France also provided coopérants (trainers) to education systems in many parts of Francophone Africa and Asia. Many thousands of other staff from Europe and North America went to man the new university systems of South East Asia, the Caribbean and sub-Saharan Africa. There was a widespread optimism that the new states would rapidly catch up with Europe and North America.

The UNESCO conferences of the 1960s, mentioned above, were also the first vehicle for setting targets for different levels of education. It was at this time that the new discipline of the economics of education entered the debates on education and development. The optimistic targets in these first conferences underlined the euphoria about development and education's role in facilitating this.

Within only a few years from the era of independence, the discourse of optimism had been replaced by talk of crisis, especially in Africa. The target-driven plans for educational expansion were not generating the expected economic returns. Suddenly, there was talk of educated unemployment and of a *World Educational Crisis* (Coombs 1968). This ushered in a new external engagement with nonformal education and the 'discovery' of the informal sector in the very early 1970s. The excitement about high-level manpower and the development of the new universities of Africa was short lived (King and McGrath 2012). Now the talk was of "More help for the poorest" (King and McGrath 2012) and of education as a 'basic need'.

The speed with which fashions in educational aid have changed, reflecting different approaches to development, has been a continuing feature of educational cooperation. High-level manpower in support of education for national development was followed by a fascination with nonformal education for development. This provided a few years of much needed international attention to a whole range of structured education and training activities beyond the confines of the formal school. Adult education was suddenly, but briefly, on the world's education cooperation agenda.

But in all these different international aid priorities and fashions, it must be emphasised that there has often been a disconnect between what may be exercising the international educational aid community and the realities of what is happening in national ministries of education and of labour. Thus, the focus on nonformal education in the early and mid-1970s internationally may have had little impact at the national level.

1980s – a lost decade?

We will fast-forward now to 1980 and to new education priorities. On the global stage, of course, this was the moment when the neoliberals gained power, represented by the Reagan-Kohl-Thatcher triumvirate. The 1980s were widely felt to be a lost decade in terms of educational development, especially in Africa. As far as one of our principal story threads – educational aid targets – is concerned, it was the year that universal primary education (UPE) in Africa was meant to be achieved, according to the Addis Ababa commitment from the UNESCO regional conference already mentioned (UNESCO/UNECA 1961). This is an important fact to remember for the rest of this chapter, as it marked the first of a series of failures for international education targets to be met, a point of great salience as we contemplate the current round of such target making post-2015. Yet, unlike what we can see in the case of the supposed millennium development targets for 2015, this 1980 deadline for UPE to be achieved passed with little political or policy attention.

However, the 1980s did see the World Bank established as the major force in research on education and development. In turn, the Bank's education priorities influenced other aid donors. Thus, from a research perspective, it was not a lost decade at all but a very rich, albeit highly controversial, one. The Bank's new education research priorities were captured in its very influential *Education Sector Policy Paper* of 1982. This built on a series of early research studies that famously made the link between female education and reduced fertility and infant mortality (Cochrane 1979); between four years of education and farmer productivity (Lockheed, Jamison and Lau 1980; King, Palmer and Hayman 2005); and, particularly in developing African economies like Uganda, argued that inputs like textbooks would 'make a difference' to a much greater extent than in the older developed economies (Heyneman, Farrell and Sepulveda-Stuarda 1978). These studies tended to focus on primary education as a key element in delivering wider developmental benefits (cf. Colclough 1980). But it was left to Psacharopoulos to deliver the body blow in favour of primary education and against secondary and higher education through a range of cross-national rate of return studies that showed that primary education largely and consistently gave a significantly better return on investment than other forms of formal education (Psach-aropoulos 1981, 1985). These findings were criticised by many academics, but arguably they helped the Bank with what seemed a powerful economic case for support to primary education. And that made it possible for the Bank, in due course, to support Education for All (EFA) directly, as we shall see below.

Meanwhile, the Bank was also busy spreading a new message of structural adjustment to Africa and more generally. In 1981, the Bank released a report entitled *Accelerated Development in Sub-Saharan Africa* (World Bank 1981). At its heart was an argument that Africa's developmental woes were largely self-inflicted, being the result of bad governance and statism. Together with the International Monetary Fund (IMF), the Bank developed a set of conditionalities for loans to Africa (and other regions). Though their neoliberal confidence was often misplaced, the Bretton Woods institutions did paint a picture of Africa's ills that was agreed upon by many internal commentators. However, many of these also argued that forced austerity would lead to greater poverty and called for African versions of the East Asian development state (Mkandawire 1988, 1999; Onimode 1988; Olukoshi 1993).

The education parallel to structural adjustment was the World Bank's *Education in Sub-Saharan Africa* (1988). Based on the research studies to which we have referred, but also on inadequate research on the African university sector, the Bank delivered a further body blow to the already fragile university sector in Africa. Even the subtitle, *Policies for Adjustment, Revitalisation, and Expansion,* reminded the reader that this was an education parallel to economic structural adjustment. There was an articulate African critique of this World Bank report, including by the then two ministers of education in Zimbabwe (Chung 1989; Mutumbuka 1989), but this had little traction compared to the Bank report. The chapter in the Bank report relating to international cooperation made the point that despite the Bank's research studies, a great deal of foreign aid to education went to support of tertiary education in Africa. Within two years from 1988, that was about to start changing dramatically.

Jomtien and Education for All – the 1990s

To date, the most significant of all the international conferences and target-setting moments for educational aid has been the Jomtien World Conference on Education for All of March 1990. The wealth of research evidence generated by the World Bank in previous years came together with a strong human rights discourse, largely from the international NGO community, to generate a set of six suggested goals for "Education for All" (EFA) to be achieved by 2000. It is worth taking a moment to recall the breadth of the EFA goals, as that breadth subsequently has largely been forgotten.

Box 27.1. The six dimensions of EFA targets at Jomtien

- Expansion of early childhood care and development activities, including family and community interventions, especially for poor, disadvantaged and disabled children;
- Universal access to, and completion of, primary (or whatever higher level of education is considered as 'basic') by the year 2000;

- Improvement of learning achievement such that an agreed percentage of an age cohort (e.g., 80 percent of 14-year-olds) attains or surpasses a defined level of necessary learning achievement;

- Reduction of the adult illiteracy rate (the appropriate age group to be determined in each country) to, say, one half its 1990 level by the year 2000, with sufficient emphasis on female literacy to significantly reduce the current disparity between male and female illiteracy rates;

- Expansion of the provision of basic education and training in other essential skills required by youth and adults, with programme effectiveness assessed in terms of behavioural change and impact on health, employment and productivity;

- Increased acquisition by individuals and families of the knowledge, skills and values required for better living and sound and sustainable development, made available through all education channels including the mass media, other forms of modern and traditional communication, and social action, with effectiveness assessed in terms of behavioural change.

Source: WCEFA 1990.

It is important to emphasise that Jomtien's focus was not narrowly on basic education of children but more broadly on "meeting the basic learning needs" of children, youths and adults. Like with the earlier Bank education sector policy papers, Jomtien was yet another external influence impacting Africa, Asia and Latin America. The Jomtien process was driven essentially by the heads of UNICEF and of the World Bank, but its priorities were a far cry from the more inclusive spirit of the Addis Ababa conference. It did not use the words 'primary education' at all, but it did use 'basic education' 158 times in 37 pages! 'University education' was only mentioned once. So the message was clear.

One year after Jomtien, in 1991, a further external influence, in the form of the World Bank's first education sector policy on vocational and technical education and training, was issued. Its critique of public sector vocational education and training (VET) was so pronounced that it effectively weakened both the national and donor agency case for supporting VET (World Bank 1991). Despite the continuing influence of Psacharopoulos's rate of return work (see above), the Bank produced its first higher education policy paper in 1994 (World Bank 1994; King and Buchert 1995). Arguably, the Bank review of *Priorities and Strategies for Education* the following year (1995) was more influential. It claimed controversially that "the major difference between East Asia and Sub-Saharan Africa is due to variations in primary school enrolment rates" (World Bank 1995: 23).

The later part of the 1990s also saw the beginnings of attempts to move beyond structural adjustment and the Washington Consensus. At the World Bank itself, the appointment of James Wolfensohn as President in 1995, and his subsequent invitation to Joseph Stiglitz to be his Chief Economist, marked the beginning of a shift within the Bank towards a more holistic view on development; a greater emphasis on national ownership (rather than conditionalities); and a stressing of the importance of the "knowledge economy" (both in terms of internal organisation and the Bank's portfolio of projects) (King and McGrath 2004).

Recasting the goals – 2000 to the present

2000 came and went, with the EFA goals of Jomtien unmet. However, attention to this fact was largely distracted by the United Nations' declaration of a new set of Millennium Development Goals (MDGs) following the Millennium Declaration of that same year. These drew very heavily on the set of "international development targets" proposed in 1996 by the Development Assistance Committee of the Organisation for Economic Co-operation and Development (OECD). Although it is a staple of international policy rhetoric to point to the fact that the MDGs were agreed to by all governments as evidence for their Southern ownership, it is salient for this discussion of aid to stress that the real origins of the MDGs were in the OECD, an agency of the richest countries, meeting in Paris (King 2007).

The MDGs incorporated two education targets:

- Universal primary education
- Equality of enrolments by gender in primary and secondary education.

As can be seen, these reflected a considerable narrowing of the EFA agenda to one of the original Jomtien goals and another that had been added at the 10-year review meeting in the World Forum on Education for All in Dakar. Most strikingly, education had come to be seen once more as identical to schooling. Moreover, these narrower targets were now seen as requiring a further 15 years (until 2015), rather than the 10 of Jomtien, to be achieved.

The new goals produced a new drive to ensure their achievement, with investment in secretariats in both UNESCO and UNICEF; innovative funding mechanisms, such as the Fast Track Initiative (now renamed Global Partnership for Education); and a series of Global Monitoring Reports, published from UNESCO but funded externally from 2002 and led by a series of British directors until 2014. As noted above, there has also been a plethora of funded academic research in this field, including through large-scale investment by DFID. It should be emphasised that the aid funding of educational research in the North has played a key role in the influencing of education policy (King 1991).

Arguably of importance in the period since 2010 has been a return of aid donors (or of "development partners", to use the more fashionable term) to a concern about quality. Whilst the third Jomtien target had spoken of acceptable levels of minimum learning achievement, there is now a wealth of research that points to the widespread failure to achieve quality whilst driving forward on quantity during the EFA era (e.g., Hungi and Thuku 2010; Zuze and Leibbrandt 2011). It is noteworthy that though much of the literature about the learning crisis was derived from Northern sources such as Brookings (2011), there was also data generated by Asian and African assessments, such as the Annual Status of Education Report (in India) and the Southern and Eastern Africa Consortium for Monitoring Educational Quality (SACMEQ). The once donor-dominated Association for the Development of Education in Africa (ADEA) has recently focused on "Promoting critical knowledge, skills and qualifications for sustainable development in Africa: how to design and implement an effective response by education and training systems" (ADEA 2012), but the searing reality for much of Africa is that university-based research, for instance, on skills and qualifications is almost completely absent (UNESCO 2012a).

The 2000s also saw an increasing concern that a poverty reduction-only focus for development was too narrow. In particular, the spread of the discourse of the knowledge economy led to concerns that developing countries needed to focus on building knowledge-intensive industries. As a result, the importance of higher education began to be reassessed, once more, within the international aid community. Most notable here was the report of a joint UNESCO-World Bank task force (UNESCO and World Bank 2000).

Across Africa, Asia and Latin America, higher education enrolments increased markedly, but these were not aid dependent like the experiences with the first generation of universities in many British Commonwealth countries of Africa, Asia and the Caribbean. Governments invested in expanding existing universities, upgrading other tertiary institutions and opening new universities. They also reduced obstacles to private higher education, and a wave of new, local and international private providers entered into many national systems. But over the 30 years since agency and government support for higher education had been questioned in Africa and more widely in other regions, the earlier national institutions had been weakened substantially. Structural adjustment had ensured that, despite university expansion, funding had been constrained and, as a result, one-off consultancies had replaced long-term research in even the once most prestigious universities, especially in Africa.

Although VET never left the agenda in the North, the power of Foster's 1965 critique with those of Psacharopoulos, taken together with the EFA priority and the 1991 World Bank paper, had resulted in a new orthodoxy across most international development agencies that public sector VET was old-fashioned and ineffective. VET provision did continue across Africa, however, driven largely by persistent concerns about youth unemployment rather than by any rigorous reading of what industry wanted (McGrath 2011). The substantial if partial success of EFA in getting more children into schools, nevertheless, has started to push VET up the policy agenda, as has relatively high growth across a number of economies. This has led to greater international interest in the issue. Hence, 2010 saw UNESCO-IIEP publish a new account of the key issues in planning VET (King and Palmer 2010), whilst 2012 saw the draft of a new UNESCO World Report (UNESCO 2012a), an International Congress on TVET and a Global Monitoring Report on Skills (UNESCO 2012b). A range of other key actors produced global reports on skill, including the OECD, the World Bank, and the ILO, but it is an indication of the growing diversity of international players beyond traditional aid donors that the McKinsey Global Institute should also contribute to the debate on skills, work and jobs (NORRAG 2013).

The beginning of the new millennium saw increased efforts at African cooperation in constructing a regional approach to development. The African Union was established in 2002, and the New Partnership for Africa's Development (NEPAD) was inaugurated (Hayman, King and McGrath 2003). As the decade progressed and growth began to be seen in some African economies, there was a new wave of popular economics books that argued that aid was a barrier to development, the encouragement of entrepreneurship and trade being what was required (Easterly 2007; Moyo 2009).

The decade also saw the rise of another discourse that sought to stress agency in poorer countries, although from a very different ideological position than the anti-aid camp. Building on the work done at the UNDP to offer an alternative to the Washington Consensus, and especially to the use of GNP as the sole measure of development, Amartya Sen (1999) and Martha Nussbaum (2000) developed the human development and capabilities approach, which stressed the importance of individual- and community-identified views of the good life over international models of development. Until very recently, its application to education largely consisted of accepting the human rights-based drive of EFA and seeing education as a means of facilitating other capabilities and functionings (McGrath 2012). However, the discourse is beginning to have influence in international VET policy debates (McGrath and Powell 2015).

Although the very different anti-aid and capabilities accounts suggested a move away from 'big development', this was not the message of much of the agencies' continued work nor of the Director of the UN Millennium Project, Jeffrey Sachs (2005, 2008), whose rhetoric and proposals were strongly reminiscent of some of the big push development ideas of the 1960s.

Although conditionalities were declared to be dead, a new discourse of aid effectiveness emerged as agencies sought to get national buy-in to the MDGs and the policies, systems and new aid modalities deemed necessary for their achievement. The iconic policy was the Paris Declaration on Aid Effectiveness (OECD 2005). As with the MDGs, the driving force behind this new approach was the OECD, cementing its rise to a role as a central player in global policymaking, notwithstanding its official status as a membership organisation for developed countries. Although partnership was a central element of the new account, it was easy to see this, like the MDGs, as Southern participation in a Northern-devised process (NORRAG 2009).

Alongside effectiveness also came a new form of developmental positivism in which randomised control trials and systematic reviews came to be seen as the way to measure development in a way that far outstripped the World Bank's earlier research into 'what works' and that rejected as unscientific the large amounts of more interpretivist and critical research that had become dominant in fields such as African Studies and International and Comparative Education (NORRAG 2012).

In the period of three years – 2012–2014 – before the 2015 deadline, there was a tsunami of activity around recasting the millennium goals (King and Palmer 2013). Although there have been several new actors involved, including the private sector and private foundations, that were not present so conspicuously at Jomtien or Dakar, nevertheless the traditional development partners, bilateral and multilateral as well as NGOs, have continued to be very influential. Arguably, this is because securing a stand-alone education goal and a particular set of targets for post-2015 will be vital to the future financing of educational aid, whether by bilateral or multilateral agencies or by international NGOs. Thus, in the field of education, UNESCO and UNICEF remained very visible right through this period, along with key bilaterals such as DFID.

Aid-related themes in the education-development relationship

A great deal of the research published in at least one of the key journals serving the community of international and comparative education, the *International Journal of Educational Development (IJED),* is probably ultimately dependent on aid funding, whether through research grants or consultancies from development partners. Many of the themes covered by a journal such as IJED are those to which we have already alluded above as being closely linked to aid concerns.

In a review of the first 30 years of the *International Journal of Educational Development,* McGrath noted areas of continuity in writing about education and development (McGrath 2010). In 1981, IJED's first issue comprised a series of reviews of the UNESCO target-setting regional conferences of the 1960s, including papers from Fredriksen (1981) and Thompson (1981). McGrath also noted how issues of access and quality were reflected in a large number of more recent IJED articles. In turn, these were strongly influenced by DFID's decision to launch three large education research programmes on access, quality and outcomes, which ran from 2006 to 2010. However, as we have seen above, these three concerns have been central to many development agencies' agendas in the last 20 and more years.

It is crucial both for policy and research on education's role in development to consider why these three themes continue to be so salient. One reason clearly has to do with the way that access became the dominant thread in much donor discourse after Jomtien and then fully 15 years later was suddenly confronted by a great deal of research, much of it aid-supported, that children and young people were not actually learning the basics. The aid fashion switched from access to a focus on learning, learning outcomes and assessment. As early as 2006, the vital need for a learning goal to measure "real progress in education" had been identified by three economists all associated with the World Bank (Filmer, Hasan and Pritchett 2006). This concern about learning outcomes was bolstered by USAID's work on Early Grade Reading Assessment (EGRA), especially in Africa, as well as by regional assessments in Africa and Asia to which we have already alluded (cf. Bartlett and Frazier, this volume).

There has also been a growth of research about pedagogies, which has developed into a rich debate about the extent to which Western learner-centred approaches are an international 'best practice' (NORRAG 2007) or are beyond the resource capacities of poor countries and/or are culturally inappropriate in other contexts (Schweisfurth 2011). One issue that emerges from this literature is the powerful effect that aid projects have had on transmitting an international toolkit of best practice in this area (McGrath 2012) and the difficulty this causes in separating out aid effects from issues inherent in adapting learner-centredness in African contexts. The challenge of policy learning nationally, as opposed to policy borrowing from international best practice, is another way of expressing this.

There have also been new answers to the question of how to reach the poorest with quality education that reflect the ideological shifts from the 1960s. Instead of community self-help and nonformality being celebrated, the emphasis of much more recent literature has been on private provision of education for the poorest (Woodhead, Frost and James 2012), public–private partnerships (Amjad and MacLeod 2014), philanthropy (Srivastava and Oh 2010), vouchers (Elacqua 2012; Mizala and Torche 2012), and conditional cash transfers (Heinrich 2007). However, these answers remain contested and controversial, and there is simply no consensus on the relative roles that should be played by state, market and community in ensuring access to quality education for all. Indeed, it appears that most of the analysis flows very neatly from initial ideological and epistemological assumptions. Thus, any attempt at 'systematic review' of these increasingly copious literatures appears impossible; there is no fixed point outside the debate from which to conduct such an analysis.

The question of language use in education has remained a current one for many researchers (NORRAG 2004), although it has struggled to ever make it to the heart of the global education debate over the past 50 years, in an echo of the marginalisation of this issue at the Addis Ababa conference. There remain complex issues here, including debates about national cohesion; the costs of supporting 'minority languages'; language needs for insertion into the global knowledge economy; and learner, parent and community 'choice', mediated as it is by these other discourses. But so-called metropolitan languages remain high on the global agenda of cultural diplomacy and of support from ministries of foreign affairs, if not also of development. Whether through the Goethe Institutes, the Alliance Française, the Cervantes Institutes, the British Council, the Confucius Institutes, the Russkiy Mir Foundation, the Japan Foundation or the United States Information Agency, language remains a very high aid priority. The alternative position, on the role of local languages as media of instruction, was salient during the colonial period, especially in British colonies, but is currently hard to find except in the valuable work of the Summer Institute of Linguistics (cf. Trudell, Young and Nyaga this volume).

In education, there remains considerable scepticism regarding the merits of targets, especially global ones (cf. King and Rose 2005). We are very aware within the education field that 50 years of targets for education have not resulted in all children being in school, let alone achieving even minimum learning outcomes. We also know that a narrow focus on one part of education cannot bring about the successful development of a whole education system. Going beyond theory to policy, we see a continued faith in international targets for development, as witnessed in the latest iteration of the aid effectiveness targets and the talk of a new set of international development goals for when the MDGs are due to end in 2015.

Shifts in aid modalities: in principle or in practice?

There have been some major proposed shifts in aid modalities since the emergence of bilateral and multilateral agencies. Originally, the project approach reigned supreme in donor support to education and training, with project offices, project cars, project personnel and project budgets. The unsustainability of this approach has been known for years, yet it continues as the preferred form of aid in several key development agencies, as well as in the educational cooperation of the so-called emerging donors such as China, South Africa and India. Aid is essentially tied to the use of the donor's facilities, personnel, overseas training resources and equipment. Money is not transferred into the budget of the recipient or host country.

By contrast, the discourse of the Paris Declaration in 2005 suggested the use of country systems and the avoidance of project implementation offices. But what actually happens when donors seek to put their funds, instead, into sector budget support or general budget support, and when their aid money goes, for example, into the education sector or into the treasury? There have been major shifts over the last 15 years towards sector and general budget support, especially by DFID, but equally there have been concerns that it has proved difficult to demonstrate value-added or value for money when the specifically British contribution is merely part of the budget. And an additional problem is that it does prove possible to change the aid modalities rather substantially but without altering practice in the classrooms (King 2010). This move towards sector and general budget support has actually coincided with the requirement to show value for money. These are, to some extent, in contradiction with each other.

The Paris Declaration as well as the follow-up accords in Accra and in Busan have not had very much direct impact on the way that aid is delivered. Equally, the hugely intensive debates about education and training post-2015 have had very little to say about aid modalities. The bulk of the discussions around education and skills post-2015 has been about the overarching goal and the rationales for the different subsector targets. There has been little discussion of the ways that educational aid is being delivered. One of the key documents in this regard is the *Report of the Thematic Consultation on Education in the Post-2015 Development Agenda* (UNESCO/UNICEF 2013). It was unusual in even discussing the importance of good governance in education, but it contented itself with stressing the importance of donors meeting the 0.7% of GNP for their aid allocations (which only a handful have succeeded in reaching) and of their "delivering predictable aid" and adhering to such "internationally accepted principles as those stated in the Paris Declaration on Aid Effectiveness" (which we have just noted few actually do).

Despite the intensity of the discussions about the detailed content of any education and skills goal, there has been little appetite for discussing the educational financing, both domestic and external, that would be required to meet the ambitious, proposed education targets. All that is said with certainty by the Education for All Global Monitoring Report 2013/4 is that there is currently a massive, annual funding gap of US$26 billion needed to provide basic education to all children, youth and adults by 2015 (UNESCO 2013: 112). If the plan of including lower secondary education in the post-2015 education targets is confirmed, then the annual financing gap would rise to US$38 billion. But "the development assistance community will never be able to fund these further ambitions, even with increased domestic funding" (King 2013: 17).

The mood music in 2014 around aid to education is distinctly bleak. The conclusion of the EFA GMR of 2013/14 as far as aid is concerned restates a sorry evaluation of the 14 EFA years since Dakar 2000: "One of the biggest failures of the EFA period has been fulfilling the pledge that no country would be thwarted in achieving its goals due to lack of resources" (UNESCO 2013: 139). There is little to suggest that there will be a difference around the next set of even more ambitious education targets. The GMR continues:

> To avoid this happening after 2015, national governments, aid donors and other education funders need to be held to account for the commitments to provide the resources necessary to reach education goals. Post-2015 education goals must include a specific target for financing by governments and donors.

In other words, the aid challenge, along with the domestic challenge, is essentially about global and national governance. It is about clarity of understanding the role of a set of internationally agreed goals for education and skills if there is no financing mechanism to put them into place. What body is to hold national governments and aid donors accountable? None exists at present.

In conclusion

There have been many shifts in educational aid over the last century and over the first decade and a half of this century. The global governance approach to education and training points to there being many more players, including nonstate actors, today than there were at the time of Jomtien. Equally, there is much talk about innovative financing mechanisms beyond the traditional aid modalities (King and Palmer 2014). But in the education sector, these new financing mechanisms have not begun to take the place of the existing approaches by development partners. Nor has the discourse about the global governance of education and training really taken the place of such structures as were in place for Jomtien and Dakar. Educational targets remain the name of the game in 2014, as they were in the early 1960s. An agreed text for education post-2015 should be available by the time of the World Educational Forum in South Korea in 2015, and much of this should manage to be secured as part of the world's next development agenda, expected to be complete in September 2015.

It will continue to be important for the international education community to review what happens post-2015. For how long will the valuable EFA Global Monitoring Report be published? Will the Global Partnership for Education become more truly global? Will the OECD's benchmarking through its Programme for International Student Assessment (PISA) and other measures prove to be as globally influential as its international development targets of the 1990s or its Paris Declaration of the 2000s? Beyond agreeing on an overarching goal for education and training post-2015, will it really prove possible to agree on globally indicators that will measure the adjectives in a goal such as this: "Ensure equitable and inclusive quality education and lifelong learning for all" (UNESCO 2014)?

What does seem likely is that, despite these measurement challenges, the quality of learning outcomes will remain a dominant theme in both domestic and international discourses about education for several years to come. Development partners will continue to be engaged with this process. Predictions about the end or demise of aid will continue to be made, but it seems likely that these will continue to be premature.

Note

1 This chapter draws selectively from an unpublished paper by King and McGrath (2012) on 'Education and Development in Africa: Lessons of the past fifty years for beyond 2015', from CAS@50. Available at http://eprints.nottingham.ac.uk/1640/

References

Achebe, C., 1958. *Things Fall Apart*. Heinemann Educational Books, London.
Amjad, R., MacLeod, G., 2014. Academic effectiveness of private, public and private–public partnership schools in Pakistan. *International Journal of Educational Development* 37, 22–31.
Association for the Development of Education in Africa (ADEA), 2012. Promoting critical knowledge, skills and qualifications for sustainable development in Africa: how to design and implement an effective response by education and training systems. Triennale, Ougadougu, February 13–17, 2012.

Accessed September 29, 2014. http://www.africa-eu-partnership.org/news/adea-will-hold-2012-triennale-ouagadougou-february-13-17-2012

Brookings Institution, 2011. *A Global Compact for Learning: Taking Action on Education in Developing Countries.* Centre for Universal Education, Brookings Institution, Washington.

Chung, F., 1989. Policies for primary and secondary education in Zimbabwe: alternatives to the World Bank perspective. *Zimbabwe Journal of Educational Research* 1, 1, 22–42.

Cochrane, S., 1979. *Fertility and Education.* Johns Hopkins University Press, Baltimore.

Colclough, C., 1980. Primary schooling and economic development: a review of the evidence. World Bank Staff Working Paper No. 399, World Bank, Washington.

Coombs, P., 1968. *The World Education Crisis.* Oxford University Press, Oxford.

Easterly, W., 2007. *The White Man's Burden.* Penguin, London.

Elacqua, G., 2012. The impact of school choice and public policy on segregation: evidence from Chile. *International Journal of Educational Development* 32, 3, 444–453.

Filmer, D., Hasan, A., Pritchett, L., 2006. A millennium learning goal: measuring real progress in education. Working Paper 97, Centre for Global Development, Washington.

Foster, P., 1965. The vocational school fallacy in development planning. In: Anderson, A. and Bowman, M. (Eds.) *Education and Economic Development.* Aldine, Chicago.

Fredriksen, B., 1981. Progress towards regional targets for universal primary education: a statistical review. *International Journal of Educational Development* 1, 1, 1–16.

Hayman, R., King, K., McGrath, S. (Eds.), 2003. *The New Partnership for Africa's Development.* Centre of African Studies, University of Edinburgh.

Heinrich, C., 2007. Demand and supply-side determinants of conditional cash transfer program effectiveness. *World Development* 35, 1, 121–143.

Heyneman, S., Farrell, J., Sepulveda-Stuarda, M., 1978. Textbooks and achievement: what we know. World Bank Staff Working Paper No. 298, World Bank, Washington.

Hungi, N., Thuku, F., 2010. Differences in pupil achievement in Kenya: implications for policy and practice. *International Journal of Educational Development* 30, 1, 33–43.

King, K., 1971. *Pan-Africanism and Education.* Clarendon, Oxford.

King, K., 1991. *Aid and Education in the Developing World.* Longman, Harlow.

King, K., 2007. Multilateral agencies in the construction of the global agenda on education. *Comparative Education* 43, 3, 377–391.

King, K., 2010. The new aid architecture in Ghana: influencing policy and practice? *European Journal of Development Research* 23, 648–667.

King, K., 2013. Development assistance for education Post-2015. Regional Consultation Meeting of the Western European and North American States on Education in the Post-2015 Development Agenda, December 5-6, 2013, UNESCO, Paris.

King, K., Buchert, L. (Eds.), 1995. *Learning from Experience: Policy and Practice in Aid to Higher Education.* CESO, The Hague.

King, K., McGrath, S., 2004. *Knowledge for Development?* Zed, London.

King, K., McGrath, S., 2012. Education and development in Africa: lessons of the past fifty years for beyond 2015. Paper presented at CAS@50: Cutting Edges and Perspectives, Centre of African Studies, University of Edinburgh, June.

King, K., Palmer, R., 2010. *Planning for Technical and Vocational Skills Development.* International Institute for Educational Planning, UNESCO, Paris.

King, K., Palmer, R., 2013. Post-2015 agendas: northern tsunami, southern ripple? The case of education and skills. Working Paper No. 4, NORRAG, Geneva.

King, K., Palmer, R., 2014. Development assistance for education post-2015. *Journal of International and Comparative Education* 3, 1, 139–152.

King, K., Palmer, R., Hayman, R., 2005. Bridging research and policy on education, training and their enabling environments. *Journal of International Development* 17, 803–817.

King, K., Rose, P., 2005. Transparency or tyranny? Achieving international development targets in education and training. *International Journal of Educational Development* 25, 4, 362–367.

Livingstone, D., 1858. *Missionary Travels and Researches in South Africa Including a Sketch of Sixteen Years of Resident in the Interior of Africa.* Harper and Brothers, New York.

Lockheed, M., Jamison, D., Lau, L., 1980. Farmer education and farm efficiency. *Economic Development and Cultural Change* 29, 1, 37–76.

McGrath, S., 2010. Education and development: thirty years of continuity and change. *International Journal of Educational Development* 30, 6, 537–543.

McGrath, S., 2011. Where to now for vocational education and training in Africa? *International Journal of Training Research* 9, 1–2, 35–48.

McGrath, S., 2012. Vocational education and training for development: a policy in need of a theory? *International Journal of Educational Development* 32, 5, 623–631.

Mizala, A., Torche, F., 2012. Bringing the schools back in: the stratification of educational achievement in the Chilean voucher system. *International Journal of Educational Development* 32, 1, 132–144.

Mkandawire, T., 1988. The road to crisis, adjustment and deindustrialisation: the African case. *Africa Development* 18, 1, 5–31.

Mkandawire, T., 1999. Developmental states and small enterprises. In: King, K. and McGrath, S. (Eds.) *Enterprise in Africa. Between Poverty and Growth*. Intermediate Technology Publications, London.

Moyo, D., 2009. *Dead Aid*. Penguin, London.

Mutumbuka, D., 1989. Policies for higher education in Zimbabwe: alternatives to the World Bank perspective. *Zimbabwe Journal of Educational Research* 1, 1, 43–70.

NORRAG, 2004. *NORRAG News 34. Language Politics and the Politics of Language (in Education)*. http://www.norrag.org/en/publications/norrag-news/online-version/language-politics-and-the-politics-of-language-in-education.html

NORRAG, 2007. *NORRAG News 39. Best Practice in Education and Training. Hype or Hope?* http://www.norrag.org/en/publications/norrag-news/online-version/best-practice-in-education-and-training-hype-or-hope.html

NORRAG, 2009. *NORRAG News 42. A Safari Towards Aid Effectiveness?* http://www.norrag.org/en/publications/norrag-news/online-version/a-safari-towards-aid-effectiveness.html

NORRAG, 2012. *NORRAG News 47. Value for Money in International Education: A New World of Results, Impacts and Outcomes*. http://www.norrag.org/en/publications/norrag-news/online-version/value-for-money-in-international-education-a-new-world-of-results-impacts-and-outcomes.html

NORRAG, 2013. *NORRAG News 48. 2012: The Year of Global Reports on TVET, Skills and Jobs*. http://www.norrag.org/en/publications/norrag-news/online-version/2012-the-year-of-global-reports-on-tvet-skills-jobs-consensus-or-diversity.html

Nussbaum, M., 2000. *Women and Human Development*. Cambridge University Press, Cambridge.

OECD, 2005. *Paris Declaration on Aid Effectiveness*. OECD, Paris.

Olukoshi, A., 1993. *The Politics of Structural Adjustment in Nigeria*. James Currey, Oxford.

Onimode, B., 1988. *A Political Economy of the African Crisis*. Zed, London.

Psacharopoulos, G., 1981. Returns to education: an updated international comparison. *Comparative Education* 17, 3, 321–341.

Psacharopoulos, G., 1985. Returns to education: a further international update and implications. *Journal of Human Resources* 20, 4, 583–604.

Rist, G., 1997. *The History of Development*. Zed, London.

Sachs, J., 2005. *The End of Poverty*. Penguin, London.

Sachs, J., 2008. *Common Wealth*. Penguin, London.

Schweisfurth, M., 2011. Learner-centred education in developing country contexts: From solution to problem? *International Journal of Educational Development* 31, 5, 425–432.

Sen, A., 1999. *Development as Freedom*. Oxford University Press, Oxford.

Srivastava, P., Oh, S.-A., 2010. Private foundations, philanthropy, and partnership in education and development: mapping the terrain. *International Journal of Educational Development* 30, 5, 460–471.

Thompson, A., 1981. The Addis Ababa conference in retrospect. *International Journal of Educational Development* 1, 1, 17–31.

UNESCO, 2012a. *Transforming Technical and Vocational Education and Training: Building Skills for Work and Life*. Main Working Document for the Third International Congress on Technical and Vocational Education and Training, Shanghai, May.

UNESCO, 2012b. *Youth and Skills: Putting Education to Work. Education for All Global Monitoring Report 2012*. UNESCO, Paris.

UNESCO, 2013. *Teaching and Learning: Achieving Quality for All. Education for All Global Monitoring Report 2013/14*. UNESCO, Paris.

UNESCO, 2014. *2014 GEM Final Statement – The Muscat Agreement*. Global Education for All Meeting, UNESCO, Muscat, May.

UNESCO, World Bank, 2000. *Higher Education in Developing Countries: Peril and Promise*. World Bank, Washington.

UNESCO, UNECA, 1961. *Final Report. Conference of African States on the Development of Education in Africa, 15–25 May 1961*. UNESCO/ED/181, UNESCO, Paris.

UNESCO, UNICEF, 2013. *Making Education a Priority in the Post-2015 Development Agenda: Report of the Thematic Consultation on Education in the Post-2015 Development Agenda*. UNESCO, Paris and UNICEF, New York.

Woodhead, M., Frost, M., James, Z., 2012. Does growth in private schooling contribute to Education for All? Evidence from a longitudinal, two cohort study in Andhra Pradesh, India. *International Journal of Educational Development* 33, 1, 33, 65–73.

World Bank, 1981. *Accelerated Development in Sub-Saharan Africa*. World Bank, Washington.

World Bank, 1988. *Education in Sub-Saharan Africa*. World Bank, Washington.

World Bank, 1991. *Vocational and Technical Education and Training: A World Bank Policy*. World Bank, Washington.

World Bank, 1994. *Higher Education: The Lessons of Experience*. World Bank, Washington.

World Bank, 1995. *Priorities and Strategies for Education: A World Bank Review*. World Bank, Washington.

World Conference on Education for All, 1990. *World Declaration on Education for All and Framework for Action to Meet Basic Learning Needs*. Interagency Commission, New York.

Zuze, T., Leibbrandt, M., 2011. Free education and social inequality in Ugandan primary schools: a step backward or a step in the right direction? *International Journal of Educational Development* 31, 2, 169–178.

28

LESSONS FROM 25 YEARS OF EDUCATION FOR ALL

Pauline Rose

Introduction

Much has been achieved since Education for All (EFA) goals were set in Dakar, Senegal, in the year 2000. More children are in school than ever before, with many countries narrowing the gap in enrolment between girls and boys. However, despite progress, none of the six goals will be met by 2015 (UNESCO 2014a). This is neither an argument for complacency nor is it a reason to turn our backs on targets that aim to hold policymakers to account. It is, though, a reason to reflect on experience over the past 15 years and to learn lessons for post-2015 goals.

This chapter begins by identifying the origins of global education frameworks, showing how they have evolved over the decades. In particular, it identifies the way in which global education priorities established in Jomtien, Thailand, in 1990 were translated into more concrete goals in Dakar, Senegal, in 2000. It then presents a more detailed assessment of the Dakar goals, identifying the extent to which they succeeded in meeting the principles of clarity, measurability and the prioritisation of equity. It also assesses whether sufficient attention was paid to financing of the goals over the years.

The analysis identifies variability in the clarity and measurability of EFA goals, which was a key reason why the more narrowly defined Millennium Development Goals (MDGs) received greater attention over the past 15 years. It also shows that the lack of a specific target for the financing of education has resulted in insufficient resources available to achieve the ambitions that were set. Drawing on this experience, the chapter argues that ensuring the post-2015 global education framework meets principles of clarity, measurability and equity, and also includes specific targets on financing, will help towards achieving universal access to good quality education for all in the future.

From Jomtien to Dakar to Ichnea

Global education target setting has a long history. Its origins can be traced back to the 1948 Universal Declaration of Human Rights, which laid down the principles of free and compulsory education for all and access to higher levels of education on the basis of merit. But these principles needed to be translated into time-bound targets if they were to mean anything in reality (Colclough 2005). Such global-target setting began with regional UNESCO conferences

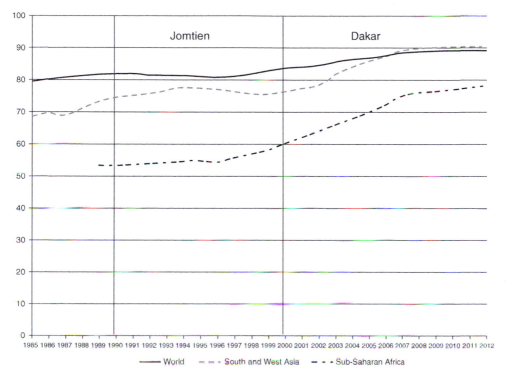

Figure 28.1   Trends in net enrolment rate, 1985–2012

Source: UNESCO Institute for Statistics database.

in the 1960s, which aimed to achieve universal primary education by 1980. However, by the mid-1980s, around one in five primary-school-aged children were not in primary school, and almost half of those living in sub-Saharan Africa were in this situation (Figure 28.1).

Subsequently, world leaders agreed on an Education for All framework at the World Conference on Education for All held in Jomtien, Thailand, in 1990, expressing an 'expanded vision' of:

- universalising access and promoting equity;
- focusing on learning;
- broadening the means and the scope of basic education;
- enhancing the environment for learning; and
- strengthening partnerships (Inter-Agency Commission for the World Conference on Education for All 1990).

The ambitious agenda seemed to have had limited impact. Over the Jomtien decade, little progress was made on even the most basic indicator of getting children into school. Between 1990 and 1999, the numbers out of school actually increased by 2 million – from 103.8 million in 1990 to 105.8 million in 1999 (Figure 28.2). In particular, there was a significant rise in the number of children out of school in the first part of the decade. This could partly be attributed to the effects of structural adjustment programmes on education in some of the poorest countries, including the charging of school fees which, alongside the other costs of schooling, were prohibitive for poor households. This negative trend began to reverse in the

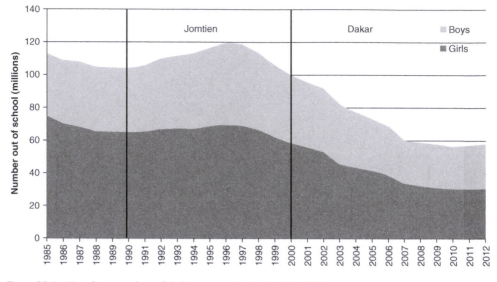

Figure 28.2   Trends in number of children out of school, 1985–2012
Source: UNESCO Institute for Statistics database.

mid-1990s, largely thanks to the abolition of primary school fees, which extended oppor-tunities to children from poor households to enrol in school (Rose 2003). In addition, the Jomtien period did not benefit from ongoing political clout to drive a visible campaign to improve education, in the context of wider development reforms that the subsequent Dakar and MDG era offered.

In many ways, the Jomtien declaration provided a springboard for the six Education for All goals that were endorsed by world leaders at the World Education Forum in Dakar in 2000 (UNESCO 2000). Without the basis provided by the Jomtien documents and the coalitions formed at that time, it is questionable whether the Dakar Framework for Action would have received as much attention. Indeed, Jomtien's expanded vision is not only reflected and rein-forced in the Dakar framework for action but is very similar to the principles set out for the development of post-2015 education goals to be agreed upon by world leaders meeting in Incheon, Republic of Korea, in 2015 (UNESCO 2014b). Education as a human right is the basis of all three frameworks, reflecting back to the 1948 Universal Declaration.

In parallel to these education world meetings and global declarations, broader development frameworks have been crafted. Notably, the UN Millennium Declaration was translated into eight Millennium Development Goals (MDGs) in 2000. These goals included one specifically on education, narrowing the broader Education for All framework to one goal on primary school completion, with education also a target within the MDG on gender.

The Dakar, and associated MDG, period has been somewhat more positive overall than the Jomtien period. The number of children out of school has almost halved, with a significant nar-rowing of the gender gap over the 15-year period (Figure 28.2). However, there are two very worrying signs: first, the numbers out of school has stagnated in the second part of the Dakar period; second, there appears to be an increase in the number of children out of school as we reach the 2015 deadline, leaving over 50 million children out of school. Continued efforts are, therefore, required to ensure that costs of schooling do not prevent children from poor house-holds attending school. These efforts need to be accompanied by targeted strategies to support the most marginalised groups, such as children with disabilities, who face specific barriers to gaining access to education.

There has been variation in progress across different parts of the world. Improvements in South and West Asia were particularly notable in the first part of the Dakar period, largely thanks to a reduction in out-of-school numbers in India. Yet, the challenge remains to reach the most marginalised 10% in the region. Sub-Saharan Africa has not been as successful in reaching the last 20%, stagnating at this level towards the end of the Dakar period. As a result, sub-Saharan Africa only reached the same level that South and West Asia had achieved by the beginning of the Dakar period.

While the recent stagnation is worrying, overall progress that has been made over the 15-year period in giving more children the opportunity to go to school should be celebrated. The global visibility of the MDGs has helped to ensure wider political attention to improving educational access. However, this progress has been accompanied by concerns over the poor quality of education, which is expected to be a more central focus of the post-2015 goals. Even so, these concerns need to take account of the fact that the quality of education was already poor before the expansion in enrolment that occurred in the Dakar period. As such, there is not an inevitable trade-off between quality and quantity, as some would claim – but, rather, the problem is rooted in a more systemic, long-term failure to tackle the causes of poor quality education.

The long history of international attempts to use goals as a way of focusing political attention on the right to education and to hold policymakers accountable for promises that they make raises a question of why we keep reiterating the same priorities: is it because we have not been successful so far? If so, do lessons from experience suggest we are doomed to fail again? Or are we learning from mistakes with the aim of building a better future?

It is perhaps not surprising that the priorities remain similar over the decades, as extending access and improving learning, with particular attention to equity, ought to be key features of any education system. They are also priorities that arguably need international attention if there is to be progress; ensuring the marginalised gain access to good quality education might otherwise not be a sufficient focus in national planning. Indeed, a review of 40 national education plans in low and lower-middle income countries identified that these rarely include strategies aimed at overcoming learning inequalities (Hunt 2015). Even fewer plans set themselves targets aimed at narrowing learning inequalities (UNESCO 2014a).

While their priorities are similar, there have been developments between each of the periods of global frameworks. One notable change in the framing of the Dakar Framework for Action was that, unlike the Jomtien one, it provided a more concrete set of six goals that could be monitored (Table 28.1). While Jomtien advocated the setting of national targets aimed at achieving basic learning needs, it shied away from prescribing these at a global level. By contrast, the six goals set at Dakar provided a framework for holding the global community accountable for their commitments. The Education for All Global Monitoring Report was instigated in 2002, tasked with the responsibility of tracking progress towards the six goals. This global monitoring is widely recognised as providing a basis for presenting an independent, evidence-based assessment of the status of the education sector.

Financing was another area that was strengthened in the Dakar Framework for Action. The Jomtien declaration recognised the need to protect education spending, in particular in light of structural adjustment programmes and debt burdens, as well as the need to identify new sources of financing but fell short of making any concrete commitments. The Dakar framework went a step further, affirming that "no countries seriously committed to education for all will be thwarted in their achievement of this goal by a lack of resources" (UNESCO 2000).

4 4 4 4 4 4 4 4 4 4 4 4 4 4 4 4 4 4 4 4 4 4 4 4 4 4 4 4 4 4 4 4 4 4 4 4 4 4 4 4 4 4 4 4 4 4 4 4 4 4 4 4 4 4 4 4 4 4 4 4 4 4 4 4 4 4 4 4 4 4 4 4 4 4 4 4 4 4 4 4 4 4 4 4 4 4 4 4 4 4 4 4 4 4 4 4 4 4 4 4

Table 28.1 Clarity, measurability and equity in the six Education for All goals

	Goal	Clarity	Measurability	Equity
Goal 1: Early childhood care and education	Expanding and improving comprehensive early childhood care and education, especially for the most vulnerable and disadvantaged children	Yes: focus on early childhood care and education	No: no target and not time bound	Yes: especially for the most vulnerable and disadvantaged children
Goal 2: Primary schooling	Ensuring that by 2015 all children – particularly girls – children in difficult circumstances and those belonging to ethnic minorities have access to and complete, free and compulsory primary education of good quality	Yes: focus on primary schooling	Yes: all complete by 2015	Yes: particularly girls, children in difficult circumstances and those belonging to ethnic minorities
Goal 3: Skills	Ensuring that the learning needs of all young people and adults are met through equitable access to appropriate learning and life skills programmes	No: life skills not defined, and focus on learning needs overlaps with goal 6	No: no target, not time bound, and data lacking	Yes: equitable access
Goal 4: Adult literacy	Achieving a 50% improvement in levels of adult literacy by 2015, especially for women, and equitable access to basic and continuing education for all adults	Yes: focus on adult literacy and continuing education	Partial: 50% improvement (although baseline date not clear) by 2015; measure for continuing education not clear	Yes: especially for women, and equitable access
Goal 5: Gender	Eliminating gender disparities in primary and secondary education by 2005 and achieving gender equality in education by 2015, with a focus on ensuring girls' full and equal access to and achievement in basic education of good quality	Yes: focus on gender disparities and gender equality	Partial: target to eliminate gender disparities by 2005, and gender equality by 2015, but measure for gender equality not specified	Yes: focus on gender

	Goal	Clarity	Measurability	Equity
Goal 6: Quality and learning	Improving all aspects of the quality of education and ensuring excellence of all so that recognized and measurable learning outcomes are achieved by all, especially in literacy, numeracy and essential life skills	Partial: literacy and numeracy clear, but not clear what 'all aspects' of quality refers to, and overlap with goal 3	Partial: learning outcomes associated with literacy and numeracy by all measurable, but other aspects not, and not time bound	No

Source: Author.

This affirmation gave the impetus for the formation of the Education for All Fast Track Initiative that was established in 2002, in part due to recognition related to the lack of progress since Jomtien that was attributed in part to insufficient donor resources and lack of effective coordination of donor efforts (Rose 2005). The EFA Fast Track Initiative was subsequently rebranded as the Global Partnership for Education, extending its role not only to mobilising resources and strengthening country planning processes with the aim of ensuring effective use of resources but also to a wider global advocacy role.

However, financing was still not included as a specific target within the Dakar Framework for Action. This omission meant that there was no possibility to know whether sufficient resources would be available for the six Education for All goals to be achieved. In reality, domestic resources increased in many of the poorest countries, but significant funding gaps remained to achieve the goals by 2015. While aid resources increased in the earlier part of the Dakar period, they began to fall by the end of the period. This left a large financing gap, estimated to reach US$26 billion per annum for the poorest countries. In addition, there were limited attempts to redistribute resources within countries to populations that were most left behind (UNESCO 2014a).

Lessons from 15 years of monitoring progress towards Education for All goals

After 15 years of monitoring progress towards Education for All goals, it is important to take stock of the challenges that have arisen in light of the way in which goals were framed. Successful goals need, first, to be clearly expressed and unambiguous in their wording; second, to be measurable and time-bound; and third, to focus on the marginalised. To what extent did the Dakar goals achieve these criteria?

Of the six goals, four could be considered to be clearly expressed (goals 1, 2, 4 and 5) (Table 28.1). Goals 3 on skills and 6 on quality did not meet this criterion, in part because they were overlapping in their intent. They also included concepts that were not sufficiently defined. Goal 3 focused on "appropriate learning and life skills", but it was not clear what would constitute "appropriate" learning, and common agreement on the meaning of "life skills" was lacking. As a result, as each edition of the EFA Global Monitoring Report illustrates, time and energy has been spent debating the meaning of this goal over the past 15 years, which has been a distraction from identifying concrete policy actions that could make a difference to the skills needed for young people to earn a decent living and lead a fulfilling life.

To address this problem, the 2012 EFA Global Monitoring Report was dedicated to the theme of skills and, for the first time, provided a framework for defining skills for the purposes of tracking progress towards goal 3. However, as the report pointed out, there were still serious deficiencies in data available to track progress towards this goal (UNESCO 2012).

Goal 6 included aspects that were clear ("recognised and measurable learning outcomes are achieved by all, especially in literacy [and] numeracy") but, similarly to goal 3, also included "essential life skills", as well as a vague aspiration to "improve all aspects of quality". As a result, the EFA Global Monitoring Report primarily assessed progress towards quality using proxy indicators, most commonly the number of pupils per teacher. The measurement of learning outcomes has mainly been confined to richer countries, which are more commonly included in internationally-comparable assessments such as PISA, PIRLS and TIMSS.[1]

In terms of the criterion of measurability, goal 2 on universal primary education is closest to providing information that allowed it to be measurable. It included a target that all children have access to and complete primary schooling and is time bound, with the expectation of achieving this target by 2015. Only two other goals included a date by which the goal is expected to be achieved – goal 4 on adult literacy and goal 5 on gender. Goal 4 also includes a specific target, namely of reducing adult literacy by 50%, although confusion arose as it has not been clear whether 1990 or 2000 levels should form the baseline.

In the case of goal 5, the specific target of eliminating gender disparities was expected to be achieved within five years; unsurprisingly, this goal was not met because this was an aspiration that was almost impossible to achieve. However, progress towards it was achieved over the 15-year period, with disparities at the primary level eliminated in some countries – including ones that had wide gender gaps in earlier years. Measures for the other aspect of goal 5, achieving gender equality by 2015, were not identified from the outset and, as a result, tracking progress was not problematic.

One of the problems with measurement of the EFA goals was that indicators and data sources were not identified at the time of developing the goals. So, while goal 4 on adult literacy was specified in a way that could be measured, poor quality data (primarily based on self-reported literacy from census data that are collected intermittently) has made tracking progress difficult.

Even the potentially more straightforward goal of universal primary education has suffered from measurement problems as indicators were not agreed to at the time of specifying the goals. As a result, different measures were used to assess progress towards universal primary school completion by the World Bank (using the gross intake rate to the last grade of primary school) and by the EFA Global Monitoring Report (primarily using the net enrolment rate). Both approaches have their flaws, overestimating the extent to which primary school completion has been achieved – and also potentially show quite different results for the same countries (UNESCO 2010).

The World Bank's measure of the gross intake rate to the last grade of primary school expresses the share of children entering the last grade as a proportion of the official age group for that grade. It tends to be inflated (with many countries displaying a rate over 100%) as it includes children who started school late or repeated grades. The EFA Global Monitoring Report's primary measure, the net enrolment rate, measures the proportion of primary school-aged children who are in school. Countries with a net enrolment rate close to 100% have most of their primary school-age children in the school system, but the indicator does not identify where they are within the system. Some countries might, therefore, have a high net enrolment rate with a large proportion of the school-aged children enrolled in early grades due to starting school late or high levels of repetition. As a result, they may still be a distance from achieving universal primary completion.

To address these shortcomings, the EFA Global Monitoring Report has developed a set of indicators using household survey data that makes it possible to assess progress through the different stages of an education system. This shows, for example, that goal 2 for primary school completion is still a long way from being achieved for the most disadvantaged groups: amongst poor rural girls in sub-Saharan Africa in 2010, 61% started school, but just 23% made it to the end of primary school (UNESCO 2014a).

A further lesson for post-2015 relates to one of the greatest failures of the current set of goals, namely for sufficient progress to be evident towards reaching the marginalised. With the exception of goal 6 on the quality of education, all included equity in their language (Table 28.1). There are two likely reasons why disadvantaged groups have not sufficiently benefited despite this focus on the goals themselves. One is that the Millennium Development Goals – which have dominated development planning – did not incorporate equity as a core principle as the EFA goals did. Another is that the lack of measurable equity targets associated with the EFA goals, and insufficient availability of data disaggregated to track progress towards achieving equality in education within countries, has let down the most marginalised, including the poorest, girls, those with disabilities, and those in rural areas or urban slums over the past decade.

As a result, until the 2010 EFA Global Monitoring Report, goals were primarily being tracked by looking at average progress across the population. The fact that poor girls living in rural areas of low-income countries only spend three years in school, on average, compared with over nine years for rich boys in urban areas, has therefore been hidden (UNESCO 2014a). This, in turn, has enabled marginalised groups to remain outside the gaze of policymakers, some of whom might feel more comfortable to report national averages so that social inequalities remain obscured (Watkins 2012). This is precisely why post-2015 goals and targets should take an approach that aims to achieve equity in educational opportunities by tracking progress of the disadvantaged.

This lesson is also being learnt, resulting in recent improvements in the availability of disaggregated household survey data and approaches to measurement. In education, the World Inequality Database on Education (WIDE),[2] developed by the EFA Global Monitoring Report team, is an example of a tool that is being used by civil society organisations, think tanks and researchers to draw attention to the extent of education inequalities such that groups who were previously invisible now cannot be ignored by policymakers.

Finally, each of the EFA goals has not received equal attention, in part because the framework did not show sufficient prioritisation. As a result, those devising the broader MDG agenda narrowed down the education goals that met the criteria of being clear and measurable, namely primary school completion and gender parity in enrolment. Given their simplicity, aid donors, and so in turn national governments receiving funds from them, drew on the MDGs rather than the EFA framework to shape their development programmes (King and Rose 2005a, 2005b). This narrowing is widely recognised as resulting in insufficient concern for the quality of education that children receive (Colclough 2005; Filmer, Hasan and Pritchett 2006).

One potential consequence of the failure to give sufficient attention to the broader Education for All agenda is that an estimated 250 million children are not able to achieve the basics in reading and mathematics, at least half of whom have spent at least four years in school (UNESCO 2014a). This implies that the quality of education is so poor that children are not learning even if they are in school. The poor quality of education most affects those who are already marginalised due to circumstances at birth. These children are more likely to be attending schools that are poorly resourced, with too few teachers and thus large class sizes, and have dilapidated classrooms lacking basic facilities such as regular electricity supplies.

An aim of future global goals should therefore be to turn the spotlight on policy failures of this kind. They should emphasise the need for governments and the international community to ensure the marginalised have access to school and tackle the poor quality of education they receive. By drawing attention to the large numbers of children not learning the basics, hopefully a future generation will be saved from a similar fate.

Looking forward to 2030

Proposals for post-2015 goals suggest that some of the lessons over the past 25 years of Education for All have been learnt. Unlike the Jomtien framework, they aim to present time-bound targets. While the precise wording of proposed post-2015 goals and targets varies in different official UN proposals, all include equity, quality and learning as an overarching goal (Rose 2014).[3] Unlike with the Dakar EFA goals and MDGs, which were set up as parallel processes, efforts have been made to ensure coherence across the education and broader sustainable development frameworks this time around.

The lesson on the need to develop indicators has been learnt for the post-2015 goals, with preparations made in education to identify appropriate indicators along with the proposals for goals and targets this time around. Notably, a Technical Advisory Group, chaired by the UNESCO Institute for Statistics and including technical experts from the EFA Global Monitoring Report, OECD, UNESCO, UNICEF and the World Bank, has been established with responsibility for identifying indicators to track progress towards proposed targets (EFA Steering Committee Technical Advisory Group 2014). These developments should ensure that indicators present metrics, drawing on comparable, robust data to make it possible to show whether a target has been met. To be effective, indicators should be able to track progress for disadvantaged groups in ways that are easy to communicate and signal actions that need to be taken for them to achieve the targets.

While progress is being made in developing indicators this time around, the task is not yet over. Notably, continued efforts will be needed to collect good quality data on learning – there are still large gaps in data available for some countries, and national assessments are not always carried out on a sufficiently regular basis to assess progress. In addition, data are still not systematically collected for some groups of the population, notably people with disabilities, nomadic populations, or those living in urban slums. Even so, it is encouraging that these gaps are increasingly recognised and steps are being taken to fill them.[4]

The collection of data on learning outcomes should not, however, primarily be for global tracking – this should be an additional benefit. National data on school enrolment collected for planning purposes within countries have been collated by the UNESCO Institute for Statistics in a way that has allowed them to form the basis of global tracking of universal primary education. Similarly, national assessment data should be collected with the main aim of strengthening planning within countries. Identifying ways to enable comparability of these data for global tracking is the next step. Such an approach will help to avoid the dangers that global assessments (such as PISA) risk encouraging, such as the promotion of internationally standardised curricula that do not take account of local realities.

In taking these steps, it will be important to be mindful of potential risks and unintended consequences that can accompany student testing. One danger is that a stronger focus on measuring learning outcomes could result in teaching to the test, diverting attention from the broader purposes of education, which are not easily measurable (Goldstein 2004; Barrett 2011a,

2011b). Failure to avoid such dangers could not only limit the achievement of the targets themselves but also further undermine the broader objectives that education systems should seek to accomplish.

A final step to rectify previous omissions is the importance of including a financing target, both aimed at increasing domestic resources for education as well as ensuring donors show commitment to promises that no country should be left behind due to lack of resources this time around.

Conclusion

Global frameworks agreed in Jomtien in 1990 and Dakar in 2000 have striking similarities, and many of their priorities will be carried forward towards 2030 when world leaders meet in Incheon in 2015. Yet this chapter argues that the continued search for universal access to good quality education should not be understood as a failure of previous decades. Rather, over time, there has been strengthening of the frameworks – with improvements in their clarity, measurability and equity.

It is, therefore, important to take the lessons from the past 25 years of global education frameworks forward into the future. Notably, developments in the use of data for tracking the progress of disadvantaged groups should be a key aspect of holding world leaders accountable for promises they make in ways that ensure no one is left behind. In setting targets and measuring progress towards them, greater attention needs to be given to making sure all children, regardless of their circumstances, are not only in school but also that the quality of education offers them the chance to learn. Furthermore, for countries to have sufficient resources to fulfil their promises, concrete financing targets are needed. These steps will help to ensure that a future generation of children and young people receive the quality of education they deserve.

Notes

1 PISA stands for Programme for International Student Assessment; PIRLS – Progress in International Reading Literacy Study; and TIMSS – Trends in International Mathematics and Science Study.
2 http://www.education-inequalities.org/
3 These official processes include the EFA Steering Committee agreement agreed at Muscat in May 2014 (UNESCO 2014b); the UN High Level Panel report in May 2013 (United Nations 2013); the Open Working Group proposal for Sustainable Development Goals in July 2014 (United Nations 2014); and the Sustainable Development Solutions Network in June 2014 (Sustainable Development Solutions Network 2014).
4 The Washington Group on Disability Statistics in particular has made great progress in developing measurement approaches and integrating them into survey instruments.

References

Barrett, A., 2011a. An education Millennium Development Goal for quality: complexity and democracy. *Compare* 41, 1, 145–148.

Barrett, A., 2011b. A millennium learning goal for education post-2015: a question of outcomes or processes. *Comparative Education* 47, 1, 119–133.

Colclough, C., 2005. Rights, goals and targets: How do those for education add up? *Journal of International Development* 17, 101–111.

EFA Steering Committee Technical Advisory Group, 2014. *Towards Indicators for a Post-2015 Education Framework*. UNESCO Institute for Statistics, Montreal.

Filmer, D., Hasan, A., Pritchett, L., 2006. A millennium learning goal: measuring real progress in education. CGD Working Paper 97, Center for Global Development, Washington.

Goldstein, H., 2004. Education for all: the globalisation of learning targets. *Comparative Education* 40, 1, 7–14.

Hunt, F., 2015. Review of national education policies: teacher quality and learning outcomes. *Prospects* (in press).

Inter-Agency Commission for the World Conference on Education for All, 1990. *Meeting Basic Learning Needs. A Vision for the 1990s.* UNICEF, New York.

King, K., Rose, P., 2005a. Transparency or tyranny? Achieving international development targets in education and training. *International Journal of Educational Development* 25, 362–367.

King, K., Rose, P., 2005b. International development targets and education: towards a new international compact or a new conditionality. *Journal of International Development* 17, 97–100.

Rose, P., 2003. From the Washington to the post-Washington consensus: the influence of international agenda on education policy and practice in Malawi. *Globalisation, Education and Societies* 1, 1, 67–86.

Rose, P., 2005. Is there a fast track to achieving the Millennium Development Goal in education? *International Journal of Educational Development* 25, 4, 381–394.

Rose, P., 2014. New proposals on post-2015 education goals. How do they compare? Global Partnership for Education blog, June 10, 2014. http://globalpartnership.org/blog/new-proposals-post-2015-education-goals-how-do-they-compare

Sustainable Development Solutions Network, 2014. *An Action Agenda for Sustainable Development. A Report for the United Nations Secretary-General.* Sustainable Development Solutions Network, New York.

UNESCO, 2000. *The Dakar Framework for Action. Education for All: Meeting Our Collective Commitments.* UNESCO, Paris.

UNESCO, 2010. *Education for All Global Monitoring Report. Reaching the Marginalised.* UNESCO, Paris.

UNESCO, 2012. *Education for All Global Monitoring Report. Youth and Skills: Putting Education to Work.* UNESCO, Paris.

UNESCO, 2014a. *Education for All Global Monitoring Report. Teaching and Learning: Achieving Quality for All.* UNESCO, Paris.

UNESCO, 2014b. *Joint Proposal of the EFA Steering Committee on Education Post-2015.* UNESCO, Paris.

United Nations, 2013. *A New Global Partnership: Eradicate Poverty and Transform Economies through Sustainable Development. The Report of the High-Level Panel of Eminent Persons on the Post-2015 Development Agenda.* United Nations, New York.

United Nations, 2014. *Open Working Group Proposal for Sustainable Development Goals.* United Nations, New York.

Watkins, K. 2012. The power of circumstance. A new approach to measuring education inequality. Center for Universal Education Working Paper 5, Brookings Institution, Washington.

29

EDUCATION AND THE POST-2015 DEVELOPMENT AGENDA

Simon McGrath

The post-2015 development agenda seems set to reinforce the focus on quantitative global goal setting that characterised the Millennium Development Goal (MDG) era. This has led, in education as in other sectors, to a strong focus on ensuring "a place in the sun" by getting key sectoral and/or subsectoral priorities included within the goals architecture. However, at the time of writing this chapter a year before the goals are due to be finalised, there remain justifiable concerns about the whole project of making goals central to development policy and practice; the quality and coherence of the goals, both generally and in the specific field of education; and the potential consequences for international education of the process. Overall, it appears that the MDGs and the Sustainable Development Goals (SDGs) that will succeed them are part of the rise of new technologies of development that have overwhelmed more philosophical and theoretical debates and have threatened spaces for practical action. These concerns are the focus of this chapter.

It consists of three main parts. First, I look back at the 15-year history of the MDGs to review the critiques that have been advanced of the impacts and effects of the MDGs and their associated set of practices and ways of structuring development discourse and knowledge production. These issues are considered both at the level of the MDGs in general and the education goals and sector in particular. Second, I move forward in time to the current (2013–14) debates regarding the post-2015 goals for a similar, but inevitably future-looking, analysis of the general and the education specific. Given the timing of writing, this section focuses on the two major official contributions of draft goals of 2013–14: the High Level Panel (HLP) goals of May 2013 and the zero draft Open Working Group (OWG) goals of July 2014. Third, I ask what this case tells us about the emergence (or lack thereof) of a new account of education for development, the role of key actors in the shaping of the international education agenda, and the nature of the political economy of knowledge production for education and development.

Perhaps the greatest challenge of writing this chapter lies in knowing that it runs the risk of being out of date by the time it is published. This cannot be avoided insofar as some of the detail of the second section in particular is concerned. However, at this point it seems implausible that there will be a radical shift in the overall approach to either development planning or the orthodox view of education's place therein. Thus, the bulk of the argument of the chapter seems likely to be pertinent regardless of the actual detail of the eventual SDGs.

Critiques of the MDGs

An overall evaluation

It is important to acknowledge that there has been progress against the targets of the MDGs and that this progress reflects a great deal of real improvement of the lives of poor people globally (cf. Rose, this volume). However, even here there have been two main critiques of the MDGs' quantitative impact. First, it is noted that considerable statistical sleight of hand was involved in maximising the claimed impact of the MDGs. Pogge (2004, 2010), for instance, notes that the approach to measurement of MDG 1: halving extreme poverty by 2015 was constructed in such a way as to require less than 40% of the reduction in the number of extremely poor that had been promised at the 1996 World Food Summit. Second, he also shows how this statistical move allowed China's massive economic growth of the 1990s to count towards achievement of a goal set in 2000. In this analysis, widely shared by other critics, the claimed impact of the MDGs needs to be deflated, and the implied causality of the MDGs being the sole cause of positive change needs to be rejected.

Box 29.1. The MDGs

1. Eradicate extreme poverty and hunger
2. Achieve universal primary education
3. Promote gender equality and empower women
4. Reduce child mortality
5. Improve maternal health
6. Combat HIV/AIS, malaria and other diseases
7. Ensure environmental sustainability
8. Global partnership for development

Source: www.un.org/millenniumgoals.

Beyond this quantitative impact on the primary goal of the halving of extreme poverty, a range of analysts have shown concern regarding the wider impacts of the MDGs. A summary of such impacts generally and across a range of sectors is given by the Power of Numbers project, led by former Human Development Report director Sakiko Fukuda-Parr and Alicia Yamin (harvardfxbcenter.org/power-of-numbers).

Their overall argument is that the MDGs had a distorting effect, emphasising certain sectoral and subsectoral priorities at the expense of others; undermining a range of existing people-centred development practices; and ignoring the development achievements and needs of a large number of countries (Fukuda-Parr, Yamin and Greenstein 2013, 2014). The MDG approach to development was highly reductionist. Many of the more political issues agreed at the world conferences of the 1990s and featured in the Millennium Declaration were downplayed or excised from the development agenda through the MDGs. These include peace and security, human rights, democracy and good governance, the protection of the most vulnerable, decent work, and reproductive rights. Indeed, they note that Goal 3 on gender equality only focused on one out of 13 points in the Beijing Platform for Action, whilst Goal 5 on maternal mortality sidestepped much of the larger sexual and reproductive rights debate of the Cairo Conference.

They argue further that the MDGs undermined the vibrant democratic debates that accompanied the world conferences of the 1990s and the emergent cross-sectoral thinking of that decade. Rather, the MDGs had their origins in the OECD's international development targets (IDTs) of the mid-1990s. Designed originally merely as a reporting tool, these moved within a decade to become the central tools of global development governance (Davis et al. 2012). However, they are performative, technocratic and (allegedly) value-free.

Moreover, even as a technical exercise, the MDGs can be criticised. Pogge's critique of the statistical manipulations involved in the "success" of Goal 1 have been noted above. More generally, the MDGs only measure that which can be measured but often do this badly.

Several indicators were conceptually weak as explanatory factors for underdevelopment or had serious issues of data availability and/or reliability. For instance, maternal mortality ratios were widely believed to be flawed (Yamin and Boulanger 2013) and measles (indicator 4.3) was a relatively insignificant cause of under-5 mortality (Diaz-Martinez and Gibbons 2013), whilst the undernourishment target (1B) focused on calorie consumption and weight for age at the expense of broader (and more political) dimensions of food insecurity (Fukuda-Parr and Orr 2013).

Moreover, the IDTs were designed to be a way for multilateral and bilateral agencies to manage their global portfolios, not as measures of the performance of individual developing countries. Many supposed target countries had met or were close to meeting some or all of the targets, whilst others were so far away from the targets that they had no chance of meeting them. Thus, the goals were of limited value for many countries but became a central part of national development policies due to aid conditionalities and the disciplining effects of the global development discourse.

In this view, the MDGs were neither a development planning blueprint nor a theoretical model of how development is achieved. Whilst claiming that the MDGs were intended to be more ambitious, one of their key architects, Vandermoortele, is forced to conclude that:

> [T]he MDGs were meant to broaden the development narrative beyond the narrow growth paradigm . . . [but] the search for a broader interpretation of development has failed. The MDGs have been misconstrued and distorted to make them fit with the orthodox policy framework. As a result, the global debate remains dominated by the implicit formula: faster economic growth + more foreign aid + better governance = MDGs.
>
> (Vandermoortele 2011: 13)

Nonetheless, the period since 2000 has seen the power of the MDGs rise as part of a wider emergence of "governing by numbers" (Rose 1991). It is now apparently self-evident that policies must be based on and evaluations of performance focused upon measurable indicators. More recently, the rise of new communications technologies (particularly blogs and tweets) and the "evidence-based" and media-savvy infographic have allowed the rise of a new wave of global advocacy led by a Northern-based development technocratic elite, which makes the case for a post-2015 settlement that is "more of the same but better".

The MDGs and education

In her contribution to the Power of Numbers project, Unterhalter (2013) echoes the project's overall conclusions that the MDGs were instrumental, impoverishing and distorting, showing the specific dynamics of this in the education sector. Summarising much of the education and development debate of recent years, she notes how the Jomtien agenda was narrowed to fit into the MDGs.

The most powerful empirical justification for focusing largely on primary education at Jomtien, whilst acknowledging the importance of other levels of education, had come from the World Bank's work on rates of return to education (e.g., Psacharopoulos 1981, 1985), which had shown that the highest returns to education were at this level. This had a crucial effect given the distribution of national government and official development assistance spending on education at the time (King 1991). Through the 1990s, as part of Education for All, and then even more so from 2000 under the MDGs, the simple political message of getting children into school came to dominate national and international education policy thinking, buttressed by the methodology of rates of return, which considered years of notional school attendance as its core variable, rather than any measure of input quality or learning attainment. Thus, considerations of educational quality, visible in the Jomtien text, were abandoned. Indeed, the massive and often unplanned growth of primary schooling in a number of countries (most famously Malawi and Uganda) had a depressing effect on educational quality as schools were overwhelmed by the precipitous growth in enrolments. Millions of children were badly served as they supposedly achieved a key human right but in ways that undermined that right, its supposed effects in empowering them more widely, and their ability to voice the effective absence of this right. Too often, the right to schooling was little more than the right to experience unacceptably poor, frequently demeaning and often unsafe learning environments. As Unterhalter stresses, gender violence in particular was ignored, as was inequality and its often intersectional nature.

Education was narrowed to being about children and schools. The wider education sector, the learning of adults and informal learning were all marginalised (Rogers, this volume). Educational planning became obsessed with the targets and rise of payment by results, including conditional cash transfers to parents, teacher salary and school funding reforms, and aid disbursements, which led to pernicious distortions that often moved funding away from the most vulnerable and needy.

As with the wider MDGs, Unterhalter argues that the education sector experienced a disempowerment of actors at the local and national levels. The approach ignored the realities of many Southern states where the MDGs did not reflect their particular educational achievements and challenges. This was particularly the case for the small island developing states (Crossley and Sprague 2014).

This brief review of elements of the critical literature on both the MDGs and their education elements should serve as a reminder that the real education and development challenge around the post-2015 goals is neither simply about getting the best education goals nor fighting the corner for a particular subsector of education. Rather, it should not be assumed that education goals or broader development goals are necessarily desirable.

The post-2015 debate

Global architecture

Thus far, the overall list of goals, and accompanying texts, being discussed are less reductionist than the MDGs, with a wider range of issues being considered. However, there are serious absences and flaws in both the two main official statements of draft goals.

The High Level Panel report (UN-HLP 2013) was stronger on economic development than the MDGs, with a clearer sense of the role of work, technology and industry being important elements of development. However, it was particularly disappointing with respect to sustainable development. There was some rhetoric around "sustainable consumption and production" but the concept remained vague and the aspiration for "rapid, inclusive and sustainable growth" appears to demonstrate the hope that hard choices can be avoided. Decent work was also explicitly downplayed in the text, as I have noted previously (McGrath 2013):

> The ILO's concept of "decent work" . . . sets a high standard toward which every country should strive. However, it has become clear that there can be middle ground for some developing countries, where "good jobs" . . . are a significant step.
>
> (UN-HLP 2013: 46)

In a document full of aspirational (and often unrealistic) rhetoric, such a note of pragmatism seems particularly stark and indicative of a lack of seriousness about the decent work agenda.

Box 29.2. The HLP goals

1. End poverty
2. Empower girls and women and achieve gender equality
3. Provide quality education and lifelong learning
4. Ensure healthy lives
5. Ensure food security and good nutrition
6. Achieve universal access to water and sanitation
7. Secure sustainable energy
8. Create jobs, sustainable livelihoods and equitable growth
9. Manage natural resource assets sustainably
10. Ensure good governance and effective institutions
11. Ensure stable and peaceful societies
12. Create a global enabling environment and catalyse long-term finance

Source: UN HLP 2013.

Overall, the HLP did not fix much that was wrong with the MDGs. It was based squarely on the setting of goals, but many of these were underdeveloped and unworkable. Beyond an overall rhetoric, there had been no real engagement with the lack of national focus of the MDGs. Broader democratic ownership of the process and the draft goals was limited. Sectoral silos were not successfully broken down, with an overall rhetoric of integrated development giving way to highly sector-specific goals.

The zero draft of the sustainable development goals by the UN Open Working Group is in some ways an advance on the HLP report. It further improves the economic and environmental aspects of HLP and also emphasises culture more. However, it has also come under criticism for perpetuating many of the failings of both the MDGs and the HLP report.

Box 29.3. The SDGs (07/14 draft)

1. End poverty everywhere
2. End hunger, improve nutrition and promote sustainable agriculture
3. Attain healthy lives for all
4. Provide quality education and lifelong learning opportunities for all
5. Attain gender equality, empower women and girls everywhere
6. Ensure availability and sustainable use of water and sanitation for all
7. Ensure sustainable energy for all
8. Promote sustained, inclusive and sustainable economic growth, full and productive employment and decent work for all
9. Promote sustainable infrastructure and industrialization and foster innovation
10. Reduce inequality within and between countries
11. Make cities and human settlements inclusive, safe and sustainable
12. Promote sustainable consumption and production patterns
13. Tackle climate change and its impacts
14. Conserve and promote sustainable use of oceans, seas and marine resources
15. Protect and promote sustainable use of terrestrial ecosystems, halt desertification, land degradation and biodiversity loss
16. Achieve peaceful and inclusive societies, access to justice for all, and effective and capable institutions
17. Strengthen the means of implementation and the global partnership for sustainable development

Source: OWG 2014: 3.

Kenny (2014) argues that the document has a crisis of identity, not having a clear purpose and not being fit for any of the multiple purposes it appears to be trying to address. He suggests that it is too narrow to be a vision statement about the "world we want"; too thin on implementation to be a planning and financing tool; too big a shopping list to serve as a meaningful set of priorities and too vague on who the priorities are for; too ambitious and vague to hold governments effectively to account; and inadequate in its coverage of either key development issues or the range of global public goods relevant to a global policymaking process.

Raworth (2014) notes that the social targets are much sharper linguistically than the environmental ones. She highlights the continued inadequacy of engagement with the challenge of balancing growth and sustainability, noting that the need to address this is acknowledged but not adequately addressed. She also argues that voice is the most obvious gap in the SDGs. This reflects a wider failure for the human development and capabilities approach to gain a place at the heart of the development agenda in spite of its significant influence on development theory.

The OWG also fail to engage satisfactorily with the issue of global versus national goals. It argues that:

> They [the SDGs] are . . . global in nature and universally applicable to all countries, whilst taking into account different national realities, capacities and levels of development and respecting national policies and priorities. . . . Targets are defined as global

targets, with each government settings its own national targets guided by the global level of ambition but taking into account national circumstances.

(UN–OWG 2014: 2)

It is clear here that the global level has primacy, further limiting the possibilities for voice and agency.

New educational goals

The draft goals for education can be criticised for many of the failings of the overall goals, whether these are the MDGs or the draft SDGs. They have many technical problems, and it is unclear whether these are all surmountable in the year remaining from the time of writing. As with other goals, they have been driven by a global technocratic elite of staff from bilateral and multilateral agencies, international NGOs and Northern think tanks.

The HLP education goal was "provide quality education and lifelong learning". As King and Palmer (2012) and McGrath (2014) have noted, this is a return to the broader language of Jomtien and can be welcomed as such, whilst remaining mindful of how Jomtien's relative breadth was lost in the subsequent operationalisation of EFA and the MDG process. In this light, the subgoals are less positive.

Box 29.4. HLP education goals (including economic subgoal on NEETs)

Goal 3: Provide quality education and lifelong learning

3a. Increase by x% the proportion of children able to access and complete preprimary education

3b. Ensure every child, regardless of circumstance, completes primary education able to read, write and count well enough to meet minimum learning standards

3c. Ensure every child, regardless of circumstance, has access to lower secondary education and increase the proportion of adolescents who achieve recognised and measurable learning outcomes to x%

3d. Increase the number of young and adult women and men with the skills, including technical and vocational, needed for work by x%

8b. Decrease the number of young people not in education, employment or training by x%

Source: UN HLP 2013: 30–31.

Together, these give a broader sense of formal education than even the Jomtien goals, notwithstanding the continued exclusion of higher education. There is also a strong return to concerns about learning outcomes, reflecting the learning of lessons about the failings of the access obsession of the EFA-MDG era. However, the focus is even more strongly on young people and schooling, with adult literacy being marginalised. Though admittedly draft targets, they are strikingly poorly conceptualised and offer considerable measurement problems.

Strikingly, the shift towards a focus on learning outcomes rather than school enrolments is based on the same literature as the previous approach. In the two pages that support the education goals, the key text is Psacharopoulos and Patrinos (2004), which updates the Psacharopoulos studies used to such effect in the Jomtien debates. This is striking. Even if a human capital approach is still an important way of thinking about education and development (cf. Thomas and Burnett, this volume), then the past decade has seen two moves in that field that are important for policy debates. First, changes both in the global labour market and in education enrolments (in response in part to the Psachoropoulos research) have led to significant changes in relative rates of return to different levels of education. Hence, Colclough, Kingdon and Patrinos (2010) show that mean global rates of return to primary education are now lower than for higher levels of education. In any case, the new goals are moving away from an argument that primary education should be the predominant focus. Second, and of huge significance for a discussion of learning quality rather than quantity, human capital theory has become more sophisticated in its treatment of learning, with a far stronger emphasis on cognitive and noncognitive skills acquisition (e.g., Hanushek and Wössmann 2008). This is much more in line with the thrust of the goals and much of the wider debate stressing quality learning outcomes. To base the discussion of the future role of education in development on old evidence that does not argue for the main premises of the proposed goals is remarkable.

The argument behind the HLP education goals remains highly instrumental. It is taken as unproblematic that education has measurable developmental benefits and that these justify an investment in education (cf. McGrath 2014). A paper from the Brookings Institution, a recently emerged major player in the education and development debate, exemplifies the approach in a paper subtitled "Why learning is central to the post-2015 global development agenda". In this, it is argued that education:

- increases wages, leading to reduced poverty
- reduces vulnerability to shocks
- reduces inequality
- increases employability
- improves life skills for participation in society
- improves reproductive health
- reduces fertility, leading to population sustainability
- raises civic awareness and political participation
- improves social integration and cohesion
- increases productivity
- enhances political stability
- reduces criminality (Adams 2012).

The introduction of the NEET notion in the economic subgoals is also redolent of the instrumentalisation of education and replays a long-standing view of "youth as problem". NEET is a deficit, nonagentic and ultimately Northern concept with little purchase in most countries' definitions of employment or training. It accepts a narrow version of employability that has long been critiqued across a range of literatures (cf. McGrath and Powell, this volume).

Whilst the proposals restore the importance of learning, they are poor on inequality and how the two intersect. The strange looking-back to an earlier phase of human capital literature is part of a "rather backward-looking stance is one in which education's economic and contraceptive purposes remain at the forefront and education continues to be seen as a mixture of silver bullet and black box." (McGrath 2014 9).

The OWG text slightly modified the HLP goal: "provide quality education and lifelong learning opportunities for all". "For all" was implicit in the HLP wording and perhaps served a symbolic purpose in being explicit. However, "opportunities" is potentially a more significant addition. Whereas the implicit sense of the HLP wording was towards stressing access and outcomes, the shift in wording seems to soften both to a mere provision of opportunities to access. Indeed, strictly it is the opportunities that need to be of quality, not the learning outcomes. This is presumably an issue of weak drafting rather than intention.

Box 29.5. Education goals in the OWG zero draft

"Provide quality education and lifelong learning opportunities for all"

4.1. By 2030 provide all children access to quality early childhood care and preprimary education

4.2. By 2030, ensure all girls and boys complete free, equitable and quality primary and secondary education leading to relevant and effective learning outcomes

4.3. By 2030 ensure equal access for all to affordable quality tertiary education, including university

4.4. By 2030 promote lifelong learning, provide employable skills especially to young women and men, and increase by at least x% adult literacy and basic numeracy

4.5. By 2030, eliminate gender disparities and ensure equal access to all levels of education and vocational training for people in vulnerable situations, including persons with disabilities

4.6. By 2030 integrate into education programs knowledge and skills necessary for sustainable development, human rights, gender equality, promoting a culture of peace and nonviolence and culture's contribution to sustainable development

4.a. By 2030 increase by x% the supply of qualified teachers, including through international cooperation for teacher training in developing countries, and ensure safe, inclusive and effective learning environments for all

4.b. By 2020 expand by x% globally the number of scholarships for students and government officials from developing countries in particular LDCs to enrol in higher education, including vocational training, programmes in developed countries and other developing countries

4.c. Build and upgrade education facilities that are child and gender sensitive and provide safe and inclusive learning environments.

Source: OWG 2014: 6.

Goal 4.1. was more ambitious in scale than its HLP equivalent in terms of scale, moving from x% increase to universal coverage. However, it was also far less ambitious in that it retreated to an access measure rather than combining this with a focus on completion. The language of access, as with the HLP goals, remains apparently simplistic, with no hints of the development of the notion by Tomasevski (2001) when she was UN Special Rapporteur on the Right to Education.

Goal 4.2. combined and extended two of the HLP goals, moving to a language of complete secondary education rather than just lower and including notion of free education. It was also more ambitious on learning outcomes, moving from "minimum learning standards" (HLP 3b) and "recognised and measurable learning outcomes" (3c), to "relevant and effective learning outcomes". Rather than focusing on increasing percentages (unspecified) of coverage, again the ambition was raised to universality.

Goal 4.3. introduced tertiary education as a goal for the first time, stressing affordability. This is striking, going beyond Jomtien. However, serious questions remain regarding what equal access to tertiary education for all actually means, particularly when primary and secondary full access have not been achieved yet.

Goal 4.4. brought in adult literacy and numeracy, an element of the Jomtien settlement that had been lost in subsequent formulations. Here it was placed alongside employable skills. This subgoal raises a series of issues that were not answered adequately in the EFA era regarding definitions, measures and reliable data sets. The language of employable skills may be pointing towards new approaches to the testing of individual skills, as in the World Bank's Skills Toward Employment and Productivity programme and the OECD's Programme for the International Assessment of Adult Competencies. However, whilst the schooling learning metrics approach (cf. Anderson and Winthrop, this volume) is being pursued relatively transparently, the current debate about adult skills testing is being pursued entirely as a technical debate in a group of agencies that have limited democratic traditions.

Goal 4.5. is a poorly worded subgoal that began with gender but also threw in "people in vulnerable situations" and "persons with disabilities". Whilst the focus on equity is to be welcomed, this was clumsily done, being about equitable access rather than outcomes, and even lacked the references to quality provision present elsewhere. This is particularly worrying since the formulation was not about education but "education and vocational training". This raises the possible danger of equity being achieved by channelling certain target groups into poor-quality vocational training. It is also unfortunate that the only references to "vocational" (here and in 4.b.) are to "vocational training", a language not used by UNESCO and implicitly far narrower than conventional formulations that insist on talking about "vocational education and training".

Goal 4.6. is highly ambitious and contentious, making a set of ideologically-laden and contested concepts (sustainable development, peace, human rights, gender equality, culture) appear to be uncontroversial and about skills delivery and acquisition, rather than a matter for public dialogue in different settings. It is far from clear that these are actionable and measurable.

The format of the OWG zero draft is to follow the main subgoals with a set of more enabling subgoals. There are three in the case of education.

Goal 4.a. included teachers in the goals language for the first time (drawing on the proposals from the Global Coalition on Education). However, it implied a focus on initial teacher education when much of the challenge is about upgrading the skills and knowledge (and addressing the attitudes) of existing teachers. This subgoal still lacked quantification, marking the first appearance in this education goals text of the "x%" formulation. It also conflated teacher qualifications and teaching and learning quality. Moreover, the concern about teacher qualifications was merged into one goal with safe learning environments. This also appeared in another goal – another example of bad drafting. Measurement of safe, inclusive and effective learning environments is far from being straightforward. All three terms are contestable and overlapping, and questions of measurement are large, including a very big set of questions around whose ratings count.

Goal 4.b. continued the theme of including higher education by making the intriguing proposal that higher and vocational education scholarships should be the subject of development goals. This is remarkable given 25 years of neglect of the scholarship issue due to the orthodoxy that higher education is elitist and costly, again drawing in part from Psacharopoulos and rates of return. Whilst I would argue that the areas of international cooperation in higher education and capacity development are important, this still feels like a surprising expansion of the education goal agenda and a rather questionable specific focus for this expansion. It could be asked why the focus is on a rather traditional notion of scholarships rather than developing joint programmes, regional programmes or strengthened national programmes, as might be expected from a reading of the more recent literature in this area. There are also issues about what is being taught and learnt in such programmes, as Crossley (2014) has recently noted.

Goal 4.c. even finds a place for architecture in the goal architecture. This is an issue of some importance (cf. Uduku, this volume) but, again, it is a surprising inclusion in such a high level of text. Moreover, there is no quantification at all of this subgoal.

Elsewhere in the text, the NEET subgoal has been lost, whilst broader aspirations regarding decent work have been significantly strengthened.

Overall, the OWG zero draft has a significantly broader educational focus than the HLP, cutting across much of the sector, including higher education, and linking the headline goals to targets on supporting infrastructure. However, the text is still predominantly formally focused. It remains to be seen whether the breadth is excessive. Some of the infrastructural emphases seem to be too specific.

It is generally stronger on inequality. However, there is still too much of a language of access, even when couched in terms of quality and equality. Indeed, there has been some backsliding from HLP in terms of going beyond access. What "equal access" means is absolutely central to the discussion, but there is little sense here of a rich understanding of access, such as that of Tomasevski.

There has been a significant shift in the treatment of vocational education and training. This appears to have been moved away from the Ministry of Education and supply-side focus of HLP, but the notion of employable skills requires more attention. Whilst the rest of the text suggests a shift away from a narrow youth unemployability focus, there is no sense of a strong notion here of how education and work link. The education text still appears to be operating in a silo, with other parts of the text going far beyond MDGs and HLP on issues of production, technology and work.

There are major technical issues with the subgoals in terms of drafting, definitions, available data and methodologies. Whilst these may be solved in subsequent drafts, this cannot be assumed given the history of previous goals. There are also major unanswered questions regarding contested issues, such as about inequality and appropriate values to be inculcated by education. The OWG goals mark an even stronger move towards measuring individual learning outcomes than the HLP ones in that they seem to imply more in the way of testing the skills of adult and youth. This area has seen major new developments in the very recent past, but there has been very little academic or public debate about these developments thus far.

Implications of the post-2014 agenda for education and development

This final substantive section explores what this case tells us about the emergence (or lack thereof) of a new account of education for development, considers the rise of new key actors in the shaping of the international education agenda, and revisits the political economy of knowledge production on education and development.

Towards a new account of education and development?

Taken together, the HLP and OWG proposals point to relatively minor revisions of the education for development orthodoxy. Education is still overwhelmingly valued in these documents for its instrumental value. Of course, this is hardly to be wondered at. The game afoot in the goal-setting process is one of playing up the centrality to development of a range of sectors. Given the weak external understandings of education's purposes and value elsewhere in the development community (McGrath 2010) and worries early in the post-2015 process about education's potential marginalisation within, and even exclusion from, the core goals (cf. Burnett 2012), it is particularly unsurprising that the international education community have made strong claims for education's developmental value.

However, it does need restating that the education goals are still narrowly human capital oriented. Yet, whilst they are economistic in this sense, they are also disappointingly unengaged with the increasingly sophisticated discussions of work, technology and industry that are taking place elsewhere in the post-2015 discussions. There is a missed opportunity to engage with evolutionary and institutional economics accounts, particularly over the vocational and higher education aspects of the proposed subgoals. Overall, the account is still stuck too firmly in an educational silo.

This silo thinking perhaps explains some of the limitations of the move towards considering inequality, welcome though it is at the level of principle. Although there has been a shift away from a model that was essentially stripped down to "primary schooling for development", there is still an excessive focus on formal schooling as opposed to multiple modes of learning. Unsurprisingly, there is no sense of the dark side of education in perpetuating multiple forms of violence.

In spite of the rise of education research on human development (reflected in a number of chapters in this Handbook) and its wider salience in the development literature, there is no sense in either set of goals of notions of human freedom and flourishing, agency, voice or public dialogue and how these matter when thinking about education's purposes. The goals remain deeply technocratic and elite driven.

A changing set of actors?

Much has been made in discussions about development and the post-2015 settlement that the actors involved would necessarily change. Given the relative decline in the importance of ODA to many Southern countries; the emergence of a new range of philanthrocapitalist foundations and countries with new development programmes; and a general shift towards market solutions, amongst other factors, it was assumed that the post-2015 goals would be constructed in a very different way from the MDGs.

What has happened since 2000 is the partial reordering of the international development community. The OWG process does reflect some greater influence for Southern governments, but this serves to reinforce the role of states, alongside multilateral membership organisations and UN structures, as the core of the goal-setting community. However, much of the process has been about the development of goals within a technocratic community in which agencies have been joined by a small group of influential think tanks and international NGOs (cf. Magrath, this volume). The Power of Numbers project notes how the NGO activism centred on the debates around the world conferences of the 1990s was largely dissipated by the rise of the MDGs. However, it is the case that the MDGs did offer new spaces for NGOs within the development settlement as long as they became more like their funders in the ODA world: focused increasingly on policy, scale and delivery. Amongst think tanks, the rise since 2010 of the Brookings Institution as a player in education goal development has been particularly noteworthy. Within the UN specialist agencies with an education focus (UNESCO and UNICEF), the most obvious shift has been to a higher profile for more technical units – the externally-funded Global Monitoring Report team within UNESCO headquarters and the UNESCO Institute for Statistics, based in Montreal. At the same time, the OECD's increasing profile as a development agency has been strongly reflected in the education and skills sector.

A shifting political economy of knowledge production?

As has already been noted, the MDGs can be seen in the light of the rise of what Rose (1991) termed "governing by numbers". In turn, this has led to the strengthening of the relative power within the development debate of those organisations with the strongest competences in working with hard data. The proposed new goals will require a further huge effort in developing meaningful targets, setting up and operationalising system for gathering data, and building up analyses and analytical capability. All of these are likely to strengthen further the power of the development technocratic elite.

The post-2015 debate appears to continue the rise of new languages of performance and delivery, which includes such technologies/discourses as evidence-based practice, nudges, metrics, conditional cash transfers and randomised control trials (cf. Ozga 2009; McGrath and Lugg 2012; Lawn 2013; Meyer and Benavot 2013; Crossley 2014; Unterhalter 2013 on the international disciplining of education policy and practice by performative technologies).

Crossley raises the likelihood that these processes are likely to further undermine local ownership of policies. He argues that where national research capacities are weak:

> [A]s in many poor or small countries, the potential for the control or mediation of internationally inspired policy interventions is often significantly reduced. This can lead to more direct forms of policy transfer, importation or imposition – and to the limited degrees of success that have repeatedly been well-documented at the level of implementation.
>
> (Crossley 2014: 19)

Allied to the new technologies of performance, the education and development debate has seen the rise of technologies of persuasion. The rise of Twitter and infographics create a spurious certainty as complex, contested and contextualised realities are compressed into brief and universally true "killer facts". McGrath (2014) selects a handful of 2013 tweets from the GMR team to illustrate this trend:

The odds of children carrying malaria is one-third lower if their mothers have a secondary education than if their mothers have no education

Every \$1 spent on education generates \$10–15 in economic growth

If all students in low income countries left school with basic reading skills, it would result in an almost one-seventh cut in world poverty

One additional year of maternal education would decrease child deaths from pneumonia by 14%

Alongside a relative shift of international education research priorities towards more positive traditions from economics, political science, psychology and health science researchers, these technologies of performance and persuasion contribute to a broader threat to the Sadlerian comparativist position that favours deeper anthropological, sociological and political economy readings of particular cases (Crossley 2014; McGrath 2014).

Conclusion

In this chapter, I have attempted to do three things. First, I have considered both educational and wider critiques of the MDGs in terms of their impacts and effects on development and their structuring of development discourse and knowledge production. I follow a line that argues that the MDGs have had distorting effects on what counts as development (and education for development); have served to depoliticise and domesticate key issues about inequality, quality and violence; and have marginalised voices from outside the development elite (cf. Fukuda-Parr, Yamin and Greenstein 2013, 2014; Unterhalter 2013). A key conclusion here is that there is insufficient evidence that goals work and that the post-2015 goals will be able to avoid the distorting effects of the MDGs.

Second, and where this chapter is more original, I have examined current (2013–14) debates regarding the post-2015 goals focusing on the two major official contributions of draft goals of 2013–14: the High Level Panel (HLP) goals of May 2013 and the zero draft Open Working Group (OWG) goals of July 2014. Overall, the OWG zero draft has a significantly broader educational focus than the HLP, cutting across much of the sector, including higher education, and linking the headline goals to targets on supporting infrastructure. However, the text is still predominantly formally focused. It is generally stronger on inequality than either the MDGs or HLP, but there is still too much emphasis on access, without a rich understanding such as that of Tomasevski (2001). The education text still appears to be operating in a silo, with other parts of the OWG text going far beyond MDGs and HLP on issues of production, technology and work. Finally, the OWG goals mark an ever stronger move towards measuring individual learning outcomes that may be desirable but requires stronger academic and public debate and deliberation. Overall, even when looking within the paradigm, the goals remain poorly formulated and are unlikely to produce useful enough data.

Third, I follow on from earlier parts of my own work (e.g., McGrath 2001, 2010, 2014; McGrath and Lugg 2012) to explore some of the wider implications of the emergent post-2015 agenda on education for its potential reshaping of the dominant account of education for development and what it might mean for the nature of the political economy of knowledge production for education and development. I argue that the goals need to be seen as part of a broader set of technologies of performativity and persuasion that threatens democratic debate and undermines agency and voice at multiple levels (cf. Fukuda-Parr, Yamin and Greenstein 2013, 2014). Moreover, from the specific perspective of the education and development field, I argue (as does Crossley 2014) that these pernicious effects threaten to undermine what limited current space for qualitative education research to engage in critical dialogue with policy in favour of a further strengthening of positivist and technocratic approaches to research and policy transfer.

How the international education research community seeks to resist, subvert or ameliorate the threats described here may define its future.

References

Adams, A., 2012. The education link: why learning is central to the post-2015 global development agenda. Center for Universal Education Working Paper 8, Brookings Institution, Washington.

Burnett, N., 2012. Are we becoming irrelevant? Reflections on the international education community's current approaches. Background note for DFID-UKFIET dialogue 11 December 2012 on Education and Development to 2015 and Beyond. Results for Development Institute, Washington.

Colclough, C., Kingdon, G., Patrinos, H., 2010. The changing pattern of wage returns to education and its implications. *Development Policy Review* 28, 733–747.

Crossley, M., 2014. Global league tables, big data and the international transfer of educational research modalities. *Comparative Education* 50, 1, 15–26.

Crossley, M., Sprague, T., 2014. Education for sustainable development: implications for small island developing states. *International Journal of Educational Development* 35, 86–95.

Davis, K., Kinsbury, B., Merry, S., Fisher, A., 2012. *Governance by Indicators: Global Governance through Quantification and Ranking.* Oxford University Press, Oxford.

Diaz-Martinez, E., Gibbons, E., 2013. The questionable power of the Millennium Development Goal to reduce child mortality. FXB Working Paper, Harvard University.

Fukuda-Parr, S., Orr, A., 2013. The MDG hunger target and the contested visions of food security. FXB Working Paper, Harvard University.

Fukuda-Parr, S., Yamin, A., Greenstein, J., 2013. Synthesis paper – The Power of Numbers: A critical review of MDG targets for human development and human rights. FXB Working Paper, Harvard University.

Fukuda-Parr, S., Yamin, A., Greenstein, J., 2014. The power of numbers: a critical review of MDG targets for human development and human rights. *Journal of Human Development and Capabilities* 15, 2–3, 105–117.

Hanushek, E., Wössmann, L., 2008. The role of cognitive skills in economic development. *Journal of Economic Literature* 46, 3, 607–668.

Kenny, C., 2014. What's the Point of the Post-2015 Agenda? http://www.cgdev.org/blog/what%E2%80%99s-point-post-2015-agenda

King, K., 1991. *Aid and Education*. Longman, London.

King, K., Palmer, R., 2012. Education and skills in the Post-2015 global landscape: history, context, lobbies and visions. NORRAG Working Paper No. 1, Graduate Institute for International Development, Geneva.

Lawn, M. (Ed.), 2013. *The Rise of Data in Education Systems*. Symposium, Oxford.

McGrath, S., 2001. Research in a cold climate. *International Journal of Educational Development* 21, 5, 391–400.

McGrath, S., 2010. The role of education in development: an educationalist's response to some recent work in development economics. *Comparative Education* 46, 2, 237–253.

McGrath, S., 2013. Skills, Work and Development: Initial Reactions to the High Level Panel's Post-2015 Vision. http://norrag.wordpress.com/2013/06/03/skills-work-and-development-initial-reactions-to-the-high-level-panels-post-2015-vision

McGrath, S., 2014. The Post-2015 debate and the place of education in development thinking. *International Journal of Educational Development* 39, 4–11.

McGrath, S., Lugg, R., 2012. Knowing and doing vocational education and training reform: Evidence, learning and the policy process. *International Journal of Educational Development* 32, 5, 696–708.

Meyer, H., Benavot, A. (Eds.), 2013. *PISA, Power and Policy*. Symposium, Oxford.

Open Working Group on Sustainable Development Goals, 2014. Introduction and Proposed Goals and Targets on Sustainable Development for the Post-2015 Development Agenda. Zero Draft rev 1. http://sustainabledevelopment.un.org/content/documents/4044zerodraft.pdf

Ozga, J., 2009. Governing education through data in England: from regulation to self- evaluation. *Journal of Education Policy* 24, 149–162.

Pogge, T., 2004. The first UN Millennium Development Goal: a cause for celebration? *Journal of Human Development* 5, 3, 377–397.

Pogge, T., 2010. *Politics as Usual*. Polity, Cambridge.

Psacharopoulos, G., 1981 Returns to education: an updated international comparison. *Comparative Education* 17, 3, 321–341.

Psacharopoulos, G., 1985. Returns to education: a further international update and implications. *Journal of Human Resources* 20, 4, 583–604.

Psacharopoulos, G., Patrinos, H., 2004. Returns to investment in education: a further update. *Education Economics* 12, 2, 111–134.

Raworth, K. 2014 Will These Sustainable Development Goals Get Us into the Doughnut (aka a Safe and Just Space for Humanity)? http://oxfamblogs.org/fp2p/will-these-sustainable-development-goals-get-us-into-the-doughnut-aka-a-safe-and-just-space-for-humanity-guest-post-from-kate-raworth/

Rose, N., 1991. Governing by numbers: figuring out democracy. *Accounting, Organizations and Society* 16, 7: 673–92.

Tomasevski, K., 2001. Human rights obligations. http://www.righttoeducation.org/content/primers/rte_03.pdf

UN High Level Panel 2013. A New Global Partnership: Eradicate Poverty and Transform Economies through Sustainable Development. http://www.un.org/sg/management/pdf/HLP_P2015_Report.pdf

Unterhalter, E., 2013. Education targets, indicators and a post-2015 development agenda: Education for All, the MDGs, and human development. FXB Working Paper, Harvard University.

Vandemoortele, J., 2011. If not the Millennium Development Goals, then what? *Third World Quarterly* 32, 1, 9–25.

Yamin, A., and Boulanger, V., 2013. From Transforming Power to Counting Numbers: The evolution of sexual and reproductive health and rights in development; and where we want to go from here. FXB Working Paper, Harvard University.

30

AID FOR HUMAN RESOURCE DEVELOPMENT

The rise of Asia

I-Hsuan Cheng and Sheng-Ju Chan

Introduction

This chapter explores the constructs and contents of international education aid provided by emerging Asian donors for human resource development (HRD). Specifically, this chapter presents analyses of the role that HRD can play in fostering economic and social equality for the disadvantaged and poor and sheds light on the potential value of education in international development in the post-Education for All (EFA) age.

As the amount of Official Development Assistance (ODA) provided by traditional Development Assistance Committee (DAC) donors decreases, emerging Asian donors have become more influential in international education aid. Educational ODA allocated by traditional DAC donors declined from US$14.4 billion in 2010 to US$13.4 billion in 2011 (UNESCO 2013a). Despite the vibrant and prominent role that traditional DAC donors have played in promoting EFA, the promise that these donors stated at the World Education Forum in Dakar, Senegal, in 2000 that no country will lack the resources to achieve EFA goals is unlikely to be fulfilled (UNESCO 2013b). Contrary to traditional DAC donors and their conformity to internationally agreed goals, the aid experience of bilateral development actors from emerging Asian states including India, South Korea and Taiwan is strongly rooted in HRD. HRD has recently received more attention from these Asian ODA providers, partially because of the key role that HRD has played in the success of developing Asian countries' national and regional development and partially because HRD is widely perceived by these Asian countries as a bridge for effectively linking both the demand and supply sides of education in the post-EFA age.

Concepts and conceptualisation of human resource development in the context of international development

The term "human resource development" (HRD) was first introduced by Leonard Nadler in 1969 at the Annual Conference of the American Society for Training and Development in Miami, Florida, United States. He defined HRD as "the learning experiences organised for a definite time period, and designed to increase the possibility of behavioural change and job performance growth" (Nadler and Nadler 1989). The concept of HRD historically originates from a field of education and training that is "for and about work" (Swanson and Holton 2001). HRD emphasises the employment and economic values of education; thus, HRD attracts the technical and vocational skills development (TVSD) community. The United Nations Development Programme (UNDP) (UNDP 1991) expanded the concepts and definition of HRD by adding:

> [P]olicies and programmes that support and sustain equitable opportunities for continuing acquisition and application of skills, knowledge and competencies which promote individual autonomy and are mutually beneficial to individuals, the community and the larger environment of which they are a part.
>
> (p. 19)

Based on this definition, HRD is a broad concept encompassing all aspects of human development, and human resources is considered one of three vital pillars (in addition to capital resources and natural resources) that supports a nation's socioeconomic development. Mankind is not only an economic resource but also a resource for social development. The meanings and ideas of HRD have been expanded to refer to the competence and skill development of employees within a corporation or an organisation for the purposes of job performance, cooperative productivity, and organisational competitiveness and are concerned with individual, organisational, and national levels of sustainable development through education and training (Rao 1996). In summary, HRD has been perceived as a method of empowering people by nurturing the capacities that they can use to improve their quality of life and that of their organisation and society. Developing human resources supports a nation's economic competitiveness and sustainable development and fulfils individuals' socioeconomic needs.

However, the UNDP's definition of HRD is vague. It is mainly because the meanings and purposes embedded in the UNDP's definition are too broad and continuously scaled up, ranging from individual productivity and autonomy to national socioeconomic development and self-reliance, from economic competitiveness to future sustainable development. Accordingly, ambitious and ambiguous languages are found in relevant policy documents, sometimes leading to everywhere but nowhere. Although HRD is unlikely to convey a homogeneous and singular meaning in the extant literature on international development, the lack of a standard definition has caused inconsistent ideas and practices to be pursued by groups with distinct interests in varying organisational settings and societal contexts.

In the context of international development, HRD has evolved from focusing on individual capacities and economic contributions at the organisational level to developing individual, organisational, and national capacities through international cooperation, educational aid, internationally agreed-upon sustainable development goals and targets (such as EFA goals and targets and the ongoing discussion about post-2015 goals for education), and extending opportunities for education and training to underprivileged groups and individuals in societies (UNDESA n.d.). Recently, global consultations and discussions amongst the intergovernmental Open Working Group (OWG) on Sustainable Development Goals and the Education for All Steering Committee (EFA SC) have produced proposals for HRD-related targets, such as "skills for employment" and "skills for work", in a post-2015 educational development framework (Palmer 2014). Both the OWG and EFA SC proposals stress the skills necessary for employment, including technical and vocational training. The OWG target specifically emphasises the skills required for employment, including vocational, information and communications technology (ICT), technical, engineering, and scientific skills. By comparison, in addition to the skills required for employment, the EFA SC target entails facilitating the development of knowledge and skills through technical, vocational, upper secondary, and tertiary education and training to increase the quality of work and life, placing particular emphasis on gender equality and the most marginalised populations (Anderson and Quint 2014). The following questions are rooted in the origin of education and training for and about work: 1) Can the evolution and expansion of HRD ideas contribute to the current fundamental tensions regarding various proposals concerning the definition of skills and methods for evaluating and measuring skill-related targets? 2) If individuals' "skills for employment" (OWG proposal) or "skills for decent work and life" (EFA SC proposal) are unable to be separated from the overall long-term development plans and strategies of a nation to which individuals belong, can the understanding of HRD aid and its emphasis on capacity and performance growth at the individual, institutional, and national levels provide a broad and strategic perspective on the current proposals for skill-related targets?

As global labour markets both influence and adapt to the emerging occupational structures of formal and informal economies, international HRD aid encounters increasing challenges in balancing the demands of new employment sectors with the supply of required skills (UNDESA n.d.). International HRD aid is concerned not only with the formal schools and ministries of education of aid-recipient countries but also a complex world-level concept in which:

> [P]ublic institutions (under various ministries and spanning all education levels), private providers, non-formal provision and informal learning, and enterprise-based training in both formal and informal economies [operate]. Not only are sites, modes and levels diverse, but structured vocational learning may be certificated or not, with these certificates being attached to programmes of a few hours or several years.
>
> (McGrath 2014)

This chapter focuses on the logic, governance, strategies, and approaches used by emerging Asian (South Korean, Taiwanese, and Indian) donors to intervene in the HRD sector. It concludes with implications for the future effectiveness of aid delivery and cooperation as well as for reconsidering the relationship of education with international development in post-EFA society.

From recipient to donor: South Korea and Taiwan's approach to developing human resources

Widely regarded as successful development stories by the international community, South Korea and Taiwan transformed from agricultural and low-skill-based economies to technologically and educationally advanced societies in the past four decades. One of the frequently cited "secrets" of these countries' ongoing success is the emphasis on educational systems and skill development (Sorensen 1994). These two countries have become emergent donors and shared their approach with developing countries. Such an approach is highly relevant to the mainstream belief in the enhancement of human resources. Examination of the aid policy for education and HRD in South Korea and Taiwan indicated that the approach these countries undertake is based on their pasts. Aid expenditure on HRD is prior and ranked first in South Korea. The concrete strategies and measures used to enhance human resources in developing countries are threefold: providing universal basic education to all citizens, improving technical and vocational skills of industrial workers, and creating long-term societal leaders. This design is beneficial to various levels of socioeconomic structure and can improve personal and organisational abilities in every aspect. Unlike the MDGs or EFA fully endorsed by most multilateral and bilateral organisations, South Korea and Taiwan highly emphasise intermediate skill development and cultivation of societal leaders. The experiences of South Korea and Taiwan indicate that, in developing countries, HRD should comprise three layers, namely basic education, the skills of technical workers, and training of societal leaders. The post-2015 development agenda should incorporate these new elements and consider these three layers as a whole.

History and the role of human resources

One of the most frequently mentioned factors for explaining the successful development of South Korea and Taiwan over the past four decades is the emphasis on the investment in education and human resources (Sorensen 1994). Numerous researchers believe that this factor compensates for the drawbacks of other factors required for effective development, such as natural resources, a solid infrastructure, and abundant capital. South Korea and Taiwan are two examples demonstrating the value of human capital and resources in overcoming or removing barriers embedded in local and national settings. The main strategies and mechanisms for cultivating human resources that both countries adopted in the 1950s and 1960s comprised three dimensions. First, leaders in South Korea and Taiwan established primary and secondary schools to provide the younger generation with universal access to public schooling. Second, vocational and technical training systems were initiated to nurture workers' basic and intermediate industrial skills. Finally, leaders in both countries understood the value of high-end talent in long-term national development. Several upper-class citizens and professionals in various industries were sent to study abroad and learn about the most recent technology, best practices, and advanced knowledge. In hindsight, these measures seem effective in promoting development. When these two countries became donors, their previous experiences became valuable assets or baselines for enacting aid policies and strategies.

Rationales

Adopting a similar stance to undertake international aid, South Korea and Taiwan emphasised the importance of past developmental experiences in the following excerpts from their ODA policies: "integrating Korea's development experience and comparative advantages into development cooperation projects/programmes" (Korean International Cooperation Agency – KOICA 2008a) and "drawing on Taiwan's comparative advantages [and] responding to partners' needs" (ICDF 2014a). As stated by the KOICA, the official aid organisation in South Korea, "education has played a critical role that links all the items on the international development agenda such as poverty reduction, health, technology sharing, environment, gender equality, democracy and governance improvement" (KOICA 2008b). KOICA even allows "the redistribution of income by expanding the scope of opportunities". Education is fundamental for other social and economic achievements and links all Millennium Development Goals (MDGs) as interrelated agendas. Adopting a similar stance but with a more instrumental purpose than that of KOICA, the Taiwan International Cooperation and Development Fund (ICDF) (2014b) indicated that:

> [T]he development of human resources is often the key to economic growth and social development. In addition to being constrained by poor infrastructure, health care systems and gender inequality, economic growth in such countries can be inhibited by poor institutional capacity, the quality of human resources, the poor performance of basic education, high unemployment and a lack of a professional workforce.

The value of human resources is to become the "engine" and "enabler" for other social and economic sectors. Therefore, the ICDF regards "capacity building as a new aid strategy for human development". The main goal of facilitating HRD is to raise the capacity, competence, and ability of individuals, organisations, and entire nations. Therefore, capacity building entails "addressing the problem of individuals or organizations whose capacity is weak or insufficient by making a sustained investment in all stakeholders (including governments, NGOs, and professionals, community leaders, academics and other persons)". The long-term goal of capacity building is to "develop problem-solving abilities and raise potentials" (ICDF 2014b) to achieve self-governance and sustainable development in recipient countries.

Volume of aid to education and human resources

After the histories, rationale, and logic for HRD aid in South Korea and Taiwan were analysed, results regarding expenditure allocation according to sector were presented, and whether education and HRD received sufficient support, as previously emphasised, was assessed. Judging from the available statistics, both countries allocated substantial amounts of the budget to education and HRD. In 2012, South Korean aid focused on education (27%), health (16%), governance (15%), and industry and energy (13%). These are sectors that comply with the MDGs of South Korea, sectors in which South Korea possesses a comparative advantage and sectors for which partner countries have demands (KOICA 2012: 16). Education, as the largest sector, comprises more than a quarter of the annual budget, indicating that the HRD approach is empirically supported. Moreover, according to statistics obtained in 2011, primary and secondary education (mainly technical and vocational education and training) respectively account for 30% and 49% of the total sectorial educational distribution. This indicates a strong motivation for raising the quality and competence of human resources. This pattern also appears to be based on the successful experiences of South Korea and Taiwan, where comprehensive schooling and vocational and technical training were emphasised.

In agreement with the international development community's agreement on EFA and MDGs, Taiwan has prioritised agriculture, public health, education, ICT and environmental protection (ICDF 2013: 17). Therefore, education has been emphasised for its value in the social and economic development of developing countries. The most recent expenditure statistics from 2012 indicated that the highest percentage of a national budget is allocated to management and general affairs (34%), followed by international education and training (18%) and technical cooperation (18%). Humanitarian assistance, lending, and investment account for 5% (ICDF 2013: 61). This distribution indicates that human resources is a valuable sector, despite accounting for a moderate proportion. In addition to education and training, technical cooperation is highly related to knowledge sharing in the form of "capacity building", with the goal of enhancing individual or organisational competence. This category has critical implications for HRD. If knowledge sharing were considered a form of HRD, then much higher ratios of Taiwanese ODA expenditure would be used for education and human resources.

Strategic measures for increasing human resources

As mentioned previously, both South Korea and Taiwan possess experience in transforming human resources into a critical catalyst for social and economic development. The strategic HRD aid measures that both countries implement reflect their past experiences. This section reviews the recent aid projects that South Korea and Taiwan have provided to developing countries to identify the primary features and traits of these aid policies.

South Korea

After exploring the aid model for skills development, Chun and Eo (2012: 7) indicated that the main strategies employed by South Korea for enhancing HRD were establishing a training infrastructure, providing a quality training environment, and enhancing capacity building. In this study, descriptions of the aid projects provided by the KOICA (KOICA 2008b) were examined to determine that the conclusions provided by KOICA are correct. First, the major task of the South Korean government is to increase universal access to basic education. A large amount of the national budget was allocated to the construction of primary and secondary schools. To compensate for the insufficient supply of basic education in recipient countries, South Korea established more schools in those countries. In addition, several projects concentrated on producing teachers' guides and textbooks, which are essential elements for improving teaching and learning. Moreover, physical facilities and equipment were stressed in South Korean aid. This approach was consistent with the objectives of EFA and the MDGs supported by major multilateral and bilateral organisations. Second, another primary focus of South Korean aid in HRD was the "training of skilled workers". By launching vocational training centres and systems, prospective workers received more training and enhanced their skills, competencies, and abilities. Several African and Asian countries (e.g., Bangladesh) have acquired such centres or systems through the promotion of South Korean aid projects. In addition, South Korea has focused on improving institutions and the rules and regulations of TVSD as well as establishing a national qualification system (Chun and Eo 2012). One concrete example of the introduction of such a national qualification system is that of Vietnam in 2010. Using its comparative advantage in industry, South Korea emphasised the introduction of automobile-related training centres and systems for developing countries, attempting to enhance the capacity of this industry through this cooperative mechanism.

Capacity building is the main strategy for "fostering advanced human resources". South Korea helped establish distance-learning institutions through recent technology such as ICT and the Internet. Examples include cyber universities in the Association of Southeast Asian Nations region, open universities in Bangladesh, and even ICT schools at the National University of Rwanda. To enhance capacity building, South Korea supported the construction of an HRD centre in the Philippines. Finally, a fellowship programme entitled the "Capacity Improvement and Advancement for Tomorrow" was launched in 2012 to "share important technical skills and knowledge as well as to develop capacities for sustainable socioeconomic development" (KOICA 2008c). Professionals and technical staff members of recipient countries were invited to learn about the development of South Korea and acquire new technical and managerial skills. Approximately 50,000 participants have participated in this fellowship programme. This programme includes short-term, mid-term, and long-term periods (more than one year, including scholarship programmes). To enhance the capacity of public administration, the KOICA jointly cooperated with Seoul National University to launch master's degree programmes in public administration and international studies.

Taiwan

Like South Korea, Taiwan emphasised HRD aid. The most common measures employed include professional workshops and seminars, scholarship programmes, and support for basic education. As stated previously, these are measures used by both South Korea and Taiwan for social and economic development. Since 1962, Taiwan has shared developmental experiences with less developed countries through professional workshops. The themes of these workshops initially focused on agriculture and industry training. Recently, the focus of these workshops covers an increasingly wide range of global and contemporary development concerns such as health care, the environment, social development, trade and economics, agriculture and aquaculture, and management (ICDF 2013: 47). Up to 20 professional workshops and seminars are conducted annually by the ICDF. Every year, approximately 500 trainees who are high-level officials in the governments of developing countries and the staff of nongovernmental organisations (NGOs) participate in the workshops. The subjects of these workshops are typically related to experiences of economic development in Taiwan, including experiences in agriculture, small- and medium-sized enterprises, and technical and vocational education and training. The main objective is to teach participants how to train others and to assist partner countries in overcoming specific concerns by using a pragmatic approach. All of these measures are used to increase capacity (ICDF 2013: 47). The International Higher Education Scholarship Programme was created in 1998 to support the increasing demand for highly skilled human resources in partner countries. Students from developing countries received a full scholarship to study in Taiwan. All courses were taught in English. Like the Capacity Improvement and Advancement for Tomorrow programme implemented in South Korea, this programme was conducted in cooperation with domestic universities, and students from developing countries were invited to enhance their technical knowledge and skills. All participants were required to return to their home country after graduation. In 2013, more than a quarter of the students chose business administration (27%) and engineering (26%), 20% chose public health and medicine, 16% chose agriculture, and 10% chose social sciences and humanities. This student distribution revealed that the main focuses were on administration and governance abilities, technical skills, and knowledge transfer in productive industries. By studying these subjects, students' skills and knowledge could improve substantially and be applied to their national contexts. In addition, Taiwan provided financial support to improve primary and secondary schools. By cooperating with NGOs such as World Vision, the ICDF established a scholarship programme sponsoring subsidised tuition, school meals, and materials for disadvantaged children in Mongolia. From 2011 to 2013, a similar programme in Burkina Faso was conducted to help poor, underprivileged children living in or around gold mines and quarries through cooperation with the Terre des Hommes Lausanne Foundation. Such programmes were implemented to provide children of various socioeconomic statuses with access to primary and secondary education. Concurrently, these children were expected to enhance their long-term abilities and skills.

South-South cooperation: India's approach to developing human resources

India has experienced unique national development and economic growth since gaining its independence in 1947. India's economic growth was largely triggered by its economic reforms to market openness enacted in 1991, catalysing the transformative status of India from an aid recipient to an aid donor. Other factors also contribute to the uniqueness of India. First, India is regarded as an "emerging" donor, but it historically played a donor role by providing aid to neighbouring countries in the region. Second, India has become a knowledge-based society recognised for its excellence in soft power and elite education. The increasing scale of India's knowledge-based economy is widely recognised, but India contains the highest number of out-of-school children of all Asian countries. Finally, with the dual role of being an aid donor and an aid recipient, India has developed its own philosophies and methods for providing overseas assistance to other countries based on its abundant experience with North-South and South-South cooperation. Therefore, this section reviews India's overseas HRD assistance. Based on the conceptualisation of HRD mentioned in Section 1, the term "HRD" in India encompasses a broader meaning that particularly focuses on the educational and skills development of a nation (Dutt 2010).

Recipient reflection: how does India develop its human resources with external aid?

To emphasise the strategic role and function of education in the India's overall national development, the Ministry of Human Resource Development was established in 1985, replacing the original Ministry of Education in the Government of India (GoI). Recognising that India perceives and repositions HRD as the engine of growth and self-development (Dutt 2010) is essential for understanding how India copes with external aid for developing human resources and how India provides aid for developing human resources of other countries. Over the 60 years that India has been an aid recipient, the country has increased scepticism regarding the necessity for external aid and has required more domestic financing to achieve its educational policy goals. Such scepticism increased substantially after India's economic growth in 1991. The Bharatiya Janata Party discovered in 2003 that the national capacity and confidence of India was gradually undermined and degraded by a supply-driven North-South relationship. Since then, the country has attempted to reduce reliance on donors. According to UNESCO (2013b), only eight Development Assistance Committee (DAC) donors substantially disburse bilateral ODA for education in India. External aid in India must be provided directly to the central and state governments of India to support national five-year plans (FYPs), including the National Programme Universalisation of Elementary Education (also called Sarva Shiksha Abhiyan) in the 10th FYP (2002–2007), Universalisation of Secondary Education (also called Rastriya Madhyamic Shiksha Abhiyan), and Skills Development in the 11th FYP (2007–2012). As an example, India's National Skills Development Policy, launched in 2009, reflected the HRD ambition announced in the 11th FYP to educate and cultivate 500 million Indian people by 2022 (IMaCS 2013). To achieve this ambitious policy goal, bilateral assistance (such as from Britain and Germany) and multilateral resources (such as the European Union and World Bank) have been used and directly controlled by the GoI. The experience of India in managing external aid can explain why India acts as an "emerging" aid donor and prefers to disburse its own ODA resources directly through recipient governments, unlike the traditional DAC donors who typically disburse their bilateral ODA through their own governments or as unearmarked aid through multilateral development organisations. According to India's ideology and logic of aid effectiveness, the most vital concern is the ownership of recipient countries and how skilfully recipient countries manage external aid, rather than how aid delivery is regulated by OECD DAC norms and principles.

Donor experience: how is Indian ODA used to develop the human resources of other countries?

The first method by which India seeks a role as a donor is to share its distinct HRD experiences in the form of South-South cooperation and triangular cooperation because HRD is considered the engine of domestic growth and development in India. At least three international agreements have provided a foundation for South-South cooperation and shaped the ideology and philosophies of Indian overseas assistance. The first is the Panchsheel Agreement signed by India and China in 1954. In this agreement, both nations endorsed five principles, namely mutual respect for territorial integrity and sovereignty, mutual nonaggression, mutual non-interference, equality and mutual benefit, and peaceful coexistence. Second, the Asian–African Conference in

Bandung, Indonesia, in 1955 (also called the Bandung Conference) produced the Declaration on the Promotion of World Peace and Cooperation and engendered the famous Non-Aligned Movement. The third is the Technical Cooperation between Developing Countries (TCDC) established at the Buenos Aires Conference, which was attended by all UN member states, and, accordingly, the Buenos Aires Plan of Action for Promoting and Implementing TCDC, which was adopted by the UN General Assembly in 1978 (Agrawal 2012; OECD 2012). However, India's donor status as a partner and peer in mutually beneficial relationships with its partner countries, rather than a donor-recipient relationship, distinguishes India from traditional DAC donors and their North-South technical transfer. India provides ODA according to the principle of not interfering in the domestic affairs of partner countries. In addition, commonalities between India and other traditional DAC donor countries can be observed because both traditional and emerging donors have economic, geopolitical, and diplomatic motivations for their official aid provision. Geopolitically and diplomatically, India has long history of donating to its neighbouring countries in the South Asian region, such as Bhutan, Sri Lanka, Nepal, Bangladesh and Maldives, and in the 1960s, India expanded its aid to African countries by sharing technical knowledge, expertise, and experience. India further expanded its strength as a regional leader and world-class knowledge hub through economic cooperation and technical assistance provided to Afghanistan, Myanmar, and other nations (as seen in Table 30.1). Economically, India's trade interests and commercial motivation constantly determine which partner countries should be selected and prioritised for aid.

In addition to economic cooperation, Indian aid is generally provided in the form of technical cooperation. India assists partner countries in improving the acquisition of technical expertise, capacity building, and the development of institutions and human resources to facilitate long-term self-development (OECD 2012). Although no single centralised agency in India develops and implements ODA strategy and policies, the specialised Technical Cooperation Division (TCD) of the Ministry of External Affairs established in 1964 is currently responsible for coordinating the majority of skills development and education programmes for Indian

Table 30.1 India's ODA (including loans) to other countries

Country/Region	2009/2010	Country/Region	2010/2011	(USD million)	
				Country/Region	2011/2012
Bhutan	235	Bhutan	311	Bhutan	366
Afghanistan	52	Afghanistan	56	Afghanistan	52
Nepal	27	Nepal	27	Maldives	49
Africa	23	Africa	27	Nepal	27
Mongolia	23	Sri Lanka	16	Africa	22
Sri Lanka	14	Myanmar	16	Sri Lanka	24
Myanmar	10	Eurasia	5	Myanmar	20
Eurasia	4	Maldives	2	Eurasia	5
Bangladesh	0.68	Latin America	0.72	Bangladesh	1
Maldives	0.63	Bangladesh	0.54	Latin America	0.36
Latin America	0.36	Others	64	Mongolia	0.09
Others	37			Others	49
Total	**426**		**527**		**618**

Source: Adapted from OECD (2012: 6).

ODA. Three schemes administered by the TCD were formulated to channel India's bilateral ODA, mainly concentrating on training programmes, the deployment of Indian experts, and the sharing of knowledge and expertise with more than 160 partner countries worldwide. These schemes were separately named the Technical Cooperation Scheme under the Colombo Plan, the Indian Technical Economic Cooperation (ITEC) Programme, and the Special Commonwealth Assistance for Africa Programme (SCAAP). According to the OECD statistics (2012), at least 5,500 participants from partner countries annually participate in more than 230 training courses (as seen in Table 30.2) provided by 42 Indian institutions in the fields of ICT, management, technical and vocational skills, accounting and banking, English skills, environment and renewable energy, and enterprise skills. In some situations, triangular cooperation is employed as a cost-effective method that involves encouraging other donor countries and multilateral development organisations to financially support Indian institutions that provide training programmes to personnel and students from partner countries. Every year, Indian experts are deployed to partner countries to share knowledge and expertise. Study trips are organised to invite officials and professionals from partner countries to visit India.

In the ongoing transformation from a recipient to a donor, India's perception and practices regarding HRD aid, including aid for developing the human resources of other countries and managing external aid for education and skill development, are based on the concept of mutual benefit and the goals of capacity building and developing the institutions and human resources of a nation. India's HRD aid indicates the trends, methods, and problems of India's South-South cooperation and provides an alternative approach to the conventional North-South technical transfer as well as existing OECD DAC norms and principles regarding aid effectiveness. However, some researchers have criticised India by stating that the boundary between aid activities and trade and investment is unclear in Indian ODA. Despite India's commitment to avoid interfering in the domestic politics and affairs of partner countries, the geopolitical, diplomatic, and commercial self-interests of Indian ODA are a political choice and cannot be easily justified according to the noninterference principle. Therefore, more skilful coordination; more transparent accountability; and a centralised, professionalised aid agency in India that mobilises ODA resources is required. Finally, as Agrawal (2012) indicated, further development of India's long-term aid policy goals, rather than short-term goals, is necessary. India has gained substantial experience by playing a dual role as an aid receiver and provider, and, thus, the power of Indian HRD aid is a result of India's readiness to assist partner countries in strategic planning of HRD rather than to provide ad hoc, tactical, or transactional HRD projects in exchange for partner countries' temporary economic, political, or diplomatic support.

Table 30.2 Courses offered under ITEC and SCAAP

Courses	*% of the total number*
Technical Skills	28 %
IT, Telecom, English	15 %
Environment and Renewable Energy	13 %
SME/Rural Development	9 %
Management	6 %
Accounts, Banking, Finance	6 %
Other	23 %

Source: Adapted from Agrawal (2012:12).

Concluding note

HRD aid has received great support from emerging Asian countries and has been perceived as an effective method for reducing the gap between the demand and supply sides of education. India, South Korea, and Taiwan have demonstrated the positive relationship between HRD and national development, which catalysed their transformation from aid recipients to aid donors. South Korea and Taiwan are no longer aid receivers, but India still maintains a dual role. India, South Korea, and Taiwan attribute their specific HRD donor experience to (1) the abundance of previous recipient reflection and (2) successful methods for HRD implemented in their own national development.

Unlike traditional DAC donors who fully endorsed the MDGs and EFA goals, India, South Korea, and Taiwan have allocated a substantial amount of resources to and emphasised the strategic role of education and skills development in increasing the capacity, competence, and confidence of individual, organisational, and national self-development of partner countries. Unlike traditional DAC donors who align their strategies for providing aid with OECD DAC norms and principles, emerging Asian donors more emphasise the importance of how to improve the national capacity, ownership, and sovereignty of partner countries; how to reduce partners countries' aid dependency how partner countries organise and manage external aid; and how to maintain mutually beneficial relationships with partner countries. In the post-EFA era, emerging Asian donors' practices in education will involve not only assisting partner countries in continually engaging in HRD by using long-term strategic planning and goals but also assisting partner countries in fully using the potential of human resources to benefit partner countries' individuals, communities, and societies. Under the emerging Asian donors' reconceptualisation of aid for HRD, HRD is purposed to achieve a large scale of development changes. Such large-scale changes can neither rely on a single source from a single donor nor afford high transaction costs of mobilising aid resources. Accordingly, in the post-2015 aid landscape, emerging Asian donors' practices in aid effectiveness might exhibit less convergence but more cooperation with traditional DAC donors than they did previously.

References

Agrawal, S., 2012. Technical training, curriculum support and education initiatives: An assessment of India's overseas aid in skills development. Background paper prepared for the Education for All Global Monitoring Report 2012, UNESCO, Paris.

Anderson, A., Quint, R., 2014. A User's Guide to the Post-2015 Agenda Education Targets. http://www.google.com.tw/url?sa=t&rct=j&q=&esrc=s&source=web&cd=1&ved=0CBsQFjAA&url=http%3A%2F%2Fwww.brookings.edu%2Fblogs%2Feducation-plus-development%2Fposts%2F2014%2F06%2F18-post-2015-agenda-education-targets-anderson&ei=Sl_FU6aHL87jkAWlwID4BQ&usg=AFQjCNGqB84LhhYy7OeWjHb3KJvC3jr6Aw

Chun, H.-M., Eo, K.-C., 2012. Aid for skills development: South Korea case study. Background paper prepared for the Education for All Global Monitoring Report 2012, UNESCO, Paris.

Dutt, M., 2010. Development and HRD in India. Presented at IDEAS 20th Anniversary, Tokyo, March.

ICDF, 2013. *2013 Annual Report: International Cooperation and Development Fund.* ICDF, Taipei.

ICDF, 2014a. Core Strategies. http://www.icdf.org.tw/ct.asp?xItem=8111&CtNode=30181&mp=2

ICDF, 2014b. Education. http://www.icdf.org.tw/ct.asp?xItem=12412&ctNode=29860&mp=2

IMaCS, 2013. Human resource and skill requirements in the education and skill development services sector. Study on mapping of human resource skill gaps in India till 2022. Report prepared for the National Skill Development Corporation, New Delhi.

KOICA, 2008a. Policies and Strategies. http://www.koica.go.kr/english/koica/policies/index.html

KOICA, 2008b. Education. http://www.koica.go.kr/english/aid/education/index.html

KOICA, 2008c. Training Program. http://www.koica.go.kr/english/schemes/training/index.html

KOICA, 2012. *2012 KOICA Annual Report.* KOICA, Gyeonggi-do.

McGrath, S., 2014. A Post-2105 Skills Sub-Goal: Confusion Still Reigns. http://www.ukfiet.org/cop/2014/a-post-2015-skills-sub-goal-confusion-still-reigns/

Nadler, L., Nadler, Z., 1989. *Developing Human Resources.* Wiley, Hoboken.

OECD, 2012. Trade-related south-south cooperation: India. OECD, Paris.

Palmer, R., 2014. Skills for Work Is High on the Post-2015 Agenda, but Are We Still on Track for Another Vague Target? http://norrag.wordpress.com/2014/05/19/skills-for-work-is-high-on-the-post-2015-agenda-but-are-we-still-on-track-for-another-vague-target/

Rao, T., 1996. *Human Resource Development.* Sage, Thousand Oaks.

Sorensen, C., 1994. Success and education in South Korea. *Comparative Education Review* 38, 1, 10–35.

Swanson, R., Holton, E., 2001. *Foundations of Human Resource Development.* Berrett-Koehler, San Francisco.

UNDESA, n.d. United Nations Office for ECOSOC Support and Coordination Human Resources Development. http://www.un.org/en/development/desa/oesc/humanresources.shtml

UNDP, 1991. Inter-sectoral approach to human resource development for the 1990s and beyond. Bureau for Programme Policy and Evaluation, UNDP, New York.

UNESCO, 2013a. Schooling for millions of children jeopardized by reductions in aid. Education for All Global Monitoring Report Policy Paper 9, UNESCO, Paris.

UNESCO, 2013b. Trends in aid to education: lessons for post-2015. Education for All Global Monitoring Report Policy Paper 11, UNESCO, Paris.

31

THE ROLE OF CIVIL SOCIETY IN EDUCATION FOR DEVELOPMENT

Bronwen Magrath

Introduction

Education policy in both "developed" and "developing" countries is increasingly shaped by decisions made at the global level. International frameworks like the Education for All agenda and the Millennium Development Goals are forged by diverse stakeholders – international organisations, national governments, aid organisations, civil society and the private sector – who come together at global megaconferences to debate the future of the international and development education field. This poses significant methodological and theoretical challenges for the field, as the traditional unit of analysis for education policy studies has been the nation-state. I will attempt to meet this challenge through a focus on global-level decision making and through a critical analysis of the role civil society plays in global educational governance.

This chapter explores the emergence of a global advocacy movement centred on the "education for all" agenda. I examine how different political opportunities have emerged for civil society advocacy in international education governance and how civil society organisations have themselves shaped and created these opportunities. I then move on to analyse a number of dominant critical themes in the literature on civil society and global governance, both within and outside the field of education. Here I concentrate particularly on how large international nongovernmental organisations often dominate global advocacy networks and the role global normative discourse plays in imbuing these organisations with authority. In the final section, I explore the links between global discourse and governance power by analysing the adoption of the Rights-Based Approach to development at ActionAid International.

Civil society organisations and global educational governance: a brief history

In this section, I offer a brief history of the evolving role civil society organisations have played in education for development. In particular, I explore how civil society organisations (CSOs) have become involved in global educational governance – decision making concerning education policy that is carried out at the global level by a host of international, governmental and nongovernmental organisations. The idea that CSOs should participate in social policy decisions is quite a recent development. The traditional role for civil society in international education and development has been one of service-delivery: CSOs have been involved in constructing schools, running nonformal education centres, training teachers and developing innovative pedagogy. BRAC Education Programmes in Bangladesh, Escuela Nueva in Columbia and Action-Aid's REFLECT literacy method are but a few examples of the pioneering education service delivery work carried out by civil society organisations around the world. Based on their experience and expertise in providing education to underserved populations, CSOs have begun to assert a stronger voice in the decisions that impact the communities in which they work.

The origins of global educational governance

The idea that some decisions regarding education policy should be made at the global level first emerged in the wake of the Second World War, part of a wider trend in multilateralism typified by the creation of the United Nations and Bretton Woods systems. In this emerging multilateral system, education was seen not simply as a matter for national governments but as a means to establish global cooperation and development. Postwar concerns with peace and prosperity were firmly linked to education, as reflected in UNESCO's constitution: "Since wars begin in the minds of men, it is in the minds of men that the defences of peace must be constructed" (UNESCO 1945). The right to education was enshrined in the UN Declaration of Human Rights, which urged governments to provide free elementary education "directed to the full development of the human personality and to the strengthening of respect for human rights and fundamental freedoms" (UN 1948: Article 26).

It was not just UN agencies that expressed an interest in global-level education decision making. A host of institutions, including multilateral organisations such as the World Bank and the OECD, as well as bilateral organisations such as the US Agency for International development (USAID) and UK Department for International Development (DFID), saw value in promoting education as a global good. For many of these organisations, education was valued as a driver of economic growth rather than of peace and human rights. Human capital theory, which linked education with national economic growth, emerged as a dominant part of global education discourse beginning in the early 1960s and led to a huge expansion of education systems in both developing and developed countries in this era (Resnik 2006). Cold War politics served to encourage bilateral rather than multilateral education aid, allowing donor governments to use education to further their geopolitical goals and to promote the neoliberalising of education in developing countries (Robertson and Dale 2006).

From the 1950s through the 1980s, civil society organisations had a very small role in global educational governance. These organisations were valued for their ability to deliver education services to needy and underserved populations. By the 1980s, the number of civil society organizations involved in education development had expanded considerably. This expansion was due in part to the growth of neoliberal discourse in international development, which sought to limit government spending on social services and to promote the private sector as a more efficient and cost-effective deliverer of public goods. Service-oriented CSOs worked to fill the gaps left by declining government provision, and this role was championed by many bilateral aid organisations and international financial organisations for its efficiency and efficacy (Chabbott 1999).

The emergence of the education for all consensus

By 1990, however, a new global consensus on development education began to emerge, beginning with the World Conference on Education for All. This conference, which was convened jointly by the World Bank and a host of UN agencies, championed universal basic education as a fundamental human right and as a key part of economic and social development (UNESCO 1990a). The Jomtien Declaration produced from this conference emphasised that achieving basic education for all was a global as well as a national responsibility, requiring "international solidarity" and the revitalisation of partnerships "between government and non-governmental organisations, the private sector, local communities, religious groups, and families" (p. 7). Thus, in discourse at least, the WCEFA placed significant importance of forging partnerships with civil society in order to fulfil the basic learning needs of all. This opened the door for civil society organisations to voice their opinions in global educational governance.

Despite this rhetoric about partnerships for achieving EFA, there has been significant academic criticism of the role given to civil society organisations during and after the 1990 conference. Chabbott (2003) and Jones (2007) have shown that the participation of civil society at the conference was severely limited by the sponsoring agencies. CSOs were virtually shut out of the policymaking process, their influence restricted to a single premeeting. The result was a lack of cohesion among participating CSOs, many of whom had no prior relationship to each other, which drastically curtailed their potential to create a cohesive civil society voice at the conference.

Furthermore, Mundy and Murphy (2001) have pointed out that the role for civil society envisioned by the EFA multilaterals remained one of service provider rather than policy advocate. This was made clear in the Framework for Action, which outlined the potential roles of CSOs within EFA:

> These autonomous bodies, while advocating independent and critical public views, might play roles in monitoring, research, training and material production for the sake of non-formal and life-long educational processes.
>
> (UNESCO 1990b: 5)

The same document praised CSOs for:

> [T]heir experience, expertise, energy and direct relationships with various constituencies are valuable resources for identifying and meeting basic learning needs. Their active involvement in partnerships for basic education should be promoted through policies and mechanisms that strengthen their capacities and recognise their autonomy.
>
> (p. 12)

Although most governments and multilateral organisations were unwilling to see civil society organisations move beyond their roles as service providers, the expanding interest in international education programming did indirectly create new political opportunities for CSO advocacy. The increased donor support and funding for CSOs carrying out education service delivery led to a number of organisations expanding their basic education programmes as well as new CSOs entering the field. The growing density of education-related CSOs as service providers opened the door to legitimising these organisations as political advocates based on their experience in the field (Minkoff 1994). The EFA mandate also provided an advocacy target – assessing whether or not governments were living up to the international commitments – around which civil society could organise.

The global campaign for education: a CSO advocacy coalition

By the late 1990s, a number of large nongovernmental organisations had launched education advocacy initiatives. These initiatives focused on highlighting the decoupling between promises made at Jomtien and the failure of national governments and the international community to translate these into educational change. Three prominent organisations with interest in advocating for EFA came together in 1999 to form the Global Campaign for Education (GCE) on the eve of the 2000 World Education Forum in Dakar – ActionAid, Oxfam and Education International.

In the lead-up to the Dakar Conference, the Global Campaign for Education engaged in a number of strategic activities designed to leverage more political opportunities for CSOs within the EFA movement. This included a letter to the World Bank President criticising the failure of the interagency EFA forum and demanding greater participation of civil society groups in EFA policymaking; a Global Week of Action to engage teachers unions as well as other civil society organisations whose work touched in some way on education related issues; and hosting an NGO conference at the Africa regional EFA preconference meetings. By March of 2000, the GCE had grown to over 400 member organisations (Mundy and Murphy 2001).

On the eve of the Dakar Conference, the Global Campaign for Education created a nine-point platform to be used as the basis of advocacy efforts. This was circulated widely among CSOs and the media as well as members of national delegations. Again, we can see that although formal political opportunity structures were limited, the very nature of the EFA consensus created political opportunities that the GCE and its affiliates were able to exploit. By creating a coherent and widely owned advocacy platform, the GCE raised its profile in the run-up to Dakar, highlighting that:

> [T]he more a movement can aggregate popular interests into concrete policy demands, the more effective it should be at coordinating global strategy and utilising the political opportunities created by intergovernmental organisations.
>
> (Smith, Pagnucco and Chatfield 1997: 69)

Despite the increasing advocacy activities on the part of civil society organisations, or perhaps because of it, the interagency steering committee sought to limit CSO influence at the Dakar Conference. Only 55 official invitations were given out, as compared to 125 in 1990. The conference did offer a few key venues for CSO advocacy, including the presence of civil society representatives – many of whom were members of the GCE – on the Dakar Declaration drafting committee. The final document included a number of points based on the GCE's platform: it referred to "free" rather than "affordable" education; maintained language around education as a right; and included a statement on civil society actors as partners in policy dialogue, planning and monitoring, rather than just as service providers (Mundy 2012).

The civil society platform also emphasised the need for concrete financing plans to achieve Education for All, and this was a major lobbying point for the Global Campaign for Education. The conference facilitated GCE access to the World Bank, by far the largest donor to development education, and the GCE took this opportunity to push its education financing agenda. In 2002, the World Bank developed the Fast-Track Initiative for education financing, based largely on the recommendations of Oxfam and the GCE, indicating that the campaign had been successful in leveraging the political opportunities made available by the Dakar Conference (Kitamura 2007; Mundy 2012).

New partnerships post-Dakar

It was widely recognised at the Dakar Conference that the failings of Jomtien were directly related to the lack of strong partnerships among governments and intergovernmental and nongovernmental organisations to achieve Education for All (Jones 2007; Kitamura 2007). Post-Dakar, a number of mechanisms were introduced to facilitate the access of NGOs to the EFA follow-up process, influenced by recommendations made by civil society organisations at the conference (ActionAid 2000). These include the EFA High Level Group Meeting, the Working Group Meeting on EFA, and the Collective Consultation of NGOs on EFA (CCNGO/EFA).

There were also new financial opportunities created for, and by, civil society advocacy in the post-Dakar EFA agenda. The largest of these was the Commonwealth Education Fund, launched by DFID in 2002, and the Civil Society Education Fund, which replaced the CEF in 2009 and is financed by the multilateral Global Partnership for Education. Both of these funds were/are designed to support national civil society organisations in developing countries to become effective development partners, particularly as monitors of EFA progress at national levels. This represents a growing trend in aid architecture: multilateral and bilateral donors have increasingly called on the participation of civil society actors as watchdogs who can monitor the implementation of the poverty reduction strategies and use of donor funds at the country level. In this way, funding civil society advocacy can be seen as a donor strategy to counterbalance support to developing country governments, a way to minimise the risk of financial mismanagement or corruption (Collinson 2006; Tomlinson and Macpherson 2007). But these funds also provide political and financial opportunities for CSOs to monitor governments and hold them to account for the commitments they have made.

The Commonwealth Education Fund was carried out using a collaborative management structure with three British INGOs – ActionAid, Oxfam and Save the Children – acting as the fund's managing committee and overall strategy coordinators. These three organisations, and particularly ActionAid, were instrumental in establishing the Civil Society Education Fund and play an active role in the global secretariat and each regional funding committee. Again, this is a growing trend in the international development field: many large funds targeting civil society are managed and dispersed by large international NGOs, keeping the funding agency at arm's length. But this mechanism raises some considerable issues of power between local advocacy groups and the INGOs who control their funds (Collinson 2006; Tomlinson and Macpherson 2007). The following section explores this theme in more depth by discussing some major currents in the literature on civil society advocacy, both inside and outside the international and development education field.

Civil society advocacy and global social policy: critical viewpoints

The growing role of civil society in social policy formation is heralded by many as a way to democratise global governance (Held and Koenig-Archibugi 2005; Scholte 2007; Glasius 2008; Bexell, Tallberg and Uhlin 2010). This perspective rests on the idea that civil society organisations could serve to reinvigorate international political and economic structures by holding state and nonstate actors to account, by bringing the voices of the citizenry into the international policy process, and by placing social and moral issues on the international agenda (Collingwood and Logister 2005), a process that has been described as "globalisation from below" (Appadurai 2000). Among the leading advocates of this process is David Held (1995, 2004), who has suggested a reforming of the United Nations system to incorporate new actors, including INGOs, whose links to local and grassroots governance would help create a "global cosmopolitan democracy".

However, many scholars warn against the perspective that NGOs are "doing good" by virtue of their nonprofit, nonstate status (Kaldor 2003; Anderson 2011). These organisations have no direct legal ties to the citizenry on whose behalf they claim to speak (Gordenker and Weiss 1995), and many have argued that upward accountability to donors often takes precedence over downward accountability to the populations on whose behalf an NGO works. Furthermore, those that are able to have their voices heard in global policy fora are often Northern-based, well-funded NGOs with direct ties to international organisations, leaving smaller civil society groups underrepresented (Bexell, Tallberg and Uhlin 2010). This important critique will be discussed in more depth shortly.

In the field of international and comparative education, scholars have been relatively positive about the impact civil society organisations are having on global educational governance. In their wide-ranging study of national education coalitions affiliated with the Global Campaign for Education, Verger and Novelli (2012) have found that these coalitions "have made significant symbolic, procedural and political impacts on their respective national educational landscapes over the last decade" (p. 173). Case studies drawn from Southeast Asia and Latin America have shown that civil society organisations play a role in promoting local participation in education policy, gathering alternative data on education access and quality, and advocating for a holistic understating of Education for All that encompasses lifelong learning (McCormick 2012; Schnuttgen and Khan 2004).

At the same time, research indicates that the impact civil society has on decision making is limited by the fact that some governments and donors continue to view civil society organisations primarily as educational service deliverers (Schnuttgen and Khan 2004; Mundy 2008; Strutt and Kepe 2010). Furthermore, the capacities and capabilities of nationally based CSOs vary considerably from one context to another, with many organisations lacking the resources or training necessary for genuine engagement in policy formulation (Mundy et al. 2010).

The dominant perspective in the literature appears to be that national civil society organisations can best improve their advocacy capabilities by forming coalitions with other in-country CSOs and linking with regional and national NGOs and coalitions like the Global Campaign for Education. These coalitions are celebrated for strengthening the voice of civil society, increasing its credibility in the eyes of donors and governments, providing resources and training, and facilitating information sharing. Nationally based groups that are unable to exert pressure on their own governments may find linking with international NGOs advantageous, as these bigger players can help put international pressure on noncomplying national governments, a process known as the "boomerang model" of advocacy (Keck and Sikkink 1998).

It is important to bear in mind, however, that entering coalitions can entail a degree of risk for the autonomy of national civil society organisations. Although terms like "partnership" and "community participation" have become central to international development discourse, there has been considerable effort to critique how these terms mask unequal power relations with a false sense of representation (Ferguson 1990; Escobar 1995; Vavrus and Seghers 2010). Questions arise about who is empowered to speak for whom and who has the authority to set the agenda for advocacy campaigning. When coalitions span North-South divides, we need to think additionally about the flow of resources and the problems of representation. In their study of Ghana's national education coalition, Strutt and Kepe (2010) found that dependency on donor funds and INGO support meant that the organisation's focus moved more in line with these international players than the local populations on whose behalf they work. This led the authors to argue that:

> [T]he system remains entrenched in a notion of power hierarchy so deep that relinquishing implementation has done nothing to erode the paramount role that decision making and funding continue to play. Thus, while development may now be implemented by the nationals of developing countries, there has been no willingness on the

part of donors, international organisations, and INGOs to relinquish, or at least share, their decision-making power.

(p. 376)

This perspective has been echoed outside the field of education, most notably by scholars adopting a "firm analogy" to the study of advocacy organisations (Prakash and Gugerty 2010). Arguing against the assumption that advocacy groups are motivated primarily by principled beliefs "that cannot easily be linked to rationalist understanding of their 'interests'" (Keck and Sikkink 1998: 9), the firm perspective views these organisations as largely motivated by instrumental needs such as financial security and brand awareness. Rather than assuming that coalition formation is an effective and impactful way to engage in political advocacy, Prakash and Gugerty have argued that civil society organisations are as likely to compete as to collaborate with other actors in their advocacy field.

In this way, advocacy organisations are seen as special types of firms that operate in a "policy market" characterised by a high degree of competition to "supply distinct products to well-defined constituencies" (Prakash and Gugerty 2010: 3). Bob (2010) argues that, within this marketplace, big international NGOs play a crucial mediating role by gathering data and testimony about human rights violations and "selling" it to donors. The competitive nature of transnational advocacy funding means that a handful of powerful and highly strategic organisations dominate most advocacy issue areas. These organisations, which are generally based in wealthy Western countries, build on past success with funders through demonstrable impacts and personal connections.

Advocacy networks in the education field are similarly dominated by a few international NGOs like Oxfam and ActionAid, and this raises important issues about how smaller civil society organisations are represented. The various EFA conferences, consultations and meetings discussed previously have been criticised for being donor driven and for privileging northern INGOs at the expense of southern civil society groups (Torres 2001; Kitamura 2007; Newman 2012). A significant criticism levelled against the Commonwealth Education Fund, for example, was that power imbalances were implicit in its design, which accorded so much control to the INGOs who managed it – Oxfam, ActionAid and Save the Children – at the expense of national coalitions (CEF 2005; Tomlinson and Macpherson 2007; Woods 2009; Hart 2009).

The mandates and missions statements of most INGOs, and certainly of ActionAid, Oxfam and Save the Children, express a deep commitment to establishing equitable and accountable partnerships with CSO partners operating at country level. ActionAid in particular has been praised for its work to address unequal power relations in its organisation, for example through its Accountability, Learning and Planning System (Scott-Villiers 2002; David, Mancini and Gujit 2006). Yet these INGOs continue to dominate advocacy coalitions and networks. They are able to capitalise on political opportunities and to leverage the resources and the channels of influence necessary to engage in political advocacy.

There are many reasons why INGOs hold such power in global advocacy networks, and accounting for the authority of any single organisation would require a thorough analysis of its history, membership, funding base, leadership structure and personal ties to policymakers – an analysis beyond the scope of this chapter. One factor that will be considered is how INGOs use discourse and espouse norms that align with the interests of international organisations and donors. These INGOs are led and staffed by highly educated individuals, many of whom received graduate degrees from Western universities and have been trained to understand and speak the language of national and global policymaking (Kitamura 2007; McCormick 2012).

This phenomenon has been termed "elite cohesion" (Weiss 2003), and it can help us understand why some organisations are particularly successful at getting their voices heard.

The NGOs who lead the Education for All advocacy movement appear to be genuinely committed to working with and through country-level staff and partners. But balancing between their role in global governance and their desire to work alongside locally based civil society organisations is not a straightforward task, as the norms and discourse espoused at the global level are not always in harmony with local reality. As the next section will illustrate, working within a global advocacy paradigm entails a degree of "elite cohesion" that can create tension between INGOs headquarters and its grassroots network.

Global discourse and "people-centred advocacy": a case study of the rights-based approach

The rights-based approach to development, which emerged in the late 1990s, has become arguably the dominant way to frame international development interventions. Although the idea that all individuals hold certain inalienable, universal rights was not new in the 1990s, this decade saw a profound growth in international attention to human rights law and the application of a rights-based approach (RBA) to a number of issues areas – including education and development. Particularly key for the growth of RBA was the 1993 Vienna Conference on Human Rights, which emphasised the integration of economic, cultural and social rights and brought together a diversity of civil society organisations, including some involved in international development work. This was followed by the 1995 World Social Development Summit, which saw some of these CSOs form a "development caucus" that spearheaded a rights-based approach to development (Cornwall and Nyamu-Musembi 2004). Human rights were mainstreamed into all UN programming beginning in 1997, and RBA is official policy in all UN agencies that work in the development field. UNESCO, the lead agency in Education for All, identifies their mission as "to promote education as a fundamental right, to improve the quality of education and to facilitate policy dialogue, knowledge sharing and capacity building" (www.unesco.org).

For many NGOs, framing underdevelopment and poverty as human rights abuses has been an extremely powerful discursive strategy because it highlights to the public that poverty is neither natural nor inevitable but is the result of specific injustices. Framing underdevelopment as a violation of human-rights norms is also very powerful as a strategy of political leverage: it invokes international legal agreements to convince states, bilateral donors and aid organisations that they have a duty to safeguard the well-being of marginalised populations (Offenheiser and Holcombe 2003; Cornwall and Nyamu-Musembi 2004).

It is important to emphasise that rights-based discourse represents a major sea change in development, ostensibly shifting development programmes away from the tradition of needs-based service delivery. That so many national and international NGOs as well as UN agencies and other international organisations so quickly latched on to the discourse of rights-based development is remarkable. The extent to which this discourse is carried out in practice is another topic altogether, and not one that can be adequately discussed here. The essential point, however, is that the ascendancy of the rights-based approach represents an example of elite cohesion and of wide-reaching "frame alignment" (Snow et al. 1986), whereby organisations deliberately link their discourse to that of prospective members, allies and resource providers. As the following case study of ActionAid's rights-based approach to education will illustrate, the desire to speak the language of global normative frameworks does come at the expense of representing the grassroots constituents on whose behalf INGOs claim to work.

The rights-based approach at ActionAid

ActionAid was an early-adopter of the rights-based approach, formally integrating RBA across all sectors and country programs in 1999 (ActionAid 1999). This was a major organisational as well as a discursive change: where previously ActionAid had provided services like education and health care to "needy" underserved populations, it was now committed to help these populations assert their right to publicly funded social services (see Magrath 2014 for a fuller discussion of how the rights-based approach was integrated at ActionAid).

In 2001, ActionAid's International Education Team (IET) convened a workshop to assess its progress instituting RBA and to prepare for a major organisation-wide review of its education programmes. This workshop brought together education leaders and consultants from four country programmes (AA Nepal, AA Ethiopia, AA Ghana and AA Nigeria). The workshop report made clear that RBA was a locally owned and people-centred endeavour, something demanded at the grassroots that changes the locus of power from ActionAid to the communities in which it works. RBA is associated with decentralisation as opposed to service delivery, which is said to require more centralised planning and control: "(RBA) involves constant seeking to avoid creating dependency and working to make ourselves redundant . . . (service-delivery) makes communities dependent" (ActionAid 2001: 7).

Surveys carried out the following year revealed that many country programmes were not adhering to rights-based principles despite the fact that RBA was designed to be "people-centred" and "locally owned". Many country-level staff and partners argued that widespread poverty made the application of human rights-based approaches difficult to understand and to administer. Communities were used to ActionAid delivering social services, and these services were more important to them than an abstract notion of rights:

> The rights-based approach is proving difficult to be understood by both implementers, partners and recipients of development initiatives. The service delivery approach has always been preferred by people at all levels as tangible results can be produced through this approach . . . it is difficult to sustain community motivation for such a time consuming effort like the rights-based approach.
>
> (Consultant, Nepal, quoted in ActionAid 2002: 30)

> The conflict situation in which we have been working for 8 years has blocked everything.... The context is not suitable to have a rights based approach to education.
>
> (Programme Coordinator, Burundi, quoted in ActionAid 2002: 31)

Based on these survey results, ActionAid acknowledged that "poor communities are often unable to see the broader picture and gains of the rights-based approach as against service delivery" (p. 30). This serves to undermine ActionAid's insistence that RBA is about "locally owned" and "people-centred" advocacy. In fact, rights-based approaches to development were something emanating entirely from global-level discourse espoused by other INGOs and UN agencies. In order to be part of this global dialogue, ActionAid needed to push RBA on its country-level programmes, many of which were sceptical about its applicability to their situation.

This entailed a significant conundrum for ActionAid leadership: on the one hand, the organisation was establishing itself as an international leader in educational advocacy, in no small part because of its pioneering approach and deep commitment to rights-based development (Cornwall and Nyamu-Musembi 2004; Nelson and Dorsey 2008). On the other hand, it was dedicated to a decentralised organisational model that placed power in the hands of local ActionAid programme offices and civil society partners (ActionAid 1999; 2002). But many of these programmes and partners were still carrying out traditional service-delivery programmes, such as running nonformal education centres (ActionAid 2002: 9), and thus working against ActionAid's full-scale adoption of RBA. Despite its stated commitment to bottom-up decision making, ActionAid was clear that service-delivery programmes needed to be reformed to fit its rights-based mandate:

> If, having mobilised demand for education, we respond by simply delivering the services ourselves, this defeats the purpose, reduces government responsibility and acts to demobilise people. In those cases where we are already engaged in service delivery without a clear rights-based framework and without clear means for achieving wider change or impact, projects may need to be phased out or closed down.
>
> (ibid: 79)

In 2005, ActionAid's International Education Team devised a new five-year strategy that brought the organisation further in line with an international rights-based framework. The *Education Strategic Plan 2005–2010* incorporated six strategic goals, the first of which stated "we will secure constitutional rights to basic education where these are not in place and ensure they are enforceable in practice" (ActionAid 2005). These goals were elaborated with a number of indicative activities, for example "working with national parliaments and the media to place the right to education on the national agenda"; "undertaking targeted legal work to enforce rights"; "building sustained pressure on international donors"; and "challenging IMF/World Bank imposed macroeconomic norms" (pp. 3–4).

Rather than espousing a notion of rights that is rooted in local definition and experience, ActionAid was adhering to a legalistic understating of rights based on national and international laws. This is an important distinction, as organisations using RBA are somewhat divided over whether rights should be understood as universal and based on international legal frameworks or whether they should be rooted in local contexts and focus on empowering individuals and communities (Newman 2012). ActionAid officially opted for an approach that straddled both positions (ActionAid 1999; 2007), but critical analysis of its discourse reveals very little emphasis on local understanding of rights and a heavy reliance on the language of international legal norms (Magrath 2014).

In 2007, the IET published *Education Rights: A Guide for Practitioners and Activists*, which offered further guidance on how to accomplish the goals set out in the *Education Strategic Plan 2005–2010*. This handbook was essentially a toolkit to help ActionAid staff, and partners use a legal rights framework, encouraging them to frame their work in terms of international conventions and national legislation and to build alliances with human rights organisations and lawyers (p. 18). Fully ten pages of the handbook are dedicated to preparing a legal case for the right to education, including steps to take a case to the international level if domestic governments are unresponsive (p. 43–53).

Although these documents indicate that ActionAid was chiefly concerned with using national and international legal frameworks to campaign for education rights, there was also an emphasis on basing rights activism in local experience. *Education Rights* stipulated that national and international campaigning should be clearly linked to grassroots advocacy efforts, arguing that "grassroots experience enhances the impact and legitimacy of work at national and international levels" (p. 11). However, throughout this document there is substantially more focus on local-level activities that feed into national and international campaigns than on activities whose main focus is community empowerment. So, for example, school budget analysis is linked with monitoring national education spending and understanding the impact of IMF policies; local school committees are linked with national coalitions, which are linked regionally and globally.

One of the more interesting elements of Education Rights in the context of this chapter is the emphasis it placed on working with and through teachers unions. ActionAid had been forging strong links with teachers' unions through Education International the GCE. The Parktonian Recommendations, created by ActionAid and a range of national teachers unions, had strongly linked public education and professional teaching with the EFA goals (ActionAid 2007: 56). Education Rights recommended that ActionAid staff and partners should gather data on nonprofessional teaching in their area in order to directly challenge NGOs involved in nonformal education: "The local group could look at the impact of NFE provision, exploring the level of provision. Asking how NFE provision has impacted on public education provision as well as looking at who are the teachers and what training they have received" (p. 36).

This recommendation stands in stark contrast to the actual activities carried out by ActionAid country programmes, many of whom were supporting nonprofessional teachers and running nonformal education centres (Newman 2012). A review undertaken in 2009 indicated that for nearly 25% of ActionAid partners, the majority of funding went to supporting education service provision (Sayed and Newman 2009). The implication is that ActionAid's advocacy strategies were shaped by its increasing ties to international organisations and to the global Education for All movement, not to the experience of its country-level staff and civil society partners. By using the language of legal rights and union solidarity, ActionAid was aligning itself with the dominant discourse and normative framework of its international allies in the Global Campaign for Education at the expense of representing the interests of its grassroots network.

The 2009 *Education Review* revealed that the International Education Team had been highly successful in introducing RBA to its country-level staff and CSO partners: 20 of 22 country offices indicated that "all programmes are designed using RBA" (p. 42). The survey also revealed considerable convergence in terms of how RBA was defined by staff and partners, with almost full agreement that rights are universal and inalienable, and that the state is primarily responsible for safeguarding these rights (p. 37–38). The survey also made clear that ActionAid was responsible for introducing rights frameworks to its CSO partners: over half of the respondents had never heard of RBA before it was introduced by ActionAid International, and only 25% had previously carried out rights work. This indicates a more top-down approach to RBA than ActionAid's "locally owned" discourse suggests.

The *Education Review* survey indicated a continued tension between applying a rights-based approach and continuing traditional education service delivery. Many local civil society partners continued to carry out nonformal education services, and nine of 22 considered service delivery as "a crucial element of the Rights Based Approach" (p. 42), a statement that directly contradicted the definition of RBA promoted by ActionAid. A number of respondents indicated that they supported the idea of rights-based advocacy in theory, but in practice, service provision was often what communities required. This perspective was particularly strong among respondents from Africa:

> ActionAid Somaliland is a resource poor country programme and mainly implements teachers' training, capacity building of school management, school construction and provision of teaching and learning materials. . . . Establishing non-formal centres and supporting public schools to increase access to basic education is the most significant innovation of our education work.
>
> (AA Somaliland staff, quoted p. 39)

If children need to go to school and a government is not able or unwilling, and if AAI has the means (through resources raised in the name of children), they are morally and duty-bound to give children education from their own money.

(AA Zambia staff, quoted p. 40)

The transition of ActionAid from a deliverer of services to an organisation which empowers individuals and communities to demand their rights presents the most challenge to AAG. All of the individuals and organisations I met were in complete agreement with the change of direction but also strongly believed it should not be an either or choice. . . . For the continued credibility of AAG and in order to maintain the trust, confidence and commitment of communities the RBA must be delivered alongside an element of service delivery.

(ActionAid Ghana Trustee, p. 40)

In the *Management Response to Education Review* (ActionAid 2009), the International Education Team recognised that by framing the rights-based approach as largely against service-delivery work, they had allowed a divide to emerge between their policy advocacy work and the activities of their country offices. In an apparent reversal of policy, the IET acknowledged that the two approaches need not work in opposition and that services could be delivered within a rights-based approach. This would require more of a focus on RBA methods as well as a "strong capacity development plan for education colleagues across the organisation" (p. 4). At the same time, there was a caveat that any new approaches should not "open the floodgates to the comfort zone of simple infrastructure projects which are wrapped up in rights based rhetoric" (p. 4). How this will be accomplished remains to be seen: ActionAid's new strategy, *Peoples Action to End Poverty 2012–2017*, is still in its early days. The new strategy was introduced after the field work for this research was completed, and thus I cannot offer an analysis of how ActionAid continues to balance between its role in global educational governance and its commitment to people-centred advocacy.

Conclusions

Since 1990, civil society organisations have played an increasingly prominent role in global educational governance. New political opportunities for civil society advocacy have emerged at the national and international levels, part of a broader trend towards international cooperation in development and a shifting attitude towards civil society organisations. No longer valued just for their ability to provide social services, policymakers and donors are increasingly recognising their role in monitoring programmes and policies, holding governments to account, providing data on educational access and quality, and generating new policy initiatives.

Civil society organisations have created and exploited many of these opportunities, particularly in the lead up and follow up to the Dakar conference, when organisations came together to create the Global Campaign for Education coalition. A number of large international NGOs have taken the lead in setting the agenda for the Education for All movement: ActionAid and Oxfam in particular have been at the forefront of most global educational advocacy efforts, including establishing the GCE, creating the Fast-Track Initiative framework, and managing major funds like the Commonwealth Education Fund and the Civil Society Education Fund.

The entry of civil society organisations into global educational governance must be treated with a degree of caution, however. As scholars in the fields of international relations and human rights have argued, we cannot automatically assume that these organisations represent the interests of the communities on whose behalf they speak; CSOs have multiple lines of accountability, including to donors and to diverse stakeholders. International NGOs often dominate advocacy networks due to their size, financial capacities, highly educated staff and personal ties to international organisations. One of the ways NGOs assert themselves as legitimate policy actors is through the use of globally accepted discourse.

Through a process of what Snow et al. (1986) term "frame alignment", many civil society organisations, and particularly large international NGOs, have begun to use the language of universal rights to frame their advocacy work. ActionAid was a pioneer in applying rights-based approaches to all areas of programming, including their work in the education sector. This was not simply a discursive shift: it was a radical change involving the overhaul of educational programming carried out by ActionAid country-level staff and partners, not all of whom were convinced of RBA's benefits. The use of rights-based discourse by ActionAid's International Education Team reflected its growing ties to global Education for All governance and its role as a lead agency in the Global Campaign for Education. But the adoption of RBA required ActionAid to overlook the fact that many country-level programmes continued to operate in the service-delivery mode and to ignore staff and partners who felt that RBA was not relevant to their contexts. This case study thus offered an illustration of how large INGOs dominate advocacy networks operating in the international and development education field and the role that discourse plays in reinforcing this power imbalance.

References

ActionAid, 1999. *Fighting Poverty Together 1999–2005, ActionAid Strategic Plan.* ActionAid, London.

ActionAid, 2000. Proposal for new Education for All structures and mechanisms. Internal document.

ActionAid, 2001. Report of education review workshop. Internal document.

ActionAid, 2002. *Global Education Review 2002.* International Education Unit, ActionAid, London.

ActionAid, 2005. *Education Strategic Plan, 2005–2010.* International Education Unit, ActionAid, London.

ActionAid, 2007. *Education Rights: A Guide for Practitioners and Activists.* Global Campaign for Education, Johannesburg.

ActionAid, 2009. Education review: IET management response. Internal document.

Anderson, K., 2011. Accountability as legitimacy: global governance, global civil society and the United Nations. Washington College of Law Research Paper No. 2011–28.

Appadurai, A., 2000. Grassroots globalization and the research imagination. *Public Culture* 12, 1, 1–19.

Bexell, M., Tallberg, J., Uhlin, A., 2010. Democracy in global governance: the promises and pitfalls of transnational actors. *Global Governance* 16, 1, 81–101.

Bob, C., 2010. The market for human rights. In: Prakash, A. and Gugerty, M. (Eds.) *Advocacy Organisation and Collective Action.* Cambridge University Press, Cambridge.

Chabbott, C., 1999. Development INGOs. In Boli, J. and Thomas, G. (Eds.) *Constructing World Culture: International Non-Governmental Organizations Since 1975.* Stanford University Press, Stanford.

Chabbott, C., 2003. *Constructing Education for Development.* Routledge, New York.

Collingwood, V., Logister, L., 2005. State of the art: addressing the INGO "legitimacy deficit". *Political Studies Review* 3, 175–192.

Collinson, H., 2006. *Where to Now? Implications of Changing Relations Between DFID, Recipient Governments and NGOs in Malawi, Tanzania and Uganda.* ActionAid International and CARE International, London.

Commonwealth Education Fund, 2005. Global midterm review. Internal document.

Cornwall, A., Nyamu-Musembi, C., 2004. Putting the rights-based approach to development into perspective. *Third World Quarterly* 25, 8, 1415–1437.

David, R., Mancini, A., Gujit, I., 2006. Bringing systems into line with values: the practices of the accountability, learning and planning system (ALPS). In: Eyben, R. (Ed.) *Relationships for Aid.* Institute for Development Studies, Brighton.

Escobar, A., 1995. *Encountering Development: The Making and Unmaking of the Third World.* Princeton University Press, Princeton.

Ferguson, J., 1990. *The Anti-Politics Machine: "Development," Depoliticization and Bureaucratic Power in Lesotho.* Cambridge University Press, Cambridge.

Glasius, M., 2008. Does the involvement of global civil society make international decision-making more democratic? The case of the international criminal court. *Journal of Civil Society* 4, 1, 43–60.

Gordenker, L., Weiss, T., 1995. Pluralising global governance: analytical approaches and dimensions. *Third World Quarterly* 16, 3, 357–387.

Hart, J., 2009. *Commonwealth Education Fund: Final Report.* Commonwealth Education Fund, London.

Held, D., 1995. Democracy and the international order. In: Archibugi, D. and Held, D. (Eds.) *Cosmopolitan Democracy.* Polity, Cambridge.

Held, D., 2004. *Global Covenant.* Polity, Cambridge.

Held, D., Koenig-Archibugi, M. (Eds.), 2005 *Global Governance and Public Accountability.* Blackwell, London.

Jones, P., 2007. WCEFA: a moment in the history of multilateral education. In: Baker, D. and Wiseman, A. (Eds.) *Education for All: Global Promises, National Challenges.* Emerald, Bingley.

Kaldor, M., 2003. Civil society and accountability. *Journal of Human Development* 4, 1, 5–27.

Keck, M., Sikkink, K., 1998. *Activists Beyond Borders.* Cornell University, Ithaca.

Kitamura, Y., 2007. The political dimensions of international cooperation in education. In: Baker, D. and Wiseman, A. (Eds.) *Education for All: Global Promises, National Challenges.* Emerald.

Magrath, B., 2014. Global norms, organisational change: framing the rights-based approach at ActionAid. *Third World Quarterly* 35, 7, 1273–1289.

McCormick, A., 2012. Whose education policies in aid-receiving countries? A critical discourse analysis of quality and normative transfer through Cambodia and Laos. *Comparative Education Review* 56, 1, 18–47.

Minkoff, D., 1994. From service provision to institutional advocacy: the shifting legitimacy of organisational forms. *Social Forces* 72, 4, 943–969.

Mundy, K., 2008. From NGOs to CSOs: social citizenship, civil society and "Education for All": an agenda for further research. *Current Issues in Comparative Education* 10, 1, 32–40.

Mundy, K., 2012. The Global Campaign for Education and the realization of Education for All. In: Verger, A. and Novelli, M. (Eds.) *Campaigning for Education for All: Histories, Strategies and Outcomes of Transnational Advocacy Coalitions in Education.* Sense, Rotterdam.

Mundy, K., Haggerty, M., Sivasubramaniam, M., Cherry, S., Maclure, R., 2010. Civil society, basic education, and sector-wide aid: insights from Sub-Saharan Africa. *Development in Practice* 20, 4–5, 484–497.

Mundy, K., Murphy, L., 2001. Transnational advocacy, global civil society? Emerging evidence from the field of education. *Comparative Education Review* 45, 1, 85–126.

Nelson, P., Dorsey, E., 2008. *The Rights Advocacy: Changing Strategies of Development and Human Rights NGOs.* Georgetown University Press, Washington.

Newman, K., 2012. *Challenges and Dilemmas in Integrating Human Rights-based Approaches and Participatory Approaches to Development: An Exploration of the Experiences of ActionAid International.* PhD dissertation, Goldsmiths College, University of London.

Offenheiser, R., Holcombe, S., 2003. Challenges and opportunities in implementing a rights-based approach to development: an Oxfam America perspective. *Nonprofit and Voluntary Sector Quarterly* 32, 268–301.

Prakash, A., Gugerty, M. (Eds.), 2010. *Advocacy Organisation and Collective Action.* Cambridge University Press, Cambridge.

Resnik, J., 2006. International organizations, the "education–economic growth" black box and the development of world education culture. *Comparative Education Review* 50, 2, 173–195.

Robertson, S.L., Dale, R., 2006. New geographies of power in education: the politics of rescaling and its contradictions. In Kassem, D., Mufti, E. and Robinson, J. (Eds.) *Education Studies: Issues and Critical Perspectives.* Open University Press, Maidenhead.

Sayed, Y., Newman, K., 2009. Education review 2005–2009: full report. ActionAid Internal document.

Schnuttgen, S., Khan, M., 2004. Civil society engagement in EFA in the post-Dakar period: a self-reflective review. Working Paper for the Fifth EFA Working Group Meeting, 20–21 July 2004. UNESCO, Paris.

Scholte, J.-A., 2007. Civil society and the legitimation of global governance. *Journal of Civil Society* 3, 3, 305–326

Scott-Villiers, P., 2002. The struggle for organisational change: how the ActionAid accountability, learning and planning system emerged. *Development in Practice* 12, 3–4, 424–435.

Smith, J., Pagnucco, R., Chatfield, C., 1997. Social movements and world politics: a theoretical framework. In: Smith, J., Chatfield, C. and Pagnucco, R. (Eds.) *Transnational Social Movements and Global Politics.* Syracuse University Press, Syracuse.

Snow, D., Burke Rochford, E., Worden, S., Benford, R., 1986. Frame alignment processes, micromobiliza-tion, and movement participation. *American Sociological Review* 51, 4, 464–481.

Strutt, C., Kepe, T., 2010. Implementing Education for All: whose agenda, whose change? The case study of the Ghana National Education Campaign Coalition. *International Journal of Educational Development* 30, 369–376.

Tomlinson, K., Macpherson, I., 2007. *Funding Change: Sustaining Civil Society Advocacy in Education.* Com-monwealth Education Fund, London.

Torres, R., 2001. What happened at the World Education Forum? *Adult Education and Development* 56, 45–68.

United Nations, 1948. *Universal Declaration of Human Rights.* United Nations, New York.

UNESCO, 1945. *UNESCO Constitution.* UNESCO, Paris.

UNESCO, 1990a. World Declaration on Education for All. Adopted by the World Conference on Edu-cation for All: Meeting Basic Learning Needs. Jomtien, Thailand, March 5–9, 1990. UNESCO, Paris.

UNESCO, 1990b. Framework for Action to Meet Basic Learning Needs. Adopted by the World Con-ference on Education for All: Meeting Basic Learning Needs. Jomtien, Thailand. 5–9 March 1990. UNESCO, Paris.

Vavrus, F., Seghers, M., 2010. Critical discourse analysis in comparative education: a discursive study of "partnership" in Tanzania's poverty reduction policies. *Comparative Education Review* 54, 1, 77–103.

Verger, A., Novelli, M. (Eds.), 2012. *Campaigning for 'Education for All': Histories, Strategies and Outcomes of Transnational Advocacy Coalitions in Education.* Sense, Rotterdam.

Weiss, L. (Ed.), 2003. *States in the Global Economy: Bringing Domestic Institutions Back In.* Cambridge Uni-versity Press, Cambridge.

Woods, E., 2009. Commonwealth Education Fund final evaluation report. Internal document.

32

PUBLIC-PRIVATE PARTNERSHIPS AND INTERNATIONAL EDUCATION POLICIES

Alexandra Draxler

Introduction

The use of the term public–private partnership (PPP) to describe the involvement of the private sector in the delivery of public services, in this case education, has become widespread during the last 20 years. Any specificity that was originally attached to the concept has become fuzzy over time: "partnership" has become part of the descriptive vocabulary of a wide variety of activities such as public sector contracts with the private sector, publicly-subsidised private education, philanthropy and some governance mechanisms.

The claim that PPPs for education have demonstrated their potential as positive forces for expanding access as well as improving delivery and quality of basic education in developing countries is widespread in both academic and policy literature. While private education has long been a part of the education landscape in countries all over the world, private providers of services or operators of educational institutions have only since the 1990s, and principally on the urging of international bodies and corporations, come to be considered both at the international and national levels as "partners" in the formulation of development policy and the push to provide quality education for all.

Depending on how one interprets information about PPPs in developing countries, they constitute either a marginal phenomenon with powerful advocates or a growing trend that has the potential to radically change the face of education. Although precise figures are hard to come by, it is clear that, as a proportion of aid or national budgets, PPPs are hardly weighty. Nevertheless, if one looks at the increase in private education worldwide, one can see that demand is growing and that government subsidy to private provision is also growing significantly. For-profit private education, including at the basic level, is regarded approvingly by a number of governments and funding sources. In international cooperation, the corporate sector now has a seat at almost every table alongside the nonprofit private sector as represented by nongovernmental organisations (NGOs).

There are numerous reasons for the emergence of PPPs as delivery mechanisms. Funds available for development assistance to education are stagnating or shrinking, and many donors want to spread the effort and responsibility for assistance to education. The United Nations system has embraced partnership with the private sector in the hope that this will enhance funding and broaden commitment to overall development goals. In a number of donor countries, domestic policies currently favour subcontracting or abandoning large parts of the provision of public services to the for-profit sector, including in education. Donor behaviour quite naturally mirrors domestic policies and concerns of its taxpayer funders. In poor countries, the inability of governments to expand provision and quality in function of demand for education has encouraged, for some, the belief that private sector involvement can act as a stimulant and at the same time take pressure off the public sector. Finally, corporations find that blurring the distinction between for-profit and not-for-profit private provision by the use of the big-tent partnership concept can provide enhanced market opportunities with the added value of loose regulation and public sector subsidy.

This chapter will examine some of the principal claims and aims of public-private partnerships, focusing on trends in policy and practice of international development institutions. While the topic does not lend itself to sweeping generalisations, some trends can be described and policy conclusions drawn from evidence so far.

What follows is not a comprehensive overview of programmes and practice but rather a look at policies through illustration and examples. It is framed by four questions: What are the imagined and real-world roles for public-private partnerships in meeting the goals of education for all? How do they measure up to public sector provision in terms of quality, equity and efficiency? What are some examples? What are some possible trends, and what issues do they raise?

Background and definition

What actually constitutes a public-private partnership, including in education, is a more matter of perception than of agreed definition. Historically, the involvement of for-profit entities in education has been described in contractual terms or simply called private education, even when public sector subsidies were involved. The actions of NGOs and foundations that were previously labelled philanthropy have been increasingly grouped under the partnership label. The vocabulary of international cooperation between rich and poor states has been sanitised to eliminate notions of hierarchy or power and to favour terms that imply equality and alliance. Originally applied to infrastructure projects, where governments could avoid constraints on public borrowing by making a long-term contractual arrangement with private entities for the provision of public services, public-private partnership has morphed into a catchall term for private involvement in policy formulation and delivery of public services.

In the United Nations system, initiatives to include the public sector in both discourse and initiatives concerning development began in the 1990s. The Jomtien Framework for Action (World Conference on Education for All 1990) mentioned the private sector as a partner and a potential source of additional financing. Agenda 21 (United Nations Environment Programme 1992), which emerged from the Rio Conference, gives a prominent place to business and industry as partners in sustainable development and includes a specific chapter on strengthening the role of business. Since then, the suggestion that the private sector is an essential partner in the social contract of the international community has underpinned initiatives in almost all areas of public services, including education. Under the impetus of the UN and the World Bank, several development institutions have increased their emphasis, both in policy documents and in practice, on including corporations and foundations among the stakeholders in development (Martens 2007). Corporations are participants in global fora such as the various coordination mechanisms for Education for All (EFA) or the Global Partnership for Education (GPE). They have their own framework and forum within the UN, the Global Compact (UN Global Compact 2012), they are consulted extensively by UN initiatives such as the post-2015 process (UN

High Level Panel 2013) and there is mutual representation between the UN and the World Economic Forum at key conferences.

PPP in education, therefore, is now used to cover almost any involvement of the private sector with the public one, whether through privatisation, contract for specific services, or philanthropy (LaRocque and Lee 2008). Broader groupings of partners that include both for-profit and not-for-profit participants are called multistakeholder partnerships (MSPs). Corporations like using the terms PPP (or MSP), as they imply shared values, objectives and risks and are less in disfavour than the somewhat discredited designation "privatisation" (Wong and Unwin 2012).

The way in which PPP is defined, then, is one indicator of a highly ideological divide about the role and place of education in societies (Education International 2009). Critics have viewed PPPs as merely a convenient shorthand for privatisation of public services and therefore a big setback to the obligation of the state to ensure a human right (Robertson 2008). Those in favour often describe PPPs as a new way of doing things (shared risk, responsibility and benefit, in the classic definition of partnership) that can be a win–win situation for all sides (Latham 2009). And finally, shifts in terminology have resulted in the frequent inclusion of private education (both for profit and not-for-profit) under the umbrella of PPPs (LaRocque and Lee 2008).

Still, even though it is impossible to give a strict definition in view of changing usage, some terminological definitions follow here:

The *public sector* includes any entity that is representative of government, at the international, national or subnational level.

The *private sector* principally refers to the for-profit sector. However, since many coordination mechanisms or programmes include representatives of both for-profit and not-for-profit entities, trying to keep them separate would ignore the permeability between, for example, corporations and nonprofit entities (foundations or NGOs) entirely financed by them.

The term *nonstate sector* or expressions that communicate a broad range of actors such as "partnerships across the public-private spectrum" (Department for International Development 2013) have also come into usage to refer to all institutions that are not the state, whether for profit or not for profit, and including religious organisations.

Public-private partnership is an arrangement whereby the entities involved mutualise –through formal or informal agreements – investment, risk, responsibilities and benefits. There can be more than two partners, in which case the term *multistakeholder partnership* is used. Observers generally agree that the principal distinctions between pure contracting and partnership lie in the joint design of objectives and solutions, sharing of risk, and financing methods that include concession or lease (Grimsey and Lewis 2004). It is common in the literature, but less so in practice, to find an insistence on a definitional and programmatic differentiation between partnerships and contractual arrangements or between PPPs and MSPs (Draxler 2008; LaRocque and Lee 2008).

The common definitional features of PPPs or MSPs – shared purpose, responsibilities and risk – are somewhat loosely defined and/or applied in most cases (see Figure 32.1).

Although shared purpose is often claimed by all partners, the reality is more complex. The public sector is responsible for the general welfare of all. The for-profit private sector is responsible to specific constituencies, that is owners or shareholders, who quite naturally want profit maximisation. Win–win situations in which profit maximisation and the public good spontaneously converge can exist, but one cannot assume them to be spontaneous or frequent. In the case of nonprofit entities, whether NGOs, religious organisations or foundations, delegation of public sector responsibility for subsectors of broad constituencies has long existed and of course makes sense, subject to regulatory measures that ensure the public good.

As for responsibilities, many observers acknowledge that in PPPs responsibilities can be diluted as the nature of partnerships removes decision making and accountability further away

The World Bank *(World Bank Institute and Public-Private Infrastructure Advisory Facility (PPIAF) 2012)*	"a long-term contract between a private party and a government agency, for providing a public asset or service, in which the private party bears significant risk and management responsibility"
Organisation for Economic Co-operation and Development (OECD) *(Organisation for Economic Co-operation and Development (OECD) 2012)*	"… a long term agreement between the government and a private partner where the service delivery objectives of the government are aligned with the profit objectives of the private partner. The effectiveness of the alignment depends on a sufficient and appropriate transfer of risk to the private partners."
United Nations UN General Assembly, 60th Session, Report of the Secretary General. UN Doc A/60/214.	"Partnerships are defined as voluntary and collaborative relationships between various parties, both State and non-State, in which all participants agree to work together to achieve a common purpose or undertake a specific task and to share risks and responsibilities, resources and benefits."
World Economic Forum/UNESCO *(Ginsburg, Brady et al. 2012)*	"… the pooling and managing of resources, as well as the mobilization of competencies and commitments by public, business and civil society partners to contribute to expansion and quality of education …"

Figure 32.1   Some definitions of public-private partnerships

from both constituencies and beneficiaries (Buse and Walt 2000). Where these PPPs are under-taken with corporations, the profit-maximisation objective can take precedence, for example, in lowering teacher salaries below a living threshold (Lewin 2013) or in pushing the introduction of technologies that are either not cost-effective or not scalable (Trucano 2014).[1]

And finally, equal risk-sharing in PPPs is very rare. Many reports of PPPs underline the fact that sustainability is entirely dependent on public funding that attenuates or eliminates private sector risk.

Agreement is general that PPPs for education are controversial. Critics argue that empirical evidence shows outcomes do not match claims, that investment in PPPs is not more efficient overall than public sector provision and that PPPs leach public money as well as staff away from state education and in consequence weaken education systems (Education International 2009; Ginsburg et al. 2012). Indeed, case studies point to the fact that when absenteeism is tolerated in the public sector, teachers will frequently moonlight or engage in simple double employment in private schools (Osorio and Wodon 2014). Advocates tend to focus on the inherent virtues of market forces and on ways to ensure these operate optimally as well as the virtues of choice and diversity of provision, while often recognising there are both reputational and evidential weak-nesses with PPPs (Ginsburg et al. 2012). Most observers and stakeholders agree that empirical evidence on outcomes as compared to alternatives is quite thin. Finally, although private education is widespread and even highly significant in a few countries, public-private partnerships in fact do not currently play a weighty role in the delivery and assessment of learning in developing countries.

Scale

The lack of benchmarks and pertinent financial data make it very difficult to assess the scale of public-private partnerships. There is no systematic collection of comparable data about the extent of private education or the level of government subsidy or partnership with the private sector. The estimates communicated by the EFA Global Monitoring Report, based on an earlier survey of giving from US foundations and Fortune 500 companies, indicates some US$683 million a year going to education in developing countries (UNESCO 2013a). The bulk of this amount goes to higher education and is concentrated in a handful of countries. A few large philanthropic organisations, such as Azim Premj or Aga Khan, which are not in the United States, are left out of this equation, but even they are influential more by the way they target specific groups than through system-wide impact.

Similarly, international aid to private provision of education, whether defined as PPP or not, is not very large in scale. The education portfolio of the International Finance Corporation (IFC) in 2013 was US$650 million, a very small percentage of its total portfolio. Numerous analysts have estimated that World Bank spending on PPPs and private sector initiatives for education are included as elements in less than 20% of its projects and even there are only a modest proportion of project spending, in spite of the Bank's analytical and rhetorical emphasis on the virtues of private education (Mundy and Menashy 2012a). While the principal bilateral agencies that advocate for private education and PPPs, namely USAID, AusAID and DFID, give policy emphasis to private financial flows, a reading of their strategies and selected project information does not give a picture of large proportions of funding to nongovernment spending.

When one looks at reviews of PPPs or MSPs, it is impossible to get a clear picture of how much funding comes from outside the public sector for these partnerships. World Bank publications often describe programmes for which the private sector is the operator but the investment comes from the public sector (including World Bank loans or grants). The World Economic Forum gives no funding breakdowns for its education initiatives (Wong and Unwin 2012). Other reviews describe collaborative programmes (Education International 2009) with little funding attached or programmes for which it is difficult to assess the size of financing or distribution between government investment through private entities and actual private investment.

It seems clear, nevertheless, that both demand for private education and supply of private education are gradually growing all over the world (see Figures 32.2 and 32.3) and in a few countries significantly (Bjarnason et al. 2009; Patrinos, Barrera-Osorio and Guáqueta 2009), much of it substantially subsidised by public funds. It is also safe to say that, with a few exceptions, these sums represent no more than a small portion of national education spending.

The impact of funding for education in developing countries coming from outside government budgets nevertheless has an outsized impact compared to its relative financial weight because of its capacity to shift priorities for innovation and experimentation. Private sector representatives can participate in policy and funding discussions in international and national bodies, having an impact far beyond their financial participation (van Fleet 2011). Therefore, policy bias that comes with education funding in the form of advocacy for PPPs may have impact much more significant than its monetary value would suggest.

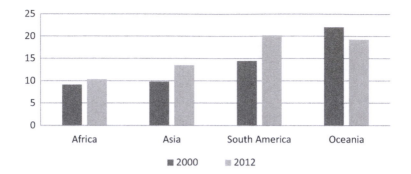

Figure 32.2 Percentage of enrolment in primary education in private institutions
Source: Author's calculations based on UNESCO Institute of Statistics data.

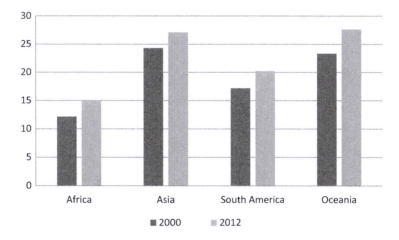

Figure 32.3 Percentage of enrolment in secondary education in private institutions
Source: Author's calculations based on UNESCO Institute of Statistics data.

Development institutions and partnerships

The UN has established a number of fora that are intended both to favour and to frame relations with the business sector. Some of these are established bodies. Others are managed by memoranda of understanding or similar relatively informal founding documents.

In particular, the UN has been committed since the year 2000 to engaging the business sector in the achievement of the Millennium Development Goals (MDGs) through its Global Compact. In education, a recent "framework" developed by UNICEF and UNESCO, aimed at the business sector (UNESCO 2013b), identifies a number of "drivers" for business engagement in education and affirms that "Regardless of the type of engagement or rationale – either philanthropic or commercial – corporate activities have the potential to create shared value and advance education goals when done well." All the specialised agencies and funds of the UN have specific programmes of collaboration with the private sector.

However, critics within the UN system also exist. These include the observation that the UN has maintained an overly casual approach to collaboration with the private sector (Martens

2007). Contrary to its structured relationships with NGOs, the UN dealings with business are based on the assumption of shared objectives, mutual trust and voluntary reporting. Within the Global Compact, reporting is voluntary, nothing is legally binding, and there are no regulatory features (UN Global Compact 2007).

Led by the World Bank, USAID and DFID, a number of multi- and bilateral development institutions have moved to promoting publicly supported private education and the use of PPPs for a wide range of education initiatives in the developing world. At the same time as conditionality for aid has crept out of the development vocabulary, the conditionality of private sector involvement has crept into aid programmes through linking funding to private sector involvement. The now largest single-funding mechanism for education, Global Partnership for Education (GPE), has the corporate education giant Pearson as a voting representative of the private sector on its board (although the private sector has yet to channel any funds through this mechanism).

USAID and IADB have matching funds programs that require partnership formats (Mann, Pier and Yasin 2009: 3). DFID funds voucher schemes and provides other kinds of support (including research and evaluation) to private education in Ghana, India, Kenya, Nigeria and Pakistan (DFID 2013).

Beginning in the 1980s, the World Bank recommended the introduction of market mechanisms in schooling at all levels through higher parental "participation" and more private schools (Mundy and Menashy 2012a). Until around 2000, the Bank's strategy was formulated thus:

> The underlying principle is that strengthening the private sector's role in non-compulsory education over time will release public resources for the compulsory (primary) level.
>
> (Sosale 2000: 15)

But more recently, it has broadened out its discourse to include basic education as an area for private sector action. Its most recent education strategy points out that "since 2001, when the International Finance Corporation (IFC) started to focus on the education sector, it has invested $500 million in 46 private education projects" (World Bank 2011). It also repeatedly included "nonstate" actors and the private sector as important levers for attaining education for all and details World Bank-sponsored subsidies provided for private education in countries such as Mozambique, Pakistan, Vietnam and the Arab region (in conjunction with the Islamic Development Bank). The Bank also flags its collaboration with corporations and private donors (often philanthropic arms of these same corporations) to provide technologies for management and delivery of education in a variety of countries. Its data collection and measurement tool for education policies, Systems Approach for Better Education Results (SABER), includes a methodology for looking at policies governing the private sector involvement in basic education. Similarly to other aid agencies, the actual distribution of funding has not entirely followed the discourse, with only a slight increase in recent years of the number of projects containing a component of support to private sector participation (Mundy and Menashy 2012b: 126).

PPPs have also been created by development agencies as general frameworks for collaboration and norm setting. An international ICT Competency Framework for Teachers (CFT) was developed and issued in 2008 by UNESCO, Microsoft, Cisco, Intel and other partners (UNESCO 2008). UNESCO and UNICEF have a number of memoranda of understanding with private sector partners, including those mentioned above. The Global Business Coalition for Education, founded in 2012, brings together some 115 companies that develop partnerships in a wide range of countries. GBC-E organised a panel on the role of business in transforming education at the 2014 replenishment conference of the Global Partnership on Education and clearly intends to remain at the table of major events and decision-making bodies where possible. A recent policy brief issued by GBC-E carries the somewhat ambiguous title "Cooperating with Multilaterals for Global Education: Opportunities for the Business Community".

Typical partnership formats

Public support to private education

Many countries in all parts of the world have a significant proportion of fee-paying private education that operates with support from the public sector. This type of private schooling both responds to demand and generally costs less in public funding per student than public schooling. In many poor countries, religious or other not-for-profit organisations also fill a gap that the public sector is not yet equipped to fill, sometimes with fee-free schooling. While international and national test results for private school learners are often higher than those in the public system, most studies show that when adjustments are made for socioeconomic status of learners, private schools perform no better than public schools (OECD 2011). Still, demand is high, and the perceived factors leading parents to make financial efforts to send their children to private schools all over the world are similar: better environment and peer group, safety, teacher regularity, and quality of instruction. High demand persists even when these factors are partially or totally absent, and parents are prepared to make large sacrifices even when they are very poor (Heyneman and Stern 2014). Indeed, important outcomes of private schooling that compare favourably to public are better school-life expectancy and higher private rates of return. Whether these are due to self-selection factors or not, they are convincing for those users who favour private schooling.

What is relevant to the new interest in public-private partnership is the growing support on the part of donors and other international partners (including large corporations) for private schooling of various types operated and managed by for-profit entities with public support. Public support can take the form of tax breaks, land concessions, vouchers and other kinds of cash transfers, easing of regulatory restrictions, or management and teacher training. A recent review of issues around low-cost private schools internationally and case studies in Jamaica, Kenya, Tanzania, Ghana, Indonesia and Pakistan found evidence that such schools enjoy community support and approval and provide services not available otherwise. Recommendations included more attention by both governments and donors to ensuring the gathering of statistics on these schools, working on the regulatory environment and carrying out targeted interventions to improve quality and management (Heyneman and Stern 2014).

The largest network of private schools in Latin America, Fe y Alégria, is faith based and caters to approximately one million children in twenty countries, focusing on disadvantaged groups. Governments pay teachers' salaries, and the Fe y Alégria Federation (which receives both national and international donations) and community support provide the rest. A recent World Bank study of the network (Osorio and Wodon 2014) found excellent results for costs comparable to those of the public system. Unfortunately, one of the features pointed to as a key to success is "labour market flexibility", which means no unions and no retirement benefits for teachers, many of whom "also work in the public schools simply to gain retirement benefits".

According to a recent review of potential for expanding the resource base for universal education in Africa, public support to private education can increase access but only marginally. In terms of quality, private and public education serve different populations, but when research controls for socioeconomic status, there is no major difference between the two. Low-fee private schools require government subsidy to remain solvent, and private education at all levels receives direct and indirect subsidies, thus effecting reverse redistribution of educational funding and opportunity towards higher socioeconomic groups.

> Disentangling . . . the privatisation process reveals a mix of foreign aid, government subsidy, and private investment. Doing so indicates that investment in private schools at best provides little new education revenue and focuses that revenue on learners already better served by the education system.
>
> (Samoff and Irving 2014: 61)

Vouchers

In Latin America and the Caribbean, the two most significant vouchers schemes, much studied, are in Chile and Colombia. In Pakistan, there have been determined efforts in Sindh and Punjab to provide state, and donor, support to low-cost private schools.

The longest-standing and largest voucher programme was introduced in Chile in 1981. It has continued until now, with approximately 80% of school children receiving vouchers and "for-profit institutions account[ing] for a third of the total national primary and secondary enrolment, [receiving] state subsidies on equal terms with not-for-profit private and public institutions" (Bellei 2014). It continues to act as a bellwether for the ideological divide between advocates and critics of state support to for-profit basic education. Research has shown that Chile's progress is slower than comparable countries and that socioeconomic status has a higher influence than elsewhere on student achievement as measured by PISA. Even advocates of private sector participation in education are cautious to make claims of its success in the light of very mixed research results (Lewis and Patrinos 2012). Some critics find evidence that the nationwide voucher programme has increased stratification (González, Mizala and Romaguera 2004). Indeed, the Chilean government has recently announced sweeping reforms that are designed to cease all government subsidy for private for-profit education in the face of student protests, evidence of increased socioeconomic stratification in education and widespread corruption (Bellei 2014).

Colombia implemented a voucher system with World Bank support from 1991 to 1997, called PACES (Plan de Ampliación de Cobertura de la Educación Secundaria). Both the design of the system (targeting poorest, assignment by lottery, government payment by pupil to private operators) and the evaluations highlight the aims of equity, quality and cost-effectiveness (40% less expensive per pupil than public schools) and scale (140,000 children) (Lewis and Patrinos 2012). Research has found some positive differences in learning outcomes and further study for lottery winners (LaRocque and Lee 2008). However, with a change of government, and presumably the end of World Bank funding, the system was shut down, so it did not meet the aim of sustainability. There has not been any documented attempt to assess the disruptions caused by ending the programme.

In Pakistan, private schools cater to more than a third of children in school, with government direct and indirect subsidies through tax incentives, scholarships and vouchers. The World Bank provides support, channelled through quasigovernmental foundations, to vouchers and low-cost private schools in both Sindh and Punjab catering to several million children and claims these give better results than the public school system (World Bank 2013). Critics claim that these schools, supported with public money, do not significantly expand access, reach the poorest or drive up quality by increasing choice (Lewin 2013). Other critics point to the arbitrary selection of schools for implementation of vouchers schemes, loopholes in the distribution of vouchers, and imperfect reporting (Naeem 2012).

Vouchers can improve learning outcomes for beneficiaries and often also increase household costs. Private voucher schools also tend to attract students with more advantaged backgrounds, leaving behind those with lower socioeconomic backgrounds. Although critics of voucher systems point to increased stratification as a negative effect, there is little research that looks specifically at the impact on the public system of increasing private schooling in the developing world (International Initiative for Impact Evaluation 2010).

Measurement, testing and evaluation

During recent years, several OECD countries such as the United States, the UK, Australia and New Zealand, have begun to encourage shifts in responsibility for compulsory education to private entities. They have also, in differing forms, expanded standardised testing to learners as well as increasing the use of standardised tools to evaluate both school and teacher performance. At the same time, in the United States, a cohort of wealthy private donors is encouraging education reform through wide-scale private involvement in education. This is not only through owning or operating government-subsidised schools but also through the use of standardised curricula and high-stakes testing developed and administered by private entities (Barkan 2011). 'Donor logic' (Steiner-Khamsi 2008) in the form of recommendations to recipient developing countries to follow similar paths therefore has found its way into policy documents and programmes of their aid agencies. See, for example, this statement of the virtue of the private sector from USAID that refers to the Early Grade Reading Assessment developed by several companies in the United States and implemented in more than 20 USAID recipient countries:

> The private sector can play a variety of important roles in improving reading. These include but are not limited to assessing and contributing relevant technology needs and assets, developing and providing resources and complementary learning platforms and opportunities, and providing accountability and policy advocacy as it relates to the government's role in delivering quality education to ensure that children are able to read.
>
> (USAID 2011: 11)

The UN High Level Panel Report (2013) has called for a data revolution over the following 15 years. In education, this has prompted a flurry of programmes and recommendations involving standardised international metrics, with close participation by some key corporations and US non-profit institutions with development expertise in these recommendations and their projected practical applications.

While wide-scale standardised international testing of school children is not a reality across the developing world so far, the build-up to the post-2015 development process has generated a number of initiatives to push the creation of internationally comparable standards and measurement tools. Putting in place such initiatives will inevitably open up massive market opportunities for corporate contracts with donors and developing country governments.

For example, OECD's Programme for International Student Assessment (PISA), which currently covers 65 participating economies, is preparing to expand even more through a new initiative, entitled PISA for Development, conceived to accompany the post-2015 development process. As with the original PISA, countries pay to participate. The development and administration of assessments is carried out by private entities.

Brookings and UNESCO have launched a parallel process through the Learning Metrics Task Force (LMTF 2013), cochaired by the publishing giant Pearson, that aims to build "consensus on global learning indicators and actions to improve the measurement of learning in all countries". If implemented, internationally-standardised measurement of learning outcomes will inevitably bring in the private sector at a level not seen before.

> Of course some groups benefit from global standardisation of indicators and testing, perhaps most obviously those large scale private providers who can develop common tests and offers common services on a high volume basis, removing smaller competitors and facilitating higher profits.
>
> (Archer 2014)

There exists a lively, even acrimonious, debate on the perverse effects of standardised metrics about learning (Draxler 2014). The most germane arguments for the purposes of this chapter are that proponents are mostly in industrialised countries and that the most obvious benefit of international standardisation will accrue, as Archer points out, to the providers.

Technologies

Information and communications technologies (ICTs) are natural domains for public-private partnerships. International corporations have both products and expertise for offer that the public sector doesn't possess. Demands and desires for reform and modernisation of education almost always include both the familiarisation of learners with technologies and the use of technologies as tools for learning. Development agencies, particularly bilateral ones, can be seen as doing good for development as well as supporting their own technology industries when they encourage the use of ICTs as a means of delivery, a subject matter, and a management tool. And, more simply, donors tend to support innovations and reforms in developing countries that correspond to their national systems and preferences (Steiner-Khamsi 2008).

Technology corporations, e.g., Microsoft, Cisco, Intel, Hewlett-Packard, have many of their own programmes, and they have corporate social responsibility programmes within the corporations as well as separate foundations. They partner with many educational entities in countries all over the world, both for developing technology skills and using technologies for delivery of education. These kinds of partnerships can provide real services to both small and large groups. Critics point to the fact that some partnerships can incur costs that were ignored or unforeseen in the design stage, pushing total cost of ownership beyond acceptable cost-benefit calculations (Draxler 2012).

The World Economic Forum's Global Education Initiative, which ran from 2003 to 2011 with iterations in Egypt, Jordan, Rajasthan and Pakistan, had the goal of broad education reform by means of multistakeholder partnerships. Information and communications technologies were part of the original conception in each case (Wong and Unwin 2012). Few hard facts are available about the implementation and cost breakdowns of initiatives in Egypt, Rajasthan and Pakistan. Final reports make it clear that they all began with enthusiasm, multiple partners, a loose structure, unclear objectives and correspondingly vague outcomes.

The Jordan Education Initiative (JEI), the one most written about, is a poster child for the concept of multistakeholder partnerships. It had very broad ambitions that included education reform by implementing ICTs in schools through pilots that would eventually be expanded and, as a parallel result, build up the endogenous IT industry's capacity for educational activities. It brought together up to 35 partners that included bilateral and foundation donors, as well as non-state entities from Jordan and elsewhere (McKinsey and Company 2005). The main educational activity seems to have been the installation of computer labs and the issuance of portable laptop computers and projectors to teachers for use in classrooms and guidance for the teachers for using existing software in 100 Discovery Schools in Amman. "The annualised costs of scaling up the inputs provided under JEI (excluding any additional computer laboratories and associated PCs) are \$17 724 per school, \$2 215 per teacher and \$19 per student, per year" (Light et al. 2008: 16). It operated on a loose framework and shifting budget (some reports state a total budget of \$21 million, McKinsey and Company 2005). The partnership is hailed a success in various publications and continues as a nonprofit with a range of activities. The 2008 evaluation report published by USAID concludes:

> The current success of the JEI in motivating widespread excitement and collaboration among global and local partners to support Jordanian education suggests that the JEI's vision and mission are relevant to those stakeholders. But in order for the JEI to effectively reach teachers, principals and eventually students, the JEI needs a clear message of how ICT can support teaching and learning in a language that is both meaningful to educators and aligned with the [Ministry of Education's] reforms.
>
> (Light et al. 2008: 18)

USAID has recently announced funding of US\$750,000 over two years through its Global Development Alliance[2] to a private sector partner in order to foster the reach of massive open online courses (MOOCs) in the developing world. This is in line with other ICT projects where it is assumed that early risk is borne by the public sector donor and eventually costs will come down or that going to scale will bring the unit costs to a manageable level.

Programmes that involve using technologies to help deliver learning opportunities are naturally encouraged by technology companies. While there is also widespread, and growing, enthusiasm for the use of Internet delivery of content or classroom for out-of-school use of tablets, laptops and mobile devices for learning, there is little rigorous research on impact and sustainability and even less on total costs and cost-effectiveness. A few recent randomised control trials and large-scale evaluations have not given encouraging results about their impacts on learning basic skills (Trucano 2014).

Corporate social investment

Some large corporations, typically mining or energy companies, carry out training where they operate as part of corporate social responsibility activities (UNESCO 2013b) and in partial response to always difficult and sometimes appalling working conditions in these industries in poor countries. These are frequently targeted training programmes to enhance local competencies required for the industry and have come under fire in wealthier countries when they result in company involvement in setting local curriculum narrowly targeted to industry needs. Indeed, the World Bank, on its website[3] devoted to the energy and mining industries, cautions that:

> It is important . . . not to ask the company to invest in services typically provided by the government, such as health and education, but rather, to find a public-private partnership arrangement that makes use of the company's ability to invest while not taking over government's role.

Rationale, opportunities and risks

Six criteria are essential for successful outcomes of partnerships: definition of needs, ownership by stakeholders, a conscious focus on impact, strong regulation and accountability, sustainability, and monitoring and evaluation (Draxler 2008: 16). The fundamental and overarching principle to all these is the right to education. When definitions of needs are driven by ideology or by the search to test market-driven innovations, implementation can damage equity, distort public spending in favour of relatively advantaged socioeconomic groups, and pay insufficient attention to quality of inputs and of outcomes. The search to minimise costs, a potentially positive feature of PPPs, in fact often translates into lower salaries for teachers – the overwhelming recurring cost in basic and secondary education. Often, needs are defined primarily by a supply approach driven by a assuming that outcomes will improve if market principles are applied, ignoring to reflect on unintended consequences and neglecting to take into account the long time frames for educational change and outcomes.

Advocates of PPPs point to potential benefits of both process (competition, flexibility, risk sharing (Patrinos, Barrera-Osorio and Guáqueta 2009) and outcomes (LaRocque and Lee 2008), with greater emphasis on the former.

> There is little rigorous research on the effects of contracting in education ... However, the absence of rigorous research on this important area should be taken as a clarion call for introducing more and larger scale contracting interventions that would provide an opportunity to assess the impact of such programs. It should not be used as an excuse for ignoring contracting's potential as an educational policy tool.
>
> (World Bank 2007: 3)

The process benefits mentioned include, more broadly, the hope that increased competition will result in higher standards system-wide, that additional resources will be mobilised, and that autonomy and innovation will release creativity. Desired outcomes are maintaining or improving equity, improved learning outcomes in terms of standardised tests, and economies for government budgets resulting from higher household participation in costs.

Unfortunately, research has not shown that competition through expanded public-private mechanisms improves quality as measured by standardised tests (OECD 2011; Samoff and Irving 2014). Low-cost private schools that have government subsidies, as in Pakistan, have a lower per-pupil cost than in the public system, but they operate both with external funding and offering teacher salaries that are below a living wage. In the Fey y Alegría example already cited, low salaries result in many teachers being moonlighters from the public system, definitely creating system efficiency problems. ICT innovations are appealing and find widespread support from many quarters. However, as already noted, research on both implementation and impact over time is scarce, and costs are rarely low enough to take ICT pilots system-wide.

Still, it is clear that there is demand for private education on the part of families. ICT innovations are appealing to both users and authorities. Therefore, as PPPs are implemented, the international community needs to ensure it helps governments implement regulation, cost control, respect for human rights and other international labour and environmental agreements while helping to safeguard against increased inequality by means of additional subsidies to already advantaged socioeconomic groups.

While all observers pay attention to the notion of regulation and accountability, specific reports about regulatory issues posed by PPPs are lacking. Even the most enthusiastic advocates of PPP recognise that a proper regulatory environment is fundamental to success. Yet, in countries like Pakistan, where DFID and World Bank are strongly supporting PPPs, it is precisely the poor regulatory environment that is a major contributor to keeping the public education system so troubled (Malik 2010). There is clearly more information and research required to ascertain the challenges and needs related to regulation of PPPs. While all international bodies talk about regulation, steps to make it effective and democratic are so far lacking.

Corporate motivations

Corporation motivations for public-private partnerships or multistakeholder partnerships generally include reduced risk, enhanced image, development of new markets, early access to a new customer base, easy access to public-sector decision makers, and reduced regulatory scrutiny through a partnership model (Draxler 2008). Programmes that are privately run but have government subsidy are particularly attractive for the private sector: risk is minimal, guarantees are strong, and oversight can be relatively loose. Corporate philanthropy can come with significant hidden costs to the recipient (Ginsburg et al. 2012). Cost overruns, costs for unforeseen problems, and the costs of managing partnerships are rarely if ever borne by corporations. When PPPs or MSPs are informal in nature, for example on the basis of a memorandum of understanding, risks are entirely borne by the public sector.

Naturally, there is a great deal of good done by corporate foundations, particularly in communities where corporate entities are located, or through scholarships, grants or donated expertise (van Fleet 2011). On the other hand, studies also show that alignment with international agreements, such as EFA, or national priorities can be quite weak, as corporations and their foundations pursue objectives that are necessarily related to their branding.

> The worth of "shared value" is often only assessed by the donor – not the recipient – and ignores the degree to which power relationships of donor and recipient, ideology, and rhetoric associated with the private interests can create long-term systemic inequalities or interruptions to the provision of strong public education.
>
> (van Fleet 2012: 5)

Nonprofit actors

In the recent past, new foundations with very large sums of money have been created, such as the UN Foundation, Soros Foundation Network, Bill and Melinda Gates Foundation, and William and Flora Hewlett Foundation, to name just a few. These donors, often dubbed "philanthropreneurs" with funding capacity to rival many bilateral aid agencies, have on the whole taken a policy-oriented approach, attempting to build and/or influence institutions in order to ensure sustainability of the impact of funding by way of longer-term policy shifts on the part of the public sector. While most of their giving does not go to education, the commitment to private sector ideologies and methods has nevertheless spilled over into the discourse, if not so much the practice of aid to education (Steiner-Khamsi 2008).

Several international multistakeholder partnerships have also joined the development institutions during the past decades. The Global Partnership for Education (GPE, formerly FTI) is the principal one for education. Independent assessments have underscored some of the features outlined in a recent study on international governance of MSPs, notably the need to match resources to strategies and to track progress of added value (Bezanson and Isenman 2012).

There are, as has been mentioned, a number of large nonprofit organisations that have long-established networks of private schools. Fe y Alegría (Latin America), Azim Premji Foundation (India), already mentioned, are among providers of basic education for disadvantaged children. In India, many relatively small NGOs that provide basic education but cannot survive without government support are vocal in demanding more stability of state financing. In the

Philippines, an extensive programme of PPPs includes a national programme of subsidising some 600,000 secondary students' participation in not-for-profit private secondary schools that, according to several evaluations, is both cost-effective and provides satisfactory education (Civil Society Network for Education Reforms E-Net Philippines 2012). Uganda and Venezuela provide individual grants to disadvantaged students for attending private secondary schools (LaRocque 2011). Such programmes fulfil needs; however, they can be subject to fraud, and some have been criticised for loose controls and lax accountability.

Governments

Governments typically engage in public-private partnerships in the hope of obtaining one or several of the following: additional resources or cost reductions, expertise, relevance, efficiency, diversity of approaches, innovation, and budget flexibility.

In spite of early hopes, PPPs have not brought substantial additional resources to bear system-wide in any country. Some PPPs result in cost reductions for governments, but, as we have seen, these can be passed on by the private sector to households, increasing system inequities. The managerial expertise demonstrated by the private sector in basic education has mainly been demonstrated in personnel management (less organised labour, lower salaries). In terms of relevance, specific capacity-building programmes for personnel or young people have certainly played a part in innovation and diversity, for example the JEI (World Economic Forum 2007; Light et al. 2008). Budget flexibility, whereby PPPs escape the detailed scrutiny that national education budgets undergo, have, of course, benefits and risks. In situations where overall regulatory power is weak, PPPs can be subject to all of the expected defects of corruption, low quality, and profiteering when oversight is lax. Education systems everywhere are as strong as their public backbones.

In conclusion, some possible trends

Education aims and policies are today heavily influenced by economic considerations in almost all countries. An emphasis on learning that has economic value, the marketisation of the system, and the prevalence of assessing outcomes in terms of measurable competencies (on the part of both education personnel and learners) have become prominent in the international development community. Countries all over the world are attempting to adapt the education they fund to labour market conditions, in the hope of reducing unemployment, stimulating growth and delivering "value for money". Curricula are screened for their adaptation to "21st century skills". One result has to been to give credence to the notion that the private sector has vast expertise, wisdom and legitimacy to offer the public sphere. The private sector is happy to participate in this view of things while expanding its market reach into public services. While these trends are so far relatively limited in the poorest countries of the developing world, we can expect the dominance of marketisation in the UN system and among key donors to spill over much more strongly into global governance and policies in the coming years.

Progress in achieving universal access to basic education has stalled, while quality is often so low that approximately 250 million young people cannot read even a single word, although the majority of them have attended school (UNESCO-GMR and UIS 2014). In consequence, one can safely assume that, in the search for alternative and additional solutions, development agencies and governments will continue to provide support to the involvement of the private sector in education provision in a variety of ways. At a time when external funding for education is stagnating or shrinking, the claim that private sources can fill the gap will have additional appeal. Private education will likely continue to increase in its share of provision, including at the basic level, as will pressure from private institutions and development agencies for the provision of public subsidies for private entities involved in basic education.

Data collection and analysis are moving from being background technical supporters of social policy to being the drivers of social policy. We should not underestimate the impact this will have on the role of the private sector in education. Big data requires big tools, and these tools are mostly affordable to international corporations: we can, as a matter of course, expect large corporations to play a bigger and bigger role in the future, including in delivery of aid to education in developing countries. As corporations move into provision of a broad range of education services, from design and delivery of standardised tests and other data tools to training and certification of teachers to owning and operating institutions in non-OECD countries, we will undoubtedly see more cross-national standardisation of curricula, methods and assessment – with the high volumes of single products that produce the greatest profits – promoted by large corporations and supported by aid and development agencies.

At the same time, experiences in OECD countries with privatisation have revealed some of the flaws and unintended consequences of market-based solutions to public policies: inflated costs, increasing inequality, narrowing of curriculum, decrease in the prestige (and therefore the pool of applicants) of the teaching profession are some of these. Without government support, the private sector will not assume or sustain high-risk ventures or extend services to the most difficult populations to reach or teach. In a few developed countries, widespread high-stakes testing, a cash cow for a handful of large corporations, is already under intense critical scrutiny. We can anticipate that calls for more effective regulation and less high-stakes testing will become louder and more persistent. At the same time, corporations that develop materials for teaching and testing are seeking to expand their markets, particularly as some of the flaws of high-stakes testing and corporate influence on education policy become evident in countries like the USA and resistance seems poised to slow down growth.

While ownership of learning materials and data on education and on learners have not so far been significant subjects of scrutiny in developing countries, if PPPs expand in the form of large franchises of education institutions and large-scale data collection by private entities, two other issues will certainly arise: one is policies about ownership of learning materials created by private entities with public funds, and the second is creation of appropriate safeguards for confidentiality of data collected on learners and learning. In countries where regulatory systems and experience with these issues are weak, development agencies need to help build capacity and make sure their own policies do not allow bad decisions and poor regulation.

Finally, we are facing what could be called a teacher paradox that will be significantly influenced by the growth, if that is the case, of PPPs. Research increasingly shows that individual outcomes of schooling are based predominantly on factors outside of schools. However, both scholarly research and international efforts such as PISA highlight the importance of a confident and well-trained teaching corps for long-term quality of education systems. And yet, the desire to quantify efficiency can lead to attempts to limit teacher initiative and increase direction and control. As private sector involvement gains strength and influence, the bargaining power of teachers is often weakened, as is, over time, the status of the profession. Thus, we can expect new tensions between the ideologies of quantification, control and rapid feedback and those that give priority to longer-term visions and human interaction.

Notes

1 There is relatively little analytical work on scalability and cost-effectiveness of technologies in schools in developing countries, but both UNESCO and the World Bank are quite cautious on the subject. See,

for example, the well-sourced World Bank InfoDev page on costs of ICTs in education; http://www. infodev.org/articles/icts-education-costs

2 http://www.usaid.gov/work-usaid/get-grant-or-contract/opportunities-funding/global-development- alliance-annual-program

3 http://web.worldbank.org/WBSITE/EXTERNAL/TOPICS/EXTOGMC/0,,contentMDK: 20246101~menuPK:509413~pagePK:148956~piPK:216618~theSitePK:336930,00.html

References

Archer, D., 2014. *Critical Reflections on the Learning Metrics Task Force.* ActionAid, London.

Barkan, J., 2011. Got Dough? How Billionaires Rule Our Schools. *Dissent.* http://www.dissentmagazine. org/article/got-dough-how-billionaires-rule-our schools

Bellei, C., 2014. Sweeping Reforms Set to End For-Profit Education in Chile. The Conversation. http:// theconversation.com/sweeping-reforms-set-to-end-for-profit-education-in-chile-26406

Bezanson, K., Isenman, P., 2012. Governance of new global partnerships challenges, weaknesses, and lessons. Center for Global Development Policy Paper No. 14, Washington.

Bjarnason, S., Cheng, K.-M., Fielden, J., Lemaitre, M.-J., Levy, D., Varghese, N., 2009. *A New Dynamic: Private Higher Education.* UNESCO, Paris.

Buse, K., Walt, G., 2000. Global public-private partnerships: part II – what are the health issues for global governance. *Bulletin of the World Health Organization* 78: 699–709.

Civil Society Network for Education Reforms E-Net Philippines, 2012. *Assessing Public-Private Partnership in Education from the Perspective of the Marginalized Sectors.* Civil Society Network for Education Reforms E-Net Philippines, Manila.

Department for International Development, 2013. *Education Position Paper: Improving Learning, Expanding Opportunities.* DFID, London.

Draxler, A., 2008. *New Partnerships for Education: Building from Experience.* UNESCO and World Economic Forum, Paris and Geneva.

Draxler, A., 2012. International PPPs in education: new potential or privatizing public goods? In: Robertson, S., Mundy, K., Verger, A. and Menashy, F. (Eds.) *Public Private Partnerships In Education: New Actors and Modes of Governance in a Globalizing World.* Edward Elgar, Northampton, MA.

Draxler, A., 2014. Metrics on Policies and Learning Outcomes for Post-2015: Some Words of Caution. NORRAG Newsbite. http://norrag.wordpress.com/2014/07/11/metrics-on-policies-and-learnin g-outcomes-for-post-2015-some-words-of-caution/

Education International, 2009. *Public-Private Partnerships in Education.* Education International, Brussels.

Ginsburg, M., Brady, K., Draxler, A., Klees, S., Luff, P., Patrinos, H., Edwards, D., 2012. Public-private partnerships and the global reform of education in less wealthy countries–a moderated discussion. *Comparative Education Review* 56, 1, 155–175.

González, P., Mizala, A., Romaguera, P., 2004. *Vouchers, Inequalities and the Chilean Experience.* Center for Applied Economics, University of Chile.

Grimsey, D., Lewis, M., 2004. *Public Private Partnerships: The Worldwide Revolution in Infrastructure Provision and Project Finance.* Edward Elgar, Cheltenham.

Heyneman, S., Stern, J., 2014. Low cost private schools for the poor: What public policy is appropriate? *International Journal of Educational Development* 35, 3–15.

International Initiative for Impact Evaluation, 2010. Subsidising education: are school vouchers the solution. 3ie Brief No. 16, International Initiative for Impact Evaluation, London.

LaRocque, N., 2011. *Non-State Providers and Public-Private Partnerships in Education for the Poor.* Asian Development Bank and UNICEF, Manila.

LaRocque, N., Lee, S., 2008. *Public-Private Partnerships in Basic Education: An International Review.* CfBT Education Trust, Reading.

Latham, M., 2009. *Public-Private Partnerships in Education.* International Finance Corporation, Washington.

Learning Metrics Task Force (LMTF), 2013. *Toward Universal Learning: Recommendations from the Learning Metrics Task Force.* UNESCO Institute for Statistics and Center for Universal Education, Brookings Institution, Montreal and Washington.

Lewin, K., 2013. Making Rights Realities: Does Privatising Educational Services for the Poor Make Sense? http://www.periglobal.org/role-state/news/article-making-rights-realities-does-privatising-edu cational-services-poor-make-sens

Lewis, L., Patrinos, H., 2012. Impact evaluation of private sector participation in education. CfBT Education Trust, Reading.

Light, D., Method, F., Rockman, C., Cressman, G., Daly, J., 2008. *Evaluation of the Jordan Education Initiative: Synthesis Report.* USAID, Washington.

Malik, A., 2010. *Public-Private Partnerships in Education: Lessons Learned from the Punjab Education Foundation.* Asian Development Bank, Manila.

Mann, G., Pier, D., Yasin, K., 2009. *Multi-Stakeholder Partnerships in Education: The Escuela Nueva Program in Colombia.* USAID, Washington.

Martens, J., 2007. *Multistakeholder Partnerships: Future Models of Multilateralism?* Friedrich-Ebert-Stiftung, Berlin.

McKinsey and Company, 2005. *Building Effective Public-Private Partnerships: Lessons Learnt from the Jordan Education Initiative.* World Economic Forum, Geneva.

Mundy, K., Menashy, F., 2012a. The World Bank and the private provision of K-12 education: history, policies, practices. Education Support Program Working Paper Series, Open Society Foundation, Geneva.

Mundy, K., Menashy, F., 2012b. The World Bank, the International Finance Corporation, and private sector participation in basic education: examining the Education Sector Strategy 2020. *International Perspectives on Education and Society* 16: 113–131.

Naeem, M., 2012. Public Private Partnerships for Education Provision in Pakistan: How Does Punjab Education Foundation Address Equity? http://www.periglobal.org/justice-and-equality/document/public-private-partnerships-education-provision-pakistan

OECD, 2011. Private schools: who benefits? PISA in Focus No. 7, OECD, Paris.

Osorio, J., Wodon, Q. (Eds.), 2014. *Faith-Based Schools in Latin America: Case Studies on Fe y Alegría.* World Bank, Washington.

Patrinos, H., Barrera-Osorio, F., Guáqueta, J., 2009. *The Role and Impact of Public-Private Partnerships in Education.* World Bank, Washington.

Robertson, S., 2008. The new global governance paradigm in education: public-private partnerships and social justice. Education and Development Working Paper No. 6, University of Amsterdam.

Samoff, J., Irving, M., 2014. Education for All: A Global Commitment Without Global Funding. http://www.periglobal.org/role-state/document/education-all-global-commitment-without-global-funding

Sosale, S., 2000. Trends in private sector development in World Bank education projects. Policy Research Working Paper 2452, World Bank, Washington.

Steiner-Khamsi, G., 2008. Donor logic in the era of Gates, Buffett, and Soros. *Current Issues in Comparative Education* 10, 1/2, 10–15.

Trucano, M., 2014. Two New Rigorous Evaluations of Technology Use in Education. http://blogs.world bank.org/edutech/IDB-research 2014

UNESCO, 2008. *ICT Competency Standards for Teachers Policy Framework.* UNESCO, Paris.

UNESCO, 2013a. Private sector should boost finance for education. GMR Policy Paper No. 5, UNESCO, Paris.

UNESCO, 2013b. *The Smartest Investment: A Framework for Business Engagement in Education.* UNESCO, Paris.

UNESCO-GMR, UNESCO Institute for Statistics, 2014. Progress in getting all children to school stalls but some countries show the way forward. GMR Policy Paper No. 14, UNESCO, Paris.

United Nations Environment Programme, 1992. *Agenda 21: Environment and Development Agenda.* UNEP, New York.

United Nations Global Compact, 2007. *After the Signature: A Guide to Engagement in the United Nations Global Compact.* UNGC, New York.

United Nations Global Compact, 2012. *Business, the Millennium Development Goals, the Post-2015 Development Framework and the UN Global Compact.* UNGC, New York.

United Nations High Level Panel on the Post-2015 Development Agenda, 2013. *A New Global Partnership: Eradicate Poverty and Transform Economies through Sustainable Development.* Development Agenda. UN, New York.

USAID, 2011. *Education Opportunity Through Learning. USAID Education Strategy 2011–2015.* USAID, Washington.

Van Fleet, J., 2011. A global education challenge: harnessing corporate philanthropy to educate the world's poor. Center for Universal Education Working Paper No. 4, Brookings Institution, Washington.

Van Fleet, J., 2012. Private philanthropy and social investments in support of Education for All. Background paper prepared for the Education for All Global Monitoring Report 2012: Youth and skills: Putting education to work. UNESCO, Paris.

Wong, A., Unwin, T., 2012. Insight report: Global Education Initiative retrospective on partnerships for education development 2003–2011. World Economic Forum, Geneva.

World Bank, 2007. *Enhancing Accountability in Schools: What Choice and Contracting can Contribute.* World Bank, Washington.

World Bank, 2011. *Learning for All: Investing in People's Knowledge and Skills to Promote Development. The World Bank Group Education Strategy 2020.* World Bank, Washington.

World Bank, 2013. *Using Low-Cost Private Schools to Fill the Education Gap: An Impact Evaluation of a Program in Pakistan.* Human Development Network, World Bank, Washington.

World Conference on Education for All, 1990. *World Declaration on Education for All.* UNESCO, Paris.

World Economic Forum, 2007. *Global Education Initiative.* World Economic Forum, Geneva.

Conclusion

33

LOOKING BEYOND 2015

The future of international education and development research

Simon McGrath and Qing Gu

Introduction

This Handbook has considered many of the substantive and theoretical debates facing international education and development in 2015. In this final chapter, we will shift our gaze more explicitly to the challenges and possibilities for research in the field. The future of international education and development research is clearly powerfully structured by the emergence of a new development settlement, as this begins to shape the definitions of education and development, and their interrelationship; define key development challenges to be researched; and influence the allocation of money to particular research challenges and even methodologies. Our discussion also needs to be located within the global political economy of knowledge production, as McGrath's chapter notes.

In this chapter, we will consider five issues. First, we will begin with the future of debates about the purpose and nature of education, which we explored mainly in Section 1 of this Handbook. Second, we will move on to the substantive debates on education, largely explored in Sections 2 and 3. Third, we will push rather further than the Handbook has done thus far into debates about which models of development should be explored in relationship with education. Fourth, we will look at what the issues discussed in Section 4, regarding the future of international cooperation, imply for international education and development research. In so doing, we will also reflect on the rise of approaches to the global governance of education and the ways in which national educational decision making may be reshaped by forces beyond the usual international education and development debates. Fifth, and finally, we draw these discussions together through a consideration of the future of the field of international education and development, including methodological possibilities, units of analysis and the representation of varied voices in the literature.

Dealing with values

There are chapters in this Handbook that contain arguments that will be strongly disagreed with by other authors and by wider readers. Such arguments will go beyond issues of whether they agree on the merits of a theoretical construct or item of analysis to questions about the value and values of education. It seems important to spend a little time reflecting on this. At one level, the divisions within the field of international education and development might seem unnecessarily strong and acute. Whether coming from libertarian or critical theory backgrounds, those working in the field are largely motivated by a view that poverty needs to be overcome. In this sense, they are motivated by the same goal, even if their ways of working towards it (such as advocating more private schooling for the poor or critiquing the rising marketisation of education) are markedly different. It may be that a little more respect for other positions, whilst retaining theoretical, methodological and analytical robustness, would serve the field well.

Nonetheless, the Handbook, and the wider literature, points to important challenges regarding the values that education should be inculcating and demonstrating. First, we will focus on the values that education should be demonstrating. This is where arguments about the appropriateness of market and state involvement in education, and what types of involvement, become pertinent. If getting the poorest into quality education is the ultimate goal, then is it of great significance who delivers, pays for and oversees this? Or, instead, is it fundamental that education is a public good that should be delivered by a state or that markets are inherently better at both efficiency and equity than governments?

One discussion that this Handbook has not engaged in is that about religious schooling. Again, there are extreme secularist and religious views on the issue, but there may be more interesting debates to explore regarding how religious organisations may or may not be effective in their delivery of quality learning. The parameters of this discussion may well need reconsideration in the light of the new values elements of the education subgoals. The OWG zero draft subgoal 4.6 states:

> [B]y 2030 integrate into education programs knowledge and skills necessary for sustainable development, human rights, gender equality, promoting a culture of peace and non-violence and culture's contribution to sustainable development.
>
> (OWG 2014: 6)

Are religious schools, or some types thereof, likely to be particularly effective or ineffective in the provision of these values? What might particular religious traditions have to contribute through their particular perspectives on creation and stewardship, nonviolence or justice and peace? What obstacles might religious schooling present in terms of views about sexual rights or gender equality? These are important questions for the international education and development community, but it has been too secularist in its world view to engage seriously enough with these issues to date.

There are important questions, too, about the value of education and its ultimate purpose. A number of chapters in this Handbook question how the current orthodoxy combines rights-based and instrumental languages about why education is important. Inevitably, the case made for education to remain as an important part of the global development goal architecture has tried to argue from a combined rights and investment perspective. However, it is important to continue to ask what this might do to the weight of arguments about education's importance. Does it matter that there is a tendency, even within the human development tradition, to stress education as a building block for the achievement of other rights, capabilities and functionings, rather than a key aspect of freedom in and of itself?

The big issues in international education and development after 2015

Many of the current major issues in international education and development will not go away in the near future. Indeed, some may be genuinely perennial. However, it is apparent both from the previous chapters and from ongoing debates about education post-2015 that other issues are likely to come further to the fore.

If the EFA era, crudely put, was about getting children into primary schooling, then the draft SDG for education points to a likely new core focus for the next period *on quality across educational levels and forms*, although just how inclusive a vision of lifelong learning will emerge seems highly debatable. Of course, and rightly, quality will not be understood by the international education and development community in isolation from continued concerns with inequality of access, retention and acquisition. Tomasevski's insistence on the "four A's of access" seems to continue to be of great relevance but now applied much more expansively to forms and levels of education and with an even more explicit focus on the quality of the education accessed. There is likely to be more attention in the next period to work that looks at her concepts of availability of provision at the systemic level; access in practice; acceptability in terms of quality, process and content; and adaptability to the needs of individuals and groups as it applies to education beyond schooling and even informal learning (Tomasevski 2001; cf. McGrath 2012 on the 4A's and vocational education and training).

Indeed, it is to be hoped that international education and development research will be able to *push far more beyond schooling as a focus*. Section 3 of this Handbook has shown some of the vibrancy of work on other aspects of education, but there is far too little research of real quality on these other aspects and even less appreciation of an interest in nonschooling research by the mainstream of international education and development researchers. Yet, as schooling expands, so does participation in tertiary education, as we noted for higher education in Africa in our introductory chapter. When Ethiopia grows its higher education system twelvefold and India commits to upskilling 500 million youth and adults, these are not marginal educational issues of concern only to specialists in those narrow areas.

In cultivating what are still the outlying fields of international educational research, there is a particular need to get outside the formal frame of reference. In his contribution to this Handbook, Rogers rightly insists on the importance of informal learning of children as underpinning their learning in schools. However, this should be read alongside his stress on the learning of adults that largely take place outside formal education spaces. One of the most important learning spaces globally is the workplace. Whilst there is a history of research on work-based learning in the South – most notably on learning in traditional apprenticeships and informal enterprises (e.g., King 1977; Lave 1977) – the mainstream journals have carried very little of such work in recent years. The official development agenda, at least rhetorically, talks of lifelong learning, but there is much more to be done from the research side to ensure that this is also understood as lifewide.

Even within the schooling mainstream, there are clearly new challenges. Some of these are at *the intersections between technology and society*. There have long been efforts to introduce new technologies into schooling in the South, with the latest frontier here being the use of tablet computers. However, the discussion here has been too concentrated within a further specialism, that of educational technology, with little mainstream discussion of either the affordances of new technologies in different contexts or the possible more negative effects of the introduction of such technologies into settings where learning is fragile and where teachers are struggling. From anthropological and sociological traditions, there is a keen awareness that new technologies are adopted in ways that often adapt them to fit existing relations of power, particularly of gender, but there is too little in the way of a conversation between traditions that explore how the emancipatory potential of new technologies may be best ensured.

Similarly, emphases on informal and virtual learning do not undermine the continued salience of *physical, formal learning spaces*. A welcome contribution to this Handbook is Uduku's architectural perspective. Here again, there is real scope for interdisciplinary engagement about what supports and obstructs quality and inclusive learning in varying contexts.

The recent attention to *learning quality* is welcome insofar as it seeks to open up the black box of educational practice, which has tended to be neglected by official and research focus on years of education as if these were devoid of context and content. The SDG subgoal interest in education for sustainable development, peace, etc. can be usefully extended to reopen a discussion about the content of education. Equally, the attempt to break free of development silos in the post-2015 debate has led to some interesting initiatives, such as the Global Monitoring Report team's attempt to map education onto some of the other draft SDGs (UNESCO 2014a). We need a new debate about which educational content supports which forms of development, and with which potential consequences for equity, remembering Tomasevski's concerns with acceptability and adaptability, as well as historical patterns of gender and other stereotyping about which subjects are "suitable" for which learners. As was hinted at in the previous section of this chapter, the SDG ambition to use schooling to inculcate a set of "universal values" must be a major focus of international education and development research in the near future.

Alexander's chapter points to another area that needs more attention in the future international education and development research agenda. *Pedagogy* is a central element of educational practice, yet, he argues, it has been relegated to the margins of international education debates, in spite of there being major developments in pedagogical research in the North. Again, we need to think about pedagogies in terms of both quality and equity.

Assessment has come back into both policy and academic debates in a dramatic way in the current decade, as is reflected in the chapters starting Section 2. This is likely to grow in importance as an area of study. The chapters point to the technical challenges involved but also some of the manifestations of power that are embedded in international initiatives. Beyond the coverage of the chapters and the spread of models such as EGRA and the ambitions of the Learning Metrics Task Force, there are also powerful trends at play between the attempted spread of PISA (and, arguably, OECD power and influence) to the South and the rise of largely internally funded national learning assessments.

A stronger focus on curriculum, pedagogy and assessment seems necessary for a medium-term agenda for international education and development research. In all of these areas, *the quality of teachers* is a key factor. There is established evidence in educational research that shows that teachers' classroom practices have the largest effects on student learning and achievement (e.g., Rockoff, 2004; Hallinger 2005; Rivkin, Hanushek and Kain 2005; Leithwood et al. 2006; McKinsey 2007, 2010). Given this, we believe that every student in every school in every country of the world has an entitlement not only to the provision of educational opportunities but also to be taught by knowledgeable, committed and pedagogically effective teachers. However, in many countries in the South where school enrolment is on the rise, an acute shortage of primary teachers continues to represent one of the greatest hurdles to providing education for all school-age children (UNESCO 2011). A lack of resources and financial incentive packages to attract qualified personnel into teaching has meant that quantity, rather than quality, continues to be a primary concern in their efforts to provide basic education. This has also meant, unfortunately, that children in countries needing teachers the most tend to be taught by the least-qualified personnel (UNESCO 2006, 2014b).

It is perhaps not surprising then that the skills and roles of teachers, on the one hand, and the dynamics of the teaching workforce, on the other, have seen renewed (but often polarised) attention in recent years. The Global Monitoring Report for 2014 (UNESCO 2014b) and the draft SDGs (OWG 2014) highlight the importance of qualified teaching workforce at the same time as there are drives globally to deskill teachers. The latter is often linked to portrayals of teachers' unions as being an obstacle to learning quality. Whilst some of this is obviously ideological in motivation, it is clear that teachers' unions do have to manage a tension between acting in the interests of their members and in the interests of learners, for the two will not always coincide. However, rather than the current unhelpful disputes over teacher unionism, it is worth considering whether there are ways of supporting teachers' unions as legitimate and necessary organisations so that they better combine their dual functions of supporting their members as workers with rights and as professionals with a commitment to improving learning (cf. Stevenson [2012] in the English context). There is potential, too, for building on other more fruitful and educationally more meaningful approaches to thinking about teachers' work, lives and effectiveness (Day and Gu 2010, 2014). Day and Gu argue that greater attention should be paid to the personal, workplace and broad policy factors that enable many teachers to maintain committed to their own learning and the learning and achievement of their pupils. This is, in essence, a *quality* retention issue because, as Johnson and her colleagues (2005: 2) have argued, the *physical* retention of teachers, "in and of itself, is not a worthy goal". The international education and development field has seen some recent research using the capability approach to think about teachers' work (Buckler 2011; Tao 2014), and this appears a fruitful line for further enquiry.

Inevitably, consideration of teachers and teaching leads us on to matters of *leadership, school improvement and effectiveness*, and *decentralised educational governance*. The positive impact of strong leadership on student learning through building supportive school culture and creating favourable working conditions for teachers is well documented in the Northern teacher development, school improvement and school effectiveness literature (e.g., Johnson 2004; Leithwood et al. 2004, 2006; Day et al. 2011; Sammons et al. 2011). There is also evidence that points to strong and positive associations between school leaders' administrative support and low teacher retention rates (Ladd 2009; Boyd et al. 2011). In addition, a strong sense of staff collegiality has been found to be crucial in building intellectual, emotional and social capital in schools so that teachers, and especially those working in schools serving socioeconomically deprived communities, are able to maintain their integrity and commitment in times of change (Allensworth et al. 2009; Day et al. 2011; Holme and Rangel 2012). More importantly, we know from research that pupils of highly committed teachers are more likely to perform better academically (Day et al. 2007). This Handbook is relatively silent about these issues, which are less well researched in the South, but they need more attention in thinking about international education and development. One challenge here is to build a better engagement between such concerns, which are typically addressed in rather technical ways, and evolving debates about education's role in sustainable development and the reduction of inequality (cf. Bosu et al. 2011).

What model(s) of development is education "for"?

The bulk of international education and development research is based in one of two development paradigms, or in a mixture of the two. Either the grounding is in economic development or a human rights approach to basic needs, largely concentrated on education, health and poverty reduction. In practice, both approaches have a view that investments in education lead to wider developmental benefits of the kind McGrath cites in his chapter:

- increases wages, leading to reduced poverty
- reduces vulnerability to shocks
- reduces inequality
- increases employability
- improves life skills for participation in society

- improves reproductive health
- reduces fertility, leading to population sustainability
- raises civic awareness and political participation
- improves social integration and cohesion
- increases productivity
- enhances political stability
- reduces criminality (Adams 2012, cited in McGrath, this volume).

However, there are other views that can be found within the education and development literature that point to different perspectives on the nature of development. These include approaches to economic, human and sustainable development.

The neoclassical and human capital groundings of the current orthodoxy offer only one perspective on the nature of economics and economic development (Chang 2014). A particularly fruitful approach to thinking about education and development might be to consider more

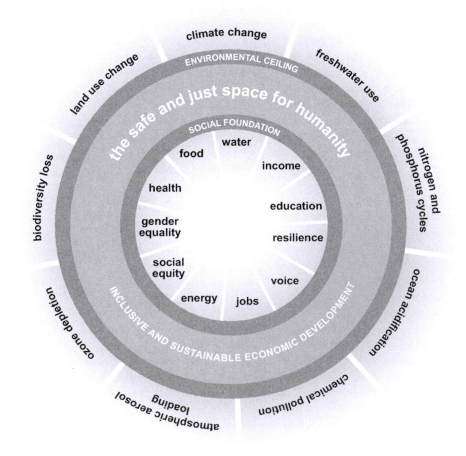

Figure 33.1　Raworth's development doughnut

deeply the role that work, technology and innovation play in economic development, drawing on the evolutionary economics tradition and sectoral systems of innovation (Kruss et al. 2014). This approach focuses on the challenges that firms and economies have in learning how to technologically innovate and transform their productive capabilities and offers a more plausible account of how development has taken place in East Asia than does the orthodoxy, a point made by Lauder in his chapter. There is need, too, for educational researchers to take far more seriously the challenge of decent and sustainable work, as McGrath and Powell's chapter argues.

There are versions of human development that are entirely compatible with the orthodox view that health and education are the underpinnings of either economic development or capabilities and functionings (depending on which form of human development thinking is being considered). However, the human development and capability approach also contains a strand that is opposed to the linear instrumental view of education as foundation, preferring to stress the importance of agency, freedom and voice. In this view, whilst education may indeed be supportive of the achievement of other individual development goals, the value of education does not reside in this facilitative function but in whatever value the individual accords to it.

Challenges also lie ahead in building a stronger engagement between the education for sustainable development movement and the international education and development community, which have tended to operate in largely unarticulated ways (see Sprague's chapter). The decision that sustainable development is to be the core concept of the official international development agenda from 2015 has profound implications for the future of international education and development research. New frontiers here might include education research engagement with the notion of the doughnut (Raworth 2012) between the planetary boundaries at which human futures become unsustainable and the social foundations captured by the SDGs. It is between these two boundaries that Raworth suggests lies an environmentally safe and socially just space.

Again, education is present as one element of the social foundation, but the real research opportunity lies in exploring its interactions with other elements of the social foundation and with the planetary boundaries.

Education, globalisation and international cooperation

There has been much talk in recent years about the end of aid. If true, this will have profound implications for international education and development research. It will impact on the issues to be researched and on sources of funding. Change certainly is happening in this area, but the situation is highly complex. Official development assistance to education from the Development Assistance Committee (DAC) members has declined (UNESCO 2013), but there has been a rise of funding from new bilateral actors. These have different perspectives than the DAC donors on what forms of education matter for development and about what development is, as Cheng and Chan's chapter notes. However, this different paradigm is often tacitly understood and has not been the subject of significant research. Thus, one potential research agenda for the next period would be to explore the implications of new donors both on the systems that they are funding and on the overall discourses and theories of education for development.

At the same time, the old donors have often significantly changed their views about education and development. Although the Washington Consensus is arguably less pervasive at the multilateral level, a number of bilateral agencies have developed huge enthusiasm for market solutions. Part of this may be seen in a new form of tied aid, where agencies, such as DFID, are now seeking to promote the interests of major private sector education organisations, such as Pearson, in building new markets in the South. There are also new trends in aid prioritisation that influence the education and development research agenda. These include recent attention to rising powers and growing middle classes internationally, as well as focus on the "bottom billion" (Collier 2007) and postconflict settings. The latter in particular highlights the rising challenge of education's relationship with the growth of securitisation, whilst the focus on the inculcation of global values in the new education goals cannot easily be separated from a consideration of education's role in the "war on terror".

This export-led development assistance of new public-private partnerships is part of a complex mix of Northern education exports. The rise of national qualifications frameworks internationally, for instance, has seen national public education organisations from the North play an active service provider role in setting up new systems (McGrath 2010a). For organisations such as the Scottish Qualifications Authority, this export work is part of the requirement under new public management for them to develop stronger cost-recovery models. As several chapters in Section 3 illustrate, the public higher education institutions of Britain and Australia have been particularly active in exporting Northern higher education to the South. This exportation of educational services has been mirrored at lower levels of the education system, with elite private schools opening branch campuses in East Asia and vocational institutions seeking to attract greater numbers of international students and, more occasionally, enter into joint delivery models overseas.

The global education agenda is also being shaped increasingly by the rise of philanthrocapitalism and the emergence of venture capitalist interest in the possibilities of making profits from investments in education in the South. The picture here is made even more complex as some of these actors are part of diasporas who have returned from successful careers in OECD countries to do development at home. These new actors are interesting in part for their tendency to favour more experimental approaches to funding, marking a move away from logical framework-type approaches to project planning and monitoring and introducing different models of development cooperation in practice.

As Magrath's chapter reminds us, the past 25 years have also seen the rise of civil society organisations as players in the global education governance system, even though their real ability to influence the agenda needs to be seen as very constrained. There are complexities of interactions within these networks that require further exploration.

There are established literatures on the internationalisation of higher education and on international schools, many of which, of course, are Southern-owned but offering programmes in colonial languages and with qualifications that are accepted in the North. Critics argue the unprecedented expansion of international education has played an important role in reinforcing the inequalities in flows of knowledge and skills between the North and the South and also in enhancing the social origins and family habitus of middle-class students in the society. However, these literatures have tended to be bracketed off from the international education and development literature.

Moreover, there are new frontiers for research on the globalisation and internationalisation of education, as the above discussion demonstrates. The range of actors and forces has grown hugely and diversely, and this has major research implications. Even as aid diminishes in importance (rather than really ends), it is clear that new conditionalities are emerging as part of global governance trends. In a new context, there is still need for research that critically considers whose power, voices and interests are represented in new national and international processes.

The future of the field

All of the discussion thus far in this chapter points to a range of new dynamics and opportunities for international education and development research. However, in this section, we want to zoom in on the research dimension more sharply.

As noted above, any movement "beyond aid" will have huge implications for education research. Even within the aid context, concerns have been raised about the status of education. A number of agencies have reduced their educational investment and staffing considerably, and aid funding has concentrated on an ever smaller group of countries.

On the other hand, there are undoubtedly real possibilities for international education and development research from the new development agenda. As noted earlier in this chapter, the new development discourse suggests new research directions towards thinking about such issues as innovation, work and environmental sustainability. A useful first step in thinking about how education is located within the new development agenda has been produced by the Global Monitoring Report team (UNESCO 2014b). This takes the existing wider benefits of education arguments (see the list cited above) and starts to try to strengthen the environmental dimension of this in particular. This short think piece highlights possible new directions for educational research in looking at education's role in addressing the challenges of water and energy use (draft goals 6 and 7); urban development (goal 11); and the range of environmental protection goals (12–15).

This is a useful starting point, although it is rather school-centric. As well as this exploring of how education is important to other sectors, there is a parallel need to understand better how education is perceived by actors in other sectors as contributing to their sectoral goals. This is itself an issue requiring research, but there are broader possibilities for new interdisciplinary research programmes on development that include education. However, in embarking upon this attempt, we need to remain mindful of the ways in which education has been downplayed in many mainstream development accounts and the power of beliefs that we know all that it is necessary to know about education's role in development (cf. McGrath 2010b, 2014 for critiques of these positions).

One challenge facing international education research at the moment, which could be exacerbated by interdisciplinary collaborations, lies in debates about hierarchies of research evidence. Many funders seem increasingly sure about the relative value of different methodologies. Some international development agencies appear to accept a medical view of the gold standard of randomised control trials, with systematic reviews coming next, and a long way ahead of ethnographic approaches. Some, more academic, funders seem to be influenced by implicit rankings of disciplines, with education often near the bottom and/or value quantitative over qualitative research. All of this poses very serious challenges for the Sadlerian comparative tradition, which has been so influential in international education and development research (cf. Crossley 2014; McGrath 2014).

However, there are also new and exciting methodological possibilities that could arise from better interdisciplinary conversations and from new technological developments. There may be particular possibilities in exploring mixed-methods approaches that can maintain and refresh qualitative approaches in genuine dialogues with other traditions.

Alexander's chapter, for one, notes the limited way in which the international education and development literature is attuned to breakthroughs in the mainstream education literature. As we have noted in this chapter, there are also a number of other education literatures that tend not to have an interaction with the international education and development field. These include research on the internationalisation of higher education, international schools, the global governance of education and education for sustainable development. As well as building interdisciplinary bridges, there is much scope for building new research alliances within the wider education research community.

As education becomes more transnational, decentred, globalised and internationalised, new questions arise as to the distinctiveness of the development context as a useful concept. There are important questions, too, about appropriate units of analysis. There are clearly differences between the disciplinary traditions that are involved in international education and development regarding how such issues are tackled. These include debates about whether the primary unit of analysis is the individual or the collective. There are now long-standing questions about the conceptual and methodological importance of nation-states under globalisation. Moreover, and perhaps more interestingly, there are theoretical and policy dynamics that point towards greater emphasis on analysing global networks, cities, economic sectors, etc. as important educational units of analysis. In all of this, it is important to remember that issues of scale and units of analysis are themselves constructed (Jessop 2002).

A final, crucial concern for many in the international education and development field are questions of whose voices and theories are represented in the field's outputs. Such concerns are sensitive to the problems of the increasingly powerful disciplining effect that performative cultures, the global political economy of knowledge production, and the dominant status of English have on hierarchies of outputs. This has led leading Northern-based journals, such as the *International Journal of Educational Development* and *Compare*, to actively seek to increase the numbers of Southern scholars amongst their authors. Building Southern research capacity in international education and development remains vital to the health of the field and to the improvement of policy and practice (Crossley 2012, 2014).

There are still concerns amongst many in the field about claims to universality of Northern theory and methodology. This strand of thought is sympathetic to indigenous and Southern critiques of Northern knowledge (e.g., Smith 1999; Connell 2007). However, the field is operating within the performative logics of contemporary academia and its place within the broader global capitalist system, and the scope for radical action is clearly constrained. Nonetheless, the field does need to continue to address the challenges and possibilities of serious engagement with Southern theories and methodologies and attempt to become more plurilingual.

Conclusion

This Handbook has covered just a fraction of the fertile thoughtscape of international education and development, pointing to the richness of a field informed by multiple disciplines, issues and contexts. There clearly are many challenges ahead for the field as we move into a new global development phase post-2015. The pluralism of the field is something to celebrate, but it also requires work in a number of ways. These include seeking to ensure that Southern voices are well represented in the visible outputs and debates of the field and cultivating far more of a conversation between the different traditions within the field, and between it and broader education, and development debates. There are opportunities to develop innovative new theories and methods to address existing and emerging issues. In all of this, reflection on and commitment to a strong ethical framework will be essential. International education and development will continue to aspire to be social science that makes a difference and must reflect critically and creatively on its practice of pursuing this.

References

Adams, A., 2012. The education link: why learning is central to the post-2015 global development agenda. Center for Universal Education Working Paper 8, Brookings Institution, Washington.

Allensworth, E., Ponisciak, S., Mazzeo, C., 2009. The Schools Teachers Leave: Teacher Mobility in Chicago Public Schools. http://ccsr.uchicago.edu/publications/CCSR_Teacher_Mobility.pdf

Bosu, R., Dare, A., Dachi, H., Fertig, M., 2011. School leadership and social justice: evidence from Ghana and Tanzania. *International Journal of Educational Development* 31, 1, 67–77.

Boyd, D., Lankford, H., Loeb, S., Ronfeldt, M., Wyckoff, J., 2011. The role of teacher quality in retention and hiring: using applications-to-transfer to uncover preferences of teachers and schools. *Journal of Policy Analysis and Management* 30, 88–110.

Buckler, A., 2011. Reconsidering the evidence base, considering the rural: aiming for a better understanding of the education and training needs of Sub-Saharan African teachers. *International Journal of Educational Development* 31, 3, 244–250.

Chang, H.-J., 2014. *Economics: A User's Guide*. Pelican, London.

Collier, P., 2007. *The Bottom Billion*. Oxford University Press, Oxford.

Connell, R., 2007. *Southern Theory*. Polity, Cambridge.

Crossley, M., 2012. Comparative education and research capacity building: reflections on international transfer and the significance of context. *Journal of International and Comparative Education* 1, 1, 4–12.

Crossley, M., 2014. Global league tables, big data and the international transfer of educational research modalities. *Comparative Education* 50, 1, 15–26.

Day, C., Gu, Q., 2010. *The New Lives of Teachers*. Routledge, London.

Day, C., Gu, Q., 2014. *Resilient Teachers, Resilient Schools: Sustaining Quality in Testing Times*. Routledge, London.

Day, C., Sammons, P., Leithwood, K., Hopkins, D., Gu, Q., Brown, E., with Ahtaridou, E., 2011. *School Leadership and Student Outcomes: Building and Sustaining Success*. Open University Press, Maidenhead.

Day, C., Sammons, P., Stobart, G., Kington, A., Gu, Q., 2007. *Teachers Matter: Connecting Lives, Work and Effectiveness*. Open University Press, Maidenhead.

Hallinger, P., 2005. Instructional leadership and the school principal: a passing fancy that refuses to fade away. *Leadership and Policy in Schools* 4, 3, 1–20.

Holme, J., Rangel, V., 2012. Putting school reform in its place: social geography, organizational social capital, and school performance. *American Educational Research Journal* 49, 2, 257–283.

Jessop, R., 2002. The political economy of scale. In: Perkmann, M. and Sum, N.-L. (Eds.) *Globalization, Regionalization and Cross-Border Regions*. Palgrave Macmillan, Basingstoke.

Johnson, S., 2004. *Finders and Keepers*. Jossey-Bass, San Francisco.

Johnson, S., Berg, J., Donaldson, M., 2005. *A Review of the Literature on Teacher Retention*. Harvard Graduate School of Education, Harvard.

King, K., 1977. *The African Artisan*. Heinemann, London.

Kruss, G., McGrath, S., Petersen, I.-H., Gastrow, M., 2014. Tertiary education and development – the central role of technological capabilities. Paper presented at the Higher Education and Development conference, London, October.

Ladd, H., 2009. Teachers' perceptions of their working conditions: how predictive of policy-relevant outcomes. Working Paper No. 33, National Center for Analysis of Longitudinal Data in Education Research, Washington.

Lave, J., 1977. Cognitive consequences of traditional apprenticeship training in Africa. *Anthropology and Education Quarterly* 7, 177–180.

Leithwood, K., Day, C., Sammons, P., Harris, A., Hopkins, D., 2006. *Seven Strong Claims about Successful School Leadership*. National College for School Leadership, Nottingham.

Leithwood, K., Seashore Louis, K., Anderson, S., Wahlstrom, K., 2004. How leadership influences student learning. Center for Applied Research and Educational Improvement, St. Paul.

McGrath, S., 2010a. Beyond aid effectiveness: the development of the South African further education and training college sector, 1994–2009. *International Journal of Educational Development* 30, 5, 525–534.

McGrath, S., 2010b. The role of education in development: an educationalist's response to some recent work in development economics. *Comparative Education* 46, 2, 237–253.

McGrath, S., 2012. Vocational education and training for development. *International Journal of Educational Development* 32, 5, 623–631.

McGrath, S., 2014. The post-2015 debate and the place of education in development thinking. *International Journal of Educational Development* 39, 4–11.

McKinsey, 2007. *How the World's Best-Performing School Systems Come Out on Top*. McKinsey & Co., London.

McKinsey, 2010. *How the World's Most Improved School Systems Keep Getting Better*. McKinsey & Co., London.

Open Working Group on Sustainable Development Goals, 2014. Introduction and Proposed Goals and Targets on Sustainable Development for the Post-2015 Development Agenda. Zero Draft rev 1. http://sustainabledevelopment.un.org/content/documents/4044zerodraft.pdf

Raworth, K., 2012. *A Safe and Just Space for Humanity: Can We Live Within the Doughnut?* Oxfam, Oxford.

Rivkin, S., Hanushek, E., Kain, J., 2005. Teachers, schools and academic achievement. *Econometrica* 73, 2, 417–458.

Rockoff, J., 2004. The impact of individual teachers on student achievement: evidence from panel data. *American Economic Review Papers and Proceedings* 94, 2, 247–252.

Sammons, P., Gu, Q., Day, C., Ko, J., 2011. Exploring the impact of school leadership on pupil outcomes. *International Journal of Educational Management* 25, 1, 83–101.

Smith, L., 1999. *Decolonising Methodologies.* Zed, London.

Stevenson, H., 2012. Teacher leadership as intellectual leadership: creating spaces for alternative voices in the English school system. *Professional Development in Education* 38, 2, 345–360.

Tao, S., 2014. Using the capability approach to improve female teacher deployment to rural schools in Nigeria. *International Journal of Educational Development* 39, 92–99.

Tomasevski, K., 2001. Human Rights Obligations. http://www.right-toeducation.org/content/primers/rte_03.pdf

UNESCO, 2006. *Teachers and Educational Quality: Monitoring Global Needs for 2015.* UNESCO, Paris.

UNESCO, 2011. *The Global Demand for Primary Teachers – 2011 Update.* UNESCO, Paris.

UNESCO, 2013. Schooling for millions of children jeopardised by reductions in aid. Education for All Global Monitoring Report Policy Paper 9, UNESCO, Paris.

UNESCO, 2014a. *Sustainable Development Begins with Education.* UNESCO, Paris.

UNESCO, 2014b. *Education for All; Global Monitoring Report 2014. Teaching and Learning: Achieving Quality for All.* UNESCO, Paris.

INDEX

Note: Page numbers with *f* indicate figures, those with *t* indicate tables, and those with *b* indicate boxes.